# Legal Orderings and Economic Institutions

*Legal Orderings and Economic Institutions* addresses the lively interaction between the disciplines of Law and Economics. The traditional boundaries of these two disciplines have somehow inhibited a full understanding of the functioning of and the evolution of economic and legal systems. It has often been the case that these boundaries have had to be reshaped, and sometimes abolished, before either one of the two disciplines could successfully clarify the real-life problems arising from the complex institutions of contemporary societies.

The contributions to this volume encompass some of the core controversial issues in Law and Economics arising from interactions between legal orderings and economic institutions. They include (1) the nature of institutional and legislative change and the emergence of strong institutional complementarity in legal positions, (2) the relationship between private orderings and the role of the state in enforcing contracts and defining property rights, (3) the nature and dynamics of endogenous enforcement, and (4) the analysis of governance models and corporate ethics.

**Fabrizio Cafaggi** is Professor in Law at the European University Institute, Italy.

**Antonio Nicita** is Associate Professor of Economics at the University of Siena.

**Ugo Pagano** is Professor of Economics at the University of Siena and Visiting Professor at the Central European University, Budapest.

## Routledge Siena Studies in Political Economy

The Siena Summer School hosts lectures by distinguished scholars on topics characterized by a lively research activity. The lectures collected in this series offer a clear account of the alternative research paths that characterize a certain field. Different publishers printed former workshops of the school. They include:

**Macroeconomics: A Survey of Research Strategies**
*Edited by Alessandro Vercelli and Nicola Dimitri*
Oxford University Press, 1992

**International Problems of Economics Interdependence**
*Edited by Massimo Di Matteo, Mario Baldassarri and Robert Mundell*
Macmillan, 1994

**Ethics, Rationality and Economic Behaviour**
*Edited by Francesco Farina, Frank Hahn and Steffano Vannucci*
Clarendon Press

Available from Routledge:

**The Politics of Economics and Power**
*Edited by Samuel Bowles, Maurizio Franzini and Ugo Pagano*

**The Evolution of Economic Diversity**
*Edited by Antonio Nicita and Ugo Pagano*

**Cycles, Growth and Structural Change**
*Edited by Lionello Punzo*

**General Equilibrium**
*Edited by Fabio Petri and Frank Hahn*

**Cognitive Processes and Economic Behaviour**
*Edited by Nicola Dimitri, Marcello Basili and Itzhak Gilboa*

**Environment, Inequality and Collective Action**
*Edited by Marcello Basili, Maurizio Franzini and Alessandro Vercelli*

**Inequality and Economic Integration**
*Edited by Francesco Farina and Ernesto Savaglio*

**Legal Orderings and Economic Institutions**
*Edited by Fabrizio Cafaggi, Antonio Nicita, and Ugo Pagano*

# Legal Orderings and Economic Institutions

Edited by
Fabrizio Cafaggi, Antonio Nicita,
and Ugo Pagano

Routledge
Taylor & Francis Group
LONDON AND NEW YORK

First published 2007 by Routledge
2 Park Square, Milton Park, Abingdon, Oxon OX14 4RN
52 Vanderbilt Avenue, New York, NY 10017, USA

*Routledge is an imprint of the Taylor & Francis Group, an informa business*



Typeset in Baskerville by
Newgen Imaging Systems (P) Ltd, Chennai, India



*British Library Cataloguing in Publication Data*
A catalogue record for this book is available from the British Library

*Library of Congress Cataloging in Publication Data*

Legal orderings and economic institutions / edited by Fabrizio Cafaggi, Antonio Nicita, and Ugo Pagano.
p. cm.
Includes bibliographical references and index.
1. Law and economics. 2. Law–Economic aspects. I. Cafaggi, Fabrizio. II. Nicita, Antonio. III. Pagano, Ugo, 1951–

K487.E3L44 2006
330–dc22 2005029106

ISBN13: 978–0–415–32942–2 (hbk)
ISBN13: 978–0–203–39132–7 (ebk)

**To Letizia Gianformaggio**

# Contents

# Illustrations

## Figures

## Tables

# Contributors

**Luca Anderlini** is Professor of Economics at the Georgetown University.

**Alberto Battistini** is Assistant Professor in Economics at the University of Siena.

**Fabrizio Cafaggi** is Professor of Law and the European University Institute and Professor of Private Law at the University of Trento.

**Francesco Denozza** is Professor of Corporate Law at the University of Milano.

**Francesco Farina** is Professor of Economics at the University of Siena.

**Leonardo Felli** is Professor of Economics at The London School of Economics and Political Science.

**Nancy Gallini** is the Dean of the Faculty of Arts and Professor of Economics at the University of British Columbia, Vancouver.

**Nita Ghei** is Assistant Professor of Law at the George Mason University.

**Katsuhito Iwai** is Professor of Economics at the University of Tokio.

**Antonio Nicita** is Professor of Economic Policy at the University of Siena and faculty member of CLEIS Center for Law and Economics and Economics of Institutions Siena.

**Douglass C. North**, Nobel Laureate, is Emeritus Professor of at the University of Washington.

**Ugo Pagano** is Professor of Economic Policy at the University of Siena and Director of the Siena PhD programme in Economics.

**Francesco Parisi** is Professor of Law and Economics at the University of Minnesota.

**H. Peyton Young** is Professor of Economics at the Johns Hopkins University.

**Lorenzo Sacconi** is Professor of Economic Policy at the University of Trento and Director of EconomEtica.

**Ernesto Savaglio** is Professor of Economics at the University of Pescara.

**Alan Schwartz** is Sterling Professor of Law at the University of Yale.

**Suzanne Scotchmer** is Professor of Economics and Public Policy at the University of California, Berkeley.

**Thomas S. Ulen** is Professor of Economic analysis of Law and Director, Illinois Program in Law and Economics at the Universiy of Illinois.

# 1 Law, economics, and institutional complexity

## An introduction

*Fabrizio Cafaggi, Antonio Nicita, and Ugo Pagano*

### The way ahead

Law and economics is more than the lively interaction between two disciplines. It has grown from the awareness that the traditional boundaries of the two disciplines do not make significant steps towards a full understanding of the functioning and of the evolution of economic and legal systems. They needed to be often reshaped, and sometimes abolished, if either of the two disciplines would deal successfully with the real-life problems arising from the complex institutions of contemporary societies.

The law and economics movement has spread widely in recent years.[1] As Mercuro and Medema (1997) have pointed out,

> Law and economics has developed from a small and rather esoteric branch within economics and law to a substantial movement that has helped to both redefine the study of law and expose economics to the important implications of the legal environment.[2]

Law and economics has appealed to legal scholars and practitioners and has had such an important impact on legal doctrine because it offers an attractive method to describe how people are likely to respond to law and how they make normative judgments about legal rules and institutions (as remarked by Ulen in his contribution to this volume (Ch. 2)).

In the midst of so much success, one way to understand the way ahead for further research at the intersection of law and economics is to be aware of what has already been successfully challenged. For too many scholars, law and economics were two separate Nirvanas.[3] This separation was, however, necessary to prevent the downfall to Earth of the two disciplines. The Nirvana fallacy of each discipline was, indeed, based on unrealistic assumption about the other discipline.

In the European Kelsenian tradition, the lawyers' Nirvana was based on the assumption that law was *consistent* and *complete*. According to that tradition, the legal scholar could check the validity of each legal rule by interpreting it in the framework offered by the other rules and in particular by those legal rules that were hierarchically superior. This consistency and completeness of the law required that its production and enforcement were not bounded by the availability of human and other natural resources and that there was no standard economic tradeoff that limited the building of the realm of law. Lon Fuller had aptly observed that if this assumption was removed, law became simply an enterprise to subject human behavior to the observance of rules – an enterprise that could aim at but never achieve the total consistency and completeness of the rules. Standard legal theory was not just simply demanding that an unrealistic amount of resources be dedicated to the setting and enforcement of rules, but also that humans did not face any constraint due to bounded rationality.[4] Thus, the resulting *legal Nirvana* was sustained by an implicit assumption about a sort of *economic Nirvana* where the production and the enforcement of law did not consume scarce economic resources.

Paradoxically, with all their emphasis on economic scarcity, most economists were most unlikely to challenge the lawyers' assumptions. Their own Nirvana depended on a legal Nirvana that was totally consistent with the lawyers' approach. The standard orthodox microeconomic approach assumed, and often still assumes, a world of well-defined property rights that are verified and enforced by a costless third party.[5] This legal Nirvana was, indeed, necessary to obtain the standard efficiency results concerning competitive markets. Thus, with surprising symmetry, the economic Nirvana was sustained by an implicit assumption about a legal Nirvana where property rights could be defined, enforced (and, sometimes, even exchanged) at zero costs.

The categorizing of law and economics into two separate but mutually supporting Nirvanas was indeed based on an assumption of minimum institutional complexity. Most lawyers did not appreciate the institutional complexity of the economic processes underlying the process of production and enforcement of law as well as the (sometimes unexpected) economic consequences of legal rules. At the same time, standard economic theory did not see property rights as institutionally complex legal interactions among people but rather as simple relations among individuals and things to be exchanged (possibly at zero transaction costs).

Since there are many ways of dealing with institutional complexity, it is not surprising that there are many law and economic schools. However, they have all shared the task of removing the traditional disciplinary boundaries that inhibited an appropriate analysis of the relation between legal orderings and economic institutions. In this respect, the outcome of the downfall from Nirvana has been especially rewarding if one considers the nature of the problems that all social scientists had to face in the past two decades.

A massive wave of liberalization and privatization occurred in the 1990s across Europe and more recently in transition economies and in some developing countries together with the enduring processes of regulatory reforms in corporate governance in almost all the developed countries, this has highlighted the need for an interdisciplinary approach aimed at setting out a comprehensive theoretical framework in order to outline the dynamics of the complex interaction between legal orderings and economic institutions. "law and economics" appears to be the sole well-defined field of research capable of addressing these challenges. While traditional "law and economics" covers a number of long investigated topics (such as the economic analysis of contract law, property law and torts, criminal law, competition law, and corporate governance), most scholars would nowadays also include in the list topics such as the theory of the firm, the theories of institutions and regulation, the evolution of norms and behavior, and so on. The resulting picture outlines the need to go beyond the Chicagoan tradition, and even beyond the standard results of the New Institutional Economics approach, in order to assess the full range of interdependencies between legal rules, economic behaviors, motivations, and institutional change. In spite of lively disagreement on many topics,[6] the seminal works by Aaron Director, Ronald Coase, George Stigler, Richard Posner, Frank Easterbrook, Gordon Tullock, Guido Calabresi, Harold Demsetz, and Oliver Williamson among others share the fundamental merit of having outlined the critical role played by an interdisciplinary approach at the intersection of law and economics in order to properly understand "the very stuff of economic policy."[7]

However, many issues are still very controversial and are open for the research agenda. They include the role of rational maximizing agents;[8] the assumption of *homo economicus* with exogenous preferences;[9] the implicit idea of markets always in equilibrium;[10] the role of property rights in providing optimal incentives and the efficiency of markets in realizing Coasean exchanges through well-defined property rights;[11] the relative dominance of public versus private orderings; the optimal role of enforcers (both public and private) as social wealth maximizing agents;[12] the impact of legal origins and institutional diversity and the (im)possibility of the emergence in the long run of efficient legal rules and economic organizations;[13] and the structuring of power relations and of (in)efficient subversion of rules in legal systems, markets, and organizations.[14]

The attention to these controversial themes has not only marked a departure from the legal and economic Nirvanas but also, in some way, a return of both Law and Economics to earlier intellectual traditions where they dealt actively with the problems arising from institutional complexity. As Hodgson (1998) has pointed out, some of these issues were at the heart of the Old Institutionalist tradition of Thorstein Veblen and John R. Commons, a tradition that has been almost neglected by successive developments in economic analysis.[15] Especially, some recent results reached by the so-called behavioral law and economics approach seem surprisingly consistent with the main messages of Old Institutionalism on the role of preferences, motivations, and the nature of property rights.

The contributions to this volume encompass some of the core controversial issues arising from interactions between legal orderings and economic institutions. They include (1) the nature of institutional and legislative change and the emergence of strong institutional complementarity in legal positions, (2) the relationship between private orderings and the role of the state in enforcing contracts and defining property rights, (3) the nature and dynamics of endogenous enforcement, and (4) the analysis of governance models and corporate ethics.

The book is divided into four parts that focus on these stimulating developments. In the following sections of this introduction, we will briefly consider how each of the chapters contained in this book tries to make its contribution to shape the way ahead for the new, lively discipline that has be fallen on earth.

## Complexity and evolutionary paths in framing markets and legal rules

Under the ideal type of perfect competitive markets, there is no role for public, private, or social enforcement of contracts. As in the magic world with zero transaction costs depicted by Coase just as a provocative example in his 1960 article, contracts are simply the exchange of goods and services and the mere fact of economic exchange is an automatic response to the existence of potential gains from trade. In the absence of transaction costs of any kind, goods and services produced and sold at any point in time and in any geographical market will instantaneously end up in the hands of those agents who value them the most, so that "eternity can be experienced in a second."[16] In the neoclassical ideal type, property rights and markets are thus coëxtensive: for every possible use of a resource a property right is defined and, consequently, a corresponding market for exchange. This assumption has guaranteed the traditional results about the optimality of markets: in a world in which transaction costs are absent and property rights are well defined, market exchange tautologically ensures allocative efficiency. Once the neoclassical fiction is abandoned, however, we are faced with a world in which, on the one hand, markets can exist for bundled incomplete property rights, that is for rights in which a relevant part of the potential/available uses of some economic goods has not been defined, and, on the other hand, the real effectiveness and force of "nominal" rights for holders are often defined and/or limited by the extension of corresponding markets, that is by the governance mode and by the degree of competition that characterizes them in a relationship of interdependence and complementarity. In one case, we can have some potential markets inhibited by the process of bundling uses in property rights (as in the case of an intellectual property right very wide in scope). In the other, we can have the case in which having a property right over an asset for which there is no demand at all, or for which there is a monopsony, strictly affects the market value of the right or even the existence of a market for that good.

In a non-neoclassical world, the competitive functioning of markets can – in some instances – be limited by the exercise of rights and, at the same time, the effectiveness of property rights can essentially depend on the characteristics of their market. The interdependence between property rights and markets appears therefore to be a complex and endogenously determined relationship, over which some further research is needed. Starting from the seminal work of Coase (1960), the Chicagoan tradition has been mainly focused on an attempt to design the minimal legal standards aimed at restoring the effectiveness of the market mechanism in maximizing social wealth. According to Posner (1995), "the law tries to make the market work and, failing that, tries to mimic the market."[17] In this attempt, legal rules are complementary to the existing institution of the market. In a sense, the market is an institution which preexists to legal and public intervention, and the task of law (through the *ex ante* legislative process and/or the *ex post* intervention of courts) is simply to fill those gaps in existing markets so as to restore efficiency.[18] Under Posnerian law and economics,[19] the dimension of markets, their functioning, or their equilibrium are somehow independent of legal intervention, apart from the minimal intervention aimed at completing the existing market process. A similar attitude towards the market is expressed by Coase (1937) and Williamson (1988). In New Institutional Economics the market is seen as being an institution complementary to private orderings such as firms and economic organizations. However in this approach there is an internal inconsistency. From one side, firms and economic organizations do emerge as an efficient response to market failure due to high market transaction costs; from the other, property rights allocations within firms always occur in an efficient and costless way so that the firms' control is under the hands of those agents with the highest skills in governance. The outside market is quite often depicted, in New Institutional Economics, as an equilibrium market,[20] and the market for corporate control does not seem to be suffering from the same transactions costs to be which induced the emergence of firms with respect to market transactions. Under the New Institutional approach, the extent of quasi-rents gained by agents by bringing their market transactions within firms, strictly depends on the super-additivity conditions characterizing internal production in firms, whereas the market value of generic transactions is always assumed to be determined by a constant equilibrium price.[21] The main consequence of this approach is that it tends to neglect the impact of power on economic relations, and on the structuring and evolution of private as well as public orderings.[22]

Several chapters in this volume challenge the mainstream view that the market is a given institution that preexists to legal intervention and to public definition of legal rules, procedures, and enforcement devices. In his contribution to this volume, Ulen (Ch. 2) speculates on the future course of scholarship in law and economics. He identifies four areas in which future work is likely to concentrate: the filling-in of gaps in our economic understanding of particular areas of private and public law; the unification of the economic theory across five areas in the law; the expansion of empirical work; and the emendation of the rational choice theory. Under an evolutionary perspective, Douglass North (Ch. 3) provides historical background to the development of economics and its relationship to law and to the growth of a legal system. In particular, Professor North explores the emergence of markets and the way they have evolved. His contribution shows, on one side, how such evolution has been depending upon the ability to have impersonal exchange while on the other, he argues that the evolution of impersonal exchange has required in turn the development of a complex institutional structure of which the rule of law has been a critical part. The main lesson to be drawn is that market dynamics and the degree of legal intervention are co-evolving entities embedded in a complex institutional environment which simultaneously shapes the nature and the extent of legal rules and the way in which markets develop. In this respect, according to North, there is no unique efficient development path in setting legal rules, as in the Posnerian vision of the evolution of the common law system, but rather several potential paths are equally possible according to the relative power exercised by legal origins, interest groups, political pressure, and technological shocks.[23] The nature and the extent of property rights enforcement and even the "mining" of property rights depend on the particular evolutionary path which has been followed in a given institutional system.[24]

Moreover, as Nicita and Savaglio show in their contribution (Ch. 7), while the Coasean approach has deeply emphasized the role of *ex post* transaction costs in absorbing externalities by mutual exchange of rights in the market, the crucial analysis of the role played by *ex ante* transaction costs in inhibiting the *ex ante* definition of property rights is still in its infancy. They point out the fact that, when a reciprocal externality does emerge, it is because there are competing claims between rival uses of a given resource for which clear property rights have not been defined in the first instance. As a consequence, any failure in defining *ex ante* property rights (i.e. rights to exclude non-owners and correlate duties to abstain from interference) would result in a subsequent market failure. Thus, the market as an institution requires as a pre-requisite an authority that, at the very least, is in charge of defining universally some bundle of property rights: an outcome which completely reverses the Posnerian approach to Law and Economics.

This argument is further magnified if we consider not only the definition of property rights but also, more generally, the wide range of legal positions (such as rights, duties, liberties, powers, liabilities, and immunities)[25] that actually characterize a legal system. In his chapter (Ch. 4) Pagano shows how legal positions are linked together by strong institutional complementarities.[26] Legal positions should be interpreted as strong institutional complements since they do not merely satisfy the usual conditions of "weak" institutional complementarity stemming from the fact that legal positions that "fit" each other do marginally better than the ones that do not. Legal positions also define legal equilibria characterized by the social scarcity constraint that is typical of positional goods.[27] Indeed, they can be considered as positional goods defining equilibrium conditions that may be violated *ex ante* but that must hold *ex post* as accounting identities. In this sense, according to Pagano, they define "strong institutional complementarities" supported by the "tight glue" of social scarcity. The positional nature of legal relations implies, in turn, that *ex ante* disequilibrium is very likely to arise and to generate a constant oversupply of positions such as rights and powers with respect to correlated positions such as duties and liabilities. This is especially so when we remove the assumption of perfectly competitive markets in which a right (and its related market) is defined over all possible uses of any asset. At the same time, once we become aware of the emergence of institutional complementarities among legal positions, then we can also explain the structuring of institutional diversity[28] and the evolution of institutions over time according to the complex ruling of legal positions. In Pagano's view, alternative systems of capitalism are characterized by the interplay of the "strong" and "weak" "institutional complementarities" existing among different legal positions, and the other characteristics of the system such as the technology and the nature of the resources. In this way, the *ex ante* disequilibrium, due to the positional nature of legal relations, can spill over to other parts of the economic system. The emergence of institutional complementarities in legal systems affects the conditions that might generate or delay innovation in legislation. Legal systems may thus be characterized by efficient equilibria or inefficient development paths according to the specific way in which institutional complements are crafted.

One instance of inefficient development of the legal system is pointed out by Parisi and Ghei's (Ch. 5), though in a framework rather different from Pagano's. The two authors analogize the process of implementing new laws in an environment of social change to the process of making investment decisions under uncertainty. In their contribution to this volume, Parisi and Ghei outline how in any society that is not totally static, the lawmaker faces uncertainty about its evolution, given that he cannot know with certainty what the appropriate law will be in the future, and therefore cannot know with certainty what the future stream of benefits from the law will be. In addition, implementing a new law requires the outlay of resources in formulating and enforcing the law, just as investment in a new project does. The costs of implementing a new law are largely sunk and irreversible and thus cannot be recovered if the law turns out to be inappropriate in any way. Thus, according to Parisi and Ghei, the lawmaker faces a decision akin to an irreversible investment under uncertainty in which timing of the investment is therefore a critical issue. As a consequence, when the lawmaker chooses to invest in the new law, he gives up the option of waiting to implement the law at some future time. This option is the opportunity cost of investing today. At the same time, there is a cost in delaying the implementation of new laws, due to the decreasing effectiveness of the old laws in the changing social environment. That is, in Parisi and Ghei's view, there is an "opportunity benefit" in investing today. In determining the optimal timing of adoption of new laws, the value of the option of waiting must be taken into account. Parisi and Ghei present a formal model drawn from the investment literature to demonstrate the value of waiting and discuss its implications in the context of two real-world legislative problems, environmental laws and privacy regulations. In both cases, there might be a cost in delaying investment in new laws, in that the damage to the environment or privacy could be irreversible. On the other hand, the benefits of the laws are hard to estimate. In addition, compliance costs might be very large and the value of waiting correspondingly important in the decision to invest in lawmaking.

## Private orderings, legal rules, and the role of the state

Legal positions are also influenced by the way in which private orderings emerge to internalize market transactions. While there is now a broad economic literature on the specific and isolated impact of alternative enforcement mechanisms against free-riding and opportunism in agency relations and incomplete contracts (concerning respectively public enforcement, private enforcement through long-term contracts and hierarchy in firms, implicit contracts, and social norms), few attempts have been made to analyze the impact of both public and private (both judicial and informal) enforcement mechanisms in shaping agents' incentives and motivations when several enforcement rules are jointly at work. In this respect, the study of the emergence of institutional complementarities in a setting in which rules and motivations co-evolve over time could shed new light towards a full understanding of the complex interaction among distinct enforcement devices shaping the institutional environment within which agents make their choices and of the evolution of institutional diversity in alternative economic systems. Indeed, the second part of the volume is dedicated to the analysis of the interdependence between private and public orderings.

The chapter by A. Schwartz (Ch. 6) singles out the proper role of public enforcement of private agreements. Schwartz questions why the state should enforce private agreements and what roles the state should play regarding private agreements in addition to legal enforcement. Public enforcement of private agreements allows parties operating in relatively large economies to make credible promises to perform their agreements. In the absence of public enforcement, the inability to make credible promises would severely limit parties' ability both to make short-term supply contracts in volatile markets and to make long-term supply contracts. In addition, the resulting contractual incompleteness would also severely limit parties' ability to contract for investments that are more productive in a given contractual relationship than elsewhere. According to Schwartz, the poor performance of transition economies with weak legal enforcement underpins the importance of being able to make credible promises to perform. In his view, in Western countries the state perform three roles in connection with enforceable contracts: (1) it regulates the contracting process, (2) it supplies parties with a stock of default rules to govern transactions, and (3) it interprets private agreements in the course of resolving disputes. Schwartz argues that the second function is trivial and suggests how the first and third of these functions should be best performed.

As mentioned, Nicita and Savaglio (Ch. 7) emphasize an additional role for the state that is not explicit in Schwartz's trichotomy: the function of governing the process of continuously defining and redefining property rights when competing claims over rival uses do emerge as a reciprocal negative externality. Nicita and Savaglio compare the Sen's paradox on the Paretian Liberal (1970) and the standard version of the Coase Theorem (1960). The comparison of the two theorems is somehow puzzling: if we accept Sen, then we have to abandon Coase, and vice versa. Nicita and Savaglio formulate a definition of right and of externality which shows a *possibility result* for a Paretian Liberal by applying the Coase Theorem in its textbook version. They formulate the notion of a Coasean Liberal in which well-defined rights always follow social preferences. Then they show an *impossibility result* for a Coasean Liberal by applying the Sen Theorem in a world of incomplete or undefined rights. What generates a possibility result for a Paretian Liberal thus shows also the conditions for an impossibility result for a Coasean Liberal, unless any hierarchy of social preferences is introduced by any allocation of complete rights in order to induce social preferences to follow rights. As a consequence, when agents fail to properly define a set of rights over the social choice domain, a Coasean Liberal is inhibited even in a world of zero (*ex post*) transaction costs. The state, as a producer of public ordering, thus can assume several distinct forms of regulation, and the degree of market regulation very often rises with liberalization process as long as the process of market creation always requires a correlated process of rights redefinition. Hence in a world of incomplete definition of rights, externalities abound and redefinition of rights by a hierarchical authority is necessary in order to reach socially optimal outcome.

One very clear example of the question concerning the process of unbundling and redefinition of property rights is given by the current debate regarding the governance of intellectual property (IP) rights. Controversies over what should constitute intellectual property swirl around business methods, computer software, research tools in the biomedical industry, and genetic sequences. Gallini and Scotchmer's (Ch. 8) reviews what economists have said about incentive schemes to promote R&D, including intellectual property. In some of the examples provided, the incentive mechanisms alternative to intellectual property involves social costs that recourse to the latter would avoid. Gallini and Scotchmer thus comment on whether the design recommendations of economists can actually be implemented and argue that IP regimes should be designed so that the subject matter of each one has relatively homogeneous needs for protection, thereby reversing one of the main conclusions of standard analysis of IP in law and economics. In reviewing the most recent contributions on the characteristics of the optimal design of IP rights, Gallini and Scotchmer highlight the crucial role that private contracting plays in affecting the determination of optimal policy. The question of whether economic agents are able to bargain over the transfer and rearrangement of rights over their intellectual creations deeply affects the effectiveness of IP-induced incentives, especially in a context of cumulative innovation. This suggests the opportunity of different policy options when confronting issues at the interface between IP and antitrust legislation.

The interaction between private ordering and public ordering and the degree of intervention by the state is often affected by considerations regarding not only efficiency requirements but also fairness attributes. While recent contributions[29] outline how the assessment of a legal policy should depend exclusively on its effects on individuals' welfare, Denozza emphasizes in his piece (Ch. 9) how the opposite could in some cases be necessary. According to Denozza, the analysis of Kaplow and Shavell's argument confirms that welfare economics cannot provide autonomous criteria to assess legal policies. Neither the scrutiny of the preferences of the affected individuals nor simple computations (as the sum of several distinct well-beings) are able to deliver unequivocal suggestions to policy analysts and decision makers. Resorting to external value judgments (with respect to welfare economics) is unavoidable according to Denozza, and for any usual meaning of the word, fairness provides the appropriate framework within which these value judgments have to be considered. Fairness and welfare do not lie on the same level playfield. While welfare can provide a descriptive framework for classifying different states of the world, only fairness is able to provide a normative framework for assessing legal policies, that is to say for choosing among possible states of the world characterized by different distributions of welfare. In this sense, in Denozza's view, fairness and welfare should not be intended as competing values.

## Contractual incompleteness and the nature of endogenous enforcement

The incompleteness of contracts constitutes a sort of paradigm for law and economics,[30] since the questions it poses cut across almost all economic problems that entail a legal solution. This is why the incomplete contract framework has been applied to a wide range of research fields in law and economics, covering, among other issues, the theory of the firm and economic organizations, the study of corporate governance and finance, the design of liberalization and privatization policies, the governance of IP, and international trade. Since incompleteness raises relevant transaction costs, incomplete contracts are a potential source of market failure. In order to minimize transaction costs, an appropriate institutional environment has to be designed in order to enforce parties' obligations against opportunism and renegotiation. The law and economics of incomplete contracts thus is a privileged field of research for the compared analysis of transaction costs associated with the legal rules and the private solutions meant to guarantee parties' performance.

One way of clarifying some essential features of incomplete contracts is to distinguish between exogenous and endogenous incompleteness.[31] Roughly speaking, exogenous incomplete contracts refer to a dimension of contractual unverifiability that is independent of parties' actions. On the contrary, endogenous incomplete contracts refer to the idea that the degree of (un)verifiability in a contract could be also explicitly determined by contractual parties who may deliberately decide to leave unspecified some essential contractual terms in the presence of uncertainty.[32] This distinction is important since it outlines two opposite and somehow contradictory, effects of contractual incompleteness on parties' attitudes to perform contractual obligations. When the degree of unverifiability is exogenous, it has the effect of weakening the probability for parties to achieve a contractual agreement in the first place, given that at least one party could be exposed to the counterpart's post-contractual opportunism at the renegotiation stage (opportunism). When the degree of unverifiability is explicitly agreed upon by parties, it may support contract formation and encourage parties' performance (adaptation).

Part III of this volume contains several chapters aimed at uncovering new relevant features of contractual incompleteness. While Anderlini and Felli show how in a Coasean framework incompleteness may result in a recursive hold-up problem, the chapter by Farina outlines possible solutions to incompleteness, based on game theory applications, suggesting how some design of legal rules may overcome the dramatic problem of hold-up. Peyton Young's and Battistini's contributions, on the other side, emphasize the role of customs, social norms, and local institutions in creating an institutional environment that overcomes the pervasive risk of post-contractual opportunism.

The model provided by Anderlini and Felli (Ch. 10) refers to a framework in which two parties have each to pay an *ex ante* cost to be able to draw up a contingent contract that allows them to share risk. They show that this situation may give rise to a basic "hold-up" problem that will generate under-investment in the *ex ante* contractual costs. This in turn may cause the resulting contract to be incomplete. Anderlini and Felli verify this claim both in a setting in which the choice of *ex ante* costs is "lumpy" and in a model with a continuous choice of *ex ante* costs. They also analyze a static and a dynamic principal–agent model in which the basic hold-up problem may give rise to contracts that are incomplete in a well-defined sense.

Farina (Ch. 11) provides a game-theoretic – sequential or multi-period – representation of the current definitions of contractual incompleteness with particular reference to cases in which the nature of incompleteness stems from the fact that a court cannot complete the contract, and thus there is no way in which the parties' strategies and beliefs could be consistently aligned. Farina shows the case in which the parties, by using the game-theoretic solution concept of "mixed strategies," may reduce the occurrence of litigation in the implementation of the contract, thus providing a conceptual framework for explaining endogenous enforcement even when a strong notion of incompleteness has characterized market exchange.

The standard New Institutionalist analysis of opportunism in an incomplete contract framework is mainly based on the assumption of self-interested agents with exogenous preferences. This approach thus replicates standard "nirvana" assumptions of perfect competitive markets. As Bowles and Gintis (1993) have pointed out, "the Walrasian general equilibrium model is based on an artificially truncated concept of self-interested behavior, depicting a charming but utopian world in which conflicts abound but a promise is a promise."[33] The idea that moral commitment may act as an enforcement device in incomplete contract has been studied, among others, by Kreps (1990), Crémer (1993), Lazear (1995), and Hodgson (1996), who emphasized the role played by reputation in favoring implicit and self-enforcing cooperation in repeated interactions.[34] In many situations, the endogenous enforcement devices represented by trigger strategies and optimal penal codes in infinitely repeated prisoner dilemmas might even be cheaper than building detailed and complicated contracts. Given that with trigger strategies players' deviations from cooperating are punished by other players' refusal to cooperate in the future, a "good reputation" represents a powerful tool to minimize transaction costs in incomplete contracts[35] and to enhance reciprocal trust. In this respect, firms should be interpreted as repeating players who may develop an internal system of contractual enforcement based on reputation and on "corporate culture," that is, on a dominant set of norms which guides the way in which work is accomplished within the organization.

The contribution by Peyton Young (Ch. 12) analyzes the emergence of an endogenous enforcement device in the form of a customary contract. A customary contract is a set of terms that is standard in a given local area for a given economic purpose. Once established, such a standard tends to perpetuate itself because it creates expectations about what is fair and appropriate in a given type of economic bargain. Peyton Young proposes a dynamic model of how contractual customs form endogenously. Agents are situated in a geographical or social space, and they recontract periodically based on expected returns, focal properties of the contract, and its conformity with local practice. The model predicts that the most likely geographic pattern consists of "patches" where contractual terms are nearly uniform, separated by boundaries where contractual norms jump from one set of terms to another. Differences in regional customs are roughly related to average differences in economic fundamentals, but they mask the considerable amount of heterogeneity that exists within regions. Finally, Peyton Young compares these predictions with contractual practice in contemporary Illinois agriculture and finds considerable support for the model's predictions.

A similar perspective is offered by Battistini in his contribution (Ch. 13). The chapter introduces a notion of intermediate degree of specificity in order to explain the combination between market and non-market coordination mechanisms typically associated with the local industrial systems governance structure in a context of incomplete contracts. More specifically, it is shown that, when investments are in principle imitable, a group of investors may find it profitable to reduce the hold-up risk by making investments that are *not* specific to their particular relationships with their individual counterparts (taken one by one), but are specific to the *set* of their relationships with their counterparts (taken as a group). Then, the corresponding grouping form of economic organizations is presented as a way to reduce the organizational cost of specificity without depressing the *ex ante* incentives to invest. An independent result of the analysis consists of clarifying to what extent asset specificity can be thought of as creating value.

## Governance models and corporate ethics

The incomplete contract framework also helps in explaining the emergence of diversity in corporate governance models. In recent years, an extensive body of work has dealt with the issue of convergence versus diversity in corporations' ownership and control in contemporary economic systems. Most of these works have compared corporate governance models under the lens of the New Institutional Economics theory of the firm, stressing the role of the legal nature of corporations beside the traditional agency costs theories (Allen and Gale, 2000; Becht *et al.*, 2002). The main question addressed recently by a wide scholarly literature is whether one or another national corporate governance system possesses some relative competitive advantage in the global market so as to overcome national diversities and to move towards a global model of governance which shapes markets and firms. According to this literature two main systems of corporate governance might be distinguished (Bratton and McCahery, 1999; Allen and Gale, 2000): a *market system* characterized by dispersed shareholding and thick, liquid trading markets, and a *hierarchical control system* characterized by a hard control exerted over the management by a principal or a coalition of principals (banks, families, etc.) and thin trading and noncontrolling stakes. While the former system may be found in the USA and the UK, the latter has been experienced, although with many differences, in Germany, Italy, and Japan, among other countries. Some of these systems, such as the German and the Japanese systems, are now subject to economic and institutional crises. This leaves unsolved the problem of convergence *versus* diversity in corporate models.

Recent works have emphasized the role of historical conditions and legal origins in shaping path-dependency and diversity in corporate governance patterns (Djankov *et al.*, 2003; Nicita and Pagano, 2003; Bebchuk and Roe, 2004; Becht and Delong, 2004; Schmidt and Spindler, 2004), while some others have announced "the end of history" in corporate governance models (Hansmann and Kraakman, 2004).

Part IV of the book tries to contribute to the debate by analyzing the structuring of corporate governance models in several distinct frameworks and by outlining the main function that a firm performs in reproducing internal quasi-judicial structures beside public orderings. Iwai (Ch. 14) begins his chapter with a question, "what really is a corporation?" In his view, the law speaks of a corporation as a "legal person," that is, as a subject of rights and duties capable of owning real property, entering into contracts, and suing and being sued in its own name separate and distinct from its shareholders. For many centuries there has been heated controversy between corporate nominalists and corporate realists as to the "essence" of this soulless and bodiless person. The first purpose of Iwai's chapter is thus to end this age-old "corporate personality controversy" once and for all. This is done, however, not by declaring victory for one side or the other, but by declaring victory for both. The key to this claim is the observation that an incorporated firm is composed of not one but two ownership relations: the shareholders own the corporation and the corporation in turn owns the corporate assets. The corporation thus plays, in Iwai's view, a dual role of a "person" and a "thing" in the system of law. Iwai then shows how this person–thing duality of a corporation is capable of generating two seemingly contradictory corporate structures, one "nominalistic" and the other "realistic." He also suggests that these two variants of corporate structure respectively correspond to an American-style corporation that is expected to maximize the returns to shareholders and a Japanese-style corporation that strives to reproduce its organization as a going concern. Iwai also reexamines the theory of corporate governance. The fact that an incorporated firm is characterized by a two-tier ownership structure implies, for Iwai, that corporate managers cannot be regarded as agents of shareholders, rather they should be considered to be "fiduciaries" of the corporation. Iwai's conclusion is thus to advocate the return to the pre-law-and-economics orthodoxy, maintaining that the foundation of every corporate governance system should be the managers' fiduciary duties to the corporation and that the law governing these duties should be essentially mandatory. The variety of corporate governance systems across countries is thus due, in Iwai's view, to the difference in governance mechanisms that supplement the costly implementation of fiduciary law by courts.

In a similar line of reasoning, Fabrizio Cafaggi outlines in his contribution (Ch. 15), various ways in which juridical systems uphold the relevance of differing interests in private organizations, especially corporations and, to a lesser extent, nonprofit organizations. The chapter specifies that different legal devices are used to protect these interests and then it frames the issue of governance within the debate on the combined use of social norms and legal rules. Cafaggi questions the current understanding that organizations, due to their hierarchical structure, use social norms more than legal rules to define their governance structures by pointing out that protection of relevant stakeholders is generally assured by contracts and that social norms operate within these relationships in the framework of contracts that are generally incomplete. He thus approaches the question of governance as a crucial issue in relational interdependencies. The incompleteness of corporate contracts in Cafaggi's view is affected by, and itself affects, incompleteness of financing, supply, customer, and labor contracts. In this respect, the issue of the choices among different models of corporate governance should be addressed in terms of a comparative assessment of the best "technologies" of contracts completion. In the third section of the chapter Cafaggi shows that the debate has developed within a dominant, vertically integrated, model of the firm, and thus different conceptual lenses and legal devices should be used when networks of firms are considered. In particular, he explores the difficulties of applying the stakeholder/shareholder debate to networks of firms, and of defining fiduciary duties as granting accountability of the network and of the firms participating in the network. It redefines the content of loyalty and care in a fairly unstable environment, where cooperation and competition often complement each other. Cafaggi concludes with a research agenda to examine the web of relationships of a juridical nature operating in a network of firms.

Lorenzo Sacconi (Ch. 16) closes the final part with a submission analyzing under a new perspective the question of authority and control in a firm under an incomplete contract framework. According to Sacconi, ownership and control structures respond to a need for minimizing some transaction costs, but he also admits the potential risk of abuse of authority. Both empirical investigation and theoretical deduction from the theory of firms suggest that corporations need systems of self-regulatory norms of behavior like codes of ethics exactly because of the "abuse of authority" problem. According to Sacconi, a code of ethic conduct should at least answer the question of how whoever holds authority in the firm may undertake commitments over events and situations that cannot be ex ante contractible nor describable. Sacconi suggests thus a first modeling of unforeseen contingencies in terms of fuzzy sets theory. Incomplete knowledge about unforeseen contingencies is captured in his chapter by defining some events as fuzzy sub-sets of the set of unforeseen states of the world. Such events correspond to terms of the *ex ante* language used to define the domain of general abstract principles. The cost of their all-encompassing nature is vagueness. This approach opens the route to define domains of abstract principles as fuzzy sets of unforeseen states of the world.

* * *

The main message coming from the contributions collected in this volume suggests that the relationship between legal orderings and economic institutions is far from being understood under the traditional lens of law and economics and new institutional economics. Transactions occur in a given institutional framework, in which economic, legal, and organizational issues are bundled in a complex institutional order, shaping all the relevant agents and their actions. The impact of legal change needs to be assessed and predicted under a wide and enlarged framework according to actual behavior of real-life agents. This approach could thus be employed to analyze the emergence of self-enforcing, path-dependent equilibria in the governance of transactions between economic and legal domains, so as to explain the variety of legal systems, and the structuring of alternative governance systems for transactions according to historical local conditions. When legal relations are inconsistent this does not simply mean that there is a better alternative where they would fit (that defines a case of weak complementarity) but also that the consequent mismatch in the expectations of the agents will cause some costly conflict in the economic system (that defines a case of strong complementarity). Both public and private orderings are costly and imperfect systems to align expectations *ex ante* and avoid costly conflicts *ex post.* Their institutional comparative advantage depends on the relations of complementarity that exist between the legal system and other domains where individuals exercise their choices and, in turn, the relative efficiency of these other institutional domains depends on the arrangements that prevail in the other domains. No one of these domains must be assumed to be an independent Nirvana that could support the efficiency of the other domains.[36] It is the absence of this Nirvana assumption that, in our opinion, should set the future research agenda for law and economics. A complex approach towards a full understanding of legal and economic rules shaping transactions dynamically is still in its infancy.

## Acknowledgment

We would like to thank for helpful comments Roberto Galbiati, Matteo Rizzolli, Alessandra Rossi, and Riccardo Vannini.

## Notes

1 See Backhaus (1999), Mercuro and Medema (1997), and Shavell (2004).
2 Mercuro and Medema (1997), pp. ix–x.
3 See Nicita and Pagano (2005a).
4 According to Fuller (1969 p. 44) when human societies aspire to subject human behavior to the governance of rules, "the principle of marginal utility plays an increasing role in our decisions." In this case, "something like an economic calculation may become necessary when a conflict arises between the internal and the external morality of law."
5 For a critique to standard definition of property rights in law and economics and the need for a theory of the incompleteness of property rights see Nicita and Rizzolli (2004).
6 For a review of the differences among Coase, Posner, and Williamson, see Coase (1993a,b), Posner (1993), and Williamson (1993).
7 See Coase (1988), p. 31.
8 See for a critique, Sunstein (2000).
9 See Bowles and Gintis (1993).
10 See Franzini (1993).
11 See Usher (1998).
12 See Maki (1998).
13 See also Mattei and Cafaggi (1998).
14 Pagano (1993), Pagano and Rowthorn (1996), Bowles and Gintis (1993), and Glaeser and Shleifer (2003).
15 It is really surprising that two main textbooks in law and economics, such as Cooter and Ulen (1997) and Shavell (2004), do not even quote these eminent scholars.
16 Coase (1988), p. 15.
17 Posner (1995), p. 416.
18 Pagano (2000).
19 Posner (1993) and Williamson (1993).
20 Franzini (1993).
21 Nicita (2001).
22 See Bowles *et al.* (1999).

23 A similar argument has been recently developed by Glaeser and Shleifer (2003). According to Glaeser and Shleifer, "whatever law enforcement strategy the society chooses, private individuals will seek to subvert its workings to benefit themselves. The efficiency of alternative institutional arrangements depends in part on their vulnerability to such subversion."
24 See also Cole and Grossman (1999).
25 See Commons (1924) and Cole and Grossman (1999).
26 See also Aoki (2001), Topkis (1998), Milgrom and Roberts (1990).
27 See Hirsch (1978) and Pagano (1999).
28 Pagano (2001).
29 Kaplow and Shavell (2001) and Kaplow and Shavell (2003).
30 See Hart (1995) and Nicita and Pagano (2005a).
31 See Shavell (2004).
32 See Nicita and Pagano (2005a).
33 Bowles and Gintis (1993).
34 Kreps (1990), Crémer (1993), Lazear, (1995), and Hodgson (1996).
35 Hermalin (1999).
36 See Nicita and Pagano (2005b).

## References

Allen, F. and D. Gale (2000), *Comparing Financial Systems*, MIT Press, Cambridge, MA.

Aoki, M. (2001), *Toward a Comparative Institutional Analysis*, MIT Press, Cambridge, MA.

Backhaus, J. (1999), "Introduction," in J. Backhaus (ed.), *The Elgar Companion to Law and Economics*, Edward Elgar, pp. 1–4.

Bebchuk Lucian and Roe Mark J. (2004), "A theory of path dependence in corporate ownership and governance," in Gordon Jeffrey N. and Roe Mark J. (eds), *Convergence and Persistence in Corporae Law*, Cambridge University Press, Cambridge, pp. 69–114.

Becht Marco and DeLong J. Bradford (2004), "Has there been so little block holding in America," in Morck Randall K. (ed.), *A History of Corporate Governance around the World. Family Business Groups to Professional Managers*, The University of Chicago Press, Chicago, IL and London, pp. 613–660.

Becht, M., P. Bolton, and A. Röell (2002), "Corporate governance and control," *ECGI Finance Working Paper* 02.

Bowles, S. (2003), *Microeconomics: Behavior, Institutions, and Evolution*, Princeton University Press, Princeton, NJ.

Bowles, S. and H. Gintis (1993), "The revenge of *homo economicus*: post-Walrasian economics and the revival of political economy," *Journal of Economic Perspectives*, 7(1): 83–102.

Bowles, S., Franzini, M., and Pagano, U. (2000), "The politics and economics of power," *The Economics Journal*, 110(467): F764–F765.

Bratton, W. and J. McCahery (1999), "Comparative corporate governance and the theory of the firm: the case against global cross reference," *Columbia Journal of Transnational Law*, 38: 213–297.

Brousseau, E. and J.M. Glachant (eds) (2002), *The Economics of Contracts*, Cambridge University Press, Cambridge.

Coase, R. (1937), "The nature of the firm," *Economica*, November: 386–405.

Coase, R. (1960), "The problem of social costs," *Journal of Law and Economics*, 3.

Coase, R. (1988), *The Firm, the Market and the Law*, The University of Chicago Press, Chicago, IL.

Coase, R. (1993a), "Coase on posner on coase and concluding comment," *Zeitschrift für die Gesamte Staatswissenschaft (Journal of Institutional and Theoretical Economics)*, 149(96): 360.

Coase, R. (1993b), "Law and economics at Chicago," *Journal of Law and Economics*, 36: 239–254.

Cole, D. and P. Grossman (1999), "The meaning of property rights: law vs. economics?" forthcoming in *Land Economics*.

Commons, J.R. (1924), *Legal Foundations of Capitalism*, Transaction Publ. and D. Cole and P. Grossman (1999).

Commons, J.R. (1934), *Institutional Economics*, University of Wisconsin Press, Madison, WI.

Commons, J.R. (1970), *The Economics of Collective Action*, University of Wisconsin Press, Madison, WI.

Cooter, R. and T. Ulen (1997), *Law and Economics* (2nd edition), Addison-Wesley, Reading, MA.

Crémer, J. (1993), "Corporate culture and shared knowledge," *Industrial and Corporate Change*, 2(3): 351–386.

Djankov, Simeon, Edward Glaeser, Rafael La Porta, Florencio Lopez-de-Silanes, and Andre Shleifer (2003) "The new comparative economics," *Journal of Comparative Economics*, Elsevier, 31(4): 595–619.

Franzini, M. (1993), "The market as complex institutional order," *Quaderni del Dip.to di Economia Politica*, University of Siena.

Fuller, L.L. (1969), *The Morality of Law* (revised edition), Yale University Press, New Haven, CT and London.

Furubotn, E. and R. Richter (1997), *Institutions and Economic Theory*, University of Michigan Press, Ann Arbor, MI.

Glaeser, E. and A. Shleifer (2003), "The rise of the regulatory state," *Journal of Economic Literature* XLI (June): 401–425.

Hansmann Henry and Kraakman Reinier (2004), "The end of history of corporate law," in Gordon Jeffrey N. and Roe Mark J. (eds), *Convergence and Persistence in Corporate Law*, Cambridge University Press, Cambridge, pp. 33–68.

Hart, O. (1995), *Firms, Contracts and Financial Structure*, Oxford University Press, Oxford.

Hermalin, B.E. (1999), "Economics & corporate culture," SSRN, Mimeo. Data accesso.

Hirsch, F. (1978), *Social Limits to Growth*, Routledge, London.

Hodgson, G. (1996) (prima? Dopo? O mai questa virgola?) "Corporate Culture and the Nature of the Firm," in J. Groenewegen (ed.), *Transaction Cost Economics and Beyond*, Kluwer Academic Press, Boston, MA.

Hodgson, G.M. (1998), "The approach of institutional economics," *Journal of Economic Literature*, 36(1): 166–192.

Kaplow, L. and S. Shavell (2001), "Fairness versus welfare," *Harvard Law Review*, 114: 961.

Kaplow, L. and S. Shavell (2003), "Fairness versus welfare: notes on the pareto principle, preferences, and distributive justice," *Journal of Legal Studies*.

Kreps, D. (1990), "Corporate culture and economic theory," in J. Alt and K. Shepsle (eds), *Perspectives on Positive Political Economy*, Cambridge University Press, Cambridge.

La Porta, R., F. Lopez-de-Silanes, A. Shleifer, and R.W. Vishny (1998), "Law and finance," *Journal of Political Economy*, 106(6): 1113–1155.

Lazear, E.P. (1995), "Corporate culture and the diffusion of values," in Horst Siebert (ed.), *Trends in Business Organization*, Tübingen, Germany, J.C.B. Mohr (Paul Siebeck).

Maki, U. (1998), "Against Posner against Coase against Theory," *Cambridge Journal of Economics*, 22(5): 587–595.

Mattei, U. and F. Cafaggi (1998), "Comparative law and economics," in P. Newman (ed.), *The New Palgrave Dictionary of Economics and the Law: Volume 1*, Macmillan, London and Basingstoke, pp. 346–352.

Mercuro, M. and S.G. Medema (1997), *Economics and the Law. From Posner to Post-Modernism*, Princeton University Press, Princeton, NJ.

Milgrom, P. and J. Roberts (1990), "Rationalizability, learning and equilibrium games with strategic complementarities," *Econometrica*, 59: 511–528.

Nicita, A. (2001), "The firm as an evolutionary enforcement device," in A. Nicita and U. Pagano (eds), *The Evolution of Economic Diversity*, Routledge, London, pp. 240–270.

Nicita, A. and U. Pagano (2003), "Corporate governance and institutional complementarities: the co-evolution of 'finance' and 'technology,'" Paper presented at the thirteenth Annual Meeting of the American Law and Economics Association, September 20–21, 2003.

Nicita, A. and U. Pagano (2005a), "Incomplete contracts and institutions," in *The Elgar Companion to Law and Economics* (2nd edition), J. Backhaus (ed.), Edward Elgar.

Nicita, A. and U. Pagano (2005b), "Law and economics in retrospect," in E. Brousseau and J.-M. Glachant (eds), *New Institutional Economics. A Textbook*, Cambridge University Press, Cambridge.

Nicita, A. and M. Rizzolli (2004), "Much ado about the cathedral. Property rules and liability rules when rights are incomplete," *Siena Memos and Papers in Law and Economics*, SIMPLE 22/04, University of Siena.

Pagano, U. (1993), "Organisational equilibria and institutional stability," in S. Bowles, H. Gintis, and B. Gustafson (eds), *Markets and Democracy*, Cambridge University Press, Cambridge.

Pagano, U. (1999), "Is power an economic good?" in S. Bowles, M. Franzini, and U. Pagano (eds), *The Politics and Economics of Power*, Routledge, London.

Pagano, U. (2000), "Public markets, private orderings and corporate governance," *International Review of Law and Economics*, 20: 453–477.

Pagano, U. (2001), "The origin of organizational species," in A. Nicita and U. Pagano (eds), *The Evolution of Economic Diversity*, Routledge, London, pp. 240–270.

Pagano, U. and R. Rowthorn (1994), "Ownership, technology and institutional stability," *Structural Change and Economic Dynamics*, 5(2): 221–243.

Pagano, U. and R. Rowthorn (1996), "The competitive selection of democratic firms," in Pagano U. and R. Rowthorn (eds), *Democracy and Efficiency in the Economic Enterprise*, Routledge, London.

Posner, R. (1993), "The new institutional economics meets law and economics," *Journal of Institutional and Theoretical Economics*, 149(1): 73–87.

Posner, R. (1995), *Overcoming Law*, Harvard University Press, Cambridge, MA, p. 416.

Schimdt Reinhard and Spindler Gerald (2004), "Path dependence and complementarity in corporate governance," in Gordon Jeffrey N. and Roe Mark J. (eds.), *Convergence and Persistence in Corporate Law*, Cambridge University Press, Cambridge, pp. 114–128.

Shavell, S. (2004), *Foundations of Economic Analysis of Law*, Harvard University Press.

Sunstein, Cass, R. (ed.) (2000), *Behavioral Law and Economics*, Cambridge University Press, Cambridge.

Topkis, D.M. (1998), *Supermodularity and Complementarity*, Princeton University Press, Princeton, NJ.

Usher, D. (1998), "The Coase theorem is tautological, incoherent or wrong," *Economics Letters*, 61: 3–11.

Williamson, O.E. (1985), *The Economic Institutions of Capitalism*, The Free Press, New York.

Williamson, O.E. (1988), "Corporate finance and corporate governance," *Journal of Finance*, 43: 567–591.

Williamson, O.E. (1993), "Transaction cost economics meets Posnerian law and economics," *Journal of Institutional and Theoretical Economics*, 149(1): 99–118.

# Part I

# Complexity in law and economics

# 2 The future of law and economics

*Thomas S. Ulen*

## Introduction

Law and economics has been one of the most successful innovations in the legal academy in the last century. This intellectual revolution began modestly in the 1960s and 1970s with a few important and innovative articles[1] and a comprehensive, masterful text,[2] that showed the possibilities of the field. Then, in the 1980s the field exploded into respectability and prominence – becoming a regular course in the curricula of the best law schools, a vibrant legal research style that figured in a torrent of important books and articles, a force that transformed many faculty from exclusive practitioners of traditional doctrinal research to practitioners of a more social-science-oriented research, and a substantial justification for important public policy changes.[3] By the early 1990s, economic analysis suffused a modern legal education, even one devoid of an explicit course in law and economics.

This Symposium at the University of Wisconsin School of Law is a particularly appropriate occasion on which to take stock of the current state of law and economics and to speculate on its future. First, both the state and this school have a century-long tradition (the "Wisconsin idea") of close cooperation between scholarly innovations and good government, a tradition of which, I believe, law and economics is a modern manifestation. Second, the University of Wisconsin School of Law has its own distinguished tradition of innovation in legal scholarship.[4] Several of its renowned faculty have made important contributions to law and economics,[5] and others have contributed to – indeed, led – another important modern innovation in legal scholarship, the law and society movement.[6]

I speculate in this chapter on where the field of law and economics is headed. It helps to begin such an enterprise by seeing where the field has been, and so I start with a very brief statement of what I take to be the central tenets of law and economics and of some of the defining conclusions of the law-and-economics literature in selected areas of the law. Then, I turn to my main points about the future of law and economics. Let me state those points and thereby explain my title.

I believe that there are four central developments that will occur in law and economics in the near future. First, the existing gaps in our economic understanding of legal rules, processes, and institutions will be filled. These gaps run from relatively minor ones – such as minor tidying-up in some aspects of, say, contract law – to far broader ones – such as an economic understanding of comparative law and of the appropriate relationships among the market, private law, and public law.[7] Second, I speculate that economic theory will prove to be the force that provides a unifying theory among the now-distinct areas of private law, between private and public law, between law and social norms, and between different national legal systems. Third, I am confident that law and economics, in conjunction with law and society, will foster the empirical study of legal rules and institutions. Fourth, I am hopeful that law and economics will lead to a richer descriptive theory of human decision-making than any now in use in the social sciences. Taken together, these four developments will place the law and law and economics on far firmer ground than they now inhabit.

## The present of law and economics

Before we can speculate about the future of law and economics, we need to have a sense of where it is at the moment. I do not mean to give an exhaustive overview of the field but rather to focus on a few isolated areas, a few selected snapshots, as it were, in order to take stock of where the field has brought us. I shall begin with some very generally distinguishing characteristics of the use of economic analysis of law and then turn to some examples of disparate areas of the law.

### *Generally*

The single most important contribution that law and economics has made to the law is the use of a coherent theory of human decision-making ("rational choice theory") to examine how people are likely to respond to legal rules. A closely related contribution, but one that does not rise to the level of originality of the use of rational choice theory, is the emphasis that law and economics puts on examining legal rules from an *ex ante* perspective. The *ex ante* perspective asks of a legal rule or institution, "How will a rational actor behave when confronted with this rule or institution?" Let me briefly comment on both of these contributions, laying more emphasis on the novel aspects of rational choice theory as the central innovation of law and economics.

Prior to the advent of law and economics, the study of the law did not have a coherent theory of decision-making, largely because it did not need such a theory. Law was an autonomous discipline.[8] Doctrinal research, the scholarly manifestation of this autonomy, does not pay particular attention to how people respond to legal rules, nor to the policy issues raised by law. Therefore, doctrinal research had no need to theorize about decision-making. In criticism, the legal realists stressed, among other things, the social consequences of law, but their attempts to be clear about those consequences were never fully realized, in part because of their inability to provide a theory of how actors might respond to legal rules.

Because law and economics (and law and society) laid such great stress on the social consequences of law, and because they began their inquiries from a social scientific model, these fields inevitably required a theory of how actors respond to legal rules and institutions and, quite naturally, turned to contiguous social-science disciplines for help.[9] And there was a theory ready-to-hand: rational choice theory. Whatever flaws we might ultimately find in that theory, it is not at all mysterious as to why the theory caught on in the law so quickly: it has the great virtues of providing a coherent account of human decision-making and of being a useful guide to predicting a wide range of human behaviors.

The second and, I think, lesser innovation of law and economics – the *ex ante* perspective – is also foreign to doctrinal analysis, although perhaps not so foreign as is rational choice theory. The *ex ante* perspective focuses attention on how a rational actor would respond to a given legal rule, process, or institution.[10] There are both positive and normative aspects to this perspective. The positive aspect is merely descriptive; it perceives legal rules, processes, and institutions as creating "prices" on behaviors and analyzes the likely responses to those prices using rational choice theory. For instance, if the monetary damages imposed on a contract breacher constitute the "price" for engaging in breach of contract, the *ex ante* perspective asks how contractual parties will respond to changes in that relative price.[11] By contrast, the normative *ex ante* perspective seeks to establish the socially optimal (efficient) price to be contained in legal rules.[12] A normative analysis of contract breach could determine the socially optimal amount of breach and suggest what remedy would be most likely to lead to that amount of breach.

We turn now to examples of how rational choice theory and the *ex ante* perspective have been used to analyze legal rules, processes, and institutions.

### *The Coase Theorem*

One of the threshold questions that any legal analysis must answer is whether a legal rule is necessary to achieve a social end or whether other social devices – such as the "market" or prevailing social norms – are better able to guide decision-makers to the desired social end. It could be that the self-regarding motives of voluntary transactors are a sufficient basis on which to achieve social goals; that is, private ordering through consensual agreements between rational actors could cause the internalization of all externalities and other market imperfections.[13] If that were the case, then the law could add little to the ability of voluntary exchange to achieve efficiency (save, perhaps, by facilitating consensual agreements). Indeed, law might impede the process, by, for example, causing actors inefficiently to spend resources getting around the legal constraints or by inducing unintended (and inefficient) consequences. One of the important lessons of law and economics is the recognition that this reliance upon market transactions to achieve social ends can occur only when the costs of effectuating these transactions are very low – so low that, whenever there is a cooperative surplus between any two potential transactors, they will find a means of splitting that surplus and thereby mutually benefiting. This is, of course, the famous Coase Theorem.[14]

The applications of these important insights are legion and widely familiar. As an illustration, consider the famous Calabresi–Melamed extension of the

Coase Theorem to the issue of choice of remedy.[15] They argue that a court should choose between compensatory money damages (what they call a "liability rule") and equitable relief (such as an injunction or an order for specific performance, which remedies they call "property rules") on the basis of the transaction costs between the disputants. Specifically, if the transaction costs are low, then a property rule is the more efficient remedy, and if the transaction costs are high, then a liability rule is the more efficient remedy. An application of this observation is that the remedy for environmental harms, if those are dealt with as private wrongs, should generally be a payment of compensatory money damages because the transaction costs between the wrongdoer and the victims are likely to be so high that a mutually satisfactory solution to the wrong by consent is beyond the reach of the parties. An injunction prohibiting the environmental wrong might result in an inefficiency: the victims may collectively value the right to be free from the wrong less than the wrongdoer values the right to continue the wrong, but the injunction would never foster a bargain in which the polluter pays those harmed and continues to pollute, a result that may be socially desirable.[16] That is, there is a cooperative surplus to be divided, but that surplus will not be realized unless the parties perform the hypothetical market transaction implied by an award of compensatory money damages.

The general lesson to be drawn from the Coase Theorem has to do with the likelihood of private parties' dividing up a cooperative surplus and, closely related, the appropriate social division of authority as between voluntary exchange and legal regulation. Operationalizing the theorem consists largely in developing a facility at identifying factors that cause the costs of reaching voluntary agreements to be high – such things as the number of people involved and the uniqueness or fungibility of the item or performance at issue. The theorem's analysis is important, clear, and straightforward in application.

### *Contract law*

Turn now to the consideration of rational choice theory in another area of the law – contracts. Recently, law and economics has viewed the rules of consensual agreements as illustrating what is called the "default-rule paradigm."[17] That view begins from the proposition that, if transactions were costless, there would be no need for contract law. Just as in property law, costless transactions imply that voluntary exchange can resolve any issue of potential contracting parties without third-party help (as through a special set of legal rules). It follows that potential contractors need assistance in structuring agreements only when the costs to them of arranging those agreements are high. That could happen because of the limited abilities of the parties to guard against opportunistic breach, to make a credible commitment so as to assure one's contractual partner that he can safely rely upon her cooperation, and to foresee frustrating contingencies.[18]

On this reading, contract law is a set of rules that reduces the costs of structuring agreements in the presence of transaction costs.[19] Rational parties would agree, *ex ante* any particular consensual agreement, on what these default rules ought to be, which of them ought to be modifiable by the parties, and which immutable.

### *Tort law*

Law and economics explains tort law as that body of rules designed to minimize the social costs of accidents, defined as the sum of prevention, accident, and administrative costs.[20] By holding out the possibility of imposing liability on a party for the costs of accidents, tort law seeks to get both potential injurers and potential victims to internalize the costs that their actions or failures to act may impose on others.[21] This possibility induces rational parties to take all cost-justified care – that is, to purchase precaution up to the point at which the marginal benefit of that precaution (in terms of the reduced probability and severity of an accident) equals the marginal cost.[22] Doing so minimizes the social costs of accidents.

Consider this view as applied to the economic analysis of negligence. Negligence is the more efficient tort liability standard in situations of bilateral precaution (situations in which both the potential injurer and the potential victim can take precaution to reduce the probability and severity of an accident).[23] Imagine a situation in which it is not clear beforehand who will be a victim and who will be an injurer – automobile accidents, for example. Because anyone who is driving might be a victim or an injurer, there needs to be some method of inducing *every* driver to take care. Negligence does just that. A rational driver recognizes that he might be an injurer or a victim. He calculates that, if he should be an injurer, he will be liable under the negligence standard if he fails to take cost-justified precaution (as interpreted by the modern formulation of the Hand Rule noted above). Therefore, being a rational cost-minimizer or utility-maximizer, he will take all cost-justified precaution and thereby escape liability as an injurer.

Now consider the way that same rational driver decides how to behave if he should happen to be a victim. He reasons that if someone should injure him in an accident, that person will be rational and will have reasoned that he should take all cost-justified precautions so as to escape liability to the victim. As a result, the accident costs will be visited upon the *victim*. This potential victim will further reason that he must take all cost-justified precautions himself because he will have to bear the financial burden of any accident losses that arise.

In sum, negligence induces socially optimal care by both potential victims and injurers, both presumed to be rational actors, in situations of bilateral precaution.[24]

### *Criminal law*

Law and economics hypothesizes that rational actors commit crime and that rational actors inhabit the criminal justice system.[25] Criminals compare the costs and benefits of legal and illegal action. Specifically, they compute the expected benefit of committing a crime (the probability of successful completion of the crime times the monetary and non-pecuniary value of the crime) and the expected costs of the crime (the probability of detection, arrest, and conviction times the monetary value of the sanction that will be imposed on them, and the loss in reputation (in some instances, possibly, a gain in reputation), the loss of future legitimate employment prospects, and so on). Then, subject to limitations dictated by his risk preference, the rationally self-interested criminal commits the crime if the expected benefit exceeds the expected cost and refrains if the reverse is true.

The practical implications of this theory are straightforward. Society can direct its crime-deterrence efforts at policies designed to raise the expected cost or lower the expected benefit of crime. For example, society might lower the expected benefit of crime by making the returns to legitimate work greater or more certain. Or society might raise the expected cost of crime by increasing the probability of detection, arrest, and conviction or by raising the level of the sanction imposed.[26]

### *Other areas of the law*

For my final example of rational choice theory (and the *ex ante* perspective) as applied to the law, let me turn to the set of public law issues surrounding Acquired Immune Deficiency Syndrome (AIDS). This requires an explicit consideration of expected utility theory, the theory of rational decision-making under uncertainty, a theory that we have mentioned only implicitly thus far. That theory holds that each individual has attitudes towards risk, forms consistent probabilistic estimates (whether subjective or objective) of the various outcomes of a risky decision, and takes that course of action that maximizes his or her expected utility.[27]

Consider a rational-choice-theory analysis of AIDS and legal policy towards AIDS.[28] The Human Immunodeficiency Virus (HIV) that causes AIDS is transmitted between human beings through either sexual intercourse or the sharing of hypodermic needles by intravenous drug users. Individuals contemplating sexual relations in which AIDS may be a risk may evaluate the probability-adjusted costs and benefits of alternative practices – specifically, safe sex *versus* unsafe sex. Safe sex is typically not as enjoyable as unsafe sex, or, put in economic terms, there are costs to foregoing unsafe sex. A rational decision-maker can presumably evaluate the probability of infection if there is unsafe sex and can make some estimate of the discomfort or disutility of the infectious disease. The rational decision-maker compares the expected cost of unsafe sex with the (subjective) benefits of unsafe sex and pursues whichever course maximizes his or her expected utility.[29]

The policy implications for AIDS policy of this view of sexual relations are profound. First, notice that the socially optimal amount of AIDS is probably *not* zero, even though this is a fatal infectious disease. This is because the social costs of eradicating the disease may exceed the social benefits of eradication. As a result, a public policy prescription in favor of reducing the amount of AIDS to zero would not be a rational policy to pursue and might even make matters worse.[30] Second, the particular policies that might be adopted in the effort to reduce the incidence of AIDS may lead to perverse results. To see this second point, recall how rational decision-makers will take the risk of AIDS into account. Depending on their tastes and preferences and on their probability estimates, rational decision-makers will substitute away from the possibility of a fatal infectious disease, just as they avoid other risky situations. Ultimately, the behavior of those seeking sexual relations will alter to take into account the heightened risk of AIDS, so that the spread of the disease is likely to be limited by rational self-regard.[31]

The policy question is whether or not rational people will take too little precaution against the disease and might, thereby, impose uncompensated costs on others. That is, are there negative externalities from individual decisions about unsafe sex? An if so, what policies will induce rational actors to internalize those externalities? There are negative externalities – specifically, the fact that someone who is infected could pass the disease on to someone who is *not* infected – that normally make a *prima facie* economic case for legal intervention in private decision-making. But the extent of these externalities may well be minimal: the incentive for rational decision-makers to take account of the fact that the person with whom they are having sex might have AIDS are extremely strong.

In addition, rational people, who know that others value unsafe sex, will want to find a credible way to signal to potential partners that they are HIV-free and, therefore, suitable partners for unsafe sex. Voluntary HIV testing accomplishes this end. If everyone knows that rational people will voluntarily test for the disease and will inform their potential partners about the results of that testing, is it not rational to presume that one will be told if one's partner is HIV-positive and to believe that information? And then, depending on each individual's degree of risk aversion, to practice unsafe sex only with those who can credibly signal that they are HIV-free? The implication is that the socially-optimal amount of voluntary testing for HIV will occur without legal compulsion. It follows that a program of subsidized testing or even of mandatory testing will be (unless universal) unnecessary and possibly counterproductive. If the law requires mandatory testing and everyone believes that mandatory testing is being followed, then rational people will mistakenly believe that unsafe sex is less risky than it in fact is. As a result, mandatory testing may actually *increase* the spread of the disease – again, unless it is universal.[32]

A similar analysis applies to the policy of subsidized public education about AIDS. Rational people have just as strong an incentive to inform themselves about the disease and its prevention as they do to take the risks of disease into account. Therefore, resources devoted to spreading that information are likely to be wasted, because those who are at risk have already informed themselves and those who are not at risk do not care. It is even possible, although a remote possibility, that subsidization of information about AIDS may lead to an increase in the disease, because it dispels fears and thereby induces more unsafe sex among low-risk groups, leading to the spread of the virus to that group.[33]

The free distribution of condoms is another policy that may well have social benefits but can, under certain circumstances, increase rather than decrease the spread of the disease.[34] Similarly for a policy of the distribution of clean hypodermic needles for intravenous drug users. That latter policy may increase some people's incentive to abuse drugs, which has the obvious direct social costs and the less obvious indirect social costs of inducing more unsafe sex among those abusers and thereby increasing the spread of AIDS.[35]

My point here is not to argue in favor of the Philipson–Posner view, although I find it intriguing, but rather to show another example of how rational choice theory applies to an important legal policy.[36]

## Two criticisms of law and economics

The examples of rational-choice based law and economics that we have just seen have excited both admiration and profound skepticism in the legal community. Because my ultimate purpose is to speculate on the future of law and economics, I do not want to devote too much time to addressing the skeptics. But I do want to address *some* of the causes of skepticism about law and economics. My principal reason for this brief digression is to try to set to one side those criticisms that I believe are misplaced (the two criticisms addressed in this section) so as to bring to the fore those criticisms that I believe need to be taken more seriously in the future (the two criticisms addressed in the following section).[37]

### *The scientific method as being inappropriate to the law*

Some commentators have objected to law and economics' attempt to construct a *theory* of legal rules and institutions on the ground that law is inherently an inductive discipline, slowly growing from case to case and eschewing grand theories.[38]

Take the scientific method to consist of the three steps of articulating a set of simplifying assumptions, specifying logically consistent hypotheses, and confronting those hypotheses with data for confirmation or refutation. Economics aspires to apply this method to its subject matter (namely, market relationships and, increasingly, non-market relationships).[39] Law and economics adopts the methodology of economics – and, thereby, the scientific method – into the study of legal rules and institutions. Why should this scientific method excite skepticism among traditional lawyers? One reason is, of course, the novelty of the idea. This method has never been used before in the study of law, and most lawyers and law students are not familiar with scientific method. But there is another and, I believe, more important reason for the unease – a clash of cultures. The theory-based social sciences proceed from the general to the particular, from theory to example. The law (particularly the common law) moves from the particular to the general. The first method, the deductive, focuses on getting the theory, the general account, correct and is less fastidious about getting the particulars (the facts) correct. Indeed, being spectacularly but interestingly wrong is also valuable.[40] The second method, the inductive, focuses on getting the particulars correct and is less concerned about generating a general, unifying account correct.[41] The point I want to stress about the law is that it is always grounded in practicalities, as theorizing is not. The difference is more one of degree than of kind, but it is, nonetheless, an important difference.

Even though these methods *are* different, that does not mean that they are antithetical, that one is correct and the other is wrong for the study of law. Rather, I perceive one of the intriguing strengths of law and economics to be its joint use of what are, for the law, complementary methodologies – the deductive and the inductive. Indeed, I believe that the use of economics to study legal rules, processes, and institutions has given rise to a new set of analytical skills that does not seem to me to exist anywhere else in the social sciences – the ability to combine theoretical insights with close attention to practical details.

In brief, I find this criticism (that the scientific method is inappropriate to law) to be wholly wrong and, what is worse, to miss one of the great novelties and strengths of law and economics. Whatever else the future of law and economics may hold, it will *not* see an abandonment of the scientific method. Quite to the contrary, I shall argue later that the future of law and economics is likely to reveal an elaboration of the scientific method in the aspect of more empirical work in the study of law.

### *Failure to attend to justice issues*

One of the most common criticisms of law and economics is that it does not devote enough attention to justice. At an extreme, this criticism holds that law and economics goes beyond mere inattention to disparage justice as a legal norm and to assert that economic efficiency is, or ought to be, the principal or only legal norm.[42]

This criticism is easy to address. Efficiency is certainly a valid legal norm, but there are others. There is not much to be gained from arguing about the rank ordering of these various legal norms. My intuition is that what norm receives primacy is a matter for case-by-case analysis and the exercise of judgment. There is no meta-rule to resolve this matter.

One can say more about the seeming inattention by law and economics to distributive justice issues. First, economics has little settled learning on the issues of fairness and justice.[43] But it is perhaps not so well known outside of formal economic training that this lack of settled learning is not for want of trying. There have been numerous attempts by notable economists to deal with equity. Second, this alleged inattention is exaggerated. Efficiency and distributive justice are rarely in conflict and often in accord. The most common result of a law-and-economics examination of a legal topic is that the prevailing law, presumably favored in traditional analysis by its just result, is efficient. For instance, in tort law economic analysis generally reaches the conclusion that negligence ought to be the more common liability rule, with strict liability reserved for circumstances in which the injurer is clearly the party who can realistically act to reduce the probability or severity of an accident. That is, roughly speaking, the same result as that reached by more traditional scholars of tort liability standards. Law and economics, therefore, frequently serves to provide an additional argument in support of traditional justice analysis.

Because I do not think that this criticism has much bite, I do not believe that the future of law and economics will see notable efforts to use economics to discuss distributive justice. But I may be wrong. If there *is* such a development, it is likely to come from some advance in economics, which is one reason that I suggest, in my conclusion, that the field of law and economics should make a point to keep in touch with the economics profession.

## The future: putting law and economics on firmer ground

I turn now from criticisms of law and economics that do not have much bite to those that do. My contention in this section is that these are criticisms of which the field of law and economics is aware. The future of law and economics will consist, I think, in addressing these criticisms.

I shall deal with these points in what I believe to be their increasing order of importance. The first section – on gap-filling, a more unified account of law, and empirical work – describes in a very general way the subject matter of work that scholars in the field are likely to engage in. The final section describes what I think is the most exciting prospect for the future of law and economics: the elaboration of a more complex and realistic theory of human decision-making than that contained in rational choice theory.

## *Filling gaps in the economic theory of law*

The sweep of the literature in law and economics is stunning in its comprehensiveness. There are broad theories of property law, whose economic purpose is to maximize the efficient use of society's scare resources; of contract law, whose economic purpose is to foster mutually beneficial agreements; of tort law, whose economic purpose is to minimize the social costs of accidents; and more. These theories have achieved thoroughness, coherence, and a wide degree of professional acceptance.

The future of law and economics scholarship will surely consist of further gap-filling and extension around this central core of accepted theory. But let me venture beyond that bland and incontrovertible statement to speculate on particular areas of scholarly gap-filling. In property law there is still clarity to be brought to the troubled subject of taking and regulatory taking.[44] The rough outline of an economic analysis of those topics is evident, but there is still room for improvement. In addition, we need to be clearer about which entitlements are best protected by a rule of inalienability and why. In contract law there is what strikes me as a surprisingly large amount of ground still to be cleared. For example, there is still confusion about which rules for the enforceability of consensual agreements should be default and which immutable rules. Nor is it entirely clear when the justification for a default rule lies in the fact that it is what the parties themselves would have wanted but would typically be unable to achieve because of high transaction costs and when the justification is a "penalty" rule designed to induce one of the parties to divulge information to the other party.[45] There are also some contract defenses for which the economic analysis is thin, notably, those having to do with the exchange of information at formation time. In addition, notwithstanding my argument about the shortcomings of economics as a method of looking at distributive issues, law and economics needs to provide a better account of the circumstances under which a court ought to void or amend a contract on the ground of unconscionability.[46] In tort law there is general consensus about the economic analysis of the core areas. But there is work yet to be done on the effect of different tort liability standards on the activity levels of the victim and injurer. Another area in which there is a great deal of interest by public policy decision-makers but in which there has been only scattered work by law-and-economics scholars is the appropriate relationship between tort liability and administrative agency regulation.[47]

There are also much bigger gaps in the literature having to do with entire fields of the law – specifically, public law. There has been, it is true, a long and distinguished literature on the economics of regulation, but that literature has not been much informed by the newer law-and-economics literature. As a result, employment law, corporation law, securities regulation, family law, regulation of the legal profession, constitutional law – these and other public law areas generally have not been analyzed with the thoroughness that has been lavished on the private or common-law areas. That is to say, there is no broad consensus among law-and-economics scholars about a core theory of public law matters in the same way that there is among them about private law matters. The future will, no doubt, generate such a theory of public law and, importantly, an overarching theory encompassing both private and public law, a topic about which I shall say a few words in the following section.

Finally, there are two methodological gaps in law and economics that future scholars will fill. The first is to complete the game-theoretic analysis of legal rules. Heretofore, law and economics has relied upon the standard tools and insights of marginal analysis. But just as microeconomic theory is being re-done in game-theoretic terms, so, too, should the economic analysis of law be reworked in the newer methodology. The principal reason for this methodological update is not simply to be *au courant.* It is, rather, to gain the incremental explanatory and predictive power of game theory for the end of better understanding legal rules and processes. The gain in law and economics from this update to game theory may be large. After all, much of the focus of the law is on strategic interaction, and it makes sense, therefore, to examine those interactions using a tool designed for those purposes. The process of recasting law and economics in terms of game theory has begun, principally in contract and tort law,[48] but there is still much to be done.

The second methodological gap in law and economics that requires filling-in the future is its relative dearth of empirical work. This is such an important gap that I shall take this topic up at greater length in the section after next.

## *A more unified account of private and public law*

I have already referred to my belief that the future of law and economics will contain a more unified account of public and private law. That is not the only unification that I believe will occur. In this section I want to elaborate briefly on the five areas of law in which I believe that economics will serve to provide unification. One is unification across the common law areas; another is unification within the areas of public law; a third is unification of the theory distinguishing private law and public law; another is unification across law and other methods of channeling individual and group behavior, such as adherence to social norms; and yet another is the unification across national legal systems. By "unification" I mean the articulation of a theory that reaches across subject-matter boundaries in such a way as to make a consistent and coherent whole of those otherwise disparate areas. As an illustration, recall that physics is seeking a grand unified theory to bridge the gap between quantum mechanics (a theory that explains subatomic matter) and classical mechanics (a theory that explains very large objects, such as planets). Economics is also seeking to find a unifying theory that makes the now-disparate realms of micro- and macroeconomics consistent. On this understanding, economics would have "unified" contract and tort law if it had shown that the same general theory explained both areas.

The first unification that I believe will occur is that among the common-law fields. While traditional, doctrinal analysis asserted that "law is a seamless web," it, nonetheless, perceived fairly rigid boundaries among property, contract, and torts. Inherently, this cannot be the case in law and economics. The field begins, as we have seen, from a shared paradigm of human decision-making, and the implicit presumption is that the decisions of legal actors regarding ownership claims to and protection of resources, consensual agreements, purchases of precaution, commission of a crime or pursuit of legitimate work, the choice between safe or unsafe sex – all these are made according to the same theoretical model of human decision-making, rational choice theory. Accordingly, distinguishing among property, contracts, torts, crime, corporations, family law, and other areas is, for law and economics, not a matter of creating new theories but of applying the same theory. Just as economists explain differences between national and regional economies (in terms of their configurations of industry, service, employment and other economic characteristics) using the same underlying microeconomic theory, so, too does law and economics explain the different areas of the law as mere variations on or instantiations of the same microeconomic theory.[49]

We are close to having this unification among the core private law areas. But we are not quite there. As I indicated above, there are still gaps in the economic theories of each of those core areas. That fact, in combination with the fact that most scholars prefer dealing with specific issues to synthesizing other people's work into a coherent whole, implies that a unified theory of private law may be some years away.[50]

The second legal area in which economics should bring unification is public law. This is an area that has not received as much law-and-economics attention as has private law. Perhaps that is attributable to the fact that it was precisely in the private law areas that the novelty of the economic analysis was greatest and, therefore, attracted the most energy. Public law areas – particularly such statutory realms as antitrust, governmental regulation, and taxation – had been natural arenas for interaction with economics in the past. As a result, there was little of the attraction of novelty to induce further consideration of those areas in light of the work of the 1970s and 1980s. This has changed in the past decade, with much new scholarship in the public law areas already mentioned and much in areas (such as corporations, employment law, securities regulation, and regulation of the legal profession) for which economic analysis was new. Syntheses of public law areas are rare but not unknown,[51] but there have been almost no textual treatments of the entire public law area from an economic viewpoint.

The third area in which economics will, I believe, provide unification should be obvious – between public and private law.[52] Here I have in mind the problem of clarifying the appropriate general relationship between *ex ante* and *ex post* forms of regulation.[53] By *ex ante* regulation I mean administrative agency regulation. And by *ex post* regulation I mean regulation by exposure to private causes of action. For example, should society encourage safety in the design, manufacture, and production of automobiles by specifying standards with which manufacturers must comply before a car may be legally marketed or by letting those who have been injured bring private causes of action for recovery of damages against the manufacturers? In theory, these two methods might be equally effective at inducing manufacturers to internalize the costs that failure to take care might otherwise shift to innocent victims. If so, then society could choose whichever method of regulation is more effective or cheaper. But in practice *ex ante* administrative agency regulation and *ex post* regulation through exposure to civil actions are not equal. They have different strengths and weaknesses. Administrative agency regulation is more comprehensive but less flexible and is subject to being gamed by those whom it ostensibly seeks to control. Private causes of action are more context sensitive but achieve their laudable social ends only if, among other things that must occur, victims bring actions and fact-finders get issues of liability and damages correct. As Komesar rightly puts it, *ex ante* and *ex post* regulation are "imperfect alternatives." Law and economics needs to think this issue through so as to give a clear and coherent account of the choice between private and public law.[54]

The fourth area in which law and economics will provide unification is between law and social norms. The recognition that there are unwritten social norms that govern behavior has generated some of the most exciting new scholarship in law and economics.[55] One reason for this excitement is that it seems as if the evolution and effectiveness of social norms is particularly amenable to economic analysis. Much as the "invisible hand" directs individuals bent on pursuing their own interests to do what is in society's best interests, social norms may appear, command respect, direct behavior toward socially desirable ends, and adapt without the conscious effort of any social participant. None of these possibilities is settled; they are all still very much contested and speculative.[56] Still, they have an immediate intellectual appeal to law and economics. Moreover, to the extent that social norms prove to be a method of social control, as they surely are, then they should figure in a unified theory of social governance alongside the market, regulation, the common law, and constitutional law.

The fifth and final area in which I believe law and economics will bring unification is in the study of the various national legal systems. Comparative law has been largely immune from law and economics,[57] and so my prediction about unification in this area is entirely speculative. I suspect that when law-and-economics scholars turn their attention to comparative law they will do so in two waves that imitate the waves of scholarship that have already occurred (or will occur) in the economic analysis of private and public law. The first wave will feature the use of economics to examine narrow topics, for instance, to understand why the law in a particular area – for example, contract remedies – is different in two national legal systems, one common law, the other civil law. And, here is the important point, scholars will look to microeconomic theory for the explanation for the difference.

For example (I now speculate even more wildly), civil law countries tend to favor specific performance over money damages because of a general reluctance to give judges too much power; common-law countries tend to favor money damages over specific performance precisely to maintain the primacy of judges in the hierarchy of legitimate law-givers. That is, the civil law countries perceive the costs of giving judges greater discretion to resolve contract disputes to exceed the benefits, and the common-law countries perceive the reverse to be true.

As exciting as I expect the use of economics in the study of comparative law to be, I also expect its acceptance and its flowering to be many years away. Comparative law already makes demands on its students that are, perhaps, greater than the demands placed on those who specialize in one area of national law – namely, familiarity with at least two national legal systems. To ask comparatists also to add knowledge of economics is to ask a great deal.

### *Inadequate empirical support for efficiency assertions*

The future of law and economics holds far more empirical work than is currently the case. In large part this will occur because, as the economic theory of legal rules, processes, and institutions becomes better articulated and more complete, the focus will inevitably shift to attempts to confirm, refute, and fine-tune the theory through confrontation with data. Law and economics has not progressed very far in this aspect. The number of empirical studies in the field is few.[58] But I think that the rate of change is strongly positive.

If empirical work is to become a more routine part of law and economics, then two things must change. First, the legal system must somehow be prodded to do a far better job of gathering relevant data than it currently does. We need to know, as a matter of course, far more about who sues when and why and for how much and what the results are, and we need to know this for both the federal courts and the state courts. We need to have comprehensive records of those potential disputes that did *not* ripen into a claim. We need to know why and how some disputes settle and which disputes those are. To see the daunting tasks involved, consider that in order to assess the deterrent value of exposure to tort liability, we ought to know how many accidents did *not* take place as a result of tort rules.[59] To exaggerate only slightly, we currently know only those accidents that *did* take place and that resulted in a report. The reason why these and other legal data have not been gathered in the past is obvious: no one was interested. There are reasons for suspecting that collection will not be significantly better in the near future. One reason is that the data to be gathered are a public good, and, as a result, we are all content to let someone else incur the cost of gathering. The solution of this collective action problem will entail some concerted action in the profession.

Second, practitioners of law and economics must equip themselves to do professionally acceptable econometrics.[60] Some, of course, are so equipped, and others can become so more easily today than they could in the past because of the widespread availability of sophisticated computer programs for doing statistical analysis.

### *Deepening rational choice theory*

Recall the bare bones of the rational choice theory. Decision-makers are rationally self-interested; they have complete, transitive, and reasonably stable preferences; they can learn about and compute the costs and benefits to them of alternative courses of action; and they seek to maximize as many of their preferences as they feasibly can. Where the outcomes of current action lie in the future, rational actors compute the probability of the various outcomes, evaluate the utility to them of those outcomes, and choose that action that promises the maximum expected utility.

Few people are concerned about the application of the theory of rational choice to market behavior – buying and selling, choosing a career or a job, investing in stocks and bonds, the introduction of a new product, and so on. The power and utility of economics in explaining market behavior is patent and virtually uncontested. But controversy and resistance arise in the application of rational choice theory to non-market behavior, such as to voting behavior,[61] sexual behavior,[62] relations within the family,[63] aging and old age,[64] and behavior in the law.[65] Why the controversy and resistance? In part, it is a defensive reaction by a settled corps of scholars to the importation and seeming triumph of new scholarly methods that appear to denigrate their own, older methods. In part, it is a skepticism about the description of human beings as rational actors in non-market settings. Here I want to survey, very briefly, why this skepticism makes sense. I shall go beyond mere fulmination of the "People don't behave that way" school to look at the professional literature that is systematically and empirically critical of rational choice theory. As I review a few aspects of that literature, I shall show the implications of these criticisms for the legal examples I gave earlier in this Chapter. Finally, I shall speculate on how law and economics will incorporate these criticisms in the future.

Recall the Coase Theorem: that a Pareto-efficient bargain to divide a cooperative surplus will always result if transaction costs are zero. The legal implication is that in circumstances of low transaction costs voluntary exchange (the "market") functions perfectly to achieve socially efficient ends and does not require legal supplementation. But there is a vigorous literature that suggests that this is too sanguine a view of bargaining.

Consider the literature on the ultimatum bargaining game. The game is an economic experiment to test bargaining behavior in idealized circumstances. Experiments have conducted the game in many different countries in many different configurations, but the results are almost always the same. In the simplest version of the game there are two players who never meet. One of the players is the Proposer; the other is the Responder. The game consists of the division of $20 between the players according to these rules:

1 the Proposer suggests a division of the $20 between the players;
2 the Responder either accepts the proposed division, in which case the players actually receive the proposed division, or rejects the proposed division, in which case neither party gets anything.

The expectation is that, because both players are rational actors, the Proposer will suggest a one-sided division of the $20 (say, $18 for him and $2 for the Responder), knowing that the Responder will reason that $2 is better than nothing and accept the suggestion. That is, rational choice theory predicts a lop-sided initial offer that will be accepted.

The results are not what rational choice theory predicts. The modal response is a fifty–fifty split of the $20; the mean response was a split of 70% for the Proposer and 30% for the Responder. However, Responders rejected 25% of the proposed divisions, principally because they felt that the proposed split was unfair.[66] The implication of this literature is that fairness matters so much that people will refuse to participate in the division of a cooperative surplus if they deem the division to be too one-sided or unfair.

How does this relate to the Coase Theorem and its legal use? The results of the ultimatum bargaining game experiments point out that there may be circumstances in which a bargain will *not* occur *even though, on Coasean grounds* – that is *where there is a cooperative surplus and zero transaction costs, we should expect a bargain to take place.* Therefore, we may wish to be less sanguine about the scope of unregulated behavior and more aggressive about legal intervention in order to prevent over-reaching in bargaining situations. We have already discussed several law-and-economics results that may need to be re-thought in light of this observation. For instance, the Calabresi and Melamed suggestion for choosing between property and liability rules as methods of protecting entitlements solely on the basis of transaction costs may need to be amended in light of the results of the ultimatum bargaining game experiments.[67] And, perhaps, the view of contract law as a set of off-the-shelf default rules may need rethinking in this regard, too.

Recall that expected utility theory describes the behavior of rational actors when considering action that has uncertain future consequences. There has been substantial work to suggest that, when confronted with uncertain outcomes, people behave in ways that are not consistent with expected utility theory. Let me describe one attempt to propose an alternative theory that seems to be a better description of decision-making under uncertainty and then show its implications for the tort law, criminal law, and AIDS policy examples of law-and-economics analysis given above.

Prospect theory proposes that decision-making under uncertainty has two central aspects that are different from the assumptions of expected utility theory.[68] First, in considering actions with probabilistic outcomes, people take the *status quo* as their benchmark. As a result, they evaluate actions as either gains or losses from their current income or wealth situation. Second, people evaluate gains and losses differently. Specifically, they are risk-averse with respect to gains and risk-seeking with respect to losses. Put a person to a choice between a sure gain of $50 and an uncertain gain of either $100 with probability 0.50 or $0 with probability 0.50. (The expected value of both prospects is the same – $50.) The vast majority of people prefer the sure gain of $50. Now put that same person or a similar person to the choice between a sure *loss* of $50 and an uncertain loss of either $100 with probability 0.50 or \$0 with probability 0.50. The vast majority of people prefer the uncertain prospect of loss. (The expected value of both prospects is the same – (\$50).) Kahneman and Tversky call this attitude "loss aversion."[69]

The implications of this alternative to expected utility theory for the sort of legal topics I examined earlier are profound. In the examples from tort law, criminal law, and AIDS policy the presumption was that rational actors incorporated risky outcomes in the manner predicted by expected utility theory. But if they do so in the manner predicted by prospect theory, then the legal analysis may need rethinking. As an example, consider the implications for AIDS policy. Actors behaving in the way predicted by expected utility theory calculate the risks of safe and unsafe sex and behave in such a way as to make the case for legal intervention in private decision-making where AIDS may be a risk weak. But if prospect theory describes decisions about safe *versus* unsafe sex, an implication is that the loss of well-being from unsafe sex may trigger risk-taking behavior, rather than the risk aversion assumed by expected utility theory. This fact alone (but there are, of course, other relevant facts) would broaden the argument in favor of legal intervention in private decision-making where AIDS is a possibility. In professorial fashion, I leave as an exercise for the reader the demonstration of how the examples of tort and criminal law[70] might be amended if one presumes that prospect theory is the appropriate behavioral decision theory.

I have shown how only two, very plausible alterations in the assumptions of rational choice theory can lead to dramatic changes in the economic analysis of the law. The two alterations I have given are not the only ones that one might make. There are numerous others. A large and growing number of articles now appearing take these alternative views of human decision-making into account in making an economic analysis of the law.[71]

Let me not be misunderstood on the subject of rational choice theory. I find that theory to be a powerful and useful guide to much of human decision-making. The advances in economic, legal, political scientific, and other learning that has come from its application rank among the great scholarly accomplishments of the twentieth century. I am certainly not saying that economics or law and economics should or will abandon rational choice theory. What I am saying is that rational choice theory is in for a change – an emendation and, perhaps, replacement – and with that change, there will have to be a rethinking of the social science that is premised on rational choice theory as we now know it.

Let me use an analogy to suggest one possible future development for rational choice theory. Until the early part of this century the theory of classical mechanics – Newtonian mechanics – described and predicted the behavior of most physical phenomena reasonably well. But then anomalies appeared. Classical mechanics was found to be inadequate in explaining the behavior of either very small bodies – for example, atomic and subatomic particles – or very large bodies – for example, galaxies and the universe. Over the course of the twentieth-century physicists have elaborated alternative theories – quantum mechanics, which explains and describes the subatomic world, and the theory of relativity, which describes immense scale phenomena – that explain the realms in which classical mechanics was inapposite.

Interestingly, classical mechanics has continued to be useful for most phenomena between the very large and the very small.[72]

As a theory of human decision-making, rational choice theory may be analogous to classical Newtonian mechanics: it describes and predicts much of routine human decision-making. For instance, all the consumers in a particular market – for example, all the consumers of bicycles – when taken together, behave in the fashion that the theory predicts, even if some of them behave irrationally.[73] But, as we have seen, in a wide variety of individual choices, people do not behave precisely as the theory predicts. And, to complete the analogy to physics, some larger aggregates, such as national and international economies, do not necessarily behave in the fashion that rational choice predicts. We may need a separate theory from rational choice, the equivalent of quantum mechanics, to explain individual behavior and another theory, the equivalent of relativity, to explain the behavior of large aggregates. And, of course, like physics, we shall continue to look for a grand unifying theory that then accommodates all these realms. And then we shall examine whether or not, as a result of a richer theory of human decision-making, our economic analysis of legal rules, processes, and institutions should change.

## Conclusion

I have in this chapter speculated on the future of law and economics. I identified these four areas in which I think that the field could most profitably direct its energies:

1. filling-in the gaps in our understanding of particular areas of private and public law – for example, the economic theory of information that should be divulged and that may be kept secret in contract negotiations;
2. unification of the economic theory across five areas in the law: a unified theory of private law, of public law, of private and public law, of all forms of law and social norms, and of comparative law;
3. empirical work to supplement the theoretical insights of law and economics – for example, richer work on the deterrent effect of exposure to tort liability or to liability for breach of contract;
4. emendation of rational choice theory to incorporate (or be replaced by) a theory of human decision-making that takes account of the observed patterns of behavior – for example, overconfidence, devotion to fairness ideals, and loss aversion.

I want to close by sounding a cautionary note. Law and economics must maintain its ties to the economics profession. An element of the attraction of law and economics in the law has been its non-technical nature; typically, an undergraduate (or first-year graduate) knowledge of microeconomic theory suffices to do research in the field. While there will be an incentive to import new economic learning as it is deemed necessary in the future, I worry that the lines of communication between the legal and the economics professions are not being tended to. Because, as seems evident, law and economics is increasingly focused in law schools and less likely to hire PhD economists, the field may become isolated from one of its disciplinary homes. This raises the danger that the economics used by professional economists may proceed in one direction and the economics used in law and economics in another.[74] While recognizing that the economics in the two professions *are* different, I, nonetheless, am concerned that an unbridgeable gulf may arise between the two. We must take care that this does not happen.

## Acknowledgment

I thank Rob Spencer for his excellent research assistance.

## Notes

1 Ronald A. Coase, "The Problem of Social Cost," *Journal of Law and Economics* (1960), 3: 1; Harold Demsetz, "Toward a Theory of Property Rights," *American Economic Review* (1967), 57: 347; Robert Birmingham, "Damage Measures and Economic Rationality: The Geometry of Contract Law," *Duke Law Journal* (1969), 49; John Barton, "The Economic Basis of Damages for Breach of Contract," *Journal of Legal Studies* (1972), 1: 277; Guido Calabresi, "Some Thoughts on Risk Distribution and the Law of Torts," *Yale Law Journal* (1961), 79: 499; Guido Calabresi, "*The Costs of Accidents: a Legal and Economic Analysis*," (1970); Richard A. Posner, "A Theory of Negligence," *Journal of Legal Studies* (1972) 1: 29; and John Prather Brown, "Towards an Economic Theory of Liability," *Journal of Legal Studies* (1973), 2: 323.

2 Richard A. Posner, *Economic Analysis of Law* (1973), now in its fourth edition, 1993.

3 For an example of the impact of law and economics on important policy debates, see the United States Sentencing Commission's report on individual and organizational sentencing for federal crimes, and the American Law Institute Corporate Governance Project. Appointments to the federal bench in the past fifteen years have included many distinguished law-and-economic scholars – for example, Justices Antonin Scalia and Stephen Breyer of the United States Supreme Court and Judges Guido Calabresi, Frank Easterbrook, Alex Kozinski, Ralph Nelson, Richard A. Posner, and Stephen Williams of various United States Courts of Appeal. For an attempt to measure the effect of law and economics on both scholarship and legal practice, see William Landes and Richard Posner, "The Influence of Economics on Law: A Quantitative Study," *Journal of Law and Economics* (1993), 26: 385.

4 See, for example, John R. Commons, *Legal Foundations of Capitalism* (1957); James Willard Hurst, *Law and Economic Growth: The Legal History of the Lumber Industry in Wisconsin, 1836–1915* (1964); Lawrence Friedman, *Crime and Punishment in American History* (1993); Stewart Macaulay, John Kidwell, William Whitford, and Marc Galanter, *Contracts, Law in Action* (1995).

5 For example, see Neil Komesar, "Injuries and Institutions: Tort Reform, Tort Theory, and Beyond," *New York University Law Review* (1990), 65: 23.

6 See, for example, David M. Trubek, "Protectionism and Development: Time for a New Dialogue?" *New York University Journal of Legislation and Public Policy* (1993), 25: 345; Marc Galanter, "Lawyers in the Mist: The Golden Age of Legal Nostalgia," *Dickinson Law Review* (1996), 100: 549; Marc Galanter and Thomas Palay, "The Many Futures of the Big Law Firm," *South Carolina Law Review* (1994), 45: 905; Marc Galanter and Thomas Palay, *Tournament of Lawyers: The Transformation of the Big Law Firm* (1991); Howard Erlanger, "From Common Law Property to Community Property: Wisconsin's

Martial Property Act Four Years Later," 1990 *Wisconsin Law Review* 769; and Hendrik Hartog, "Marital Exits and Marital Expectations in Nineteenth Century America," *Georgetown Law Journal* (1990), 80: 95.

7 This last area is one that has been most cogently defined by Neil Komesar. See Komesar, *Imperfect Alternatives: Choosing Institutions in Law, Economics, and Public Policy* (1994).

8 The demise of this idea is cogently presented in Richard A. Posner, "The Decline of Law as an Autonomous Discipline," *Harvard Law Review* (1987), 100: 761.

9 It is an interesting question, but one I cannot answer here, as to why doctrinal scholarship gave way to the alternatives so completely and quickly. The fall of communism was no more sudden or unexpected than was the fall of doctrinal scholarship.

10 Doctrinal analysis was, of course, aware of the *ex ante* perspective. My impression, for it is no more than that, is that doctrinal scholars pay attention to the *ex ante* effects of law only with respect to constitutional law, procedural rules, and, perhaps, a few other public law areas. They do not pay attention to *ex ante* effects with respect to common law areas and criminal law. There may well be articulable reasons for this selectivity in the application of the *ex ante* perspective in doctrinal research, but if these have been made, I am not aware of them.

11 The "price" for committing breach is relative to the price of available alternatives, such as performance.

12 The criterion that economists use to judge social optimality is efficiency, specifically, Pareto efficiency or Kaldor-Hicks (or Pareto-potential) efficiency.

13 For example, will the constraints of competition alone induce profit-maximizing firms to seek such desirable social ends as employment stability, product and technique innovation, and community responsibility? Or ought society to foster the attainment of those social goals by intervening into the decisions of private profit-maximizing firms (through, for example, wage subsidization, tax benefits for hiring certain workers, affirmative action guidelines, and criminal and civil liability)? This is, I believe, an overly simplified view of the alternatives, but it captures the sense of the debate. One may find proponents of these two views within the law-and-economics community: Richard Epstein, *Simple Rules for a Complex World* (1995), argues for the view that intervention into private decision-making ought to be relatively rare and light-handed, and Cass Sunstein, *Free Markets and Social Justice* (1997), argues for a more expansive intervention into private decision-making.

14 Coase, *supra* Note 2. See Robert D. Cooter, and Thomas S. Ulen, *Law and Economics* 79–93 (2nd edn, 1997).

15 Guido Calabresi and Douglas Melamed, "Property Rules, Liability Rules, and Inalienability: One View of the Cathedral," *Harvard Law Review* (1972), 85: 1089. Additional articles on this tremendously important economic hypothesis may be found in A. Mitchell Polinsky, "Resolving Nuisance Disputes: The Simple Economics of Injunctive and Damage Remedies," *Stanford Law Review* (1980), 32: 107; James Krier and Stewart Schwab, "Property Rules and Liability Rules: The Cathedral in Another Light," *New York University Law Review* (1995), 70: 440; and Louis Kaplow and Steven Shavell, "Property Rules Versus Liability Rules: An Economic Analysis," *Harvard Law Review* (1996), 109: 713.

16 See *Boomer v. Atlantic Cement Co.*, 309 *N.Y.S.*2d 312, 257 N.E.2d 87 (Ct. of Appeals of NY, 1970) and the discussion of that case in Cooter and Ulen, *supra* Note 15, at 144–146.

17 For an excellent review of the literature on this topic, see Ian Ayres, Randy Barnett, Lisa Bernstein, Richard Craswell and Lawrence B. Solum, "Symposium on Default Rules and Contractual Consent," *Southern California Interdisciplinary Law Journal* (1994), 3: 1. For other able summaries of the law and economics literature on contracts, see Alan Schwartz, "The Law and Economics Approach to Contract Theory" (Working Paper No. 123, The Center for Law & Economic Studies, Columbia University School of Law, 1996) and Edward A. Bernstein, "Law and Economics and the Structure of Value

Adding Contracts: A Contract Lawyer's View of the Law and Economics Literature," *Oregon Law Review* (1995), 74: 189.

18 For an elaboration, see Cooter and Ulen, *supra* Note 15, at 167–202.

19 There may be other reasons for specifying the particular contract rules. Ian Ayres and Robert Gertner, "Filling Gaps in Incomplete Contracts: An Economic Theory of Default Rules," *Yale Law Journal* (1989), 99: 87, argue that the defaults should be considered not just in their role as filling contractual gaps in ways that the parties themselves would want to fill those gaps but also as methods of inducing parties to reveal information that they would otherwise keep hidden. They call a default rule that has this aim a "penalty default" rule.

20 This statement of the economic role of tort liability comes from Richard A. Posner, *supra* Note 2. For an elaboration, see Cooter and Ulen, *supra* Note 15, at 270–292.

21 Consensual agreements cannot generally assign liability *ex ante* an accident because the transaction costs of doing so are prohibitively high. One does not often know whether he or she will be a victim or an injurer or whom he or she will injure or by whom he or she will be injured. (The exceptions to this last observation – such as product, and personal service-related torts – are telling.)

22 This is the modern law-and-economics formulation of the famous Hand Rule. For the original formulation, see *U.S. v. Carroll Towing Co.*, 159 F.2d 169 (2d Cir. 1947). For an elaboration of the modern formulation, see Cooter and Ulen, *supra* Note 15, at 281–283.

23 Strict liability is the more efficient liability standard in situations of unilateral precaution (in which only the potential injurer can realistically take precaution to reduce the probability or severity of an accident).

24 I have, of course, left out much of the nuance of the theory. One important oversight is the analysis of how different liability standards might affect the activity levels of potential injurers. For a summary, see William Landes and Richard A. Posner, *The Economic Structure of Tort Law* (1987), 64–71. The original statement of the activity level argument was Steven Shavell, "Negligence versus Strict Liability," *Journal of Legal Studies* (1980), 9: 1.

25 See Gary Becker, "Crime and Punishment: An Economic Analysis," *Journal of Political Economy* (1968), 76: 169. See, also, Cooter and Ulen, *supra* Note 15 at 387–406, for a fuller exposition of the theory and its extensions.

26 There is general agreement about which of these policies is likely to be more efficient. Raising the probabilities of detection, arrest, and conviction costs real resources (more monitors, more police, more courts, more prosecutors), and increasing the returns to or prospects of legitimate work also costs real resources. However, raising the level of sanction is generally costless. All that is required is that the legislature agree to, say, double all existing sanctions. Therefore, the economic theory generally recommends raising the level of sanctions as the efficient method of deterring crime.

27 Expected utility theory is consistent with *any* attitude toward risk. However, in practice most analysts assume that people are risk-averse, which means that they have a declining marginal utility of income. Put somewhat differently, but what amounts to exactly the same thing: a risk-averse person prefers a *certain* outcome to an uncertain outcome of equal expected monetary value. That is, he prefers the certainty of $100 to the uncertainty of receiving $1,000 with probability 0.01 or $0 with probability 0.99.

28 The material in this section comes from Tomas J. Philipson and Richard A. Posner, *Private Choices and Public Health: The AIDS Epidemic in an Economic Perspective* (1993).

29 Ibid., at 32–33.

30 Ibid., at 14.

31 Ibid., at 31–42.

32 Ibid., at 133–142. This is a common phenomenon in safety regulation. For instance, it could be that regulations requiring the use of seat belts may not reduce the number or severity of automobile accidents because drivers, feeling themselves less at risk,

drive more recklessly and more frequently. The regulations may, however, lead to more serious injuries for pedestrians struck by the now more recklessly driven cars.

33 The material in this section comes from Tomas J. Philipson and Richard A. Posner, *Private Choices and Public Health: The AIDS Epidemic in an Economic Perspective* (1993), at 155–174.

34 Ibid., at 174–177.

35 Ibid., at 177–179.

36 The book by Philipson and Posner has been reviewed in David Charny, "Economics of Death," *Harvard Law Review* (1984), 107: 2056; Ronald Bayer, Lawrence O. Gostin and Devon C. McGraw, "Trades, AIDS, and the Public's Health: The Limits of Economic Analysis," *Georgetown Law Journal* (1994), 83: 79; and William N. Eskridge and Brian D. Weimer, "The AIDS Epidemic in an Economic Perspective," *University of Chicago Law Review* (1994), 61: 733. While each of these reviews is critical of the authors' analysis, none of them offers the sort of criticism of the use of rational choice theory in this context that I develop later.

37 There is, of course, a vast literature critical of law and economics and responding to those criticisms. Those looking for some thoughtful recent entries in this literature should see Gregory S. Crespi, "The Mid-Life Crisis of the Law and Economics Movement: Confronting the Problems of Nonfalsifiability and Normative Bias," *Notre Dame Law Review* (1991), 67: 231 and Jane B. Baron and Jeffrey L. Dunoff, "Against Market Rationality: Moral Critiques of Economic Analysis in Legal Theory," *Cardozo Law Review* (1996), 17: 431. Dean Anthony Kronman, The Lost Lawyer: Failing Ideals of the Legal Profession (1993), 225–240, sharply criticizes law and economics for its alleged role in fostering the demise of the prudential lawyer. I address that particular criticism in "The Prudence of Law and Economics: Why More Economics Is Better," *Cumberland Law Review* (1996), 26: 773.

38 See Kronman, *supra* Note 38, at 229–233.

39 There has been criticism of economics as a pseudo-science. See, for example, Steven Rhoads, *The Economists' View of the World: Government, Markets, and Public Policy* (1985) and Alexander Rosenberg, *Economics – Mathematical Politics or Science of Diminishing Returns?* (1992).

40 For example, Robert William Fogel, a recent Nobel Laureate in Economic Science, in *Railroads and American Economic Growth* (1964), argued that the railroads were not essential to United States economic growth and, in *Time on the Cross: The Economics of American Negro Slavery* (1984), that economic forces ameliorated the horrors of slavery in the antebellum United States. Neither of those spectacular hypotheses now commands widespread professional acceptance, but there is no doubt of the great value to the scholarly enterprise that resulted from the diligent efforts of professional economists to refute Fogel and of Fogel's and others' attempts to defend the hypotheses. Legal scholars seem to place a far higher value on being correct than being interestingly wrong. See Dan Farber, "The Case Against Brilliance," *Minnesota Law Review* (1986), 70: 917, and "Brilliance Revisited," *Minnesota Law Review* (1987), 72: 367.

41 These distinctions between economics and the law are themselves a simplification but, I believe, useful ones. I am well aware of the importance in legal education of logical consistency and of refining if–then hypotheticals and of the close connection between those skills and the ones of crafting general models.

42 A recent example is Tom Baker, "The Genealogy of Moral Hazard," *Texas Law Review* (1996), 75: 237. "Moral hazard" describes the diminished incentive to take care that an insured party has simply because she or he is insured. For example, in the absence of insurance against auto theft, an auto owner will bear the entire loss of theft and is likely, therefore, to take extraordinary care against theft. But once that same owner acquires theft insurance, her or his incentive to take care diminishes, making theft more likely. Baker does not like the fact that some law-and-economics scholars have used the notion of moral hazard to argue against some redistributive policies on the ground that those benefited by the redistribution will no longer have the same incentive to take care.

43 There is a growing literature aimed at broadening the scope of welfare economics to link up with philosophical conceptions of the good and the right. For a summary, see Daniel M. Hausman, and Michael S. McPherson, "Taking Ethics Seriously: Economics and Contemporary Moral Philosophy," *Journal of Economic Literature* (1993), 31: 671. A wonderful example of scholarship that combines sophisticated economics, statistics, philosophy, and distributional concerns is Partha Dasgupta, *An Inquiry into Well-Being and Destitution* (1994).

44 Notable recent attempts to do that are William A. Fischel, *Regulatory Takings: Law, Economics, and Politics* (1995) and Thomas J. Miceli and Kathleen Segerson, *Compensation for Regulatory Takings: An Economic Analysis with Applications* (1996).

45 See Ayres and Gertner, *supra* Note 20.

46 For an excellent beginning, see Eric Posner, "Contract Law in the Welfare State," *Journal of Legal Studies* (1995), 24: 283.

47 See Charles Kolstad, Gary Johnson, and Thomas Ulen, "Ex Ante and Ex Post Regulations: Complements or Substitutes?" *American Economic Review* (1990), 80: 888.

48 For example, see Douglas Baird, Robert Gertner, and Randall Picker, *Game Theory and the Law* (1994); Avery Katz, "When Should an Offer Stick? The Economics of Promissory Estoppel in Preliminary Negotiations," *Yale Law Journal* (1996), 105: 1249; and Tai-Yeong Chung, "The Efficiency of Comparative Negligence: A Game Theoretic Analysis," *Journal of Legal Studies* (1993), 22: 395. One of the main innovations of the second edition of Cooter and Ulen, *supra* Note 15, is its far greater use of game theory than was the case in the first edition.

49 Robert D. Cooter, "Unity in Tort, Contracts, and Property: The Model of Precaution," *California Law Review* (1985) 73: 1, is an attempt to show the underlying economic similarities in different areas of the law.

50 It is interesting to me to note that while there have been two book-length treatments of tort law (Landes and Posner, *supra* Note 25, and Steven Shavell, *An Economic Analysis of Accident Law* (1987)), there have been no similar syntheses of contract law and property law.

51 For example, see Frank Easterbrook and Daniel Fischel, *The Economics of Corporation Law* (1991).

52 I should, perhaps, include here the possibility of regulation by means of constitutional law. There have been, as with all the other areas noted, studies from an economic point of view of specific constitutional issues, but there is no grand synthesis of the economics of constitutional law, nor much on the appropriate division of responsibility for social issues among private law, public law, and constitutional law.

53 That is, I am assuming that *some* form of legal regulation is necessary. A broader perspective than this would compare private law, public law, constitutional law, and the unregulated market. That comparison has been beautifully done in Komesar, *supra* Note 8.

54 Another possibility is that *ex ante* and *ex post* regulation could be used together but to have their coverage tailored so as to cover the weaknesses of the alternative regulatory method. This is the suggestion in Kolstad, Johnson, and Ulen, *supra* Note 48.

55 For an introduction to the topic, see Jon Elster, "Social Norms and Economic Theory," *Journal of Economic Perspectives* (1989), 3: 99; Cass R. Sunstein, "Social Norms and Social Rules," *Columbia Law Review* (1995), 96: 906; Timur Kuran, *Private Truths, Public Lies: The Social Consequences of Preference Falsification* (1995); and "Symposium: Law, Economics, and Norms," *University of Pennsylvania Law Review* (1996), 144: 1643. Still one of the most instructive pieces on this topic is Robert C. Ellickson, "Of Coase and Cattle: Dispute Resolution Among Neighbors in Shasta County," *Stanford Law Review* (1986), 38: 623. Ellickson shows that custom, not the black-letter law, governed the relationships between cattle owners and ranchers in Shasta County, California, in respect of damage done by stray cattle.

56 Consider two open issues. First, spontaneously and unconsciously generated social norms may be inefficient, but if so, we need to have elaboration on how that process

works. Norms that prohibited women from seeking careers or from participating in competitive sports were socially costly. Second, it may be possible to manufacture norms. Sunstein, *supra* Note 14, at 33, argues that some groups create beneficial social norms. As an example, he cites a strong norm against cigarette smoking among young African-Americans. Sunstein further argues that government should assiduously manufacture desirable social norms.

57 There are only a few exceptions. For instance, Ugo Mattei, "Efficiency in Legal Transplants: An Essay in Comparative Law and Economics," *International Review of Law and Economics* (1994), 14: 3.

58 However, see Ian Ayres, "Fair Driving: Gender and Race Discrimination in Retail Car Negotiations," *Harvard Law Review* (1991), 104: 817; the empirical work on criminal justice summarized in Cooter and Ulen, *supra* Note 15, at 413–430; Trubek, *supra* Note 7; Galanter, *supra* Note 7; Galanter and Palay, *supra* Note 7; Marc Galanter, "Real World Torts: An Antidote to Anecdote," *Maryland Law Review* (1996), 55: 1093; Michael Saks, "Do We Really Know Anything About the Behavior of the Tort Litigation System – And Why Not?" *University of Pennsylvania Law Review* (1992), 140: 1147; James A. Henderson and Theodore Eisenberg, "The Quiet Revolution in Products Liability: An Empirical Study of Legal Change," *University of California Los Angeles Law Review* (1990), 37: 479; Edward Snyder and James Hughes, "Litigation Under the English and American Rules: Theory and Evidence," *Journal of Law and Economics* (1995), 38: 225; Paul Weiler, *Medical Malpractice on Trial* (1993); Donald Dewees, David Duff, and Michael Trebilcock, *Exploring the Domain of Accident Law* (1996); and Gary T. Schwartz, "Reality in the Economic Analysis of Tort Law: Does Tort Law Really Deter?" *University of California Los Angeles Law Review* (1994), 42: 377.

59 This has been precisely the problem in seeking to measure a deterrent effect for capital punishment – namely, we need to know how many murders did *not* take place that would have taken place but for the execution of the death sentence. See Cooter and Ulen, *supra* Note 15, at 425–430. Ehrlich's original study of the deterrent effect purported to show that each execution of capital punishment deterred seven subsequent homicides. Isaac Ehrlich, "The Deterrent Effect of Capital Punishment: A Question of Life and Death," *American Economic Review* (1975), 65: 397.

60 For a wonderfully lucid introduction to econometrics and its application to legal issues, see Alan O. Sykes, "An Introduction to Regression Analysis" (Law and Economics Working Paper No. 20 Old Series, October, 1993, The Law School, University of Chicago).

61 See, for example, Peter Ordeshook, *Game Theory and Political Theory: An Introduction* (1986).

62 See Richard A. Posner, *Sex and Reason* (1993).

63 See, for example, Gary Becker, *A Treatise on the Family* (2nd edn. 1991). See, also, Professor Becker's address on winning the Nobel Memorial Prize in Economic Science, "The Economic Way of Looking at Behavior," *Journal of Political Economy* (1993), 101: 385.

64 Richard A. Posner, *Aging and Old Age* (1995).

65 See, for example, Cooter and Ulen, *supra* Note 13, and Richard A. Posner, *Economic Analysis of Law* (4th edn), (1993).

66 See Richard Thaler, *The Winner's Curse* (1993); Daniel Kahneman, Jack Knetsch, and Richard Thaler, "Fairness as a Constraint on Profit Seeking: Entitlements in the Market," *American Economic Review* (1986), 76: 728; and Kahneman, Knetsch, and Thaler, "Fairness and the Assumptions of Economics," *Journal of Business* (1986), 59: 285.

67 There are other results that have suggested that we should not be over-optimistic about the success of unregulated bargaining – the presence of strategic behavior (Robert D. Cooter, "The Cost of Coase," *Journal of Legal Studies* (1982), 11: 1) and of *status quo* bias (Russell Korobkin, "Policymaking and the Offer / Asking Price Gap: Toward a Theory of Efficient Entitlement Allocation," *Stanford Law Review* (1994), 46: 663).

68 See Amos Tversky and Daniel Kahneman, "Advances in Prospect Theory: Cumulative Representation of Uncertainty," *Journal of Risk and Uncertainty* (1992), 5: 297.

69 Indeed, they find that the degree of willingness to take risks with respect to losses is greater than the aversion to risk for gains. Ibid., at 297–298.

70 See, for example, James Q. Wilson and Alan Abrahamse, "Does Crime Pay?" *Justice Quarterly* (1992), 9: 359. The authors sought to measure the extent to which criminals make decisions to commit crimes in the manner suggested by rational choice theory. Recall that theory posits that rational potential criminals compare the expected costs and benefits of crime and, subject to their attitudes toward risk and other factors, commit crime if the expected benefits exceed the expected costs. Wilson and Abrahamse found, in a careful study of the behavior of habitual criminals, that those criminals make systematic errors in the way they compute the expected costs and benefits of crime and of legitimate employment. Specifically, most habitual criminals exaggerate the benefits (for example, the returns to successful crime) of crime and underestimate the costs (for example, the likelihood of being detected, caught, and convicted) of crime. If habitual criminals make these computational errors repeatedly, then the ability of society to deter them through imposing ever-harsher sanctions may be limited.

71 See, for example, Edward J. McCaffery, "Why People Play Lotteries and Why It Matters," 1994 *Wisconsin Law Review* 71; Edward J. McCaffery, Daniel Kahneman, and Matthew Spitzer, "Framing the Jury: Cognitive Perspectives on Pain and Suffering Awards," *Virginia Law Review* (1995), 81: 1341; Jody Armour, "Stereotypes and Prejudice: Helping Legal Decisionmakers Break the Prejudice Habit," *California Law Review* (1995), 83: 733; Jody Armour, "Race Ipsa Loquitur: Of Reasonable Racists, Intelligent Bayesians, and Involuntary Negrophobes," *Stanford Law Review* (1994), 46: 781; Jeffrey Rachlinski, "Gains, Losses, and the Psychology of Litigation," *Southern California Law Review* (1996), 70: 113–185; and Kim Kamin and Jeffrey J. Rachlinski, "Ex Post ≠ Ex Ante: Determining Liability in Hindsight," *Law and Human Behavior* (1995), 19: 89.

72 Ian Stewart, *Does God Play Dice? The Mathematics of Chaos* (1989), 9, and Ivar Ekeland, *Mathematics and the Unexpected* (1988). As I noted earlier, physicists are looking for a Grand Unified Theory (GUT) that adequately brings together quantum mechanics, classical mechanics, and relativity.

73 This was the point of Gary Becker, "Irrationality and Economic Theory," *Journal of Political Economy* (1962), 13: 59–83.

74 I was struck by the divide between the professions of law and of economics when my colleagues at the University of Illinois College of Law brought to my attention a survey article on the state of the economics discipline: John Cassidy, "The Decline of Economics," *The New Yorker* (Dec. 2, 1996). Because the portrait there of economics is of a profession in disarray (for example, the article suggests that the Nobel Memorial Prize in Economic Science should be abolished because the economics profession has no legitimate claim to scientific status), I am fearful that my colleagues would infer that, if economics is as flawed as the article suggests and if law and economics is premised on this flawed discipline, law and economics is fatally flawed. (The portrait of economics drawn in that article is generally accurate but, importantly, needs some friendly, nuancing commentary.) On the other side of the divide, I know that most economists' knowledge of the law is premised on equally flawed sources, such as LA Law and re-runs of Perry Mason, and their conception of legal scholarship extends no further than the, to them, horrifying notion that law reviews are student-edited, not peer-reviewed.

# 3 Law and economics in historical perspective

*Douglass C. North*

In order to provide a historical perspective to law and economics we must provide a framework by which we can interpret the world we live in. Unfortunately the tools of social science that we possess are not up to the task. The reason is fourfold:

1 The theory we possess – neoclassical economic theory – is static and we need a dynamic theory to explain change over time.
2 Neoclassical theory derived its methodological inspiration from the physical sciences – physics in particular – rather than evolutionary biology, which is more akin to the theory we need to model dynamic economic change on.
3 The behavioral assumption we use – the rationality assumption – does not provide us with a means of explaining the way individuals make choices except in the most simple and obvious contexts where humans possess complete information and their motivation is unambiguous. We must understand how the brain and mind work if we are to explain the nature of making choices which is at the very core of economics.
4 The theory we possess is a historical but history matters. The choices we make today cannot be understood without an understanding of the historical/cultural context within which we made them.

We must start afresh, building a framework which is more comprehensive than neoclassical theory but incorporates its micro-economic insights. In the process we will see the basic connection between law and economics. We must begin by asking how we understand the world around us. There is no objective reality which we can draw upon; rather the mind and brain construct an explanation to interpret "reality." Those humans in a position to shape the human environment create a structure consistent with their beliefs about that reality. As those humans perceive new problems they (usually incrementally) alter that structure, which in turn leads to revised reality and in consequence revised beliefs, in a never ending process of change. Before we go on we must explain who "those humans" are and put the story in historical/cultural context. To explain the former issue we need to begin with the latter issue. At any moment of time we have inherited the complicated structure we live in from our past. That structure which includes a set of decision rules radically constrains the choices available to us. Let's examine in more detail the nature of that structure.

# I

Institutions are the structure humans create to order their environment and make it more predictable – that is to reduce the ubiquitous uncertainty that characterizes the human condition. They are composed of formal rules (constitutions, laws, regulations), informal constraints (conventions, norms of behavior, and self-imposed codes of conduct), and their enforcement characteristics. The formal political rules define the way choices will be aggregated and by whom. In turn the polity specifies the formal economic rules of the game (property rights, regulations) and the structure of the legal system. Outcomes are a function of the kind of property rights put in place (do they encourage productive and creative activity?), the degree to which the informal norms of behavior supplement the formal rules, and the effectiveness of the enforcement of the institutions.[1] It should be clear from this very brief summary that there is an intimate connection between law and economics.

Institutions are altered either by changes in the formal rules deliberately undertaken, or by alterations in the informal constraints which typically evolve gradually. Formal rules change because those in a position to alter the rules perceive that they could do better (given their utility function) by changing them. We know less about the way informal constraints change. They do reflect evolving beliefs of the participants about standards of human interaction. Broadly speaking, the culture of a society reflects the admixture of beliefs, formal rules, and informal constraints that have evolved over time, reflecting – as Hayek has reminded us – the cumulative learning of the society. But the enormous disparity in the performance of economies makes clear that economic change is not necessarily evolutionary progress. Let us see why.

# II

The sequence of change goes reality>beliefs>institutions>policies>altered reality>altered beliefs, and so on. But widely divergent views of reality and equally divergent beliefs exist at any one time. And as for the institutions – we alter the formal rules but we do not know how to deliberately change the informal constraints and it is both in collaboration with enforcement that determine outcomes. We do get it wrong and have been doing so throughout history far more often than getting it right. A brief account of the rise and fall of the Soviet Union will illustrate the nature of this overall process.

Marx and Engels provided the belief system that was Lenin's inspiration (explaining both the way the world was and the way it should be). The circumstances of the war-torn Russia of 1917 provided an unusual opportunity for abrupt institutional change. While Marx provided no blueprint for the transformation or construction of a socialist society, the fundamental ideological building blocks of Marx (particularly with respect to the concept of property) remained guiding principles (and constraints) of Soviet leaders. When dire necessity had forced a retreat from the principles and led to the creation of the NEP in 1921, the first five-year plan in 1928 returned to ideological orthodoxy. In the early years, there was substantial discussion of alternative strategies and hence institutions to build socialism. The gradual accretion of the complex institutional matrix that did result led to perceived successes (such as in heavy industry) and failures (such as in agriculture) and attempts to correct the failures within Marxist orthodoxy. As the economy grew and underwent the devastating torment of the Nazi invasion (and the lengthy reconstruction process), the institutional matrix was continually modified by external stimuli (war) or internal perceptions of needed institutional alterations guided by a belief system that evolved within the ideological limits of Marxism. The result throughout the 1950s, 1960s, and early 1970s was rapid growth in physical output (particularly in heavy industry), military technology, and scientific knowledge (in certain areas deemed to be strategic), and the advent of superpower status. Because almost half the world became socialist or communist in this era this development was widely perceived to be the wave of the future. But then growth began to slow down, the problems of agriculture became ever more acute, and efforts at institutional reform proved ineffectual. Following the ascendancy of Gorbachev in 1985, the policies of the next six years led to absolute decline and, in 1991, the demise of the Soviet Union – perhaps the most striking case of rapid demise without outside intervention in all of history.

What went wrong? It was the failure of feedback to correct institutional changes that did not produce the desired results. Was it a failure to comprehend the reality of the system, the inflexibility of the belief system, or the institutional rigidities of the polity and economy? All have been factors in the endless decline and/or stagnation of societies in history.

## III

In the historical success stories of institutional adaptation, the belief system of the players filtered the information from current experiences and interpreted it in ways that induced choices leading to the modification, alteration, or adoption of institutions that in turn resolved existing problems or improved competitive performance.

In early modern Europe, for example, the lack of large-scale political and economic order created the environment essential to political/economic development. In that competitive, decentralized environment lots of alternatives were pursued as each society confronted its own unique external environment. Some worked, as in the cases of the Netherlands and England; some failed as in the cases of Spain and Portugal; and some such as France fell in between. Even the relative failures in Western Europe played an essential role in European development and were more successful because of competitive pressures.

The last point deserves special emphasis. It was the dynamic consequences of competition among fragmented political bodies that resulted in an especially creative environment. Europe was politically fragmented; but it was integrated in having both an overall belief structure, derived from Christendom, and information and transportation connections that resulted in scientific, technological, and artistic developments in one part spreading rapidly throughout the others. To treat the Netherlands and England as success stories in isolation from the stimulus received from the rest of Europe (and to a lesser degree from Islam and China) is to miss a vital part of the explanation. Italian city states, Portugal, and the Germanic states all fell behind the Netherlands and England; but banking, artistic development, improvements in navigation, and printing were just a few of the obvious contributions that the former states made to European advancement.

Throughout Western Europe, competition among the evolving nation states was a deep underlying source of change and equally a constraint on the options available to them. Competition forced Crowns to trade rights and privileges – including protection of property rights – for revenue. Most fundamental was the granting to representative bodies – variously Parliament, States General, Cortes – of control over tax rates and/or privileges in return for revenue.

The critical factor in the successful evolution of the Netherlands and England – and indeed the key to successful modern growth – was the shift from personal to impersonal exchange in both economic and political markets. The wealth of nations is a function of the size of markets as Adam Smith reminds us, but as markets get beyond the personalized exchange of small markets the result is to radically alter the exchange process. To use game theory language, personal exchange provides a setting in which it typically pays to cooperate. Impersonal exchange is just the antithesis and necessitates the development of institutions to alter payoffs in favor of cooperative activity.

In the case of economic markets, recent historical research has provided analytical accounts of the evolution of institutions that undergirded long distance trade in the Middle Ages (Greif, 1993), that led to the development of merchant codes of conduct that became the foundation of commercial law (Milgrom *et al.*, 1990); that converted uncertainty into risk, leading to the development of marine insurance (deRoover, 1945); and that provided the foundation of an impersonal capital market with the development of the bill of exchange and the growth of the early banking organization. By the end of the sixteenth century these and other institutional/organizational innovations had created the first modern economy in Amsterdam and the Seven Provinces that formed the Netherlands.

But the creation of efficient economic markets is only half, and the less puzzling half, of the story. It is much more difficult to account for and explain the growth of "efficient" political markets that are a necessary precondition to the development of efficient economic institutions. It is the polity that specifies and enforces the economic rules of the game, and our knowledge of the essential conditions for the creation of such political institutions has not progressed much beyond the insightful observations of James Madison in the Federalist Papers.

However, the historical evidence cited above provides essential clues to the evolutionary process in early modern Europe. The growing need for revenue in the face of the rising costs of warfare forced monarchs to create "representative bodies" – Parliament, Estates General, Cortes – and cede them certain rights in return for revenue. But at this point the stories diverge between the Netherlands and England on the one hand and much of the rest of Europe on the other. In the former the combination of internal and external constraints led to the strengthening of the powers of the representative body; elsewhere in Europe the internal and external constraints led to a decline in their powers and the failure (at least in the short run) to create polities that would undergird efficient economic organization.

The contrasting subsequent histories of the New World bear striking testimony to the significance of path dependence. In the case of North America, the English colonies were formed in the century when the struggle between Parliament and the Crown was coming to a head. Religious and political diversity in the mother country was paralleled in the colonies. The general development in the direction of local political control and the growth of assemblies was unambiguous. Similarly the colonies carried over free and common socage tenure of land (free simple ownership rights) and secure property rights in other factor and product markets. Independence did not cause a fundamental change in the dominant organizations and therefore was accomplished with a minimum of disorder.

The Spanish Indies conquest came at the precise time that the influence of the Castilian Cortes was declining and the monarchy of Castile, which was the seat of power in Spain, was firmly establishing centralized bureaucratic control over Spain and the Spanish Indies. The conquerors imposed a uniform religion and bureaucratic administration on already existing agricultural societies. When revolution led to colonial independence from Spain in the early nineteenth century, wealth maximizing behavior by organizations and their entrepreneurs (political and economic) entailed getting control of, or influences over, the bureaucratic machinery; a struggle for power was the inevitable result. The result was ongoing internal disorder, which plagued Latin America throughout much of the nineteenth century as conflicting interest groups struggled for supremacy. One cannot make sense out of the subsequent history of the Americas north and south of the Rio Grande river without taking into account this historical background.

## IV

Whatever lessons there are from history come from the fundamentals of human interaction over time. Let me draw some specific implications from the previous two sections that can form an agenda for future research as well as a backdrop for this conference.

We can deal briefly with economies that have failed to develop. These are cases in which the belief system, reflecting the historical experiences of an economy, fails to create institutions, economic and political, that will permit impersonal exchange. Markets remain local and/or poorly developed. As these economies become exposed to the larger world economy the institutional matrix typically spawns the development of organizations whose profitable opportunities predominantly favor redistributive activities. Political organizations in such cases will appear similar to those of the classic Virginia school of political economy, in which the state is little more than a theft machine. We do not have to look very far to see instances of such polities in Africa or, with some modification, in Latin America.

The success stories have been briefly described in the preceding outlines of the Netherlands and England, where external experiences reinforced evolving belief systems in the direction of productive activities by the economic organizations. Political organizations in these cases have evolved strong informal constraints – norms of behavior – that have constrained the behavior of the polity. This point deserves special emphasis. The gradual development of informal norms of behavior that become deeply imbedded in society provides the stable underpinning to the adaptive efficiency characterizing Western economies with a long history of growth. Adaptive efficiency refers to a process of institutional change that occurs with changes in the dominant organizations and manages to still maintain order and stability.

This last point can serve as an opening wedge to explore some fundamentals of human interaction. What underlies the formation and evolution of institutions? It is the ubiquitous human drive to reduce uncertainty – to create order from disorder – that leads humans to "scaffold" both the mental models they possess, that is, belief systems, and the external environment, that is, institutions. But the very structure of the scaffolding is the key to whether this process of change can be orderly, and in the case of economic growth, can produce productivity growth as well.

Part of the scaffolding is an evolutionary consequence of successful mutations and is therefore a part of the genetic architecture of humans; part is a consequence of cultural evolution. Just what the mix is between the genetic architecture and the cultural heritage is in dispute. Evolutionary psychologists have stressed the genetic architecture in the scaffolding process at the expense of the role of the cultural heritage. Others such as Stephen J. Gould have suggested that there is a lot of slack in the genetic architecture, which gives greater scope to cultural evolution. Certainly many of our personal preferences, hunger, thirst, sex, and perhaps some of our beliefs, are genetically determined; but some preferences and most beliefs surely must be acquired.

Ken Binmore maintains that our genes probably do not insist that we prefer or believe certain things but that they do organize our cognitive processes in terms of preferences and beliefs. He maintains that we come equipped with algorithms that not only interpret the behavioral patterns we observe in ourselves and others in terms of preference-belief systems but actively build such models into our own operating systems. The evolutionary advantage of such an inductive process is that new behaviors are tested against past experience in our internal laboratory. Humans enjoy the benefits of having the potential to learn a second best strategy in any game. Interactive learning is a two-stage affair in which we first receive a social signal that tells us how to behave and then test the behavior against our preferences to see whether we wish to follow its recommendation.[2]

An issue then is the extent to which the mind is adapted by several million years of genetic encoding versus cultural evolution; another obviously related issue is just how the mind works. Both are central to dealing with the issues posed at the beginning of this chapter and we are far from settling them in either evolutionary psychology or cognitive science. Therefore what follows is tentative, more the intuitions of an economist reading in both of these fields than any settled conclusions.

It is easier to be convinced of the genetic aptitude of human beings for language, a subject on which there is a lot of interesting research, than to be similarly convinced of the genetic aptitude for cooperation. No, that is too strong. There is evidence of the innate drive for cooperation. Recent research in experimental economics has reinforced the findings of evolutionary psychologists that human beings are preprogrammed to achieve cooperative outcomes in social exchange environments. Cooperation increases with communication, observability, opportunities to punish cheaters even at one's own expense, and the ability to signal intentions without direct communication. In a recent paper by Elizabeth Hoffman, Kevin McCabe, and Vernon Smith summarizing a large number of experimental game results, they report:

> people invoke reward/punishment strategies in a wide variety of small group interactive contexts. These strategies are generally inconsistent with, but more profitable than, the noncooperative strategies predicted by game theory. There is, however, consistency with the game theoretic folk theorem which asserts that repetition favors cooperation, although we observe a substantial use of reward/punishment strategies and some achievement of cooperative outcomes even in single play games.[3]

The problems of impersonal exchange suggest that whatever drive exists for innate cooperation must be supplemented by cultural factors for successful impersonal political and economic markets. Creating cooperative frameworks of political and economic impersonal exchange is at the heart of solving problems of social, political, and economic performance.

We do not know how to create such frameworks over night. Historically they have evolved over long periods of time, a process involving the development of a sound legal framework; a structure of legal enforcement which must become embedded in the political/economic structure (DeRoover (1945), Early Examples of Marine Insurance) if it is to survive the shocks and changes that are an inevitable part of societal change. The contrasting stories of North America and Latin America attest to the powerful influence of the past institutional framework in shaping the present. While the right formal rules are a necessary part of creating such frameworks, it is the informal constraints embodied in norms of behavior, conventions, and internally imposed codes of conduct that are an essential supplement.

## Notes

1 See North (1990) for a much more complete discussion of this framework.
2 Ken Binmore (1997).

3 This research is summarized in a working paper entitled "Behavioral Foundations of Reciprocity: Experimental Economics and Evolutionary Psychology" by Elizabeth Hoffman, Kevin McCabe, and Vernon Smith, University of Arizona, June 1995.

## References

Binmore, K. (1997), *Game Theory and the Social Contract II*, vol. 2, Cambridge: MIT Press.

deRoover, F. (1945), "Early Examples of Marine Insurance," *Journal of Economics History*, 5: 172–200.

Greif, A. (1993), "Cultural Beliefs and the Organization of Society: A Historical and Theoretical Reflection on Collectivist and Individualist Societies," *Journal of Political Economy*, 102(5): 912–950.

Hoffman, E., K. McCabe, and V. Smith (1995), "Behavioral Foundations of Reciprocity: Experimental Economics and Evolutionary Psychology," Working Paper, University of Arizona.

Milgrom, P., D. North, and B. Weingast (1990), "The Role of Institutions in the Revival of Trade: The Law Merchant, Private Judges, and the Champagne Fair," *Economics and Politics*, 2: 1–23.

North, D. (1990), *Institutions, Institutional Change and Economic Performance*, Cambridge: Cambridge University Press.

# 4 Legal positions and institutional complementarities

*Ugo Pagano*

## Introduction

Rights and liberties belong to everyday political language. From the political use of the terms one may get the idea that human history is characterized by a constant advancement of both rights and liberties that does not pose any sort of trade-off between them. In this chapter we would like to argue that such a trade-off exists and that it is related to basic equilibrium conditions that rights and liberties must satisfy.[1] The rights of some individuals must often be jointly consumed with duties (i.e. an absence of liberties) of other individuals. The same rights that are enjoyed as an output or a good by some agents must be experienced as duties (as an input or as a bad) by other agents. In other words, the legal relations defining rights, duties and liberties involve the experience of opposite legal positions by agents consuming the same objects with opposite signs and may usefully be regarded as positional goods. A similar argument applies to second-order jural relations involving powers, disabilities, liabilities and immunities.

In the following section we consider Hohfeld and Commons' theories of legal positions and we introduce the concept of *legal equilibrium*. In the section 'Positional goods and social scarcity' we introduce the concepts of positional goods and of social scarcity and we argue that legal relations may be best interpreted in the light of these concepts. A result of the analysis is that there is a natural tendency of the system to accumulate *legal disequilibria* and fail to satisfy the *strong institutional complementarities* that are required by the correlative nature of legal positions. In the section 'Strong institutional complementarities' we consider some actual cases of those complementarities that characterize different systems of legal positions. We show that the positions characterizing alternative models of capitalism satisfy in different ways the social scarcity constraint underlying legal equilibria. Finally, in the last section we consider the relations of institutional complementarity that characterize the relationship between rights and the technologies. Also in this case we have multiple institutional arrangements due to the mutually reinforcing relations between different types of rights and technologies. However, we argue that the multiplicity of *organizational equilibria* that characterizes these relations is due to *weak institutional complementarities*.[2] Organizational equilibria need not satisfy the social scarcity constraint that characterizes relations among legal positions.

We conclude by arguing that an understanding of alternative systems of legal relations could benefit from both the analysis of the *strong institutional complementarities* characterizing the internal relations among legal positions and the analysis of the *weak institutional complementarities* such as those existing among alternative legal entitlements, the nature of resources and other features of the society in which these entitlements are embedded.

## Legal equilibria

Ships that are in danger enjoy the legal right to be helped by other ships. This right is necessarily correlated with the duty of other ships not to leave when another ship is in danger. This duty also necessarily entails that other ships do not have the liberty to leave, and that the ship which is in danger is not exposed to the liberty of other ships to refuse help. This example shows how, in order to be effectively enjoyed, some rights necessarily entail limitations of some liberties. By the same token, my liberty to direct my ship where I want is limited by the right that other ships have to be helped in situations of danger. As we will see in the next section, the economic trade-off among liberties and rights arises from a situation of social scarcity that cannot be appropriately studied if we concentrate only on private and public goods or bads. The understanding of social scarcity requires the introduction of positional goods.

For the time being, let us consider the analysis of legal relations that, originally introduced by Hohfeld (1919), was later developed by Commons (1924) and is one of the most important contributions of American Institutionalism.[3]

To simplify the argument we shall consider only the transactions between two agents i and j. According to Hohfeld, 'first order' jural relations define some necessary relations between the two agents i and j. For instance i may have (not have) the claim that j saves him when his ship is in trouble (Action A) and j may be deprived of the corresponding liberty to leave without assisting.

In other words we have that:

1 Claim (right) of i <----> Duty of j; or, in other words, an agent i has legal claim towards an agent j that j does the action A if and only if j has with respect to i the duty to do A.
2 No right (exposure) of i <----> Liberty (no duty) of j; or, in other words, an agent j has a legal liberty towards an agent i to do A if and only if i has no right towards j to prevent j from doing A and is, therefore, exposed to the liberty of j.
Of course, similar relations hold for the claims of j and the liberties of i:
3 Claim (right) of j <----> Duty of i;
4 No right (exposure) of j <----> Liberty (no duty) of i.

In this simple two-individual-relation the set of actions for which i has rights do not just define the duties of j. They also define the remaining actions for which j has the liberty to act (i.e. the set of actions for which i has no right to interfere and

*Table 4.1* First-order jural relations

| | |
|---|---|
| Right of i | Duty of j |
| Exposure of i | Liberty of j |

is exposed to the liberties of j). In other words, in this simple framework, the jural relations entail that the boundary between the rights and the exposures of i should coincide with the boundary between the duties and the liberties of j and vice versa.

Thus, concentrating our attention on relations (1) and (2) we have the following Table 4.1 concerning first-order jural relations.

In terms of our sinking ship example, the boundary between the right of i to be saved and the exposure of i to the liberty of the other ship not to help should coincide by definition with the boundary between the duty of the other ship to help and its liberty to leave.

In Hohfeld's original scheme, rights and duties – quite as much as the elements in each of the other three pairs of legal positions – were always correlative *by definition* (Kramer, 1998, p. 24):

> [Hohfeld] did not draw his Correlativity axiom as a contingent conclusion from empirical data. He posited the correlativity of Rights and Duties in such a way that each entails the other; each is the other from a different perspective, in much the same way that an upward slope viewed from below is a downward slope viewed from above. Hence, the adducing of empirical counter-examples is a task as pointless as the adducing of empirical counter-examples to the proposition that all bachelors are unmarried.
>
> (Kramer, 1998, pp. 24–25)

However, an *ex post/ex ante* distinction may be useful.[4] *Ex post* rights and duties can be regarded as accounting identities. In a way similar savings and investments, their retrospective values must necessarily coincide. *Ex post* if i benefited from the right to be saved, j had necessarily to bear the burden of exercising the duty to help and could not have exercised a liberty to leave the sinking boat. In this case, as in the case of an accounting identity, rights and duties are really like a slope seen with opposite signs from different standpoints. However, *ex ante* i's boundary between rights and exposures may well differ from j's boundary between duties and liberties in the sense that i and j may have different perceptions about their relative positions. For instance, i may believe that, under some circumstances, he has the right to be helped while under the same circumstances j believes that he has the liberty to leave. In this sense an important task of law-making, conceived as purposive activity which has the object of subjecting human conduct to the governance of rules (Fuller, 1969), is to reduce the gap between inconsistent expectations and, as a consequence, the gap between the prospective and retrospective views of the individuals about their entitlements. In other words, the purpose of law is to eliminate 'legal disequilibrium' and to induce agents to hold relative legal positions that are *ex ante* consistent (i.e. a situation of 'legal equilibrium').

When i and j have different interpretations of their relative positions, and therefore different *ex ante* expectations, either the rights of i or the liberty of j is going to be sacrificed. According to the tradition of positive law inaugurated by Kelsen, analysis of this type of problems is the central theme of law. In the absence of law, no agent can state which one of the perceptions entailed by the two ships is 'valid', and inconsistent rules followed by the agents may easily arise.

The elimination of these inconsistencies and the establishment of the validity of the rules was, according to Kelsen,[5] the fundamental purpose of law. The analysis of the validity of law implied that eventual inconsistent interpretations of the rules had to be settled by referring to rules of superior order. This approach did not only assume the necessity of an agent (the state) having the monopoly of enforcement but also the existence of a constitutional grundnorm. Such grundnorm is necessary to provide an end to an otherwise potentially infinite regress in the analysis of the validity of rules.

A limitation of the Kelsenian approach is that the existence of legal rules can only be thought of within the framework of a developed legal system. By contrast, common expectations about rights, duties and liberties can often arise also in absence of the intervention of the state.

In this respect a meaningful development of the positivist approach to legal theory was due to Hart (1958, 1961)[6] who used an evolutionary approach to explain the formation of real-life legal systems. However, he retained the Kelsenian idea that the validity of law is the central concept of positive law. A primitive society could well develop a system of 'primary' rules without the intervention of central authority and some 'grundnorm' from which the validity of the other rules could be logically derived. However, such a system will be upset by uncertainty because in many cases the agents will maintain that different rules exist or should be applied in particular cases. It will also be static because, besides custom and tradition, nobody has the power to change the rules even when it may be urgent to do so. Moreover the system will be characterized by numerous contrasts and by an inability to impose sanctions that go beyond a system of private revenge. For this reason any such social arrangements will tend to evolve a system of 'secondary' rules that can provide a solution to the problems encountered by the system of 'primary' rules that we have just considered. A rule of 'recognition', establishing the 'Kelsenian' validity of the primary rules, is the first attribute that a proper legal system should evolve. In order for the other shortcomings of a system of primary rules to be overcome, rules of change and of adjudication and sanction imposing rules must also be included in the system of secondary rules. Thus, a proper legal system is necessarily based on the existence of 'second-order' jural relations that give to some agents the power to identify clearly, change quickly and enforce efficiently those primary rules that may also emerge in a primitive society.

The institution of second-order jural relations requires that some agents invest in the ability to verify and enforce *ex post* the rights and corresponding duties among the different individuals. In this way, they can also create the conditions for expectations that are consistent *ex ante.*

In other words, independent of whether these agents belong to the 'private' or the 'public' sphere, they make an important contribution to the elimination of the 'disequilibrium' between the rights and duties of the individuals. Or, in other words, the role of the 'second-order' jural relations can be thought of as that of creating the conditions for the existence of 'legal equilibria' among the rules defining the rights, duties, liberties and exposures of the different individuals. Such a role must entail the power to define the first-order relations and requires analysis of the nature of such power.

It is not surprising that, like rights and liberties, powers and immunities also necessarily limit each other. If, because of the existence of a Bill of Rights the state has no power to change legal entitlements and restrict my liberty of speech (Simmonds, 1986, p. 132), this means that in this respect I have no liability towards the state or, in other words, an immunity[7] against its power that is correlated with the corresponding disability of the state. Second-order legal relations also should be characterized by the fact that some boundaries must be aligned if the powers of the State are really to hold or the immunities of the individual really respected. In particular, in a two-agent-economy, the boundary between powers and disabilities of one agent must be aligned with the boundary between liabilities and immunities of the other agent.

Thus second-order jural relations are characterized by the following relations that are analogous to those that we have considered above:

1 Power of i <----> Liability of j; or, in other words, i has a legal power over an agent j to bring about a particular legal consequence C for j if and only if some voluntary actions by i would be legally recognized to have this consequence for j.
2 Disability of i <----> Immunity of j; or, in other words, an agent j has a legal immunity with respect to an agent i from a specific legal consequence C if and only if i does not have the legal power to do any action that according to the law would have the consequence C for j.

Again, similar relations hold for the powers of i and the immunities of j:

3 Power of j <----> Liability of i.
4 Disability of j <----> Immunity of i.

Second-order jural relations also entail symmetric correlation between the positions of the two agents. In this case too, the boundary between the powers and the disabilities of i should coincide with the boundary between the liabilities and the immunities of j and vice versa. Again, concentrating our attention on relations (1′) and (2′), we obtain Table 4.2 concerning the second-order legal relations.

Both first-order and second-order jural relations have a prominent role in Commons' analysis of transactions and, in particular, in his distinction between authorized and authoritative transactions.

*Table 4.2* Second-order legal relations

| | |
|---|---|
| Power of i | Liability of j |
| Disability of i | Immunity of j |

According to Commons the minimum description of a transaction involves the two transacting agents, the two agents who are the next best transacting alternatives for each agent and the working rules according to which the transaction takes place.[8] The working rules of the transaction include the definition of the rights, duties, liberties and exposures of the agents or, in other words, their entitlements. However, there is no guarantee that the working rules of the transactions satisfy the relations considered above.[9] If we concentrate our attention on the two agents i and j that are involved in the transactions, the two agents may well hold different views on their entitlements. For instance, the rights of the agent i may not match the duties of j and the liberties of j may not match the exposures to these liberties of i. In other words, the limit between the rights and the exposures of i may not coincide with the limit between the duties and the liberties of j. An 'authorized transaction' occurs when, because of the activity of a fifth agent (the public authorities), the limit between the rights and the exposures of each agent coincides with the duties and the liberties of the other agent.

However, 'authorized transactions' cannot be taken for granted. They require 'authoritative transactions' and second-order jural relations. In other words, a legal system can help to guarantee a perfect fit between the entitlements of the different agents.

As in the case of the first-order jural relations, authoritative transactions may also occur in a situation of 'disequilibrium' where the boundary between the powers and the disabilities of one agent does not coincide with the liabilities and immunities of the other agent. Commons observes how, from the Magna Carta[10] onwards, legal systems have progressed towards the establishment of an increasingly clear correlation between powers and liabilities on the one hand, and disabilities and immunities on the other.

The type of transactions considered by standard economic theory requires a complex equilibrium that involves both 'authorized' and 'authoritative' transactions. For instance, the boundary between the claims and the exposures of i must coincide with the boundary between the powers and the disabilities that public officials have to enforce in terms of his entitlements with respect to j. In a similar way, the limit between the duties of j and his liberties must coincide with the limit between the relative liabilities and immunities that j has with respect to public officials. Similar 'equilibrium' relations must hold for the entitlements of j with respect to i.

Concentrating on the entitlements of i with respect to j, Table 4.3 describes a situation of 'legal equilibrium' that is a set of *ex ante* consistent first- and second-order legal positions.

*Table 4.3* Legal equilibrium

| | | | | | | |
|---|---|---|---|---|---|---|
| Power of i via p.o. | <------> | Right of i | <------> | Duty of j | <------> | Liability of j via p.o. |
| --------- | | --------- | | --------- | | --------- |
| Disability of i via p.o. | <------> | Exposure of i | <------> | Liberty of j | <------> | Immunity of j via p.o. |

*Table 4.4* Legal disequilibrium

| | | | |
|---|---|---|---|
| Power of i via p.o. | Right of i | Duty of j | Liability of j via p.o. |
| -------------------- | ----------- | ----------- | -------------------- |
| Disability of i via p.o. | Exposure of i | Liberty of j | Immunity of j via p.o. |

In a legal equilibrium the broken line separating the rights and the exposures of i coincides with the power and the disabilities that are granted to public officials (p.o.) to enforce her rights. It also coincides with the broken line separating the duties and the liberties of j, which in turn coincides with the broken line that defines the boundary between the liabilities and the immunities that j has towards public officials.

However, the broken lines of Table 4.3 do not necessarily need to be aligned. In reality a situation of legal disequilibrium, such as that considered in Table 4.4, may well arise.

In Table 4.4, the broken line, defining the boundary between the rights and exposures of i, does not coincide with that defining the boundary between the duties and the liberties of j. In this case the powers of and the liabilities towards public officials fail to match the legal entitlements of the two agents. By contrast, a well working legal system, equilibrating the power and liabilities that agents acquire through public officials, tends also to equilibrate their rights and duties or, in other words, tends to achieve the legal equilibrium considered in Table 4.3.

According to Commons, the correlation between the entitlements of i and j requires a corresponding correlation of the second jural relations between the two agents and public officials. While Kelsen sees the unity and the consistency of the legal system as a pure matter of logic and concentrates on the analysis of the validity of rules, Commons points out how the jural relations considered by Hohfeld cannot be taken for granted. They notably require the costly intervention of public officials who attribute corresponding powers and liabilities to the agents (via public officials) and, in this way, also equilibrate their rights and duties. The limits to the powers and to the liabilities of public officials (or their disabilities to act in the interest of i and the immunities of j from their intervention) also equilibrate the exposures and the liberties of the agents. In other words, while both first and second jural relations may well be in disequilibrium, with the help of public officials a good legal system tends towards the realization of a complex legal equilibrium where the conditions considered above are satisfied.

While Commons does not use the term legal equilibrium (or the term legal disequilibrium), perhaps, this term can usefully catch the originality of his contribution and his distance from the Kelsenian tradition of the analysis of the validity of legal rules.[11]

In the Kelsenian tradition the 'consistency' of rules is purely a matter of logic and eventual discrepancies have to be solved by stating which rule is hierarchically superior. For instance, if under some circumstances the rules simultaneously stipulate the right of i to be assisted and liberty of j to do something else, the matter has to be logically solved by checking which of the two rules has priority. In a way, inconsistency never arose for scholars who were aware of the logical rules governing the system and could easily judge the validity of each single rule.

In contrast, according to Commons the consistency of a legal system is only an ideal goal of such a system and some degree of disequilibrium is a permanent feature of the working of a legal system.[12] Moreover, in Commons' view, the elimination of disequilibrium is not a pure matter of logic which requires a 'corner solution' stating the priority of the rights of i over the liberties of j or vice versa. The costly elimination of disequilibrium is a real process that may either involve 'corner solutions' or 'intermediate solutions' characterized by some dilution of the rights of i and of the liberties of j.

According to Commons, elimination of legal disequilibrium cannot be carried out only by public officials but, as Fuller (1969) also emphasized, it must also be performed by the many agents that have a similar function in the private sphere. In particular, firms may be seen as 'going concerns' where some working rules are established by private agents who bear the costs of setting up a 'private' legal equilibrium which is specifically tailored to certain types of transactions. Similarly, arbitrators and the private orderings of many other institutions contribute to the costly elimination of legal disequilibrium.[13] Each one of these institutions has some relative advantages that depend on the type of action that has to be governed. The more specific is the nature of the relations among the individuals, the more specific are the skills and the knowledge that are required to eliminate legal disequilibrium. In this sense, the first-order specificity of the positions of the individuals involves a comparative advantage of second-order specific investments aimed at their efficient governance. The costs of investments, which public courts make to verify and enforce private contracts, can only be recovered when they are applied to a wide range of legal relations. Thus public courts are more likely to have a comparative advantage in the general purpose investments in human capital that are required for the *ex post* governance of standard contracts. Arbitrators, intermediaries and firms' managers may be interpreted as private orderings that, thanks to second-order specific investments in human capital and their familiarity and involvement with the relations among the agents, can govern better than public courts relations characterized by first-order specific investments. In such cases private internal organization is likely to replace some of the institutions of public markets.[14]

## Positional goods and social scarcity

The correlative nature of legal positions implies that these positions are characterized by some form of social scarcity that is associated with the fact that each position is available to an individual only if a corresponding position (but, to use the analogy of Kramer mentioned above, with an 'opposite slope') is occupied by some other individual.

The same action belongs to the rights of one individual only if, at the same time, it is a duty for some another individual. The set of actions that defines the rights of individual i imposes duties for some individual(s) j, limiting the set of actions that define the liberties of j. The same action (the sinking boat of i being saved by j) is consumed with opposite signs as a desired output by i and as a costly input by j, and any increase in the rights of i necessarily limits the liberties of j.

In a similar manner, the same action belongs to the powers of one individual if it constitutes a liability for another individual. The powers of i limit the immunities of j and no increase in the set of powers of i can be obtained without decreasing the set of immunities of j. Again, the same action is consumed with opposite signs as a power by i and as a liability by j (or as disability by i and as an immunity by j).

Rights, Liberties, Powers and Immunities have some characteristics that distinguish them from other goods. We can easily imagine a society where everyone consumes large quantities of goods such as rice, cars and housing space. It is much harder to imagine a society where everyone consumes 'large quantities' of rights, liberties, powers and immunities. For some individuals the exercise of their rights must be limited by the liberties of others (that imply that they are not bound to perform the duties corresponding to these rights). Similarly, for some individuals the exercise of their powers must be limited by the immunities of other individuals (that imply that they are not subject to the exercise of these powers).

Any positive amount of rights and powers must be jointly consumed with negative quantities of other goods. It is impossible to exercise a right or a power if somebody is not subject to the exercise of these rights and powers: positive amounts of rights and power must be jointly consumed with negative amounts of liberties and immunities (that is with duties and liabilities).[15]

Unlike traditional economic goods, rights and powers inevitably involve different *positions*[16] of the individuals with respect to other individuals; for this reason, following Fred Hirsch's terminology, we can call goods like power and prestige *positional goods*.

In traditional economic theory we usually consider two types of goods (and their intermediate combinations): private and public goods.

Pure private goods are characterized by the fact that other individuals consume a *zero amount* of what each individual chooses to consume. The other individuals are excluded from the consumption of private goods that do not belong to them and their position with respect to the consumption of these goods is not altered by the consumption choices of the other agents. In all cases they are excluded from the consumption of the goods consumed by other individuals.

This exclusion is impossible in the case of a pure public good. In the case of a pure public good, each agent must consume the *same positive amount* that other agents decide to consume. Here the position of each of the two agents is not relevant in the sense that in the case of the consumption of a public good all individuals are in the very same position. In a similar way in the case of a public bad the positions of the individuals are irrelevant because all the individuals must consume the *same negative amount* of the public bad.

In an economy consisting of two individuals, a pure positional good is a good such that, given the consumption choice of one agent, the second agent must consume *a corresponding negative amount* of what the first chooses to consume. In this respect, positional goods define a case polar to that of public goods.[17] Unlike the case of private goods, here the consumption choices of the agents are interdependent and, unlike the case of public goods, the consumption of the goods differs between individuals having *different positions* (negative and positive consumption) relative to the good.

A visit to Robinson Crusoe's island, though unoriginal, may clarify the difference between these goods. In this island Crusoe will not perceive the difference between the public and the private goods that he is consuming. At the same time, he will not consume any positional goods. In particular, he does not enjoy any right, liberty, power or immunity and he has no duty, exposure to liberty, liability or disability. Only when Friday arrives the distinction between private and public goods will become clear and negative and positive consumption of positional goods will become possible. Before the arrival of Friday only *economic scarcity* can be perceived. Both private and public goods may be consumed in limited quantities because either these goods, or the inputs that are necessary for their production, may be available in fixed supply. However, after the appearance of Friday, a new type of scarcity – *social scarcity* – is experienced by Robinson (and even more by Friday!).

Social scarcity is not due to the fact that the consumption of the two agents cannot exceed some given amount that is fixed by technology and/or limited by the natural availability of resources. Instead, it is due to the fact that whatever one individual consumes as a positive quantity must be jointly consumed by the other individual as a negative quantity. The constraint is not anymore (or, at least, not only) fixed in terms of a positive maximum quantity. It is rather due to the fact that aggregate consumption must be equal to zero.

Like a slope viewed from above and below, the same action must be jointly consumed as a positive quantity (i.e. as a right or as a power) and as a negative quantity (i.e. as duty or as a liability). The rights that are enjoyed by Robinson may imply numerous duties by Friday and squeeze his liberty. The power consumed by Robinson may be so extensive as to give him the possibility of interfering with all the possible actions that Friday may carry out, and eliminate any sort of immunity. While Friday may be granted by Robinson some liberties, he may enjoy no immunity against the unlimited power of Robinson to restrict them.

In the case of legal positions (and, in general, in the case of positional goods) the main limitations do not arise from a situation of *economic scarcity*, that is from a positive limited amount of resource availability. Instead they derive from a form of *social scarcity*, that is from the fact that the aggregate consumption of positional goods by the two individuals must be equal to zero. This implies that, while for private goods the consumption choices of each individual are independent of each other, and for public goods and bads they must move in the same direction, in the case of positional goods consumption must move in opposite directions. Thus, the different categories of goods may be characterized in terms of the following table:

| | Robinson | Friday |
|---|---|---|
| Public good | + | + |
| Private good | + | 0 |
| Private good | 0 | + |
| Positional good | + | – |
| Positional good | – | + |
| Public bad | – | – |

*Positional competition* is much harder, and sometimes more violent, than competition for 'private' goods.

Consider the case that if all the individuals work harder they may all consume more private and public goods. The same is not true for positional goods like power and prestige. If we all work harder none of us can consume more of them. *Social scarcity* constrains the welfare of humankind much more than *natural scarcity*.

Conflicts may easily arise even in cases where voluntary agreement has been reached about their supply.

In the case of private goods such agreement would separate a public sphere where the agreement takes place and a private sphere where consumption is carried out without affecting the welfare of the other individuals.

In the case of public goods the agreement should be such that the free riding problem is overcome and the good is supplied; however the consumption of pure public goods and bads is not conflictual because everyone consumes the same quantity of the good.

By contrast, in the case of positional goods, reaching an agreement about their supply cannot move their consumption to a non-conflictual sphere. Positive and negative consumption are not separable and conflicts may easily arise. Take the case of the sinking boat example. It involves all the seamen and women enjoying a safety gain by agreeing *ex ante* that each one of them has the right to be saved. However, the *ex post* consumption of this right can be conflictual because it must be jointly consumed with the corresponding duty.

It is not surprising that the problems of positional goods are the reverse of those of public goods. It is very likely that we will have over-investment in positional goods when all the agents try to consume positive amounts of these goods. A well-known example of this problem is social status. Social status is a typical positional good. It involves a shared feeling of the superiority of some individuals and of the inferiority of some other individuals. The Veblenian theory suggests that important consumption decisions are not motivated by the desire to enjoy the private benefits of these goods but rather by the desire to consume more positive status. However, the positive consumption of status by some individuals implies the negative consumption of status by other individuals and a reaction to try to maintain their status. 'Keeping up with the Jones' involves an over-consumption that is wasteful because both consumers spend a lot of their resources to consume unchanged status and could be better off by reaching a cooperative agreement where they both limit their consumption.

Rights, liberties, power and immunities may often share a similar characteristic of oversupply. Typically, politicians prefer to speak the language of rights, liberties, immunities and powers while they know that the language of duties, expositions to liberties, disabilities and liabilities is much less popular. However, in each society there is a very *strong institutional complementarity* between the structure of rights, liberties, powers and immunities and the structure of duties, exposition to liberties, liabilities and disabilities. This is due to the fact that a consistent legal equilibrium is necessarily governed by the constraint of social scarcity typical of positional goods.

In a sense, this type of strong institutional complementarity is a particular case of the concept of institutional complementarity. Standard conditions of institutional complementarity are defined by the two following circumstances:

1 the additional benefit of having institution $X_1$ instead of institution $X_2$ in some domain X is greater when institution $Y_1$ (instead of institution $Y_2$) is chosen in the domain Y.
2 the additional benefit of having institution $Y_2$ instead of institution $Y_1$ in some domain Y is greater when institution $X_2$ (instead of institution $X_1$) is chosen in the domain X.

These propositions considered by Aoki (2001) re-state in terms of institutional choices the supermodularity conditions among strategies considered by Milgrom and Roberts (1990) and are concerned with the property of incremental pay-offs with respect to a change in parameter value. They do not exclude the possibility that the level of the pay-off of one rule is strictly higher than that of the other for the agents of one domain or of both domain(s) regardless of the choice of rule in the other domain. There is the possibility of a unique equilibrium. However, under the supermodularity condition, there can be two pure Nash equilibria (institutional arrangements) for the system comprised in X and Y that is $(X_1,Y_1)$ and $(X_2,Y_2)$. When such multiple equilibria are possible, we say that domains X and Y are institutional complements of each other and that:

1 $X_1$ and $Y_1$ are institutional complements
2 $X_2$ and $Y_2$ are institutional complements.

The relations that define legal equilibria imply some sort of institutional complementarity in the sense outlined above.

Consider X and Y as two different domains where the rights ($X_1$,$X_2$) and the duties ($Y_1$,$Y_2$) are respectively chosen. Assume that ($X_1$,$Y_1$) and ($X_2$,$Y_2$) satisfy the conditions necessary for a legal equilibrium in the sense that individual i has the legal claim $X_1$ towards an agent j, that j does the action A if and only if j has the duty $Y_1 = -X_1$ with respect to i to do A (and vice versa for the rights of the individual j and duties of the individual i). In this sense, any increase in the rights of i (j) is perfectly matched by a decrease in the liberty of j (i). Or, in other words, ($X_1$,$Y_1$) satisfy (as an equality) the social scarcity constraint. Assume that similarly ($X_2$,$Y_2$) are rights and duties that satisfy (also as an equality) the social scarcity constraint for each couple of individuals i and j.

Legal disequilibrium is costly in a double sense. Being outside the set of feasible arrangements defined by the constraint implies costly social conflict. Being at a point within the interior of this feasible set implies that the rights or the powers of j can be increased without a sacrifice of the liberties or the immunities of j. For this reason, it is clear that the additional benefits arising from the system of rights $X_1$ with respect to the system $X_2$ are larger when the corresponding system of duties $Y_1$ (instead of $Y_2$) is chosen in the other domain Y. In a similar way the additional benefits arising from the system of duties $Y_2$ with respect to $Y_1$ are the greatest when the system of rights $X_2$ (instead of $X_1$) is chosen in the other domain X.

Thus, in some sense legal equilibria can be regarded as cases of institutional complementarity. However, they are a case of *strong institutional complementarity* in the sense that hybrids (such as $X_1$,$Y_2$ and $X_2$,$Y_1$) are particularly unstable. Indeed, when rights and duties are not aligned *ex ante* in terms of the expectations of each other's behaviour they must still satisfy *ex post* the social scarcity constraint as an accounting identity and this social constraint makes hybrids particularly fragile. Take again the sinking boat example. The agents may have different expectations concerning their rights to be saved and their liberties to sail away. However *ex post*, if a right has been really enjoyed, the corresponding duty must have been consumed, while if the liberty to sail away has been really taken, the sinking boat must have been exposed to the consequences of this liberty. While the legal system provides various mechanisms to link the different domains and eliminate disequilibrium *ex ante*, the failure of the formal legal system to eliminate disequilibrium is not the end of the story. *Ex post*, the nature of positional goods implies that legal positions must match as accounting identities. This *ex post* adjustment can have several solutions. For instance, rights may adjust to duties, or duties may adjust to rights. However all sorts of intermediate non-corner solutions may also arise *ex post*[18] and involve some dilution of rights and some partial limitations of liberties. Indeed, Norberto Bobbio (1990) has claimed that the latter type of *ex post* adjustment towards intermediate solutions has become a fundamental mechanism in creating new generations of rights. Rights – especially social rights – are claimed and enacted without stating the corresponding duties and/or the corresponding powers of enforcement hoping that some intermediate compromise may later take place thanks to a partial enhancement of these duties.[19]

In the case of legal relations the diachronic linkages between the domains of rights, liberties, powers and immunities and the domains of duties, exposures to liberties, liabilities and disabilities are stronger than the linkages that are usually implied by institutional complementarities. While individuals may sometimes use strategically the social scarcity constraint and other times may be unaware of it, this constraint is endowed with its own *ex post* ways of shaping legal and social relations.

Bobbio's statement expresses two important characteristics of the production of law.

The first characteristic is that the production of law is often characterized by disequilibrium due to the oversupply of the 'positive side' of positional goods.

The second characteristic is also due to the positional nature of legal relations. Infringement of the social scarcity constraint and legal disequilibrium are not without consequences. The strong institutional complementarities that characterize legal positions may be violated *ex ante* only at the cost of some form of *ex post* adjustment.

While these two characteristics reinforce Bobbio's point that legal disequilibrium has become an integral part of the production of law, the convergence to some equilibrium should not be taken for granted, especially in case of widespread and dramatic inconsistency among the *ex ante* legal positions of the agents. A strong and persistent disequilibrium may discredit the entire legal system and, in some cases, lead to the collapse of the legal system.[20]

## 'Strong institutional complementarities' and alternative systems of legal positions

As Simmonds points out:

> The right of ownership is really a complex bundle of claim-rights, liberties, powers and immunities. An owner of land, for example typically enjoys (*inter alia*) the claim-right that others not trespass on his land, the liberty to walk on his land, the powers to transfer title to others, and immunity against having his title altered or transferred by the act of another.
>
> (1986, p. 132)

The assignment of private property rights involves the establishment of a legal equilibrium. The right of exclusive use of assets by some individuals has to be correlated with the duties of others not to consume these resources and the liberty that the owners have to choose among different uses of the resources has to be correlated with the exposure of others to these liberties. Similarly, the power that the private owner has to transfer his title has to be aligned with the liability that the other agents have towards these transfers of property, while the immunity of the owner against having his title altered or transferred by the act of another has to be aligned with the disability of others to perform these acts. In other words, the constraints due to the existence of social scarcity necessarily characterize the institution of private property rights.

A system of well-defined private property rights involves the condition that no disequilibrium exists between all these legal positions. When standard economic theory assumes that such a system exists and considers the equilibrium conditions that hold for the competitive exchange of private property rights, it is also implicitly assuming that no economic resources were expended to establish this legal equilibrium. In contrast, the establishment of the legal equilibrium that is necessary to define private property rights is very costly and valuable economic resources must be expended by the private and public orderings that are engaged in this enterprise.[21] Moreover, transacting rights is also costly and constitutes a fact essential to perceiving some of the fundamental advantages of private property that do not make sense in the standard framework.

In the case of 'pure private goods', private property allows an optimal decentralization of decisions because no individual is exposed to the liberty to choose of other individuals. Each new set of uses that improves the utility of the owner of the private good necessarily leads to Pareto improvements. This characteristic of private property holds independently of exchange. This quality of private property cannot be seen in a world of zero transaction costs where individuals take consumption and exchange decisions together. In the traditional setting one misses the main quality of private property, which is the possibility of taking decisions without incurring the costs of transacting with other people.[22]

The cost of transacting may be such that the assignment of private rights may be worthwhile even when the liberty that an individual is entitled to with respect to her private property involves exposures among which other individuals are not indifferent.

In the case of positional, public and complementary goods, the assignment of private property rights cannot 'separate' consumption decisions from transactions with other individuals. An externality can be seen as the impossibility of private property rights eliminating interference between the 'liberties' of different individuals. However, if such interference involves sufficiently limited losses of welfare, unfettered private property may still be convenient because the costs of organizing the relative transactions may well offset the gains obtained when each individual takes into account the exposures correlated with the exercise of his liberties.

In this respect, the assignment of private property rights in physical assets is an important way in which economic decisions are decentralized to other individuals. In the case of 'pure private goods', rivalry in use implies that it is desirable to assign an exclusive right to somebody (and such that the corresponding duties do not interfere with others). Otherwise, costly conflicts will necessarily arise. At the same time, complete exclusion from the benefits and the damages (another important characteristic of 'pure private goods') implies that the other agents are not affected by the way in which the owner exercises her liberty to consume and allocate the good among different uses. For this reason, in the case of 'pure private goods', exposure to the liberties of the owners has no effect on other individuals and it is best to grant them to the owners. Similarly, third parties are not affected by the identity of the owner and, for this reason, it is best to grant the owner the power to transfer her title as well as the immunity against having her title altered by others.

While in a world of positive transaction costs the virtues of decentralization of private property may make its institution desirable in circumstances outside the strict limits of 'pure private goods', in many cases the opposite is true.

Some goods seem to belong to a private sphere and seem to be subject to a perfect definition of private property rights. However, a more careful analysis shows that it is impossible to claim that private property rights can be easily defined in the sense that we have considered above. We will be here concerned with the difficulty of defining 'private property rights' in human labour and the implications of this difficulty for other rights and liberties that are related to it by 'strong institutional complementarity' associated with the existence of social scarcity.

In neo-classical theory human activity is divided into two parts. One part is an argument in the utility function and is called leisure. The other part is an argument in the production function and is called work.[23] In the standard framework there is no difference between human activity and other commodities and, in both cases, similar rules govern the definition and the exchange of private property rights. While it is generally recognized that human capital cannot be bought and sold, in standard economic theory the rental of human capital is not substantially different from the rental of other resources.

Indeed, in a famous passage Samuelson has argued, 'In a perfectly competitive economy it doesn't really matter who hires whom.' (1957, p. 894) – a statement that underlies the perfect symmetry that exists in neo-classical theory between human and non-human assets as well as its irrelevance for relations between the nature of the firm, its ownership, and the type of technology, division of labour and labour process which take place within it.

Samuelson's sentence can be understood by observing how in orthodox economics, perfect competition brings about the same efficient allocation of resources independently of the initial distribution of property rights including those rights that the individuals have in the firms.[24]

Neo-classical economics considers a perfectly competitive economy, where the prices for all goods exist, property rights in these goods are well defined and the agents can exchange these rights without any transaction cost. In this economy the individuals will sell their rights to those agents who can employ the goods, over which the rights are defined, in the uses where a marginal unit of them is most highly valued. As a consequence, under perfect competition, the final allocation of property rights is Pareto efficient: the value of production is maximized and it is impossible to improve the welfare of an individual without worsening the welfare of other individuals. The techniques and organization will be optimal independent of the initial distribution of property rights. The initial distribution of property rights matters in determining the distribution of wealth but is irrelevant for the nature of the organization of production. For, a perfectly competitive market economy determines endogenously an efficient final allocation of any initial distribution of property rights.

In this framework questions like 'who owns the firms' and 'who hires whom' also become irrelevant: the techniques and organization of production will not change because, in any case, they will be efficiently determined by the competitive system.

Take the case in which capital owns the firm and hires labour. The workers will rent their labour to the 'capitalists' who can employ their labour power in the uses where it is at the margin most productive and can therefore be paid the highest wage. The 'capitalists' will have an interest in employing not only the labour that they hire but also their own capital in those uses where its marginal productivity is highest.

Consider now the case in which labour owns the firm and hires capital. The capitalists will now rent their capital to those workers' cooperatives that can employ it in those uses where it is most productive at the margin and that can therefore pay them the highest rent. The workers will have an interest in employing not only the capital that they rent, but also their own labour, in those uses where its marginal productivity is highest.

In both cases, at equilibrium the organization of production will be such that the marginal productivity of each factor is the same in each use and, as a consequence, such that the productivity of each factor is maximized.[25] In a competitive economy each rational agent has an incentive either to employ or to make other agents employ its resources in those uses where they yield the highest benefits. This holds for either workers cooperatives or capitalist firms acting in a competitive economy and implies the equivalence and the efficiency of these alternative institutions. A competitive economy always brings about an efficient organization of production. In this sense, who owns what and who hires whom do not matter.

However, the symmetry between capital and labour is a joint result of three assumptions:

1 the costless definition and enforcement of private property rights
2 the costless transfer of these rights
3 the division of human activity into leisure and work.

The third assumption implies that humans can be treated in the same way as other non-human resources. The welfare of individuals is only assumed to be affected by the time that they keep for themselves but not by the time that is used by others in the production process. Thus, individuals are assumed to be sensitive only to working more or less but not to be affected by the allocation of their time in production among different uses (as long as the amount of leisure is unchanged).

In this framework, there is a perfect symmetry between labour and other non-human resources. The only difference becomes that human resources can be used in an additional production process by which one unit of labour can be transformed into one unit of leisure. Once this fictitious production process is added to the economy, labour should be allocated among different production processes in the same way as steel, iron or buildings – that is, in such a way that the marginal productivity is the same in all the possible uses. In other words, the third assumption implies that the part of human time that is hired by others can be allocated by a simple profit maximizing rule. Employers can acquire temporary private property in the human labour of the other individuals; in particular, they can obtain an exclusive right to the use of other individuals' labour and a liberty to allocate it according to their interests that parallels the private property rights that they have in non-human assets. However, there is a fundamental difference between non-human assets and labour: one cannot rent out one's labour power to others and walk away. Workers cannot be indifferent towards the allocation of labour time because it is the allocation of themselves (the very same individuals to which preferences are attached in the traditional framework!). Thus, in the case of human labour, the 'temporary private property' arising from the fact that capital hires labour cannot imply the same liberties that the hiring agents would have in the case of non-human assets. Workers necessarily suffer from the exposure to this sort of liberty. This point becomes very evident when we add also that humans can also be exposed either to a virtuous process of *learning by doing* or to a vicious system of *deteriorating by doing*. An exposure to the unfettered liberty of employers may have not only short-term consequences but also lasting effects on the well-being of the workers.

The distinguishing characteristics of human labour become even more important when they are coupled with two other important points that are usually not adequately considered in standard neo-classical analysis: that the definition and enforcement of rights as well as their transfer are usually costly. If these costs (that may be grouped under the label of transaction costs) were absent, then it would be possible to have a separate transaction for each possible use of labour power. However, when this solution is not possible, some 'voice' should be given to the preferences of the workers for the allocation of their labour and for their need to invest in a working environment that favours a process of learning by doing. The allocation of labour cannot then be seen as a private exercise of some rights giving the employer the liberty to dictate working conditions. When this unfettered liberty is granted, we have a Marxian model of *classical capitalism* where the alienation of labour and the underinvestment in human capital can be two undesirable consequences of institutions assimilating the employment relationship with the other transactions of the private sphere.

A possible alternative institutional arrangement to *classical capitalism* may rely on the transfer of control rights from the owners of machines to the workers who could either rent the machines or borrow money and buy them. This solution is tantamount to transferring the bundle of rights that the employers have in the machines and in the labour that they hire to the workers. In this case the workers, having acquired the liberty to decide on the use of their own labour power, could take due account of their preferences for good work and skill enhancing production processes. In many cases[26] this could be a good solution. However, it may turn out to be very problematic in industries that make intensive use of difficult-to-monitor and/or specific capital. In this case capital-owners would be exposed to the liberty of management and workers to use (and abuse) their capital.[27]

For this reason, the protection of workers has often not been based on the transfer of some bundles of rights from capitalist owners to workers. It has rather taken the form of an unbundling of some property rights and their redistribution to different agents. Such unbundling and redistribution can be seen as a different type of legal equilibrium that is characterized by different legal positions of capitalist owners and workers. These legal positions must also be linked together by the strong institutional complementarities that are associated with social scarcity.

In real-life capitalist economies the workers have often acquired two types of rights with respect to the work that they perform. In some cases (that are very frequent in the 'company workers' type of capitalism' characterizing the Japanese economy) they have the right to some unspecified job in a particular organization for a long time and, in some cases, until retirement. In some other cases (that are typical of 'the unionised type of capitalism' that has been developed in the German economy) a union of workers can have the exclusive right to perform some well specified jobs in all organizations but the single worker does not have the right to a job in a particular organization; the specification of the content of these jobs and the associated training is agreed by the unions and employers' associations.

The cases, considered above, correspond to different types of 'unbundling' and redistribution of rights in physical assets from those existing under 'classical Tayloristic capitalism'[28] where the workers do not have any of these rights. However, even more relevant is that the conditions of legal scarcity that characterize a legal equilibrium imply that this unbundling of rights involves a re-definition of the relations that define private property in physical assets under classical capitalism.

Consider first the case of 'company workers capitalism'. If a worker has a right to job security, the owners of the physical assets do not have the liberty to employ the assets of the firm without that worker. Therefore, employers do not have a liberty in the use of physical assets that they have under 'classical capitalism'. Thus, 'company workers capitalism' involves the 'unbundling' and redistribution of a liberty in physical assets that belongs to the employers under 'classical capitalism'.

Likewise, in the case of 'unionized capitalism,' if only workers having certain qualifications and belonging to a certain union have the right to work in a certain trade, the owners of assets do not have the liberty to employ the asset with other workers. Moreover, if the employers' associations and the unions have the right to specify and standardize the nature of the jobs across firms, then the ownership of physical assets does not entail the liberty to employ the assets with any type of organization of production. Thus in a way similar to 'workers capitalism', under 'unionised capitalism' some rights held under 'classical capitalism' by the owners of the assets are 'unbundled' and redistributed.

Observe how hybrid types of organization would involve a violation of the conditions of social scarcity that characterize legal equilibria. Such a situation would arise if the workers expect a right to job security and/or to the exclusive access to and co-definition of some occupation while, at the same time, the owners of physical assets expect to have the unfettered liberty to employ their assets with any worker. While other liberties (such as the possibility to change the allocation of machines in such a way as to change the product mix) can still be held by the employers, one particular liberty must be unbundled and replaced by a duty. Otherwise, the rights of the workers would fail to be in equilibrium with the duties of the employers and the first would be exposed to the unfettered liberty of the latter.

A financial system that is based on the mechanism of take-overs as an *ex post* control mechanism for inefficient managerial choices may require such an unfettered liberty to be exercised by the new owners after a take-over. These liberties would be in a situation of legal disequilibrium with respect to the rights of workers that characterize unionized or workers' company capitalism.

By contrast, the bank-based financial system, which relies on a 'contingent property right system' of financiers (Aoki, 2000), may be in equilibrium with these rights. In a bank-based financial system the liberty of the financiers to interfere is limited to the case in which the incumbent management and the workers of the company are not able to repay their debts.

Thus, financial and labour markets must satisfy *strong conditions of institutional complementarity* related to the social scarcity constraint that characterizes legal equilibria. The two domains are also related together by *weak conditions of institutional complementarity* in the double sense that:

1 in the financial market domain a bank-based system is marginally better than a share-holder dominated system when some forms of rights are given to insiders in the labour market domain (instead of the absence of rights typical of the classical system);
2 in the labour market domain the absence of rights is marginally better than insiders' rights when a shareholder-based system prevails in the financial market domain (instead of the bank-based system).

The *weak conditions of institutional complementarity* also follow from the fact that each of these arrangements must satisfy the conditions of *strong institutional complementarity* characterizing legal equilibria. When shareholders' liberties and insiders' rights are coupled together, the social scarcity constraint is not satisfied and costly conflicts arise. Similarly, when a bank-based system and no-insider rights prevail, the liberties of interference of the financiers could be increased without decreasing the rights of the workers. Here, the inefficiency of an unsatisfactory institutional fit arises from the fact that we would be in an interior point of the feasible set defined by the social arrangements satisfying the social scarcity constraint. The supermodularity conditions would follow from the fact that we are worse off when we are either inside or outside the set of feasible arrangements satisfying the social scarcity constraint that characterizes legal equilibria.

## 'Weak' institutional complementarities and organizational equilibria

While the relations of strong institutional complementarity associated with legal equilibria also imply the existence of weak institutional complementarities among legal positions, in general *weak institutional complementarities* can also well exist independently of *strong institutional complementarities*. In particular, each system of legal positions may be linked by weak relations of complementarities to the type of resources (i.e. the technology) over which the legal relations apply. These relations are only weak in the sense that they do not have to satisfy the social scarcity constraint that characterizes legal equilibria. However, they otherwise have a very important role in determining the economic feasibility of a particular legal equilibrium.

The relations between rights and technology have traditionally been very controversial. It was the core of the Marxian theory of history and has recently attracted the attention of both New-Institutional and Radical Economists who have stressed one of the two possible directions of causation between rights and technology. However, these two approaches should rather be seen as two complementary ways in which the 'double-neutrality assumption' that characterized Samuelson's statement can be challenged. Both can contribute to the conclusion that different systems of rights and technologies can be institutional complements and bring about the existence of multiple organizational equilibria.

In a world of positive transaction costs technology ceases to be neutral. The employment of different factors is likely to be associated with different agency costs because some factors will be relatively more costly to monitor and to safeguard against the hazards of specific investments. Consider the case in which we have only two factors: factor 1 and factor 2. The agency cost that factor 1 has to sustain to hire factor 2 will in general be different from the cost that factor 2 has to bear when it hires factor 1. Define now by $T_1$ and $T_2$ two technologies such that $T_1$ contains a higher intensity of agency costs of factor 1 relative to $T_2$. Denote now by $P_1$ the system of property rights where 1 hires 2 and denote by $P_2$ the system of property rights where 2 hires 1. The choice between $P_1$ and $P_2$ occurs in a domain P where actors such as financiers, stockbrokers and various types of investors search for the best system of property rights given the prevailing technology. By contrast, the choice between $T_1$ and $T_2$ occurs in a domain T where agents such as production managers, engineers and all sorts of technologists search for the best technology given the prevailing system of property rights.

We can now show that the relations between technologies and property rights satisfy the following conditions:

1 the additional benefit of having the property right system $P_1$ instead of the property right system $P_2$ in the domain P is greater when the technology $T_1$ (instead of the technology $T_2$) is chosen in the domain T.
2 the additional benefit of having the technology $T_2$ instead of the technology $T_1$ in the domain T is greater when the property right system $P_2$ (instead of the property right system $P_1$) is chosen in the domain P.

In other words, we are now going to argue that the conditions (1) and (2) discussed in this section satisfy the supermodularity conditions discussed in the section 'Positional goods and social scarcity'.

Indeed, the condition (1) discussed in this section coincides with what may be denoted as the 'new-institutional assumption.[29] A property right system $P_1$ is marginally better than $P_2$ if factor 1 can save a bit more on agency costs. This occurs when in the domain T the prevailing technology is $T_1$ (instead of $T_2$). Since under the technology $T_1$ the agency cost faced by 2 when it employs 1 is higher than under technology $T_2$, under the former technology agent 1 can save marginally more on agency costs than under the latter technology. Thus, the relative advantage of $P_1$ over $P_2$ increases when $T_1$ (instead than $T_2$) is employed in domain T.

The economic meaning of this condition (2) (discussed in this section) is also quite straightforward and coincides with what in some papers[30] we have denoted as the 'radical assumption'. In an analogous manner a technology $T_2$ is marginally better than a technology $T_1$ if it allows us to save a bit more (or to waste a bit less) on agency costs. When the property right system $P_2$ (instead of $P_1$) prevails in the domain P, (parts of) the agency costs of employing factor 2 are saved, whereas the agency costs of employing factor 1 are (completely) paid. Thus, the relative advantage of technology $T_2$ over $T_1$ increases when $P_2$ (instead of $P_1$) is adopted in domain P.

Thus, ($P_1$ $T_1$) and ($P_2$ $T_2$) satisfy the supermodularity conditions and can give rise to multiple organizational equilibria[31] or, in other words, they can be institutional complements.

Observe the self-reinforcing character of these equilibria. $P_1$ is reinforced by the existence of $T_1$ in domain T and $T_1$ is reinforced by the existence of $P_1$ in domain P. Similarly, $P_2$ is reinforced by the existence of $T_2$ in domain T and $T_2$ is reinforced by the existence of $P_2$ in domain P. While our analysis has been framed in a 2 factor world, this self-reinforcing characteristic is not lost when the complexity of the system is augmented by more factors, more technologies and by more sophisticated systems of property rights.

In general, the unbundling and redistribution of rights (i.e. typical of forms of non-classical capitalism that we have considered in the preceding section) is likely to dilute the incentives of capital-owners to invest in high-agency-cost physical assets whose user-induced depreciation cannot be easily monitored and which cannot be easily re-allocated to alternative uses.

However, the same unbundling and redistribution of rights is likely to have positive incentive effects on the agency costs of human capital. In the case of 'company workers capitalism' job security can favour investments in firm-specific human capital that is safeguarded against the threat of 'unfair' termination. And, in the case of 'unionized capitalism' the standardization of jobs across firms, safeguarding the generality of the learning acquired by doing, favours investments in human capital that can be utilized in other firms in case of job termination (or, in other words, this system of rights creates a market for skilled workers).[32] In both cases, the sense of belonging to a firm or to a craft union and the satisfaction of learning by doing should make 'difficult-to-monitor' jobs less costly.

Thus, technologies characterized by easy-to-monitor and generic unskilled labour and high intensity of specific and difficult-to-monitor capital do marginally better than alternative technologies when the system of rights of *classical capitalism* prevails against alternative forms of property rights in the property rights domain, while this is not true under the latter systems of rights. In this sense, we may think that direction of causation from rights to technologies holds also for more complex cases. However, the opposite direction of causation is also likely to hold and a self-reinforcing mechanism generating multiple organizational equilibria may easily arise.

Observe that the 'unbundling' and redistribution of rights is likely to shape the nature of resources in a self-sustaining manner.

Under both company workers and unionized capitalism the truncation of the rights of asset-owners may cause the under-employment of high-agency-cost physical capital. In turn, this under-employment may make the asset-holders value less those rights in the physical assets that have been redistributed to the workers. If the new rights are allowed to survive for a sufficiently long period then, after some time, we would have a lower intensity of high-agency-cost capital that is consistent with the new rights.

A similar self-reinforcing process between the nature of human capital and rights will take place either under 'company workers capitalism' or under 'unionized capitalism'. In the first case, the increased employment of firm-specific human capital will, in turn, increase the value of the firm-specific job rights for the workers. In the second case, the increased employment of general purpose (but trade-specific) human capital will, in turn, induce the workers to give greater value to the rights that their union has in that particular trade.

Under both systems the workers will have a greater incentive to acquire the knowledge that can be useful to perform their jobs; by contrast, the incentives of managers and asset-holders to acquire the knowledge to direct the labour process will become weaker. In other words, in both cases, the unbundling and redistribution of rights in the physical assets will also tend to induce a different complementarity technology characterized by a different distribution of specificity characteristics and asymmetric information. At the same time, these alternative types of technologies may make the unbundling and the redistribution of rights more or less convenient and may favour complementary systems of rights.

## Conclusion

While the rights prevailing in the financial markets domain and the labour market domain must satisfy the conditions of *strong institutional complementarity* that characterize legal equilibria, the relationship between the financiers' and workers' rights and the technology of each system is likely to satisfy only conditions of *weak institutional complementarity*.

In the first case, the supermodularity conditions follow from the fact that the social scarcity constraint that characterizes the relations of legal positions implies that legal disequilibrium is costly. The different positions do marginally better in each domain when they match *ex ante* in a *legal equilibrium* with the legal positions existing in other domains. Otherwise, costly disequilibrium will arise *ex post* and will decrease the benefits arising from those legal positions.

In the second case, different legal positions (taken as a whole and possibly defining a legal equilibrium), do marginally better in their own domain when they fit together in a consistent *organizational equilibrium* with the nature of the technology and the characteristics of the resources (that are shaped by decisions taken in some other domain). Here, the supermodularity conditions do not follow from the costs of (*ex post*) conflicts but from the fact that the benefits arising from a certain set of legal positions are marginally greater when they are matched by a certain technology (instead of some other technology) and vice versa. In this case, the mismatch between rights and technologies, or *organizational disequilibrium,* is only indirectly costly. Individuals do not directly experience the conflicts of some costly disequilibrium but they may realize that they could be better off by moving to situations where the choices made in the different domains fit each other. In this sense we have referred to these as cases of *weak institutional complementarity* and, in our opinion, they can be usefully distinguished from the strong cases of *institutional complementarity* that arise from social scarcity.

However, one should consider some higher levels of institutional complementarity where all these 'strong' and 'weak' complementarity relations influence each other. We have seen that the positional nature of legal relations implies a constant creation of inconsistent claims and costly legal disequilibrium. Such a *legal disequilibrium* may often induce *organizational disequilibrium* and bring about processes that are not limited to the relations existing among different legal positions. In a similar way technological change may often induce situations of organizational disequilibrium with a certain attribution of rights. While it is possible that the system moves in an orderly way to a new consistent attribution of rights that fits the new technology, it can also happen that organizational disequilibrium induces legal disequilibrium.

In other words, the system may easily undergo fairly complex dynamics where both 'weak' and 'strong' complementarities interact with each other. In contrast, this chapter has examined each institutional complementarity independently from the other. In this sense, it can at most offer some preliminary material for the study of these complex interactions.

## Acknowledgements

Preliminary versions of this chapter were presented at the EAEPE annual meetings held in Siena in November 2001 at the Sorbonne University in February 2002 and at the joint Hamburgh–Siena conference held in Hamburgh in June 2002.

I thank the participants of both seminars for useful comments. I also thank, for their suggestions, Masahiko Aoki, Samuel Bowles, Marcello De Cecco Eric Brousseau, Jean-Michel Glachant, Mathew Kramer, Antonio Nicita, Hans-Bernd Schäfer Gregory Valatin and Carlo Zappia. The responsibility for mistakes is entirely mine.

## Notes

1 However, in some cases we can be below some efficiency frontiers and be able to increase the rights and the powers of an individual without decreasing the liberties and the immunities of other individuals.

2 On the concept of Institutional Complementarity see Milgrom and Roberts (1990) and Aoki (2001). Pagano (1993) and Pagano and Rowthorn (1994) introduce the concepts of Organizational Equilibria and Institutional Stability. In spite of the different terminology Aoki (2001, p. 396) has generously acknowledged that '[a]lso Pagano (1993) and Pagano and Rowthorn (1994) are two of the earliest analytical contributions to

institutional complementarity'. According to the terminology used in this chapter, both organizational equilibria and institutional complementarities are 'weak' cases of institutional complementarity.

3 Parts of this section are based on Pagano (2000).

4 The concepts of *ex ante* and *ex post* were introduced in economics in the 1930s by the famous Stockholm School that included Gunnar Myrdal and Erik Lindahl. For a brief (and fairly unsympathetic) account see Steiger (1987).

5 Kelsen (1992) considered the validity of the law or its consistency (not its justice or its efficacy) as the proper object of legal studies and argued that the validity of legal rules should be distinguished from their justice and efficacy. If some final 'grundnorm' was transcendentally given, the unity, consistency and completeness of the legal ordering could be established by checking the consistency of the rules with the hierarchical superior rules. Only the rules that satisfied this consistency test were valid rules of the legal system. Ferrajoli (1993) has distinguished between a concept of validity based on consistency with hierarchically superior norms and a procedural concept of validity meaning that the norms were promulgated by legitimate procedure. This distinction helps understanding that existing norms may be valid in the sense that they have been produced by a legitimate procedure but invalid in the sense that they are inconsistent with superior norms.

6 Hart also 'diluted' the Kelsenian separation between ethics and law. For other authors, like Finnis (1980), even a partial separation is impossible. The final 'grundnorms' at least must be based on some ethical principles.

7 Simmonds (1986, p. 132) points out that while 'the exact limit of such immunities is, of course, a controversial matter . . . American 'civil liberties' differ from their British equivalents precisely in their status as immunities'. In Britain the enjoyment of freedom of speech could in principle at any time be abridged by parliament. 'Freedom of speech in Britain is enjoyed as a Hohfeldian liberty, not an immunity.'

8 In other words, Commons' notion of transaction costs not only includes the traditional *enforcement costs* that characterize relations with another agent, it also includes the cost of the public institutions and *competition costs* to be sustained by the agents when they seek to exclude their competitors from the market. On this point see Nicita (1999, 2001) who introduces the notion of *cross competition* that arises when both the assumptions of zero enforcement and competition costs are removed.

9 Commons (1924) observes that Hohfeld transactions can also be interpreted as ethical relations between the agents which may also be supported by traditional beliefs. However, Commons observes,

> There is, however, a difficulty with these ethical mandates. They are mental processes and therefore as divergent as the wishes and the fears of individuals. Hence, when they emerge into action they are individualistic and anarchistic. They are unrestrained in action by an actual earthly authority to whom each party yields obedience.
>
> (1924, p. 85)

The lack of subjective correlation may express itself in the fact that one agent considers that the boundary of his rights differs from the related boundary of the duty of the other agent. For this reason, according to Commons,

> It seems that the only procedure that will *collerate* the wishes and fears of each and prevent anarchy is to resort to a third person of an earthly quality whom each consents to obey, or each is compelled to obey.
>
> (1924, p. 86)

Wellman (1978) has indicated how Hohfeld relations can be interpreted as both ethical relations and jural relations, and that they can be written as two sets of independent propositions. Bobbio (1990) points out that ethical rights can only logically imply ethical duties and not legal obligations. According to him we can cause much confusion when we mix ethical and jural relations.

10 However, Commons points out how the role of the Magna Carta was somehow limited. 'When, in the Magna Carta, the barons claimed their "liberties" they were claiming personal privileges, or the right to exercise the powers of sovereignty. ... In short, "liberty meant, not liberty nor property, but political privilege"' (Commons, 1924, p. 51).

11 In some respects, the Kelsenian concept of the validity of rules establishing the complete consistency of lawful behaviours is analogous to the Walrasian concept of economic equilibrium. On this point see Pagano (1995). However, the level at which this consistency is established is different. As Gianformaggio (1993) has pointed out, lawful behaviour is made of normative statements that are not intended to represent the actual behaviour of the individuals.

12 Like most economic relations, legal relations become *ex post* simple accounting identities. *Ex post*, if x was exercising some rights, y was necessarily observing some duties. However, the existence of these *ex post* accounting identities does not imply that there was *ex ante* equilibrium between the perceptions of x concerning her rights and the perceptions of y concerning his duties. In other words, *ex ante* disequilibrium is consistent with the *ex post* identity between rights and duties (or between liberties and exposures etc.).

13 The importance of private orderings and of the other many institutions that may contribute to subject human behaviour to the observance of law has been forcefully pointed out by several authors such as Fuller (1963, 1969), Hayek (1973), Leoni (1980) and Williamson (1985).

14 We mean by *public markets*, markets where the task of eliminating legal disequilibrium is mainly performed by public courts. In contrast, as Williamson observes, the

> implicit contract law of internal organization is that of forbearance. Thus, whereas courts routinely grant standing should there be disputes over prices, the damages to be ascribed to delays, failures of quality and the like, courts will refuse to hear disputes between one internal division and another over identical issues. Access to courts being denied, the parties must resolve their differences internally. Accordingly, hierarchy is its own court of ultimate appeal.
>
> (1996, p. 98)

In this sense, in the case of firms, one of the roles of management is to act as a substitute for public courts.

15 Parsons (1986) disagrees but, as Aron (1986) maintains, he seems to be confusing the power over somebody with the power to do something. The former (and obviously not the latter) is a zero-sum good. This implies that the exercise of power may decrease overall welfare because 'one may well experience being subject to the power of another as a welfare loss' (Bowles *et al.*, 1999, p. 6). At the same time, the exercise of power can be Pareto efficiency enhancing if its exchange is agreed on a competitive market and it helps to solve the problem of contractual incompleteness. On this point see Bowles and Gintis (1999). On the concept of power see also the other essays collected in Lukes (1986).

16 Such positions are more generally the fundamental ingredient of a social system. A social system can be conceived as a set of structured processes of interaction characterized by networked, internally related positions with associated rules and practices, while an institution may be defined as those structured processes of interaction 'that are relatively enduring and identified as such' (Lawson, 1997, p. 318). While this chapter focuses on the relations between 'formal' systems of private and public orderings, the study of these systems cannot be abstracted from the informal rules, the customs and the ethical codes that have evolved in different countries and have a fundamental role

in determining the positions of the individuals. As Hodgson (1988, p. 160) points out 'The vision of a "pure" market or capitalist system which has driven out all vestiges of habit and tradition is both theoretically implausible and unrealisable in practice.' For this reason the stream of institutional economics related to Commons' work should be integrated with that deriving from Veblen. On the different streams of institutional economics see Hodgson (1998).

17 This definition is given in Pagano (1999). A different definition, based on rank, is given by Frank (1985). Being related to the definition of status, Frank's definition cannot be easily extended to cases of the exercise of power and to legal relations. Pagano (1999) distinguishes among different particular cases of 'semi-positional' goods. Bi-positional goods are defined by the fact that only one other individual consumes the corresponding amount while 'multi-positional' and 'pan-positional' goods are defined by the fact that many individuals consume. In what follows these definitions are not relevant because we will concentrate on a two-individual economy, but they may perhaps be useful two-distinguish among legal relations occurring 'inter partes' or 'erga omnes'.

18 The Kelsenian solution, where the conflict is resolved by appealing only to superior order norms, usually implies corner solutions. Typically, only the rights or the duties will be consistent with the superior norm. In reality non-corner solutions, as Bobbio (1990) implies, may easily arise.

19 According to Kramer (2001) these rights are not genuine rights but simply nominal rights. According to his 'Interest Theory approach' there are similarities and differences between a nominal right and a genuine legal right. A nominal right

> is a legal right because of its connection with the upholding of the people's interests through the law's setting of standards and requirements, and it is only nominal because the implementation of it by judicial and executive officials cannot go beyond the mere restating of the relevant norm or decision.
>
> (Kramer 2001, p. 73)

20 This observation has been suggested by Professor Schäfer who has also pointed out to me how such circumstances characterized the unfortunate experience of the Weimar Republic.

21 See Holmes and Sunstein (1999) and Pagano (2000).

22 Private property in physical assets is the most elementary way in which an overall legal equilibrium can be broken into simpler subsystems. This quality of private property can only be appreciated in a world of positive transaction costs where the interactions among these subsystems are costly. In a world of positive transaction costs the same quality is shared by more complex private orderings or lower-level governance structures like firms, which complement the formal norms of the legal systems. The type of legal equilibrium posited by Hohfeld's classification would be impossible if many agents working in these subsystems were not to share the burden of eliminating the legal disequilibrium.

23 This formulation is due to Walras and emerged as a compromise between the British and the Austrian stream of the marginalist revolution. While Jevons and Edgeworth had underlined the preference for and the disutility of work, Menger Bohm-Bawerk and von Wieser tended to consider human activity similar to all other non-human resources. A similar divide characterizes the classical economists, while Marx occupied an intermediate position claiming that the fulfilment of the preference for work was the fundamental aspect of communism while the same preferences did not matter under the conditions of alienated work that characterized capitalism. For the 'full story' see Pagano (1985).

24 We could argue with Coase (1937) that, in the Samuelsonian framework, the firm, as an internal allocation mechanism does not exist, and ownership of the firm by an agent simply means that this agent has hiring and firing rights. When transaction costs are taken into account the firm should also be seen as a private ordering (Fuller, 1969).

On the substantial equivalence between the views of Coase and Fuller see Pagano (2000). A very early criticism of the fact that neo-classical theory did not allow a comparative analysis of alternative organizations of production was put forward by Rowthorn (1974).

25 When the preferences for alternative uses of labour power are properly taken into account, the condition that the marginal productivity of a factor is the same should be changed into that requiring that the sum of the marginal utility and the marginal productivity of labour should be the same in each use. Moreover, under these conditions, the maximization of productivity and technological efficiency are not necessary conditions for the overall maximization of the welfare of the individuals and the latter implies an allocation of labour that does not coincide with that maximizing profits. On this point see Pagano (1983, 1985).

26 The advantages of this solution are considered by Bowles and Gintis (1998). Some comments on their claims are advanced in Pagano (1998).

27 Similarly, in these industries financiers who have lent their capital against difficult-to-monitor and specific collateral would be exposed to expropriation hazards.

28 For a more precise definition of 'classical capitalism', 'company workers' capitalism' and 'unionised capitalism' see Pagano (1991a). For a (very short) explanation of the reasons why the major three Western economies have developed alternative 'organizational equilibria,' see the concluding section of Pagano (1993).

29 It is clearly related to the seminal works of Alchian and Demsetz (1972) and Williamson (1985).

30 For instance see Pagano (1991b, 1993, 2001), Pagano and Rowthorn (1994, 1996).

31 Organizational equlibria define situations where the technology is optimal given the current property rights and property rights are optimal given the current technology. The formal analysis of organizational equilibrium shows the precise conditions under which we can have multiple organizational equilibria and how the set of agency costs for which multiple equilibria arises increases with the elasticity of substitution among factors. The properties of institutional stability to shocks in agency costs are also dependent on the value of the elasticity of substitution. See Pagano (1991b, 1993) and Pagano and Rowthorn (1994, 1996).

32 Thus, the unions and the employers' associations that are usually seen as impediments to the unfettered working of efficient markets can, at the same time, be institutional preconditions for a system of property rights that allows the existence of markets for skilled labour. On this point see section 4 of Pagano (1991a).

## References

Alchian and Demsetz (1972) Production, Information Costs and Economic Organisation. *American Economic Review*, vol. 62, pp. 777–795.

Aoki M. (2000) *Information, Corporate Governance, and Institutional Diversity*. Oxford University Press, Oxford and New York.

Aoki M. (2001) *Towards a Comparative Institutional Analysis*. MIT Press, Cambridge.

Aron R. (1986) Macht, Power, Puissance: Democratic Prose or Demoniacal Poetry? In S. Lukes (ed.) *Power*. Blackwell, Oxford, pp. 173–201.

Bobbio N. (1990) *L'età dei diritti*. Einaudi, Torino.

Bowles S. and H. Gintis (1998) Efficient Redistributions: New Rules for Markets, States and Communities. In S. Bowles and H. Gintis (eds) *Recasting Egalitarism*. Verso, London and New York.

Bowles S. and H. Gintis (1999) Power in Competitive Exchange. In S. Bowles, M. Franzini and U. Pagano (eds) *The Politics and the Economics of Power*. Routledge, London, pp. 13–31.

Bowles S., M. Franzini and U. Pagano (1999) Introduction: Trespassing the Boundaries of Politics and Economics. In S. Bowles, M. Franzini and U. Pagano (eds) *The Politics and the Economics of Power*. Routledge, London, pp. 1–11.

Coase R.H. (1937) 'The Nature of the Firm' *Economica*, vol. 4, pp. 386–405. Reprinted in R.H. Coase (1988) *The Firm, the Market and the Law*. University of Chicago Press, Chicago, IL, pp. 33–57.

Commons J.R. (1924) *Legal Foundations of Capitalism*. Augustus M. Kelley Publishers, Clifton reprinted, 1974.

Ferrajoli L. (1993) Il Diritto come sistema di garanzie. *Ragion Pratica*, no. 1, pp. 143–162.

Finnis J. (1980) *Natural Law and Natural Rights*. Clarendon Press, Oxford.

Frank R.H. (1985) The Demand for Unobservable and Other Non-Positional Goods. *American Economic Review*, vol. 75, pp. 101–116.

Fuller L.L. (1963) Collective Bargaining and the Arbitrator. *Wisconsin Law Review*, pp. 3–46.

Fuller L.L. (1969) *The Morality of Law* (revised edition). Yale University Press, New Haven, CT and London.

Gianformaggio L. (1993) *Diritto e ragione fra essere e dovere essere. In le ragioni del garantismo. Discutendo con Luigi Ferrajoli*. Giappichelli, Torino.

Hart H.L. (1958) Positivism and the Separation of Law and Morals. *Harvard Law Review* vol. 71. Reprinted in J. Feinberg and H. Gross (1991) *Philosophy of Law*. Wadsworth Publishing Company, Belmont, CA, pp. 48–81.

Hart H.L. (1961) *The Concept of Law*. Clarendon, Oxford.

Hayek F. (1973) *Law, Legislation and Liberty*. The University of Chicago Press, Chicago, IL.

Hodgson G.M. (1988) *Economics and Institutions*. Polity Press, Oxford.

Hodgson G.M. (1998) The Approach of Institutional Economics. *Journal of Economic Literature*, vol. XXXVI, pp. 166–192.

Hohfeld W.N. (1919) *Fundamental Legal Conceptions*. Yale University Press, New Haven, CT and London.

Holmes S. and C.R. Sunstein (1999) *The Costs of Rights: Why Liberty Depends on Taxes*. W.W.W. Norton & Company, New York and London.

Kelsen H. (1992) *Introduction to the Problems of Legal Theory*. A translation of the first edition of the *Reine Rechtlehere*. Clarendon Press, Oxford.

Kramer M. (1998) Rights without Trimmings. In M. Kramer, N.E. Simmonds and H. Steiner (eds) *A Debate over Rights*. Oxford University Press, Oxford.

Kramer M. (2001) Getting Rights Right. In M. Kramer (ed.) *Rights, Wrongs and Responsibilities*. Palgrave, Basingstoke and New York.

Lawson T. (1997) *Economics and Reality*. Routledge, London and New York.

Leoni B. (1980) *Scritti di scienza politica e teoria del diritto*. Giuffré, Milano.

Lukes S. (ed.) (1986) *Power*. Blackwell, Oxford.

Milgrom P. and J. Roberts (1990) Rationalizability, Learning and Equilibrium Games with Strategic Complementarities. *Econometrica*, vol. 59, pp. 511–528.

Nicita A. (1999) Endogenous Outside Options, Incomplete Contracts and the Nature of the Firm. *Quaderni del Dipartimento di Economia Politica*, no. 250, Università di Siena.

Nicita A. (2001) The Firm as an Evolutionary Enforcement Device. In A. Nicita and U. Pagano (eds) *The Evolution of Economic Diversity*. Routledge, London, pp. 240–270.

Pagano U. (1983) Profit Maximization, Industrial Democracy and the Allocation of Labour. *The Manchester School*, No. 2, pp. 159–183.

Pagano U. (1985) *Work and Welfare in Economic Theory*. Basil Blackwell, Oxford.

Pagano U. (1991a) Property Rights, Asset Specificity, and the Division of Labour under Alternative Capitalist Relations. *Cambridge Journal of Economics*, vol. 15, no. 3. Reprinted in G. Hodgson (1993) *The Economics of Institutions*. Edward Elgar, Cheltenham, pp. 121–147.

Pagano U. (1991b) Property Rights Equilibria and Institutional Stability, *Economic Notes*, vol. 2, no. 2, pp. 189–228.

Pagano U. (1993) Organizational Equilibria and Institutional Stability. In S. Bowles, H. Gintis and B. Gustafson (eds) *Markets and Democracy*. Cambridge University Press, Cambridge, pp. 86–166.

Pagano U. (1995) Diritto. In A. Boitani and G. Rodano (eds) *Relazioni pericolose. L'avventura dell'economia nella cultura contemporanea*. Laterza, Bari, pp. 291–315.

Pagano U. (1998) Redistributions of Assets and Distributions of Asymmetric Information. In S. Bowles and H. Gintis (eds) *Recasting Egalitarism*. Verso, London and New York, pp. 319–322.

Pagano U. (1999) Is Power an Economic Good? Notes on Social Scarcity and the Economics of Positional Goods. In S. Bowles, M. Franzini and U. Pagano (eds) *The Politics and the Economics of Power*. Routledge, London, pp. 63–85.

Pagano U. (2000) Public Markets, Private Orderings and Corporate Governance. *International Review of Law and Economics*, vol. 20, no. 4, pp. 453–477.

Pagano U. (2001) The Origin of Organizational Species. In A. Nicita and U. Pagano (eds) *The Evolution of Economic Diversity*, Routledge, London, pp. 21–48.

Pagano U. and R. Rowthorn (1994) Ownership, Technology and Institutional Stability. *Structural Change and Economic Dynamics*, vol. 5, no. 2, pp. 221–243.

Pagano U. and R. Rowthorn (1996) The Competitive Selection of Democratic Firms in a World of Self-Sustaining Institutions. In U. Pagano and R. Rowthorn (eds) *Democracy and Efficiency in the Economic Enterprise*. Routledge, London, pp. 116–145.

Parsons T. (1986) Power and the Social System. In S. Lukes (ed.) *Power*. New York: New York University Press, pp. 94–143.

Rowthorn R. (1974) Neo-classicism, Neo-Ricardianism and Marxism. *New Left Review*, vol. 86, pp. 63–82.

Samuelson P. (1957) Wage and Interest: A Modern Dissection of Marxian Economic Models. *American Economic Review*, no. 47, pp. 884–912.

Simmonds N.E. (1986) *Central Issues in Jurisprudence. Justice, Law and Rights*. Sweet & Maxwell, London.

Steiger O. (1987) Ex-Ante and Ex-Post. In J. Eatwell, M. Milgate and P. Newman (eds) *The New Palgrave. A Dictionary of Economics*, Macmillan, London, pp. 199–201.

Wellman C. (1978) A New Conception of Human Rights. In E. Kamenka and A.E.S. Tay (eds) *Human Rights*. Edward Arnold, London.

Williamson O.E. (1985) *The Economic Institutions of Capitalism*. The Free Press, New York.

Williamson O.E. (1996) *The Mechanisms of Governance*. Oxford University Press, Oxford.

# 5 Legislate today or wait until tomorrow?

## An investment approach to lawmaking

*Francesco Parisi and Nita Ghei*

### Introduction

Changes in laws are inevitable in any dynamic society. As social and economic customs change over time, often in response to or in conjunction with technological change, the old laws become increasingly ineffective in their application, giving rise to a need for legal change that will permit efficient transactions to take place in the new environment. Thus, for example, the real property laws that were appropriate in a feudal system became increasingly irrelevant and cumbersome over time, say, at the time of the Industrial Revolution, when continuing growth required the law to recognize a society where the population was increasingly mobile. The restraints on alienability of land that were appropriate during feudal times acted as a constraint on growth during the Industrial Revolution. The laws had to change to accommodate the changed technology and customs. A modern example is found in the debate on regulating privacy on the Internet. In this case, the change in technology has permitted the gathering of personally identifying information in a manner never possible before. The European Union has chosen to comprehensively regulate the collection of such information, while the US is still waiting.

The issue of privacy regulation is a striking illustration of the notion that lawmaking is essentially an investment decision. This investment decision – in lawmaking – has several important characteristics. First, since the lawmaker does not know exactly how the environment will change in the future, this is investment under uncertainty. Second, the investment is largely irreversible (i.e. sunk). Third, the lawmaking intervention can be delayed, giving the lawmaker an opportunity to acquire new information concerning the expected costs and benefits of its proposed intervention. The EU has already undertaken the investment, and its costs are sunk. The US is still waiting; it has chosen to retain the option to invest in lawmaking in this area. The purpose of this chapter is to highlight the value of this option of waiting to invest in a social environment with change.

As the emerging investment theory literature has amply shown (e.g. Pindyck, 1991), the ability of an investor to delay an irreversible investment profoundly affects the logic underlying the decision on whether to invest. These results change the conclusions of standard neoclassical investment theory, in the application of the net present value rule. Ignoring the value of the option in the optimization calculation results in investment being undertaken too soon. In the context of lawmaking, these results alter the traditional conception of optimal time to legislate, according to which a rational lawmaker should enact a new rule (or modify an existing rule) when the present value of the expected benefits from the legal innovation are at least as large as its cost.

The structure of the chapter is as follows. In the section "Lawmaking as investment," we expand on the notion that the lawmaking decision is analogous to the decision to undertake an irreversible investment, and that the choice of optimal timing in lawmaking should be derived considering the option-like characteristics of lawmaking decisions. In the section "Optimal timing in the adoption of a new legal rule," we will set out a simple dynamic model of lawmaking under uncertainty to characterize the optimal timing of adoption of a new legal rule. In the section "The costs of waiting," we consider two specific instances of legislative decision-making: privacy regulation on the Internet, and the adoption of new environmental standards as an illustration of the value of waiting to legislate, as well as the costs of waiting. In the section "The value of not waiting," we will explore the significance of these results for the understanding of the optimal timing of lawmaking, considering the implications of the model for legislative and judicial policy. We consider some extensions to the simple model more attuned with the variety of real-life lawmaking problems and then discuss some of the implications for regulatory policy. Some of these results generate conclusions that are qualitatively aligned to the results reached by Heiner (1986) in the context of judicially driven legal innovation[1] and the general wisdom in the political economy of regulation stressing the importance of stability and certainty in the legal system.[2] In the section "The timing and specificity connection," we explore the relationship with the timing issue discussed here, and the issue of specificity of laws analyzed in the law and economics literature. Ultimately, the timing and specificity decisions are intertwined, and a joint analysis would be a valuable contribution in future research. We conclude by contemplating the hypothesis that legal systems, through evolved institutional constraints, have devised instruments that induce courts and lawmakers to take into account the option value of a lawmaking investment.

## Lawmaking as investment

This chapter suggests that the legal problem of optimal lawmaking can be analogized to an investment problem. In this context, the legal and economic analysis of the issue should greatly benefit from the methodological premises and substantive findings of modern investment theory. Economics defines investment as the choice of incurring a present cost in the expectation of future benefits (Dixit and Pindyck, 1994). Viewed from this perspective, legal systems can be regarded as making investment decisions when incurring present lawmaking costs that will generate benefits over time.

Like most other investment decisions, lawmaking investments share, in varying degrees, three important attributes:

1 First, there is often uncertainty over the future benefits of the legislation. Chosen rules may prove ineffective or changes in the social or economic

circumstances may render them obsolete over time. Given such uncertainty, some estimation of the probabilities of alternative outcomes may be necessary.
2 Second, the initial lawmaking costs are at least partially sunk: lawmaking costs cannot be recovered if the enacted rule proves to be ineffective or undesirable at a later time. In this sense, lawmaking investments are partially or completely irreversible.
3 Third, as in any investment decision, there is the choice of the timing of the investment. Lawmakers need to choose the timing for legal intervention. Given uncertainty about future returns, investment can be postponed to acquire more information. Likewise, legal intervention or revision of current rules can be postponed. But delays in such investment decisions often come at a cost, given the forgone benefits of the investment in the immediate future.

According to our hypothesis, these three characteristics interact to determine the optimal decisions of legal planners. Building upon investment theory under uncertainty and recent contributions in option pricing theory, this chapter focuses on the optimal timing of legal intervention illustrating the interaction among the above factors in identifying the optimal patterns of lawmaking.

As the emerging investment theory literature has amply shown (e.g. Pindyck, 1991), the ability of an investor to delay an irreversible investment profoundly changes the logic to be followed in reaching a decision on whether to invest. Traditionally, investment theory under uncertainty suggested that given such tradeoff of costs and benefits, an investment should be carried out whenever it generated a net increase in present value. These conclusions have been revisited in light of option pricing theory (McDonald and Siegel, 1985; Pindyck, 1991) which revealed that the optimal choice of an investment under uncertainty is not the one generated by net present value calculations, but the one generated taking into account the full value of the option to invest.[3] The results of the investment literature have important implications for the choice of optimal timing in lawmaking.

## *Lawmaking costs as sunk costs*

Several of the results that are presented in this chapter are driven by the assumption on the sunk nature of the lawmaking investment. Given the important role played by this assumption in the model presented in the section "Optimal timing in the adoption of a new legal rule," it may be desirable to offer a few words of explanation and justification of the irreversibility assumption in the present context.

In the context of lawmaking, irreversibility merely implies that the legislative (or judicial) costs that bring about a legal innovation are at least partially sunk and cannot be recovered if the enacted rule proves to be undesirable over time.[4] In general, there are a variety of sunk costs in lawmaking. First, there are the obvious costs of legal intervention, which include the direct legislative and political costs, lobbying costs, publication and notice costs. Second, there are the learning costs for courts, enforcement agencies, lawyers and general public. These costs may be substantial and are for the most part irreversible, given the complete dissipation of lobbying and preparatory costs of a law, and the limited value of having learned a law, once the law is repealed. Third, there may be sunk costs of legal innovation whenever there is a change in the existing set of legal entitlements, given the change in equilibrium that is likely to take place as a result of legal changes. Prospectively, lack of stability in legal environments may discourage specific investments, and the forgone benefits of these investments can similarly be regarded as the sunk cost of expected legal change, under rational expectations. Finally, there may be institutional costs involved in the change in the legal rule. For example, there may be sunk costs associated with the discontinued operation of an existing rule, given the lost value in the specialization of legal operators and other sunk investments by law enforcement agencies.

The irreversibility of lawmaking costs has important implications for our understanding of optimal lawmaking behavior. It makes lawmaking especially sensitive to various forms of uncertainty over the future costs and benefits derived from the enforcement of the new rule and the rate of change of the regulated environment that may induce obsolescence in the enacted rule.

Quite notably, any model of optimal lawmaking that fails to consider the option value of delaying innovation is necessarily assuming – explicitly or implicitly – that the legal system can avoid all the above sunk costs, and can abrogate and enact laws without sunk expenditures. For most real-life applications, however, there are likely to be substantial sunk costs involved in regulatory or legal innovation, which necessitate a revision of the net present value rule in the context of lawmaking.

### *The possibility of waiting*

There may be important exceptions to the existence of an option to delay intervention. As public choice theory tells us there are several strategic and institutional constraints that affect the timing of legal intervention. For example, there can be several situations in which strategic concerns render it important for a legislative coalition to act promptly in order to preempt possible intervention by alternative coalitions. Likewise, even though judicial bodies have full control on the decision of whether to overturn a precedent, they do not have the privilege of postponing decision-making in the case at bar. Thus, whenever they are presented with a novel legal issue, the court's obligation to provide a decision in the specific case implies their lack of freedom in the choice of timing for the creation of a new precedent. But, in spite of such institutional or strategic constraints, in most cases, delay in legal intervention remains to a large extent feasible.

Obviously, there are costs to delaying legal intervention. In an ideal world, lawmakers would weigh the benefits of waiting for new information against the cost of postponing lawmaking. However, there is likely to be a difference between the private and social costs of delaying legal intervention. This difference will result in a possible discrepancy between the socially optimal timing for legal intervention and the timing chosen by actual lawmakers. Some of the waiting costs are, in fact, social costs (e.g. the lost opportunity to govern a specific area of the law in the short term) and some other costs are private costs that are only relevant for the specific lawmakers (e.g. the lost of opportunity for individual legislators to enact laws that may benefit their reputation or their leverage with specific interest groups) or for the specific judges (e.g. the lost opportunity to generate a law-changing legal precedent).

### *Timing of legal intervention and the option pricing analogue*

The opportunity to delay an irreversible lawmaking investment can be analogized to a financial call option.[5] In our lawmaking investment application, we should note that unlike most financial options, the lawmaking opportunity is always available, and thus is comparable to a perpetual option with no expiration date.[6] As with financial options, the opportunity to delay legal intervention is intrinsically valuable whenever the future benefit from the lawmaking investment is uncertain. If the expected benefit from legal intervention rises over time, the net payoff from lawmaking increases accordingly. If the proposed legislation loses some of its appeal over time – so that the expected benefits are more than outweighed by the expected costs of legal intervention – then the lawmaker need not intervene and would thus avoid incurring a loss from an irreversible investment.

When a lawmaker decides to legislate, she exercises (or "kills") her lawmaking option, giving up the possibility of waiting for new events and information that might influence the desirability of the legislative innovation. By deciding to intervene, the lawmaker dissipates the full option value. Such opportunity cost should be included in the cost–benefit analysis of the lawmaking decision.

Legal innovation should be carried out only when the expected value of lawmaking exceeds the lawmaking costs by an amount equal to the value of keeping the lawmaking option alive. In the presence of uncertainty, this result modifies considerably the traditional results of the net present value rule, which would suggest proceeding with legal innovation any time the expected present value of lawmaking exceeds the expected costs of lawmaking. Indeed, in the presence of sunk costs and uncertainty, the application of the net present value rule would always lead to non-optimal decisions.

Lawmaking guidelines that ignore the "value of waiting" principle can be grossly in error. Most importantly, as we will show in the next section, the "value of waiting" in lawmaking is an increasing function of (1) the level of uncertainty in the regulated environment and variance of the expected benefits from legal intervention, and (2) the extent that lawmaking expenditures are sunk.

## Optimal timing in the adoption of a new legal rule

The present section sets forth a dynamic analysis of lawmaking, building upon the results of the investment theory literature. In particular, we present a formal model examining the choice of timing of the adoption of a legal rule in a world of uncertainty. This model is formulated keeping in mind that the investment in promulgating laws is generally irreversible, that is, the costs are sunk and not recoverable.[7]

Consider a world with a single supreme adjudicator, with sole lawmaking authority. For the purposes of this section all laws are the same type; there is no discretion on the part of the lawmaker on the choice of legislative instrument or degree of specificity of the rule.[8] The external environment is changing, at a stochastic rate. As time passes, the lawmaker has the option of changing the law. We assume that the new law is a better fit with the new environment, and is thus more efficient. The date and type of change in the external environment is not known to the lawmaker. There is always the option of waiting, rather than changing the law now, since the environment changes in a stochastic pattern.[9] This timing choice will be exercised in light of two important considerations. First, lawmaking investments are partially or completely sunk (i.e. lawmaking costs cannot be recovered if the enacted rule proves to be ineffective or undesirable at a later time). Second, given the existing political and institutional constraints in legislation, changing the law now often means giving up an option of changing later. That is, the choice of timing is irreversible.

The law production function has the form

$$L(v, \Theta) = \Theta v^{a}, \quad 0 < a < 1 \tag{5.1}$$

where $\mathbf{v}$ is a variable input (such as enforcement cost) and $\mathbf{\Theta}$ is the rule parameter whose value is determined stochastically. Assume that $\mathbf{p}$ is the fixed value of the benefit of the law, per unit, and $\mathbf{w}$ is the fixed unit cost of the variable input, enforcement cost. We consider a dynamic model with an infinite time horizon. At time 0, the state of the law is designated by

$$\Theta = \Theta_0 \tag{5.2}$$

Over time, as the external environment evolves, this parameter changes. Assume that this follows a jump process such that

$$d\Theta = dq, \quad \Theta(0) = \Theta_0 \tag{5.3}$$

where

$$\begin{aligned} dq &= u \quad \textit{with probability } \lambda dt \\ &\phantom{=}\ 0 \quad \textit{with probability } 1 - \lambda dt \end{aligned}$$

For simplicity, we assume that $\mathbf{u}$ is distributed uniformly, across the interval $(0, u^*)$. Adopting a new legal rule means incurring a sunk cost of $\mathbf{I}$, which is assumed to remain constant.

The general problem facing the lawmaker is choosing the right moment to switch to the new law. One extreme possibility is that the lawmaker change the law every time there is a change in the external environment; the other extreme is never to change the law. The former option would mean incurring the sunk costs for each switch, which could be prohibitive. The latter could result in laws that are in effect obsolete and inefficient, since they do not address the needs of the society they are designed to serve. In between the two extremes, there should be a range of points where the benefits of the switch exceed the sunk cost of making the switch.

According to traditional neoclassical investment theory, the optimal timing of the investment should be the one that maximizes the net present value of the benefits from the legislative switch. Such a present value calculation, however, has been shown to ignore the option value of the investment decision (Pindyck, 1991). We will utilize a similar intuition to show the use of present value calculations in legislative decisions omits to take into proper account the value of waiting in lawmaking.

In this section, we consider the simple case of a single switch. There has been a change in the external environment. The lawmaker could continue with the current law or could adopt a new law. If the lawmaker adopts the new law, the value of this new law is given by

$$V(\Theta_1) = \int_{t=0}^{\infty} \max(p\Theta_1 v^a - wv)e^{-rt}dt = \int_{t=0}^{\infty} f(\Theta_1)e^{-rt}dt = \frac{f(\Theta_1)}{r} \tag{5.4}$$

where $\mathbf{f}(\boldsymbol{\Theta})$, the net benefit from the new law, is defined as

$$f(\Theta) = \max(p\Theta v^a - wv) \tag{5.5}$$

The value of $\mathbf{v}$ that maximizes the term above is given by

$$v^* = \left(\frac{ap\Theta}{w}\right)^{1/(1-a)} \tag{5.6}$$

This means that f($\Theta$) is

$$f(\Theta) = (1-a)\left(\frac{a}{w}\right)^{a/(1-a)} p^{1/(1-a)}\Theta^{1/(1-a)} \tag{5.7}$$

This can be re-written as

$$f(\Theta) = \phi\Theta^b \tag{5.8}$$

where

$$\phi = (1-a)\left(\frac{a}{w}\right)^{a/(1-a)} p^{1/(1-a)} \tag{5.9}$$

and

$$b = 1/(1-a) > 1 \tag{5.10}$$

From Equations 5.5 and 5.8, we obtain the following:

$$V(\Theta) = \frac{\phi\Theta^b}{r} \tag{5.11}$$

The termination payoff from adopting the new rule, is equal to V($\Theta$) – I.

To derive the optimal switching level, $\Theta^*$, we have to consider the case $\Theta^* - u^* \leq \Theta \leq \Theta^*$, so that there is a positive probability that changing the law will be optimal after the next environmental change. First, we need to derive the Bellman equation. Combining the Bellman equation at $\Theta = \Theta^*$, and the value-matching condition (see Dixit and Pindyck, 1994) at the same point, we can arrive at the equation from which the optimal switching level can be calculated. The Bellman equation is

$$F(\Theta) = f(\Theta_0)dt + \frac{1}{(1+rdt)}E[F(\Theta + d\Theta)] \tag{5.12}$$

where

$$E[F(\Theta + d\Theta)] = F(\Theta) + \lambda dt\left[\int_{u=0}^{\Theta^*-\Theta} F(\Theta + u)\frac{1}{u^*}du + \int_{u=\Theta^*-\Theta}^{u^*}(V(\Theta + u) - I)\frac{1}{u^*}du - F(\Theta)\right] \tag{5.13}$$

$$(1 + rdt)F(\Theta) = f(\Theta_0)dt + F(\Theta) + \lambda dt\left[\int_{u=0}^{\Theta^*=\Theta} F(\Theta + u)\frac{1}{u^*}du + \int_{u=\Theta^*-\Theta}^{u^*}(V(\Theta + u) - I)\frac{1}{u^*}du - F(\Theta)\right]$$

Ignoring terms of dt with higher powers than one, the two equations give the following:

$$F(\Theta) = \frac{f(\Theta_o)}{(r+\lambda)} + \frac{\lambda}{(r+\lambda)}\left[\int_{u=0}^{\Theta^*=\Theta} F(\Theta + u)\frac{1}{u^*}du + \int_{u=\Theta^*-\Theta}^{u^*}(V(\Theta + u) - I)\frac{1}{u^*}du\right] \tag{5.14}$$

Dividing by $(r + \lambda)$, we get

$$F(\Theta^*) = \frac{f(\Theta_o)}{(r+\lambda)} + \frac{\lambda}{(r+\lambda)}\int_{u=0}^{u^*}(V(\Theta^* + u) - I)\frac{1}{u^*}du \tag{5.15}$$

From this we can derive the Bellman equation for $\Theta = \Theta^*$.

The value-matching condition indicates that, at this critical point, the lawmaker would be indifferent between adopting a new law now, or waiting to adopt a more efficient rule later. Contrast this to the net present value rule. From Equation 5 we know that the value of using the law $\Theta$ is $V(\Theta)$. The net present value method yields the following rule for the optimal switch level, $\Theta^*$ PV

$$V(\Theta^*_{PV}) - I = V(\Theta_0) \tag{5.16}$$

Using Equation 5.11 we get

$$\frac{\phi(\Theta^*_{PV})^b}{r} - I = \frac{\phi(\Theta_0)^b}{r} \tag{5.17}$$

The threshold under the net present value rule is lower than that obtained when the value of the option of waiting is taken into account. We can now proceed in the present "qualitative" analysis to explore the idea of evolution of laws in a dynamic framework.[10]

This model captures two essential elements in the adoption of a new legal rule. First, the sunk costs in the legislative change are irreversible. The costs associated with promulgating a new legal rule include the costs of acquiring information, as Kaplow (1992) and Erlich and Posner (1973) postulate. In addition, the process of rule-making through the private legislature, explored by Schwartz and Scott (1995), can be taken into account. There is also the cost of passing the law, and disseminating information about the new law, the latter being the focus of Kaplow (1992). Once the law is formulated and promulgated, these costs cannot be recovered. That is, the switch in the legal rule is analogous to an irreversible investment in a new technology.

Second, when the new legal rule is adopted, the lawmaker gives up the option of making the switch at some other time, using those same resources. Given some binding budget, time, or political constraint on the part of the legislature, there is an opportunity cost of adopting a new rule, represented by the forgone possibility to enact a new rule in the subsequent time period. It should be noted that this additional element brings the model closer to real-life politics, where frequent amendments of the same rule are either infeasible or impose severe reputational costs, given the unavoidable public dislike of unstable legislation. Furthermore, legislators face a binding resource and a time constraint in their activity, which renders the ideal models of unconstrained optimization hardly descriptive of real-life legislative problems.

As a result of these factors, the option to enact a new law (or amend an existing law) has a value, an opportunity cost.[11] If the analysis is extended to include the effects of such constraint-driven opportunity cost, the optimization problem should consider the forgone value of the option. Using a simple discounted, net present value rule would, in fact, yield an incorrect result of the optimal time to switch the rule, since it does not take into account the option value of the legislative choice.

The importance of the option in this context depends on the fact that, by waiting, the legislator preserves the opportunity of making a better (or more informed) legislative change in the future, and not just that of not amending at all, as would be the case if the random events give new value to the existing legal rule. One implication of a non-zero, positive value to this option of waiting is that the change in legal rules will in fact be slower than would be predicted under a net present value rule.

On the other hand, there can be benefits that will be forgone by waiting. The longer the lawmaker waits, the greater is the divergence between the actual law and the law required due to social change. For example, in cases such as environmental policy and privacy, as we discuss below, further damage can occur during the waiting period. Thus, information will already be disseminated, or the numbers of an endangered species might fall so low as to render regenerating infeasible. This cost of waiting can be added quite simply to the model. We discuss this in the specific context of privacy and environmental legislation in the following section. Further, there are more subtle issues to consider as well. In many cases laws can be enacted incrementally, and there can be valuable learning during the process. These benefits of acting now would act to set off the value of waiting. We explore the implications of sequential lawmaking and learning by doing in the section "The value of not waiting."

## The costs (and value) of waiting: illustrations

In the real world there can be costs as well as benefits to waiting. In this section we will consider two illustrations, in an attempt to provide flesh to the abstract model discussed above. Environmental policy has been the subject of growing attention from investment theorists, one of the most recent being Pindyck (2002). Academic analysis of the issue of privacy regulation has largely been confined to discussion by legal scholars, such as Murphy (1996), Volokh (2000) and Kobayashi and Ribstein (2001). But both have striking similarities in the costs and benefits of waiting, and in the decision to legislate. Both environmental and privacy regulation are undertaken in an environment of uncertainty on several levels. First, the lawmaker does not know the extent of environmental damage that will occur or its full cost. Second, the lawmaker does not know exactly how costly implementation of the new environmental standard will be. Similarly, the lawmaker does not know the extent of privacy violation in the future, and its cost. Nor does the lawmaker know the cost of implementation of a legislated privacy regime. In each case, the cost of investment will be largely irreversible. We discuss each in greater detail below.

### *Environmental legislation*

As Pindyck (2002) points out, in the context of environmental regulation, society faces the following question: at what point in time should society adopt a costly policy to limit environmental damage?[12] As a concrete example, consider the case of global warming. There is considerable debate about implementing new standards – through legislation and regulation – to reduce the threat of global warming. A simple net present value rule, which involves a standard cost–benefit analysis in capital budgeting terms, will likely bias legislators in favor of adoption. But such a rule fails to take into account the uncertainty in future costs and benefits, and the issue of irreversibility of investment.

There is a great deal of uncertainty about the costs and benefits of adopting any particular legislation. The first source of uncertainty is the magnitude of the problem of global warming. There is no consensus among scientists on whether there is such a phenomenon. Second, if in fact global warming is taking place, there is no scientific consensus about the effectiveness of reducing emissions of greenhouse gases in limiting the rise in temperature. Finally, the economic impact of higher global temperatures is uncertain.[13]

There are at least two kinds of irreversibilities that Pindyck identifies in such cases. The costs of adopting new environmental standards are largely sunk. If the government imposes stricter emission standards, manufacturers will have to invest in the appropriate technology – which is costly. There is another cost that is sunk, which Pindyck does not consider explicitly, the cost of legislation itself.

The process of enacting laws and implementing regulations is costly, requiring outlay of government resources. The affected agents incur information costs in learning about the new legislation, and revising all related decision-making. All these costs are sunk; they cannot be recovered at a later time if the regulation is found to be inappropriate. Reversal of the policy in the future will require further outlay of resources. Reversal might also be complicated by standard public choice problems. Once a regulation is in place, reversal can be made more difficult by the presence of interest groups and other political constraints.[14] Thus, for example, if scientists determine, say, twenty years from now, that either global warming has not occurred, or that it does not in fact harm the environment, it might be difficult to revise the emissions standards upwards then. In any case, all affected parties would already have invested in the technology needed for the lower emissions at that point, and the costs are not recoverable. These sort of sunk costs increase the opportunity cost of enacting new legislation now, and increase the value of waiting. If in fact global warming is not a problem, then doing nothing is the most efficient outcome, in that these costs would be avoided. In this case, the option to legislate environmental standards would not be cashed in.

On the other hand, there is also what Pindyck terms a "sunk benefit" to enacting new legislation now rather than waiting due to the other irreversibility that need to be considered. Specifically, environmental damage can be irreversible, either partially or totally. Thus, limiting greenhouse gas emissions in the future might only limit further global warming, but not reduce the warming that has already occurred. Or, the damage to the ecosystem as a result of the global warming would already have occurred during the time the legislators chose to wait, and it might not be possible to reverse the damage. For example, some species of plant or animal might have become extinct in the interim, as legislators waited. Adopting the new environmental standards now, that is, cashing in on the option to wait, will allow society to capture these sunk benefits.

The two irreversibilities work in opposite directions. The ultimate decision on the timing of adoption of new environmental standards by law needs to take both into account, as well as the uncertainty about future costs and benefits.

### *Regulating privacy on the Internet*

Privacy regulation is another policy area where many of the issues of uncertainty and irreversibility make it wise to consider the value of waiting. The issue of privacy regulation has arisen largely due to a technological change that made it extraordinarily easy to gather personally identifiable information. This technology has resulted in a profound economic and social change, and sharpened concerns about how this information was being acquired and used and by whom.

One of the earliest proposals in dealing with the issue was by Murphy (1996), who suggested creating property rights in such information. However, as Volokh (2000) has pointed out, at least in the US, such proposals might be constitutionally problematic. The discussion of privacy regulation has been confined to two broad areas. First, the nature of the regime, and second, the implementing authority.

Broadly speaking there are two sorts of regulatory regimes. In an "opt-in" regime, personally identifiable information can be used only when the person whose information it is gives explicit consent to such use.[15] In an "opt-out" regime, the person who has acquired the information is free to use it, unless the person whose information it is explicitly forbids the use, that is, opts out of the information sharing. In the US, the choice of implementing authority is between the federal government or the states. Ribstein and Kobayashi (1996) have suggested that it might be better for the states to legislate on the issue, in that competition among the states will ensure that the most efficient laws will survive. Apart from the possible constitutional problems, these problems fail to account for the uncertainty and the irreversibilities inherent in the situation, and the corresponding value of waiting.

We would suggest that the problem should first be posed as a timing one: when, if ever, should the government legislate to regulate privacy on the Internet? The costs and benefits of such legislation, including the choice of regime (opt-in or opt-out), are uncertain. At least one study, by Staten and Cate (2002), suggests that the adoption of an opt-in regime might impose significant costs on both business and consumers. But neither the costs nor the benefits of any regime can be known with any degree of certainty.

Privacy regulation also faces the same sort of irreversibilities discussed in the context of environmental legislation. The actual costs of enacting legislation are irreversible. Once the legislation has been enacted, the affected parties incur information costs in learning about the new legislation. In addition, they will incur compliance costs, such as updates on computer systems.[16] These costs are sunk, and cannot be recovered if the legislation is repealed in the future. Thus, there is a value to waiting, to see whether the benefits are large enough to justify cashing in the option of legislating.

On the other hand, there is a sunk benefit to adopting the legislation now. There might be damage from use of the information that might later be irreversible. Once the information is available in the public domain, it might be impossible to recover the privacy of the individual. The damage to the individual from the loss of privacy thus is irreversible. This damage would be prevented by the adoption of regulation today. That is, the sunk benefit would be captured by cashing in the legislation option.

In the context of privacy, the EU has cashed in the option, in enacting the Privacy Directive. The US has chosen to taken a different approach, by legislating incrementally.[17] Currently, the federal government has acted to legislate only with respect to information where there is a heightened expectation of privacy, in the form of medical information and financial records, or where the individual is especially vulnerable, such as children on the Internet. So far, the federal government has chosen to retain the option to wait in legislating privacy with respect to other Internet traffic.

There is some evidence that this might be the efficient solution. As markets forces encourage innovation, to the extent that customers demand privacy and security of their information, there is evidence that suppliers are responding to such concerns. As of the current date, virtually all the large Internet retailers have some sort of privacy policy in place. At the same time, new software has been developed and marketed that gives the individual much greater control over securing his or her own personal information, and preventing unauthorized use. In waiting to legislate, the government can now take these developments into account, which will result in a more accurate assessment of the costs and benefits of further regulation. It might well be that costs of new legislation to further regulate privacy on the Internet exceed the benefits. If this in fact turns out to be the case, the option to legislate will not be cashed in, and new legislation will not be adopted.[18]

## The value of not waiting

The model presented in the section "Optimal timing in the adoption of a new legal rule" illustrates how a proposed legal change can be viewed as an option and valued accordingly. However, we ignored some of the possible benefits of acting immediately, that is, of not waiting. In the following pages, we will explore some of them. While no mathematical models are included for these extensions, the relevant optimization problems are plainly presented and some tentative conclusions are discussed.

### *Sequential lawmaking decisions*

Many regulatory objectives involve multistage legal intervention that needs to be carried out in sequence (e.g. several programmatic laws require implementing legislation and/or subsequent governmental intervention, international treaties require ratification and subsequent implementation and harmonization at the national level, etc.).[19] Sequential lawmaking processes like these can take substantial time to complete. Furthermore, they can be temporarily or permanently abandoned midstream if the expected net benefit of the final legal innovation declines, as might be the case of the privacy regulation discussed in the previous section.

How does the existence of multistage regulatory objectives (when the benefits of undertaking each step are uncertain) change the results of the one-time legal intervention discussed above? Under plausible assumptions, the sequential lawmaking problem will show an increased importance of the effects of uncertainty and irreversibility. The longer it takes for a legal enactment to come into force (be such delay due to a time lag in legal implementation or to a complex multistage regulatory process) the greater is the uncertainty regarding the value of the innovation at the time of entry into force of the final regulation. Because the value of the law upon completion is more uncertain, an even higher expected discounted benefit from regulation will be necessary to justify legal intervention.[20]

### *Learning from legal experimentation*

In our model of lawmaking, no learning takes place in the sense that future benefits from legal intervention are always uncertain, and the degree of uncertainty depends only on the time horizon. Our model thus fails to account for the possible informational benefits generated by legal experimentation. In real life, even an unsuccessful legal innovation can occasionally generate informational benefits, since it discloses the intrinsic value of attempted legal solutions and reduces the risk of similar legislative errors in the future. Legislative experimentation may indeed provide valuable information about the net benefits (or lack thereof) of alternative legal rules.

The informational value of past legislative errors affects the results reached in the section "Optimal timing in the adoption of a new legal rule" of the present chapter, since present legal innovation yields information that reduces the uncertainty over the value of future legal alternatives.[21] The consideration of the value of learning may lead to counterintuitive results. For example, paradoxically, even legal proposals that have a negative expected present value may be worth carrying out, given the external informational benefits generated by such form of legal experimentation.

These results may partially offset the tendency suggested by option pricing theory. As we have seen above, in the absence of learning, option pricing theory yields a test for the optimal timing of legal innovation which is stricter than the net present value rule. We called this result the "value of waiting" in lawmaking. If we take into account the value of learning from past errors, the above result may be considerably changed in the diametrically opposite direction. With learning, we may have a more permissive test concerning the optimal timing of legal innovation, given the external informational benefits from past experience. We may call this the "value of experimentation" in lawmaking. Neither case coincides, however, with the net present value rule that, in these cases, may be viewed as an intermediate benchmark against which to evaluate the desirability of legal change.[22]

The implied and most crucial assumption of models with learning is that the underlying reality does not evolve stochastically. The identity of the best legal rule may not be known (at least until all possible rules have been tried), but the identity of such rule, whichever it may be, does not evolve stochastically over time. In this limit case if the only source of information comes from actual trial and error, there is no gain from waiting and, to the contrary, there is an opportunity cost to delaying experimentation, given the informational value of innovation.[23]

## The timing and specificity connection

There are two interrelated issues concerning the adoption of legal rules: the timing of adoption of legal rules, and the degree of specificity of the rule. Law and economics scholars have treated these issues as independent, often concentrating on the question of optimal degree of specificity (i.e. rules versus standards, etc.) and assuming no degree of freedom in the choice of timing in the implementation of legal rules. Such simplifying assumption, while useful for rendering the problem more tractable, should be relaxed to unveil the important interrelation between timing and specificity of legal rules. In the present chapter we have considered the related problem of optimal timing in the adoption of legal rules. In doing so, we have undertaken a different simplification, treating the level of specificity of legal rules as a constant. While the analysis of the tradeoff between timing and specificity of legislative intervention falls beyond the scope of the present chapter, we think it relevant to offer some preliminary insight on this important extension.

In the existing literature, the problem of optimal degree of specificity of legal rules was first discussed by Erlich and Posner (1973) and Schwartz and Scott (1995) who structured their seminal papers around the dichotomous distinction of rules versus standards. Erlich and Posner (1973) offer a formal optimization model that is static. Schwartz and Scott (1995) model rule-making in the context of private legislatures as a single-shot, multistage game. However, as Kaplow (1992) points out, (in the only other study on the topic with a similar degree of rigor, though from a different angle), it is possible to have a complex rule and a simple standard. This, in effect, uses a different definition of what is a rule and what is a standard. Kaplow (1992) takes the choice of legal rule as a given, and considers the problem of whether an individual will choose to acquire information about the existing law.

Building upon these contributions, the problem of optimal specificity can be reassessed in a dynamic fashion, considering a world where there is a single supreme lawmaker whose business it is to create law. Along the lines of the model presented in the section "Optimal timing in the adoption of a new legal rule," we should, however, give the lawmaker two control variables: first, the option to innovate (or delay intervention); second, the choice of either fully specifying the rule *ex ante* (i.e. choosing a "rule" in Erlich and Posner's terminology) or to state the law in general terms, which requires an *ex post* interpretation of the law (i.e. choose a "standard" in Erlich and Posner's terminology).

The choice of a well specified rule is likely to require a larger up-front investment, but has lower operating costs later. Enacting a rule requires a large outlay in the initial acquisition of information, but because the rule is simple to understand and apply, the operating costs are low. A standard requires a smaller investment initially, as it requires less information and legislative detail to enact a standard. However, it requires larger outlays in its enforcement, in that it is more costly for individuals to acquire information about a standard (as per Kaplow) and it requires greater implementation and interpretation efforts by the courts.

Given the different sunk investment of a rule as opposed to a standard, the option value of delaying legal intervention varies in the two cases. Thus, in the presence of uncertainty and sunk investment costs, the lawmaker is faced with a wedge between the economies of scale obtainable with the implementation of a specified rule and the increased value of the forgone option to postpone the lawmaking decision.

The dual optimization problem facing the lawmaker, then, is that of determining the optimal level of specificity and timing of intervention in consideration of the above factors.[24]

The understanding of the optimal timing problem presented in this chapter in conjunction with the optimal specificity problem presented in the existing law and economics literature (Erlich and Posner, 1973; Kaplow, 1992; Schwartz and Scott, 1995) would serve as building blocks for a more complex model of lawmaking where timing and degree of specificity are allowed to vary simultaneously. The two optimization problems can then be set up to tackle the interesting problem of the simultaneous choice of optimal timing and specificity of legal rules. Indeed, at any point in time, lawmakers decide their legislative action controlling both the timing and the degree of detail of legal rules, with a likely awareness of the important interrelationship between the two variables.

Some tentative possible conclusions can be drawn from the intuitive analysis of the above problem. In particular, it is likely that in times of high uncertainty, the expected value of investment in rules declines relative to standards, and one would expect to see more standards and fewer rules during times of instability. Correspondingly, one would expect to see detailed rules that leave little to the discretion of the rule-applier in times of stability. These are testable hypotheses that are grounds for further work.

## Conclusion

In this chapter, we have presented a dynamic analysis of the evolution of legal rules. The model draws on the work on investment theory, stressing the fact that lawmaking investments are generally irreversible and that decisions concerning legal innovation are made in a world of uncertainty. A simple model of adoption of a new legal rule in a world where the external environment was changing at a stochastic rate was developed in the section "Optimal timing in the adoption of a new legal rule." In view of the fact that investment in the new legal rule means incurring sunk costs, the switch to a new legal rule has an opportunity cost that is non-zero. Therefore, the change in the legal rule is likely to be slower than would be indicated by a simple discounted, net present value analysis.

The findings of this chapter suggest that uncertainty may be a more crucial determinant of optimal timing in lawmaking than usually believed under the net present value criterion. This is likely to have implications for the explanation and prediction of regulatory and judicial behavior and for the institutional design of lawmaking and legislative policy. In the present chapter we have focused largely on lawmaking innovations, but the principles elaborated above apply to a much broader range of problems involving legal intervention in situations of uncertainty and sunk costs. Similar issues may arise in situations where individuals, firms or institutions face short-term organizational costs when subjected to a legal change. These costs are for the most part sunk, since they cannot be recouped if the legal rule reverts to the preexisting form. In evaluating the optimal timing and frequency of change of legal rules, the lawmaker should account for such private adjustments costs and should measure the opportunity cost of investing now rather than delaying legal intervention.

The application of the "value of waiting" rule may obviously become problematic when applying this method to legal intervention concerning depletable resources and the environment, since several irreversibilities on the benefit side may be present to offset the sunk cost considerations enunciated above. Likewise, the quantification difficulties in solving a specific timing problem may be exacerbated by society's changing valuation of legal, moral or ethical principles, and the dynamic effects of legal intervention on the evolution of individual preferences and values.

In spite of these limitations and likely difficulties in giving a normative significance to our "value of waiting" principle, the above considerations have unveiled the critical role of uncertainty and irreversibility in lawmaking, and have, we hope, provided some insight into the importance of the latent opportunity costs of lawmaking.

## Notes

1 The conclusions of this chapter are not inconsistent with Heiner's (1986) economic interpretation of the doctrine of *stare decisis*, despite its very different origin.

2 As shown in the economic development literature, a major cost of political and economic instability may be its depressing effect on investment.

3 See Pindyck (1991) who stresses the equivalence between the decision to invest and the decision to exercise an option, reviewing the literature in the field. As a result of these contributions, the investment literature now generally views the investment decision as a problem of option valuation.

4 In the general Industrial Organization literature, an investment expenditure is considered irreversible whenever the capital is firm or industry specific and has a substantially lower value if used in a different firm or industry.

5 In the investment literature, this analogy was pointed out by Pindyck (1991) who observes that an irreversible investment opportunity is like a call option, which gives the holder the opportunity to pay an exercise price and receive an asset in consideration for such price. Similar to a sunk investment, the exercise of a call option is irreversible. As Pindyck (1991 p. 1111) points out "although the asset can be sold to another investor, one cannot retrieve the option or the money that was paid to exercise it."

6 One of the first models of irreversible investment was developed by McDonald and Siegel (1985) who pointed out that the investment opportunity is equivalent to a perpetual call option.

7 The analysis in this section follows Farzin *et al.* (1998). As Doraszelski (2001) has pointed out, Farzin *et al.* make an error in their derivation for multiple switch problem. Doraszelski's results suggest that the threshold accounting for the option value of waiting always exceeds the threshold implied by the net present value approach, even when technology can be switched $n < \infty$ time. This section draws from the body of work on investment under uncertainty; a survey can be found in Dixit and Pindyck (1994). For an exposition of the mathematical tools used, see Stokey and Lucas (1989).

8 In later extensions, the distinction between rules and standards should be reintroduced to study the tradeoff between the optimal timing and specificity of legal rules.

9 The model presented in this section utilizes a stochastic shift parameter, $\boldsymbol{\Theta}$. In real-life applications, it may not be always clear what the correct stochastic process is and which functional form should be substituted for $\boldsymbol{\Theta}$. For example, while the choice of a geometric random walk may be sensible for, say, some situations concerning technological innovation and new scientific discoveries, other regulated environments may be better represented by other stochastic functional forms. One could argue, for example, that over the long run, the level of unemployment or the level of criminality may follow a mean-reverting process, where the mean reflects the long-run equilibrium expected value of unemployment or criminality. While the choice of a specific stochastic form is necessary to generate precise results and is convenient for analytical purposes, the specification of the stochastic variable is not crucial for the qualitative results. For a review of the various results under different stochastic assumptions in the investment theory literature, see Pindyck (1991).

10 In the investment context, the model can be solved for greater detail to determine the efficiency level that triggers the adoption of a new technology. See Farzin *et al.* (1998) for a full solution and presentation of a general model allowing for multiple switches in technology.

11 In terms of physical or financial investment, it would be relatively easy to assign a dollar value to this option. The value of the option in the context of investment in an

asset is discussed extensively in Dixit and Pindyck (1994). See also Pindyck (1991) for a relatively non-technical treatment of the subject of irreversibility and investment. It is more difficult to do this in the context of legal change, giving up an option reduces the choices available to the lawmaker in terms of the timing of future changes to the legal rule.

12 Pindyck develops an elegant formal model to deal with the issue of optimal timing of environmental standards.

13 We offer no opinion on either side of the global warming debate here. This discussion aims at highlighting the potential issues that might be relevant to the legislator's decision in such cases.

14 Of course, the problem of narrow interest groups exists at the initial adoption as well. Small groups can organize more easily, and therefore lobby more effectively in having legislation they favor enacted. This problem was discussed by Olson (1965), and has been extensively discussed in the public choice literature.

15 Effectively, the EU Privacy Directive mandates an opt-in regime.

16 The Gramm–Leach–Bliley Financial Services Modernization Act required the affected financial institutions to mail notices to all customers. Even if the Act is repealed in the future, the cost of these mailings, which was not insignificant, is sunk and cannot be recovered.

17 See the discussion in the section "The value of not waiting" below on sequential lawmaking decisions.

18 The issue of privacy is also complicated by other factors that are much harder to quantify. For example, privacy preferences can vary, not only across individuals, but also across nations. When this possibility is taken into account, one can speculate that the mandatory opt-in regime is the optimal one for the EU, in that to European citizens the value of the benefits of protection of private information exceed the costs of the opt-in regime, while different privacy preferences might make the contract based, private law solution that seems to be emerging the optimal one for the US.

19 Much of the investment literature focuses on continuous investment variables allowing for marginalization of cost and revenue. Lawmaking rarely possesses such properties of continuity and differentiability, but this factor does not change the fundamental rule for investing. The lawmaker must account for the opportunity cost of innovating at the present time – rather than waiting to choose the optimal timing of lawmaking.

20 This problem has some similarity to the problem addressed by Majd and Pindyck (1989) where a firm invests continuously until the project is completed.

21 In the standard investment literature, Roberts and Weitzman (1981) present a model of sequential investment that allows for learning during a multistage investment process, with results that depart from the standard net present value approach as well as from the basic option pricing result.

22 Interestingly, in the absence of learning, the use of a simple net present value rule can allow legal innovation that is inefficient, given the forgone value of the option to wait. Conversely, in the presence of learning, the net present value rule can reject proposals for legal innovation that are efficient.

23 For a study of optimal investment in the absence of stochastic random walks of costs and benefits, see Roberts and Weitzman (1981), with application to research and development and exploration projects.

24 A related question is what is the choice of technology that will be optimal. The lawmaker could choose to specialize in rules, and invest in a lawmaking technology that is best suited for that purpose. Alternatively, the lawmaker could choose to create a legal system that could incorporate both rules and standards; in effect, choose a technology that permits flexible output. In either case, we assume that the investment is irreversible, and the external environment changes in a stochastic manner. See He and Pindyck (1992) for a rigorous discussion of an analogous problem in investment – choice of technology.

## References


Dixit, Avinash K. and Robert S. Pindyck (1994), *Investment Under Uncertainty*, Princeton University Press, Princeton NJ.

Doraszelski, Ulrich (2001), "The Net Present Value Method Versus The Option Value of Waiting: A Note on Farzin, Huisman and Kort (1998)," *Journal of Economic Dynamics and Control*, Vol. 25, pp. 1109–1115.

Erlich, Isaac and Richard A. Posner (1973), "An Economic Analysis of Legal Rulemaking," *Journal of Legal Studies*, Vol. 11, pp. 257–286.

Farzin, Y.H., K.J.M. Huisman, and P.M. Kort (1998), "Optimal Adoption of Technology Adoption," *Journal of Economic Dynamics and Control*, Vol. 22, pp. 779–799.

He, Hua and Robert S. Pindyck (1992), "Investment in Flexible Production Capacity," *Journal of Economic Dynamics and Control*, Vol. 16, pp. 575–599.

Heiner, Ronald A. (1986), "Imperfect Decisions and the Law: On the Evolution of Legal Precedent and Rules," *Journal of Legal Studies*, Vol. 15, pp. 227–261.

Kaplow, Louis (1992), "Rules versus Standards: An Economic Analysis," *Duke Law Journal*, Vol. 42, pp. 557–629.

Kobayashi, Bruce H. and Larry E. Ribstein (2001), A Recipe for Cookies: State Regulation of Consumer Marketing Information (*unpublished manuscript*).

Majd, Saman and Robert S. Pindyck, "The Learning Curve and Optimal Production under Uncertainity," *The RAND Journal of Economics*, Vol. 20, No. 3 (Autumn, 1989), pp. 331–343.

McDonald, Robert and Daniel R. Siegel (1985) , "Investment and Valuation of Firms when there is an Option to Shut Down," *International Economic Review*, Vol. 26, pp. 331–349.

Murphy, Richard S. (1996), "Property Rights in Personal Information: An Economic Defense of Privacy," *Georgetown Law Journal*, Vol. 84, pp. 2381–2417.

Olson, Mancur (1965), *The Logic of Collective Action*, Harvard University Press, Cambridge, MA.

Pindyck, Robert S. (1991), "Irreversibility, Uncertainty and Investment," *Journal of Economic Literature*, Vol. 29, pp. 1110–1148.

Pindyck, Robert S. (2002), "Optimal Timing Problems in Environmental Economics," *Journal of Economic Dynamics and Control*, Vol. 26, pp. 1677–1697.

Ribstein, Larry E. and Bruce H. Koboyashi (1996), "An Economic Analysis of Uniform State Laws," *The Journal of Legal Studies*, Vol. 25, No. 1 (Jan.), pp. 131–199.

Roberts, Kevin and Martin L. Weitzman (1981), "Funding Criteria for Research, Development, and Exploration Projects," *Econometrica*, Vol. 49, pp. 1261–1288.

Schwartz, Alan and Robert E. Scott (1995), "The Political Economy of Private Legislatures," *University of Pennsylvania Law Review*, Vol. 143, pp. 595–654.

Staten, Michael E. and Fred E. Cate (2002), The Adverse Impact of Opt-in Privacy Rules on Consumers: A Case Study of Retail Credit, available at www.bbbonline.org/UnderstandingPrivacy/library/whitepapers.asp

Stokey, Nancy L. and Robert E. Lucas (with Edward C. Prescott) (1989), "Recursive Methods in Economic Dynamics," Harvard University Press, Cambridge, MA.

Volokh, Eugene (2000), "Symposium: Cyberspace and Privacy: A New Legal Paradigm? Freedom of Speech and Information Privacy: The Troubling Implications of a Right to Stop People from Talking about You," *Stanford Law Review*, Vol. 52, pp. 1049–1124.

# Part II

# Private orderings, efficiency, and the role of the state

# 6 The enforcement of contracts and the role of the state

*Alan Schwartz*

## Introduction

This chapter asks two questions: (1) Why should the state enforce private agreements? and (2) What roles regarding private agreements should the state play in addition to legal enforcement? Regarding question (1), enforcement permits parties who function in relatively large economies to make credible promises to perform their agreements. The inability to make credible promises would severely limit parties' ability to make short term supply contracts in volatile markets and to make long term supply contracts; and it would also severely limit parties' ability to contract for the making of investments that are more productive in a contractual relationship than those investments would be elsewhere. The poor performance of transition economies with weak legal enforcement evidences the importance of being able to make credible promises to perform. Regarding question (2), Western states perform three roles in connection with enforceable contracts – they (1) regulate the contracting process, (2) supply parties with a stock of default rules to govern transactions, and (3) interpret private agreements in the course of resolving disputes. These notes will argue that the second function is unimportant and suggest how the first and third of these functions should be best performed.

## Why enforce private agreements?

Parties can establish the credibility of their promises either with reputation or through legal enforcement. Regarding reputation, economic actors will not deal with persons who are known to renege on promises, or will require unfavorable terms from them, such as delivering only for cash. Hence, we say that a commercial party "stakes his reputation" on complying with the deals he makes. Reputation is a noisy signal, however. As an example, let a deal between party A and party B break up because one of them failed to perform as promised. Then the innocent party will incur costs in informing others that it was not at fault; and third parties will incur costs learning about which of the contract parties is unreliable. The larger the economy the greater are these costs. Economic actors face increasing difficulty in persuading others of the reliability of their promises as the costs of establishing and evaluating reputations increase.

The analysis that follows assumes for convenience that parties cannot establish reputations at all. Even in such cases, parties will comply with their agreements when a deal is as profitable at the time for performance as the parties expected the deal to be when they made it. Thus, to understand how the legal enforcement of promises supplements reputation in a market economy, one must ask when private parties have incentives to breach.

### *Planning*

Parties have an incentive to breach contracts in markets where prices are likely to fluctuate substantially in the interval between contract formation and the time for performance. As an example, let the contract price and market price for goods both be $1,000 when the contract was made, but let that price drop to $500 at the time of performance. The opportunity cost of performance for the buyer then is $500 – the difference between the contract and new market prices – and this cost may exceed the buyer's profit under the contract. The buyer thus would breach if he would incur neither a reputational nor a legal sanction. Anticipating this, the seller may refuse to make the contract at all, planning instead to sell in the spot market. The buyer will then be forced into that market too, but the buyer *made a contract* in order to avoid having to make spot purchases. Presumably, the buyer wanted to ensure delivery in order to facilitate his own plans. Hence, the buyer is forced to bear the cost of his possible later breach, which in this example is the cost of being forced into the wrong market. The buyer therefore would like to make a credible promise that it will accept the goods no matter what the market price later turns out to be. Making the buyer's promise to perform legally enforceable makes that promise credible to the seller. Legal enforcement also is efficient because the seller is at least as well off with enforcement as without, and the buyer is better off.

### *Encouraging investment*

A party also will have difficulty making a credible promise to perform when the contract requires her contract partner to specialize assets to the relationship. To understand this difficulty, consider a simple model. At time $t^0$, the parties make a contract that is not legally enforceable. The buyer's valuation for performance is $V$ if the seller makes an investment $I$ in tailoring the product to the buyer's particular needs. The investment is to be made at $t^1$ and will command a zero price in an alternate use. The contract price is $P$. If the deal falls through, the buyer can purchase a generic use product in a competitive market. This product will generate a value for the buyer of $V'$, it trades at price $P'$ and it costs $I'$ to produce.

We make the following assumptions: (1) $V > P > I$: tailoring the product to the buyer's needs would generate more value than it would cost; (2) $V' - P' = I' > 0$: the buyer would earn a positive profit if she purchased the generic product on the market and, because that market is assumed to be competitive, the price of the generic product equals the cost of producing it; (3) $V - P > V' - P'$: the buyer will earn a higher profit if she purchases the specialized product from the seller than if she purchases the generic product. Assumption (3) explains why the buyer wants to make the contract under study. The contract also would be efficient because a seller cannot do worse producing the specialized product than producing the generic product, where its profit is competed down to zero; and the buyer does better with the specialized product.[1]

The parties will not make the efficient contract, however. If they did make it, the buyer has an incentive to renegotiate the price downward after the seller makes the investment. To see why, bargaining theory holds that the better a party's disagreement point is the more power she has inside the bargaining relationship. In this model, if the parties fail to agree on a new lower price, the buyer will earn $V' - P'$ elsewhere, but the seller will earn zero because he has already made the investment I and I is assumed to be worth zero to anyone except the contract buyer. The buyer thus will do better if the parties cannot agree than the seller would, and thus the buyer will have the bargaining power to compel the seller to accept a lower price than P for the specialized product.

However, a commercially sophisticated seller will recognize that the buyer has an incentive to renegotiate after the seller makes the investment I, and the seller will respond by refusing to enter into the agreement initially. Rather, the seller will produce generic goods and sell them on the market. The buyer and society thus both would like the buyer to have the ability to make a credible promise to perform the contract: the buyer because he does better under the contract than he could do elsewhere; and society because the contract is efficient.

To summarize, when exchange is intertemporal rather than simultaneous, there sometimes is a question whether a party will comply with her promises. Parties want their contract partners to believe that they will perform because deals are profitable. Reputations can make promises to perform credibly in small economies, and parties form trade associations partly to shrink the size of the relevant reputational group, and thereby reduce the costs of forming and evaluating reputations. But reputations can be ineffective in large, heterogenous economies, and then parties will have strong incentives to breach in two very important situations: when price can fluctuate substantially in the interval between contract formation and scheduled performance, and when at least one of the parties is required under the contract to make an investment that is more profitable in the relationship than elsewhere. In these two cases, legal enforcement permits parties to make credible promises to perform. The ability to do this helps parties and increases welfare.

## Regulating contracts for fairness

### *Duress*[2]

Under the law, it is not duress to exploit a situation that a party did not create, but it is duress to create a situation and then exploit it. As an example, it is not duress for a seller to raise the price in a time of shortage if the seller did not create the shortage. To illustrate what duress is in a contract context, consider the aforementioned investment model. There, it was assumed that the threat of a law suit by the seller would deter the buyer from renegotiating the price downward. In some cases, the threat of a law suit would be insufficient, as when the seller is capital constrained and so could not wait for the duration of a litigation to receive at least some payment from the buyer. In these cases, the seller will perform under the modified contract, but that contract was a product of duress: the buyer created the seller's poor bargaining position by promising to perform under the original contract. Sellers, however, have the legal right later to sue to reinstate the price term in the original contract; the duress doctrine directs a court to ignore the modified contract. In this way, the law functions to *prevent the seller* from making a credible promise to perform for less than the sum in the original contract: the buyer will anticipate that the seller later will sue for the full price. The inability of sellers to make modification promises credible helps to deter buyers from exacting them – from exercising duress. Put more broadly, the duress doctrine functions to reduce the incentives of contract parties to exploit contract partners who have specialized assets to the relationship.

### *Unconscionability*

Today, the unconscionability doctrine is applied by courts to regulate contract terms in large markets that have firms on the selling side and consumers or very small firms on the buying side. The doctrine is used less than the large amount of commentary on it would suggest, and should be used much less than it is. To see why there is such a small sphere for the sensible application of an unconscionability approach, we can begin with standard form contracts that consumers cannot alter. The inability of consumers directly to affect the terms of the deal is thought to raise a public policy problem, but consumers also cannot alter the design of particular products. Thus, a consumer has a choice of stereo speakers but seldom can ask the manufacturer to make a pair of speakers just for him. No one is concerned with this state of affairs because it is widely recognized that the economies of scale flowing from standardized production are efficient. Also, that markets respond to the preferences of consumers in general rather than to the preferences of particular consumers is considered normatively acceptable. The same economies flow from standardizing contract forms and the same normative considerations apply. Hence, there should be as little concern about the inability of consumers to influence standard form contracts as there now is about the inability of consumers to influence the content of standard products.

It is wise to worry about the illustrative stereo market, however, if it is flawed by monopoly power or imperfect information, and so it is wise to worry about "contract markets" that have these flaws. But then there is the too seldom asked question whether courts can "worry" in useful ways. A judicial refusal to enforce contract terms is an ineffectual remedy: it does not get at the source of monopoly power or reduce the costs to consumers of acquiring information. As an illustration, if a court refuses to enforce a contract term that a monopolist used, the monopolist will exploit its power by using a different, unfavorable term, or by raising the price. The monopolist wants to increase demand, and so it will initially use the terms that consumers prefer, but charge higher prices for those terms than would be charged in a competitive market. Hence, when a court strikes down a term that a monopolist uses, it will usually be making matters worse for consumers; the monopolist's next move will be to use a term that consumers like even less, and to charge a supracompetitive price for that term.

Imperfect information in consumer markets takes three forms: (1) the contractual language is too complex for a consumer to understand, (2) the costs of comparing the prices or terms that different firms do or could use is too costly (thereby reducing the incentive of firms to compete), and (3) the costs of acquiring or applying the expertise to evaluate and reduce product risks is too great. Administrative agencies acting under well drafted statutes can ameliorate some of these problems. For example, providing consumers with price information facilitates competition and reduces market prices. Also, creating readable standard forms for common transactions, such as borrowing to finance a purchase, will increase the ability of a consumer to evaluate transactions. Courts cannot provide price information or create and require the use of standard contract forms.

The unconscionability doctrine is used by *courts* to decide when to enforce or strike down particular contract terms. Courts are institutionally ill equipped to diagnose when the evils that require regulation are present – for example, when monopoly power exists – and they are not equipped at all to supply appropriate remedies for these evils. As a consequence, the unconscionability doctrine should function "in reserve" to deal with highly unusual cases that no other doctrine or legal institution has anticipated, and that the limited powers of courts can improve. Just what cases these might be cannot be the subject of a generalization. To summarize, the state has an important role to play in enforcing contracts, in policing contracts for duress and in ensuring that contract markets function well. Courts are indispensable for the performance of the first two of these tasks, but are ineffective at the last.

## Supplying parties with default terms

Advanced economies would have few contract law rules if courts only enforced contracts and attempted to deter fraud and duress. The contract codes in these economies contain a fairly large number of rules for courts to apply, however. These codes are best justified as public goods. To see why, let the costs to particular contract parties of creating a term for a situation that may arise be larger than the gains the parties would reap from having the term. Then, the parties will not create the term. But suppose as well that the term could be used in a large number of similar transactions. Then the costs to a lawmaker of creating the term could be below the social benefit, and it would be efficient to create the term and put it in a code. Hence, the contract laws of Western states justifiably exist to supply parties with terms that these parties would have created for themselves had term creation been cost-justified for them.

Two related implications follow from this analysis. To understand the first of these, realize that in large economies some sets of parties will dislike particular statutory terms. For example, most contract codes require the breaching party to compensate its contract partner fully: in legal parlance, the breacher is required to pay that sum that will put its partner in the same position as if the breacher had performed. Many contract parties prefer to substitute for this broad requirement a term requiring the breacher to reimburse the other party only for a subset of breach costs, such as the cost of replacing a defective part. The statutory rule is justified as doing for parties what they would have done for themselves had the parties' cost/benefit calculus gone the other way, so it should follow that when for parties the cost of creating their own term to govern a particular situation is less than the gain to them, the parties should be permitted to supplant the state supplied rule. In brief, the rules in contract codes should be defaults, applying only when the parties' contract is silent on the issue.

The second implication of the public goods justification for a contract law relates to the grounds on which the state should choose the rules to enact. If the parties are to be free to supplant or modify the state supplied terms, it follows that the lawmaker should attempt to maximize the size of the set of parties that will find any statutory term acceptable. Put another way, the lawmaker should minimize the parties' contracting costs. From this point of view, it would be wrong of the lawmaker to enact a term that a large number of parties will dislike, because then the parties would have to expend resources drafting their own term. And while this may seem obvious, commentators and lawmakers often argue for or enact contract law rules on the ground that these rules are fair. A focus on fairness would be innocuous if the set of fair rules and the set of efficient (or party preferred) rules perfectly overlapped, but in practice these sets are partly disjointed. Then choosing a contract code on the basis of some normative conception of fairness would be wrong, in the sense that it would not increase the amount of fair contracts in the world, but it would increase the amount of contracting costs in the world, as parties contracted out of the codes. The contract lawmaker thus should ask what parties would like, not what parties should want.[3]

That contract laws are, and should be, default rules has been the principal organizing paradigm in contract law scholarship for the last two decades, but the paradigm has come under criticism in recent years. The criticism follows from two concerns. First, state rule creation itself may seldom be cost justified. Second, where there is asymmetric information state rule creation is not even possible.

### *The cost concern*

Rule creation by the state can be expensive while many solutions to contracting problems are context specific. Let a contracting problem be to specify the quality obligation that a seller's performance is to satisfy, or the nature and number of services she is to provide, or the mechanism that will determine the price in various circumstances. The solutions to problems such as these will vary from set of parties to set of parties, and the gains each set of parties would derive from a good solution seldom would exceed the lawmaker's costs. As a consequence, while contract codes contain a large number of rules, if these rules are regarded as terms in actual contracts, then the set of publicly supplied terms should be an infinitesimal fraction of the number of contract terms that are operable at any one time. This is because the principal criterion for a contract default rule is that it must be acceptable in a wide variety of situations[4] in order to justify the costs of creating the rule.

### *The asymmetric information concern*

To understand this concern, refer to the investment model above, in which the seller was to tailor a product to the buyer's particular needs. Parties will write this contract when (i) the parties can specify clearly what standards the product is to meet; (ii) the product always will meet those standards if it is made correctly; and (iii) the parties can conveniently prove to a court whether the product satisfied the contractual standards. The second of these conditions sometimes is difficult to satisfy. In such cases, the product is more likely to be valuable to the buyer if the seller made a strong effort to produce high quality, but even a strong effort may not suffice; production processes seldom are perfect. To understand the contracting difficulties that such probabilistic success can cause, it is helpful to have an information taxonomy. Let a datum of information be the effort the seller exerted in specializing the product to the buyer's needs. Then the seller's effort level will be (1) "verifiable" if the buyer can observe what that level was, and verify the level to a court at a litigation cost that is below the gain the parties could derive from being able to prove what the seller's costs were; (2) "observable" if the buyer can learn what the seller's investment level was but cannot verify that level to a third party decision maker; (3) "unobservable" if the buyer cannot observe the seller's investment at all.

Now consider two possibly optimal contracts. Contract A provides that the seller is to receive a specified price if the product turns out to be highly valuable to the buyer and a lower price if the product turns out to be less valuable. Such a contract may give the seller the incentive to exert a high effort to ensure that the buyer is satisfied with the product because the higher the effort the greater is the probability of success. The parties could not use this contract, however, if the buyer's valuation (V in the earlier model) is not verifiable. In the absence of verifiability, the contract will be affected by moral hazard. The buyer may claim that the quality was low, in order to pay the lower price, although the quality actually was high. Conversely, the seller may claim that the quality was high, in order to get the higher price, although the quality actually was low. These disputes over quality will cause Contract A to be unacceptable.

Contract B provides that the price is higher when the seller makes a strong effort to produce high quality than when the seller makes a weak effort. This contract gives the seller an incentive to make the strong effort, and the parties might use it if the seller's investment level were verifiable. This is because if the seller did invest optimally it could sue for the appropriate price, and if the seller invested suboptimally the buyer could pay only the amount actually due. Assume, however, that the seller's investment is only observable. In this case, neither party could prove to a court what the seller actually did, and this inability also would create moral hazard: the buyer might claim that investment was low when it was high, so that the buyer would have to pay only the low price; and the seller might claim that investment was high when it was low. The parties nevertheless could write the illustrative investment contract if reputation were an effective sanction because the parties, we now assume, can learn what the seller did; hence, cheating in this deal could be punished later.[5] Reputation can work poorly in large economies, however.

Assume next that the seller's investment is unobservable. Then reputation cannot work at all because no one but the seller could know whether the seller performed optimally or not. When investment is unobservable, the seller never could make a credible promise to invest optimally, and the buyer never could make a credible promise to pay honestly. And to summarize, contracts that compensate the seller on the basis of the value the product actually had for the buyer or on the basis of the seller's investment behavior could create efficient incentives when values or costs are verifiable. Parties seldom will write these contracts when investment or value is only observable, and will never write these contracts when investment or value is unobservable. A standard assumption in the industrial organization literature is that values and costs commonly are difficult to verify.

Now return to the lawmaker's task of writing default rules. The lawmaker should perform this task, it was said, by asking what contract terms would be acceptable to the widest set of potential contract parties. On this view, contract default rules that condition on the value the good has for the buyer or that require a seller to make an optimal relation specific investment would often be bad defaults. Actual parties seldom would write contracts that condition on these economic variables, even when it would be costless to do so. Consequently, parties would routinely contract out of these possible defaults.[6] And to generalize, the existence of asymmetric information further shrinks the set of situations for which contract lawmakers could create default rules that are acceptable to actual contract parties.

To summarize, there is need for default rules when contracts are "complete" – when they contain terms that govern all of the situations the parties could face. We have identified two reasons why actual parties write incomplete contracts: the costs of writing a complete contract are too high in relation to the parties' gains; and the existence of asymmetric information prevents contracts from conditioning on such economic data as cost or investment behavior. The state seldom could remedy the first cause of incompleteness and never could remedy the second (because the lawmaker cannot write a better contract for the parties than they could write for themselves). Therefore, the reasons for incompleteness in contracts actually function as constraints on the number of occasions in which state supplied contract law rules can facilitate efficient contracting. Lawmakers in advanced economies sometimes function as if they understood this analysis. Contract codes contain a tiny number of rules relative to the number of terms in actual contracts that are operative at any time, and some of these statutory rules can function well in a wide variety of contexts. Lawmakers apparently do not understand all of this analysis, however, because many of the rules in contract codes, such as the warranty and consequential rules, are helpful to few parties. Thus, real parties expend large resources in contracting out of what the state does.

## Contract interpretation

Parties sometimes will disagree over what the words they used required one or the other of them to do, and in these cases courts must say what the words meant. There is no consensus on how courts should perform this task, but the alternatives can be described. Under autonomy theories of contract, the parties' agreement has normative force because the parties actually agreed to it. The law's task is to enforce the parties' will the better to permit parties to realize their goals in commercial arenas. These theories of contract thus require courts to find out, as far as is possible, what the parties actually did mean by the words they used. All relevant evidence is admissible in the performance of this task. Not only are the words of the contract itself considered, but also prior negotiations, any course of performance of the actual contract, any prior course of dealing between the parties and any arguably relevant trade customs. Parties sometimes try to truncate such an investigatory process with "merger clauses," which provide that the written contract is to be the sole source of what the parties intended. A strong commitment to an autonomy theory of contract, such as that contained in sections of the American Uniform Commercial Code, will incline courts to find ambiguity in the application of merger clauses themselves, and in response to consider the full range of possible evidence relevant to meaning.

An efficiency theory of contract, in contrast, will accord considerable weight to the words the parties used, and will attempt to enforce merger clauses. Under the efficiency theory, the function of the state is to create, and to help the parties create, standard vocabularies for the conduct of commercial transactions. Legislatures perform this function when they enact explicit definitions for statutory terms, such as the FOB or CIS term. Parties to a particular contract may have meant something by the use of an FOB term that differs from the statutory meaning, but under an efficiency theory it is the statutory meaning that controls. Similarly, a contractual word or phrase that has been given a particular meaning in a litigated case will be given the same meaning in later cases unless the parties explicitly say otherwise. Also, courts that use the efficiency theory of interpretation tend to give words their dictionary meanings.

The efficiency theory privileges the contract's words and reads those words in the ways just set out in order to facilitate the parties' ability to plan and to resolve disputes. When a phrase has a set, easily discoverable meaning, parties who use it will know what the phrase requires of them and what courts will say the phrase requires. A search for "true" meaning – the meaning the parties actually intended – is inconsistent with the planning and dispute resolution goals. This is because, when an autonomy theory of interpretation is operative, a party for whom a deal has turned out badly has an incentive to claim that the parties meant their contract to have a different meaning than the obvious or standard one. Such a party can often find in the parties' negotiations, their past practices and in trade customs enough evidence to ground a law suit, and thus to force a settlement on terms more favorable than those the contract, under standard interpretation, would direct. If a party can impeach careful contract drafting with evidence of this type, the rewards to careful contract drafting will fall, though not the costs. In consequence, parties will less frequently write precise, directive contracts.

An autonomy theorist is willing to bear some costs of a reduced ability to plan and a higher frequency of disputes in order to ensure that parties are not held to contracts against their will. To choose a method of contract interpretation thus seems to require a choice between theories of contract. These notes are not the place to defend such a choice, so this analysis will conclude with an observation and a remark. The observation is that common law courts, at least in the US, adhere by and large to the efficiency theory of interpretation. These courts thus attempt to supply contracting vocabularies and thereby to facilitate planning. The remark, which partly explains the observation, is that the autonomy theory is more attractive when a contract is between two individuals, and the efficiency theory is more attractive when a contract is between sophisticated companies. Since contract interpretation cases more commonly arise between companies, and since contract codes commonly regulate business transactions, the efficiency theory thus is more relevant to students of contract.

## Conclusion

Recent evidence from the former communist states and other emerging market countries strongly supports the claims made here, that courts perform the crucially important roles in advanced economies of enforcing contracts and policing contracting processes for fraud and duress. Courts that use an efficiency theory of contract interpretation also perform the important function of helping to supply parties with "contracting vocabularies" the better to write clear and enforceable contracts. Legislatures also contribute to the vocabulary supplying function, and have the resources to improve competitive conditions in markets, or to create administrative agencies to improve those conditions.

Today, courts sometimes attempt to improve market performance with contract law doctrines such as unconscionability, and this is a mistake: courts using contract law cannot create the conditions under which competition can flourish, and they seldom can ameliorate bad conditions. Much of contract law in Western countries, however, does not focus on enforcing contracts or policing contracting processes, nor on supplying parties with commercial vocabularies. Rather, this law attempts to supply parties with rules that function as implied terms in actual contracts. For the reasons given here, the state can supply an extremely small percentage of the terms that are useful to actual parties. Codes and contract law doctrines regrettably supply many more rules than these. As a consequence, most of what today is called contract law is irrelevant to commercial life, except in so far as commercial parties are compelled to contract out of inefficient legal rules.

## Notes

1 For those who like proofs, social welfare under the contract for the specialized product is $W_k = V - I$; social welfare with the generic product is $W_g = V' - I'$. Assumption (2) implies that $W_g = V' - P'$; assumption (3) implies that $V - P > V' - P'$; and assumption (1) implies that $V - I > V - P$. Therefore, $V - I > V' - I'$, and so $W_k > W_g$. It is efficient to contract for the specialized product.

2 These notes discuss duress but courts also police contracts for fraud. No one disputes that policing against fraud is useful.

3 Scholars have identified a set of default rules that are termed "information forcing," because these rules create incentives for parties to disclose relevant information to their contract partners. The rule providing that a party cannot recover damages for breach unless those damages were foreseeable to the other party is information forcing; it creates an incentive for the party fearing breach to disclose the extent of the damages it would suffer to the other party. Information forcing rules fall within the analysis above because parties can create such rules on their own. For example, a seller can propose a contract that disclaims liability for consequential damages. Her contract partner then can remain silent and sign the contract or propose a clause that would compensate him for elements of these damages. The proposed contract serves an information forcing function, because it creates an incentive for the informed party to offer an amendment to the contract and thereby to disclose his possible damages.

4 The rule requiring a contract breacher to pay damages equal to the difference between the contract and market prices at the time of breach is a good example of such a rule. The rule is convenient to state and is efficient in application in many disparate contexts.

5 Reputation also could save Contract A, which conditions on the product's actual value.

6 Contract damage rules do condition on the value that the goods actually have for the buyer, because they permit buyers to sue for consequential damages – the difference between the good's value and the price. In sales of goods where consequential damages can be large, parties very frequently contract out. Typical contracts substitute for consequential damages verifiable cost elements, such as the cost of replacing a defective product. Hence, the consequential damage rules appear to be bad defaults.

## Bibliography

Anderlini, Luca and Leonardo Felli, "Incomplete Written Contracts: Undescribable States of Nature," 109 *Quarterly Journal of Economics* 1085–1124 (1994).

Anderlini, Luca and Leonardo Felli, "Incomplete Contracts and Complexity Costs," 46 *Theory and Decision* 23–50 (1999).

Anderlini, Luca and Leonardo Felli, "Costly Bargaining and Renegotiation," 69 *Econometrica* 377–412 (2001).

Anderlini, Luca, Leonardo Felli, and Andrew Postlewaite, "Courts of Law and Unforseen Contingencies," manuscript (2001).

Battigalli, Pierpaolo and Giovanni Maggi, "Rigidity, Discretion, and the Costs of Writing Contracts," unpublished manuscript (2001).

Bernstein, Lisa B., "Merchant Law in a Merchant Court: Rethinking the Code's Search for Imminent Norms," 144 *University of Pennsylvania Law Review* 1765–1821 (1996).

Bernstein, Lisa B., "The Questionable Empirical Basis of Article 2's Incorporation Strategy: A Preliminary Study," 69 *University of Chicago Law Review* 710–780 (1999).

Bernstein, Lisa B., "Private Commercial Law in the Cotton Industry: Creating Cooperation through Rules, Norms and Institutions" manuscript (2001).

Blum, Brian A., *Contracts* (at 331) (2nd Edition 2001).

Brennan, James and Joel Watson, "The Renegotiation–Proofness Principle and Costly Renegotiation," unpublished manuscript (2001).

Bull, Jesse, "Costly Evidence Production and the Limits of Verifiability," unpublished manuscript.

Bull, Jesse and Joel Watson, "Evidence Disclosure and Verifiability," UC San Diego Economics Working Paper 2000–2016 (2000).

Calfee, John E. and Richard Craswell, "Deterrence and Uncertain Legal Standards," 2 *Journal of Law, Economics and Organization* 279–304 (1986).

Che, Yeon-Koo and Donald B. Hausch, "Cooperative Investments and the Value of Contracting," 89 *American Economic Review* 125–147 (1999).

Che, Yeon-Koo and Alan Schwartz, "Section 365, Mandatory Bankruptcy Rules and Inefficient Continuance," 15 *Journal of Law, Economics and Organization* 441–467 (1999).

Coase, Ronald, "The Nature of the Firm," 4 *Economica* 386–405 (1937).

Craswell, Richard, "Do Trade Customs Exist?," in *The Jurisprudential Foundations of Corporate and Commercial Law* 118–148 (J. Kraus and S. Walt, eds, 2000).

De Fraja, Gianni, "After You Sir. Hold-Up, Direct Externalities, and Sequential Investment," 26 *Games and Economic Behavior* 22–39 (1999).

Dye, R. A., "Costly Contract Contingencies," 26 *International Economic Review* 233–250 (1985).

Edlin, Aaron and Stefan Reichelstein, "Holdups, Standard Breach Remedies, and Optimal Investment," 86 *American Economic Review* 478–501 (1996).

Eggleston, Karen, Eric A. Posner, and Richard Zeckhauser, "Simplicity and Complexity in Contracts," University of Chicago Law School Working Paper 93 (2nd series, 2001).

Goldberg, Victor and John R. Erickson, "Quantity and Price Adjustment in Long-Term Contracts: A Case Study of Petroleum Coke," 30 *Journal of Law and Economics*. __ (1987).

Gray, Jo Anna, "On Indexation and Contract Length," 86 *Journal of Political Economy* 1–18 (1978).

Grossman, Sanford and Oliver Hart, "The Costs and Benefits of Ownership: A Theory of Vertical and Lateral Integration," 94 *Journal of Political Economy* 691–719 (1986).

Grout, Paul, "Investment and Wages in the Absence of Binding Contracts: A Nash Bargaining Approach," 52 *Econometrica* 449–460 (1984).

Hart, Oliver, "Financial Contracting," forthcoming, *Journal of Economic Literature* (2001).

Hart, Oliver and John Moore, "Incomplete Contracts and Renegotiation," 56 *Econometrica* 755–786 (1988).

Hermalin, Benjamin E. and Michael L. Katz, "Moral Hazard and Verifiability: The Effects of Renegotiation in Agency," 59 *Econometrica* 1735–1753 (1991).

Holmström, Bengt, "Moral Hazard in Teams," 13 *Bell Journal of Economics* 324–340 (1982).

Huberman, Gur and Charles Kahn, "Limited Contract Enforcement and Strategic Renegotiation," 78 *The American Economic Review* 471–484 (1988).

Jolls, Christine, "Contracts as Bilateral Commitments: A New Perspective on Contract Modification," 26 *The Journal of Legal Studies* 203–238 (1997).

Klein, Benjamin, R. A. Crawford, and Armen A. Alchian, "Vertical Integration, Appropriable Rents, and the Competitive Contracting Process," 21 *Journal of Law and Economics* 297–326 (1978).

Lewis, Tracy R. and David E. M. Sappington, "Inflexible Rules in Incentive Problems," 79 *American Economic Review* 69–84 (1989).

MacLeod, W. Bentley, "Complexity and Contract," 92 *Revue d'Economie Industrielle* 149–178 (2000).

MacLeod, W. Bentley and James Malcomson, "Investments, Holdup and the Form of Market Contracts," 83 *American Economic Review* 811–837 (1993).

Maskin, Eric and John Moore, "Implementation and Renegotiation," 66 *Review of Economic Studies* 39–56 (1999).

Maskin, Eric and Jean Tirole, "Unforseen Contingencies and Incomplete Contracts," 66 *Review of Economic Studies* 83–114 (1999).

Schmitz, Patrick W., "The Hold-Up Problem and Incomplete Contracts: A Survey of Recent Topics in Contract Theory," 53 *Bulletin of Economic Research* 1–25 (2001).

Schwartz, Alan, "Legal Contract Theories and Incomplete Contracts," in *Contract Economics* 76–108 (L. Werin and H. Wijkander, eds. 1992).

Schwartz, Alan, "Incomplete Contracts," 2 *The New Palgrave Dictionary of Economics and the Law*, 277–283 (1998).

Schwartz, A. and Scott R. E. "Contract Theory and the Limits of Contract Law," *Yale Law Journal* 113:541 (2003).

Schwartz, A. and Watson J. "The Law and Economics of Costly Contracting," *Journal of Law Economics and Organizations* 20:2–31 (2004).

Segal, Ilya and Michael Whinston, "The Mirrlees Approach to Mechanism Design with Renegotiation (with Applications to Hold-Up and Risk-Sharing)," *Econometrica*, forthcoming (2001).

Snyder, David V., "The Law of Contract and the Concept of Change: Public and Private Attempts to Regulate Modification, Waiver, and Estoppel," 1999 *Wisconsin Law Review* 607–686 (1999).

Spier, Kathryn E., "Incomplete Contracts and Signalling," 23 *RAND Journal of Economics* 432–443 (1992)

Tirole, Jean, "Incomplete Contracts: Where Do We Stand?" 67 *Econometrica* 741–781 (1999).

Tirole, Jean, "Corporate Governance," 69 *Econometrica* 1–35 (2001).

Townsend, Robert, "Optimal Contracts and Competitive Markets with Costly State Verification," 21 *Journal of Economic Theory* 265–293 (1979).

Watson, Joel, "Contract and Game Theory: Basic Concepts for Settings of Complete Information," unpublished manuscript (2001).

Watson, Joel, "Contract, Mechanism Design, and Technological Detail," unpublished manuscript (2001).

Williamson, Oliver, "Transactions-Cost Economics: The Governance of Contractual Relations," 22 *Journal of Law and Economics* 233–261 (1979).

Williamson, Oliver, *The Economic Institutions of Capitalism: Firms, Markets, Relational Contracting*, New York: Free Press (1985).

# 7 Minimal liberty and the 'Coasean Liberal'

## Boundaries and complementarities between the state and the market

*Antonio Nicita and Ernesto Savaglio*

Zeus on Olympus dispenses many things.
Gods often contradict our fondest expectations.
What we anticipate does not come to pass.
What we don't expect some God finds a way to make it happen.
(Euripides, Medea)

## Introduction

The Coase Theorem (Coase, 1960) has been traditionally interpreted[1] as a theory of the superiority of free market exchange over state regulatory intervention for externalities' absorption. As Coase (1988) has later pointed out, his 1960 article has been widely cited and discussed only with reference to the first part of the analysis (concerning a world with zero transaction costs), 'neglecting other aspects of the analysis'[2] such as those remarking 'the fundamental role which transaction costs do, and should, play in the fashioning of the institutions which make up the economic system'. The Coase Theorem, which thus covers only a part of a more general argument, could be formulated in the following way: 'if transaction costs were assumed to be zero and the rights of the various parties well defined, the allocation of resources would be the same' independently of the initial allocation of rights. The consequence of this assertion is that

> how the rights will be used depends on who owns the rights and the contractual arrangements into which the owner has entered. If these arrangements are the result of market transactions, they will tend to lead to the rights being used in the way which is the most valued, but only after deducing the costs involved in making these transactions. Transaction costs therefore play a crucial role in determining how the rights will be used.

The mere existence of an externality (which in Coase's terms is simply defined as 'harmful effects') therefore 'does not imply that there is a *prima facie* case for governmental intervention (taxation or regulation)'. Sometimes, 'if with governmental intervention the losses also exceed the gains from eliminating "externality" it is obviously desirable that it should remain'. It could happen that when externalities occur, 'the only reason individuals and private organizations do not eliminate them is that the gain from doing so would be offset by what would be lost (including the cost of making the arrangements necessary to bring about this result)'. It comes out that the Coasean boundary between market decentralized exchange and governmental intervention (and, more generally, the choice among alternative economic institutions) should be essentially referred to the dimension of transaction costs and to the potential distortions attributable to public centralized intervention.

As some authors have noticed (Cooter, 1987; Allen, 1991; Parisi, 1999; Usher, 1999), under the Coasean framework, the notion of transaction costs could be expanded so as to include every potential source of market failure in allowing efficient bargaining over an externality, thus including not only all kinds of *ex post* transaction costs sustained for the exchange of given rights, but also all the *ex ante* transaction costs to be sustained for the definition of rights and/or for contracting over the initial allocation of rights (Bernhölz, 1997; Anderlini and Felli, 2006). Cheung (1983), for instance, has argued that in the absence of transaction costs 'the assumption of private property rights can be dropped without in the least negating the Coase Theorem'.

In this chapter, we argue that the distinction between *ex ante* transaction costs (as the costs of well-defining rights over uses), and *ex post* transaction costs (as the costs of exchanging rights over uses), should be maintained so as to reveal a relevant feature of the boundaries between market decentralized exchange and governmental intervention. In our view, the original Coasean intuition, which outlined two separate assumptions for the Coase theorem to work (zero transaction costs *and* well-defined rights), should be preserved and investigated in detail (Nicita and Rizzolli, 2004). What does it mean to state that rights should be well defined? This question involves the following ones: who is entitled to define rights in the first instance? How is she selected? How are rights maintained and enforced over time? What is the consequence of not having well-defined rights at all, even in a world of zero *ex post* transaction costs?

A possible answer to the above questions may rise from the comparison of the Sen paradox on the Paretian Liberal[3] and the (standard version) of the Coase theorem (1960). We show that this comparison is somehow puzzling: if we agree with the Coase theorem we have to abandon the Sen paradox, and vice versa.

This conclusion leads us to show

1 a possibility result for a Paretian Liberal by applying the Coase theorem (defined as 'Coasean Liberal')[4];
2 an impossibility result for a 'Coasean Liberal' by applying the Sen result to the problem of absorbing Pareto-relevant externalities by the market exchange in a world of incomplete rights.

Our argument proceeds as follows. In a world of zero *ex ante* transaction costs, rights are well defined and complete, in the sense that there is a clear right for every possible use (Pagano, 2000; Nicita and Rizzolli, 2004) and agents are able to write complete contracts over those uses. As a consequence, not only, as Cheung (1986) has stressed, are private property rights irrelevant for the Coase theorem to work, but also, and even more important, in a world with zero *ex ante* transaction costs there will be no externality at all, since for every use there will be a right to be exchanged and a related market price. In real-word economic and legal systems (property) rights are far from being complete (in the sense of defining all possible uses).[5] As a consequence, as Coase (1988) refers, we have to think of 'what is bought and sold as consisting of a bundle of rights'. It is for this reason that externalities do emerge as conflicting preferences over rival uses not already 'unbundled' in specific and distinct rights. In a world of complete rights (a world of complete contracts over resources' uses), such a conflict will never appear as rights to uses will be immediately acquired by those agents who value them the most, so that 'eternity can be experienced in a second' (Coase, 1988 p. 15).

On the contrary, when agents fail to define a system of complete rights (to write complete contracts over all possible resources' uses) they may fail in introducing *any* allocation of rights over the relevant set of choice among uses for which conflicting preferences do emerge. As a consequence, conflicting preferences over those uses will tend to persist and the impossibility of a Paretian Liberal will rapidly extend to a 'Coasean Liberal' as well.

The relevance of *ex ante* property rights definition for a Coasean market to work leads us to stress, following Coase (1988), the institutional nature of the market, and the constant need, besides the market, of a regulatory authority that is able to properly define rights whenever an externality does emerge and that grants rights' enforcement against non-holders' interference.

This conclusion, which does not depend on the existence and on the dimension of *ex post* transaction costs, throws new lights, in our view, on the definition of state–market boundaries stressing their complementarity. State intervention for externalities' absorption should thus be referred not only to direct intervention on rights' allocation (as in the Pigouvian case), but also on rights' definition and re-definition over time. The impossibility of a Coasean Liberal shows how this form of direct intervention requires a *maximal authority* instead of a minimal state, as in the Nozick theory (1974). The state has not only to enforce every contract performing rights' exchange in the market but it has also to define and re-define a system of rights which allows market exchange over emerging externalities. While the Coasean argument is directly referred to state–market trade-off emerging with positive *ex post* transaction costs, our argument emphasizes that state intervention plays a crucial role in minimizing *ex ante* transaction costs and, consequently, in increasing market's performance. The analysis of the Coasean Liberal thus reveals a wider institutional environment which outlines both the boundaries and the complementarities between the state and the market.

## Minimal liberties and tragic choices: the impossibility of a Paretian Liberal

In 'the Impossibility of a Paretian Liberal', Sen (1970) argues that 'in a very basic sense liberal values conflict with the Pareto principle. If someone takes the Pareto principle seriously [. . .] then he has to face problems of consistency in cherishing liberal values'. As a consequence, 'if someone does have certain liberal values, then he may have to eschew his adherence to Pareto optimality'. Sen (1970) defines liberal values as personal liberty over certain matters in which each person should be free to decide what should happen, no matter what others think, so that the choice of that person over those matters must be taken to be the better for the society as a whole. Liberal values thus imply, according to Sen (1970), that each person, for at least certain matters, should be protected against others' externality over his choice domain: 'given other things in the society, if you prefer to have pink walls rather than white, then society should permit you to have this, even if a majority of the community would like to see your walls white'.

According to Sen (1970, 1976), a consequence of his famous example on the two readers of *Lady's Chatterley's Lover* (henceforth *LCL*), is that it is not possible to link together individual liberty and Pareto principle. If we want thus to preserve liberal values we have to abandon the Pareto principle; if we want to keep the Pareto principle we have to renounce individual liberty (hence, 'the impossibility of a Paretian Liberal').

Since defending individual liberty on the 'protected sphere' seems quite reasonable, Sen argues that the Pareto principle, often invoked by economists, might not always reveal an optimality feature in terms of the social choices selected according to it. Individual liberty, also defined as minimal libertarianism, is, in such a framework, defined by Sen as a right to choose in the 'protected sphere'.

Let us illustrate the conflict between liberal values and the Pareto principle by using an example suggested by the famous Euripides tragedy Medea.

The story takes place in the years just before the Trojan War (about 1300 BC). Medea, daughter of Aietes, king of Colchis, left her native city to travel to Greece with her lover Jason. Medea helped Jason to take the Golden Fleece and then escaped with him. Medea was credited with knowledge of potions and witchcraft which she used to help Jason. She not only betrayed her father, but also killed her brother. And all this, she did for Jason. Once they got the Golden Fleece, Jason and Medea settled in the Greek city of Corinth, and when the Euripides' play opens they have been living in Corinth for some time, long enough to have had two little sons, maybe 6 or 7 years old. At this point, however, the king of Corinth, Creon, asked Jason to marry his daughter, Creusa. Creon had no sons, so he proposed a deal to Jason: marrying Creusa would have given Jason the kingdom of Corinth. Seeking the chance to become the future king, Jason agreed to marry Creusa, forgetting Medea in just one second.

When Medea found out that Jason was going to marry Creusa, she became quite angry: Medea thought they were 'de facto' married (Greeks had no marriage ceremony).

Desperate, she opposed Jason's decision unsuccessfully, but the decision was taken: after all, Jason said, they were never married, since a barbarian like Medea was not entitled to marry a Greek like Jason. As a consequence, Jason invited Medea to accept his decision and to leave Corinth and their sons.

At that point Medea got even more angry than she was before. She made a beautiful magic dress for Creusa, and sent her sons to take it to Creusa. When Creusa dressed in it, it suddenly turned into fire and burned her up together with the royal palace. But thing turned even worse. Medea also killed her sons: if she could not have them, Jason could not either. The tragedy then explodes with all its sadness: Jason and Medea lose everything in one shot: the glory, the family, the love.

Let us try to understand why Jason ($\mathcal{J}$) and Medea ($M$) were not able to avoid such bad consequences of their actions at the very beginning of the story.

We have here three social states:

- *romantic choice*, $W_{\mathcal{J}}$: Jason ($\mathcal{J}$) refuses the proposal of King Creon and remains with Medea ($M$) and his sons;
- *opportunistic choice*, $W_M$: Jason accepts the proposal to marry Creusa and to leave Medea;
- *tragic choice*, $W_T$: Medea's vengeance against Jason's marriage.

We have also the choices available to Jason and Medea:

- $\mathcal{J}$ has to choose between the romantic and the opportunistic choice, that is, between remaining with Medea or marrying the daughter of the king;[6]
- $M$ has to choose between retaliating with her murderous revenge, or not retaliating notwithstanding Jason's decision to abandon his family to marry Creusa.

Let us assume the following preference ordering $\succ$:

$$\begin{aligned} &\text{for agent } \mathcal{J}, \quad W_M \succ W_{\mathcal{J}}, \\ &\text{for agent } M, \quad W_T \succ W_M. \end{aligned}$$

Since the actions of Medea are strictly dependent on the choice of Jason, we can assume that Medea would not have acted if Jason had decided to remain with her. So we can write the following preference ordering for Medea, $W_{\mathcal{J}} \succ W_T \succ W_M$.

Now let us assume that Jason ignores the tremendous project of Medea (i.e. he ignores that a state of the world like $W_T$ is possible), being quite confident that she will accept his decision to marry the daughter of the king, Creusa. Being rational, Jason will thus marry Creusa, since $W_M \succ W_{\mathcal{J}}$. However, at that point, since for Medea $W_T \succ W_M$, a tragedy would happen and a state of the world like $W_T$ will close the scene.

The moral is that Jason, by ignoring a possible relevant state of the world, has made a decision not consistent with a 'complete' list of possible contingencies or externalities coming from his choice: his *ex ante* decisions were made in a world with zero-externalities (i.e. in a world where the proud Medea simply accepted Jason's decision). However the *ex post* consequences of his choices, if expected *ex ante*, would probably have induced Jason to continue his relationship with Medea rather than marry the daughter of the king, since, according to Jason's preferences, $W_M \succ W_{\mathcal{J}} \succ W_T$.

## Liberties, externalities, and *Deus ex machina*

In the earlier example, the Pareto principle should therefore be viewed as a sort of the *Deus ex machina* rule that prevents the tragic outcome. A *Deus ex machina* rule implies that the externality produced by Medea's action is anticipated in the first instance so as to enrich Jason's *ex ante* domain choice. In a sense, anticipating Medea's *ex post* action increases Jason's *ex ante* liberty of choice. Once the externality generated by Medea has been taken onto account, Jason may re-formulate his choices so as to prevent the worst *ex post* social outcome. This leads us to formulate the following question: is the emergence of an *ex post* externality really a 'limitation' of Jason's *ex ante* liberty? Is the possibility of becoming aware of emerging externalities a 'reduction' of Jason's liberty even if it gives Jason with a richer choice domain? What is the relationship between liberties and externalities?

Let us assume first, as in Sen's paradox, that Medea's action is in fact a limitation of Jason's liberty to marry Creusa (which is a typical personal matter). As a consequence, in order to preserve Jason's liberty we should design a world in which *ex post* consequences do not affect *ex ante* Jason's preferences and choices $W_M \succ W_J$ (i.e. a non-regret assumption over Jason's behaviour). However, this assumption contradicts our hypothesis that an outcome like $W_T$ is possible such that for Jason $W_J \succ W_T$. The only way of preserving Jason's *ex ante* liberty is to limit Medea's *ex post* liberty. That is an important result, quite neglected in Sen's analysis. The externality produced *ex post* by Medea is not a direct impediment on Jason's *ex ante* liberty (Jason has the full possibility to decide on his personal matter, to marry Creusa), whereas preserving Jason's liberty from *ex post* externalities is a direct impediment on Medea's liberty to implement her tragic plan. In order to preserve the minimal liberty assumed by Sen, we have therefore to inhibit every possible *ex post* externality (an assumption which has been called *Paretian Epidemic*[7]).

Let assume now that externalities are ubiquitous. What is the meaning of liberties in the presence of externalities? Is a liberty which ignores externalities and fails to face them a full liberty? If Jason had known that by choosing to marry the daughter of the king he would have generated a tragedy, he would probably have corrected his choice in the first instance. In this respect, when liberty is faced with externality, Jason's (*ex post*) liberty would simply imply the decision not to marry the daughter of the king. Why should we thus prefer *ex ante* liberty to *ex post* liberty, if it is the latter one which (*ex post*) leads to the optimal outcome? The tragedy here is therefore generated by Jason's inability to anticipate *ex post* externalities induced by his action. In this sense, *ex post* externalities induce liberty to choose among the *ex post* relevant situations. In such a context, liberty is accrued, and not reduced. Put it differently and recall Sen's example; if I prefer to have pink walls rather than white in my house, liberal values imply that society should not affect this decision: however, if all my friends hate pink enough to decline any invitation to my party, I may want to take this externality onto account. Should I prefer a pink house without friends to a white happy house full of people? And in case I decide to change the colour of the walls, are others' preferences over my walls really a limitation of my liberty? Or is the decision to change the colour, taking onto account others' preferences, the very expression of my liberty? After all, I can still be free to have pink walls in an empty house. What is hence the relationship between liberty and externality? When agents' choices do not produce *ex post* externality (I do not care about having pink walls in an empty house) *ex ante* minimal liberty is preserved. When agents' choices produce reciprocal externalities, the consequence is simply a re-definition of the original choice domain over which choices are expressed, so as to preserve *ex post* minimal liberties.

## Coase Theorem as a *Deus ex machina* rule

In the earlier example, Jason's liberty is indicated by his decision to marry or not to marry the daughter of the king. Medea's preferences do not interfere directly with this choice, but produce, according to Medea's liberty, some *ex post* outcome which was simply ignored *ex ante* by Jason. In order to avoid the worst outcome, Jason may *credibly* have decided to renounce marriage to the daughter of the king, so as to prevent murder by Medea. This decision implies that in order to internalize *ex post* externalities Jason renounces his right to marry the princess (which impels Medea to renounce the her tragic decisions). In other terms, the *Deus ex machina rule* allows agents to reach the *ex post* optimal social state, which is the same as selected according to the Pareto principle. What the *Deus ex machina* does here in fact is simply apply the Coase theorem: given their reciprocal externalities, $J$ and $M$ bargain with each other in order to reach the outcome $W_J$. The bargaining between $J$ and $M$ requires $J$ to exchange his right to choose between $W_M$ and $W_J$ with Medea's right to choose between $W_T$ and $W_M$. Thus, in this setting, not only do externalities not limit liberties, but liberties (to exchange and alienate rights) are necessary in order to absorb *ex post* externalities.

In what follows, we define claim-rights (and correlative duties), which erase non-holders' preferences such that they imply that non-holders' preferences ordering is subject to acquiring a claim right over that ordering. If individual $i$ has a claim right to choose over two options $(A, B)$, $j$'s preferences over $(A, B)$ might emerge only by acquiring $i$'s claim right. In such a case, as Gibbard (1974) has shown, if minimal liberties are defined as an alienable right to choose over a given choices domain, then minimal liberty is consistent with the Pareto principle. The reason why this is possible is simply explained by the standard Coase theorem: given an externality, if alienable rights are well defined and transaction costs are zero, then parties' bargaining will produce an outcome which is Pareto-efficient, independent of initial rights' assignment.

Now in order to define minimal liberty, let $\succeq_j$ be the preference ordering of individual $j$, and following Gibbard (1974), let us propose a *revised* version of his definition.[8]

**Definition 1 (Alienable Right).** *Individual $J$ has an alienable right to $W_M$ over $W_J$ if*

1 $W_M \succ_J W_M$

2 $\nexists W_Z : W_J \succ_J W_Z$ and $W_Z \succ_I W_M \forall I \neq J$
$\Rightarrow W_M \succ W_J$.

This definition simply asserts $J$ has an alienable right to $W_M$ over $W_J$ if $J$ prefers $W_M$ to $W_J$ (*ex ante* choices domain) and there is no $W_Z$ such that $J$ prefers $W_J$ to $W_Z$ (*ex post* choices domain) or is indifferent between them, and if others claim $W_Z$ over $W_M$ (externality), then $W_M \succ W_J$. This definition links the *ex ante* and the *ex post* sets of choices and externalities.[9] The intuition behind Definition 1 is that $J$ has a right to choose as long as his choice does not conflict with an externality (others' preferences). However, when others' preferences modify $J$'s set of choice $J$'s. If this externality does not occur then the *ex ante* and the *ex post* sets of choice are the same and social preferences reveal that right. When the externality occurs, on the contrary, $J$ will not have anymore a right to choose between $W_M$ and $W_J$. However, what is hidden in this definition is the alienability character of the *ex ante* right. The reason why, once an externality has grown $J$ has no rights over the *ex ante* choice domain is that given $W_Z$, and the preference over Z and $W_J$, $J$ has alienated his original right over $W_M$ and $W_J$, in order to obtain at least $W_J$. This is exactly why, after an externality has emerged, the consequence of having a right over $W_M$ and $W_J$, that is $W_M \succ W_J$, does not hold anymore. According to Gibbard, thus, what generates Sen's impossibility of a Paretian Liberal is the idea of having defined minimal liberties as *inalienable* rights[10] to choose between two alternative states of the world (so that $W_M \succ W_J$ even when an externality $W_Z$ has emerged) or, recalling the Coase theorem, the idea that high transaction costs inhibit efficient rights' alienability in order to absorb externalities.[11] Suppose that either Jason is not able to renounce $W_M$ (the king forced him to marry Creusa against his will) or Medea is not able to renounce $W_T$ (she was possessed by a cruel and foolish desire for a murderous revenge in any case).[12] In that case, nobody could restore the Pareto optimality. The Sen's paradox, in this case, implies therefore that one of the two agents would be a prisoner of his or her liberty, obliged to play the piece as Euripides wrote it. Minimal liberty in this case would go against *ex post* preference orderings and agents would not have the *liberty to limit their liberty* (by alienating the right to choose a given state of the world, they would credibly commit themselves not to exert their liberty to choose that state in the first instance).

Let us assume, in the earlier example of Euripides' Medea, that the agents lack a definition of alienable rights in the first instance. In the absence of any right, social preferences will show a cycle $W_M \succ W_J \succ W_T \succ W_M$. In fact, a system of alienable rights breaks the cycle at the step where the Pareto principle is invoked (Gibbard, 1974).

In Figure 7.1, for agent $J$ to have a right over $(W_J, W_M)$ means to impose a duty on $M$ and society to allow $J$ to exert that right. The same applies for agent $M$ over $(W_M, W_T)$. In both cases community choice should reflect the holder's preference orderings. However, if agent $J$ gives up his right over $(W_J, W_M)$ in exchange for the right of agent $M$ to give up her rights over $(W_M, W_T)$,[13] then, in each rights domain, the opposite preference ordering will prevail so that a social situation like $W_J$ arises.

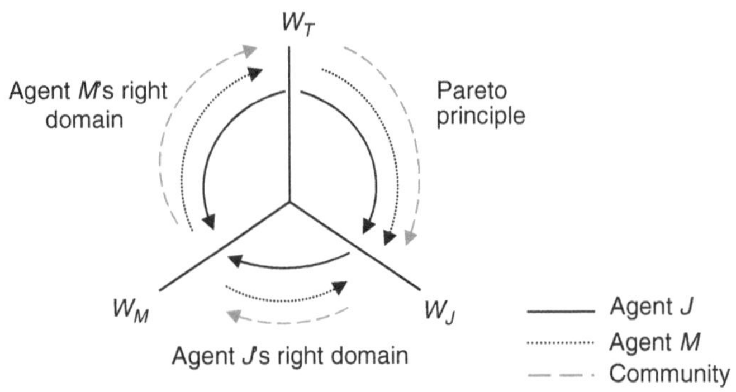


*Figure 7.1* Social preferences cycle.

The tragic outcome is thus generated by the parties' inability to appropriately use (and alienate) their liberties according to *ex post* preferences orderings. They are somehow sort of 'prisoners' of their *ex ante* preferences orderings, which would have been made in an isolated context (i.e. assuming no externalities). Liberty in this case is at the same time the opposite of liberty and something more than just liberty: it is a blind non-renegotiable commitment to choose according to *ex ante* preferences orderings. The above example of Jason and Medea thus shows how the Sennian impossibility result depends on a very restricted idea of rights, defined as the liberty to choose only *ex ante* preference orderings, without considering the impact of externalities on an agent's preferences.[14]

## Conditions for a 'Coasean Liberal'

The definition of alienable right suggests that, given an alienable right, others' preferences will follow the preferences of the right's holder (*social preferences will follow rights*).[15] At the same time, given an externality the preferences of the right's holder will follow others' preferences by exchanging alienable rights (*rights will follow social preferences*). In both cases, *minimal liberty and Pareto principle will be consistent*: when there is no externality the right's holder will reveal his right according to his preference orderings, aligned with social preference orderings; when there is an externality, the right's holder will reveal his preference orderings by alienating his right, according to the Coase theorem prediction.

What is needed, as in the Coase Theorem, is that at the very starting point, there has been a notion of rights to choose over all the relevant states of the world. *Given the Coase Theorem, thus, an appropriate definition of alienable rights seems to be a sufficient condition in order to obtain Paretian Liberal: a possibility result for a Paretian Liberal is thus obtained by simply applying the Coase Theorem.*

A social configuration in which minimal liberty (defined now as the liberty to acquire, exert and alienate individual rights) and the Pareto principle are made consistent through market exchange of alienable well-defined rights might be defined as *Coasean Liberal.*[16] Roughly speaking, Coasean Liberal is based on the very common idea that a right is quite different from the notion of minimal liberty provided by Sen. A right is something that assigns to the holder a liberty that is preserved from others' interference. A (property) right of individual *i* always implies that individual *j* has a correlated duty to allow *i* to exercise her right.[17] In a sense, a (property) right of *i* erases *j*'s (opposite) preferences over the exercise of that right. When there is a right for *i*, her preferences over the use of that right are all that matter in order to properly define that right. So why should one takes onto account *j*'s preferences over *i*'s exercise of her own right? In the *LCL*'s Lover case, if there is just one book and one owner, the non-owner's preferences over the use of the book simply should not matter in order to define the owner's liberty over the use of the book. In a sense, rights assignment aligns owner's preferences with the Pareto principle. If we define, in Sen's setting, libertarian claims as the above *i*'s claim-rights, then conflicting preferences simply do not matter and a possibility result is always obtained (social preferences follow rights). Social preferences cycles are thus broken by rights assignment (see, for example, Gibbard, (1974)). Assigning thus a right over a pair, gives more than just minimal liberty over that pair: it gives a 'bundle' of rights over all pairs of possible social situations. What is important to stress here is that the Coasean interpretation of the Sen theorem reveals why liberal values generally invoke the free market mechanism as an efficient tool to defend liberties. In this respect, the inability to define alienable rights over social states, inhibits Pareto optimality. Indeed, suppose that alienable rights are not defined in the first instance, so that it is impossible to determine, in agents' right domain, whose rights social preferences have to follow. As a consequence, agents might even ignore what is the relevant set of choice (i.e. what are the two alternative situations over which a choice is possible), when an externality is emerging and how to behave in order to select the *ex post* socially optimal outcome. In a world in which alienable rights are not defined, externality would emerge and each ordering over a pair of alternatives by an agent will conflict with at least another agent's orderings. As a consequence, when agents fail to introduce any well-defined allocation of property rights over the relevant resources, conflicting preferences persist and the impossibility of a Paretian Liberal will extend to a Coasean Liberal as well, leading thus to the impossibility of a Coasean Liberal, an outcome which is independent of the level of transaction costs: when the Coase theorem holds, the Sen's paradox fails, and vice versa.

All in all, in this setting, the emergence of alienable rights has the purpose of solving any conflict among preferences over a pair of alternatives. The definition of an alienable right assigns to the holder a set of choices that may not be violated by any other agent. Only the right holder may indeed decide to renounce that set of choices, when the emergence of an externality (others' claim over another option) redefines his set of choices so as to induce him to alienate that right.

## Transaction costs and the role of the state in supporting rights' exchange

The discussed argument has been conducted so far without considering the role played by transaction costs in inhibiting the exchange of well-defined rights, as in Coase (1960).

We will distinguish two possible sources of transaction costs:

1 *ex ante* transaction costs in defining alienable rights;
2 *ex post* transaction costs in exchanging alienable rights.

*Ex ante* transaction costs are here referred to the parties' inability to define any rights allocation over the social choice domain. That means that *ex ante* transaction costs in defining rights generate a social configuration in which *every* choice produces externalities, since agents do not dispose of a relevant own domain of choices which is preserved from other agents' interference. The Sen Paradox here is ubiquitous since we face a social configuration in which neither minimal liberties nor the Pareto principle hold.

*Ex post* transaction costs are referred to a situation in which potential socially optimal outcomes could not be reached even if rights are well defined and parties may desire to internalize externalities by rights exchange.

Whereas case (1) seems consistent with measures which reduce *ex ante* transaction costs through a hierarchical definition of any system of alienable rights, case (2) seems consistent with interventions aimed at minimizing *ex post* transaction costs so as to increase the role of parties' bargaining through market exchange.

The minimal liberty defence thus seems twofold. From one side, it requires minimization of the role of the market (when alienable rights are not defined) and increase in an authoritative intervention aimed at introducing a system of alienable rights; from the other it requires enhancement of the role of market exchange (when alienable rights are well defined), and minimization of any interference of the state.

The first requirement seems to outline the state primacy over the market, in the sense that market creation always requires a state intervention in order to properly define alienable rights and to 'defend' minimal liberty through market exchange; the second requirement seem to confirm the liberal market primacy over the state (which has only to intervene in order to reduce transaction costs).

The emergence of the impossibility of a Coasean Liberal shows that the optimal attributes of (perfect competitive) markets, as their allocative efficiency, always require as a pre-condition, a well-defined system of alienable rights, that is a state which, for every possible action or issue defined over all possible contingencies, provides a system of property rights, a system of rules for market exchange, and a system of public enforcement when controversies come out.[18] As Coase (1988) stresses,

> for anything approaching perfect competition to exist, an intricate system of rules and regulations would normally be needed. [...] Markets such as

> those that exist today require more than the provision of physical facilities in which buying and selling take place. They also require the establishment of legal rules governing the rights and duties of those carrying out transactions in these facilities. [...] Those operating in these markets have to depend, therefore on the legal system of the State.[19]

The necessity of a pre-existing state as a pre-condition for having well-functioning markets and obtaining the possibility of a Coasean Liberal, rarely might be obtained in a Lockean world in which rights originally come with (and within) individuals before that something recalling the state is created. As we have shown above, individual rights are always *social* rights, in the sense that they need mutual recognition: any right implies a correlative duty, so as to eliminate conflicting preferences over the exercise of that right. Why, thus, should natural rights have always this social connotation without an enforcement system that imposes duties against rights? And if natural rights require an enforcement system, how does one realize a system of 'social rights' in a world of conflicting preferences? Nozick's critique of Sen's argument reflects a conception of rights which from one side gives to holders a very powerful instrument to choose among alternatives; but from the other is obtained without a pre-existing enforcement system. Thus the question is how, in Nozick's world, conflicting preferences over the same pair of alternatives are solved so as to let social preferences follow individual rights. Nozick's solution is to build a system of social ordering as a residual choice. As Nozick outlines, with reference to Sen's argument

> the trouble stems from treating an individual's right to choose among alternatives as the right to determine the relative ordering of these alternatives within a social ordering. [...] A more appropriate view of individual right is as follows. Rights are always co-possible: each person may exercise his rights as he chooses. The exercise of these rights fixes some features of the world. Within the constraint of these fixed features, a choice may be made by social choice mechanism based upon a social ordering; if there are any choices left to make.[20]

In this theory, a right is 'enforced' by a 'first choice' mechanism: first comers become holders, erasing latecomers'[21] preferences over the same pair of alternatives, and there is never interdependence, or externalities, among agents' actions. For the same reason Nozick's system seems to propose a sort of Paretian Epidemic or *the tyranny of first choice*: who chooses first determines a certain amount of world features which are consistent with his first choice: the consequence is that late comers' liberty is subject to first comers' liberty and rights co-possibility ends up to the illiberality of this system of rights. Moreover, it is not clear how to enforce such a system: why should latecomers (whose rights are co-possible in the first instance) accept belonging to a world in which first comers decide quite everything? If latecomers do not accept a given feature of the world they may want to exercise their rights in an opposite direction (as if rights were not well defined in the first instance): how do agents face the emergence of externality? Rights exchange may be successful only if rights are well defined; that is, only if rights are not co-possible but alienable, and impose on non-holders a duty not to interfere. However, for a system of alienable rights to work well, a pre-existing system, which properly defines what a right is, is needed. In a world of alienable rights first comers and late comers solve their conflicts through market exchange, according to the Coase theorem, and the socially optimal outcome is independent of being the first comer or the late comer. When rights are simply described as the possibility to choose among alternatives (and not as a right which imposes a correlative duty over others not to interfere), then conflicting preferences lead to the Sen Paradox and to the impossibility of a Coasean Liberal, thus hindering not only the emergence of a minimal state but even the emergence of a well-functioning market.

As a consequence, in Nozick's theory, economic liberties (i.e. the market) cannot be defined outside of a system of coercion (i.e. the state) and minimal liberties require maximal authorities (state). As a consequence, thus, market efficiency always requires a maximal authority that, defining alienable rights, realizes the prerequisites for the market to perform its function and reach a Pareto-efficient outcome. Moreover, this process of rights defining is not something that is needed only at the very beginning, rather it is a continuous process of definition and re-definition of rights, bundling and unbundling of the same issues as Coase (1988) outlines, since 'people can always negotiate [. . .] to acquire, subdivide, and combine rights.' The state can assume several distinct forms showing how the degree of market regulation very often rises with liberalization process as long as the process of market creation always requires a correlated process of rights re-definition. Hence, in a world of incomplete rights definition, externalities abound[22] and re-definition of rights by a hierarchical authority is necessary in order to reach socially optimal outcome of the pervasive complementarities occurring between the state and the market.

Such a claim here has been addressed revising the well-known impossibility result of Sen (1970), showing thus an interesting and new direction of research which goes beyond the traditional dichotomy between the state and the market, which has been for a long time at the core of the liberal tradition in the law and economics field.

## Notes

1 The Stigler's version, as Coase (1988 p. 12) refers.
2 The following quotations refer to Coase (1988 pp. 12–13).
3 Notice the Pareto principle is defined by Sen (1970) as follows: if everyone in the society prefers a certain social state to another, then the choice of the former must be taken to be better for the society as a whole.
4 For a formalization of the results see Savaglio and Nicita (2003).
5 Pagano (2000).
6 Thus *romantic* and *opportunistic* choices are mutually excludable.
7 See Sen (1982).

8 See also Binmore (1994), Sugden R. (1985) and Mueller (1989).
9 Notice that Nicita and Savaglio (2003) provide an alternative framework for a definition of alienable right.
10 To say that $J$ has an *inalienable right* to $W_M$ over $W_J$ is to say the following. If $J$ prefers $W_M$ to $W_J$ then $W_M \succ W_J$, independent of any others' claim $W_Z$ over $W_M$.
11 This conclusion, however, does not undermine the argument provided by Sen (1970) as he argues, 'the difficulties in achieving Pareto optimality in the presence of externalities are well known. What is at issue [...] is the acceptability of Pareto optimality as an objective in the context of liberal values, given certain type of externalities'.
12 This is equivalent to the assumption of no-regret.
13 In the above example, however, it seems sufficient that only one of the two agents gives up his rights.
14 Hillinger and Lapham (1971) have shown that in conditions of interdependence, as in the case of externality, 'we cannot conceive of any "principle of liberalism" which would govern what actions are to be left to individuals independently of the majority preferences of the individual concerned'.
15 This is the Pareto-consistent libertarian claim provided by Gibbard (1974). See Gibbard (1974) for a proof.
16 See Nicita and Savaglio (2003) for a formal proof of the above statement.
17 See Pagano (2000).
18 On this point see also Pagano (2000) and Nicita and Rizzolli (2004).
19 Coase (1988 p. 10).
20 Nozick (1974 pp. 165–166). See also Sen's critique to the above (1976).
21 Here latecomers extend also to first comers new choices over the past pair of alternatives.
22 See also Nicita and Rizzolli (2004).

## References


Allen, D.W. (1991) 'What are Transaction Costs'? *Research in Law and Economics*, 14, 173–195.

Anderlini L. and L. Felli (2006) in this volume, Chapter 10.

Bernhölz, P. (1997) 'Property Rights, Contracts, Cyclical Social Preferences, and the Coase Theorem: A Synthesis', *European Journal of Political Economy*, 12, 419–442.

Binmore, K. (1994), 'Toward a History of Game Theory. Annual Supplement to the History of Political Economy, Vol. 24, by E. Roy Weintraub', *Economica*, New Series, 61(241) (February), pp. 118–119.

Cheung, S. (1986) 'Property Rights and Invention', *Research in Law and Economics*, 8, 5–18.

Cheung, S.N.S (1983) 'The Contractual Nature of the Firm', *Journal of Law and Economics*, 26, 1–22.

Coase, R. (1960) 'The Problem of Social Costs', *Journal of Law and Economics*, 3, 433–476.

Coase, R. (1988) *The Firm, the Market and the Law*, Chicago, IL, Chicago Press.

Commons, J.R. (1924) *Legal Foundations of Capitalism*, New York, Macmillan.

Cooter, R. (1987) 'Coase Theorem', *Palgrave Dictionary of Economics*, London, Palgrave, 457–459.

Gibbard, A. (1974) 'A Pareto-Consistent Libertarian Claim', *Journal of Economic Theory*, 7, 388–410.

Hayek, F.A. (1960) *The Constitution of Liberty*, London, Routledge.

Hillinger, C. and V. Lapham (1971) 'The Impossibility of a Paretian Liberal: A Comment by Two Who are Unreconstructed', *Journal of Political Economy*, 79, 1403–1405.

Hohfeld, W.N. (1913) 'Some Fundamental Legal Concepts as Applied in Judicial Reasoning', *Yale Law Journal*, 51, 951–966.

Mueller, M. (1989) 'Reviewed Work(s): The Process of Technological Change: New Technology and Social Choice in the Workplace by Jon Clark', *The Business History Review*, 63(4) (Winter), pp. 988–990.

Nicita, A. and M. Rizzolli (2004) 'Much Ado About the Cathedral. Property Rules and Liability Rules When Rights are Incomplete', *Siena Memos and Papers in Law and Economics*, SIMPLE 22/04, University of Siena.

Nicita, A. and E. Savaglio (2003) 'Minimal Liberty and the Coasean Liberal: A Solution for a Tragedy'? Mimeo.

Nozick, R. (1974) *Anarchy, State and Utopia*, Oxford, Blackwell.

Pagano, U. (2000) 'Public Markets, Private Orderings and Corporate Governance', *International Review of Law and Economics*, 20(4), 453–477.

Parisi, F. (1999) in J. Backhaus (ed.) *The Elgar Companion to Law and Economics*, Edward Elgar.

Sen, A. (1970) 'The impossibility of a Paretian Liberal', *Journal of Political Economy*, 78, 152–157.

Sen, A. (1976) 'Liberty, Unanimity and Rights', *Economica*, 43, 217–245.

Sen, A. (1982) *Choice, Welfare and Measurement*, Oxford, Basil Blackwell.

Sugden, R. (1985) 'Why be Consistent? A Critical Analysis of Consistency Requirements in Choice Theory', *Economica*, New Series, 52(206) (May), pp. 167–183.

Usher, D. (1998) 'The Coase Theorem is Tautological, Incoherent or Wrong', *Economics Letters*, 61, 3–11.

# 8 Private orderings and intellectual property

## What is the best incentive system?[1]

*Nancy Gallini and Suzanne Scotchmer*

### Introduction

Intellectual property (IP) is the foundation of the modern information economy. It fuels the software, life sciences and computer industries, and pervades most other products we consume. Although most inventors consider it essential, it is currently under attack by some academics and policy makers. One complaint is that IP rewards inventors beyond what is necessary to spur innovation. Another is that IP is a drag to innovation, rather than a spur, since it prevents inventions from being used efficiently, especially in creating further innovations. A third complaint is that some inventions should not be protected at all but, instead, should be supported by public sponsors.

Controversies over what should constitute IP swirl around business methods, computer software, research tools in the biomedical industry, and genetic sequences. However, this is not new; controversies have swirled around every new technology in the twentieth century. A sampler might include the question of whether player piano rolls should receive copyright protection, whether "purification" of chemical compounds constitutes "invention" for purposes of patent law, and whether mathematical algorithms such as public key encryption should be patentable subject matter. Technologies that fall outside the subject matter of patents and copyrights have sometimes received *sui generis* protections, such as computer chips under the Semiconductor Chip Protection Act.

For all these technologies, the same questions arise: are there natural market forces that protect inventors so that formal protections or other incentives are not necessary? If not, is IP the best incentive system, or would the technology more appropriately be developed by a public sponsor and offered freely in the public domain? How should IP be designed so as to minimize deadweight loss due to monopoly pricing without undermining incentives to innovate?

Our objective in this chapter is to review what economists have said about incentive schemes to promote R&D, including IP. While we focus on environments in which other forms of protection are not available, we note that other protections can obviate the need for any formal reward system. For example, encryption offers the potential to protect digitally distributed products such as music, movies, and software, even in the absence of IP (National Research Council, 2000). In the realm of databases, for which formal protections have been mandated in Europe and proposed in the US Congress, vendors are protecting their data with both clever business strategies and technology (Maurer, 1999; Maurer and Scotchmer, 1999). In markets with network effects, there may be natural barriers to entry, so that a vendor may capture the entire market even without formal protection (Farrell, 1995). And, of course, trade secrecy can be an important protection, especially when firms devise clever nondisclosure agreements that enable them to license without leaking the secret to unauthorized users (e.g. see Anton and Yao, 1994). In some of these examples, the alternative protection involves social costs that could be avoided by formal IP. But if not, the case for IP may be weak.

In the section "Alternative mechanisms for rewarding innovation," we compare IP to alternative incentive schemes. Without losing the thread of the chapter, the reader who is only interested in the design of IP (as opposed to other incentive schemes) could skip the last three subsections of this section. In the section "Optimal design: the case of a single innovation," we review optimal design issues for IP, especially the question of patent breadth, and in the section "Optimal design: the case of cumulative innovation," we turn to the special problems that arise when innovation is cumulative. In the last section, we summarize the arguments for and against IP. We comment on whether the design recommendations of economists can actually be implemented, and argue that IP regimes should be designed so that the subject matter of each one has relatively homogeneous needs for protection.

## Alternative mechanisms for rewarding innovation

Competitive markets will not generally be conducive to innovation, for a reason that was well articulated by Arrow (1962). Inventions are "information" and information is a public good. An invention such as a wireless palmtop is a combination of tangible embodiments and an intangible idea, as well as information about how to manufacture it. Typically, both the information and the tangible embodiments are costly to the inventor, but only the tangible components are costly to a rival. Without some sort of protection or reward, the inventor will therefore be at a market disadvantage relative to rivals, and will possibly be dissuaded from investing.

Arrow explained why *some* incentive scheme is needed, but not *which* scheme. Many schemes have been used in practice. In the seventeenth century, for example, a prize was offered in France for developing a workable water turbine (Reynolds, 1983 p. 338). For about a century in the same era, a prize was outstanding for developing a method to calculate longitude at sea (Sobel, 1995). In the modern era, R&D is sponsored to a large extent by government grants. According to the National Science Foundation (2000), in 1998 about 30% of US research was funded by the federal government. These examples raise the following question: in what environments are there better incentive schemes than IP?

We shall use the term "intellectual property (IP)" to mean an exclusive right to market an invention for a fixed time period. It includes copyrights, patents, plant patents, protection under the Plant Variety Protection Act, and other *sui generis* types of protection. By a "prize" we mean a payment funded out of general revenue that is made to a researcher conditional on delivering a specified invention. Prizes can either be tailored individually to firms, depending on their efficiency characteristics, or can be offered symmetrically to any firm that wants to compete, just as a patent is. By "procurement," we mean a mechanism to solve the problem of getting an invention at minimum cost, in a timely manner, or otherwise efficiently (e.g. Laffont and Tirole, 1986, 1987). A simple procurement mechanism would be an auction for the right to be paid when the invention is delivered.

A form of procurement commonly used in government-sponsored research appears, on its face, to be a fixed-price contract. For example, the National Institutes of Health give funding in advance for projects that are described in the proposals. Funds are not withheld if the output is not delivered, since the idea of the contract is to pay costs as they accrue. If such funding were a one-time event for each researcher, researchers might be inclined to "take the money and run." This moral hazard problem is overcome because future grants are contingent on previous success. The linkage between previous success and future funding seems even more specific in the case of the National Science Foundation. Fixed-price contracts thus operate much like prizes, with the wrinkle that a researcher must convince the sponsor in advance that his output might be worthy of a prize. For this purpose, his reputation might suffice, and in some cases, much of the research has already been completed.

We begin our analysis with a benchmark. When both the costs and values of innovations are publicly observable to both firms and a public sponsor, IP is not the best incentive scheme. A better scheme is for a public sponsor to choose the projects with the largest net social benefits, and pay for them on delivery, using funds from general revenue. With IP, projects are funded out of monopoly profits. Monopoly pricing is equivalent to taxing a single market, which is generally thought to impose greater deadweight loss than the broad-based taxation that generates general revenue. Thus, to justify IP, there must be some type of asymmetric information about the costs and benefits of research programs.

We first make some comparative remarks about IP, prizes and procurement contracts. These remarks are much in the spirit of Wright (1983), who gave the first formal treatment of how asymmetric information should inform our choice among incentive mechanisms. In the subsections that follow, we then show that these three mechanisms can generally be improved upon.[2]

IP has an obvious defect as well as obvious virtues. The defect is the deadweight loss due to monopoly pricing. The virtues are several. Most importantly, if the costs and benefits of R&D investments are known only to firms, and not to government sponsors, firms will use their superior knowledge to screen investments. A sponsor does not need to decide in advance which investments are meritorious. An investor knows that he will be punished by the market if he does not invest wisely. Another obvious virtue is that the prospect of valuable IP might incite higher levels of effort than those generally associated with sponsored research. For example, much has been made of the human genome project, whose completion was accelerated by a private firm hoping to win IP rights on gene sequences. Finally, an IP system imposes the costs of an invention on its users. In other incentive mechanisms, the costs are borne more generally by taxpayers. Taxpayers might rightfully revolt if asked to bear the costs of developing, say, computer games.

Lest these advantages of IP be overstated, however, we note that prizes have many of the same virtues. If an investment's prospective value is known to the sponsor (or defined by the sponsor, as in the case of military wares), the sponsor can screen projects himself. A prize system then seems superior to IP. It avoids deadweight loss, and can be as good as IP at inciting effort.

Moreover, IP will not work as an incentive mechanism unless third parties can observe at least some aspects of value. A rightholder must be able to defend his right against potential infringers. He must be able to prove in court that his IP meets the standard for protection, and that an alleged infringer is marketing a product that falls within the breadth of his claims. Aspects of the invention's value must therefore be observable *ex post*, although typically at the high cost of litigation and discovery.

The *ex post* observability requirement will typically impose less cost under an IP system than under a prize system. Under an IP system, the costs of discovery are incurred only if there is litigation. In contrast, for a prize, costs would have to be incurred for every invention in order for the sponsor to set a payment commensurate with the value.[3] Therefore, our distinction is not really between "observability" and "nonobservability," but rather a distinction on whether the value is known to the sponsor without incurring cost. The most natural example is when the sponsor defines the value of the invention himself, as in military procurement.

Recently the World Health Organization and the World Bank have suggested prizes for developing vaccines that would not be developed or might not be widely enough distributed under a system of proprietary rights. The problems are great: how to assess whether a vaccine merits a prize; how to ensure that the prizes are not given prematurely before higher-quality vaccines are brought forward; how to ensure that the prizes are actually given, when it is easy to manufacture reasons to withhold them. Prizes can be organized so that worthy projects need not be identified in advance, but administering the prize then becomes particularly burdensome. The problems are particularly acute where innovation is cumulative. See Kremer (2000) for a thoughtful and detailed analysis of how such a system might work.

Unlike IP, a procurement contract would typically not be offered to all comers. Instead there would be a negotiation phase in which the procurement officer tries to sort out which firm(s) are more efficient, and only offers the "prize" to those firms. A mechanism that allows such flexibility is more effective by definition than a prize offered to all comers. As for prizes, the sponsor must identify worthy projects. For traditional government procurement, such as for fighter jets, this is automatic. For medical research, the sponsor may solicit open-ended proposals, which entails administrative cost. In addition, the negotiation required for procurement might be politically infeasible, as well as costly.

In the next subsections, we investigate optimal incentive mechanisms in specific research environments, with a view toward understanding how optimal mechanisms relate to IP, prizes and simple reimbursements. We focus on environments in which no alternative mechanisms for protection (private or market) are available, and on single inventions that do not lead to future innovations. Following Scotchmer (1999b), we stylize the allocation problem as having three facets, which are intertwined. The first is the *decision* problem: should a project be undertaken? The second is the *delegation* problem: by which firms, or how many, and at what rates of investment? The third is the *funding* problem: can the deadweight loss of monopoly pricing be avoided?

### *The problem of aggregating information*

To solve the decision, delegation and funding problems jointly, all the information that is decentralized among firms might have to be aggregated. IP, prizes and simple procurement mechanisms such as fixed-price contracts and auctions cannot aggregate information, and are therefore flawed at the outset.

To see this, consider a well-defined project, such as finding an AIDS vaccine or developing supersonic transport. Suppose that there are two potential researchers, $i = 1, 2$, and that each researcher $i$ has an efficiency parameter $c_i$ for this project, interpreted as the cost of success. The product will have a common value $v$ regardless of which firm develops it, and each firm has a signal $v_i$ of this value. The underlying value would typically be determined by the extent of demand or anything else that affects monopoly profit and social welfare. Because each $v_i$ is a noisy signal of an underlying common value, it is natural to suppose that the signals $\{v_1, v_2\}$ are correlated. It is less obvious whether the cost parameters $\{c_1, c_2\}$ would be correlated. We shall assume that they are independent draws from a known distribution.

To make an efficient investment decision, each firm would like to know the other firm's signal. For example, a firm with a low signal of value, $v_1 = L$, might invest if it knew the other firm had a high signal of value, $v_2 = H$, but not otherwise. But neither the value nor its best estimate is known *ex ante* to either firm since neither can observe the other's signal.

The importance of aggregating information is revealed in the following special case in which both the costs and the signals take on binary values: $c_i \in \{l, h\}$, $v_i \in \{L, H\}$. Suppose that the first-best, full-information rule for allocative efficiency is that the project should be undertaken unless (1) both firms have high costs, regardless of the signals of value or (2) both firms have low signals of value, regardless of costs. The project should be undertaken by a single firm if (3) at least one firm has low cost and at least one firm has a high signal of value or (4) both firms have high cost and both have high signals of value.

Suppose $(c_1, v_1) = (l, L)$. Firm 1 should invest if $(c_2, v_2) = (h, H)$ but not if $(c_2, v_2) = (h, L)$. Without knowing firm 2's information, firm 1 could not make an efficient decision. Such could be the case under a patent system. Firm 1 may fail to invest because it is pessimistic about value, $v_1 = L$, and firm 2 may fail to invest because its costs are too high, $c_2 = h$. If the firms could share their information, firm 1 would invest based on firm 2's propitious information about the market. To some extent, the firms should be able to learn each other's private information by observing each other's investments. However, even if the firms know each other's costs, they might get stuck in an inefficient, but self-reinforcing, equilibrium where each invests because the other is investing, and each incorrectly thinks the other has a high signal of value (or vice versa) (Minehart and Scotchmer, 1999). When the firms have different, unobservable costs, the difficulties of making inferences from investment behavior are compounded. A firm that invests could either be investing because it has low cost or because it has very propitious private information about the market. The observing firm cannot distinguish between these two cases.

Neither IP nor prizes nor simple procurement mechanisms (e.g. auctions) can cope with the problem of aggregating information. Scotchmer (1999b) describes a procurement mechanism that bears little resemblance to auctions, prizes or IP, but can achieve as good an outcome as when the signals of value are known, provided the firms' signals of value are correlated.[4] While the mechanism described will delegate efficiently, it may not be realistic given the constraints of government procurement. The mechanism might entail payments from firms to the government, or payments to firms that are not asked to invest. Such payments would be difficult to enforce.

The problems with the efficient procurement mechanism may explain the use of prizes, IP, and simple procurement mechanisms but, under the conditions presented in this example, no one has studied their relative merits as second-best mechanisms. In order to identify the relative merits of the simple schemes and other more realistic mechanisms, we now consider the decision and delegation problems separately.

## *The delegation problem*

We isolate the problem of optimal delegation by assuming that the sponsor already knows the optimal decision, namely, to invest. That is, the sponsor knows the value of the project and that it exceeds the cost of delivery, but it does not know which firm(s) is (are) more cost-efficient. Optimal delegation has two components: choosing the most efficient firm or group of firms, and motivating the firm(s) to invest at efficient rates.

If the sponsor faced only a problem of selecting the more efficient firm(s), then the delegation problem would be easy to solve, for example, by auctioning the right to invest. In contrast, IP and prizes could lead to inefficiency. If the market has room for only one firm, there is no reason that the lower-cost firm would be the entrant, especially when the relative efficiencies of the firms are not publicly observable.

But even an auction will not perform well when there is also a problem of inciting the right amount of effort, so that the invention is delivered in a timely manner. The appropriate rate of progress is key to the economics of R&D: how much additional cost should be tolerated in return for a higher rate of progress?

A firm's willingness to accelerate invention at higher total cost depends on the "prize" it will receive, conditional on delivering the product. Thus the size of the prize determines the rate of investment. However the optimal size of prize (and the optimal rate of investment) depend both on the researcher's "efficiency" and on his efficiency relative to other firms. For an inefficient firm, the optimal rate of investment might be zero if it is possible to delegate to a more efficient firm, but positive if the other firm is even less efficient. Thus, the problem is to tailor prizes both to the firms' *individual* efficiencies and to their *relative* efficiencies.

Gandal and Scotchmer (1993) study this problem, and show that the sponsor should offer a menu of options with both fixed fees and firm-specific prizes.[5] The menu serves two purposes. It gets the firms to reveal their relative efficiencies and, once the contracts are awarded, it gets the firms to invest at the efficient rates. The difficulty is in the coordination: each firm's efficient rate depends on both firms' efficiency parameters. A simple patent or prize system, where the IP or prizes are not tailored to the firms' relative efficiency, will not ensure that only the most efficient firm(s) invest, or at the efficient rates. And a simple fixed-price contract might not create incentives to invest fast enough, even if the contract is auctioned to the more efficient firm.

The message here is that, even when the value of the prospective invention is known prior to the investments, optimal procurement requires a mixture of prizes and fixed payments, rather than a "pure" prize system, a patent system or an auction. Simple mechanisms can be resurrected as "best" in very simple contexts. An auction performs well when the only issue is to choose the most efficient firm, but there is no issue of inciting the right amount of effort. A simple prize performs well when there is a single firm qualified to undertake the research. If the prize is set equal to the social value, the firm will have the same objective function as society and will invest efficiently. Since the "best" simple mechanisms are different for different simple contexts, it is no surprise that complicated research environments with several firms call for mechanisms that combine instruments.

In the next section we focus on the optimal decision problem, assuming that the value of the innovation is unknown.

## *The decision problem*

We have just pointed out that if there is a single firm qualified for the research program, the optimal mechanism is a prize set equal to the social value. The firm's private incentives are then aligned with social incentives. However, to set such a prize, the sponsor must know the social value in advance or observe it *ex post*. Since IP automatically reflects the social value, at least to some extent, IP looks like an attractive alternative to a prize when the social value is unobservable. We now investigate whether this justification for IP holds up.

Kremer (1998) proposes a system to create a prize equal to the social value, even when the sponsor cannot observe it in advance. His proposal involves IP, but avoids deadweight loss by turning a patent into a prize. He proposes that the patent authority take possession of the patent, and auction it to the highest bidder, assuming that every firm can observe the value *ex post.* The rules of the auction are that with very small probability the patent will actually be sold to the highest bidder, and otherwise the invention will be put in the public domain. Firms will bid the true value, hence revealing it. The social value is estimated from the revealed private value, and the inventor receives a "prize" equal to the social value, paid out of general revenue. He will thus invest if the social value exceeds his cost, as is efficient. [6]

Another scheme to avoid deadweight loss is proposed by DeLaat (1996). To illustrate his idea in a very simple model, suppose that a potential R&D project is described by a pair $(c, v)$, where $c$ is the cost, which is observable to the sponsor, and $v$ is the value, which is not. But if the cost $c$ is observable to the sponsor, he can ask the researcher to report the prospective value $v$, and then give a fixed-price contract to reimburse the cost $c$ if and only if the prospective value exceeds the cost. Since the researcher earns zero profit whatever he reports (he is only reimbursed the cost), he will report the value truthfully to the sponsor, who will make the efficient decision whether to invest. Thus, IP would be unnecessary.

But this scheme only seems credible if (contrary to the premise) the value of the invention is observable *ex post*, or if the sponsor can verify that the researcher is investing exactly as he promised (as deLaat assumes explicitly).[7] If not, the researcher could use the contract money for other purposes and deliver a shoddy product; there is a disabling problem of "moral hazard", which IP could overcome.

Nevertheless, we can conclude from the arguments of Kremer and deLaat that if either cost or value is truly observable to a sponsor, there may be a better mechanism than IP. Consistent with this view, Scotchmer (1999a) justifies patents by assuming that both the cost and value are both unobservable. A similar interpretation can be made for Cornelli and Schankerman (1999). The latter present a model where the value of an invention is endogenous to the firm's investment effort which, in turn, depends on an unobservable efficiency parameter. In effect, neither cost nor value is observable to the sponsor. Thus it is hard to see how any mechanism short of IP could be effective. Since the value of the patent increases with the value of the invention, a patent system gives the firm at least some incentive to spend more resources to create a product of greater value. Cornelli and Schankerman show how this incentive can be increased by using a patent renewal system.

The patent renewal system is a menu of options (F, T), where F is a payment from the patentholder to the sponsor and T is a patent life.[8] The fee F increases with the patent life, and might start out negative (a subsidy). The patentee can then "buy" a longer patent life by paying renewal fees. The value of the patent automatically increases with the value of the invention, but increases more for higher-value inventions, since those are the ones that will be renewed in return for fees. Thus the incentive to develop higher-value products is compounded.

Scotchmer (1999a) derives the renewal system as a multi-dimensional screening mechanism for ideas $(c, v)$, where both are unobservable. Again, it is the higher-value ideas that will be renewed the longest, compounding their value. Thus the cost, $c$, that firms are willing to bear may go up faster than linearly with the value of the innovation, $v$.

As mentioned, the renewal system could start with subsidies, which are then reduced as firms pay fees in return for a longer patent life. Subsidies are advocated by Shavell and van Ypersle (1998) on grounds that they are a more efficient way to reward innovators than IP. Subsidizing low-value innovations allows the protection on high-value innovations to be shorter (thus reducing the deadweight loss), without jeopardizing incentives to innovate.

The problem with subsidies, of course, is that they may be exploited by opportunistic firms, which could collect the subsidy and either not invest, or produce something worthless. To avoid this problem, subsidies, like their close kin, prizes, must be contingent on some aspect of the resulting invention, such as its value. Thus it seems reasonable to suppose that subsidy schemes will not be used if the invention's value or success cannot be verified *ex post*. But then we have a contradiction. If subsidies are possible, it must be because some aspect of value is observable *ex post*. If so, IP should not be used at all, since prizes (rewards, fixed-price contracts) dominate. IP and prizes can serve the same screening function, and can incite firms to the same levels of effort, but prizes avoid the deadweight loss. Consistent with this caveat, renewal schemes seen in practice do not provide for subsidies. (See Calandrillo, 1998 for a broader set of criticisms of subsidies.)

In conclusion, IP can be justified in two ways. First, it can be justified as a screening mechanism to encourage investment in high-value projects, which may also have high cost. Second, it can be justified as a means to increase the rate at which firms invest, either to increase value or to accelerate progress. Without a means to link prizes to social value, there is no alternative to achieve these results. These virtues of IP should be weighed against the aggregation problems described earlier when more than one firm is capable of the research.

Assuming that, in a second-best analysis, IP would prevail, we now ask how the right should be designed. We have already discussed the benefits of a renewal system. But how broad and long should protection be?

## Optimal design: the case of a single innovation

Perhaps the most influential work on patent design was that of Nordhaus (1969), who explained why patents (or other IP) should have finite length. If the sole concern is to encourage innovation, then IP should last forever. And if the sole concern is to avoid deadweight loss that occurs through proprietary prices, then IP should not exist at all. A finite length of protection balances these two concerns. Longer protection would encourage more innovation, but only by prolonging the deadweight loss on inventions that would be made anyway.

Nordhaus' simple framework spawned a large literature on the design of IP, with consideration of patent races, imitation by rivals, technology licensing, and how the design question changes when technology is cumulative. In this section we focus on the design question of *breadth* (also called *scope*), which has occupied considerable journal space in the 1990s. In the next section we turn to sequential or cumulative research, where breadth plays a different role.

We begin with Gilbert and Shapiro (1990) who introduced the notion of patent scope into the Nordhaus analysis. They define patent scope as the price p that the innovator is able to charge for the product that embodies the innovation. Thus a patent policy is (T, p), where T is the patent life. While such a definition is far removed from what a court might use, the analysis that arises from using it is still informative, as discussed below. Maximizing social surplus over all combinations of (T, p) that yield enough revenue to cover the cost of research, Gilbert and Shapiro find that optimal patent length is infinite, with the patent scope set at the level that just covers R&D investment.[9] That is, the optimal design is for the patent to be narrow and long.

Gallini (1992) reversed this design conclusion in a model where patent breadth determines the ease of entry into the protected market. She defined scope technologically, as the cost K that rivals must incur to imitate the invention without infringement. Thus a patent policy is a pair (T, K). The lower price that results from narrow scope arises from rivals' attempts to "invent around" the patent, rather than from some type of regulatory or antitrust action, as assumed by Gilbert and Shapiro. In contrast to Gilbert and Shapiro, the innovator's profit does not strictly increase with patent life since a long patent life will encourage imitation (hence competition) before the patent expires. An increase in patent life provides incentives for wasteful imitation but not for productive innovation.

For a given imitation cost K, a sufficiently long patent will attract imitators, resulting in oligopoly pricing instead of monopoly pricing. Conversely, for a given patent life T, a sufficiently narrow scope will attract entrants. Patent life and scope are complementary in that *both* instruments must be increased or reduced to achieve most efficiently the required reimbursement to the innovator.

With imitation, the social cost of a patent may have two components: deadweight loss and the cost of imitation. The optimal patent policy minimizes these costs. Gallini shows that the optimal design is to avoid entry entirely by making the patent broad and short, in contrast to that proposed in Gilbert and Shapiro. That is, the patent should be just long enough to generate the required revenue for the monopolist patentholder, and broad enough to prevent imitation.

However, this reversal depends on an assumption about licensing, or, rather, its absence. In the Gallini model, if the patent is too long or too narrow, the innovator is assumed to sit back passively and watch imitators erode her market share. Maurer and Scotchmer (1998) point out that the duplicative waste could be avoided voluntarily through licensing rather than by adjusting patent policy, which can again reverse the optimal design. Whatever the market outcome without licensing, the innovator and potential entrants can achieve the same market outcome (price and number of entrants) through a licensing agreement with appropriate royalties and other fees. Since both the innovator and potential entrants can jointly save the imitation costs, they prefer licensing to imitation. The innovator can do even better by fine-tuning the number of entrants.

An important point of agreement among Gilbert and Shapiro, Gallini, and Maurer and Scotchmer is that a narrow patent reduces market price. However, their arguments differ. Gilbert and Shapiro have in mind some sort of regulatory mechanism; Gallini argues that price reduction will occur through duplicative entry; and Maurer and Scotchmer argue that price reduction will occur through licensing to prevent duplication. In addition, the analyses of social cost differ, leading to different prescriptions about optimal length and breadth. Since Gilbert and Shapiro do not recognize imitation costs, they simply ask whether the deadweight loss of monopoly pricing is smaller with a long patent and low price, or a short patent and high price. Gallini argues that if the social cost includes the cost of imitation, the optimal policy should be aimed at avoiding it. Maurer and Scotchmer argue that the imitation costs will not be borne in practice if licensing is available, so that the Gilbert and Shapiro type of analysis is restored.

It is worth expanding on why licensing will lower the market price, by considering what would happen if there were a single potential entrant. The latter situation was analyzed by Gallini (1984), who first pointed out that licensing can prevent entry. With a single potential entrant (or a fixed number), the optimal licensing strategy is to sustain the profit-maximizing (monopoly) price with high royalties, and to share the revenues by using other fees. The licensor has an incentive to keep the market price high regardless of the cost of imitation. In contrast, in the argument above, the licensor is worried about imitation by *non*licensees as well as by licensees; there is always an unlicensed potential entrant. The patent holder commits to a low market price precisely to reduce the attractiveness of entry by nonlicensees, who can be numerous and unidentifiable *ex ante*. This point impresses the significance of potential entry to the welfare analysis of licensing and, therefore, to the optimal design of IP.

The foregoing discussion shows that private contracting can dramatically alter the optimal design of patents, and that public and private instruments may be complementary in reducing social costs. Patent scope governs the market price in the proprietary market, and licensing prevents wasteful imitation. In this environment where goods are homogeneous, licensing determines the design of patent policy: If licensing is available, a case can be made for narrow and long patents; if licensing is not available, the analysis points to patents that are broad and short.

Licensing may not occur for a variety of reasons, in which case we need a more thorough investigation of the relative merits of the Gilbert and Shapiro and the Gallini arguments, in broader economic environments than they address. Such an analysis has been provided by Denicolò (1996). He explains that narrow (and long) or broad (and short) patents depend on the concavity or convexity, respectively, of the relationship between social welfare and post-innovation profit. Situations in which relatively short broad patents are optimal include costly imitation; Cournot duopoly with constant marginal costs; and horizontally differentiated firms and linear transportation costs, as in Klemperer (1990).

We now turn to cumulative innovation in which subsequent research activity is directed toward the development of improvements or applications of a previous innovation.

## Optimal design: the case of cumulative innovation

In the earlier discussion, IP is designed for isolated innovations that may be imitated. In reality, research is cumulative. Innovations build upon each other, and subsequent research activity is directed toward improvements or applications of previous discoveries. This fact changes the problem of patent design in interesting and complex ways.

The first and most fundamental complexity, articulated by Scotchmer (1991), is that early innovators lay a foundation for later innovations. The later innovations could not be made without the earlier ones. So that the first innovator has enough incentive to invest, she should be given some claim on profit of the later innovations; otherwise, early innovators could be under-rewarded for the social value they create. This is particularly evident in the case of a research tool for which all the social value resides in the innovations it facilitates. If the innovator could not profit from the later products, she would have no incentive to create the tool. The incentive problems are particularly vexed in the case of "creative destruction," discussed by Schumpeter (1934): an innovator's descendants can actually become the instruments of their destruction.

The Schumpeterian perspective highlights an important problem that arises in the cumulative context: that of dividing the profit between innovators in a way that respects their costs. If, for example, only one pot of money is available for distribution between two innovators and most is allocated to the first firm, the second inventor's incentive for research is reduced and vice versa. Green and Scotchmer (1995) argue that because of the difficulties in dividing profit, patent lives will have to be longer than if the whole sequence of innovations occurs in a single firm. *Ex ante* licensing – licensing before investments are made – is a way of mimicking the latter outcome. As in the case of a single invention, the availability of private contracting influences the optimal patent scope when innovation is cumulative.

Cumulativeness changes the design instruments that are relevant to the length of protection. The statutory life can be irrelevant when a noninfringing substitute, such as an improvement, can displace a protected product. What matters is the *effective* life, that is, the time until the noninfringing substitute appears (Scotchmer, 1991; O'Donoghue *et al.*, 1998). The effective life is determined by patent *scope* or*leading breadth*, which is interpreted as the minimum quality improvement that avoids infringement. As in the case of costly imitation discussed earlier, the effectiveness of patent life as an instrument for R&D may be limited when subsequent innovation can undermine profitability.

Finally, cumulativeness makes a third instrument – the minimum standard for protection, or minimum inventive step – relevant to the optimal design of IP. For copyrighted works the standard for protection is low (as is the breadth of protection), while for patents, the patentability standard (or novelty requirement) can be quite stringent. In our discussion of isolated inventions above, we assumed that the invention was protectable, since there would be no incentives to innovate if there were no IP or other incentive instruments. But in the cumulative context, patentability on second-generation inventions is less essential, since an innovation can be protected by an exclusive license on a previous patent it infringes, rather than by its own patent. Leading breadth and the standard for patentability together determine the level of "forward protection" each innovation has.

Several arguments favoring both weak and strict standards for IP protection have been advanced. Green and Scotchmer (1995) argue with caution for a weak standard (a weak "novelty requirement"), so that firms are encouraged to disclose every small bit of progress. While these disclosures could speed up invention by giving a technological boost to competitors, they warn that the weak novelty requirement could also encourage firms to choose trade secrecy over patents. In contrast, a tightening of the standards for patentability can encourage firms to be more ambitious in the improvements they attempt to develop (O'Donoghue, 1998) or can direct their investments toward more socially useful inventions (Eswaran and Gallini, 1996). Even when the standard for protection does not reorient research efforts, it can affect the division of profit among sequential researchers. Scotchmer (1996) argues that the strictest novelty requirement (no protection) on second-generation products would tilt the joint profit of a sequence of innovations in favor of earlier innovators without jeopardizing second-generation advances. A second-generation product can be protected by an exclusive license on the infringed patent of the earlier generation. Denicolò (2000b) makes a case for a patent policy with a weak patentability standard and narrow leading breadth. In a model in which firms race for the first- and second-generation patents, he shows that tilting profits in favor of earlier innovators might only encourage a socially wasteful patent race at the stage of basic research and underinvestment in the second stage.

Although the complexities of cumulativeness seem to defy clear, unqualified design implications, one lesson is clear: the optimal design of IP depends importantly on the ease with which rights holders can contract around conflicts in rights. Contracting is especially relevant to the question of breadth, which determines the likelihood that a follow-on innovation will infringe a prior patent.

A danger of IP that has been debated from its inception to the present (see Machlup and Penrose, 1950) is that IP can stifle innovation and slow progress. Merges and Nelson (1990) link this danger to breadth, using examples from the aircraft, radio, and pharmaceutical industries to argue for narrow patents. An earlier example concerned steam engines. James Watt refused to license his patents for improvement, with the result that there was a flood of pent-up invention when his patents expired in 1800 (Derry and Williams, 1993, p. 324).

In contrast, Kitch (1977) argues that broad patents are socially beneficial precisely *because* they stimulate further developments. Scotchmer (1991) and Green and Scotchmer (1995) take the same point of view, but focus on how *ex ante* contracting affects division of profit. With *ex ante* contracting, the role of breadth is not to determine whether subsequent products are made (they will be made if they add to joint profit), but rather to determine how the profit is divided. This theme is also carried forward in later papers, for example, Merges (1998, 1999), Scotchmer (1996), O'Donoghue *et al.* (1998), Schankerman and Scotchmer (2001). Matutes *et al.* (1996) and Chang (1995) argue for broad patents even without assuming that *ex ante* contracts can be made.

To some extent, broad patents are also supported by the arguments of O'Donoghue *et al.* (1998), who study breadth in a model with an infinite sequence of improved products (quality ladder). If patents are relatively narrow, the effective life of each patent ends when a noninfringing improvement arrives, and is thus endogenous. But if the patent is broad, then the statutory life is also the effective life: every subsequent innovation on the quality ladder infringes during the statutory life and must be marketed under license. To achieve the same rate of progress under both regimes, the effective patent life with a narrow patent must be longer than the (effective) statutory life with a broad patent. Broad, short patents are more efficient at rewarding innovators along the quality ladder because less of the total profit in the system accrues to high-value innovations that would be made in any case, and more goes to the innovators who need additional incentives.

Thus, with some caution, we can extract from the literature a case for broad (and short) patents. Broad patents can serve the public interest by preventing duplication of R&D costs, facilitating the development of second-generation products, and protecting early innovators who lay a foundation for later innovators. However, these benefits disappear if licensing fails. Heller and Eisenberg (1998) argue that licensing will likely fail when researchers must negotiate multiple licenses, as now occurs in the biomedical industry. Mazzoleni and Nelson (1998) caution that these transaction costs may limit the use of contracts for coordinating innovations that follow from a broad patent.

Another problem with licensing is that it can lessen competition both in "innovation markets"[10] and in product markets. It thus raises antitrust issues, even in the simpler context where there is no cumulative aspect. One of the difficult issues is that *ex ante* mergers of research activities can be either efficient or inefficient from a social perspective. On the efficiency side, *ex ante* mergers can enable firms to avoid duplicated costs and to delegate efficiently, much as discussed in the section "Alternative mechanisms for rewarding innovation." But on the inefficiency side, *ex ante* mergers can retard progress, for example, by nullifying the acceleration that would otherwise come from a patent race. See Gilbert and Sunshine (1995) for a discussion of these issues. One of the thorny questions that arises is whether competition policy should view licensing practices more leniently than otherwise if incentives to innovate are at stake. See Gallini and Trebilcock (1998) for a discussion of these issues.

The cumulative context raises another issue. Above we focused on the salutary effects of licensing, namely that *ex ante* licensing can ensure investment in infringing follow-on products that would add to joint profit. Turning this argument on its head, licensing can stifle noninfringing follow-on products that would *detract* from joint profit. Gallini and Winter (1985) analyzed a situation where a potential competitor is licensed *ex ante* in order to dissuade him from investing in a noninfringing cost reduction that would have lowered prices in the market. Such licensing clearly reduces product-market competition relative to what the Congress apparently intended in designing patent law. If such licensing occurred *ex post* to prevent production of the cost-reducing innovation after it had been developed, it would presumably be an antitrust violation. Chang (1995) analyzes precisely that type of *ex post* collusion and advocates a strict antitrust rule against collusion. For a discussion of how principles of competition policy might be formulated to distinguish *ex ante* licensing that is procompetitive from that which is anticompetitive, see Scotchmer (1998).

Besen and Maskin (2000) argue that if firms do not license in a way that takes full advantage of their IP, for example, because of antitrust restrictions, then licensing may reduce industry profits below those available without licensing, and the broad patents that support such licensing are counterproductive. However a caveat is in order: the licensing terms that are prohibited in the authors' model may not be prohibited by the Department of Justice, Federal Trade Commission's guidelines. Broadly speaking, the guidelines do not prohibit licensing terms unless they lessen competition relative to no license. In this sense, Besen and Maskin's paper is consistent with the above observation that impediments to contracting may strengthen the case for narrow patents.

In light of these qualifications, what conclusions can we make for patent design in the cumulative context? One interpretation is that, when research is cumulative, relatively broad patents may be efficient if *ex ante* contracting is available. However we prefer to be cautious; the jury is still out.

What is conclusive is the importance of private contracting. Whether property rights are helpful or counterproductive in encouraging innovation depends on the ease with which innovators can enter into agreements for rearranging and exercising those rights, as constrained by the rules of antitrust law.

## Conclusions

In the past two decades, academic interest in the economics and law of IP has exploded. The renewed interest has been fueled by controversies surrounding new technologies, by international agreements, and by changes in the nature of protection; for example, see Mazzoleni and Nelson (1998). It is generally thought that IP rights have been strengthened. Contrary to the apparent intent, such strengthening is thought by some commentators to impede research rather than to promote it (Heller and Eisenberg, 1998). In this environment, economists have had much to say about both the optimal design of IP and the advisability of substituting other incentive mechanisms.

Although it comes as no surprise that a property system has defects, we hope we have illuminated some offsetting virtues, and some circumstances where other mechanisms, such as prizes, fixed-price contracts and auctions can dominate. Our main conclusions on the effectiveness of IP are that

1. IP is probably the best mechanism for screening projects when value and cost are not observable by the sponsor, since the private value of IP automatically reflects the social value, and firms automatically compare some measure of value to the cost of innovation. In addition, IP encourages firms to accelerate progress, since the reward is conditional on success. Prizes could serve the same purposes if the size of the prize could be linked to the social value and without the deadweight loss of monopoly pricing.
2. Neither IP nor prizes can aggregate the information that is decentralized among firms, and neither will be completely effective at delegating research effort efficiently. A procurement system that restricts prizes to certain firms, or differentiates prizes according to firms' relative efficiencies, can improve on a simple prize system or patent system, but then there must be an *ex ante* negotiation to select the favored firms.

For circumstances where IP is justified, we asked how the property right should be designed. Every IP regime has provisions on length, breadth and the standard for protection. The economics literature on design of IP concerns the appropriate choice of these provisions. The optimal length, breadth, and standard for protection depend on the economic environment, for example, the shape of the demand curve, the rate at which improvements to existing technologies are developed, and the relative costs of sequential innovators.

How much flexibility is there in designing IP rights differently for different economic environments? In fact, there is a lot of flexibility. Different IP regimes are targeted at different subject matters, and the subject matter is an important defining aspect of the IP regime. Copyright has traditionally been targeted at literature, other printed matter, and art. Patents have traditionally been targeted at manufactured items. The subject matters of *sui generis* laws typically have very specific subject matter, for example, the Plant Patent Act, the Plant Variety Protection Act, the Semiconductor Chip Protection Act, and the proposed database legislation.

The IP regimes that cover different subject matters are noticeably varied in the three important features, length, breadth and standard for protection. On the matter of length, copyrights last essentially forever; patents last twenty years; and chip protection lasts ten years. On the matter of breadth, copyright protection is restrained by fair use exemptions and by the fact that the underlying "ideas" are not protected; patents have the doctrine of equivalents; and copying of chips is allowed for some uses but not others. We thus believe that it is incorrect to criticize the economic design arguments on grounds that, in IP, "one size fits all." While we do not think it would be appropriate to define new IP regimes for every small category of technology, we wish to emphasize that the Congress can exercise as much flexibility as it wishes, and that courts also have some flexibility.

Each IP regime should cover subject matter with similar needs for protection, especially if heterogeneous needs cannot be remedied by courts. Many controversies arise because of heterogeneity within IP regimes. For example, business methods probably do not need the strong protection provided by the Patent Act, even though such protection is appropriate for other patentable subject matter. A new regime could have been created for business methods, but protection under the Patent Act could alternatively be weakened through the courts' interpretation of novelty and nonobviousness.

Finally, there are the design recommendations themselves. We have not been specific in this review about the exact ways in which length, breadth and standards for protection should reflect the economic environments, and refer the reader to the underlying papers for more detail. Instead, we have emphasized a message of a different sort: the optimal design of the property right should depend on whether firms contract with others for the use of their protected innovations. With fluid contracting, policies that otherwise would be inefficient may be optimal. For example, licensing can avoid wasteful imitation, making an otherwise inefficient narrow patent optimal. In the cumulative context, there is a danger that broad patents will inhibit future innovators from making product improvements. But with contracting, the patentholder can profit from, instead of being threatened by, new improved products, and will ensure that they arise even if they are infringing. The most striking message of the literature is that IP and private instruments may be complementary in reducing social costs from an over-reaching or insufficient protection regime.

However, contracting also has the potential to undermine competition in ways that were not anticipated or approved by the Congress when designing IP. Contracting that we have not covered includes cross-licensing and patent pools. We have also not discussed joint ventures and other alliances for avoiding litigation, duplicated efforts and hold-ups. A recurring theme, especially evident in these contexts, is that despite the efficiencies that contracting can ensure, contracting may also facilitate anticompetitive behavior. See Hall and Ham (1999), Shapiro (2000), Denicolò (2000a). To understand whether the property system is too strong, too weak, or necessary at all requires us to understand the incentives for contracting, and its potential anticompetitive consequences.

## Notes

1 This chapter will also appear in *Innovation Policy and the Economy*, A. Jaffe, J. Lerner, and S. Stern (eds), vol. 2, MIT Press, 2002, Cambridge, MA, 51–74.

2 For example, in the environment discussed by Wright (1983), none of the three mechanisms is optimal. The first best can be achieved with a mechanism similar to the one mentioned in Note 4.

3 But prizes might also require enforcement. John Harrison's longitude prize was delayed for decades while the prize committee attempted to prove that astronomical solutions were superior to his clock. Harrison eventually sought redress in Parliament, and was partially rewarded.

4 She suggests a two-part procedure. First the sponsor asks the firms to reveal their information on value and then, if warranted, employs the best procurement mechanism to delegate to the least cost firm(s). Following Cremer and McLean (1988), it is costless to get the firms to reveal their correlated information on value. They are asked to report their signals of value, and then rewarded if they agree, and punished if they disagree. Due to the correlation, an equilibrium is to report truthfully, and the payments can be chosen so that each firm makes zero expected profit.

5 A related problem is studied by Bhattacharya *et al.* (1998). Instead of assuming that firms have different efficiency parameters, they assume that firms have different "knowledge" about the cost of achieving an innovation. If the knowledge is revealed, then all firms have the same cost. Their mechanisms also use payments conditional on delivery (prizes).

6 We caution, however, that the Kremer scheme is only efficient if there is a single researcher. A prize equal to the social value could easily attract other firms to a race in which the firms overinvest (Loury, 1979). Not only is there a problem of overinvesting, but inefficient firms as well as efficient firms may invest. This is the problem avoided by the more complex procurement mechanism discussed above, where prizes are tailored to the firms' relative efficiency in order to make sure that the investment effort is undertaken by the more efficient ones.

7 In deLaat's model, the sponsor chooses the "size of the invention," which is observable, given the firm's report of the market size (value), which is unobservable to the sponsor. DeLaat assumes that the sponsor can verify which invention is made but not the market conditions (e.g. demand) for the invention.

8 For recent empirical investigations of how firms exercise their option to renew, and implications for the values of innovations, see Lanjouw (1997) and Schankerman (1998).

9 The intuition for this result can be found in the familiar economic principle that underlies Ramsey pricing. Ramsey pricing solves the problem of maximizing consumer surplus in multiple markets subject to the constraint that revenues cover cost. The solution is to set prices below monopoly prices so that the markup of price in each market is inversely proportional to the elasticity of demand in each market. In the patent problem, the different time periods are parallel to different markets and since the demands are assumed to be constant over time, the markup of price over cost in each period is identical.

10 See the US Department of Justice, Federal Trade Commission's *Antitrust Guidelines for the Licensing of Intellectual Property* (1995) for a discussion of innovation markets.

## References

Anton, J. and D. Yao (1994), "Expropriation and Inventions – Appropriable Rents in the Absence of Property Rights," *American Economic Review*, 84(1), 191–209.

Arrow, K. (1962), *Economic Welfare and the Allocation of Resource of Invention*, NBER, The rate and direction of inventive activity: Economic and social factors, 609.

Besen, James and Eric Maskin (2000), "Sequential Innovation, Patents and Imitation," MIT Working Paper No. 00-01, January.

Bhattacharya, S., Arnoud W.A. Boot, and Anjan V. Thakor (1998), "The Economics of Bank Regulation," *Journal of Money, Credit and Banking*, 30(4), November, 745–770.

Calandrillo, Steve (1998), "An Economic Analysis of Intellectual Property Rights: Justifications and Problems of Exclusive Rights, Incentives to Generate Information, and the Alternative of a Government-run Reward System," Fordham *Intellectual Property Media & Entertainment Law Journal*, 9, 301, 602–603.

Chang, H. (1995), "Patent Scope, Antitrust Policy, and Cumulative Innovation," *RAND Journal of Economics*, 26, 34–57.

Cornelli, F. and M. Schankerman (1999), "Patent Renewals and R&D Incentives," *RAND Journal of Economics*, 30(2), Summer, 197–213.

Cremer, J. and R.P. McLean (1988), "Full Extraction of the Surplus in Bayesian and Dominant Strategy Auctions," *Econometrica*, 56(6), 1247–1257.

De Laat, Eric, A.A. (1996), "Patents or Prizes: Monopolistic R&D and Asymmetric Information," *International Journal of Industrial Organization*, 15(3), 369–390.

Denicolò, V. (1996), "Patent Races and Optimal Patent Breadth and Length," *Journal of Industrial Economics*, 44, 249–265.

Denicolò, V. (2000a), "Two Stage Patent Races and Patent Policy," *RAND Journal of Economics*, 31, 488–501.

Denicolò, V. (2000b), "Combination of Competing Patents and Antitrust Policy," Department of Economics, University of Bologna Working Paper No. 487.

Derry, T.K. and Trevor I. Williams (1993), *A Short History of Technology: From Earliest Times to A.D. 1900* (Dover: Mineola, NY).

Eswaran, M. and N. Gallini (1996), "Patent Policy and the Direction of Technological Change," *RAND Journal of Economics*, 27(4), Winter, 722–746.

Farrell, J. (1995), "Arguments for Weaker Intellectual Property Protection in Network Industries," in *Standards Policy for Information Infrastructure*, Brian Kahin and Janet Abbate (eds), 369, ACM Press, New York.

Gallini, N.T. (1984), "Deterrence by Market Sharing: A Strategic Incentive for Licensing," *American Economic Review*, 74, 931–941.

Gallini, N.T. (1992), "Patent Length and Breadth with Costly Imitation," *RAND Journal of Economics*, 44, 52–63.

Gallini, N. and M. Trebilcock (1998), "Intellectual Property Rights and Competition Policy – A Framework for the Analysis of Economic and Legal Issues," in *Competition Policy and Intellectual Property Rights in the Knowledge-Based Economy*, R. Anderson and N. Gallini (eds), Industry Canada Research Series, University of Calgary Press, 17–64.

Gallini, N.T. and R. Winter (1985), "Licensing in the Theory of Innovation," *RAND Journal of Economics*, 16, 237–252.

Gallini, N.T. and B. Wright (1990), "Technology Transfer under Asymmetric Information," *RAND Journal of Economics*, 21(1), Spring, 147–160.

Gandal, N. and S. Scotchmer (1993), "Coordinating Research through Research Joint Ventures," *Journal of Public Economics*, 51, 173–193.

Gilbert, R. and C. Shapiro (1990), "Optimal Patent Length and Breadth," *RAND Journal of Economics*, 21, 106–112.

Gilbert, R. and G.C. Sunshine (1995), "Incorporating Dynamic Efficiency Concerns in Merger Analysis: The Use of Innovation Markets," *Antitrust Law Journal*, 63, 569–602.

Green, Jerry and Suzanne Scotchmer (1995), "On the Division of Profit in Sequential Innovation," *RAND Journal of Economics*, 26, Spring, 20–33.

Hall, B. and R. Ham (1999), "The Patent Paradox Revisited: Firm Strategy and Patenting in the U.S. Semiconductor Industry," University of California Working Paper No. 7062.

Heller, Michael A. and R.S. Eisenberg (1998), "Can Patents Deter Innovation? The Anticommons in Biomedical Research," *Science*, 280, 698–701.

Kitch, E.W. (1977), "The Nature and Function of the Patent System," *Journal of Law and Economics*, 20, 265–290.

Klemperer, P. (1990), "How Broad Should the Scope of Patent Protection Be?' *RAND Journal of Economics*, 21, 113–130.

Kremer, Michael (1998), "Patent Buyouts: A Mechanism for Encouraging Innovation," *Quarterly Journal of Economics*, 113, 1137–1167.

Kremer, Michael (2000), "Creating Markets for New Vaccines," Conference Paper, Innovation Policy and the Economy, National Bureau of Economic Research.

Laffont, J.-J. and J. Tirole (1986), "Using Cost Observation to Regulate Firms," *Journal of Political Economy*, 94, 614–641.

Laffont, J.-J. and J. Tirole (1987), "Auctioning Incentive Contracts," *Journal of Political Economy*, 95, 921–937.

Lanjouw, J. (1997), "Patent Value in the Shadow of Litigation: Simulation Estimations of Patent Value," *Review of Economic Studies*, 233–260.

Lee, T. and L.L. Wilde (1980), "Market Structure and Innovation: A Reformulation," *Quarterly Journal of Economics*, 94, 429–436.

Loury, G.C. (1979), "Market Structure and Innovation," *Quarterly Journal of Economics*, 93, 395–410.

Machlup, Fritz and Edith Penrose (1950), "The Patent Controversy in the Nineteenth Century," *Journal of Economic History*, 10(1, 2), 1–29.

Matutes, C., P. Regibeau, and K.E. Rockett (1996), "Optimal Patent Protection and the Diffusion of Innovation," *RAND Journal of Economics*, 27, 60–83.

Maurer, S. (1999), "Raw Knowledge: Protecting Technical Databases for Science & Industry" (report commissioned by the National Academy of Sciences).

Maurer, S.M. and S. Scotchmer (1998), "The Independent Invention Defense in Intellectual Property," John M. Olin Working Paper No. 98–11, Boalt School of Law, University of California, Berkeley.

Maurer, S.M. and S. Scotchmer (1999), "Database Protection: Is it Broken and Should We Fix it?," *Science*, 284, May 14, 1999, 1129–1130.

Mazzoleni, Roberto and Richard R. Nelson (1998), "The Benefits and Costs of Strong Patent Protection: A Contribution to the Current Debate," *Research Policy*, 27, 273–284.

Merges, R.P. (1998), "Antitrust Review of Patent Acquisitions: Property Rights, Firm Boundaries, and Organization," in *Competition Policy and Intellectual Property Rights in the Knowledge-Based Economy*, Robert D. Anderson and Nancy T. Gallini (eds), University of Calgary Press, Calgary, 40–63.

Merges, R.P. (1999), "Intellectual Property Rights, Input Markets and the Value of Intangible Assets," UC Berkeley Working Paper No. 97-016.

Merges, R.P. and R.R. Nelson (1990), "On the Complex Economics of Patent Scope," *Columbia Law Review*, 90(4), 839–916.

Minehart, D. and S. Scotchmer (1999), "Ex Post Regret and the Decentralized Sharing of Information," *Games and Economic Behavior*, 27(1), 114–131.

National Research Council, *The Digital Dilemma: Intellectual Property in the Information Age*, Committee on Intellectual Property Rights and the Emerging Information Infrastructure, Computer Science and Telecommunications Board, National Academy Press, 2000, Washington, DC.

National Science Foundation, *Science and Engineering Indicators 2000.*

Nordhaus, W. (1969), "Invention, Growth and Welfare: A Theoretical Treatment of Technological Change," MIT Press, Cambridge.

O'Donoghue, T. (1998), "A Patentability Requirement for Sequential Innovation," *Rand Journal of Economics*, 29, 654–667.

O'Donoghue, T., S. Scotchmer, and J.F. Thisse (1998), "Patent Breadth, Patent Length and the Pace of Technological Progress," *Journal of Economics and Management Strategy*, 7, 1–32.

Reynolds, T. (1983), *Stronger than a Hundred Men: A History of the Vertical Water Wheel.* Baltimore, MD: Johns Hopkins Press.

Schankerman, M. (1998), "How Valuable is Patent Protection? Estimates by Technology Field," *RAND Journal of Economics*, 29, 77–107.

Schankerman, M. and S. Scotchmer (2001), "Damages and Injunctions in Protecting Intellectual Property," *The RAND Journal of Economics*, 32, 199–220.

Schumpeter, J. (1943), *Capitalism, Socialism and Democracy*. London: Unwin University Books.

Scotchmer, S. (1991), "Standing on the Shoulders of Giants: Cumulative Research and the Patent Law," *Journal of Economic Perspectives*, 5(1), Winter, 29–41.

Scotchmer, S. (1996), "Protecting Early Innovators: Should Second-Generation Products Be Patentable?," *RAND Journal of Economics*, 27, 322–331.

Scotchmer, S. (1998), "R&D Joint Ventures and other Cooperative Arrangements," in *Competition Policy and Intellectual Property Rights in the Knowledge-Based Economy*, R. Anderson and N. Gallini (eds), University of Calgary Press, Industry Canada Research Series, 203–222.

Scotchmer, S. (1999a), "On the Optimality of the Patent Renewal System," *RAND Journal of Economics*, 30, 181–196.

Scotchmer, S. (1999b), "Delegating Effort in a Common Value Project," University of California, IBER Working Paper No. E99–266.

Scotchmer, S. and J. Green (1990), "Novelty and Disclosure in Patent Law," *RAND Journal of Economics*, 21, 131–146.

Shapiro, C. (2000), "Navigating the Patent Thicket: Cross Licenses, Patent Pools, and Standard-Setting," University of California Working Paper No. 7256.

Shavell, S. and T. van Ypserle (1998), "Rewards versus Intellectual Property Rights," Harvard University, Olin Discussion Paper 246.

Sobel, D. (1995), *Longitude: The True Story of a Lone Genius Who Solved the Greatest Scientific Problem of his Time*. New York: Walker.

*US Department of Justice-Federal Trade Commission Antitrust Guidelines for The Licensing of Intellectual Property* (1995).

Wright, B. (1983), "The Economics of Invention Incentives: Patents, Prizes And Research Contracts," *American Economic Review*, 73, 691–707.

# 9 Fairness and welfare

## Are they really competing values?

*Francesco Denozza*

## Introduction

In this chapter I will critically examine the thesis, recently outlined – and strenuously defended – by Louis Kaplow and Steven Shavell, that the assessment of a legal policy should depend exclusively on its effects on individuals' welfare.[1]

The main argument provided by Kaplow and Shavell is that when the choice of legal rules is based even in part on notions of fairness, individuals tend to be made worse off. The main point of this argument is that if any notion of fairness is ascribed evaluative weight, there exists a real possibility that *everyone* will be made worse off in certain situations. Provided that it seems difficult to approve *ex ante* and to justify *ex post* choices that make everyone worse off (or that give up making everyone better off), it seems in the same way difficult to accept fairness (which could impose such unwanted outcomes) as an appropriate standard to assessing political and legal action.

This reasoning has the form of an argument, though, as it was already pointed out;[2] it is no more than a tautology: if weight is given to something other than well-being, then it is obvious that situations may be conceived of in which well-being has to be sacrificed in the balance.

As a tautology it demonstrates nothing whatsoever. Actually its function is not that of proving the superiority of the normative framework defined by the reference to human welfare, rather that of calling up the intuitive idea that to make everyone worse off is not a good thing.

The cases in which the possibility exists of improving everyone's well-being are in fact neither frequent in practice nor theoretically relevant. One could even maintain that problems of fairness arise just and only where resources are scarce, and it would be impossible to increase in equal parts everyone's well-being.[3] Thus the interesting part of the Kaplow and Shavell thesis is the extension of their claim (that welfare is a more appropriate criterion for assessing legal policy than fairness is) from the case in which it is possible to increase the well-being of everyone, to the case in which it is possible to increase the overall well-being, but only by lowering the well-being of some. The latter is the more interesting case, for legal rules nearly always affect the well-being of different individuals in very different ways. A given rule usually increases the well-being of some, at the same time decreasing the well-being of others.

Kaplow and Shavell exorcise the problems that arise from the need of balancing gains and losses of different individuals, and the following concerns about equity in distribution, by the simple motion of taking no position as to how gains and losses should be balanced. Whatever trade-off society is willing to make in this regard, whatever "social welfare function" we choose, the claim is that legal rules should be selected on the basis of the simple sum of the costs and benefits that they impose on the population.

If welfare, and not fairness, is the standard appropriate to assessing the law, a corollary follows.

Given that under welfare economics social welfare is presumed to be a function of individuals' well-being and given that individuals' well-being is assessed by relying on individuals' existing preferences as revealed by their behavior, the choice of every legal rule shall be influenced only by the preferences of the individuals involved.[4] As a general rule no analyst (or policy-maker) is allowed to argue in favor of a legal reform which is contrary to individuals' current preferences. Obviously, the individuals may have a taste for particular notions of fairness. If this should be the case, analysis under welfare economics will take such tastes into account when measuring individuals' well-being, just as it will take any other taste into account.

To sum up, the main thesis defended by Kaplow and Shavell can be summarized as follows:

1 the concept of well-being, incorporating distributional concerns in whatever way social welfare function indicates can, and should, be the exclusive standard by which legal policies are assessed;
2 in order to determine the impact of their decisions on human welfare, policy analysts and, at least in principle, public decision makers (judges, legislators, regulators) have to resort exclusively to the analysis of the preferences of the affected individuals.

I believe that the Kaplow and Shavell attempt to demonstrate the above thesis is not very convincing. The analysis of their arguments rather confirms that welfare economics cannot provide *autonomous* criteria to assess legal policies. Neither the scrutiny of the preferences of the affected individuals[5] nor simple computations (as the sum of several distinct well-beings) are able to provide policy analysts and decision makers with unequivocal suggestions. The resort to external (with respect to welfare economics) value judgments is unavoidable and for any usual meaning of the word, fairness provides the appropriate framework under which these value judgments have to be considered.

Fairness and welfare do not lie on the same plane. While welfare can provide a descriptive framework for classifying different states of the world, only fairness is able to provide a normative framework for assessing legal policies, that is, for choosing among possible states of the world featured by different distributions of welfare. In this sense, fairness and welfare are not competing values.

## The role of fairness in aggregating individuals' well-being and in giving content to "welfare economics"

As I have just pointed out, "the view that it cannot be normatively good to make everyone worse off" (Kaplow and Shavell, 1015). Far from being demonstrated, it is presented by Kaplow and Shavell as an intuitive truth. But is it really so intuitive that an unfair regime with greater overall well-being is always preferable to a fairer regime with less overall well-being?

Let us imagine a situation in which ten individuals face the same probabilities of being the injurer in one out of five statistically unavoidable accidents, each one of them causing harm of $1,000 to victims. We can imagine a legal regime in which each injurer will pay for the harm of $1,000 whenever she causes it (something akin to a rule of strict liability). Alternatively we could decide to save the costs of establishing for each time who (out of the ten individuals) caused the harm, by resorting to a draw. Are we sure that the second regime, in which the individuals who must pay are picked at random, is more desirable than the first one?

Probably the answer depends on the weight we are prepared to put on the sense of suffering wrong which can be experienced by the individuals involved in this gamble. Suppose then that five out of the ten individuals perceive the draw as a great injustice, while the remaining five individuals are indifferent. Should this be the case, which regime would be adopted under welfare economics?

In the same line of reasoning we could make another example. Let us imagine a regime in which kidnap victims are allowed to pay ransom though only on the condition that, at the same time, they pay a tax that will then be employed to increase the resources used in the struggle against kidnappers. Let us suppose that this resource increase is able to exactly offset the incentive effect of the ransom payment, so that the transactions between the victims and the kidnappers have no third-party effects. Are we sure that nobody could argue against this regime and for a different regime in which kidnappers are not paid?

Obviously Kaplow and Shavell can maintain that in both cases what is at stake is still a matter of well-being: the well-being of individuals who do not appreciate losses distributed randomly or that of individuals who feel intense loathing for kidnappers. As Kaplow and Shavell underline, the concept of well-being "in the tradition of welfare economics, is a comprehensive one" which "encompasses not only the direct benefits that individuals obtain from the consumption of goods and services, but also individuals' degrees of aesthetic fulfillment, their feeling for others, and anything else that they value."[6]

However, even if we are ready to accept the above unusual formulation of the cases just presented, the problems they raise still remain unsolved. A great number of situations can be imagined in which different people may have different evaluations of social welfare and of the kind of society worth living in. In these situations, the simple computation of individuals' well-being may not provide any motivation to guide a choice amongst different conceptions of what really matters in order to define social well-being. We have to resort to the operations Kaplow and

Shavell describe in subsections 2 and 3 of Section A, of the second part (p. 985 ff.). We have to *aggregate* different individuals' well-being, not simply to *add* one's well-being with that of someone else. The two operations (*aggregating* and *adding*) are intrinsically different, for whilst in *adding* we do not necessitate further information *other than* the quantities of well-being we have to put together, in *aggregating* we need a *criterion* from which to deduce a *method* of aggregation. Individuals' well-being and social welfare, that are respectively the addenda and the sum of the computation, *cannot provide any suggestion* as to the choice of the *criterion* according to which they have to be evaluated.

Kaplow and Shavell do not perceive the problem and insist that they do not defend any specific way of aggregating individuals' well-being. Their only important point is that policy analysis "be guided by reference to some coherent way of aggregating individuals' well-being." Consequently they contrast "fairness" (any notion which gives weight to factors different from individuals' well-being) with "welfare economics" (Kaplow and Shavell, 1011). They maintain that "welfare economics," the normative framework concerned with the impact of policies on human welfare, and not "fairness," negatively defined as the set of notions which "have the property that evaluations relying on them are not based exclusively . . . on how legal policies affect individuals' well-being" (Kaplow and Shavell, 1000), provides the criteria by which legal policies ought to be assessed.

However, if, as we have seen and Kaplow and Shavell admit as much, welfare economics is not able to provide a criterion for aggregating individuals' well-being and must depend on external value judgment, it simply cannot be a normative framework for the assessment of legal policies. The normative framework is, instead, the set of the value judgments that are involved in aggregating different individuals' well-being. Fairness, understood in accordance with the usual meaning of the word, provides the appropriate framework for choosing and coordinating those value judgments. In fact, as it has been pointed out, "the choice of a social welfare function inevitably involves the adoption of a fairness analysis."

It may be that the foregoing remarks are not yet able to demolish the Kaplow and Shavell building. At the end of the day a tautology is still a tautology, and cannot be destroyed by definition. As matters stand, a Kaplow and Shavell critic could limit himself to a simple remark. The Kaplow and Shavell argument is unassailable simply because it is grounded on unusual, purpose-built definitions: a notion of fairness which is unusually narrow, and a definition of well-being which is unusually encompassing.

I think that the Kaplow and Shavell argument deserves a deeper criticism. In fact they compare and contrast two things (welfare and fairness) that lie on different levels. Welfare and well-being are individual or social states. As such they can be the *subject* of the policy makers' computations (in the sense that for every decision its impact on welfare and well-being is taken into account). But given that, as we have seen, individuals' well-beings cannot be simply added up (they have to be *aggregated*) the outcome of a well-being computation is a simple *description* of different states of the world. We know, for example that decision A shall increase the well-being of $x$ and $y$ while decision B shall increase the well-being of $w$ and $z$, but we have no standard for deciding which of the two decisions increases the overall welfare. In order to choose among the different states of the world resulting from the existing alternatives, we need a *normative* criterion. Welfare and well-being which are the *subject* of the computation, cannot at the same time provide the criteria according to which they have to be counted. So we have to resort to our conception of fairness.

To sum up: the only *normative* claim that could be founded on the reference to welfare and well-being would be that of maximizing (the social welfare). But in order to establish whether in one given state of the world there is more welfare than in another, we need a standard that the notions of welfare and well-being are not able to provide. Fairness instead provides the most appropriate framework for elaborating on normative standards. In this sense fairness and welfare lie on different planes and fairness, from a *normative* viewpoint, dominates welfare.[7]

## Distributive concerns in the choice of legal rules

Coming now to the problems arising from the fact that legal rules usually increase the well-being of some, at the same time decreasing the well-being of others, the Kaplow and Shavell basic idea, explained by resorting to the usual pie metaphor, is that whatever the preferred criterion for the division of the pie, a bigger pie is always able to provide bigger slices to everyone.

So we arrive to the central problem: legal rules usually affect simultaneously the size and the distribution of the pie (a rule of strict liability may affect the size of the pie by reducing the combined costs of precaution and damages, but simultaneously affects the division of the pie between injurers and victims). Therefore, we can easily imagine legal rules that are efficient in the sense that they maximize benefits and minimize costs, but have unwanted distributional effects.

In response to this argument Kaplow and Shavell argue that

- the welfare economics view incorporates an *ex ante* perspective. In a wide range of contexts individuals are symmetrically situated *ex ante* so that everybody in society is identically affected by the rule and no distributive issues are at stake;
- in case of asymmetric rules (rules that do not affect everyone in society identically: some people gain from the rule but others lose), efficiency should still remain the sole criterion for evaluating private law rules. Distributional concerns should be diverted from private law to tax. Legal rules should be left always in an efficient state, unsullied by distributive justice.

By insisting on the metaphor of the pie, in case of asymmetric rules we should resort to a "two tier distribution." In the first step we accept every distribution imposed by efficiency concerns. In the second step we can rearrange the first step distribution by means of corrective transfers written in the tax code.

I shall endeavor to demonstrate that:

- the "two tier" distribution is often ill-equipped to redress undesired effects of the first step distribution and may be hampered by a phenomenon that we could call "moral endowment effect."

- concerns of fairness influence the pursuit of efficiency (understood as welfare maximization) both in symmetric and in asymmetric rules.

## Two tier distribution

Many situations are conceivable in which the first allotment defines a world state. The second distribution can only work within this state of the world but cannot significantly change it. Imagine that the goods we have to assign are rights to instruction. We can obviously resort to income tax to compensate the individuals penalized by the criterion of distribution that we decide to follow. It is however obvious that we cannot compare the level of welfare we can reach by granting to some individuals rights to instruction with the level of welfare achievable by granting money to the same individuals. This consequence does not depend on the difficulties in valuing non-pecuniary factors. It depends on the fact that the relationships that educated people are able to have with the external world and with other people are completely different from the relationships that people with no education have. The point is that in a world populated by many people with no education, no monetary transfer is able to create the same living conditions that are present in a world in which the rights to education are equally distributed.

In this perspective we can consider that many other goods exist whose distribution influences not only the immediate well-being of the individuals to whom they are (or are not) assigned, but the manner in which those individuals interact with other people. Thus I think that we have to hesitate before adopting a very efficient rule which implies an attribution of pain and suffering that we plan to compensate by using income tax.

Other difficulties arise from a phenomenon that could be called "moral endowment effect." The phenomenon is very easily explained. People granted with a big slice in the first distribution of the cake may be persuaded that they received a big slice not as a consequence of a sophisticated cost benefit analysis, but simply because they deserved it. Thus they shall perceive as highly unfair any imposition of duties of compensation in favor of the individuals penalized by the cost benefit analysis which guided the first distribution. It is well known that this argument far from being an abstract speculation, describes a phenomenon that often influences the conceptions people have of their duties as taxpayers.[8]

## Symmetric and asymmetric rules

As an example of symmetric rules the case of reciprocal accidents involving uncertain harm is mentioned (Kaplow and Shavell, III.C,1).

Suppose that in this case a rule of no liability is preferable, from an efficiency viewpoint, to both strict liability and negligence rule (imposing liability involves administrative costs and taking precautions is not worthwhile).

The Kaplow and Shavell thesis is that, *ex ante*, all individuals having the same probabilities of turning out to cause an accident or of being injured in one, are made better off by the (efficient) no liability rule (obviously those who subsequently become accident victims would then prefer a different rule which would compensate them, but if one were to adopt this rule, every individual would be worse off *ex ante*).

I think that this thesis might be true only in the very rare hypothesis in which all uncompensated victims suffer the same loss of welfare. When we are confronted (as it is usual) with very rich and very poor victims, we are not allowed to presume that a regime of no liability in certain settings affects the well-being of all the injurers and of all the uncompensated victims exactly in the same manner. On the contrary we can easily imagine that poor people would prefer a regime in which injurers are compelled to compensate their victims (obviously within the limits of their property!) and victims are thereby (and within those limits) protected against unaffordable (for them) harms.

Symmetric rules are therefore conceivable only in the very rare circumstances in which the affected individuals are equally situated not only in respect of the probabilities of suffering the same harm, but also in respect of the incidence that a given harm may have on their overall well-being.

Coming now to the asymmetric rules, let us examine as an example of asymmetric rule the case of the so called cross-subsidization in contract damages.[9] Consider a rule that provides full compensation for the expectation interest of any victim of a breach of contract; suppose that this is the rule which minimizes the possible damages; finally suppose that sellers, held fully liable for all damages, raise their prices by an average amount. As a result, the buyers with larger potential losses will benefit from the rule (they will end up with full insurance for their losses while paying only an average premium in the form of a higher price) whilst the low-risk buyers could end up worse off for they have to pay the same average price for an insurance policy that, for these buyers, has a smaller potential payout.

In that case, in order to establish the efficiency of the rule of full compensation, we should demonstrate that the savings in actual damages plus the increase in well-being experienced by some buyers exceed the decrease in the well-being of other buyers. Usually the costs afforded by high-risk buyers are presumed equal to the costs afforded by low-risk buyers. So the saving in actual damages makes the difference. But if we take the notion of welfare seriously, we should weigh the effect of the rule on low-risk buyers, taking into account the legitimate suspicion that they are the less well off overall (i.e. considering all aspects of their economic lives, not just the regulatory sphere of the legal rule).[10] Thus it becomes very difficult to establish the efficiency of the rule. It is even more difficult to imagine that the tax code could be entrusted with the possible task of correcting the distribution resulting from the adoption of the full compensation rule.

The basic intuition we can extract from these reasonings is that the maximization of welfare is an attractive aim though only when it is pursued in a fair context, a context in which: (1) some basic differences have been eliminated (following the previous exemplification: all individuals forced to the role of the victim or of the low-risk buyers experience an identical welfare decrease, due to the fact that their overall well-being is more or less the same); (2) tactics able to neutralize differences have been adopted (e.g. a mandatory scheme of mutual insurance prevents the devastating effects that some accidents can have on poor uncompensated victims).

## Conclusions

Fairness dominates welfare. From a theoretical viewpoint, because fairness is a *normative* framework within which different criteria for the assessment of legal policies can be evaluated, whilst welfare is only an *object* that can be described and perhaps measured, but cannot provide any *normative* criterion. From a practical viewpoint, because welfare analysis may provide useful conceptual tools in situations in which we face problems of maximization, but the decision of maximizing, and the choice of what must be maximized, do not fall in the jurisdiction of welfare economics, but in the jurisdiction of fairness. Efficient rules that maximize welfare are welcome, though only where basic rules have created the fair context in which efficient rules can work.

## Notes

1 Kaplow and Shavell (2000, 2003).

2 Coleman (2003); Kaplow and Shavell (2003) at p. 971 admit that their argument "is in fact tautological on a general level."

3 Theories of fairness may be "considered appropriate ways of solving conflicts of interest between people" (Fleurbaey and Tungodden (2003)). According to this perspective, in situations of plenty, where everyone can be provided with more than she or he needs and conflicts of interest do not exist (or are almost immaterial), we face no problems of fairness.

4 It is dubious that recording actual preferences revealed by contingent individuals' behavior is a good starting point for improving overall welfare. Some difficulties connected with relying on individuals' preferences as revealed by their behavior, for the purpose of assessing their well-being, are considered by Kaplow and Shavell in Section VIII.B, entitled "Preferences and Individuals' Well-being"; *see also* Sunstein (1991), Hovenkamp (1994). One of the main difficulties arises from the fact that preferences are always intertwined with judgments (value judgments and judgments on facts). For example, let us suppose that today I buy apples instead of pears. What can be inferred from this act about my "preferences"? Nothing for sure that an external decision maker could rely on. Perhaps I love apples and ate pears, or may be that I foresee an increase in the price of apples, or a decrease in the price of pears, or may be that I ate apples but I am convinced that they can have the same effect spinach has on Popeye, and so on. The point is that whilst good arguments can support the choice of respecting people's tastes, arguments in favor of accepting all their judgments are not so much good. That is true even with reference to very simple choices such as that examined in the foregoing example. When we face choices pertaining to more complicated subjects, the problem of severing tastes from judgments becomes accordingly more difficult.

5 The dichotomy between two ways of evaluating legal policies (on the basis of individuals' tastes or on the basis of external conceptions of fairness) is only apparently straightforward. People may have second-order tastes.

> They may have tastes not just for fairness in the rules and results they hear about, but also for decision makers who take fairness into account in setting legal policy; for institutions that treat fairness as a criterion that matters; for processes of generating

> rules and results, which people may consider important regardless of whether the outcomes ever are known to them.
>
> (Farnsworth)

Other problems arise from the unintended consequences of many choices. Imagine that we are confronted with the choice between cars and stagecoaches and we choose cars. We are then confronted with the choice between cultivating oil or oats and we, as car owners, obviously choose oil. Afterwards comes the choice between building highways or consolidating river banks. We, as car owners, choose the highways. And so on. Are we sure that we have really "chosen" a highly polluted world with a lot of cars and overflowing rivers?

6 Kaplow and Shavell (2001).

7 Dorf (2002) at p. 850; see also Farber (2003).

8 Murphy and Nagel describe a phenomenon akin to that indicated in the text when they note,

> The feeling of natural entitlement produced by an unreflective sense of what are in fact conventionally defined property rights can encourage complacency about the status quo,as something more or less self-justifying. But it can also give rise to an even more confused criticism of the existing system on the ground that it violates natural property rights, when, in fact, these "natural" rights are merely misperceptions of the legal consequences of the system itself.
>
> (2002)

9 Quillen (1988); This case is examined, in the context of his discussion of the Kaplow and Shavell thesis, by Craswell (2003).

10 Dorf (2002).

## References

Coleman, J.L. The Grounds of Welfare, 112 *Yale Law Journal*, 1522 (2003).

Craswell, R. Kaplow and Shavell on the Substance of Fairness (Symposium on Louis Kaplow and Steven Shavell, Fairness versus Welfare), 32 *Journal of Legal Studies*, 248–275 (2003).

Dorf, M.B. Why Welfare Depends on Fairness: A Reply to Kaplow and Shavell, 75 *Southern California Law Review*, 847 (2002), p. 850.

Farber, D.A. What (If Anything) Can Economics Say About Equity, *Michigan Law Review* (2003), available at SSRN:http://ssrn.com/abstract=327020.

Farnsworth, W. The Taste for Fairness, *Columbia Law Review*, forthcoming (2006), available at SSRN:http://ssrn.com/abstract=305761.

Fleurbaey, M., B. Tungodden, and Howard F. Chang Any Non-Welfarist Method of Policy Assessment Violates the Pareto Principle: A Comment, forthcoming, *Journal of Political Economy*, 111 (December): 1382–1385.

Hovenkamp, H. The Limits of Preference-Based Legal Policy, 89 *Northwestern University Law Review* 4 (1994).

Kaplow, Louis and Steven Shavell Fairness versus Welfare, 114 *Harvard Law Review*, 961 (2001).

Kaplow, Louis and Steven Shavell Fairness versus Welfare: Notes on the Pareto Principle, Preferences, and Distributive Justice, *Journal of Legal Studies*, 32 (2003), 331–362, The University of Chicago.

Murphy, L. and T. Nagel *The Myth of Ownership*, Oxford University Press, Oxford (2002).

Quillen, G.D. Contract Damages and Cross-Subsidization, 61 *Southern Cardine Law Review*, 1125 (1988).

Sunstein, C.R. Preferences and Politics, 20 *Philosophy and Public Affairs*, 3 (1991).

# Part III

# Contractual incompleteness and the nature of endogenous enforcement

# 10 Costly contingent contracts

## A failure of the Coase theorem

*Luca Anderlini and Leonardo Felli*

## Introduction

### *Motivation*

Virtually all economic transactions are regulated by a contract of one type or another. Even when a supermarket posts a price on a can of food, it is offering its customers a contract for the purchase of the can at a given price with certain clauses attached, for instance that the food should be of "satisfactory quality"[1] and that the buyer must be "ready and willing to pay the price in exchange for possession"[2] of the food. The parties accept to execute such contract when the item is keyed in at the cash register.

Most larger economic transactions are explicitly regulated by contracts which specify, very often in writing, details of the transaction(s) to be carried out.

It is readily apparent to any observer that most contracts which regulate economic transactions are *costly*: some of the resources available are used up in the process of specifying and/or enforcing the contract between agents. If nothing else, each party to a contract has to invest a certain amount of time in drafting or simply reading the contract proposed by the other party.[3] In this chapter, we study the impact of these costs on whether a contract will or will not be drawn up, and to some extent on the "shape" of those contracts which agents decide to enter, given their costs.

Clearly, the *size* of contractual costs, relative to the possible surplus which the contract will generate, will be a contributing factor to the impact which contractual costs have: if contractual costs are large in relative terms, then their impact will be accordingly larger.[4] In this chapter, as well as in Anderlini and Felli (2001a,b), we choose to concentrate on a further issue – namely, is it the case that contractual costs will have an impact (on both the availability and the shape of possible contracts) which goes beyond what is due to their relative size? We conclude that contractual costs may matter, regardless of their relative size, for *strategic* reasons whenever it is the case that at least some of the costs associated with a contract must be paid *ex ante* – before the contract itself is negotiated by the agents.

Throughout the chapter, we concentrate on *contingent contracts*: those contracts which specify the delivery of a commodity contingent on the occurrence of an event (e.g. a state of nature or an agent's action). This is because, in our view, the presence of *ex ante* contractual costs fits this type of setting particularly well. Before a contingent contract can be negotiated, the agents must be able to conceive of, and agree on, the contingencies to which the contract refers, and on a way to specify them in the contract. If this process involves any costs at all, then (at least) these will be *ex ante* contractual costs.

Given that we concentrate on costly contingent contracts, one of the primary effects of contractual costs is to generate contracts which are *incomplete* in a well-defined sense. In our view, this is an important application of our results to a field which has received a great deal of attention in recent literature. It is clear, however, that the results we present in this chapter can be interpreted as an analysis of the impact of *ex ante* contractual costs in any setting in which (at least some of) the contractual costs are incurred *ex ante.*

In its simplest form, the basic strategic effect which drives our results below is not hard to outline.[5] Consider a contractual situation with the following features. Two agents contemplate entering a contract which yields a surplus of an arbitrary given size. Moreover, the bargaining powers of the two agents are exogenously given when the contract is negotiated, and hence the two agents' shares of the surplus generated by the contract are exogenously given. Suppose now that there are *ex ante* costs associated with the contract which the agents contemplate entering into. In particular, suppose that the agents must each pay some cost before the contract-negotiating phase begins. Then, if the *distribution* of *ex ante* costs is such that one (or both) agents will not be able to recoup the *ex ante* costs given his bargaining power, the contract will not be drawn up. This is possible even when the total of *ex ante* costs across the two agents is *less* than the surplus which the contract generates so that it would be *socially efficient* for the agents to pay the *ex ante* costs and enter the contract.[6]

Our results rely on two key ingredients: the presence of *ex ante* contractual costs, and exogenously given bargaining power in the contract-negotiating phase. After discussing the strategic impact of *ex ante* contractual costs in the simplest possible set up, we turn to the economic significance of our second key ingredient – fixed bargaining powers. In the sections "A principal–agent model with incomplete contrasts," and "An intertemporal model with short-term contracts," we show that our results apply naturally to a class of models in which the interplay of incentive constraints and limited liability "pins down" the agents' relative bargaining powers in the first tier contract-negotiating phase as the result of exogenously given economic parameters. We focus on a familiar principal–agent set up in the presence of *ex ante* contractual costs, and find that the resulting contract may induce the agent to exert a low level of effort although an incentive contract that induces a high level of effort would be socially efficient, after the *ex ante* costs are taken into account.

Our last concern is to apply our results to a multi-period model. Here, the choice of *ex ante* costs is "gradual" in the sense that a principal and an agent can choose to pay more *ex ante* in order to enter a contract with a longer horizon. We find that, in general, the contract which is drawn up is *shorter* than would be socially efficient, after the *ex ante* costs are taken into account.

### *Related literature*

It is necessary to mention at this point that the original version of the Coase Theorem (Coase, 1960) explicitly assumes the absence of any transaction costs or other frictions in the bargaining process. Indeed, Coase (1992) describes the theorem as a provocative result that was meant to show how unrealistic is the world without transaction costs.[7]

The two papers that are most closely related to the present one are Anderlini and Felli (2001a) and Anderlini and Felli (2001b).

In Anderlini and Felli (2001a) we are also concerned with the inefficiencies that arise when negotiation between two parties takes place in the presence of transaction costs. In contrast to the models analyzed here, we focus on a specific extensive form of the parties' negotiation in the presence of *ex ante* transaction costs: the leading alternating offers bargaining game with complete information, with potentially infinite rounds of negotiation in which the players discount the future at a strictly positive rate (Rubinstein, 1982). *Ex ante* transaction costs are modeled as positive costs that both parties, at each round of negotiation, must pay to participate upto that round of the bargaining game.

In this environment, we show that a whole plethora of inefficiencies may arise. First, for some values of these costs it is efficient to reach an agreement but the unique equilibrium outcome is one in which agreement is never reached. Second, even when there are equilibria in which an agreement is reached, we find that the model always has an equilibrium in which agreement is never reached, as well as equilibria in which agreement is delayed for an arbitrary length of time.

Finally, the equilibrium in which agreement is never reached is pervasive in the sense that if the parties are given the opportunity to renegotiate out of these inefficient outcomes, the only equilibrium outcome that survives is the one in which agreement is never reached, regardless of the value of the transaction costs. We model the renegotiation opportunities available to the parties by transforming the original bargaining game into a game of imperfect recall. In every period, with positive probability, the parties forget the past history of play. This gives them the opportunity to "start over" and escape from any inefficient path of play in which they may have been trapped.

In contrast to our analysis below, in Anderlini and Felli (2001b) the main focus is the *robustness* of the inefficiency that arises when the parties' bargaining power and the distribution of *ex ante* costs are sufficiently mismatched. There we work with a model in which the surplus-generating contract is not explicitly modeled. We consider the robustness of the basic inefficiency result to other specifications of the role of *ex ante* costs and to the possibility of compensating transfer between the agents. We return to these issues in some detail in the section "A Coasian solution?"

### *Overview*

In the section "A 'reduced form' model," we present the simplest possible model of the basic hold-up problem associated with the writing of a risk-sharing contract. This problem is analyzed both in the case in which the *ex ante* costs associated with the contract are discrete and in the case in which they are continuous. In the sections "A principal–agent model with incomplete contrasts," and "An intertemporal model with short-term contracts," we introduce two examples of economic environments to which our previous results apply. The model in the former section is a simple, static principal–agent model. In the latter section we analyze a dynamic principal–agent problem. In the section "A Coasian solution?" we address the question of whether a contractual solution to our basic hold-up problem is plausible. The last section offers some concluding remarks. To ease the exposition, we have relegated all proofs to the Appendix.

## A "reduced form" model

### *The co-insurance problem*

Consider the simplest possible co-insurance problem. There are two time periods $t = 0$ and $t = 1$, and the state space $\mathcal{S}$ contains only two elements, $s = 1$ and $s = 2$. In period 0, there is uncertainty about the state of nature which will be realized in period 1. The probability of state 1 occurring is denoted by $\pi \in (0, 1)$, and $s = 2$ occurs with the complementary probability $1 - \pi$.

Two risk averse agents $A$ and $B$, indexed by $i \in \{A, B\}$ have twice differentiable Von-Neumann Morgenstern utility functions of period 1 wealth $U_i : \mathbb{R}_+ \to \mathbb{R}$. We assume that for $i \in \{A, B\}$, $U_i' > 0$, $U_i'' < 0$, $\lim_{w \to 0} U_i'(w) = +\infty$, and $\lim_{w \to +\infty} U_i'(w) = 0$. The two agents are each endowed with an amount of period 0 wealth $\omega_i^0$ and with period 1 wealth which depends on the state of nature $s$. The endowment of $i \in \{A, B\}$ is therefore a vector $\omega_i = (\omega_i^0, \omega_i^1, \omega_i^2)$. We assume $\omega_i >> 0$ for both agents and we also let $\omega = \{\omega_A, \omega_B\}$. For simplicity, we assume that period 0 and period 1 wealth are *perfect substitutes* for both agents, so that the expected utility for $i$ from consuming, say, his initial endowment is simply $\pi U_i(\omega_i^0 + \omega_i^1) + (1 - \pi) U_i(\omega_i^0 + \omega_i^2)$. It is convenient to establish a piece of notation for each entry of $i$'s utility function; let $w_i^1 = \omega_i^0 + \omega_i^1$, $w_i^2 = \omega_i^0 + \omega_i^2$, $w_i = (w_i^1, w_i^2)$ and $w = \{w_A, w_B\}$.

In our environment, it is convenient to introduce a possible distinction between the agents' endowments and the *status quo*. We take the *status quo* to be the situation starting from which the agents bargain over the co-insurance contract they write. We denote the *status quo* vector for agent $i$ by $z_i = (z_i^1, z_i^2)$. We also let $z = \{z_A, z_B\}$. The distinction between the *status quo* and the agents' endowments will be necessary below since the parties may have to pay some costs before they bargain over the co-insurance contract.

To make the co-insurance problem non-trivial, we assume that both the allocation of wealth given by the agents' initial endowments and the status quo are not

Pareto efficient. In other words we assume that

$$\frac{U_A'(x_A^1)}{U_A'(x_A^2)} \neq \frac{U_B'(x_B^1)}{U_B'(x_B^2)} \tag{10.1}$$

for both $\{x_A^1, x_A^2, x_B^1, x_B^2\} = w$ and $\{x_A^1, x_A^2, x_B^1, x_B^2\} = z$.

Given (10.1) it is obvious that there are possible *gains from trade* between $A$ and $B$. The set of all possible *contingent* contracts between the agents can be simply taken to be the set of pairs $\tau = \{\tau^1, \tau^2\} \in \mathbb{R}^2$. Given $\tau$, $A$'s uncertain consumption becomes the vector $(z_A^1 - \tau^1, z_A^2 - \tau^2)$, while $B$'s uncertain consumption vector becomes $(z_B^1 + \tau^1, z_B^2 + \tau^2)$. We also let $\text{sgn}(i) = -1$ if $i = A$ and $\text{sgn}(i) = +1$ if $i = B$ so that the agents' uncertain consumption vectors can be written more compactly as $z_i + \text{sgn}(i)\tau$ for $i \in \{A, B\}$.

We say that a contingent contract $\tau$ is efficient and individually rational for the two agents if it lies in the core of the exchange economy we have defined. For any $x = \{x_A^1, x_A^2, x_B^1, x_B^2\}$, let $U_i^*(x) = \pi U_i(x_i^1) + (1 - \pi)U_i(x_i^2)$, for $i \in \{A, B\}$.

**Definition 1.** *A contingent contract $\tau \in \mathbb{R}^2$ is efficient and individually rational for $A$ and $B$ if and only if, for some $\overline{U}_B \geq U_B^*(z)$, it satisfies*

$$\begin{aligned} \max_{\tau\in\mathbb{R}^2} \quad & \pi\, U_A(z_A^1 - \tau^1) + (1 - \pi)\, U_A(z_A^2 - \tau^2) \\ \text{s.t.} \quad & \pi\, U_B(z_B^1 + \tau^1) + (1 - \pi)\, U_B(z_B^2 + \tau^2) \geq \overline{U}_B \\ & \pi\, U_A(z_A^1 - \tau^1) + (1 - \pi)\, U_A(z_A^2 - \tau^2) \geq U_A^*(z) \end{aligned} \tag{10.2}$$

Let $U_B^{**}(z)$ be the maximum value of $\overline{U}_B$ such that the feasible set of problem (10.2) is not empty. Clearly, $U_B^{**}(z)$ is the maximum level of expected utility which $B$ can achieve in any efficient and individually rational (for $B$) contingent contract without violating the individual rationality constraint of $A$.

In the simple model we have outlined, there is a one-dimensional continuum of efficient individually rational contingent contracts, which can be traced as we let $\overline{U}_B$ in problem (10.2) vary continuously from $U_B^*(z)$ to $U_B^{**}(z)$. We parameterize this set by letting $\tau(\lambda, z) = \{\tau^1(\lambda, z), \tau^2(\lambda, z)\}$ denote the solution to problem (10.2) when

$$\overline{U}_B = \left[U_B^*(z)\right]^{\lambda} \left[U_B^{**}(z)\right]^{(1-\lambda)} \tag{10.3}$$

We interpret the parameter $\lambda$ as being *exogenously* determined by the parties' relative *bargaining power*. Note that the contingent contracts $\tau(1, z)$ and $\tau(0, z)$ can be interpreted as the outcome of a take-it-or-leave-it offer by $A$ to $B$ and by $B$ to $A$ respectively.

### *Costly contingent contracts: discrete costs*

Let $c_A$ and $c_B$ be the *ex ante* contractual costs for party $A$ and party $B$, respectively. Since $c_i$ is a cost that agent $i$ is required to pay *ex ante* (if at all), we stipulate the following.

**Assumption 1.** *The ex ante cost for agent $i$ does not exceed his endowment in period $t = 0$. Formally, $c_i \leq \omega_i^0$ for $i \in \{A, B\}$.*

Unless both agents pay the cost at $t = 0$ only un-contingent contracts $\tau$ with $\tau^1 = \tau^2$ are possible, and therefore the only possible individually rational agreement is to set $\tau^1 = \tau^2 = 0$. We interpret this as a situation where *no contract* is signed.

The "reduced form" of the two stage game which represents this situation can be described as follows. At time $t = 0$, each agent $i \in \{A, B\}$ can choose to set $\alpha_i$ either equal to 1 or equal to 0. The cost that $i$ incurs at $t = 0$ is then equal to $\alpha_i c_i$. Unless both agents choose $\alpha_i = 1$, their payoffs are $\pi U_i(w_i^1 - \alpha_i c_i) + (1-\pi) U_i(w_i^2 - \alpha_i c_i)$ for $i \in \{A, B\}$.

Only if both agents set $\alpha_i = 1$ at $t = 0$ is a contingent contract possible. Notice that, after the agents have paid the *ex ante* costs, the *status quo* mentioned in the subsection "The co-insurance problem," above is *different* from the agents' initial endowments. We take the *status quo* after both agents have decided whether to pay the *ex ante* costs, to be given by

$$z_i = (w_i^1 - \alpha_i c_i, w_i^2 - \alpha_i c_i) \quad i \in \{A, B\} \tag{10.4}$$

We assume that the contingent contract which the agents write is the unique efficient and individually rational contract which the bargaining power parameter $\lambda \in [0, 1]$ yields. We therefore take $\tau(\lambda, z)$ to be the solution to problem (10.2) when $z$ is given by (10.4). Hence, if both agents choose $\alpha_i = 1$ at $t = 0$, the payoff to agent $i \in \{A, B\}$ can be written as

$$\pi\, U_i(z_i^1 + \mathrm{sgn}(i)\tau^1(\lambda, z)) + (1 - \pi)\, U_i(z_i^2 + \mathrm{sgn}(i)\tau^2(\lambda, z))$$

Clearly, if the overall *ex ante* costs associated with writing a contingent contract are sufficiently high the agents will not pay them and no contract will be written as a result. We are interested in the case in which the *ex ante* costs are sufficiently small so that it is *socially efficient* for the agents to pay them and hence to write a contingent contract.

**Assumption 2.** *The ex ante costs are sufficiently low so as to ensure that it is socially efficient for the agents to pay them and write a contingent contract. Formally, $c_A$, $c_B$, and $\omega$ are such that there exists a contract $\tau \in \mathbb{R}^2$ for which*

$$\pi\, U_i(w_i^1 - c_i + \mathrm{sgn}(i)\tau^1) + (1 - \pi) U_i(w_i^2 - c_i + \mathrm{sgn}(i)\tau^2) \geq U_i^*(w) \tag{10.5}$$

*for all $i \in \{A, B\}$, with at least one inequality strict.*

**Remark 1.** *Notice that Assumption 2 defines a property of the total ex ante cost $c = c_A + c_A$. This is apparent once we notice that if $c_A$, $c_B$ and $\omega$ satisfy Assumption 2, then $c_A'$, $c_B'$ and $\omega$ will also satisfy Assumption 2 provided that $c_A' + c_B' = c_A + c_B$.*

Notice that by Assumption 1, the maximum *ex ante* cost that each agent can pay will be bounded above by period 0 wealth. For simplicity, we assume that this bound is sufficiently large, so that it ceases to matter in the analysis that follows.

**Assumption 3.** *The array of initial endowments* $\omega$ *is such that there exists a total ex ante cost* $\tilde{c} < \omega_A^0 + \omega_B^0$ *such that* $\omega$ *and* $\tilde{c}$ *do* not *jointly satisfy Assumption 2.*

We are now ready to state our two main propositions on the co-insurance reduced form model with *ex ante* costs of a contingent contract. They are both stated in terms of lower bounds, $\underline{c}_A$ and $\underline{c}_B$, on the agents' *ex ante* costs since we want them to be robust to the possibility of one or both agents "burning money" over and above the necessary *ex ante* contractual cost.[8] Propositions 1 and 2 below are essentially a restatement of Propositions 1 and 2 of Anderlini and Felli (2001b) adapted to the model analyzed here.

Our first proposition takes as given the minimum *ex ante* costs $\underline{c}_A$ and $\underline{c}_B$, and the vector of endowments $\omega$.

**Proposition 1.** *Let* $\underline{c}_A$, $\underline{c}_B$ *and* $\omega$ *satisfying Assumptions 1 and 2 be given. Then, there exist a* $\lambda^* \in (0, 1)$ *and a* $\lambda^{**} \in (\lambda^*, 1)$ *such that, whenever* $\lambda$ *lies in* $[0, \lambda^*) \cup (\lambda^{**}, 1]$, $c_A \geq \underline{c}_A$, *and* $c_B \geq \underline{c}_B$, *the unique equilibrium of the reduced form model with ex ante costs of contingent contracts involves both agents not paying the cost, and hence yields the no contract outcome.*

Our second proposition, instead, takes as given the parameter $\lambda$ describing the contracting parties' bargaining power and the vector of endowments $\omega$.

**Proposition 2.** *Let any* $\omega$ *satisfying Assumption 3 and any* $\lambda \in (0, 1)$ *be given. Then there exists a pair of ex ante costs* $\underline{c}_A$ *and* $\underline{c}_B$ *satisfying Assumption 1 such that* $\omega$ *and* $\underline{c} = \underline{c}_A + \underline{c}_B$ *jointly satisfy Assumption 2 and such that, whenever* $c_A \geq \underline{c}_A$ *and* $c_B \geq \underline{c}_B$, *the unique equilibrium of the reduced form model with ex ante costs of contingent contracts involves both agents not paying the cost, and hence yields the no contract outcome.*

As in Anderlini and Felli (2001b), we view Propositions 1 and 2 together as implying that in the presence of *ex ante* costs of a contingent contract, if the *distribution* of *ex ante* costs across the parties does not "match" the parties' relative bargaining power, then the *ex ante* costs will generate a version of the hold-up problem which will induce the agents not to write a contingent contract even though it would be socially efficient to write one. Given that the only mutually beneficial contracts in our simple model are contingent ones, in this case the agents will end up in a situation which can be interpreted as an "incomplete" contract in a very strong sense: no contract at all.

The intuition behind our results above is simple enough. If entering a contingent contract involves some costs which are payable *ex ante*, the parties will pay the costs only if their relative bargaining powers will allow them to recoup the cost *ex post*. If the distributions of bargaining powers and that of *ex ante* costs do not "match," then one of the agents will not be able to recoup the *ex ante* cost. In this case, a contingent contract will not be entered, even though it would generate a total surplus large enough to cover the *ex ante* costs of both agents.

So far, we have assumed that the agents' *ex ante* costs are "perfect complements" in determining whether a contingent contract is possible or not. A natural question that arises at this point is whether our results so far are robust to changes in this assumption. In Anderlini and Felli (2001b) we analyze a set-up in which there are *ex ante* costs, but the surplus-generating contract is not explicitly modeled. There, we show that the basic inefficiency that arises when bargaining powers and *ex ante* costs are sufficiently "mis-matched" survives when the *ex ante* costs are substitutes and when they are *strategic* complements. The logic of these results in Anderlini and Felli (2001b) can be applied to the model that we have analyzed here to show that the basic inefficiency identified in Propositions 1 and 2 is also robust to these changes in the nature of the *ex ante* costs. The details are omitted for reasons of space.

### *Costly contingent contracts: continuous costs*

So far, we have assumed that the agents' decision regarding the *ex ante* costs is "lumpy"; a contingent contract is not possible unless both agents sink a minimum, strictly positive, *ex ante* cost. This is the reason why Propositions 1 and 2 refer to a *range* of the bargaining power parameter $\lambda$ for any given *ex ante* costs, and to a *range* of *ex ante* costs given any value of the bargaining parameter $\lambda$. In this subsection, we consider a variation of our reduced form model in which the agents can affect the probability that a contingent contract is feasible through their choice of *how much* to pay *ex ante*, and hence derive a more general inefficiency result.

We modify the model of the subsection "The co-insurance problem" to allow the agents a gradual choice of how much to pay *ex ante*. For the time being, we deliberately do this in the simplest possible set-up, which may therefore seem unappealing. We believe, however, that it suffices to make our next main point, namely that when the *ex ante* choice is sufficiently gradual, the hold-up problem generated by the *ex ante* costs of a contingent contract, will cause the outcome to be inefficient *in general*, and not just for some distributions of costs and bargaining power as in the previous subsection.[9] The results in this subsection are the analogs in our model of the general under-investment results stemming form a hold-up problem (Holmström, 1982; Hart and Moore, 1988).

The agents' utility functions and endowments are as in the subsection "The co-insurance problem." In period 0 each agent $i$ can choose a number $c_i \in [0, \overline{c}_i]$. The agents' choices of $(c_A, c_B)$ determine the *probability* that a contingent contract will be possible according to a function $p(c_A, c_B)$. We take $p$ to have the following form

$$p(c_A, c_B) = \min\{V_A(c_A), V_B(c_B)\} \tag{10.6}$$

where $V_i$ is a twice differentiable strictly increasing and concave function satisfying $V_i(0) = 0$, $V_i(\overline{c}_i) = 1$, $V_i'(0) = +\infty$ and $V_i'(\overline{c}_i) = 0$, for $i \in \{A, B\}$.

Equation (10.6) therefore embodies both the assumption that the agents *ex ante* costs are perfect complements, and the assumption that there are "decreasing returns" in the amounts paid, as well as regularity conditions which guarantee an interior choice of efforts.

The *status quo* after *ex ante* costs have been paid is again defined as in (10.4), and the contract which the parties sign, with probability $p(c_A, c_B)$, is again given by $\tau(\lambda, z)$ – the parameterized solution to problem (10.2). Given a pair $\{c_A, c_B\}$, no contingent contract is possible with probability $1 - p(c_A, c_B)$. Since the only possible mutually advantageous contracts are contingent ones, in this case each agent $i \in \{A, B\}$ ends up with an expected utility of $\pi U_i(w_i^1 - c_i) + (1 - \pi)U_B(w_i^2 - c_i)$.

The efficiency benchmark against which we will compare the equilibria of the "probabilistic reduced form" model we have just described is an obvious one.

**Definition 2.** *An outcome* $\{c_A, c_B, \tau\}$ *is efficient for the probabilistic reduced form model if and only if there does not exist another triple* $\{c'_A, c'_B, \tau'\}$ *which yields weakly higher expected utility for both agents, and strictly higher expected utility for at least one agent.*

Our next proposition states that when $p$ is as in (10.6), except for a unique value of the bargaining parameter $\lambda$, all equilibria of the probabilistic reduced form model are inefficient. Moreover, the inefficiency can be "signed": all equilibria are dominated by a triple involving a higher level of *ex ante* costs.

**Proposition 3.** *Assume that the function p is as in (10.6). Then, for all* $\lambda \in [0, 1]$, *except for a unique value* $\lambda^* \in (0, 1)$, *the following holds.*

*Fix any equilibrium of the probabilistic reduced form model. Let the pair* $c_A(\lambda)$ *and* $c_B(\lambda)$ *be the ex ante costs which the agents pay in equilibrium, and* $z(\lambda)$ *the status quo after these costs have been paid. Then the outcome* $\{c_A(\lambda), c_B(\lambda), \tau(\lambda, z(\lambda))\}$ *is not efficient according to Definition 2. Moreover, if we let* $c_A^*(\lambda)$ *and* $c_B^*(\lambda)$ *be the largest ex ante costs which agent A and B respectively pay in any equilibrium, then any equilibrium outcome is Pareto-dominated by a triple* $\{c'_A, c'_B, \tau'\}$ *which has* $c'_i > c_i^*(\lambda)$ *for all* $i \in \{A, B\}$.

The intuitive reason why the agents under-invest in their *ex ante* costs according to Proposition 3 is simple to outline. Each party's share of the surplus generated is fixed, and total surplus is an increasing concave function of both *ex ante* costs. Each agent invests in his *ex ante* costs only up to the point at which *his own* marginal net return is zero. Such point is therefore below the point at which the marginal social (across both agents) net return on his investment in the *ex ante* cost is equated to zero.

## A principal–agent model with incomplete contracts

### *Preamble*

In this section, we analyze a simple principal–agent problem in which the two contracting parties' shares of the surplus depend on actual economic parameters. Once *ex ante* contractual costs are added to this model, we obtain an example of an environment in which the basic hold-up problem that we have identified may or may not obtain, as a function of these economic parameters.

The interplay of the agent's limited liability and of the incentive compatibility constraint which the equilibrium contract needs to satisfy, endogenously determines the distribution of surplus between the principal and the agent. The key economic parameter in the analysis is the cost of the agent's effort.

## *A simple principal–agent model*

Consider a principal who hires an agent to run a very simple stochastic technology. The agent when hired may decide to exert a productive effort $e$ that may take one of the two values 0 and $\phi > 0$. We assume that the high level of effort $e = \phi$ entails a cost to the agent of size $\phi$, while the low level of effort $e = 0$ entails no cost.[10]

If the agent chooses effort $e = 0$ then output, $y$, is equal to 1 with probability $p_0$, and $y = 0$ with probability $1 - p_0$. On the other hand, if the agent exerts effort $e = \phi$, then $y = 1$ with probability $p_1$, and $y = 0$ with probability $1 - p_1$. We assume $p_1 > p_0$.

The value of $e$ is private information of the agent, while the amount of output $y$ is verifiable in court. Therefore an employment contract for the agent specifies a pair of wages $(w_0, w_1)$ depending on whether output is high $y = 1$ or low $y = 0$.

Finally, we assume that the agent has a reservation wage $\bar{w}$ normalized to be 0, and that any contract offered to the agent needs to satisfy a *limited liability* constraint specifying that the agent cannot be paid a negative amount $w_h \geq 0$, $h = 0, 1$.

Both the principal and the agent are risk neutral, and the negotiation of the employment contract takes the following form. The principal makes an offer of a contract to the agent that the agent may accept or reject. In the event of acceptance the contract is enforced. In the event of a rejection the agent gets its reservation wage while the principal obtains a payoff of 0.

## *The optimal contract*

In the contractual environment described earlier, $B$'s problem consists of choosing an employment contract $(w_0, w_1)$ for $A$ that maximizes his expected profit. This contract will depend on whether $B$ finds it profitable to offer a contract that induces $A$ to choose a high level of effort or a low one.

Assume for the time being that $B$ wants to induce $A$ to choose the effort level $e = 1$. In this case $B$'s decision problem takes the following form:

$$\max_{w_1, w_0} \quad p_1(1 - w_1) - (1 - p_1)w_0 \tag{10.7}$$

$$\text{s.t.} \quad p_1 w_1 + (1 - p_1)w_0 - \phi \geq 0 \tag{10.8}$$

$$p_1 w_1 + (1 - p_1)w_0 - \phi \geq p_0 w_1 + (1 - p_0)w_0 \tag{10.9}$$

$$w_0 \geq 0, \quad w_1 \geq 0 \tag{10.10}$$

In other words, the optimal contract is the one that maximizes $B$'s expected payoff and yields to $A$ at least his reservation wage, (10.8), induces $A$ to choose $e = \phi$, (10.9), and satisfies the limited liability constraint (10.10).

The solution to problem (10.7), $(w_0^*, w_1^*)$, is simple to characterize. It is in fact clear that $w_0^* = 0$ while the wage level associated with $y = 1$ can be obtained from (10.9): $w_1^* = \phi/(p_1 - p_0)$.

Notice that when $B$ wants to induce a high level of effort, not all three constraints (10.8), (10.9) and (10.10) are binding. In particular, in equilibrium, for any positive value of $\phi$, constraint (10.8) is *not* binding. In other words, given the limited liability constraint (10.10), in order to meet the incentive compatibility constraint (10.9) the principal has to reward the agent with a level of expected utility that strictly exceeds the agent's reservation level. In particular, this implies that the agent strictly prefers to accept the contract if no *ex ante* cost needs to be paid.

The equilibrium payoffs associated with contract $(w_1^*, w_0^*)$ are:

$$\Pi_A^* = \frac{p_0\phi}{p_1 - p_0} \tag{10.11}$$

for the agent, and

$$\Pi_B^* = p_1 \left[1 - \frac{\phi}{p_1 - p_0}\right] \tag{10.12}$$

for the principal, while the total surplus can easily be computed as

$$\Pi^* = \Pi_A^* + \Pi_B^* = p_1 - \phi$$

Consider now the case in which $B$ decides to induce a low level of effort. The principal's problem is now the following

$$\begin{aligned} \max_{w_1, w_0} \quad & p_0(1 - w_1) - (1 - p_0)w_0 \\ \text{s.t.} \quad & p_0 w_1 + (1 - p_0)w_0 - \phi \geq 0 \\ & w_0 \geq 0, \quad w_1 \geq 0 \end{aligned} \tag{10.13}$$

It is immediate to see that the solution, $(w_0^{**}, w_1^{**})$, to problem (10.13) satisfies $w_1^{**} = w_0^{**} = 0$, which of course does not satisfy constraint (10.9). The payoffs to the parties in this case are $\Pi_A^{**} = 0$ and $\Pi_B^{**} = p_0$, while the total surplus is $\Pi^{**} = p_0$.

The equilibrium contract is now obtained from the comparison of $\Pi_B^*$ and $\Pi_B^{**}$ – $B$'s payoff when the contract offered induces a high level of effort $(w_0^*, w_1^*)$, and $B$'s payoff when the contract offered induces a low level of effort $(w_0^{**}, w_1^{**})$, respectively. In general, both outcomes are possible. The following observations are in order.

First, it is *socially* optimal to induce the agent to exert high effort whenever $\Pi^* \geq \Pi^{**}$. This occurs if and only if

$$\phi \leq p_1 - p_0 \tag{10.14}$$

Second, $B$ will strictly prefer to induce high effort whenever $\Pi_B^* \geq \Pi_B^{**}$. This occurs if and only if the following condition is satisfied

$$\phi \leq \frac{(p_1 - p_0)^2}{p_1} \tag{10.15}$$

Notice next that the contract which induces high effort differs from the one which induces low effort in one crucial respect for our purposes. The contract $(w_0^*, w_1^*)$ is contingent on the value of output $y$, while $(w_0^{**}, w_1^{**})$ is not.

As an application of our general model of *ex ante* contractual costs, we now proceed to assume that the contract $(w_0^*, w_1^*)$ is only feasible if both parties, simultaneously and independently, decide to sink the *ex ante* costs $c_B$ and $c_A$ respectively. If either party decides not to pay this cost, only contracts which do not depend on output are feasible. Clearly, in this case the contract between $B$ and $A$ will simply be $(w_0^{**}, w_1^{**})$.

In what follows we restrict ourselves to values of the parameter $\phi$ such that it is both socially efficient and in the interest of the principal to induce the agent to exert a high level of effort. From (10.14) and (10.15), we know that this occurs whenever

$$0 \leq \phi \leq \frac{(p_1 - p_0)^2}{p_1} \tag{10.16}$$

Notice that for any $\phi$ satisfying condition (10.16) the total surplus will exceed $p_0$ by at least $p_0(p_1 - p_0)/p_1$:

$$\Pi^* - p_0 \geq p_0 \frac{p_1 - p_0}{p_1}$$

Therefore, (10.16) together with

$$c_A + c_B < p_0 \frac{p_1 - p_0}{p_1} \tag{10.17}$$

is enough to guarantee that it is socially efficient for the parties to sink the *ex ante* costs and write a contingent contract (this is the analogue of Assumption 2), which in what follows we assume to be the case.

It follows from (10.11) that for values of $\phi$ sufficiently close to 0, the payoff to $A$ is not high enough to induce him to sink the *ex ante* cost $c_A$. In other words, there exist values of $\phi$ which satisfy (10.16) and such that

$$\Pi_A^* = \frac{p_0 \phi}{p_1 - p_0} < c_A$$

Furthermore, from (10.12) it follows that for values of $\phi$ which satisfy (10.16) but are sufficiently close to $(p_1 - p_0)^2/p_1$ the payoff to $B$ will not be high enough to induce him to sink the *ex ante* cost associated with a contingent contract. In other words, there exists values of $\phi$ which satisfy (10.16) and such that

$$\Pi_B^* - \Pi_B^{**} = p_1 \left[ 1 - \frac{c}{p_1 - p_0} \right] - p_0 < c_B$$

We can now summarize our findings as follows. There exists two distinct values $\underline{\phi}$ and $\overline{\phi}$ of the parameter $\phi$ such that for every principal–agent problem in which $\phi \in [0, \underline{\phi}) \cup (\overline{\phi}, 1]$, the contracting parties choose to write a socially inefficient constant wage contract $(w_0^{**}, w_1^{**})$ rather than a contingent contract $(w_0^*, w_1^*)$ on the sole account that it is not strategically optimal for one of the two parties to sink the *ex ante* contractual cost.

## An intertemporal model with short-term contracts

### *Preamble*

In this section we present a further example of an economic environment to which the basic logic of our findings for the reduced form model applies. We consider a multi-period principal–agent model in which the choice of *ex ante* contractual costs determines the maximum length of the contract which the principal and the agent can write. We find that, in general, the equilibrium outcome of the model involves the parties writing a contract which is shorter than would be socially optimal, after *ex ante* contractual costs are taken into account.

### *An intertemporal principal–agent model*

We start with a description of the model without any *ex ante* contractual costs. Time is discrete, and runs for infinitely many periods, $t = 1, 2 \ldots$. The principal, $B$, hires an agent, $A$, to run a simple multi-period technology as follows. In period 1, $A$ chooses a level of effort $e$, which can take one of the discrete number of values $\{\phi_0, \phi_1, \ldots, \phi_T, \ldots, \phi_\infty\}$ with $\infty > \phi_\infty > \phi_T > \phi_{T-1}$ for all $T = 1, 2, \ldots$, and $\phi_0 = 0$. Exerting effort level $\phi_T$ has a cost for the agent, which we simply take to be equal to $\phi_T$. The agent's effort is non-contractible by assumption, so that any contract between the principal and the agent can only be contingent on output. Output is described as a sequence of i.i.d. binary random variables as follows. In each period $t$, the output $y_t$ can be either high ($y_t = 1$) or low ($y_t = 0$). If $A$ chooses effort level $\phi_0$, then in all periods $y_t = 1$ with probability $p_0$ and $y_t = 1$ with probability $1 - p_0$. If the agent chooses $e = \phi_T$, then in each period $t = 1, \ldots, T$ $y_t = 1$ with probability $p_1$ and $y_t = 0$ with probability $1 - p_1$, while for all periods $t \geq T + 1, y_t = 1$ with probability $p_0$ and $y_t = 0$ with probability $1 - p_0$. Finally, if $A$ chooses $e = \phi_\infty$, then in all periods $y_t = 1$ with probability $p_1$ and $y_t = 0$ with probability $1 - p_1$.

We assume that $p_1 > p_0 > 0$, and we denote by $h_t$ the history of realized output values up to and including period $t$, $(y_1, \ldots, y_t)$. The set of all possible histories of length $t$ is denoted by $H_t$, while $\mathcal{H}_T$ denotes $\cup_{t=1}^{T} H_t$, and $\mathcal{H} = \cup_{t=1}^{\infty} \mathcal{H}_T$. The probability of history $h_t$, when $A$ chooses effort level $\phi_T$, is denoted by $p_1(h_t, T)$.

A contract between $B$ and $A$ can now be seen as a sequence $\mathcal{W} = \{w(h_t)\}_{h_t \in \mathcal{H}}$, specifying a wage to be paid to the agent for each possible sequence of outputs $h_t$ at time $t$. For simplicity, we assume that both parties discount the future at the same rate, and denote by $\delta$ their common discount factor. Moreover, for simplicity again, we make the extreme assumption that both $A$ and $B$ are risk-neutral, although our results generalize fairly easily to the case in which the agent is risk-averse and the principal is either risk-neutral or "less risk-averse" than the agent.

Given a wage package $\mathcal{W}$ and a level of effort $\phi_T$, we can write the expected utility of $A$ as

$$\sum_{h_t \in \mathcal{H}} \delta^{t-1} p(h_t, T) w(h_t) - \phi_T$$

Therefore, $A$ will choose to set $e = \phi_T$ only if $\mathcal{W}$ is such that for all $T' \neq T$

$$\sum_{h_t \in \mathcal{H}} \delta^{t-1} p(h_t, T) w(h_t) - \phi_T \geq \sum_{h_t \in \mathcal{H}} \delta^{t-1} p(h_t, T') w(h_t) - \phi_{T'} \tag{10.18}$$

The expected payoff to $B$ when the agent chooses $e = \phi_T$ and the wage package is $\mathcal{W}$ can be written as

$$\sum_{h_t \in \mathcal{H}} \delta^{t-1} p(h_t, T) \left[y_t(h_t) - w(h_t)\right] \tag{10.19}$$

where $y_t(h_t)$ is output at time $t$, as specified in the history $h_t$.

As in the section "A principal–agent model with incomplete contracts," we assume that the agent has limited liability in the sense that the principal cannot pay him a negative wage in any eventuality. The principal's problem, under the assumption that he wants to induce effort $\phi_T$ from the part of the agent is therefore the following: maximize (10.19) by choice of $\mathcal{W}$ and $e$ subject to the constraints (10.18) and $w(h_t) \geq 0$ for all $h_t \in \mathcal{H}$. Throughout the remaining of this section, we denote the solution to this maximization problem by $\mathcal{W}^*$, with typical element $w^*(h_t)$.

In the subsections "*Ex ante* costs and the length of the contract" and "Short-term equilibrium contracts," we will be interested in the case in which the principal and the agent are *constrained* to write a contract which does not exceed a given length $\mathcal{T}$. Therefore we need to specify what the principal's problem is in this case. For simplicity, we assume that once the contract expires $B$ has all the bargaining power. This is because the agent's effort is decided once and for all at $t = 1$, and after date $\mathcal{T}$ the agent's effort is sunk. It follows that if the parties write a contract which lasts up to and including period $\mathcal{T}$, for all $t > \mathcal{T}$ the principal will pay the agent a wage of 0 in all possible eventualities. In other words, the principal's problem when the maximum contract length is $\mathcal{T}$ can be written as

$$
\begin{aligned}
\max_{\mathcal{W},\, T\in\{1,\ldots,\mathcal{T}\}} \quad & \sum_{h_t\in\mathcal{H}_T} \delta^{t-1}\, p(h_t, T)\,[y_t(h_t) - w(h_t)] + \frac{\delta^{T}}{1-\delta} p_0 \\
\text{s.t.} \quad & \sum_{h_t\in\mathcal{H}_T} \delta^{t-1}\, p(h_t, T) w(h_t) - \phi_T \\
& \quad \geq \sum_{h_t\in\mathcal{H}_T} \delta^{t-1}\, p(h_t, T') w(h_t) - \phi_{T'} \qquad \forall\, T' \neq T \\
& w(h_t) \geq 0 \qquad \forall\, h_t \in \mathcal{H}_T
\end{aligned}
\tag{10.20}
$$

Throughout the remainder of this section, we denote the solution to problem (10.20) by $\{T^*, \mathcal{W}^{*\mathcal{T}}\}$, with $w^{*\mathcal{T}}(h_t)$ a typical element of $\mathcal{W}^{*\mathcal{T}}$.

We make two assumptions on the parameters of problem (10.20). First of all we will assume that $A$'s cost of effort increases at a decreasing rate, so that its discounted value actually decreases with $T$. This is designed to ensure that the variation in social surplus from increasing the agent's effort from $\phi_T$ to $\phi_{T+1}$ is positive for all $T = 1, 2, \ldots$. Formally, we assume that

$$\exists k > 0 \qquad \text{such that} \qquad \delta^{T-1} k > \phi_T - \phi_{T-1} \quad \forall\, T = 1, 2, \ldots \tag{10.21}$$

Our second assumption guarantees that the principal finds it profitable to induce effort $\phi_1$, rather than $\phi_0$ when the maximum length of the contract is $\mathcal{T} = 1$. This coupled with (10.21) is enough to guarantee that the principal will always want to induce the agent to choose effort $\phi^{\mathcal{T}}$ when the maximum possible length of the contract is $\mathcal{T}$; in other words $T^* = \mathcal{T}$ for all $\mathcal{T} = 1, 2, \ldots$. Since our model in this section when $\mathcal{T} = 1$ is the same as the model we analyzed in the section "A principal–agent model with incomplete contracts," the condition which guarantees that this is the case is the same as (10.15) when we set $\phi = k$. Therefore we assume that

$$k \leq \frac{(p_1 - p_0)^2}{p_1} \tag{10.22}$$

We give a characterization of the solution to problem (10.20) and of the principal's problem when there is no limit imposed on the length of the contract in Lemmas A.4, A.5 and A.6 in the Appendix. Here, we limit ourselves to a summary of the features of these solutions which we will use in the next two subsections.

Let $\Pi_B^*$, $\Pi_B^{*\mathcal{T}}$, $\Pi_A^*$ and $\Pi_A^{*\mathcal{T}}$ be the principal's and the agent's expected payoffs when $\mathcal{W} = \mathcal{W}^*$ and $\mathcal{W} = \mathcal{W}^{*\mathcal{T}}$ respectively. What matters for the analysis that follows are the following three facts. First of all, we have that the optimal contract satisfies $T^* = \mathcal{T}$ ($T^* = \infty$ when there is no limit to the length of the contract). Second, the principal's payoff is strictly increasing in $\mathcal{T}$. Formally

$$\Pi_B^* > \Pi_B^{*\mathcal{T}+1} > \Pi_B^{*\mathcal{T}} \qquad \forall\, \mathcal{T} = 1, 2, \ldots \tag{10.23}$$

Finally, the agent's payoff is also strictly increasing in the maximum possible length of the contract $\mathcal{T}$. Formally

$$\Pi_A^* > \Pi_A^{*\mathcal{T}+1} > \Pi_A^{*\mathcal{T}} \qquad \forall\, \mathcal{T} = 1, 2, \ldots \tag{10.24}$$

The intuition behind this characterization of the optimal contract between the principal and the agent is simple to outline. Because (10.21) and (10.22) hold, $B$ will always want to induce the highest possible level of effort from the part of the agent given $\mathcal{T}$. Since it is always open to the principal to induce any other effort level $\phi_T$ with $T < \mathcal{T}$ by offering $A$ the wage package $\mathcal{W}^{*T}$ which would guarantee him a payoff of $\Pi^{*T}$, then it must be that $\Pi_B^{*\mathcal{T}} > \Pi_B^{*T}$ for all $T < \mathcal{T}$. Since $B$ always wants to "buy the maximum effort" from $A$, he has to give him appropriate incentives to choose $e = \phi_{\mathcal{T}}$. Because of the limited liability constraint we have imposed on the agent's payments, this guarantees that $A$'s expected payoff increases with $\mathcal{T}$.

### Ex ante *costs and the length of the contract*

We are now ready to introduce *ex ante* contractual costs in the multi-period principal–agent model we have described in the subsection "Intertemporal principal–agent model." We do so in the simplest possible way which allows us to capture the idea that longer contracts will cost the parties more than shorter ones. This can be justified in a number of ways. One obvious candidate which springs to mind is that longer contracts must specify more contingencies and hence are more difficult and complex to draw up.

We imagine that in period 0 the two parties simultaneously and independently choose numbers $t_A$ and $t_B$. If $i \in \{A, B\}$ chooses $t_i$, he incurs a cost of $c_i t_i$ (with $c_i > 0$ for $i \in \{A, B\}$) at this time. The agents' choices of $t_A$ and $t_B$ determine the maximum length of the contract which they are allowed to write. We take this to be given by the following expression.[11]

$$\mathcal{T} = \min\{t_A, t_B\} \tag{10.25}$$

The description of our intertemporal principal–agent model with *ex ante* contractual costs is now complete. We are interested in the sub-game perfect equilibria of the two stage game in which the two agents first choose $t_A$ and $t_B$ as described, and then proceed to write the optimal contract, given $\mathcal{T}$, as described in the subsection "Intertemporal principal–agent model." For simplicity we assume no discounting between period 0 and period 1.[12] Therefore, the payoff to agent $i \in \{A, B\}$ when the pair $(t_A, t_B)$ is chosen can be written as

$$\Pi_i^{*\mathcal{T}} - c_i t_i \tag{10.26}$$

where $\mathcal{T}$ is given by (10.25).

### *Short-term equilibrium contracts*

We are now ready to show that, in general, the model which we described in the subsections "Intertemporal principal–agent model" and "*Ex ante* costs and the length of the contracts" yields equilibrium contracts which are short-term in the sense that they are shorter than would be socially efficient, after the *ex ante* contractual costs are taken into account.

Given (10.25), it is clearly never socially efficient to choose $t_A \neq t_B$. Given this observation, the socially efficient length of the principal–agent contract is easy to characterize. Let $\Delta\Pi_i^{\mathcal{T}} = \Pi_i^{*\mathcal{T}} - \Pi_i^{*\mathcal{T}-1}$ for $i \in \{A, B\}$ and notice that by (10.23) and (10.24) we have that $\Delta\Pi_i^{\mathcal{T}} > 0$ for all $\mathcal{T}$, and $\lim_{\mathcal{T}\to\infty} \Delta\Pi_i^{\mathcal{T}} = 0$. The socially optimal level of $\mathcal{T}$ guarantees that the sum of the payoffs in (10.26) is highest. Let this value of $\mathcal{T}$ be denoted by $\mathcal{T}^*$. It is then easy to see that $\mathcal{T}^*$ must satisfy

$$\Delta\Pi_A^{\mathcal{T}^*} + \Delta\Pi_B^{\mathcal{T}^*} - c_A - c_B \geq 0 \quad \text{and} \quad \Delta\Pi_A^{\mathcal{T}^*+1} + \Delta\Pi_B^{\mathcal{T}^*+1} - c_A - c_B \leq 0 \tag{10.27}$$

In any equilibrium of the model, again because of (10.25), we must also have that $t_A = t_B$. Now let

$$\mathcal{T}_i = \max\left\{\mathcal{T} \mid \Delta\Pi_i^{\mathcal{T}} - c_i \geq 0 \text{ and } \Delta\Pi_i^{\mathcal{T}+1} - c_i \leq 0\right\}$$

It is then clear that the maximum length of any equilibrium contract will never exceed

$$\mathcal{T}^E = \min\{\mathcal{T}_A, \mathcal{T}_B\} \tag{10.28}$$

Comparing (10.27) and (10.28) it is immediately possible to conclude that $\mathcal{T}^E \leq \mathcal{T}^*$. Moreover, by inspection of the two conditions (10.27) and (10.28), it is also easy to see that "in general" we will have $\mathcal{T}^E < \mathcal{T}^*$, where the qualification "in general" refers to the fact that we could have $\mathcal{T}^E = \mathcal{T}^*$ either if $\mathcal{T}_A = \mathcal{T}_B$, or because of "integer problems." Aside from integer problems it is clear that, in general, the parameters of our multi-period principal–agent model will be such that $\mathcal{T}_A \neq \mathcal{T}_B$. We omit the details for reasons of space.

Our findings can therefore be summarized as follows. "In general," our multi-period principal–agent problem with *ex ante* contractual costs will yield equilibrium contracts which are shorter than would be socially optimal, after the *ex ante* costs are taken into account. The intuition behind this result is very similar to the one we described for the probabilistic reduced form model of the subsection "Costly contingent contracts: continuous costs." The inefficiency stems from the fact that the "marginal conditions" which determine each party's choice of *ex ante* cost do not, in general, coincide with the "marginal conditions" for social efficiency.

## A Coasian solution?

In our analysis so far we have argued that *ex ante* contractual costs may give rise to a version of the hold-up problem which in turn generates an inefficient outcome. As we mentioned in the Introduction, in all the previous literature of which we are aware (Grossman and Hart, 1986; Hart and Moore, 1988, 1990; among others) the *reason* a hold-up problem might arise in the first place is that the parties are *constrained* in their ability to write contracts: given that certain variables are not negotiable *ex ante* (or that only limited *ex ante* negotiation is feasible because of the constraints imposed by the possibility of renegotiation *ex post* (Hart and Moore, 1988)) the parties' "relationship specific" investment(s) will be inefficiently low.

In a model with "relationship specific" investments and incomplete contracting, the hold-up problem typically has a "contractual solution." If either the assumption that the parties are constrained to write incomplete contracts is removed (e.g. by increasing the information which the enforcing agency can verify as in N'oldeke and Schmidt (1995)), or if a contracting stage is added to the model in which the parties can write a "grand" *ex ante* contract in which either the amounts of relationship specific investment are specified or alternatively reported by the parties to the enforcing agency as in Maskin and Tirole (1999), or finally if the parties can commit to a given renegotiation procedure as in Rubinstein and Wolinsky (1992) and Aghion *et al.* (1994), then the hold-up problem is resolved, and an efficient outcome is guaranteed.

Clearly, in our analysis so far, if the contract can be fully negotiated at the same time at which the contractual costs are paid, then the hold-up problem could be resolved and an efficient outcome achieved. We have already argued that in many situations *ex ante* contractual costs will have to be incurred, so that this route to restoring efficiency will effectively be unavailable. The next natural question to ask is then whether the other type of contractual solution to the hold-up problem is generally available in the present set up. In other words: is it possible to add another stage to our model, prior to the stage in which the *ex ante* costs are incurred, in which the agents can negotiate a "grand contract," which will resolve the hold-up problem and hence restore efficiency?

The answer to the above question is trivially "yes," if a *truly grand* contract can be negotiated costlessly, which specifies everything, including the payment of the *ex ante* costs, *and* the division of the actual surplus.[13] However, as we have shown in Anderlini and Felli (2001b), the answer changes dramatically in the following, in our view appealing, scenario.

Consider a situation in which the two agents involved in the basic hold-up problem attempt to resolve the inefficiency in the following (Coasian) way. Before the *ex ante* costs are paid, they negotiate a transfer of money which will compensate the agent who is unable to recoup the *ex ante* cost for his loss, of course contingent on his paying the *ex ante* cost. Provided the sum of *ex ante* costs does not exceed the surplus generated by the contract, such transfer can always be arranged so that both agents now benefit from paying the *ex ante* costs and entering the contract.

However, the problem which then arises is that the contingent compensating transfer can itself be viewed as a contract, which will involve a new set of *ex ante* costs.

As seems compelling in many contractual situations, now make the assumption that the "second tier" contract we have described does indeed involve a new set of strictly positive *ex ante* costs. Assume also that the second tier contract and *ex ante* costs must be paid for, and negotiated, *before* the first order costs and contract are paid for, and negotiated, respectively.

It is then possible to show (Anderlini and Felli, 2001b) that the *ex ante* costs associated with the second tier contract may not be paid. In particular there always exists an equilibrium such that the contingent compensating transfer is not negotiated and therefore does not take place. Hence, the *ex ante* costs associated with the first tier contract will, in turn, not be paid, and the actual surplus-generating contract will not be drawn up. This outcome is of particular interest since it is the only one which survives when we restrict attention to "renegotiation-proof" equilibria. In other words if, in a Coasian spirit, we insist that the outcome of negotiation at every stage must yield a (constrained) efficient outcome, the overall outcome is not efficient and therefore not Coasian at all.

The argument we have just outlined is also robust to allowing further opportunities for compensating transfers. In Anderlini and Felli (1996) we show that a whole hierarchy of (finitely many) tiers of compensating transfers may be allowed without being able to escape the basic hold-up problem.

## Concluding remarks

If the parties to a risk-sharing contract need to sink some *ex ante* contractual costs before they can reach the contract-negotiating phase of their interaction, the *ex ante* costs may generate a version of the hold-up problem. If the distribution of *ex ante* costs and the distribution of the surplus generated by the contract do not "match," one of the two parties to the contract will not find it to his advantage to pay the *ex ante* contractual cost, even though the surplus generated by the contract would be sufficient to cover the total *ex ante* costs associated with it. Therefore, in equilibrium the contract will not be written. We have verified this claim in a variety of simple models.

We have also explored two examples of economic situations in which the distribution of surplus from the contract between a principal and an agent is "pinned down" by the interplay of incentive compatibility and limited liability constraints. Since the economic parameters of these two models fix the distribution of surplus, these provide two examples of economic situations which generate the hold-up problem we identified before. Our second example concerns a dynamic principal–agent model. The equilibrium contracts which we obtain in this case are short term in the sense that they are shorter than would be socially efficient, even after contractual costs are taken into account.

## Appendix

### *Proof of Proposition 1*

If $c = c_A + c_B$ and $\omega$ do not jointly satisfy Assumption 2, there is clearly nothing more to prove, since for one or both agents it will be a dominant strategy to set $\alpha_i = 0$.

Let then $c_A$ and $c_B$ with $c = c_A + c_B$ and $\omega$ satisfying Assumption 2 be given. From Problem 10.2 and equation (10.3), it is clear that for some $\lambda'(c_A, c_B) \in (0, 1)$ we will have that the expected utility of $A$ from contract $\tau(\lambda'(c_A, c_B), z)$ is precisely $U_A^*(w)$. Similarly, from Problem (10.2) and equation (10.3) it is clear that we can find $\lambda''(c_A, c_B) \in (\lambda', 1)$ which ensures that the expected utility of $B$ from contract $\tau(\lambda''(c_A, c_B), z)$ is precisely $U_B^*(w)$.

Given $\omega$ satisfying Assumption 3, let $c^* < \omega_A^0 + \omega_B^0$ be the maximum total *ex ante* cost such that $\omega$ and $c^*$ jointly satisfy Assumption 2. Now set

$$\lambda^* = \min_{(c_A, c_B) \in [\underline{c}_A, c^*] \times [\underline{c}_B, c^*]} \lambda'(c_A, c_B)$$

and

$$\lambda^{**} = \max_{(c_A, c_B) \in [\underline{c}_A, c^*] \times [\underline{c}_B, c^*]} \lambda''(c_A, c_B)$$

and notice that, whatever the configuration of $(c_A, c_B)$, for $\lambda \in [0, \lambda^*)$ it is a (strictly) dominant strategy for $A$ to set $\alpha_A = 0$. Similarly whenever $\lambda \in (\lambda^{**}, 1]$, it is a (strictly) dominant strategy for $B$ to set $\alpha_B = 0$. This is enough to prove the claim. □

### *Proof of Proposition 2*

Given $\omega$ satisfying Assumption 3, let again $c^* < \omega_A^0 + \omega_B^0$ be the maximum total *ex ante* cost such that $\omega$ and $c^*$ jointly satisfy Assumption 2.

Now let any $c_A^*$ and $c_B^*$ satisfying Assumption 1 with $c_A^* + c_B^* = c^*$ be given, and let $z_i^* = (w_i^1 - c_i^*, w_i^2 - c_i^*)$. Suppose next that, for the given value of $\lambda$, one of

$$\pi U_i(w_i^1 - c_i^* + \text{sgn}(i)\tau^1(\lambda, z^*)) + (1 - \pi)U_i(w_i^2 - c_i^* + \text{sgn}(i)\tau^2(\lambda, z^*)) \geq U_i^*(w) \tag{10A.1}$$

with $i \in \{A, B\}$, is violated. Then there is nothing more to prove since, for the given $c_A^*$ and $c_B^*$ a contingent contract is socially efficient, but either $A$ or $B$ will have as a dominant strategy not to pay the *ex ante* cost.

Suppose now, that both weak inequalities in (10A.1) are satisfied. Then, since $c_A^* + c_B^* = c^*$ and $c^*$ is the *maximum* total cost for which a contingent contract is socially efficient, it must be that both weak inequalities in (10A.1) hold with equality.

We can now choose $\underline{c}_B > c_B^*$ and $\underline{c}_A < c_A^*$ such that $\underline{c}_A + \underline{c}_B = \underline{c} = c^*$, and $\underline{c}_i < \omega_i^0$ for $i \in \{A, B\}$. Let $z_i' = (w_i^1 - \underline{c}_i, w_i^2 - \underline{c}_i)$ for $i \in \{A, B\}$.

From problem (10.2) it is now clear that

$$\pi U_B(w_B^1 - \underline{c}_B + \tau^1(\lambda, z')) + (1-\pi)U_B(w_B^2 - \underline{c}_B + \tau^2(\lambda, z'))$$
$$< \pi U_B(w_B^1 - c_B^* + \tau^1(\lambda, z^*)) + (1-\pi)U_B(w_B^2 - c_B^* + \tau^2(\lambda, z^*)) = U_B^*(w) \quad (10A.2)$$

where the equality on the right-hand side follows from the fact that (10A.1) must hold with equality for $i = B$. It follows that when the *ex ante* costs are equal to $c'_A$ and $c'_B$ respectively, a contingent contract is socially efficient, but it is a (strictly) dominant strategy for agent $B$ not to pay the *ex ante* cost. To complete the proof it is then enough to notice that if $c_A \geq \underline{c}_A$, $c_B \geq \underline{c}_B$ and $\omega$ satisfy Assumption 2, then it must be that $c_A = \underline{c}_A$ and $c_B = \underline{c}_B$. □

**Lemma A.1.** *In the probabilistic reduced form model with $p$ given by (10.6), let $\hat{c}_A(\lambda)$ (respectively $\hat{c}_B(\lambda)$) be the amount of ex ante cost which maximizes the expected utility of agent $A$ (respectively $B$), for the given $\lambda$, when agent $B$ (respectively $A$) sets $c_B = \overline{c}_A$ (respectively $c_A = \overline{c}_A$). Then, $\hat{c}_A(0) = 0$ (respectively $\hat{c}_B(1) = 0$), $\hat{c}_A(1) > 0$ (respectively $\hat{c}_B(0) > 0$), and $\hat{c}_A(\lambda)$ is strictly increasing (respectively $\hat{c}_B(\lambda)$ strictly decreasing) in the value of the bargaining parameter $\lambda$.*

*Proof.* We only prove the claim for $\hat{c}_A(\lambda)$. The proof for $\hat{c}_B(\lambda)$ is exactly symmetric. Notice that, from (10.6), it follows that since $c_B = \overline{c}_B$, then $p = V_A(c_A)$. Next, let $z(c_A)$ be the *status quo* after $A$ has paid $c_A$ and $B$ has paid $\overline{c}_B$. The expected utility of agent $A$, given $\lambda$, from choosing a particular value of $c_A$ can then be written as

$$V_A(c_A)\left\{\pi U_A\left[z_A^1(c_A) - \tau^1(\lambda, z(c_A))\right] + (1-\pi)U_A\left[z_A^2(c_A) - \tau^2(\lambda, z(c_A))\right]\right\}$$
$$+ (1 - V_A(c_A))U_A^*(z(c_A)) \quad (10A.3)$$

The first order condition for the maximization of (10A.3) is easily seen to be

$$V'_A(c_A)\{\pi U_A[z_A^1(c_A) - \tau^1(\lambda, z(c_A))] + (1-\pi)U_A[z_A^2(c_A) - \tau^2(\lambda, z(c_A))]\}$$
$$- V_A(c_A)\{\pi U'_A[z_A^1(c_A) - \tau^1(\lambda, z(c_A))] + (1-\pi)U'_A[z_A^2(c_A) - \tau^2(\lambda, z(c_A))]\}$$
$$\mathrm{d}/\mathrm{d}c_A[\tau(\lambda, z(c_A)) + 1] - V'_A(c_A)U^*[z(c_A)] + (1 - V_A(c_A))\mathrm{d}/\mathrm{d}c_A[U^*[z(c_A)] = 0 \quad (10A.4)$$

It is easy to see that the second order condition for expected utility maximization is always satisfied. Since we are assuming that $V'_A(0) = +\infty$ and $V'_A(\overline{c}_A) = 0$, the maximum is always achieved at an interior point $c_A \in (0, \overline{c}_A)$. It then follows that (10A.4) is both necessary and sufficient for the maximization of $A$'s expected utility. It is now enough to use concavity of $U_A$ and $V_A$ as well as the fact that the bargaining power of $A$ in problem (10.2) is increasing in the bargaining parameter $\lambda$, to show that $\hat{c}_A(\lambda)$ is increasing in $\lambda$ as required. To conclude that $\hat{c}_A(0) = 0$ it is enough to notice that when $\lambda = 0$ $A$'s expected utility conditional on a contingent contract being signed is precisely $U_A^*(z(c_A))$. □

**Lemma A.2.** *Let $\hat{c}_i$ be as in Lemma A.1 for $i \in \{A, B\}$. Then there exists a unique $\lambda^* \in (0, 1)$ such that $V(\hat{c}_A(\lambda^*)) = V_B(\hat{c}_B(\lambda^*))$.*

*Proof.* Recall that $V_i$ is assumed to be strictly increasing and to satisfy $V_i(0) = 0$ for $i \in \{A, B\}$. It then follows from Lemma A.1 that $V_A(\hat{c}_A(0)) = V_B(\hat{c}_B(1)) = 0$ and that $V_A(\hat{c}_A(\lambda))$ is increasing in $\lambda$, while $V_B(\hat{c}_B(\lambda))$ is decreasing in $\lambda$. This is clearly enough to prove the claim. □

**Lemma A.3.** *Fix any $\lambda \in [0, 1]$ with $\lambda \neq \lambda^*$, where $\lambda^*$ is as in Lemma A.2. Then in any equilibrium of the probabilistic reduced form model with p given by (10.6), either the left-hand side of the first order condition in (10A.4) is strictly positive, or the left-hand side of the equivalent first order condition for B is strictly positive, or both.*

*Proof.* From (10.6) and (10A.3) it is clear that in any equilibrium of the probabilistic reduced form model in which $p$ is given by (10.6), we must have that the chosen values of *ex ante* costs $c_i(\lambda)$ satisfy

$$V_A(c_A(\lambda)) = V_B(c_A(\lambda)) \tag{10A.5}$$

since otherwise one of the two agents could reduce the *ex ante* cost paid without reducing the probability that a contingent contract will be signed. Suppose now that for agent $i \in \{A, B\}$ at the given equilibrium, the left-hand side of the first-order condition (10A.4) (the analogue of (10A.4) in the case of $B$) were negative. Then $i$ could reduce the *ex ante* cost he pays by a small amount, and pay $c_i < c_i(\lambda)$ and increase his expected utility. It follows that the left-hand side of (10A.4) (the analogue of it in the case of $B$), is non-negative for $i \in \{A, B\}$ in any equilibrium. Since $\lambda \neq \lambda^*$, Lemma A.2 now directly implies the claim. □

***Proof of Proposition 3***

Let $\lambda^*$ be as in Lemma A.2, and assume that $\lambda \neq \lambda^*$. We only consider the case in which $V_A(\hat{c}_A(\lambda)) > V_B(\hat{c}_B(\lambda))$. The other case is a simple relabelling of this one. Observe that there is an equilibrium in which both $A$ and $B$ choose the largest value of *ex ante* costs, as compared to any other equilibrium. This follows easily from (10.6), and the equilibrium is for $B$ to set $c_B(\lambda) = \hat{c}_B(\lambda)$ and for $A$ to choose a $c_A(\lambda)$ such that $V_A(c_A(\lambda)) = V_B(\hat{c}(\lambda))$. Call this equilibrium the "maximal" equilibrium of the probabilistic reduced form model.

Clearly, any equilibrium of the probabilistic reduced form model which is not the maximal one, is not efficient according to Definition 2. Indeed, both agents are strictly better off in the maximal equilibrium than in any other equilibrium. This is simply because at any equilibrium which is not the maximal one, using Lemma A.3 it can be seen that a, say, equal and small increase in both $c_A$ and $c_B$ will increase both agent's expected utility.

Consider now the maximal equilibrium of the probabilistic reduced form model, and let $z(c_A(\lambda), c_B(\lambda))$ be the status quo after the *ex ante* costs in this equilibrium have been paid by both agents.

Since $c_B(\lambda) = \hat{c}_B(\lambda)$, by Lemma A.3 we now know that for $c_A = c_A(\lambda)$ the left-hand side of (10A.4) is positive. On the other hand, by construction, the analogue of (10A.4) is satisfied for $B$ at $c_B(\lambda) = \hat{c}_B(\lambda)$. It then follows that for some sufficiently small $\varepsilon$ and $\xi$, setting the *ex ante* costs to be $c_i' = c_i(\lambda) + \xi$ for $i \in \{A, B\}$ and setting $\tau' = \tau(\lambda, z(c_A(\lambda, c_B(\lambda)) + \xi$ will increase the expected utility of both $A$ and $B$. The proof is therefore complete. □

**Lemma A.4.** *Consider the multi-period principal–agent problem (10.20) described in the subsection "An intertemporal principal–agent model" for a given maximum length of the contract $\mathcal{T}$. For each $n = 1, 2, \ldots, \mathcal{T}$, let*

$$H_n^* = \left\{ h_n^* \in H_n \;\middle|\; h_n^* \in \arg\max_{h_n \in H_n} \frac{p(h_n, n)}{p(h_n, n) - p(h_n, n-1)} \right\}$$

*Then the solution to problem (10.20) satisfies the following. The agent's level of effort is the maximum possible, that is $e = \phi_{\mathcal{T}}$, or equivalently $T^* = \mathcal{T}$. Moreover, for all $n = 1, \ldots, \mathcal{T}$ whenever $h_n \notin H_n^*$ then $w^{*\mathcal{T}}(h_n) = 0$. Lastly, for all $n = 1, \ldots, \mathcal{T}$*

$$\sum_{h_n^* \in H_n^*} w^{*\mathcal{T}}(h_n^*) = \frac{p(h_n^*, n)}{\delta^{n-1}\left[p(h_n^*, n) - p(h_n^*, n-1)\right]} \xi_{\mathcal{T},n} \tag{10A.6}$$

where

$$\xi_{\mathcal{T},n} = (\mathcal{T} - n + 1)\phi_{\mathcal{T}} - \sum_{\ell=n-1}^{\mathcal{T}-1} \phi_\ell \tag{10A.7}$$

*Proof.* We start by arguing that it must be that $T^* = \mathcal{T}$. This is almost immediate if we consider problem (10.20) for two consecutive values of the maximum length of the contract, say $\mathcal{T}$ and $\mathcal{T} + 1$. When the maximum length of the contract is $\mathcal{T} + 1$ it is open to $B$ to offer $A$ the wage package $\mathcal{W}^{*\mathcal{T}}$ for all periods up to and including $\mathcal{T}$, and to make the wage in period $\mathcal{T} + 1$ only contingent on $y_{\mathcal{T}+1}$, and equal to the optimal contract when $\mathcal{T} = 1$. Because of (10.22), this both satisfies the constraint which guarantees that $e = \phi_{\mathcal{T}+1}$ and guarantees that $B$'s payoff is strictly greater than $\Pi_B^{*\mathcal{T}}$. Since the latter is the maximum which $B$ can obtain if he induces effort $e = \phi_{\mathcal{T}}$, this is clearly enough to show that if the claim is true for $\mathcal{T} = 1$ then it is true for all $\mathcal{T}$. Since (10.22) guarantees directly that the claim is true for $\mathcal{T} = 1$, this is enough to show that $T^* = \mathcal{T}$ for all $\mathcal{T}$.

Notice that since $\mathcal{T}^* = \mathcal{T}$, the incentive constraints in problem (10.20) can be re-written as

$$\sum_{h_t \in \mathcal{H}_\mathcal{T}} \delta^{t-1} p(h_t, \mathcal{T}) w(h_t) - \phi_\mathcal{T} \geq \sum_{h_t \in \mathcal{H}_\mathcal{T}} \delta^{t-1} p(h_t, n) w(h_t) - \phi_n \quad \forall\, n < \mathcal{T} \tag{10A.8}$$

Consider (10A.8) when $n = \mathcal{T} - 1$. Since $p(h_t, \mathcal{T}) = p(h_t, \mathcal{T} - 1)$ for all $h_t \in \mathcal{H}_{\mathcal{T}-1}$, this constraint can be simply re-written as

$$\sum_{h_\mathcal{T} \in H_\mathcal{T}} \delta^{\mathcal{T}-1} p(h_\mathcal{T}, \mathcal{T}) w(h_\mathcal{T}) - \phi_\mathcal{T} \geq \sum_{h_\mathcal{T} \in H_\mathcal{T}} \delta^{\mathcal{T}-1} p(h_\mathcal{T}, \mathcal{T} - 1) w(h_\mathcal{T}) - \phi_{\mathcal{T}-1} \tag{10A.9}$$

where the summations now extend only to histories of length $\mathcal{T}$. Clearly, in the solution to problem(10.20), constraint (10A.9) must bind, since otherwise $B$ could reduce $A$'s wage after some histories of length $\mathcal{T}$ and still satisfy all the appropriate constraints. Using now (10A.9) with equality, we can re-write (10A.8) when $n = \mathcal{T} - 2$ as

$$\begin{aligned} &\sum_{h_{\mathcal{T}-1} \in H_{\mathcal{T}-1}} \delta^{\mathcal{T}-2} p(h_{\mathcal{T}-1}, \mathcal{T} - 1) w(h_{\mathcal{T}-1}) - 2\phi_\mathcal{T} \\ &\quad \geq \sum_{h_{\mathcal{T}-1} \in H_{\mathcal{T}-1}} \delta^{\mathcal{T}-2} p(h_{\mathcal{T}-1}, \mathcal{T} - 2) w(h_{\mathcal{T}-1}) - \phi_{\mathcal{T}-1} - \phi_{\mathcal{T}-2} \end{aligned} \tag{10A.10}$$

Since (10A.10) must also clearly bind in the solution to problem (10.20), we can now proceed backwards to re-write all the constraints in (10A.8) together as

$$\begin{aligned} &\sum_{h_n \in H_n} \delta^{n-1} p(h_n, n) w(h_n) - (\mathcal{T} - n + 1)\phi_\mathcal{T} \\ &\quad \geq \sum_{h_n \in H_n} \delta^{n-1} p(h_n, n - 1) w(h_n) - \sum_{\ell = n-1}^{\mathcal{T}-1} \phi_\ell \qquad \forall\, n < \mathcal{T} \end{aligned} \tag{10A.11}$$

Therefore, the principal's problem is equivalent to maximizing the objective function in (10.20), subject to constraints (10A.11) and non-negative wages. Since both the objective function and the constraints in this problem are linear in wages, this is enough to show that whenever $h_n \notin H_n^*$ then $w^{*\mathcal{T}}(h_n) = 0$, and that (10A.6) and (10A.7) hold. This is enough to conclude the proof of the Lemma. □

**Lemma A.5.** *Equation (10.23) holds.*

*Proof.* The claim that $\Pi_B^{*\mathcal{T}}$ is increasing in $\mathcal{T}$ follows immediately from the fact that $\mathcal{T}^* = \mathcal{T}$ for all $\mathcal{T}$. Since the principal's problem without any limit to the length of the contract can be seen as the problem (10.20) with (infinitely many) additional constraints (setting $w(h_t) = 0$ for all $h_t$ with $t > \mathcal{T}$), it is clear that $\Pi_B^* \geq \Pi_B^{*\mathcal{T}}$ for all $\mathcal{T}$. To see that the inequality is strict, it is enough to recall that $\Pi_B^{*\mathcal{T}} < \Pi_B^{*\mathcal{T}+1}$. This concludes the proof of the claim. □

**Lemma A.6.** *Equation (10.24) holds.*

*Proof.* Recall that $\phi_{\mathcal{T}}$ is increasing in $\mathcal{T}$ by assumption. This is enough to show that $\xi_{\mathcal{T}n}$ is increasing in $\mathcal{T}$ for any given $n$. Given (10A.6) this implies that the expected wage of $A$ in any given period is increasing with $\mathcal{T}$, which is of course enough to show that $\Pi_A^{*\mathcal{T}}$ is increasing in $\mathcal{T}$. The rest of the claim follows from the fact that $\Pi_A^* = \lim_{\mathcal{T}\to\infty} \Pi_A^{*\mathcal{T}}$. We omit the details. □

## Acknowledgments

This chapter is a revised version of part of the material contained in a working paper entitled "Costly Contingent Contracts" (Anderlini and Felli, 1996). Both authors acknowledge financial support from the E.S.R.C. (Grant R000237825). We are also grateful to seminar participants at the I.S.E.R. 2000 in Siena for stimulating comments.

## Notes

1 In the UK, according Section 14 of the *Sale of Goods* Act of 1979, the definition of "satisfactory quality" includes (among other aspects of the goods in question): "(a) fitness for all the purposes for which goods of the kind in question are commonly supplied, (b) appearance and finish, (c) freedom from minor defects, (d) safety, and (e) durability" (Rose, 1987, p. 107).
2 Cf. Rose (1987) p. 112.
3 Of course, if legal experts of some kind are involved in the process, drafting and other costs can be substantial.
4 Cf. Anderlini and Felli (1999) and the discussion of this chapter in the following subsection.
5 See also Anderlini and Felli (2001b).
6 What we have just described is a version of a source of inefficiencies well known in Contract Theory as the "hold-up problem" (Grossman and Hart, 1986; Hart and Moore, 1988, 1990, among many others). The problem is particularly acute in our setting since, as we argue in the section "A Coasian solution?" below, it may be impossible to find a "contractual solution" to this hold-up problem (Chung, 1991; Rubinstein and Wolinsky, 1992; Aghion *et al.*, 1994; N'oldeke and Schmidt, 1995).
7 de Meza (1998) provides an extensive survey of the literature on the Coase Theorem, including an outline of its history and possible interpretations.
8 If both agents have constant absolute risk-aversion (homothetic indifference curves), then it is easy to show that neither will ever have an incentive to "burn money" in the sense of paying an *ex ante* cost over and above the minimum necessary to enter the contract-negotiating phase. If one agent, say $i$, has decreasing absolute risk-aversion, it is *possible* that, for *given values* of $\underline{c}_A$, $\underline{c}_B$, and $\lambda$, there exists an equilibrium in which $i$ pays *ex ante* a cost $c_i > \underline{c}_i$. This is because by doing so, he or she will effectively increase the share of the surplus which the solution to problem (10.2) assigns to him or her. In a sense, for given $\lambda$, it is as if $i$'s bargaining power has increased because he or she has become more risk-averse after spending the extra *ex ante* cost.
9 In the section "An intertemporal model with short-term contracts," we analyze another model in which the choice of how much to pay *ex ante* is "gradual" and obtain similar results in a more complex and, in our view, appealing intertemporal model.
10 In what follows we let party $B$ act as the principal and party $A$ as the agent.
11 Equation (10.25) clearly embodies the assumption that the agents' *ex ante* costs are perfect complements. We discussed the cases of partial or perfect substitutes in the subsection

on "Costly contingent contracts: discrete costs," in the context of our reduced form model. Our results for the present intertemporal model generalize fairly easily to the case of *ex ante* costs which are partial substitutes.

12 A simple rescaling of payoffs would be sufficient to take such discounting into account.

13 It is worth noticing that the contractual costs associated with this grand contract might be higher than the contractual costs associated with the initial risk-sharing contract, implying that the overall contractual costs might render the grand contract inefficient.

## References

Aghion, P., M. Dewatripont, and P. Rey (1994): "Renegotiation Design with Unverifiable Information," *Econometrica*, 62, 257–282.

Anderlini, L. and L. Felli (1996): "Costly Contingent Contracts," Theoretical Economics Discussion Paper TE/96/313, STICERD, London School of Economics.

Anderlini, L. and L. Felli (1999): "Incomplete Contracts and Complexity Costs," *Theory and Decision*, 46, 23–50.

Anderlini, L. and L. Felli (2001a): "Costly Bargaining and Renegotiation," *Econometrica*, forthcoming.

Anderlini, L. and L. Felli (2001b): "Transaction Costs and the Robustness of the Coase Theorem," Theoretical Economics Discussion Paper TE/01/409, STICERD, London School of Economics.

Chung, T.Y. (1991): "Incomplete Contracts, Specific Investments, and Risk Sharing," *Review of Economic Studies*, 58, 1031–1042.

Coase, R.H. (1960): "The Problem of Social Cost," *The Journal of Law and Economics*, 3, 1–44.

Coase, R.H. (1992): "The Institutional Structure of Production," *American Economic Review*, 82, 713–719.

de Meza, D. (1988): "Coase Theorem," in *The New Palgrave Dictionary of Economics and the Law*, P. Newmann (ed.), pp. 270–282. London: Macmillan.

Grossman, S.J. and O.D. Hart (1986): "The Costs and Benefits of Ownership: A Theory of Vertical and Lateral Integration," *Journal of Political Economy*, 94, 691–719.

Hart, O.D. and J. Moore (1988): "Incomplete Contracts and Renegotiation," *Econometrica*, 56, 755–785.

Hart, O.D. and J. Moore (1990): "Property Rights and the Nature of the Firm," *Journal of Political Economy*, 98, 1119–1158.

Holmström, B. (1982): "Moral Hazard in Teams," *Bell Journal of Economics*, 13, 324–340.

Maskin, E. and J. Tirole (1999): "Unforseen Contingencies and Incomplete Contracts," *Review of Economic Studies*, 66, 83–114.

N'oldeke, G. and K.M. Schmidt (1995): "Option Contracts and Renegotiation: A Solution to the Hold-Up Problem," *RAND Journal of Economics*, 26, 163–179.

Rose, F.D. (ed.) (1987): *Blackstone's Statutes on Contract, Tort and Restitution*. London: Blackstone Press Limited. 5th Edition.

Rubinstein, A. (1982): "Perfect Equilibrium in a Bargaining Model," *Econometrica*, 50, 97–110.

Rubinstein, A. and A. Wolinsky (1992): "Renegotiation-Proof Implementation and Time Preferences," *American Economic Review*, 82, 600–614.

# 11 Game-theoretic solutions to endogenous contractual incompleteness

*Francesco Farina*

## Introduction

In the neoclassical tradition, the Nirvana of perfectly competitive markets exempt from transaction costs warrants that all potential gains from trade are exploited and welfare maximization is reached. The Coase Theorem[1] replicates this result under milder conditions and stresses that Pareto efficiency occurs whatever the assignment of legal rights. The same tenet also applies to long-term contractual relationships. In each period of an 'ideal' long-term contract, prices and joint profits can be computed going backward from the last to the first short-term contract. Asymmetric information cannot represent a threat to the implementation of the contract, as new information will be shared and renegotiation could modify the division of the surplus. Even in case of the emergence of unforeseen contingencies or *free-riding* behaviour in the implementation of the contractual clauses, an efficient outcome is guaranteed. In fact, an 'internal enforcement' such as a punishment or a reward would be implemented.[2]

The New Institutional Economics complements this view, by underlining the importance of communication and negotiation costs involved in large-number of settings. Failure to agree on the 'internal enforcement' of the distribution of 'gains from trade' is traced back to positive transaction costs due to *exogenous* causes of uncertainty: (1) bounded computational capacity; (2) the impossibility to foresee (and assign appropriate probabilities to) all contingencies due to incomplete information – that is, the lack of information on goods, which corresponds to missing markets; (3) the impossibility to foresee (and assign appropriate probabilities to) all contingencies due to incomplete knowledge – that is, the problem of incomplete identification of all characteristics of the promised actions in each state of the world.[3] All these possible causes of uncertainty are related to 'bounded rationality', defined by Simon as the 'rational choice that takes into account limitations of both knowledge and computational capacity'. Whether or not the negotiation will be successful, and – if it is – the way that gains from trade are divided, depend on the transaction costs caused by opportunities for a *free-riding* behaviour linked to 'bounded rationality'.

To highlight these impediments to efficient bargaining, the Coase Theorem is rephrased by including positive transaction costs: *while the voluntary actions by the parties would succeed in optimally devising and implementing all the contract clauses, including the optimal definition and assignment of legal rights, positive transaction costs cause the outcome of a bargaining to be inefficient.* Yet, the category of 'positive transaction costs' is not only too vague and comprehensive, but basically deceptive, because it makes *exogenous* a series of possible causes of inefficiency actually stemming from the strategic interaction which develops in the writing and/or the implementation of the contract by the parties. In fact, the Coase Theorem with positive transaction costs overlooks the fact that strategic behaviour may cause agreements to fail even when transaction costs are zero.[4]

The Coasean account of the process leading to Pareto efficiency on the contract curve can then be contended, as bargaining among parties is not allowed to play any role in the determination of the market equilibrium. Just as in the standard Arrow–Debreu general equilibrium model, price-taking parties are supposed to negotiate a series of transactions belonging to the 'core' according to an equilibrium prices' vector that seems to exist *a priori*.[5] The unwelcome consequence is that the Pareto efficient equilibrium by no means depends on the bargaining about the surplus division.

Yet, differently from the Arrow–Debreu model of perfect competition, parties are not price-takers, but set prices by bargaining on the division of the surplus. The real world neatly witnesses that incomplete or imperfect knowledge surrounding contracts are most of the times to be traced back to the strategic environment. Since the parties tend to disguise asymmetric information and/or emit false signals (about their 'types', their actions, the evaluation of the assets, and so on), they are often unable to initially specify or subsequently renegotiate those clauses which could improve on the efficiency of the series of transactions involved. Most causes of coordination failure are *endogenous* to the bargaining process by which the efficiency and distributive outcomes of any contract are determined. Thus, both the parties and a court may find it difficult to detect the precise nature of the strategic environment and assess whether uncertainty or opportunism affects the implementation of a contract.

Contractual relationships where efficiency maximization is impeded by some information failure will be hereafter considered under the heading of 'endogenous contractual incompleteness'. One of the most controversial questions in law and economics concerns the theoretical foundations for empowering courts or regulators to look after strategic interactions the outcome of which is suboptimal. The aim of this chapter is to show that the analysis of long-term contracts in game form helps elucidate whether and when courts can solve endogenous contractual incompleteness. Solution concepts elaborated by game theory will then be adapted to cope with 'inefficient' outcomes of long-term contracts. It will be investigated where to draw the dividing line between contracts that are 'completable' by courts and contracts that are 'not completable' by courts, thus requiring a regulation scheme. In the former case, courts can complete contracts by directly interfering with both allocative efficiency and distribution of gains, that is by enforcing legal rules and procedures that reduce transaction costs and/or facilitate an improvement in the allocation of legal rights. In the latter case, regulators have to provide a frame aimed at preventing strategic interaction to cause a contract to be bound to a suboptimal implementation.

*The New Palgrave Dictionary of Economics and Law* classifies endogenous contractual incompleteness as follows:

> Recent theory shows that contractual incompleteness is often endogenous. Even when transaction costs are zero, parties will not write complete contracts either because they cannot observe relevant economic variables, because they cannot verify those variables to courts, or because they prefer not to disclose relevant information about themselves (their 'types').[6]

In this chapter, each of these three cases of endogenous contractual incompleteness will be given a game-theoretic – sequential or multi-period – representation. After the hypotheses of rational behaviour used in game theory have been summarized in the section 'Contracts in game form', the second and the third case are dealt with in the following two sections. In the section 'Contractual incompleteness as "non-verifiability" ', a sequential game is used to cast light on opportunistic behaviour stemming from incomplete knowledge not by the parties but by a court, as formalized by the New Property Rights Approach (hereafter, NPRA). In the section on 'Contractual incompleteness as asymmetric information' a repeated game is used to cast light on opportunistic behaviour stemming from asymmetric information, due to the incomplete information of one of the parties, who does not know the other party's 'type'. It is shown that in both cases of contractual incompleteness, possible opportunistic behaviour by parties can be counteracted by a court solving the problem of incomplete information. Finally, in the section 'Contractual incompleteness as absence of common beliefs' ignorance about relevant economic variables – the first case in the aforementioned definition of endogenous contractual incompleteness – is analysed. Different from the previous two cases, this is a case in which a court cannot complete a contract, as there is no way in which the parties' strategies and beliefs could be consistently aligned. However, it is shown that the parties, by using the game-theoretic solution concept of 'mixed strategies', may reduce the occurrence of litigation in the implementation of the contract. The final section provides the concluding remarks.

## Contracts in game form: the hypotheses of rational behaviour

In order to discuss contractual relationships in game form, I recall some background hypotheses of game theory when only two players are involved. Hypothesis 1: *mutual knowledge of the game* (i.e. the rules of the game, the payoff structure, etc.). Hypothesis 2: *mutual knowledge of the players' Bayesian rationality* (i.e. their behaviour conforms to the axioms of the Von Neumann–Morgenstern expected utility theory, so articulated: (1) the two players are rational; (2) each player knows that the other player is rational).[7]

In the following, it will be apparent that in some strategic interaction these two hypotheses are not sufficient to obtain an efficient solution of non-cooperative games. In game-theoretic terms, the equilibrium cannot be derived just from the two hypotheses of 'mutual knowledge of the game' and 'mutual knowledge of Bayesian rationality of the players'. These two hypotheses on the one side, and a Nash equilibrium on the other side, may not match. The efficient solution requires that not only strategies but also beliefs are in equilibrium. For strategies and beliefs to be consistently aligned: (1) each player who happens to move at a non-singleton decision node must have a probability on the other player's move; (2) each player's probability distributions on the other player's conjectures are to be correlated, so that 'subgame perfection' is respected and a perfect Bayesian equilibrium is reached.[8] Briefly, there is an 'alignment problem'. Just as in the Keynes' beauty contest, the beliefs' formation depends not only on objective information but also on the conjectures on the opponent's beliefs, so that the problem of infinite regression arises.

In order to overcome this difficulty in building expectations on the opponent's strategic behaviour, Aumann[9] has derived a formal set up by which a Nash equilibrium in strategies and beliefs is reached if and only if players with common information are mutually capable having expectations on the other player's strategies and beliefs whenever he performs his move. In other words, from common priors, common posteriors beliefs ensue. Thus, to reach the Bayesian (Nash) perfect equilibrium, hypothesis 3 of rationality has to be added: *mutual knowledge of common beliefs.*

## Contractual incompleteness as 'non-verifiability'

In the strand of literature on incomplete contracts derived from the NPRA,[10] the parties are assumed 'unbounded rational', in the sense that they are capable foreseeing all possible future contingencies at every stage and under all circumstances. The parties' obligations under all contingent states should then be satisfactorily described *ex ante*, and the *ex post* eventual renegotiation of the *ex ante* agreement should not be a problem.[11] However, the negotiation might be endangered by the impossibility of a precise description of the contract's reciprocal obligations. This assumption put forward by the NPRA should not appear in contradiction with the 'unbounded rationality' of the parties. Also strategic interaction among 'unbounded' rational individuals may be affected by imperfect information and/or knowledge. Despite 'unbounded rationality', it may happen that the actions taken by the parties implementing a long-term contract are *observable* but not *ex post verifiable* by a court, and the impossibility of 'external enforcement' makes opportunistic strategies profitable.

This case of endogenous contractual incompleteness then consists in an inefficient implementation of the contract due to opportunistic behaviour, as some actions and/or contingent clauses regulating the contract cannot be described *ex ante* and verified *ex post.*[12] In game-theoretic terms, the contract is not 'subgame

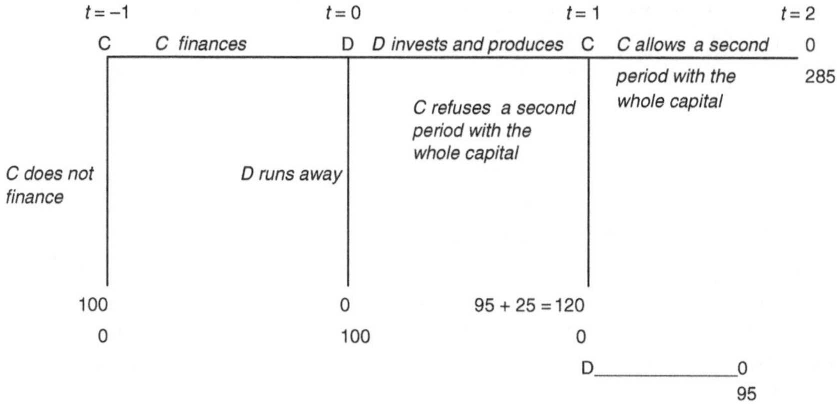


*Figure 11.1a* Long-term contract as a sequential game (non-verifiability is embedded).

perfect', so that the players cannot complete the contract due to the difficulty of enforcing a commitment not to renegotiate.

I will now analyse a contract as a sequential game among two parties, which stylizes a long-term contract in which non-verifiability is embedded. Since in the NPRA framework the parties have complete, albeit probabilistic, information about the future states of the world, they know the rules of the game, as well as payoffs and strategies available to them. The parties of the sequential game then satisfy the hypotheses of rationality 1 and 2. However, non-verifiability determines contractual incompleteness, with parties unable to *ex ante* specify – and consequently *ex post* renegotiate – those clauses which could improve on the efficiency of transactions.

Assume that a credit institution receives at time $t = -1$ a demand by an investor for financing a capital good of value equal to 100 which lasts two periods (see Figures 11.1a). The capital return $R$ – certain and known only by the two parties – is $R_1 = 95$ at $t = 1$, and $R_2 = 2\mathrm{R}_1$ at $t = 2$, and the interest rate to be paid to the creditor is $r = 20\%$ per year, while the capital good has liquidation values – certain and known only to the two parties – of $L = 50$ at the end of the first period and $L = 0$ at the end of the second period (for the sake of simplicity, the discount rate is zero). Moreover, whether or not the investor does use the capital good in his plant can be verified by a court at $t = 1$ (when its value is positive) but not at $t = 2$ (when its value is nil).

At $t = -1$, the credit institution (C) has to decide to finance the investment. If it does, at $t = 0$ the credit 100 is given to the investor. Being the debtor (D), the investor has now two possible actions. First, to run away with the finance, so that the game ends with the following payoffs: 0 for the creditor and 100 for the debtor. Yet, a court may enforce the debt restitution, being able at $t = 1$ to detect whether the capital good has been utilized in the debtor's plant. Therefore, I rule out this case. Second, to buy the capital good, put it in his production process, get the first-period product, and sell it. Granted that the certain returns $R_1 = 95$ and $R_2 = 190$ are mutual knowledge between parties since the beginning of the game, the debtor would ask the creditor to wait for debt restitution till the end of the second period, in order to avoid liquidating the capital and exploiting it also in the second period. Were the creditor to agree on the concession of the line of credit at time $t = -1$ with a promise of complete debt remission at time $t = 2$, his credit concession would be exposed to the *ex post* opportunism of the debtor. At the end of the second period the court is unable to detect whether or not the capital has been utilized, as the capital value is nil and there may be no sign of utilization in the debtor's plant. Hence, the debtor's rational action at time $t = 2$ would be to keep the whole returns ($R_1 + R_2 = 285$).

Therefore, by 'backward induction' rational behaviour prevents the creditor from subscribing to a two-period contract with the whole utilization of the capital good. The credit institution cannot accept the debtor's 'non-credible' promise to postpone debt restitution at the end of the second period, when the needed amount of returns will accrue to him. Since at time $t = 1$ the creditor cannot trust the debtor because production – and then returns – are not verifiable, in order to avoid the risk of being deceived by the debtor, the creditor refuses full capital utilization during the second period. The creditor instead asks the debtor to sell the product and to refund his debt inclusive of the one-period interest payment (120) at the end of the first period. The restitution can be done by means of his monetary returns ($R_1 = 95$) plus the return from the liquidation of one half of the residual capital value ($L = 25$). The debtor could then use the remaining half of the capital good and get the second period returns ($R_2 = 85$). However, the implementation of the contract would be inefficient, as the capital utilization would be partial and thus total returns would not be maximized.

Since the capital liquidation clause is verifiable and then enforceable, a two-period contract based on an internal enforcement can be devised, with the debtor committed to liquidate one half of the capital at the end of the first period. Accordingly, at $t = 1$, being afraid that the debtor might renege on the commitment to give back the financing, the creditor moves downward (see Figure 11.1a). By refusing to allow the utilization of the whole capital for a second period, he asks for the restitution of the finance, inclusive of the one-period interest payment. After this complete debt plus interest restitution (120) at the end of the first period, the debtor will keep utilizing the other 50% of the capital good at $t = 2$, and get the second-period return of 95 (see the lower branch in Figure 11.1a).

This mechanism of 'internal enforcement' determines an inefficient solution, as at $t = 1$ the capital is partially liquidated, despite the fact that its full utilization at $t = 2$ would yield a higher return. Indeed, it is only capable of bringing the contract to a *second best* outcome. Since the investment project has a production function with non-decreasing returns (being $R_2 = 2R_1$), the *first best* contract would stem from optimal capital utilization along the two-period contract, which would yield to the investor the return, net of debt plus interest restitution, of 145 (see Figure 11.1b), while the *second best* contract yields a return of 95. The reason for

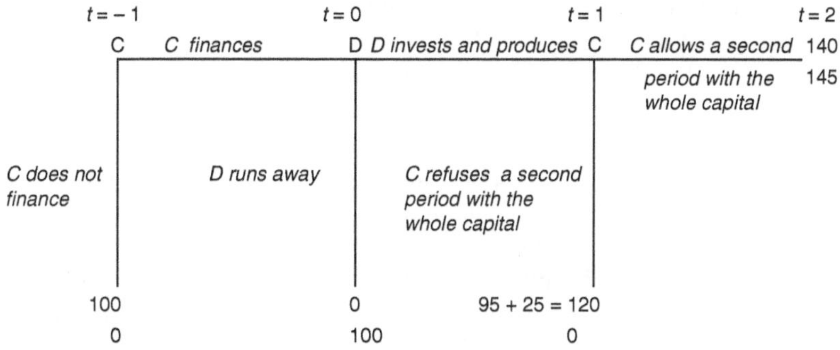


*Figure 11.1b* Opportunism or cooperation in a long-term contract.

the inefficient outcome is that the strategic environment is such that at $t = 0$ the debtor plays forward, but at $t = 2$ – were the creditor disposed to postpone debt restitution and to allow a second period with the whole capital – the debtor could pay back nothing, thus keeping, not the return (net of debt plus interest restitution) of 145, but both returns (285). In fact, a court would be unable to disguise this opportunistic behaviour. At the end of the second period there is no way to verify the debtor's return, while no debt restitution through the physical capital is possible as the value of capital has become zero.

However, game theory suggests that a court is in the position to improve on the contract. The crucial question is how to have at the same time the optimal assignment of legal rights for the debtor – so that he could utilize the full amount of capital in the second period – and the protection of the legal rights of the creditor – that is, to impede opportunistic behaviour by the debtor. Let us analyse this question in game theoretic terms. The contractual relationship is a dynamic game of complete information, but deprived by a possible Bayesian Nash equilibrium because of *ex post* non-verifiability. Although parties have common priors because hypotheses 1 and 2 are fulfilled, the efficient solution would come out only if common beliefs could be determined. Yet, in the case of subjective probabilities a direct causality nexus between an objective event and the subjective probability which refers to it is far from being granted. The problem is that in this game the players cannot mutually hold common conjectures about the other player behaving as a cooperator in the second period of the game, so that hypothesis 3 of common beliefs cannot be fulfilled.

Figure 11.1b shows the outcome of this contractual relationship when the solution of this sequential game is transformed from *second best* to *first best.* If the creditor could be shielded from opportunistic behaviour, he would not ask for the partial liquidation of the capital, so that full capital utilization during both periods would allow the debtor to give the finance back with the two interest payments $(100 + 40 = 140)$ while keeping the remaining part of returns (145). The following question can then be posed: is it possible for a court to achieve the efficient outcome, by completing the contract with clauses capable of enforcing this optimal outcome in the contractual relationship?

In Figure 11.1b, the sequential game featuring the contract replicates in its structure the 'Take or Leave' game (TOL). Just as 'backward induction' dictates to the first player of TOL game to not enter the game, the financing should be refused by the creditor due to possible opportunistic behaviour by the investor. If the first player moves 'forward', this is an out-of-equilibrium move that is considered a 'non-rational' act. Yet, contrary to the Aumann assumption that a rational player always plays equilibrium moves with certainty, it can be maintained that out-of-equilibrium moves should be admitted.[13] The occurrence of such a move implies that in the TOL game hypothesis 2 of rationality has been endogenously eliminated.[14] In fact, by playing 'forward' at the start of the TOL game, a player is rationally signalling to the other player the need to change both his strategy and his beliefs.

It has been demonstrated that the *first best* solution of the TOL game can be obtained conditional on a system of beliefs to exist such that the game is 'rationalizable': that is, weakly dominated strategies and iterated weakly dominated strategies can be eliminated, and the first player's probability distribution over the second player's moves makes it rational for both players to move 'forward' at each stage of the game.[15] To apply this reasoning to the credit contract in Figure 11.1b entails that its payoff structure must be consistent with the appropriate system of beliefs required for the first best solution. Just as in a 'rationalizable' TOL game, the creditor's probability distribution over the debtor's moves must make it rational for both players to move 'forward' at each stage of the game and achieve the *first best* outcome with whole capital utilization and payoffs of 140 for the creditor and 145 for the debtor.

However, it is unlikely that a credit contract is devised with such an appropriate payoff structure that the system of beliefs allows the *first best* solution to be reached without the creditor playing 'down' at time $t = 1$ in order not to expose himself to opportunistic behaviour by the debtor. Most of the times, the endogenous contractual incompleteness caused by *ex post* non-verifiability by a court cannot be solved by the 'internal enforcement' warranted by the appropriate system of beliefs. For the switch from the *second best* to the *first best* outcome of the credit contract to be obtained, the game-theoretic solution of 'rationalizability' has to be implemented by an 'external enforcement'.

Given that the creditor does not want to sign a contract by which the debtor is allowed full utilization of the capital at time $t = 1$, the debtor may ask a court to appoint a third party with the task of correcting the contract, by computing in accordance with the parties the payoff structure which is coherent with the system of beliefs implied by 'rationalizability'. In game-theoretic terms, the task of this third party is to determine the payoff structure capable of bridging the gap between the system of beliefs and the efficient solution. Once the 'correct' sequence of actions and payments is common knowledge between the court and the parties, the sanctioning power of the court will no longer be weakened by the *non-verifiability* of the contract. The creditor will be protected against the debtor's opportunistic behaviour by the credible threat of enforcing with a pecuniary sanction the *first best* solution, and the debtor will be allowed to efficiently use the capital.

## Contractual incompleteness as asymmetric information

A long-term contract between two parties should not be conceived *in vacuo*, that is as a bilateral monopoly, but as part of the market's search for the efficient equilibrium position or for a higher utility possibility frontier. In fact, the parties of a contract are market-takers, who continuously modify and reshuffle the market environment in which contractual relationships take place by introducing technological changes. The economics of information has convincingly demonstrated that individuals and firms are rent-seekers who compete among themselves and struggle to maximize their share of surplus by bargaining and innovation.[16] The theory of contestable markets maintains that a credible threat of entry is a sufficient condition for price competition to annul monopoly rents, due to the ubiquity of 'outside options' that are substitutes with respect to the current contractual relationship.[17] Perfectly contestable markets allow relaxation of the restriction on the number of firms, as the terms by which a bilateral transaction is set necessarily depend on the value that both parties attribute to the involved object or action *and* on whether there are outsiders eager to outcompete one of the two parties.[18] In a joint venture between a buyer and a seller of an input, when the demand for the input goes up, the higher the increase in the enforcement rent asked by the seller (for instance, a higher price of the input, to finance the capital endowment) the higher will be the price cut asked by a buyer who is in the position to exert the threat of exit towards an outside option. Generally speaking, the more the market conditions are similar to perfect competition, the lower the exit costs.[19] The conclusion is that outside options are central in the determination of the strategic setting of a PD game, because they heavily impinge on the bargaining power by which each party points to gaining an enforcement rent.

The problem is that contractual relationships are often endangered by 'bounded rationality' plaguing the strategic environment. In the long-term contract studied in this section, a revision of the parties' reciprocal obligations is needed for exogenous reasons (an increase in market demand), but endogenous contractual incompleteness is created by asymmetric information: one party does not disclose relevant information about itself (his 'type'), so that the renegotiation bargaining is stuck by the possibility of opportunistic behaviour by exit towards an outside option.

A typical game expressing the possibility of opportunism in a long-term contract is the Finitely Repeated Prisoners' Dilemma (hereafter, FRPD). In Figure 11.2, where the typical PD payoff matrix ($y > x > w > z$) in extensive form sketches the single period of a long-term contract, imperfect information is conveyed by the fact that player II – in making a move at a non-singleton information node – is unaware of the initial move by player I (left: cooperation; right: defection). In a joint venture between a buyer and a seller for the production of an input which has

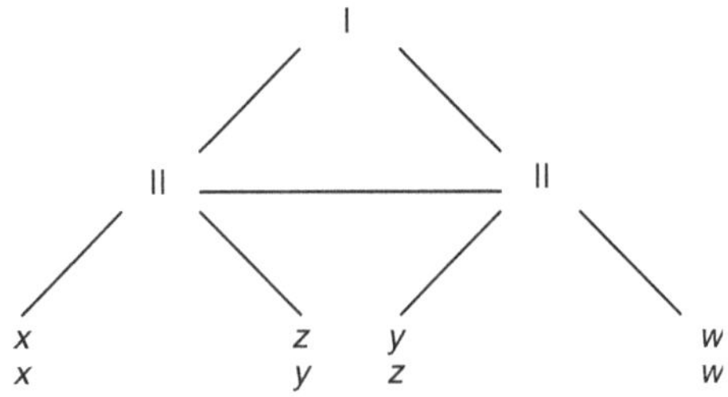


*Figure 11.2* Exit strategies.

| | | II | | |
|---|---|---|---|---|
| | | C | D | E |
| | C | x, x | z, y | m, m |
| I | C | x, x | z, y | m, m |
| | E | m, m | m, m | m, m |

*Figure 11.3* An example.

the payoff structure of Figure 11.2, assume that one of the two following 'types' applies to player I (for instance, the buyer): (1) the buyer struggles to maximize his share of surplus and looks for an outside option incorporating more technological change; (2) the buyer believes that no outside option would yield him a higher share, so that he will comply with the current joint venture that guarantees him a fair share.

Although 'backward induction' shows that in a FRPD game actions could be performed 'with guile', incomplete information may make cooperation sustainable. In fact, as a well-known analysis has shown,[20] in this game the cooperation failure explained by 'backward induction' can be overcome by the 'Harsanyi doctrine'.[21] The uncertainty on the opponent's type is interpreted by Harsanyi as a state of incomplete information which can be transformed to a state of imperfect information about the payoffs.[22] Nature is assigned the task of choosing each player's strategy among his vector of strategies, whereas the second player sets up expectations on the probability that the first player possesses one of the available strategies. Nature then communicates to player I whether he is an 'innovator' player adopting the 'maximizer' strategy, or a 'conservative' player adopting the 'Tit for Tat' (TfT) strategy. Player II has the information that player I follows the TfT strategy with probability p and the 'maximizer' strategy with probability $1 - p$. It has been demonstrated that cooperation applies up to the second-last of $n$ periods; for instance, with $n = 3$, the two players cooperate in the first two periods if the following condition is satisfied: $1 + p + z(1 - p) + py > y + z + py$.[23]

However, the inclusion in a FRPD game of the strategy of 'exit' (and join an outside option) may make the long-term contractual relationship no longer sustainable as soon as an outside option shows up. The consideration of the strategy of exit, in addition to the usual defection and cooperation strategies, consists in both players being eager to dodge the reciprocal *hold-up* externality which is typical of any joint venture. Formally, a row and a column, expressing the payoff ($m$) of the exit strategy, are to be added (see Figure 11.3). The payoffs of the exit strategy will be higher than the suboptimal equilibrium ($w, w$) corresponding to both players bearing the costs of free-riding, but lower than the costs of cooperative behaviour leading to the Paretoequilibrium. A sufficiently low exit cost – so that exit dominates defection – crowds out this latter strategy, so that in our FRPD game the exit strategy replaces the defection strategy.

As said above, assume that in our bilateral joint venture between a buyer and a seller of an input, an outside option is considered in relation to an increase in final demand which requires a higher production level of the input. The seller might ask for a higher price of the input due to the increase needed in productive capacity. In this case, the buyer will fear a hold-up by the seller, as the seller's investment is financed by the mark-up on the input's cost. Alternatively, the buyer might find an alternative, technologically more advanced and thus more profitable, joint venture. In this other case, the seller has to bear the burden of sunk costs and thus fears a hold-up by the buyer.

Let us then analyse how the buyer (B) and the seller (S) evaluate their strategies. In relation to B's exit strategy, S has to compute the payoffs relative to each of the two possible technological types of B, in order to decide whether or not to ask for a higher price of the input. To this aim, S determines the extent of market competition, that is the probability that the outside option of the buyer has a high or a low opportunity cost. Given this probability distribution on the B's types, S might decide either to pursue the aggressive strategy by asking for a higher price, or to keep on with the current price. On the other hand, the buyer's exit (towards the outside option) or cooperative strategy depends on his conjectures about these two possible strategies by the seller. In turn, the seller has to decide – for each of the two possible types of the buyer – whether the latter is switching to an outside option or cooperates, depending on his conjectures on B's belief about each of the two possible strategies available to him.

Each stage of our FRPD game can then be formalized by the two payoff matrixes of Figure 11.4a and 11.4b, respectively determined by one of the two possible technological types of the buyer. The consideration of the exit strategy (E) towards the technologically more advanced joint venture corresponds to the higher payoff for the buyer's strategy E in Figure 11.4a (while the defection strategy of S still consists in asking for a higher price). The level of exit costs can be decisive in B's choice of abandoning or keeping the joint venture with S. If the opportunity cost of B's outside option is low, B will be the new technological type A1 (see Figure 11.4a), while if it is high, B will be the technological type A2 in the joint venture with S (see Figure 11.4b).

(a)

| | | S: C | S: D |
|---|---|---|---|
| B | C | 4, 0 | 2, 1 |
| B | E | 6, 0 | 4, –1 |

(b)

| | | S: C | S: D |
|---|---|---|---|
| B | C | 4, 0 | 2, 1 |
| B | E | 2, 0 | 0, –1 |

*Figure 11.4* Technological types of the buyers.

By assumption, S does not know whether the opportunity cost of B's outside option is low or high. Thus, this is a game with incomplete information, as hypothesis 1 – common knowledge of the payoffs and thus of the rules of the game – is not fulfilled. However, the 'Harsanyi doctrine' allows switching from incomplete information to imperfect information, so that a common knowledge on the possible payoff matrices can be reached. For each of B's possible types (the low or the high opportunity cost), S has the possibility of setting up a probability distribution over the states of the world relative to B's action – the exit strategy (E) to switch, or the cooperative strategy (C) not to switch, to the alternative joint venture.

Therefore, after that Nature communicates to each player his type and the other player sets up the probability distribution on the various types, each player is aware of the common knowledge of the alternative joint ventures. S has to decide whether to adopt a free-riding strategy – by asking a higher price after the request of a higher production level – or comply with the present price. As shown above, to each possible type and to each strategy of exit or no exit for B, and to each price strategy for S, Figure 11.4a and 11.4b associate different payoff values. In case of cooperation, the FRPD will end up in the division of the quasi-rents according to the input's current price.

From the payoff matrixes it is easy to see that one should not look for a perfect Bayesian Nash equilibrium. There is a dominant strategy for each player that renders irrelevant any conjecture on the opponent's strategy. Hence, the problem of alignment of the two players' beliefs does not apply. In Figure 11.4a and 11.4b, B makes his decision independently from S's choice. Whatever strategy S follows, if B has type A1 his dominant strategy is 'exit' (E), and if B has type A2, his dominant strategy is 'cooperation' (C). Whereas S will use strategy C if the probability that B's cooperation strategy is $p < 50\%$ and strategy D if the probability that B's cooperation strategy is $p > 50\%$. Therefore, the outcome of the game ultimately depends on B's technological type, that is on whether B thinks that the opportunity cost of the outside option is low or high. If B's expectation is that this cost is low, the dominant equilibrium is (E, C), as S prefers to cooperate and not to raise the input price, but B is a straightforward maximizer and chooses the defection strategy; in the opposite case, the dominant equilibrium is (C, D), as S asks for a higher price of the input and B cooperates.

However, the implementation of this contract could be stuck by a long-lasting litigation between the parties. In case B decides to exit and start the new joint venture, S may sue B in the expectation that a court – by virtue of perfect verifiability – could force B to renounce the outside option and keep implementing the existing contract. This litigation can be evaluated from the alternative vantage points.

On the one hand, it can be maintained that a court empowered with the mandate to make a decision on the continuation or the termination of the contractual relationship, while defending the seller's right to see the contract honoured, should also take into account the improvement in efficiency warranted by the new joint venture. In this case, the payoff structure suggests that the court's verdict will be in favour of the surplus warranted by the outside option (see Figure 11.4a), which dominates the surplus of the current contractual relationship (see Figure 11.4b).

On the other hand, society may think that the equilibrium solution should not stem from the high or low opportunity cost of the outside option, but from a decision on which contract maximizes social welfare. In deciding on efficient coordination, that is whether the current or a new joint venture has to be preferred, the court relies on the game-theoretic solution that turns out from the payoff structure of Figure 11.4a, but has also to consider that the termination of the long-term relationship with the buyer may be very costly to the supplier, whose profitability might be severely endangered by the termination of the contract. In the second case, the court could ask the seller to revise the strategy of leaving constant the price of the input and promise the continuation of the contract under the condition that the seller makes this price as low as possible to guarantee to the buyer the same increase in return stemming from the technological improvement brought about by the outside option (in the payoff structures of Figure 11.4a, the increase amounts to 4). The court should appoint a qualified committee to certify that the technological conditions of the supplier are verifiable and such that the supplier may catch up.

Provided that the committee's report is positive, the court should decide in favour of the continuation of the contract. It also follows that in case B would not be willing to renounce switching to the new joint venture, damage penalties should be inflicted on B by the court. The court should also cope with the case in which the continuation of the contract is decided, but S fails to provide the input at the same quality and price of the outside option. To this extent, a clause must be inserted in the contract, stating the termination of the contract with a relevant pecuniary sanction to be paid by S to B. On the contrary, if the report maintains that the seller is unable to catch up, the court declares the exit towards another joint venture Pareto-superior with respect to the current joint venture and B is allowed to opt out and set up the 'new' joint venture. The court then solves the contractual impasse by authorizing the new joint venture and recognizing a compensation to be paid to the other party. The amount of this compensation should correspond to the foregone surplus of S which is compatible with B still finding it profitable to enter the outside option.

A well-known result in game theory is that in a bargaining between a buyer and a seller – whenever the strategic interaction is characterized by private information – there is no mechanism that is *first best* efficient.[24] Yet, when the strategic interaction between a buyer and a seller takes the shape of a long-term contract corresponding to a FRPD game with an outside option, the *second best* solution can be avoided. As was shown in this section, the *first best* outcome can be achieved by asking a court to decide on the authorization of the new contract with compensation for the losing party.

## Contractual incompleteness as absence of common beliefs

Let us finally discuss endogenous contractual incompleteness due to the impossibility of observing relevant economic variables. In the section 'Contracts in game form' it was noted that some strategic interactions impede the players of non-cooperative games from having dominant strategies, so that not only strategies but also beliefs generated by the strategies must be consistently aligned. In order to obtain a solution, the equilibrium cannot be derived just from the two hypotheses of 'mutual knowledge of the game' and 'mutual knowledge of Bayesian rationality of the players'. Aumann (1976) has indicated the condition under which the gap between these two hypotheses on the one side, and a Nash equilibrium on the other side, can be filled by hypothesis 3, that is *mutual knowledge of common beliefs*.

The problem in abiding by hypothesis 3 comes up in the proceeding of this section, where I will deal with endogenous incompleteness due to the parties' ignorance of relevant variables. Figure 11.5 shows the payoff structure of a game in which hypotheses 1 and 2 hold, the players have incentives to reach a cooperative solution, but their preferences may not match. This game has three Nash equilibria: two in 'pure' strategy and one in 'mixed strategy'.

With reference to the payoff structure of Figure 11.5, let us analyse a strategic interaction such as a long-term contract between two companies – a franchisor and a franchisee – about a line of products with a well-established demand. All products are sold in a market of monopolistic competition, and the goal to outcompete rivals is pursued by means of product differentiation based on the quality–price mix of the brand. Let us introduce the following assumptions: (1) the franchise contract is incentive compatible, as far as in each period at least a small return (payoff 1) accrues to the franchisee and at least the royalty fee (payoff 1) paid by the franchisee accrues to the franchisor; (2) all production costs are borne by the franchisor and are equal to the royalty fee; (3) since the franchisee is directly involved in some phases of the productive process and entertains tight relationships with the market, a contractual clause states that the franchisee shares with the franchisor the right to decide on the quality–price mix; (4) a conflict of interest is embedded in the cooperative enterprise, to the extent that in case of opposite conjectures on the market preference the opinion of just one of the two parties has to prevail: if the company making the decision is the franchisor, the products are sold at the high quality–high price mix, because the franchisor is mainly interested in his

| | | I | |
|---|---|---|---|
| | | A | B |
| | C | 3, 1 | 0, 0 |
| II | D | 0, 0 | 1, 3 |

*Figure 11.5* Who has the perfect information about market's preferences?

market reputation; if it is the franchisee, the products are sold at the low quality–low price mix, because the franchisee mainly points to sales maximization; (5) the franchise contract also states that net returns[25] accrue to the company winning the decision on the quality–price mix, that is the party that has succeeded in convincing the other party to agree on its own conjecture about the market's preferences on quality and price.

Given these assumptions, at each turn of a game with payoff structure in Figure 11.5, each company does its best to convince the other company to possess the 'correct' information about the market's preference in order to be decisive on the choice about the quality–price mix of the products. If the parties are unable to agree, they end up in one of two (0, 0) cells, which correspond to the coordination failure, indicating that no production will be made (this no-production outcome obviously leads to the termination of the franchise contract). Otherwise, in case of agreement as shown in the positive-payoff cells, the contract is implemented after each company has tried to foresee to what extent the other company's guess on the market's preference could find confirmation in the market and one party has finally succeeded in convincing the other party to converge on its own conjecture about the market's preference for a high or for a low quality–price mix.

This latter aspect of the agreement is crucial, as it makes the contractual relationship vulnerable to litigation in case the market's preference does not correspond to the chosen quality–price. There are two causes explaining why the products fail to match the market's preference: (1) an objective impossibility, such as 'hard uncertainty' about the market's quality–price preference; (2) an opportunistic behaviour, such as a mis-representation of the quality–price mix preferred by the market, to which the company was induced by its eagerness to be the company making the decision and catch the highest payoff.[26] Unfortunately, most of the times the company which has complied is unable to observe the relevant economic variable consisting of the reasoning put forward by the other company in making its conjecture and choice. It is then impossible to verify, both by a company and a court, whether or not the failure is due to opportunistic behaviour. When one party disastrously fails, the other party will certainly sue, but it will face many difficulties to prove its allegations because no objective evidence of misbehaviour might exist. The conclusion is that when the products fail to match the market's preferences it is very likely that the parties will be stuck in a litigation process.

The sufficient condition to avoid litigation is that the companies come up with the same beliefs about the market's preference before the quality–price mix and the production are decided. In game-theoretic terms, the requirements of subgame perfection are to be strengthened by explicitly analysing the players' beliefs, so that both strategies and beliefs be mutually consistent and a perfect Bayesian equilibrium is determined. Following the Aumann's (1987) rationale, each player was *a priori* born with an 'innate' subjective probability distribution, and is able to correct his own beliefs by getting in touch with conjectures that the other player has derived from his own information. By mutually communicating the new information and exchanging their probability distributions about possible lotteries, individuals form posterious beliefs. Hypothesis 3 might then be added to the two hypotheses of mutual knowledge: since the players have mutual knowledge of having common priors, they also have mutual knowledge of having common posterious beliefs. If this reasoning is followed, individuals entertain equal beliefs, by which they are led to a rational solution according to Aumann's theory of 'correlated equilibria'.

The problem is, however, that the two companies have a conflict of interest about their conjectures on whether the high or the low quality–price mix is preferred by the market. According to assumption (4), the franchisor is led by his preference to put more confidence in the probability of the event high quality–price mix and the franchisee in the probability of the event low quality–price mix. Savage (1954) maintains that a belief does not merely consist in a probabilistic distribution based on objective data, but the probability that an individual attributes to a certain event is also influenced by his preference. It is a tautological truth that from different information, different probabilities are deduced, but this does not warrant Aumann's conclusion – the implications of which are completely different – that from identical information the same probability distributions are obtained. Although the companies have common priors, each company might follow a different logical process. Indeed, following Savage, each company's subjective orientation towards the quality–price mix might supersede the objective information about the market's preference. Hence, from common information the two companies might infer different posterious beliefs, so that it is unlikely that they will agree on which quality–price mix, being the one preferred by the market, should be chosen for the products. If both companies stand firm and are unwilling to comply with the other company's conjecture about the market preference, each of them will stick to its preferred 'pure strategy' equilibrium. Therefore, the use of Aumann's theory of 'correlated equilibria' to force the parties to converge on the same quality–price mix does not avoid the potential for litigation on which party has to comply with the other one.

Yet, there is another way of using the Aumann procedure, which could in many cases allow the two companies to overcome the conflict of interest. The two companies could get rid of their opposite conjectures and apply Aumann's theory of 'correlated equilibria' directly to a set of beliefs that is mutually compatible between the parties. In the payoff structure of Figure 11.5 such a set of beliefs is the Nash equilibrium in 'mixed strategies'. It will now be shown that the 'mixed strategies' solution is a sensible way to avoid *ex post* litigation in case of failure to correctly forecaste the market preference. The companies should exploit the 'neutral' decision that is offered by the 'mixed strategies' solution by looking for the quality–price mix which possibly will result from their randomization. That is, the companies should attribute the 'high' and 'low' quality–price mix, respectively, to each of the two possible positive cases of a coordinated result from randomization of Figure 11.5: A, C and B, D.

Since the two players have common priors, each player is assumed to be capable of setting up a probability distribution over the other player's conjectures and their beliefs will turn out to be correlated. Given the payoff structure of Figure 11.5, to comply with expected utility maximization, the randomization by which EU (A) = EU (B) and EU (C) = EU (D) is computed by finding the optimal probability with which to choose each strategy:

$$\text{I (over II): } p_2 \times 3 + p_1 \times 0 = p_2 \times 0 + p_1 \times 1$$

$$\text{that is: } 1/4 \times 3 + 3/4 \times 0 = 1/4 \times 0 + 3/4 \times 1$$

$$\text{II (over I)}: p_1 \times 3 + p_2 \times 0 = p_1 \times 0 + p_2 \times 1$$

$$\text{that is: } 3/4 \times 1 + 1/4 \times 0 = 3/4 \times 0 + 1/4 \times 3$$

The 'mixed strategies' equilibrium solution corresponds to probabilities (3/4, 1/4). There is only one value for $p_1$ and one value for $p_2$ which makes A and B and C and D, respectively, optimal for each player. I chooses A and B with probabilities 1/4 and 3/4, respectively, and II chooses C and D with probabilities 3/4 and 1/4, respectively. According to Aumann (1987), the players' beliefs are correlated because probabilities $p_1$ and $p_2$ take the same values in each player's conjectures over the other player's move (see the equations). Thus, each player has common prior probability assessment over the event that will determine consequence A or consequence B, so that both players have the same belief regarding what player I will do. The same holds with regard to consequences C and D for player II. Probabilities $p_1$ and $p_2$ then reflect a consistency requirement with respect to the subjective beliefs that each player holds about how the other one will behave. Given their respective beliefs over the other player, both players cannot believe that the other one might play any strategy but the one which is optimal relative to their respective beliefs.

This 'correlated equilibrium' can be used as the *ex ante* mechanism design allowing the two parties of a franchise contract as sketched by the game of Figure 11.5 to avoid litigation after a failure to match the market's preference over the quality–price mix. The 'mixed strategies' Nash equilibrium can then be considered the 'internal enforcement' used by the players to agree on a common preference. The rationale is the following.

By agreeing to randomize their respective choices, the parties are renouncing their respective conjectures about the market's preference and are then able to credibly *ex ante* commit themselves to implement the quality–price mix possibly resulting from the randomization. *Ex post*, that is, after having tossed the coin, by knowing the other player's probability distribution each player is aware that he has no incentive to deviate from the choice resulting from randomization. According to the payoff structure of Figure 11.5, their results coincide with probability equal to 6/16 (joint probability is 3/4 × 1/4 for A, C plus 3/4 × 1/4 for B, D) and do not coincide with probability equal to 10/16 (joint probability is 1/4 × 1/4 for A, D plus 3/4 × 3/4 for B, C).

The application of this game-theoretic solution to a situation of disagreement among the two parties of the franchise contract is straightforward. Provided that the results of two tossing coincide (the two cases A, C and B, D), the companies will implement the corresponding quality–price mix: for instance, they might have committed to attribute to 'low quality–low price' the outcome A, C and to 'high quality–high price' the outcome B,D. On the contrary, if their results diverge, the 'mixed strategies' mechanism design will obviously be of no help in solving the disagreement and no cooperative choice of the quality–price mix will be possible. It may also be noted that the successful randomized decision about the quality–price mix is expected with probability (6/16), lower than the coordination failure stemming from the unsuccessful randomization (10/16).

The occurrence of a successful randomization, albeit with a lower probability, will allow the parties to rely on a productive decision about the quality–price mix which is litigation-free. The choice will not depend on the one or the other company's conjecture about the market's preference but on the random outcome of tossing the coin. Once the companies make recourse to this mechanism design, there no longer is a deciding company to which to attribute a failure, by raising the allegation of opportunistic behaviour in expressing views about the market preference.[27] This possible allegation is ruled out, as the choice of the quality–price mix has been made 'neutral', so that no party has any right to complain. Therefore, an important conclusion has been reached. By using the mechanism design of the 'mixed strategies' solution concept, in the positive case of a coincident randomization the two companies get rid of possible litigation in case of *ex post* divergence between their choice and the market's preference.

## Concluding remarks

Endogenous contractual incompleteness defines those forms of contractual incompleteness creating the incentive to strategic behaviour that either impedes the *first best* implementation of the contract or causes the negotiation failure. This chapter has focused on possible application of game theory to the solution of endogenous contractual incompleteness. The aim was to show that putting long-term contracts in game form helps in elucidating the question of conditions under which a court is able to enforce contractual obligations or to devise mechanisms for completing contracts. The analysis of game-theoretic examples has shown that in some cases of endogenous incompleteness a court can counteract possible opportunistic behaviour and foster the efficient outcome of the contract.

It has been shown that incomplete information by a court or imperfect information by a party are the two cases of endogenous incompleteness that may be solved when a court designs the appropriate mechanism of 'external enforcement', as indicated by the game-theoretic analysis of the long-term contract. Instead, when both parties of a contractual relationship are hampered by incomplete information as they cannot observe relevant economic variables, the coherent alignment of both strategies and beliefs which is needed for an efficient solution is more difficult to devise. If this consistency condition is missing, a court is not in a position to lead the contracting parties to the efficient outcome suggested by the game-theoretic analysis, because it cannot 'tame' a possible opportunistic behaviour. However, when the parties are able to use the 'mixed strategies' solution concept, it has been demonstrated that an 'internal enforcement' can be put forward which avoids possible in a litigation.

Therefore, the chapter suggests that the divide between contracts that are 'completable' by courts and 'non-completable' contracts has to be traced back to the existence (or the absence) of consistency between the parties' strategies and beliefs, independently from the information being 'imperfect' or 'private'. What counts for a court to complete a contract is not the degree of information as such, but how information impinges on the alignment of the parties' beliefs over their respective moves. It is also interesting to note that the impossibility for a court to complete the contract, because strategies and beliefs are not consistently aligned, does not necessarily open the way to regulation. There are contractual relationships in which parties can autonomously improve on the contract. The parties may solve the endogenous contractual incompleteness by using a game-theoretic solution concept as a mechanism design for reaching an *ex ante* agreement which *ex post* more efficient results. Indeed, this agreement is free from opportunities for a party to *ex post* put forward allegations about misconduct by the other party.

## Acknowledgements

Financial support from the Italian Ministry of University and Research (Miur) is gratefully acknowledged. I also thank Nicola Dimitri for his comments to a previous draft of this chapter.

## Notes

1 Coase (1960).

2

> Suppose the relationship lasts for two periods. In the first period, the parties reach an agreement about plant site and design (investment in specialized assets) . . . and about the share of the cost of constructing the plant each will bear. Such an agreement specifies only the immediate actions the parties will take and how they will be compensated for these. In the second period, the parties negotiate prices, possibly a fixed transfer payment, quality standards and a delivery schedule . . . in full knowledge of the circumstances then prevailing (e.g. current model year body design, demands for various models, the costs and availabilities of steel and substitute materials, and so on.
>
> (Milgrom and Roberts, 1990 p. 68)

3 These different sources of impediments have been summarized by Oliver Williamson as follows:

> Upon recognizing that all complex contracts are unavoidably incomplete (because of bounded rationality), that contract as promise is fraught with hazard (because of opportunism), and if the central problem of economic organization is that of adaption, then the object of economic organization reduces to the following: adapt

to disturbances (of both autonomous and bilateral kinds) in ways that economize on bounded rationality while simultaneously safeguarding the transactions in question against the hazards of opportunism.

(1991 p. 176)

4 The bargaining version of the Coase Theorem takes an optimistic attitude towards the ability of people to solve th(e) problem of distribution. The obstacles to cooperation are portrayed as the cost of communicating, the time spent negotiating, the cost of enforcing agreements, etc. These obstacles can all be described as transaction costs of bargaining. . . . A pessimistic approach assumes that people cannot solve the distribution problem, even if there are no costs to bargaining.

(Cooter, 1982 p. 17)

5 'The actions taken under an efficient contract do not depend on the bargaining power of the parties involved. Only the distribution of the fruits of the bargain depends on the bargaining power' (Milgrom and Roberts, 1990 p. 67).
6 Schwartz (1998 p. 282).
7 For our purposes, it is not necessary to make reference to the 'common knowledge' assumption. We will only deal with the case of two players, so that the less requiring assumption of 'mutual knowledge' will suffice. On the conditions for common or mutual knowledge to be required, see Aumann and Branderburger (1995).
8 A perfect Bayesian equilibrium is a strategy combination (s;t) and a set of beliefs $\mu$ such that for each node of the game (1) the strategies for the remainder of the game are Nash given the beliefs and strategies of the other player, (2) the beliefs at each information set are rational given the evidence appearing that far in the game (meaning that they are based, if possible, on priors updated by Bayes' rule) given the observed actions of the other players under the hypothesis that they are in equilibrium. (See Rasmusen, 1989 p. 110.)
9 Aumann (1976, 1987).
10 See Hart and Moore (1990).
11 This view has been put forward by Maskin and Tirole (1999).
12 However, there is another sense in which one can say that a contract is incomplete: it is incomplete if the parties would like to add contingent clauses, but are prevented from doing so by the fact that the state of nature cannot be verified.

(Hart and Moore, 1999 p. 134)

13 Out-of-equilibrium moves are an essential part of the game. Otherwise, 'if nothing can be said with regard to what would happen *outside* the equilibrium path, it is then obvious that nothing can be said with respect to the rationality to remain on the "backward induction" path' (Binmore, 1996 p. 136).
14 Once out-of-equilibrium moves are admitted, hypothesis 2 of mutual knowledge of rationality might be replaced with hypothesis 2': *mutual beliefs of Bayesian rationality of the players*. In other words, due to the occurrence of out-of-equilibrium moves, each player cannot *know* but just *believe* with certainty (with probability = 1) in the other player's rationality. However, if the first player – instead of the move of not continuing the game (in our example, the second period of production with the whole capital) – moves 'forward', the other player (the investor), being rational, must reject also the hypothesis of mutual beliefs of Bayesian rationality of the players. Hence follows the elimination of hypothesis 2 of rationality from a TOL game.
15 Reny (1993 pp. 112–115).
16 For a survey of these non-conventional views on market competition, see Makowski and Ostroy (2001 pp. 479–496).
17 (I)f all firms were charging the same price or paying the same wage, it might pay the last firm to charge a different price or pay a different wage; equilibrium would thus be characterized by a price or wage distribution – inducing some market

participants to spend scarce resources to search for the lowest price stores or highest wage firms.

(Stiglitz, 2000 p. 1456)

18 '(A)lmost always, social changes make some parties better off and some others worse off. This even holds for 'voluntary' exchange since in general third parties will be affected. (Hirshleifer, 1992 pp. 187–188).

19 (W)here pairs of agents engage in repeated transactions, the price and other terms of exchange often include a payment in excess of at least one agent's next alternative. The result is what we term an enforcement rent. This rent arises because it is generally suboptimal for an agent facing an enforcement problem in the process of exchange to make an offer equivalent to the trading partner's next best alternative. Should such an offer be accepted, the partner will be indifferent to the continuation of the exchange, and there would thus be means of using the threat to terminate the relationship to enforce the terms of exchange. Offering an exchange partner an enforcement rent, one using the threat of termination to ensure compliance, is what we term a contingent renewal strategy.

(Bowles and Gintis, 1993 p. 87)

20 Kreps *et al.*, 1982.

21 See Harsanyi (1967/1968, 1973).

22 Nature is assigned the task of choosing each player's strategy among his vector of strategies, whereas the second player sets up expectations on the probability that the first player possesses one of the possible strategies. However, the Harsanyi doctrine cannot impose the requirement that all players dispose of the same information set.

23 For the formal demonstration, see Gibbons (1992 pp. 224–232).

24 A bargaining game between a buyer (B) and a seller (S) of a single indivisible object, which does comply with hypothesis 1, is a game of incomplete information. Thus, B's evaluation and S' opportunity cost have been drawn from a uniform distribution on (0, 1), but each one only knows his or her own type. The two parties have an obvious incentive to misrepresent their true values for the object: B understates the offer (v), whereas S overstates the price (c). In this game there may be no trade as no Bayesian equilibrium is obtained even when $v > c$. The reason for the contract failure is the impossibility to have B (S) willing to offer (ask) an amount of money just equal to his reservation price. See the 'private information' bargaining game by Myerson and Satterthwhite (1983).

25 According to assumption (1), in Figure 11.5 total returns 4 are inclusive of the 'small return' (1) left to the franchisee (in case the franchisor is decisive) or of the royalty fee (1) paid to the franchisor (in case the franchisee is decisive).

26 The first possibility deals with the notion of observability, the second with the notion of verifiability. An outcome may or may not be observable in terms of clarity and completeness of characteristics of the facts and actions. Be it as it may, verifiability will be absent if the (*ex post*) wrong choice is due to 'opportunistic behaviour' in the perception of the market preference; that is, the company making the decision may have geared the conjecture towards its own preference. For a formal treatment of the distinction between observability and verifiability, see Dimitri (2000).

27 It can also be noted that in the case of the 'mixed strategies' Nash equilibrium for both players expected utility is lower than one, while expected utility stemming from the 'pure' Nash strategy is greater than one.

## References

Aumann, R. (1976), 'Agreeing to Disagree', *Annals of Statistics*, 4: 1236–1239.

Aumann, R. (1987), 'Correlated Equilibrium as an Expression of Bayesian Rationality', *Econometrica*, 55: 1–18.

Aumann, R. and A. Branderburger (1995), 'Correlated Equilibrium as an Expression of Bayesian Rationality', *Econometrica*, 63: 1161–1180.

Binmore, K. (1996), 'A Note on Backward Induction', *Games and Economic Behaviour*, 17: 135–137.

Bowles, S. and H. Gintis (1993), 'The Revenge of Homo Economicus: Contested Exchange and the Revival of Political Economy', *Journal of Economic Perspectives*, 7: 83–102.

Coase, R. (1960), 'The Problem of Social Cost', *Journal of Law and Economics*, 3: 1–44.

Cooter, R. (1982), 'The Cost of Coase', *Journal of Legal Studies*, 11: 1–33.

Dimitri, N. (2000), *A Characterisation of Observability and Verifiability in Contracts*, Quaderni del Dipartimento di Economia Politica, Università di Siena, n. 288.

Gibbons, R. (1992), *A Primer in Game Theory*, Hemel Hempstead, Harvester Wheatsheaf.

Harsanyi, J. (1967/1968), 'Games with Incomplete Information Played by Rational Players, Parts I, II, and III', *Management Science*, 14: 159–182, 320–334, 486–502.

Harsanyi, J. (1973), 'Games with Randomly Disturbed Payoffs: A New Rationale for Mixed Strategies', *International Journal of Game Theory*, 2: 1–23.

Hart, O. and J. Moore (1990), 'Property Rights and the Nature of the Firm', *Journal of Political Economy*, 94: 1119–1158.

Hart, O. and J. Moore (1999), 'Foundations of Incomplete Contracts', *Review of Economic Studies*, 66: 115–138.

Hirschleifer, J. (1992), 'Evolutionary Models in Economics and Law: Cooperation Versus Conflict Strategies', *Research in Law and Economics*, 4: 1–60.

Kreps, D.M., P. Milgrom, J. Roberts and R. Wilson (1982), 'Rational Cooperation in the Finitely Repeated Prisoner's Dilemma', *Journal of Economic Theory*, 27: 245–252.

Makowski, L. and J.M. Ostroy (2001), 'Perfect Competition and the Creativity of the Market', *Journal of Economic Literature*, 34: 479–535.

Maskin, E. and J. Tirole (1999), 'Unforeseen Contingencies and Incomplete Contracts', *Review of Economic Studies*, 66: 39–56.

Milgrom, P. and J. Roberts (1990), 'Bargaining and Influence Costs and the Organization of Economic Activity', in J. Alt and K. Shlepse (eds), *Perspectives on Positive Political Economy*, Cambridge, Cambridge University Press.

Myerson, R.B. and M.A. Satterthwhite (1983), 'Efficient Mechanisms for Bilateral Trading', *Journal of Economic Theory*, 29: 265–271.

Rasmusen, E. (1989), *Games and Information*, Cambridge, Cambridge University Press.

Reny, P.J. (1993), 'Rationality and Extensive-Form Games', *Journal of Economic Perspectives*, 6: 103–118.

Schwartz, A. (1998), 'Incomplete contracts', *The New Palgrave Dictionary of Economics and Law*, London, Macmillan.

Stiglitz, J.E. (2000), 'The Contributions of the Economics of Information to Twentieth Century Economics', *Quarterly Journal of Economics*, 115: 1441–1478.

Williamson, O.E. (1991), 'Economic Institutions: Spontaneous and Intentional Governance', *Journal of Law, Economics & Organization*, 7: 159–187.

# 12 Customary contracts[1]

*H. Peyton Young*

Contracts define the terms under which people enter into relationships with one another. Some contracts are explicit, such as rental agreements between tenants and landlords, or lending agreements between bankers and borrowers. Others are implicit, such as the common understandings that a couple brings to a marriage. Still others occupy a middle ground: employment contracts are usually explicit about some matters, such as the number of hours to be worked, but rather vague about others, such as the relationship between performance and pay.

Contracts often have a standard format, that is, their terms follow conventional patterns. Renters and landlords fill in the blanks of standard leases. Building contractors typically negotiate cost-plus or fixed-price contracts. Farmers either share the crop in fixed proportions with their tenants, or rent out the land at a fixed price per acre, and so forth. A standard concern in contract theory is how to structure an optimal contract based on the information available to the parties, their monitoring costs, degree of risk aversion, and the like.

Here we shall focus not on the choice of contract structure *per se*, but on the specific choice of terms, that is, on how the parties "fill in the blanks" of a given type of contract. Here too convention plays an important role by coordinating the expectations of the parties on terms that are standard in a given context. For example, cost-plus contracts employ a standard percentage markup, usually 10% or 20%. Lawyers' contingency fees are (in the US) typically one-third of the jury award. Real estate agents get 6% of the sales price of a house. Tenants and landlords often divide the harvest fifty–fifty. While opportunity costs obviously constrain the terms that rational agents will accept, there also appears to be a strong degree of inertia in contractual arrangements that results from custom and precedent.

Here we propose a dynamic model of how such contractual customs form endogenously, focusing particularly on the empirical question of why we often observe significant regional differences in these customs. We then show how the theoretical model can help to illuminate an actual case, namely, the distribution of contract terms between tenants and landlords in contemporary Illinois agriculture.

The model is an extension of the standard neoclassical framework in which principals propose contracts, which agents accept or reject depending on whether they exceed or fall short of their opportunity cost. In the standard model, the landlord proposes a contract that maximizes his expected returns subject to being acceptable to the agent. In our set-up, we assume that the parties are influenced by the local salience of the contract, that is, by the frequency with which it is used by others in the neighborhood.

To be specific, imagine that agents live at the vertices of a graph, which represent distinct locations in some social or geographical space. Let $V$ denote the set of $n$ vertices, and let $i \in V$ denote a particular vertex. If the choice of agent $j$ has an influence on agent $i$, we connect $i$ and $j$ by a directed edge $(i,j)$; the amount of influence is given by a weight $w_{ij} \geq 0$. If influence is determined by geographical proximity, then we would have $w_{ij} = w_{ji}$ for all $i$ and $j$. This *symmetry* assumption will be maintained in what follows.

Let $X$ denote the finite set of contracts that people are willing to consider. At each time $t$, the contract in force at location $i$ is denoted by $x_i^t \in X$, and the vector $x^t \in X^n$ denotes the *state* of the process. At random times governed by a Poisson random variable $\omega_i$, the principal and the agent at location $i$ renegotiate their contract. Assume that the random variables $\omega_i$ are independent and identically distributed, and that time is scaled so that, on average, there is one renegotiation per time period in each location. (Allowing differences in the rate of renegotiation at different locations does not change the results in any important way.)

Suppose that the current state is $x$, and the contract at location $i$ is about to be renegotiated. The principal offers the agent a contract, which is accepted if and only if the contract's expected utility to the agent is above the reservation utility level $u_i^0$. The value of $u_i^0$ may depend on the particular location $i$, for example, on local wages in alternative employment. We shall assume that the subset $X_i$ of acceptable contracts that meet this reservation level is nonempty for each $i$. The principal is assumed to choose a contract within the acceptable set $X_i$ that maximizes his own utility.

We treat the choice of contract at a given location as a state-dependent random variable. Let $P(x_i|\boldsymbol{x}_{-i})$ denote the conditional probability that contract $x_i$ is adopted at location $i$ when $\boldsymbol{x}_{-i}$ is the state of the other locations. We posit that $P(x_i|\boldsymbol{x}_{-i})$ is monotone increasing in three factors: the expected returns from the contract, the inherent focalness of the contract, and its frequency of use in the neighborhood. Denote the expected economic returns to the principal from contract $x_i$ by $v_i(x_i)$. The focalness of the contract will be represented by a real-valued function $f(x_i)$, whose operational meaning will become clear in a moment. The local frequency of use is given by the function $w_i(x_i, \boldsymbol{x}_{-i}) = \sum_{j \neq i} w_{ij}\delta(x_i, x_j)$, where $\delta(x_i, x_j) = 1$ if $x_i = x_j$ and $\delta(x_i, x_j) = 0$ otherwise.

A convenient functional form is to suppose that the log probability of choosing a given contract is a linear function of these three factors. In other words, for some $\beta \geq 0$, and every $x_i$ and $y_i \in X_i$,

$$\begin{aligned} &\log P(x_i|\boldsymbol{x}_{-i}) - \log P(y_i|\boldsymbol{x}_{-i}) \\ &\quad = \beta[v_i(x_i) - v_i(y_i) + w_i(x_i, \boldsymbol{x}_{-i}) - w_i(y_i, \boldsymbol{x}_{-i}) + f(x_i) - f(y_i)] \qquad (12.1) \end{aligned}$$

Equivalently,

$$P(x_i|\boldsymbol{x}_{-i}) = \frac{\exp\beta[v_i(x_i) + w_i(x_i, \boldsymbol{x}_{-i}) + f_i(x_i)]}{\sum_j \exp\beta[v_j(x_j) + w_j(x_j, \boldsymbol{x}_{-j}) + f_j(x_j)]} \tag{12.2}$$

This is known as a *log-linear response function*, and $\beta$ is the *response parameter* (Blume, 1995; Brock and Durlauf, 1995; McKelvey and Palfrey, 1995; Durlauf, 1997).

This model can be interpreted as a perturbed optimal response process in the following sense. Suppose that we represent the utility of agent $i$ in state $x$ by

$$Ui(\boldsymbol{x}) = v_i(x_i) + w_i(\boldsymbol{x}) + f(\boldsymbol{x}_i) + \varepsilon_i(\boldsymbol{x}), \tag{12.3}$$

where $\varepsilon_i(\boldsymbol{x})$ is an unobserved utility shock. Suppose that these utility shocks are independent and identically distributed according to the extreme value distribution $P(\varepsilon \leq z) = e^{-e-\beta z}$. If $i$ always chooses a contract $x_i \in X_i$ that maximizes $U_i(\cdot)$ conditional on the others' choices being $\boldsymbol{x}_{-i}$, then from the observer's standpoint it appears that $i$ is following the stochastic adoption process given by (12.2). Such models are standard in the discrete choice literature (McFadden, 1974). For purposes of empirical estimation, however, it is not the utility function but the choice probabilities that matter. In principle, these could be estimated from a sufficiently rich set of event histories that give the temporal sequence of contract adoptions at different locations.

The functional form (12.2) is a convenient way of expressing the idea that the probability of a contract at a given location is an increasing function of three factors: returns, focalness, and local frequency of use. The formula states, for example, that if two contracts $x$ and $y$ provide the same expected returns at a given location, and if they are used with the same frequency, but $x$ is more inherently focal than $y$ (say because $x$ uses a round number, like 10%, whereas $y$ involves $\sqrt{}19$), then $x$ is more likely to be adopted than $y$. Alternatively, if $x$ and $y$ have the same expected returns, and both are based on very easy fractions, but $x$ is much more commonly used than $y$ in the neighborhood, then $x$ is more likely to be adopted than $y$ is, and so forth.

The probabilistic choice model (12.2), together with the Poisson updating processes, defines a time-homogeneous Markov process on a finite state space, namely, the set of all states $\boldsymbol{x}$ that specify the contract in use at each location. This process is ergodic and has a unique invariant distribution $\mu$.

For each state $\boldsymbol{x}$, $\mu(\boldsymbol{x})$ represents the long-run relative frequency with which state $\boldsymbol{x}$ is visited in almost all realizations of the process.

In the present case the invariant distribution takes a particularly tractable form. Define the *potential* of state $\boldsymbol{x}$ to be

$$\rho(\boldsymbol{x}) = \sum_{i=1}^{n} v_i(x_i) + \sum_{i=1}^{n} f(x_i) + (1/2)\sum_{i=1}^{n} w_i(\boldsymbol{x}) \tag{12.4}$$

Potential equals the total utility from those factors that involve no social interactions, plus one-half of the utility from those that do involve social interactions.

It follows from standard arguments (see, for example, Liggett, 1985; Blume, 1995; Young, 1998a, chapter 6) that the long-run distribution of the process has the following simple form, known as a Gibbs representation

$$\mu(\boldsymbol{x}) = e^{\beta\rho(x)} \Big/ \sum_{y} e^{\beta\rho(y)} \tag{12.5}$$

It follows that, when $\beta$ is large, the probability is close to one that the process will be in a state that maximizes potential. We summarize this in the following result.

**Theorem.** *Starting from an arbitrary initial state, the long-run probability of being in any given state* $\boldsymbol{x}$ *is proportional to* $e^{\beta\rho(x)}$. *When* $\beta$ *is large but finite, the probability is close to one that the process will be in a state that globally maximizes potential. These are known as the stochastically stable states of the process.*

While the exponential form of the long-run distribution is especially convenient to work with, and depends on the log linear representation in (12.2), it needs to be emphasized that the general approach can be applied without this assumption. Suppose that the renegotiation process at each location can be represented as a stochastic choice over contracts, whose distribution is perhaps state-dependent but not time-dependent. Suppose further that, at each location, every contract in the feasible set is chosen with a probability that is bounded away from zero over all possible states. Together with the Poisson updating processes, this yields an irreducible, finite Markov chain that has a unique invariant distribution. When the variance of the individual choice probabilities is sufficiently small, the process will typically occupy a few states with high probability, and these stochastically stable states can be identified with considerable precision using the method of large deviations (see Freidlin and Wentzell, 1984; Young, 1993a, 1998a; Kandori *et al.*, 1993).

We now show how this approach can help to illuminate empirical data on contract choice that might otherwise appear to be quite puzzling. The data in question come from a sample survey conducted by the Illinois Cooperative Agricultural Extension Service in 1995. Tenants were asked to report in detail the terms of the contract they operated under, including the shares of each output and each input, cash payments (if any), and responsibilities for providing farm machinery. The stated purpose of the survey was to provide information that would enable the agency to give better advice to local farmers; individual respondents could not be identified from the data and there is no reason to think they were motivated to misreport.

Almost all of the reported contracts fall into one of two categories. *Cropsharing contracts* specify fixed shares of outputs and inputs for each party, and generally involve no cash payments. *Land rent contracts* specify a fixed rental rate per acre; the other inputs are usually provided by the tenant. Many other contracts exist in theory, including pure wage contracts and hybrid forms of rent, wage, and share contracts (Stiglitz, 1974, 1989), but it appears that they are seldom used in practice.

Of the 1,704 responses in the 1995 survey, cropsharing contracts were the most frequent (55%), land rent contracts the next most frequent (41%), and all other contract forms (mostly livestock and pasture leases) constituted less than 4%. Here we shall restrict ourselves to an analysis of the 935 cropsharing contracts.

In principle, the terms of cropsharing contracts can be extremely varied and flexible. For example, one could specify different shares for each of the major outputs (corn, soybeans, and wheat), as well as for each of the major inputs (seed, fertilizer, and machinery). But in practice very few of the possible contracts are used. Indeed, almost all of the Illinois contracts apply the same share to all of the outputs, and these shares are almost invariably expressed in denominators of two, three, or five. Furthermore, the contracts exhibit a high degree of clustering: in the northern part of the state, the standard arrangement is to divide equally between tenant and landlord, whereas in the southern part of the state the custom is for the tenant to get either 3/5 or 2/3 (see Figure 12.1). Moreover, there is a simple explanation for this shift based on economic fundamentals. The land in the south is, on average, inherently less productive than the land in the north. Hence the share for the tenant must be higher in the south if net returns to the tenants in the two regions are to be comparable.

Of course, this is very far from saying that the observed shift from $1/2 - 1/2$ to $2/3 - 1/3$ is exactly the *right amount* to compensate for the difference in average land quality. Indeed it would be quite a coincidence if $1/2 - 1/3 = 1/6$ represents just the right additional compensation necessary to equilibrate the tenant labor market between north and south. A more plausible explanation is that thirds and fifths have the most focal power when market forces push the parties away from equal division. While the quantum jump required to move from halves to fifths or thirds may bring things closer to market equilibrium, it will at best be a rough approximation. Furthermore, when we look at the distribution of contract terms within each county, we find that there is an almost complete lack of correlation between land quality and share at the local level (see Figure 12.2).

We claim that the model described above can account for these otherwise puzzling phenomena. Assume for simplicity that the only contractual variable is the agent's (tenant's) share $x$ of total output. We shall also suppose that labor input is fully monitored, and the tenant will be let go if he fails to operate the farm according to best practice. On farm $i$ the inherent productivity of the soil is given by a real number $s_i$, which is the expected output per acre, measured in dollars, under best practice. (E.g. $s_i = 80$ means that total net income on farm $i$ is, on average, \$80 per acre.) The tenant's expected income on farm $i$ is thus the contract share $x_i$ times the index $s_i$ times the size of the farm. For mathematical convenience, assume that all farms have the same size, which we may as well suppose to be unity. (This does not affect the analysis in any important way.) The tenant accepts a contract $x_i$ if and only if his expected return $x_i s_i$ is at least $w_i$, where $w_i$ is the reservation wage at location $i$. The expected return to the landlord from such a contract is $v_i(x_i) = (1 - x_i)s_i$.

Let us assume that all contracts are equally focal from an *a priori* standpoint, say $f(x_i) = 0$ for all $i$ and all $x_i$. To model the impact of custom, suppose that each of

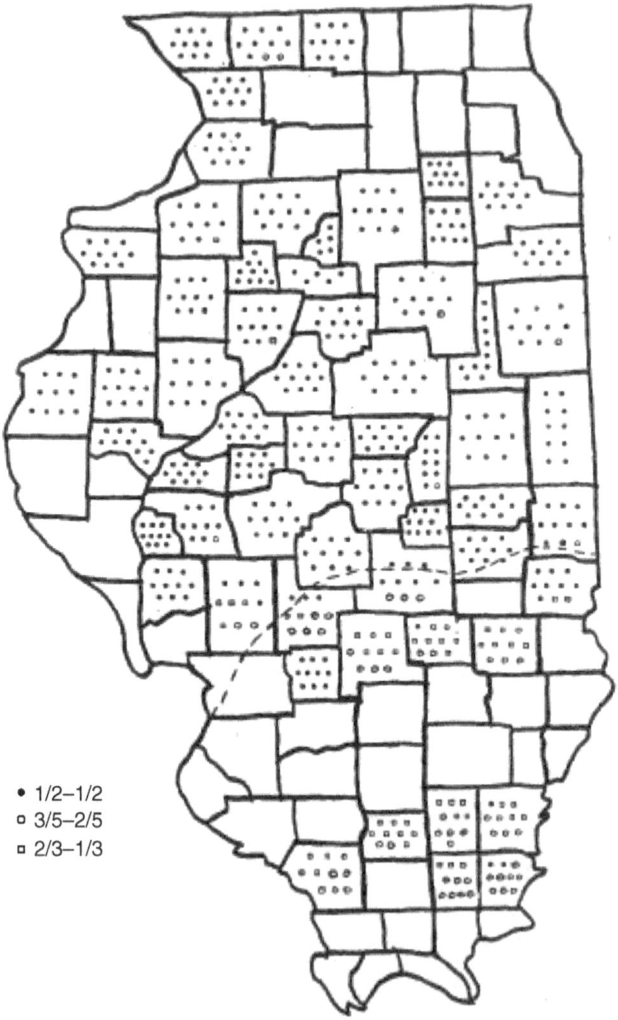


*Figure 12.1* Distribution of share contracts by county in Illinois, 1995. Blank counties had too few data to be statistically meaningful.

agent $i$'s neighbors exerts the same degree of social influence. In other words, there is a number $\gamma \geq 0$ such that $w_{ij} = \gamma$ if farm $i$ is adjacent to farm $j$, and $w_{ij} = 0$ otherwise. Let $n_i(x)$ be the number of $i$'s neighbors using the same contract as $i$ in state $x$. The potential function then takes the form

$$\rho(\boldsymbol{x}) = \sum_{i=1}^{n}(1 - x_i)s_i + (\gamma/2)\sum_{i=1}^{n} n_i(\boldsymbol{x}) \tag{12.6}$$

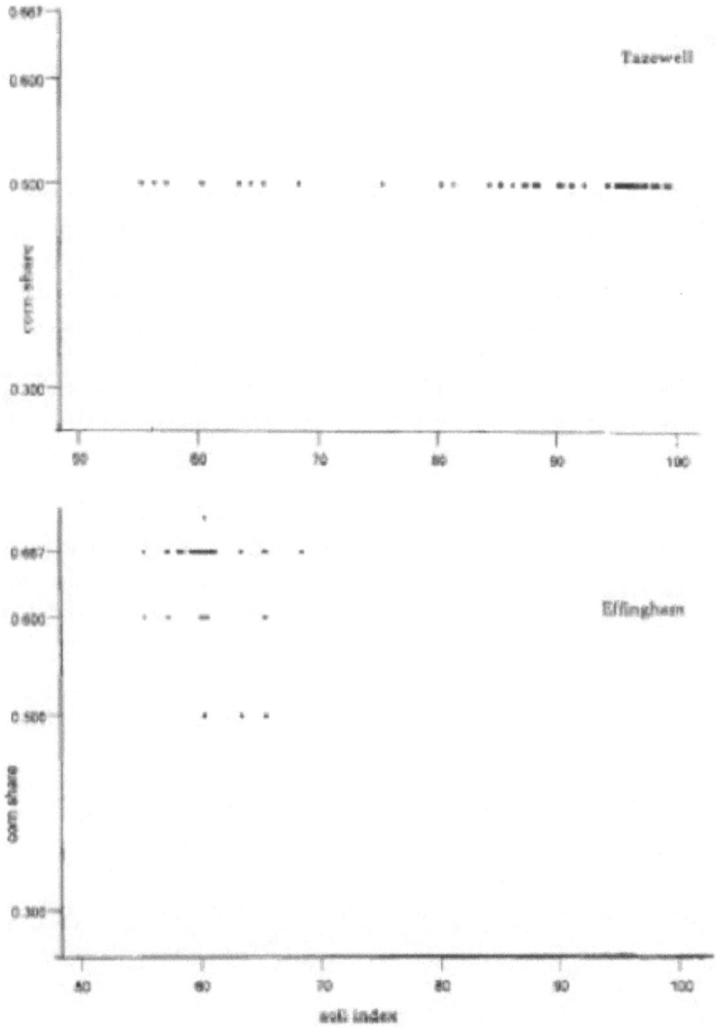


*Figure 12.2* Distribution of shares in a typical northern Illinois county (Tazewell) and a typical southern Illinois county (Effingham).

The term $\sum(1 - x_i)s_i$ is just the total return to land, which we shall denote by $r(\boldsymbol{x})$. The term $(\gamma/2)\sum n_i(\boldsymbol{x})$ is just $\gamma$ times the total number of edges (neighbor-pairs) that are coordinated on the same contract in state $\boldsymbol{x}$, which we shall denote by $c(\boldsymbol{x})$. This is the degree of local conformity in the system, and $\gamma$ is the conformity parameter. We thus obtain the particularly transparent formulation

$$\rho(\boldsymbol{x}) = r(\boldsymbol{x}) + \gamma c(\boldsymbol{x}),$$

and

$$\mu(\boldsymbol{x}) \propto e^{\beta[r(\boldsymbol{x})+\gamma c(\boldsymbol{x})]} \tag{12.7}$$

In other words, the log probability of each state $x$ is a linear function of the total rent to land plus the degree of local conformity. Given specific values of the conformity parameter $\gamma$ and the response parameter $\beta$ we can compute the relative probability of various states of the process, and from this deduce the likelihood of different geographic distributions of contracts. In fact, one can say a fair amount about the qualitative behavior of the process even when one does not know specific values of the parameters. We illustrate with a concrete example that captures some of the key features of the Illinois case. Consider the hypothetical state of Torusota shown in Figure 12.3. In the northern part of the state – above the dashed line – soils are evenly divided between High and Medium quality soils, whereas in the southern part they are evenly divided between Medium and Low quality soils. As in Illinois the soil types are interspersed, but average soil quality is higher in the north than it is in the south.

Let $n$ be the number of farms. Each farm has exactly eight neighbors, so there are $4n$ edges altogether. As in the preceding section, contracts are one-dimensional and specify the share of output for the tenant. Suppose there are nine salient contracts: $x = 10\%, 20\%, \ldots, 90\%$. (Contracts in which the tenant receives 0% or 100% are

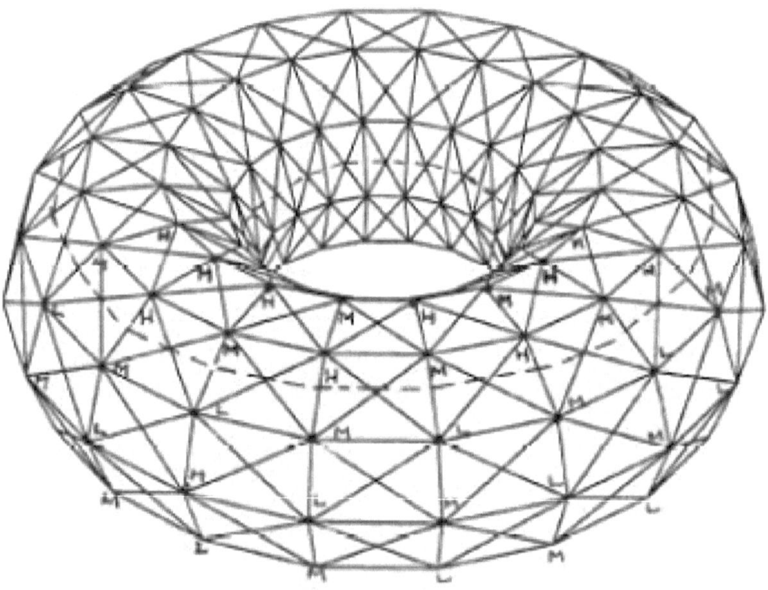

*Figure 12.3* The hypothetical state of Torusota. Each vertex represents a farm, and soil qualities are High, Medium, or Low.

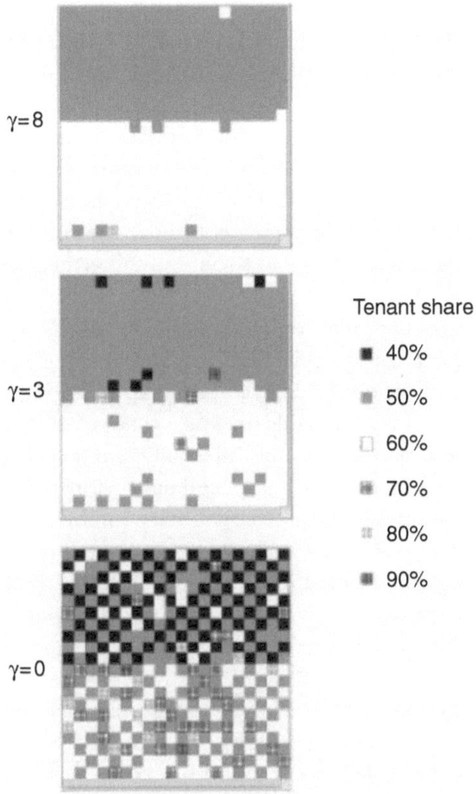


*Figure 12.4* Simulated outcomes of the process for $n = 200$, $\beta = 0.20$.

not considered.) For the sake of concreteness, assume that high quality soils have index 85, medium quality soils have index 70, and low quality soils have index 60. Let the reservation wage be 32.

The states with maximum potential will depend, of course, on the degree of conformity $\gamma$. To illustrate the behavior of the process, we simulated it for $n = 200$, $\beta = 0.20$, and three different levels of conformity: $\gamma = 0$, 3, and 8. Figure 12.4 shows the distribution of contract shares after 1000 periods have elapsed. When $\gamma = 0$ (bottom panel), the contracts are matched quite closely with land quality, and the process is close to the competitive equilibrium, which has the 40% contract on high quality soils, the 50% contract on medium quality soils, and the 60% contract on low quality soils. When the level of conformity is somewhat higher (middle panel), the dominant contract in the north is 50% and in the south it is 60%, although there are pockets here and there of other contracts. (This is similar to the Illinois case.) Somewhat surprisingly, however, a further increase in the conformity level (top panel) does not cause the two regional customs to merge into a single global custom; it merely leads to greater uniformity in each of the two regions.

Indeed, it may be shown that, when $n$ is large and $\gamma$ is sufficiently large relative to $n$, the highest potential state involves distinct regional customs in the north and in the south. The reason is that a regional custom of 40% in the north allows the landlords to capture more land rent as compared to a uniform custom, and the only cost is the loss in "social utility" on the part of those who live near the boundary. But when $n$ is large, the proportion of such people is very small. Of course, landlords could capture even more land rent under the competitive equilibrium, but this would involve a sizable loss in social utility because land quality is very heterogeneous locally.

While the details are particular to this example, the logic is quite general. Consider any distribution of soil qualities that is heterogeneous locally, but exhibits substantial shifts in average quality between geographic regions. For intermediate values of conformity $\gamma$, it is reasonable to expect that potential will be maximized by a distribution of contracts that is uniform locally, but diverse globally – in other words the distribution is characterized by regional customs. Such a state will typically have higher potential than the competitive equilibrium, because the latter involves substantial losses in social utility when land quality is heterogeneous. It will typically have higher potential than a global custom, because it allows landlords to capture more rent at relatively little loss in social utility, provided that the boundaries between the regions are not too long (i.e. there are relatively few farms near the boundaries).

In effect, these regional customs form a compromise between completely uniform contracts on the one hand, and fully differentiated contracts on the other. Given the nature of the model, we should not expect perfect uniformity within any given region, nor should we expect sharp changes in custom at the boundary. The model suggests instead that there will be occasional departures from custom within regions (due to idiosyncratic influences), and considerable variation near the boundaries. This seems to be a reasonably accurate characterization of the distribution of contracts in the state of Illinois.

## Note

1 This material is developed more fully in H. Peyton Young and Mary A. Burke (2001), "Competition and Custom in Economic Contracts: A Case Study of Illinois Agriculture," *American Economic Review*, 91(3), 559–573.

## References

Akerlof, George A. (1980): "A Theory of Social Custom, of Which Unemployment May Be One Consequence," *Quarterly Journal of Economics*, 94, 749–775.

Akerlof, George A. (1997): "Social Distance and Social Decisions," *Econometrica*, 65, 1005–1027.

Albers, Wulf and Gisela Albers (1983): "On the Prominence Structure of the Decimal System," in R.W. Scholz (ed.), *Decision Making under Uncertainty*. Amsterdam: Elsevier.

Allen, Douglas W. and Lueck, Dean (1993): "Transaction Costs and the Design of Cropshare Contracts," *RAND Journal of Economics*, 24, 1, 78–100.

Bardhan, Pranab K. (1976): "Variations in Extent and Forms of Agricultural Tenancy – I: Analysis of Indian Data across Regions and Over Time," *Economic and Political Weekly*, September 11, 1976, 1505–1546.

Bardhan, Pranab K. (1984): *Land, Labor, and Rural Poverty: Essays in Development Economics.* New York: Columbia University Press.

Bardhan, Pranab K. and Rudra, Ashok (1980): "Terms and Conditions of Sharecropping Contracts: An Analysis of Village Survey Data in India," *Journal of Development Studies*, 16, 3, 287–302.

Bardhan, Pranab K. and Rudra, Ashok (1981): "Terms and Conditions of Labor Contracts in Agriculture: Results of a Survey in West Bengal, 1979," *Oxford Bulletin of Economics and Statistics*, 43, 1, 89–111.

Bardhan, Pranab K. and Rudra, Ashok (1986a): "Labour Mobility and the Boundaries of the Village Moral Economy," *Journal of Peasant Studies*, 13, 90–115.

Bardhan, Pranab K. and Rudra, Ashok (1986b): *Agrarian Relations in West Bengal: Results of Two Surveys.* Bombay: Somaiya.

Bell, Clive and Zusman, Minhas (1976): "A Bargaining Approach to Cropsharing Contracts," *American Economic Review*, 66, 4, 578–588.

Binmore, Ken, Swierzbinski, Joe, Hsu, Steven, and Proulx, Chris (1993): "Focal Points and Bargaining," *International Journal of Game Theory*, 22, 381–409.

Binswanger, Hans P. and Rosenzweig, Mark R. (eds) (1984): Contractual Arrangements, Employment, and Wages in Rural Labor Markets in Asia. New Haven, CT: Yale University Press.

Bliss, Christopher J. and Stern N.H. (1982): *Palanpur: The Economy of an Indian Village.* Oxford: Clarendon Press.

Blume, Larry (1995): "The Statistical Mechanics of Best-Response Strategy Revision," *Games and Economic Behavior*, 11, 111–145.

Braverman, Avishay and Stiglitz, Joseph E. (1982): "Sharecropping and the Interlinking of Agrarian Markets," *American Economic Review*, 72, 4, 695–715.

Brock, William A. and Steven N. Durlauf (1995): "Discrete Choice with Social Interactions I: Theory," NBER Working Paper No. 5291, Cambridge, Massachusetts.

Burke, Mary A. and Young, Peyton H. (2000): "Terms of Agricultural Contracts: Theory and Evidence," CSED Working Paper No. 16, Johns Hopkins University.

Cheung, Steven N.S. (1969): *The Theory of Share Tenancy.* Chicago, IL: The University of Chicago Press.

Durlauf, Steven N. (1997): "Statistical Mechanical Approaches to Socioeconomic Behavior," in W. Brian Arthur, Steven N. Durlauf, and David Lane (eds), *The Economy as a Complex Evolving System.* vol. 2, Redwood City, CA: Addison-Wesley.

Fehrenbacher, J.B., R.A. Pope, I.J. Jansen, J.D. Alexander, and B.W. Ray (1978): *Soil Productivity in Illinois.* Circular 1156, College of Agriculture, Cooperative Extension Service, University of Illinois at Urbana-Champaign.

Freidlin, Mark and Alexander Wentzell (1984): *Random Perturbations of Dynamical Systems.* Berlin: Springer-Verlag.

Hayami, Yujiro and Otsuka, Keijiro (1993): *The Economics of Contract Choice, An Agrarian Perspective.* Oxford: Clarendon Press.

Illinois Cooperative Extension Service (1995): *1995 Cooperative Extension Service Farm Leasing Survey.* Department of Agricultural and Consumer Economics, Cooperative Extension Service, University of Illinois at Urbana-Champaign.

Johnson, D. Gale (1950): "Resource Allocation under Share Contracts," *Journal of Political Economy*, 58, 2, 111–123.

Kandori, Michihiro, George Mailath, and Rafael Rob (1993): "Learning, Mutation, and Long-Run Equilibria in Games," *Econometrica*, 61, 29–56.

Liggett, Thomas M. (1985): *Interacting Particle Systems.* New York: Springer-Verlag.

McFadden, Daniel (1974): "Conditional Logit Analysis of Qualitative Choice Behavior," in Paul Zarembka (ed.), *Frontiers in Econometrics.* New York: Academic Press.

McKelvey, Richard D. and Thomas R. Palfrey (1995): "Quantal Response Equilibria for Normal Form Games," *Games and Economic Behavior*, 10, 6–38.

Marshall, Alfred (1920): *Principles of Economics, 8th Edition.* London: Macmillan.

Mausel, P.W., Runge, E.C.A., and Carmer, S.G. (1975): *Soil Productivity Indexes for Illinois Counties and Soil Associations.* Bulletin 752, College of Agriculture, Agricultural Experiment Station, University of Illinois at Urbana-Champaign.

Mill, John Stuart (1848): *Principles of Political Economy.* London: Longmans Green (1929).

Murrell, Peter (1983): "The Economics of Sharing: A Transaction Cost Analysis of Contractual Choice in Farming," *Bell Journal of Economics*, 14, 1, 183–193.

Odell, R.T. and Oschwald, W.R. (1970): *Productivity of Illinois Soils.* Circular 1016, College of Agriculture, Cooperative Extension Service, University of Illinois at Urbana-Champaign.

Reid, Joseph D., Jr (1975): "Sharecropping in History and Theory," *Agricultural History*, 49, 2, 426–440.

Reid, Joseph D., Jr (1979): "Sharecropping and Agricultural Uncertainty," *Economic Development and Cultural Change*, 24, 549–576.

Robertson, A.F. (1987): *The Dynamics of Productive Relationships: African Share Contracts in Comparative Perspective.* Cambridge: Cambridge University Press.

Roth, Alvin E. (1985): "Toward a Focal Point Theory of Bargaining," in Alvin E. Roth (ed.), *Game-Theoretic Models of Bargaining.* New York: Cambridge University Press.

Roumasset, James and James, W. (1979): "Explaining Variations in Share Contracts: Land Quality, Population Pressure and Technological Change," *Australian Journal of Agricultural Economics*, 23, 2, 116–127.

Rudra, Ashok (1975): "Sharecropping Arrangements in West Bengal," *Economic and Political Weekly*, 10, A58–A63.

Schelling, Thomas C. (1960): *The Strategy of Conflict.* Cambridge, MA: Harvard University Press.

Stiglitz, Joseph E. (1974): "Incentives and Risk-sharing in Sharecropping," *Review of Economic Studies*, 41, 219–255.

Stiglitz, Joseph E. (1989): "Rational Peasants, Efficient Institutions, and a Theory of Rural Organization: Methodological Remarks for Development Economics," in Pranab Bardhan (ed.), *The Economic Theory of Agrarian Institutions.* Oxford: Clarendon Press.

Suppes, Patrick, and Richard Atkinson (1960): *Markov Learning Models for Multi-person Interactions.* Stanford, CA: Stanford University Press.

Young, H. Peyton (1993a): "The Evolution of Conventions," *Econometrica*, 61, 1, 57–84.

Young, H. Peyton (1993b): "An Evolutionary Model of Bargaining," *Journal of Economic Theory*, 59, 1, 145–168.

Young, H. Peyton (1998a): *Individual Strategy and Social Structure: An Evolutionary Theory of Institutions.* Princeton, NJ: Princeton University Press.

Young, H. Peyton (1998b): "Conventional Contracts," *Review of Economic Studies*, 65, 773–792.

# 13 Group relations and industrial districts

*Alberto Battistini*

## Introduction

One of the results most agreed upon in the large literature on local industrial systems is that their success may be attributed to an appropriate combination between cooperation and competition. Accordingly, such a combination has been investigated and explained under a variety of aspects, including socio-cultural environment, technological change and demand conditions (Piore and Sabel, 1984; Becattini, 1991; Saxenian, 1994; You and Wilkinson, 1994). In particular, a key element of this successful combination has been identified in the co-existence between innovation and imitation or, in other words, in a solution of the well-known trade-off between static and dynamic efficiency.[1]

From the point of view of organization theory, the most interesting phenomenon disclosed by this literature are the so-called clusters of firms, that is, a hybrid form of economic organization between the large integrated firm and the set of small independent firms of the neo-classical competitive model. Here, the right balance between cooperation and competition lies in the fact that the needed coordination is achieved by combining market mechanisms (such as price system) with non-market mechanisms (such as authority or rules).

This dual feature is relevant for both firms' and employer–employee relationships. As the notion of "flexible specialization" (Piore and Sabel, 1984) summarizes, highly differentiated and volatile markets require that resources are free and ready to timely move between different tasks and different firms as much as they have to be highly skilled and dedicated. In turn, this implies that the corresponding institutional arrangement is able to combine the informational and motivational role of prices with the provision of adequate appropriability conditions, that is, precisely an appropriate mix between market and non-market coordination mechanisms.

Within this framework, in this chapter I try to provide one of the possible explanations for such a hybrid organizational structure by applying the specificity-based approach to the case of investments that, in principle, could be imitated. The point is that, in this case, it is possible to formulate a definition of intermediate degree of specificity by which an investment is "intermediately" specific when it is not specific to the particular relationship between the single investor and the single counterpart individually taken, but is specific to the set of relationships between investors and counterparts taken as a group. Then, following the logic of a discriminating alignment between transactions and governance structures, this kind of "intermediately" specific assets is associated with a grouping form of economic organization which is to be intended as a stylized representation of the clustering organizational models just sketched out above.

This strategy is not new in the literature. Williamson (1991) defines an intermediate degree of specificity as a bilateral dependency "strong enough to require strict coordination, but not so strong to require full integration," and uses this notion to explain hybrid governance structures such as preferential trade, exchange agreements, and franchising. In Menard (1996), instead, "intermediately" specific assets are meant to be assets where only some of the various possible kinds of specificity (spatial, temporal, human or physical capital, etc.) are present; then the case study of the label system of the French poultry industry is taken as an illustration of the concept (among others).

Thus, the difference in respect to these contributions lies in the particular definition of intermediate degree of specificity and in the particular form of economic organization which is applied to. In addition, it should be pointed out that the focus on imitable investments allows an analysis of the consequences of the temporal sequence in which investments are usually undertaken. In this sense, the present approach can be viewed as stemming from the seminal paper by Stigler (1951) on the division of labor and the extent of the market while, from a more theoretically oriented point of view, it is aimed to clarify to what extent the degree of assets' specificity can be taken as intrinsic and invariable, or depends upon the costs and benefits of making alternative users available.

The rest of the chapter is organized as follows. In the next section I briefly review the specificity-based approach and introduce its application to the case of imitable investments. In sub-section "An example" the point is illustrated by an adaptation of famous examples drawn from the literature while, in the other two sub-sections, it is made more precise by means of a very simple entry game. The following section is concerned with some possible extensions and applications. Finally, the last section concludes.

## The specificity-based approach and its application to the case of imitable investments

By definition, when an investment is specific to a relationship, the corresponding asset is attributed with a quasi-rent, that is, an excess of its value over the next best alternative use. Since the investment is not *ex ante* contractible, however, *ex post* this quasi-rent can be appropriated by the other party. Here is the hold-up problem.

In addition to incomplete contracting and irreversibility, such a risky situation is also rooted on the implicit assumption that having more than one user for employing the asset in the same use is not economically feasible from the beginning. The consequence is that using market discipline to regulate such a relationship is a solution associated with high transaction costs and, therefore, with inefficiently low *ex ante* incentives to invest. Hence, since optimality calls for realizing the specific assets' extra value at minimum cost when specificity increases, we would observe a progressive substitution of arm's length relationships by non-market (or authoritarian) relationships.

Of course, even this solution must actually bear some relevant costs. Otherwise it would be quite difficult to understand how markets can exist at all. Not by chance, many of the possible costs of non-market relationships have been identified in the literature. The most obvious is the amount needed to compensate the party without authority for the fact that the other will presumably behave in his interest. More elaborate contributions include the impossibility of selective intervention (Williamson, 1985), the so-called "influence costs" (Milgrom and Roberts, 1988) and, most convincingly, the dilution of incentives for the party without authority (Grossman and Hart, 1986; Hart and Moore, 1990).

This last piece of the theory becomes even more important as soon as one recognizes that the degree of specificity of investments is not necessarily due to their intrinsic and invariable characteristics but simply originates from the lack of alternative users.[2] As mentioned in the Introduction, this point can be emphasized by focusing on the case of imitable investments. In this case, while the return of the investments depends on their novel character and, as such, remains unchanged until the next innovation (Schumpeter, 1911), the associated hold-up risk critically depends on the place taken in the temporal sequence in which investments are made, that is, on investing first, second, and so on. As a result, the costs of specificity and of the associated non-market relationships end up by being "organizational experimentation costs" in the sense that they will only be borne by first investors while they can be saved by later investors exploiting competition among counterparties.

In the case of *not* imitable investments, to put it another way, the above implicit assumption implies that employing an asset with different users coincides with employing that asset in different uses. Hence, one cannot obtain the investments' benefits (which come from the difference in the asset's value between alternative *uses*) without paying for their costs (which come from the difference in the asset value between alternative *users*).

When imitation is a possibility, instead, even if the above assumption is maintained, alternative users for employing the asset in the *same* use are eventually available, so that potential imitators can obtain the investments' benefits without paying for their costs. Thus, in this latter case the (initial) specificity of investments cannot be thought of as creating value but is better interpreted as a costly consequence of the fact that to invest first also means to remain (temporarily) unique, that is, to have no alternative users for employing the asset in its most valuable use.[3]

Non-cooperatively, it is quite clear that in this context the usual tendency to over- or under-invest may easily arise, and the efficiency-based reasoning is weakened. Observing specific assets and the corresponding non-market relationships is not necessarily to be interpreted as an efficient protection against the hold-up risk, for it could be an overreaching protection against the "organizational free-riding" problem.

However, in a cooperative setting, a grouping form of economic organization, to be based on market relationships within the group and non-market relationships at the level of the group, might emerge precisely as a solution to such an over- or under-investment problem. A group of investors, by making the same investment, is able to implement assets which have an extra value over the next best alternative use (as long as they maintain their novel character), but which are under a reduced threat of opportunistic behavior (since uniqueness is diluted). Being general within the group in which they have already been imitated, but specific among different groups, such assets can be interpreted as "intermediately" specific, and this is why they need the corresponding combination between market and non-market coordination mechanisms.

The next sub-section gives an illustration of this argument by an example built on the conventional story about the hold-up problem. The two main differences with respect to the literature are the introduction of an explicit structure of timing in the specific investment decision process and the addition of a real-world feature such as a bit of uncertainty about the investments' prospects.

In the following two sub-sections the point is made more precise by means of a very simple entry game. The first clarifies the non-cooperative tendency to over- or under-invest, while the second is concerned with its efficiency consequences and, in particular, with its group solution. As will be seen, the fundamental reason why it may turn out attractive is that, behaving as a group, investors are able to cooperatively internalize the adverse effects of the temporal sequence in which, otherwise, specific investments are made.[4]

## *An example*

As an illustration, consider the following adaptation of the case typically employed to explain the hold-up problem. To fix ideas, it may be useful to have in mind the very famous General Motors-Fisher Body story (see, for example, Hart, 1995) or, for the case of employer-employee relationships, a firm which is to adopt a new computer system and the related training program for its workers (Milgrom and Roberts, 1988).

At time t = 0, an element of the (finite) set X of investors, say A, must decide whether or not to make an investment in order to reduce costs or improve the quality of his product. This investment is specific because the capital will be committed irreversibly for two periods, its cost will be repaid by consumers in both periods and, to implement the investment, A needs the cooperation of B, one (but not more than one) element of the workers' set Y. Indeed, for these three reasons, at t = 1 the committed capital will have a greater value within the relationship between A and B than elsewhere but, for contractual incompleteness and the lack of alternative users, this surplus can be appropriated by B instead of being used to repay the sunk component of A's investment.

Then, as long as the investment is worth making, it is rational that, at t = 0, a two-period contract is agreed upon that gives to A authority of deciding what B has to do during their productive relationship. This contract is efficient in the sense that it maximizes the benefits to the parties involved (the investment is made at minimum cost), and such a substitution of spot market contracts illustrates the well-known effect of the hold-up risk.

Since economic organizations are hypothesized to derive from a property rights exchange process, however, it is plausible that B must be compensated in some way for accepting such a long-term contract in a subordinate position. Whatever is the reason for contractual incompleteness, the most natural interpretation of this side-payment is to think of the amount needed to make the $t = 1$ B's renegotiation threat not credible. In any case this compensation, advanced by A in $t = 0$, forms part of the surplus which is expected to obtain from consumers together with the sunk component of the investment, and is rationalized as another possible cost of non-market relationships.[5]

In respect to the literature it is important to make two additional points. The first refers to the introduction of an explicit structure of timing in the specific investment decision process. This implies that, as opposed to spot market contracts, in this example a non-market relationship with the counterparty is to be interpreted as a long-term contract (of which ownership represents the limiting case with "infinite" term). In turn, from this it follows that, thorough the chapter, the various possible ways in which production can be organized are not "discrete structural alternatives," and their differences can only be a matter of degree.[6]

The second is that to this point nothing has been said about the level of competition in the product market and, accordingly, it is possible that those making a specific investment exactly obtain what another would require for the same investment. In this sense, specific assets are not incompatible with a competitive equilibrium in the product market. So far, to put it another way, rent and quasi-rent are distinct and diverse concepts.[7]

As will be seen in a moment, by contrast, in the present story the investors' expectations about the possibility of extracting a rent from consumers are quite crucial. For the present, with these specifications we are in a position to analyze the consequences of the focus on imitable investments.

To do so, suppose that, at $t = 1$, another element of the investors' set, $A'$, is in the same situation as A. Since the investment of A is replicable, however, $A'$ now has an additional option, that of imitation. Behaving this way, that is imitating A's investment and entering the same market, $A'$ does not need to agree a long-term contract with $B'$, another element of the workers' set who is necessary to $A'$ as B is to A. Her investment too is irreversible for two periods but, in $t = 2$, the contract between A and B expires and this is a sufficient protection against the appropriation threat by $B'$.

In the case of General Motors and Fisher Body, for example, $A'$ could be any other supplier of components (FB′) that, transferring its own plant to the same geographical area as GM and FB, can easily replace its own producer of automobiles (GM′) with GM. In the case of a firm's investment in a new computer system, instead, $A'$ could obviously be any other firm which, adopting the same computer system, is indifferent between its own workers and the ones already trained by the first firm.

Thus, if A′ might confine herself to have a one-period contract with B′, she does not have to provide the corresponding compensation and is probably able to gain positive profits in spite of A, who will be easily forced to incur a loss. If instead A′ effects another investment, different from that of A and specific to B′, suppose for the moment that she is repaid the costs sustained in the case she is successful, while she expects to suffer a loss in the opposite case. Finally, if she neither invests nor imitates she will obtain nothing.

Therefore, it is clear enough that A′ will imitate and this in turn implies that, at t = 0, A will not effect his own specific investment. Imitation, diluting specificity by making alternative users available, re-establishes the attractiveness of market discipline that, in turn, allows the follower to save the costs of non-market relationships obtaining the same advantages that the leader has paid for. Of course, from this it follows that the leader will take account of it before making his own specific investment and this behavior, due to the "organizational free-riding" problem among investors, shows the possibility of an under-investment outcome.

As noted above, however, it is not necessarily true that such a free-riding risk would always be to discourage specific investments. That is, it is not always true that imitation is the dominant strategy as so far has been the case in this simple example. By making an investment different from that of the leader and specific to her own counterpart, the follower too can extract a rent which may be preferred to the profit immediately available from imitating. In turn, this implies that for the leader it may be optimal to make first his own specific investment when there are good reasons to believe that the follower will effect her alternative specific investment rather than competitive imitation. As will be seen in a moment, the addition of a bit of (real world) uncertainty about the investments' prospects suffices to allow for an over-investment outcome, and makes the example richer.

## *A very simple entry game*

Strategically, the described situation can be represented by a three-period extended form game as shown in Figure 13.1. The strategies available to the players are imitation ($i$), or high ($h$) or low ($l$) specific investment. Indicating with g the game and with g′ the sub-game in which players can imitate an existing investment, $s_x^j$ is the generic strategy available to the player j at the node x (j = A, A′; x = g, g′).

The payoffs $R$, $G$, and $L$ have the following interpretation: $R$ is the rent extractable from a (not imitated) successful investment; $G$ is the gain from imitating; $L$ is the loss from being imitated. Under reasonable conditions detailed in the Appendix, it turns out that they are all positive, with $R > G$. Respectively indicating the organizational and the technological component of the total cost of investment with $C$ and $F$, instead, the payoff $-(C + F)$ is associated with an unsuccessful investment.

Finally, $f$ is the probability of the investment's failure. This probability is assumed to be exogenously given, commonly known (or assessed) by players and, recalling that (high) specific investments last two periods, let us also assume that it

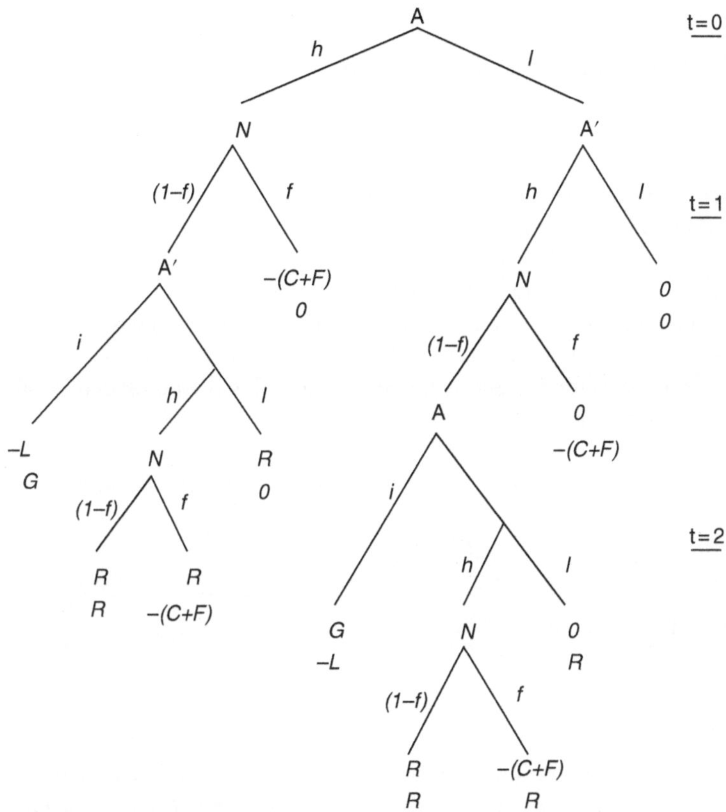


*Figure 13.1* GM and Fisher Body. A three-period extended form game.

is chosen by "Nature" ($\mathcal{N}$) after the first period (so that the uncertainty it represents vanishes in that period and, of course, only successful investments remain under the imitation threat).[8]

Now, it is not difficult to verify that the two outcomes previously discussed in words actually are the equilibria of g. Since the game is finite (see Note 9), it turns out that they can be found by backward induction critically depending on the variable representing the probability of the investments' failure.

In effect, the g′-player will choose between imitation ($i$) and high specific investment ($h$) depending on whether $G$ is (respectively) higher or lower than $-f(C+F)+(1-f)R$, that is, depending on whether $f$ is (respectively) higher or lower than $(R-G)/(R+C+F)$.

Consequently, the g-player's expected payoff from the high specific investment strategy is the following function:

$$-f(C+F)+(1-f)[-q(f)L+(1-q(f))R] \qquad (13.1)$$

$$\text{where } q = \begin{cases} 1 & \text{if } f \geq (R-G)/(R+C+F) \\ 0 & \phantom{\text{if }} f < (R-G)/(R+C+F) \end{cases} \quad (13.2)$$

indicates the probability that the g-player is imitated by the g′-player.

Accordingly, if $f \geq (R - G)/(R + C + F)$, both players play the generic investment strategy in g ($l$). For these values of $f$, the g′-player will choose the imitation strategy ($i$) and, consequently, ($l$) is the optimal choice in g. In order ($h$) is attractive in this case, in fact, the g-player's expected payoff from that strategy (eq. 13.1) would have to be positive, but $f \leq 1$ and $L > L - C - F$.

Vice versa, if $f < (R - G)/(R + C + F)$, the g′-player will choose the specific investment strategy ($h$) and so the g-player also chooses the same strategy. With $q = 0$, in fact, the g-player's expected payoff from the $h$-strategy is always positive since $R/(R + C + F) > (R - G)/(R + C + F)$.

Thus, essentially for expositional convenience, this reasoning can be summarized in the form of the following.

**Proposition 1.** *For the game g, the sub-game perfect equilibrium paths are*

$$l_g^A, l_g^{A'}(i_{g'}^A, i_{g'}^{A'}) \quad \text{if } f \geq \frac{R-G}{R+C+F'}$$

$$h_g^A, h_g^{A'}(h_{g'}^A, h_{g'}^{A'}) \quad \text{if } f < \frac{R-G}{R+L}$$

### *The group solution*

As a result of this proposition, the sequence of externalities originating from specificity determines a tendency to uniformity in the behavior of economic agents, who end up by all choosing the same strategy. Setting in an organizational framework the well-known trade-off between competition and innovation, the intermediate situation in which the investment strategy co-exists with that of imitation is not equilibrium of g.[9] Depending on the probability of failure is lower or higher than a given threshold level, either all players invest or no one invests as the likelihood of being imitated, in turn, depends on that probability and, in the present context, a necessary condition for the attractiveness of specific investments is the expectation of not being imitated before the recovery of the costs paid in advance.

Intuitively, the institutional arrangement emerging from this non-cooperative process seems to be characterized by a tendency to over- or under-invest in the sense that the benefits of specific investments are achieved at the price of a duplication of their organizational costs, or are not achieved at all. In both cases, the total costs of production (technological and organizational) would not be minimized and the corresponding institutional structure of production would not be the efficient one.

To see this point, consider an agreement between A and A′ explicitly providing the possibility of imitation, that is, an agreement linking A and A′ in a sort of business group and implementing the strategies profile $(h^A, i^{A'})$. Since the two investors make the same investment, yet B and B′ are not easily substitutable by other elements of the workers' set, but between them there is now perfect substitutability. Accordingly, in respect of the counterparts, the agreement between A and A$'$ corresponds to contracts for two periods as a group but for one period only within the group.

Compared to the outcome in which A and A$'$ invest separately $(h^{\mathrm{A}}, h^{\mathrm{A}'})$, this agreement has the advantage of alleviating the hold-up problem and, correspondingly, the compensation cost to be paid for the non-market relationships with B and B$'$. This is the case because opportunistic behavior becomes now costly since it has to be coordinated, and this reduces the amount needed to make it not credible.[10]

Compared to the outcome in which no one invests $(l^{\mathrm{A}}, l^{\mathrm{A}'})$, the A-A$'$ agreement has instead the obvious advantage that the investment is made and therefore creates its benefits, represented by the difference between the marginal costs of production before and after the investment.

Like the advantages, the disadvantages too are both technological and organizational. On the one hand, with respect to the outcome in which there are no investments, the fixed costs of the investments must be paid. On the other hand, with respect to the outcome of non-cooperative investments, to reach their agreement the two investors will have to bear some bargaining cost. Hence, the latter has the same rationale as the organizational cost paid to solve the hold-up threat with non-market relationships, but in this case it refers to the free-riding problem among investors.

Obviously, the best form of economic organization depends on the relative level of such costs and benefits in the three possible outcomes discussed so far. Adopting the joint profits of A and A$'$ in the three different situations as a measure of the efficiency of the corresponding institutional arrangement, we can write:

$$\begin{aligned}&\Pi^{\mathrm{A+A'}}(h^{\mathrm{A}}, h^{\mathrm{A}'})\\ &= 2(1-f)\left[(p-c)\sum_{t=0}^{2} Q_t - (C+F)\right] - 2f(C+F)\end{aligned} \tag{13.3}$$

$$\Pi^{\mathrm{A+A'}}(l^{\mathrm{A}}, l^{\mathrm{A}'}) = (p-\bar{\bar{c}})\sum_{t=0}^{2} Q_t \tag{13.4}$$

$$\begin{aligned}&\Pi^{\mathrm{A+A'}}(h^{\mathrm{A}}, i^{\mathrm{A}'})\\ &= 2(1-f)\left[(p-c)\sum_{t=0}^{2} Q_t - \left(F+\overline{C}+\frac{b}{2}\right)\right] - 2f\left(F+\overline{C}+\frac{b}{2}\right)\end{aligned} \tag{13.5}$$

where, $\overline{C}(<C)$ indicates the reduced compensation cost to be paid for non-market relationships with B and B$'$ in the cooperative case of the group solution,

$b$ represents the agreement's bargaining cost, and $\bar{\bar{c}}$ and $c$ are the (constant) marginal costs of production before and after the investment (with $c < \bar{\bar{c}}$).

Then, the conditions under which the A-A′ agreement is the best way to organize production can be precisely expressed in the following:[11]

**Proposition 2.** *Assume* $(C - \overline{C}) > \frac{b}{4}$ *and* $(1 - f)(\bar{\bar{c}} - c) > \overline{C} + F + \frac{b}{2}$.
*Then,* $\Pi^{A+A'}(h^{A}, i^{A'}) > \Pi^{A+A'}(h^{A}, h^{A'})$,
*and* $\Pi^{A+A'}(h^{A}, i^{A'}) > \Pi^{A+A'}(l^{A}, l^{A'})$.

Under these conditions, the (expected) reduction in both organizational and technological costs (or the quality improvement) outweighs the fixed costs of the investments and the agreement bargaining cost so that the total cost of production ends up by being lower than in the two alternative outcomes. Under these conditions, in other words, internalizing the adverse effects of the temporal sequence in which, non-cooperatively, specific investments are made, investors are able to enjoy the main advantage of the group solution, that is, to reduce the organizational cost of specificity without depressing the *ex ante* incentives to invest.

## Extensions and applications

Recalling the famous contribution by Stigler (1951) quoted in the Introduction, where he noted that firms tend to self-produce their own inputs and to vertically integrate relatively more often in infant industries rather than in mature ones, one would be tempted to conclude that the "organizational free-riding" problem and its group solution are also relevant for ownership relations. Without questioning his technological explanation in terms of increasing returns to scale, it is indeed quite easy to interpret this circumstance by referring to the preceding notion of "organizational experimentation costs" for, by definition, they only exist in the early stages of the industries' development. For productive relationships where the "uniqueness" of the parties is not intrinsically irreducible *a priori*, therefore, vertical integration could also admit a revival of interpretations giving some role to market foreclosure and other similar (not efficiency-based) considerations.

As repeatedly noted, however, in this chapter the introduction of an explicit structure of timing in the specific investment decision process suggests the adoption of an approach in which the differences between the various alternative governance structures can only be a matter of degree. As a consequence, their best empirical applications must be looked for in relationships among parties which cannot be bought. In particular, to appreciate to what extent the group solution can be seen as a stylized representation of the local industrial systems' governance structure, one could compare the above four-sided agreement with the institutional arrangement that the following quotation summarizes in the form of a slogan: "[Under flexible specialization] No firm or individual has a right to any particular place within the community, but all have a claim to some place within it" (Piore and Sabel, 1984, p. 269).[12]

Interestingly, in addition, the workers' interfirm mobility implicit in this kind of economic organization has been indicated by the more recent research as crucial to understand the way in which knowledge is therein created and exchanged.[13] Going back to the famous Marshallian observation that in industrial districts "secrets are in the air," today the idea that "thick" networks of productive relationships facilitate knowledge formation is basically formulated in terms of its tacit and (therefore) system-specific nature.

Following a reasoning in many ways similar to that of this chapter, however, there is now enough agreement on the fact that, for both theoretical and empirical reasons, the degree of tacitness is not an intrinsic and invariable character but depends upon the costs and benefits of the codification process. As a consequence, strategic considerations about who is to be included (or not) in the network become quite relevant (Cowan *et al.*, 2000; Breschi and Lissoni, 2001; see also Arcori *et al.*, 2000, for the opposite view). More directly, in a world where technology tends to make irrelevant the distinction between strong and weak ties, or between local and long distances, closure, taciturnity and even specialization could be more costly than in the past, so that the current evolution of local industrial systems would have to be eventually interpreted as moving towards a greater degree of openness and diversity (Sabel, 2001; Saxenian and Hsu, 2002).

With the appropriate modifications, the proposed framework is able to catch this point. In fact, identifying this possible new cost of grouping economic organizations in the duplication of the investments, the attractiveness of such an eventual departure from isolation and tacitness could be addressed by making explicit the relations of complementarity and substitutability between the investments' probability of failure (see Note 11).

## Conclusion

In this chapter, a notion of intermediate degree of investments' specificity has been introduced. Then, following the logic of a discriminating alignment between transactions and governance structures, this notion has been employed to give an account for a grouping economic organization which is to be intended as a stylized representation of the clustering organizational models typically associated with the network of productive relationships in local industrial systems.

Applying the specificity-based approach to the case of investments that, in principle, could be imitated (and introducing both an explicit structure of timing to the specific investment decision process and a bit of uncertainty about the investments' prospects), it has been shown that the organizational cost of specificity may be exposed to a free-riding risk and, as a consequence, a tendency to over- or under-invest may arise.

While in the first place the case for efficiency-based explanations of existing economic organizations is correspondingly restricted, on the other hand, it has been argued that a group of investors may find it profitable to internalize such an externality by making the same investment and implementing assets which are "intermediately" specific in the sense that they are not specific to the particular relationship between the single investors and the single counterparts (taken one by one), but remain specific to the set of relationships between investors and counterparts (taken as a group).

Accordingly, being general inside the group of relationships in which they have already been imitated, but remaining specific among different groups, this kind of assets has been associated to a hybrid organizational structure based on market relationships inside the group and on non-market relationships at the level of the group. As this kind of assets maintains an extra value over the next best alternative use (as long as they are not superseded by subsequent innovations), but is exposed to a reduced risk of opportunistic behavior (for their uniqueness character has been diluted), the main advantage of such an organizational form has been identified in reducing the organizational cost of specificity without depressing the *ex ante* incentives to invest.

Finally, while this advantage has been rationalized as a cooperative internalization of the adverse effects of the temporal sequence in which, non-cooperatively, specific investments are necessarily made, the eventual identification of its main cost in the duplication of investments leaves room for a discussion of the current views on the role of openness and diversity in promoting innovation in local industrial systems.

However, since a basic point of the chapter is that asset specificity unequivocally creates costs but not necessarily value, additional work to understand when a specificity-reducing strategy is simply impossible (by nature or by law), or depends upon the economics of (all) its costs and benefits, is needed.

## Appendix

To derive an analytical formula for the payoffs of the game suppose that, if not imitated, A and A′ can behave monopolistically while, if imitation occurs, they must compete *à la* Cournot. To make things interesting, suppose also that, if not imitated, a successful investment is definitely profitable ($R > 0$) but, in order that the hold-up threat is really effective, the first period only is not enough to recover its costs. More specifically, indicating with $c$ the (common) marginal cost of production, and with $p^M (p^C)$ and $Q^M (Q^C)$ the monopolistic (Cournot) price and quantity, assume:

$$2(p^M - c)Q^M \geq C + F \geq (p^M - c)Q^M, \text{ where} \tag{13A.1}$$

$F$ and $C$ respectively represent the technological and the organizational component of the total cost of the investment as in the text.

Then, as long as A′ is willing to imitate ($G > 0$), that is, as long as:

$$\frac{(p^C - c)Q^C}{2} \geq F, \tag{13A.2}$$

a sufficient condition for imitation being simultaneously harmful to A ($L > 0$) is the following:

$$C + F \geq \frac{3(p^M - c)Q^M}{2}. \tag{13A.3}$$

Since $(p^M - c)Q^M \geq (p^C - c)Q^C$, in fact, if (13A.2) and (13A.3) hold it must be that:

$$C + F \geq \left[(p^M - c)Q^M + \frac{(p^C - c)Q^C}{2}\right]. \tag{13A.4}$$

Interestingly, while condition (13A.3) could be made more restrictive by appropriately specifying the demand function, it also turns out that, since from (13A.1) it follows $(p^M - c)Q^M \geq (C + F)/2$, necessary conditions for (13A.4) are $F \leq (p^C - c)Q^C/2 \leq (C + F)/2$ and $(C + F)/2 \leq (p^M - c)Q^M \leq C$, which both imply $C \geq F$.

In other words, in the present story the organizational component of the total cost of the investment must be large relatively to the technological one, which confirms that its best applications must be looked for in productive relationships where human capital is relatively more important than physical capital.

As noted in the text, however, it is not necessarily true that such a free-riding risk would always be to discourage specific investments, that is, it is not always true that imitation is the dominant strategy. Actually, it is sufficient that $(p^M - c)Q^M \geq \frac{2}{3}C$, to have that:

$$[2(p^M - c)Q^M - (C + F)] \geq \left[\frac{(p^C - c)Q^C}{2} - F\right], \text{ that is, } R > G. \tag{13A.5}$$

## Acknowledgments

I am indebted for their useful comments and suggestions to Sam Bowles, Marco Dardi, Maurizio Franzini, Michele Grillo, Silvia Marchesi, Ugo Pagano, and two anonymous referees. The usual disclaimer applies.

## Notes

1 Clearly, the literature on technological innovation has been very influential for the present work. However, its basic issues – the role of novelty in creating value and the relationship between innovative activities and market structure – have been tackled in more detail in a related paper (Battistini, 2001).

2 See Pagano (1991) for an early analysis of the possible benefits of a specificity-reducing strategy, with applications to the German–Japanese system of industrial relations.

3 Meaning by "novelty" a difference in the asset's value between alternative uses (the new one and the old ones), and by "uniqueness" a difference in the asset's value between alternative users (the first one and the others), the point could simply be made in the

following way: in the case of non-imitable investments, novelty is a necessary *and* a sufficient condition for uniqueness, as all new assets are also unique, and all unique assets are also new; in the case of imitable investments, instead, novelty is just a necessary condition for uniqueness, for not all new assets need to be unique. From this the non-cooperative tendency to over-arises or under-invest and its cooperative solution.

4 Of course, this is only true if the number of investors is finite. In the case of an infinite number of investors the equilibrium size of the group is determined by the usual zero profit condititon.

5 It may be worth noting that this particular specification of a non-market relationships cost is not strictly necessary to the robustness of the argument. Any one of those recalled in the Introduction can play its role. Notwithstanding the differences in the context, in any case, this compensation cost is quite akin in spirit to the notion of "enforcement rent" introduced by Bowles and Gintis (1993).

6

> Once we attempt to add empirical detail to Coase's fundamental insight that a systematic study of transaction costs is necessary to explain particular forms of economic organization, we find that his primary distinction between transactions made within a firm and transactions made in the marketplace may often be too simplistic. Many long-term relationships (such as franchising) blur the line between market and the firm. Firms are therefore, by definition, formed and revised in markets and the conventional sharp distinction between markets and firms may have little general analytical importance. The pertinent economic question we are faced with is "what kinds of contracts are used for what kinds of activities, and why?"
>
> (Klein *et al.*, 1978, p. 326)

For the inadequacy of asset specificity to explain vertical integration, with particular reference to the GM–FB story, see also Casades-Masanell and Spulber (2000) and Coase (2000).

7

> An appropriable quasi rent is not a monopoly rent in the usual sense, that is, the increased value of an asset protected from market entry over the value it would have had in an open market. An appropriable quasi rent can occur with no market closure or restrictions placed on rival assets. Once installed, an asset may be so expensive to remove or so specialized to a particular user that if the price paid to the owner was somehow reduced the asset's services to that user would not be reduced. Thus, even if there were free and open competition for entry in the market, the specialization of the installed asset to a particular user (or more accurately the high cost of making it available to others) creates a quasi rent, but not a "monopoly" rent. At the other extreme, an asset may be costlessly transferable to some other user at no reduction in value, while at the same time, entry of similar assets is restricted. In this case, monopoly rent would exist, but not quasi rent.
>
> (Klein *et al.*, 1978, p. 299)

8 Note that the possibility of failure does not eliminate the irreversible character of the specific investment strategy, so that in the game players are not allowed to choose the $h$-strategy twice. This is the reason why the payoff to A$'$, after the path (h, f), and the payoff to A, after the path (l,h,f), are 0. If they try their own luck after the first mover's attempt to invest was unsuccessful, they would be imitated with certainty by their opponents. So they choose the $l$-strategy and obtain a null payoff. I am grateful to an anonymous referee for making me aware of this point.

9 Were the game's periods infinite, in addition to the pure equilibrium of Proposition 1 ($h^A h^A$), one would also be tempted of finding a mixed equilibrium in which the g-player plays $h$ and the infinite sequence of g$\prime$-players randomize between $i$ and $h$ with the probability which makes them indifferent between such strategies ($q = [f(C + F + R) + G - R]/[f(L + R) - (L + R)]$). However, this equilibrium does not exist since

$0 \geq q \leq 1$ and $0 \geq f \leq 1$ require $L > C + F$ which is not possible: the loss from being imitated, in fact, cannot be higher than the total cost of the investment.

10 Similar arguments can be easily found for the other "non-market" costs referred to in the Introduction. See also Note 5.

11 In this formulation two assumptions are implicit. With the first, the produced quantities in the three different outcomes are always the same. With the second, the probability of failure too is the same, independent of the investments being cooperatively or non-cooperatively made. Actually, both these assumptions are not very realistic. The first because in the case of non-cooperative investments the produced quantity would be greater due to a higher degree of product differentiation. The second because, depending on whether the investments are different or not, the probabilities of failure need not be independent but can also be complementary or substitute. In addition, such assumptions are not entirely innocuous since, together, they hide the duplication of investments as a possible cost of the group solution. As will be clearer in the next section, however, the focus on this possible cost of the group solution, instead of weakening its attractiveness, makes more robust the proposed applications to local industrial systems.

12 In the same spirit, describing the power and mobility of engineers in their relationships with the Silicon Valley based firms, Gilson (1997, p. 1467) points out: "The story in Silicon Valley is that they work for the Valley; they don't work for a firm." Analogously, reporting a personal interview to a founder of a now famous start-up firm, Saxenian (1994, p. 36) confirms, "There are a lot of people who come to work in the morning believing that they work for Silicon Valley."

13 In recent years several journals have devoted special issues to localized learning and knowledge creation processes. See *Regional Studies*, 1999, vol. 33 (4), *Cambridge Journal of Economics*, 1999, vol. 99, and *Industrial and Corporate Change*, 2001, vol. 10(4).

## References


Ancori, B., A. Bureth, and P. Cohendet (2000), The Economics of Knowledge: The Debate about Codification and Tacit Knowledge, *Industrial and Corporate Change*, 9: 255–288.

Battistini, A. (2001), Competizione tra organizzazioni, specificità degli investimenti e efficienza, *Economia Politica*, 3: 333–349.

Becattini, G. (1991), The Marshallian Industrial Districts as a Socio-Economic Concept. In F. Pyke, G. Becattini, and W. Semberger (eds), *Industrial Districts and Inter-Firm Cooperation in Italy, International Institute for Labour Studies*, pp. 37–52, Geneva, Switzerland.

Bowles, S. and H. Gintis (1993), The Revenge of Homo Economicus: Contested Exchange and the Revival of Political Economy, *Journal of Economic Perspectives*, 7(1), 83–102.

Breschi, S. and F. Lissoni (2001), Knowledge Spillovers and Local Innovation Systems: A Critical Survey, *Industrial and Corporate Change*, 4: 975–1006.

Casadesus-Masanell, R. and D.F. Spulber (2000), The Fable of Fisher Body, *Journal of Law and Economics*, XLIII: 67–104.

Coase, R.H. (2000), The Acquisition of Fisher Body by General Motors, *Journal of Law and Economics*, XLIII: 15–32.

Cowan, R., P.A. David, and D. Foray (2000), The Explicit Economics of Knowledge Codification and Tacitness, *Industrial and Corporate Change*, 9: 211–253.

Gilson, R. (1997), The Future of Corporate Governance in United States, *University of Richmond Law Review*, 31: 1459–1472.

Grosmann, S. and O. Hart (1986), The Costs and Benefits of Ownership: A Theory of Vertical and Lateral Integration, *Journal of Political Economy*, 94: 691–719.

Hart, O. (1995), *Firms, Contracts, and Financial Structure*. Oxford: Clarendon Press.

Hart, O. and J. Moore (1990), Property Rights and the Nature of the Firm, *Journal of Political Economy*, 98: 1119–1158.

Klein, B., A. Crawford, and A. Alchian (1978), Vertical Integration, Appropriable Rents, and the Competitive Contracting Process, *Journal of Law and Economics*, 21(2): 297–326.

Menard, C. (1996), On Clusters, Hybrids and Other Strange Forms: The Case of French Poultry Industry, *Journal of Institutional and Theoretical Economics*, 152: 154–196.

Milgrom, P. and J. Roberts (1988), Bargaining Costs, Influence Costs, and the Organization of Economic Activity. In J. Alt and K. Shepsle (eds), *Perspectives on Positive Political Economy*. Cambridge University Press (1990), 240–271.

Pagano, U. (1991), Property Rights, Asset Specificity, and Division of Labour under Alternative Capitalist Relations, *Cambridge Journal of Economics*, 15(3): 315–341.

Piore, M.J. and C.F. Sabel (1984), *The Second Industrial Divide*. Basic Books, New York.

Sabel, C.F. (2001), Diversity, Not Specialization: The Ties that Bind the (New) Industrial District, Paper Presented at the conference 'Complexity and Industrial Clusters: Dynamics and Models in Theory and Practice', Milan, June 19–20, 2001.

Saxenian, A. (1994), *Regional Advantage: Culture and Competition in Silicon Valley and Route 128*, Cambridge, MA: Harvard University Press.

Saxenian, A. and J.-H. Hsu (2002), The Silicon Valley-Hsinchu Connection: Technical Communities and Industrial Upgrading, *Industrial and Corporate Change*, 1: 893–920.

Schumpeter, J.A. (1911), *The Theory of Economic Development*, Oxford: Oxford University Press (1961).

Stigler, G.J. (1951), The Division of Labor is Limited by the Extent of the Market, *Journal of Political Economy*, 59: 185–193.

Williamson, O. (1985), *The Economic Institutions of Capitalism*. Free Press, New York.

Williamson, O. (1991), Comparitive Economic Organization: The Analysis of Discrete Structural Alternatives, *Administrative Science Quarterly*, 36: 269–296.

You, J. and F. Wilkinson (1994), Competition and Cooperation: Toward Understanding Industrial Districts, *Review of Political Economy*, 6(3): 259–278.

# Part IV

# Governance models and corporate ethics

# 14 What is corporation?

## The corporate personality controversy and the fiduciary principle in corporate governance[1]

*Katsuhito Iwai*

### Introduction

What is a corporation? The law speaks of a corporation as a "legal person" – as a subject of rights and duties capable of owning real property, entering into contracts, and suing and being sued in its own name.[2] For many centuries, philosophers, political scientists, sociologists, economists, and among all jurists and legal scholars have debated heatedly as to what constitutes the "essence" of this soulless and bodiless person. In this so-called corporate personality controversy, one of the most celebrated controversies in legal theory and legal philosophy, two competing legal theories have emerged, each advancing a diametrically opposed view on the "essence" of the corporation. They are "corporate nominalism" and "corporate realism."[3] Corporate nominalism asserts that the corporation is merely a contractual association of shareholders, whose legal personality is no more than an abbreviated way of writing their names together. In opposition, the corporate realism claims that the corporation is a full-fledged organizational entity whose legal personality is no more than an external expression of its real personality in society. And both claim to have superseded the "fiction theory," the traditional doctrine since the medieval times, which maintained that the corporation is a separate and distinct social entity but its legal personality is a mere fiction created by the state.

The rivalry between corporate nominalism and corporate realism has continued up until now. The contractual theory of the firm, be it an agency theory version or a transaction-cost economics version or an incomplete contract theory version, is a direct descendant of corporate nominalism,[4] whereas the evolutionary theory of the firm or the knowledge-base view of the firm can be interpreted as a modern reincarnation of corporate realism.[5] The former regards corporate firms as "simply legal fiction which serve as a nexus for a set of contracting relations among individuals,"[6] whereas the latter posits corporate firms as "organizations that know how to do things, ... while individual members come and go."[7] The corporate personality controversy is far from a relic of the past.

The present chapter is an attempt to "end" this age-old opposition between nominalism and realism once and for all. This is done, however, not by declaring victory for one side or the other. It is by declaring victory for both. The key to this claim is an observation that, in contrast to an sole-proprietorship firm or a partnership firm, a "corporate" form of business firm consists of not one but *two* ownership relations: the shareholders own the corporation as a legal thing and the corporation as a legal person in turn owns the corporate assets. The corporation thus plays a dual role of a "person" and a "thing" in the system of law. It is, I believe, this person/thing duality that is responsible for the long persistence of the controversy on corporate personality. Indeed, the first objective of the present chapter is to demonstrate how this person/thing duality of the corporation is capable of generating two seemingly contradictory corporate structures – one approximating corporate realism and the other approximating corporate nominalism.

The law is thus unable to determine the legal nature of the corporation even within its own system. This does not, however, imply the impossibility of a single principle unifying a variety of corporate governance systems that have evolved in different countries. The problems of "corporate" governance are literally the problems of governing the "corporate" form of business firms, not of governing sole-proprietorship firms or partnership firms. Indeed, the fact that a corporate firm is characterized by a two-tier ownership structure implies that corporate managers cannot be regarded as agents of shareholders; they are the "fiduciaries" of the corporation. The second purpose of this chapter is to demonstrate that at the foundation of every corporate governance system lie the managers' fiduciary duties to the corporation, and that the legal rules regulating these duties should be essentially mandatory. The chapter also argues that a variety of corporate governance systems across countries is due to the difference in governance mechanisms that supplement the costly implementation of fiduciary law by courts.

## Persons, things, and corporations

In the basic model of the market economy, expounded in any introductory textbook of economics, the relationship between persons and things is simple and clear. As is illustrated in Figure 14.1, persons are subjects of property right and things are objects of property right. Persons own things and things are owned by persons. There is an absolute divide between persons and things. If persons own persons, we are back to the slave economy of the ancient past. If things own persons, we are perhaps trapped in a world of science-fiction.

Capitalistic firms are founded on this simple relationship between persons and things. In the case of the traditional sole-proprietorship firm, an individual invested

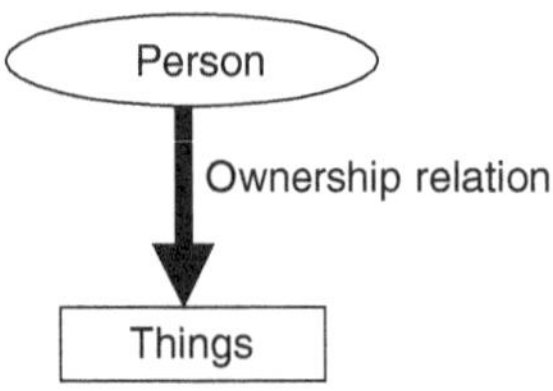


*Figure 14.1* A person and things.

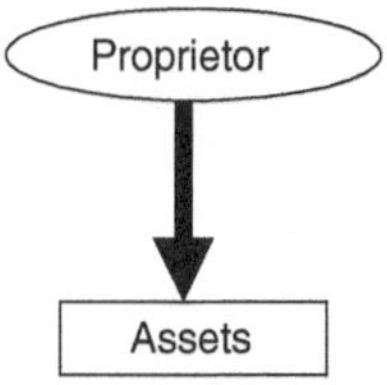


*Figure 14.2* The basic structure of a sole-proprietorship firm.

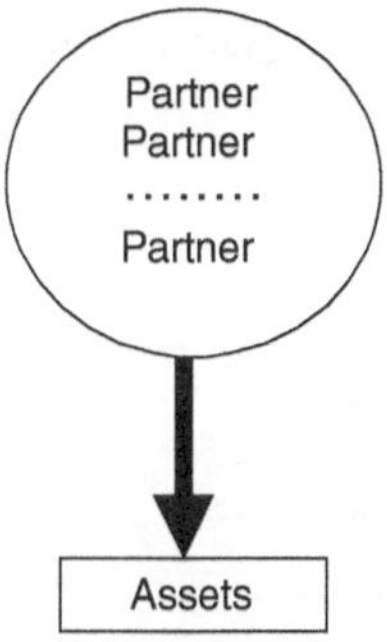


*Figure 14.3* The basic structure of a partnership firm.

his capital in productive assets in order to earn profits. As is shown in Figure 14.2, the individual capitalist was the subject of property right, whereas the assets, both tangible and intangible, were the objects of property right. They were directly opposed as a person and things.

We can draw essentially the same picture for the partnership firm. Instead of a single person owning assets, a group of individuals now own these assets jointly, as is depicted in Figure 14.3. And yet, a transition from sole-proprietorship to partnership may engender a fundamental change in the nature of the firm. As is illustrated in Figure 14.4, in capitalistic society every business undertaking must enter into numerous contractual relations with outside parties such as employees, suppliers, customers, and creditors. In the case of a partnership firm, every partner has an equal right and an equal duty to any contract it maintains. This means that whenever there is a withdrawal or a death of an old partner or an admission of a new partner, each contract has to be rewritten or at least the signatures of the partners have to be updated. To rewrite a contract *ex post* involves various kinds of transaction costs. Of course, if the number of partners is small or the scope of outside contracts is limited, it may be possible to save these transaction costs by including *ex ante* provisions for such contingencies in each contract. But, as the size of the partnership gets larger or outside relationships become numerous, these transaction costs would soon become prohibitively large, thereby rendering the

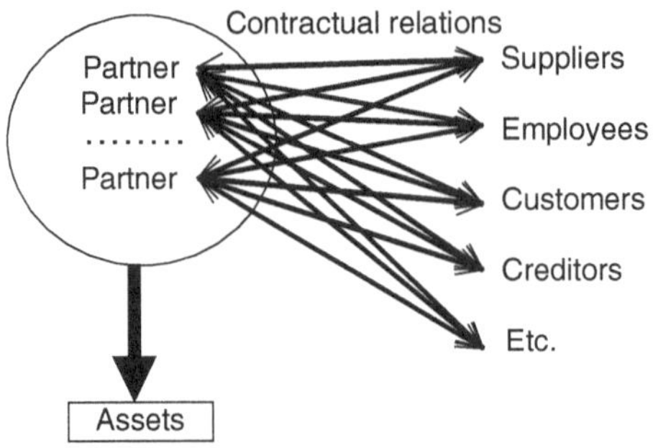


*Figure 14.4* Contractual relations between a partnership firm and outside parties.

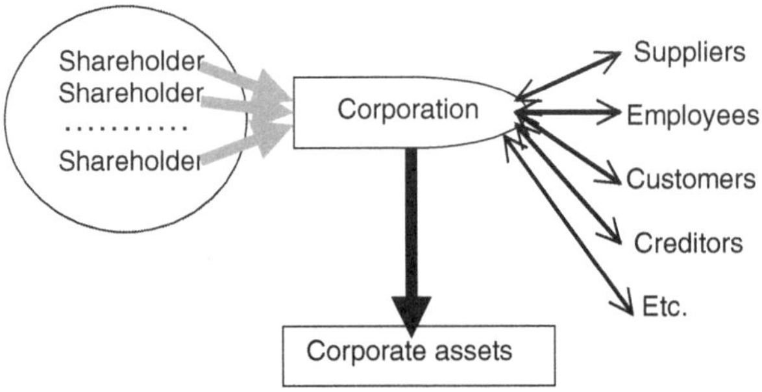


*Figure 14.5* Corporation as a legal device to simplify outside relations.

contracts necessarily incomplete. Outside parties would then be easily discouraged from entering into contractual relations with the partnership firm.

The corporation is a legal solution to this problem. How can it solve this problem? If a group of $N$ individuals decide to set up a corporation and to become its shareholders, it is like creating beside themselves the $N + 1$st person who has the same legal capacity to own real assets as they themselves have. As is illustrated in Figure 14.5, outside parties then become able to enter into a contract with this $N + 1$st person, independently of its $N$ shareholders, in exactly the same manner as they enter into a contract with the owner of a sole-proprietorship firm. Hence, the complex network of contractual relations is greatly simplified, leading to a large reduction of transaction costs for all participants. This also shields the contracting outside parties from the vagaries of the death, withdrawal or entry of its individual shareholders, thereby encouraging them to form contractual relations with the firm.

I have dwelled upon a textbook account of corporate *raison d'être* in order to bring home the central fact about the legal institution of corporation: the corporation cannot be reduced to a mere "standard form contract" among its constituting shareholders. The corporation is presented here, not as a devise to economize on the transaction costs of arranging internal organization among shareholders, but as a devise to economize on the transaction costs of arranging external relationships the shareholders have with outside parties. As the corporate nominalists have never been tired of pointing out, any innovation in the firm's organizational structure can in principle be arranged internally by a well-crafted contractual agreement among shareholders.[8] To do so may incur transaction costs, but those costs could easily be reduced by the extensive use of standard form contracts. In contrast, the corporation's legal capacity to coordinate the complex contractual relations between inside shareholders and outside parties is essentially a "social" or "inter-subjective" one. It cannot be asserted by the internal agreement among shareholders alone, no matter how skillfully they formulate the contract, unless it is acknowledged by employers, suppliers, customers, creditors, and other outsiders. A corporation is able to act as an independent owner of its own property capable of forming contractual relations with others, not because the inside shareholders will it to be so, but because, and in so far as, the outside parties recognize it to be so. Such social recognition is indispensable, and what the law does is to formalize and reinforce this social recognition in the form of legal personality. Indeed, the Latin word "persona," from which the English word "person" is derived, meant originally an actor's mask. Each persona incarnated a role in a drama, and the spectator recognized the role of each actor by the persona he wore. It is not to express his inner self through it but to act out the role incarnated by it that an actor wore a persona on his face.

To recapitulate: the corporation is introduced into the legal system as a non-contractual legal device to simplify the external relationships of a group of individuals. But we all know that there is no "free lunch" – even in the province of law. What I would like to show now is that this simplifying device also has the effect of complicating the internal ownership structure of a corporate firm.

## The corporation as a person/thing duality

Suppose you are the owner of a Mom & Pop grocery shop around the corner. Whenever you feel hungry, you can pick up an apple on the shelf and eat it right away. That apple is your property, and the only thing you have to worry about is the wrath of your spouse – your co-owner.

Suppose next you are a shareholder of a corporation, say, a big supermarket chain. Suppose further that you feel hungry. If you march into one of its stores and grab an apple from the shelf, claiming that that apple is your property, what will happen to you? You will be immediately arrested as a thief! Why? It is because corporate shareholders are *not* the owners of corporate assets. Who is, then, the owner of the corporate assets? The answer is, of course, the corporation itself as a "legal person." After all, the corporate assets are literally the corporation's assets. It is the corporation itself as a legal person that is the owner of the corporate assets. Then, what are the corporate shareholders? The answer is, of course, they are the owners of the corporation. Literally as well as legally, corporate shareholders are the holders of a corporate share – of a bundle of financial rights and participatory rights in the corporation that can be bought and sold freely as an object of property right. Indeed, to hold a corporate share is to own a fraction of the corporation as a "legal thing," independent of the remaining fraction and separate and distinct from the underlying corporate assets. It is the corporation itself as a legal thing that the corporate shareholders are the owners of.

All this is the most elementary fact about the corporation that no textbook of corporate law has ever failed to make note of. But its implications, I believe, have not been fully worked out even by legal scholars, let alone by economists. Because this observation will lead us to the most crucial characterization of the internal structure of a corporate firm. In contrast to a sole-proprietorship firm depicted in Figure 14.2 and a partnership firm depicted in Figure 14.3, a corporate firm is composed of not one but *two* ownership relations. As is shown in Figure 14.6, the shareholders own the corporation as a legal thing, and the corporation as a legal person in turn owns the corporate assets.

I have argued in the preceding section that the corporation is a legal device that simplifies the external relations a business firm has to have with outsiders. We have now seen that the same legal device has the effect of complicating the internal structure of a business firm by, so to speak, doubling the ownership relations within it. In fact, in this two-tier ownership structure the corporation is playing the dual role, of a "person" and a "thing." It owns assets and it is owned by shareholders. In other words, in regard to things, a corporation acts legally as a person, as a subject of property right; and in regard to persons, a corporation is acted on legally as a

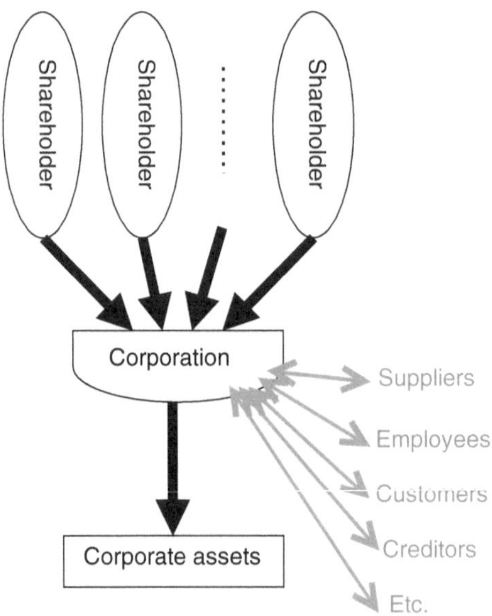


*Figure 14.6* The two-tier ownership structure of a corporate firm.

thing, as an object of property right. Of course, a corporation is in reality neither a person nor a thing. Legally, however, it is endowed with both personality and thingness.

It is my belief that it is not the personality *per se* but the person/thing duality of the corporation that is responsible for most of the confusion in the past controversy on corporate personality. In fact, if we only look at the first tier, the corporation appears merely as a thing owned and controlled by shareholders, and we draw near to the position of corporate nominalists. If we only look at the second tier, the corporation appears fully as a person owning and managing corporate assets, and we draw near to the position of corporate realists.

However, one must note that even within the province of law a corporation appears to be neither fully a person nor merely a thing. The fact that it can be owned by other persons makes it less than a person even legally, and the fact that it can own other things makes it more than a thing even legally. But what I am going to demonstrate is that there are ways to eliminate either personality or thingness from the person/thing corporation, thereby turning it into a mere "thing" or a full "person," respectively.

## How to make a "nominalistic" corporation

The way to eliminate personality from a corporation is simple: it is to have someone own more than 50% of its shares. That someone then acquires an absolute control over the corporation. The corporation is deprived of its subjectivity and turned into a mere object of property right. Legally speaking, the corporation is still the sole owner of the corporate assets, but in practice it is the dominant shareholder who can exercise the ultimate control over them. As is shown in Figure 14.7, the corporate firm is reduced *de facto* to a single ownership relation between the dominant shareholder and the assets. We are certainly in the world of the corporate nominalism here.

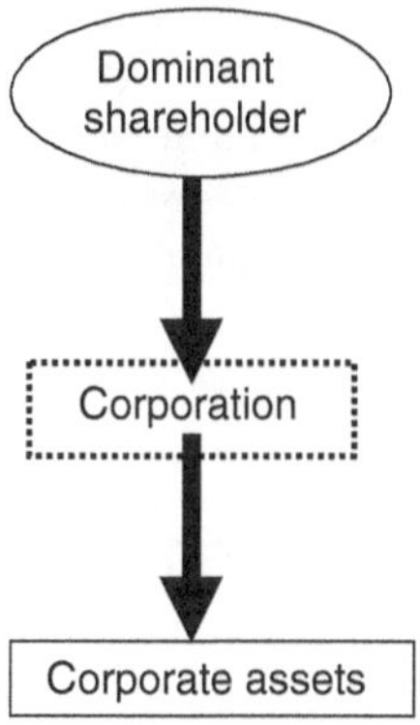


*Figure 14.7* A "nominalistic" corporation.

This is, of course, common sense. But I will now argue that the so-called corporate raiders are daily putting this legal mechanism into practice in the real economy.

That a corporate firm consists of two-tier ownership relations implies that it contains in it two kinds of "things" – the corporate assets and the corporation itself. This fact immediately implies that there are also two kinds of values residing in a corporate firm. They are, respectively, the value of corporate assets and the value of the corporation as a thing. The former can be defined as the present discounted value of the future profit stream that would accrue from the most efficient use of these assets. This can also be called the "fundamental" value of the corporation. The latter can be identified as the total share price of the corporation in the stock market.

And the business of a corporate raider is to search for a corporation whose stock market value is substantially lower than the value of the underlying assets. As soon as he has identified such a corporation, he begins a takeover bid (TOB). Suppose that a TOB was successful, then our corporate raider would gain absolute control over the use of the corporate assets.[9] He then closes off the corporation from the stock market. If he wants quick money, then he as the *de facto* owner sells off part or all of the corporate assets in second-hand asset markets. If he is patient, he replaces the incumbent managers by new and better ones, closely monitors their management, and wait for the upward turn of the performance of the purchased corporation. In any case, it is the difference between the values of corporate assets and corporate shares that constitutes the profit from this TOB operation.

We all know that money and hubris are what motivate our corporate raiders. Whatever their subjective motives, their day-to-day business in effect consists of an attempt to realize the idea of corporate nominalism in this world.

## How to make a "realistic" corporation

I am now going to demonstrate that there exists a legal mechanism which is able to eliminate thingness from the person-cum-thing corporation.

We know that as a legal person a corporation can own things, and that as a legal thing a corporation can be owned by persons. This at once suggests that a corporation as a person can in principle own another corporation as a thing. In fact, since the state of New Jersey in the US legalized holding corporations in 1889, corporations all over the world have been buying and holding the shares of other corporations. A holding corporation is a corporation that is created solely for the purpose of owning other corporations, as is shown in Figure 14.8. It thus acts as a person in regard to the corporations it owns.

In fact, the holding corporation has opened a way to an important organizational innovation: the pyramidal system of ownership and control. At the top is a capitalist family who owns a corporation as a thing. But, being also a legal person, that corporation can own another corporation as a thing, which again as a legal person can own another corporation as a thing, and so on. Such ownership hierarchy can extend *ad infinitum*. This is, however, not the whole picture. You do not

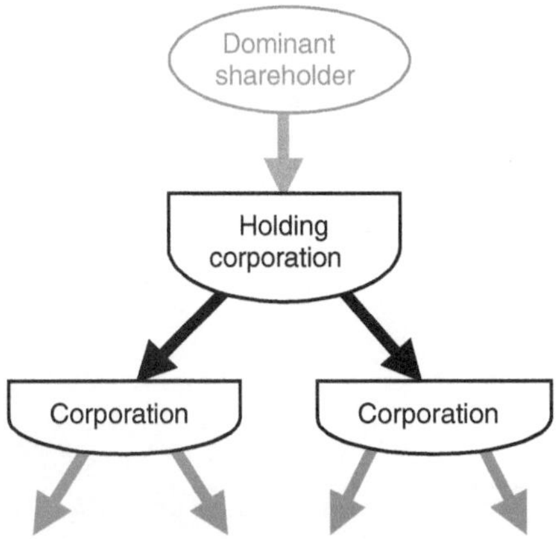


*Figure 14.8* A holding corporation and a pyramidal ownership structure.

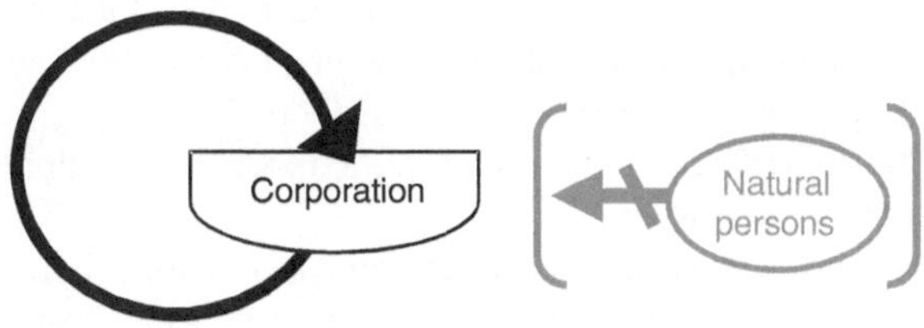


*Figure 14.9* A (hypothetical) self-owning corporation.

have to own all the shares to control a publicly held corporation. As long as minority shares are sufficiently diffused among passive investors in the stock market, only a share slightly greater than 50% is sufficient for control. This implies that one unit of capital can in principle control almost two units of capital, if each half buys a bare majority of the shares of a corporation with a capital close to one unit. It then follows that, as more and more layers are added to the ownership hierarchy, a capitalist family at the top can multiply the controlling power of their capital by the order close to $2^n$, where $n$ is the number of hierarchical layers beneath.[10] One can regard the prewar Japanese Zaibatsu and present-day Italian family empires and Korean Chaebols as typical examples of this pyramidal system of ownership and control.

Nevertheless, a holding corporation still falls short of shedding its thingness entirely, because it has its own dominant shareholders watching over it. One can, however, go a step further at least in theory. A corporation as a person can own itself as a thing. Indeed, nothing prevents us from imagining a corporation that becomes its own dominant shareholder by holding a majority block of its own shares under its own name, as is illustrated in Figure 14.9. If this were indeed

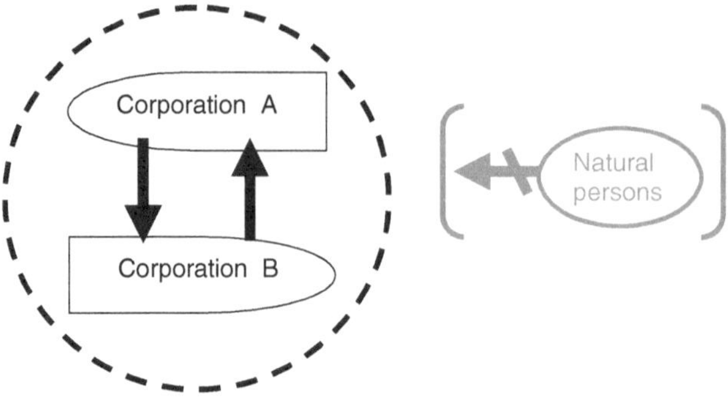


*Figure 14.10* Mutually holding corporations.

possible, that corporation would be free from any control by real human beings and become a self-determining subject. It would remove the thingness from itself and acquire a full personality in the province of law.

One might dismiss all this as idle speculation. Many countries prohibit a corporation from repurchasing its own outstanding shares. And in other countries which allow share repurchases, the repurchased shares always lose their voting rights in shareholders meetings. In the real economy, therefore, it appears impossible for the corporation to become its own owner.

There is, however, an important leeway to this. Imagine a situation where two corporations, A and B, hold a majority of each other's shares. As is illustrated in Figure 14.10, corporation A as a person owns corporation B as a thing, and corporation B as a person in turn owns corporation A as a thing. Even though each corporation does not own itself directly, it does indirectly through the intermediacy of the other corporation. Though in a much more attenuated manner than in the case of single self-ownership, we have here a pair of corporations owning themselves and becoming free from the control of any human beings.

One might still object to the practical possibility of this leeway by pointing out that some countries impose legal limits on the extent of cross-shareholdings between corporations. Equally important, many countries place ownership limits on the percentage of shares that banks and other financial institutions may own in an individual corporation. For instance, Japanese law forbids a bank from owning more than 5% of the shares of any domestic corporation.

Yet, it is possible to circumvent even these limits. Suppose that twelve corporations get together and that each holds 5% of each of the other's shares. Then, simple arithmetic ($(12 - 1) \times 5\% = 55\% > 50\%$) tells us that a majority block of each corporation's shares could be effectively sealed off from real human beings, without violating any of the aforementioned legal restrictions on cross-shareholding. As is depicted in Figure 14.11, these twelve corporations would indeed become their own owners at least as a group. It is therefore practically impossible to prevent corporations from becoming their own owners, if they so wish.

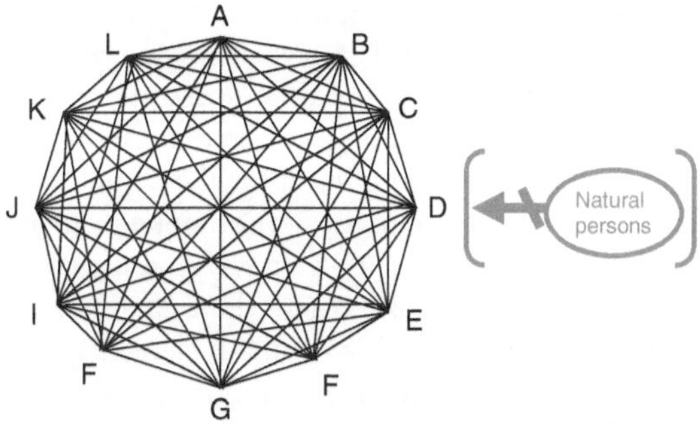


*Figure 14.11* Cross-shareholdings among twelve corporations.

We have now reached the paradigm of corporate realism. We have indeed seen that by extensive cross-shareholdings a group of corporations can get rid of their thingness and become self-determining subjects in the system of law.

## Indeterminacy principle and two capitalisms

I have thus elucidated two legal mechanisms – one turning a person-*cum*-thing corporation into a mere thing, and the other turning a person-*cum*-thing corporation into a full person.

What we have established is a sort of indeterminacy principle in law, that law is incomplete and is unable to determine the very legal nature of the corporation within its own system. Instead, the supposedly universal corporate law has unknowingly provided each society with a "menu" of corporate structures from which it can choose. Indeed, each society can choose any position along a long spectrum that runs from a purely "nominalistic" to a purely "realistic" structure, on the basis of or at least under the influence of economic efficiency, political interests, ideological forces, cultural traditions, historical evolution, and other extra-legal factors.

That the law has really served as an effective "menu" is evidenced by the well-known fact that even among advanced industrial societies the dominant corporate form varies widely from country to country – America (and Britain) with very active M&A activities in stock markets standing the nearest to the "nominalistic" pole, Japan (and Germany) with extensive cross-shareholdings among large corporations the nearest to the "realistic" pole, and most of continental European countries somewhere in between.[11]

## Corporate managers as fiduciaries of the corporation

Our picture of the corporation could never be complete without having "managers," that is, directors and officers, painted explicitly in it.[12] Even if the corporation has a full-fledged personality in the system of law, it is in reality a mere abstract entity that is incapable of performing any act except through the act of flesh and blood human beings. In fact, it is a legal requirement that the corporation must have a board of directors who hold the formal powers to act in the name of the corporation. And it is a common practice that these directors delegate part of their formal power to corporate officers for the actual management of corporate assets. It is true that there are many corporations, even among publicly held corporations, whose shareholders place themselves as directors and manage the corporate assets all by themselves. But, then, these shareholders act as board members, not as shareholders. This is once again an elementary fact in corporate law, but I have reiterated it so as to highlight a fundamental difference between managers in a corporate firm and managers in an unincorporated firm. The recent upsurge of the naïve form of corporate nominalism, under the new guise of the contractual theory of the firm, has blurred this difference completely and reduced the theory of "corporate governance" to a mere application of the theory of agency. This is a mistake.

"Agency" is, according to its leading definition, "a fiduciary relation which results from the manifestation of consent by one person [the principal] to another [the agent] that the other shall act on his behalf and subject to his control, and consent by the other so to act."[13] The control need not be total and continuous, but there must be some sense that the principal is "in charge."[14] Needless to say, the relation between an owner and managers in a sole-proprietorship firm is a paradigmatic agency relation, with the owner being the principal and the managers her agents, as is illustrated in Figure 14.12. It is the owner who unilaterally defines the objective of the relationship and maintains the power to control and direct the managers who have consented to act solely on her behalf. In fact, the owner need not hire any managers at all. She can at any time terminate the agency relation and manage her own assets by herself. If there are any problems pertaining to the governance of a partnership firm, they all arise from asymmetric information between the owner (principal) and managers (agents), in the form of adverse selection or moral hazard. And the task of governing an unincorporated firm can be reduced to that of designing an incentive system that would minimize the inefficiency (agency cost) arising from such asymmetric information. Of course, this is all in the realm

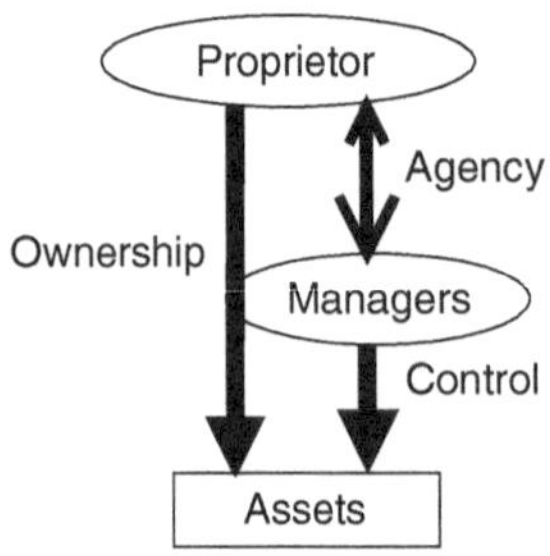


*Figure 14.12* Managers as agents in a sole-proprietorship firm.

of contractual law, and little room is left for mandatory legal rules or other forms of legal intervention.

Once, however, we turn to the problem of "corporate" governance, or of governing the "corporate" form of business firm with its characteristic two-tier ownership structure, we find ourselves on a totally different plane. The relation between shareholders and managers can no longer be identified with an agency relation. To be sure, shareholders can fire individual directors or even replace the entire team of incumbent directors at the shareholder meeting. But, they cannot dismiss the very legal institution of the board of directors, as long as a corporation remains a corporation. To be sure, shareholders can approve or veto the managers' major policy decisions at shareholders meetings. But they cannot deny the very legal power of the managers to act in the name of corporation, as long as a corporation remains a corporation.[15] Shareholders are in no sense "in charge" of the managers of their corporation.

Corporate managers are not the agents of the shareholders. If so, what are they? What is the legal status of corporate managers? They are the "fiduciaries" of the corporation. (Figure 14.13 is an attempt to visualize this relationship.) The fiduciary is a person who is entrusted to act as a substitute for another person for the sole purpose of serving that person.[16] Examples include guardian, conservator, trustee, administrator, attorney, physician, psychiatrist, fund manager, etc. A fiduciary is called an agent if he is bound by a contract (often implicit) with the beneficiary and is subject to her control. But the agent is merely a special type of fiduciary,

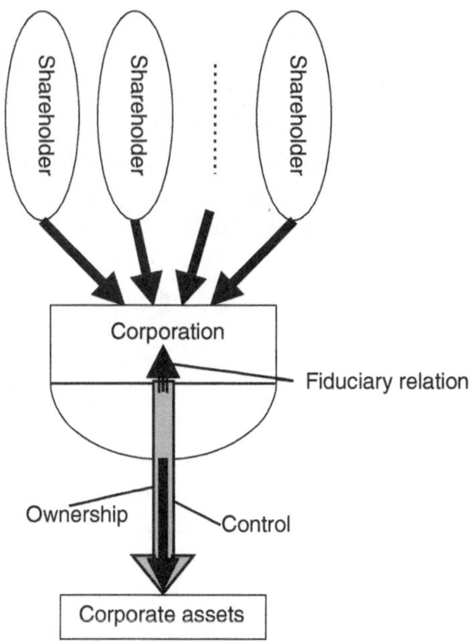


*Figure 14.13* Corporate managers as fiduciaries of the corporation.

and many of the fiduciary relations are non-contractual. Indeed, in the case of corporate directors it is the law that endows them with the fiduciary powers to act in the name of the corporation.

This at once leads us to the central problem of corporate governance: the managers' abuse of fiduciary powers. The risk that the corporate managers may not use their fiduciary powers in the best interest of the corporation stems from the very nature of the corporation as a legal person.[17] Since the corporation is a mere legal construct, its managers are the ones who actually decide whether to buy or sell, lend or mortgage, use or maintain the corporate assets, all in the name of the corporation. Any act taken by the managers as managers legally binds the corporation as the act of the corporation itself. Then, there inevitably emerges the danger of *quid pro quo*: the danger that the managers unconsciously mistake their fiduciary powers for their own powers which can be employed at their own discretion. They may not exercise these powers with enough care and prudence, such as the best interest of the corporation would demand. Worse, they may consciously appropriate these powers for the purposes of conferring a benefit on themselves, or even of injuring a particular party.

## Fiduciary principles in corporate governance

How can we prevent corporate managers from abusing their fiduciary powers? The answer to this question is by no means simple. But, I would maintain that at the foundation of the corporate governance system lie the corporate managers' "fiduciary duties" to the corporation, and that the legal rules regulating these duties should be essentially mandatory. These are no more than the orthodox principles of corporate governance before the onslaught of the contractual theory of the firm.[18] These orthodox principles are still honored among practical-minded corporate lawyers, but the current trend in legal thinking is certainly in the direction of eliminating any mandatory element from the fiduciary duties.[19] What I would like to do now is to present "proof" of the validity of the orthodoxy by means of what one might call a "legal thought-experiment." In fact, the model of the purely "realistic" corporation delineated in the section "How to make a realistic corporation" provides us with an ideal setting for that experiment.

For this purpose, let us again imagine a corporation that is its own controlling shareholder by holding a majority block of its own shares. To remove any impurities from this hypothetical self-owning corporation, let us further suppose that it has no outstanding loans from banks and other financial institutions and that its relationships with workers, suppliers and customers are all at arm's length. Then, the only flesh and blood human beings we can find within the corporate firm are the directors and officers, that is, the managers.

What would be the principles of corporate governance for this hypothetical corporation? There is only one answer: by fiduciary law. Indeed, it is simply impossible to leave the matter to private ordering. The corporation itself is unable to arrange a monitoring mechanism or a bonding scheme with the managers, except through the very managers it is supposed to discipline. The corporation itself is unable to work out an incentive system (such as performance dependent bonuses and stock options) with the managers, except through the very managers it is supposed to give an incentive to. Any attempt to control the corporate managers by means of contractual arrangements, whether explicit or implicit, would necessarily degenerate into self-dealing by managers themselves, and create the very problem it is attempting to solve. The only way to protect the interests of the corporation from such self-dealing is to have fiduciary law regulate directly the behavior of managers.

The most conspicuous feature of the fiduciary law is its highly "moralistic" tone.[20] It imposes on the fiduciaries the "duties" to perform once they have consented to act as fiduciaries. The law lists many such duties, but the most fundamental ones are "the duty of loyalty" and "the duty of care."[21] The duty of loyalty obliges the corporate managers to control the assets of the corporation in the best interest of the corporation and not in conflict of interest. It forbids them to self-deal with corporate assets, to trade corporate opportunity, and to trade on inside information; it imposes strict rules on the disclosure of information; it restrains managers from taking "excessive" compensations. The duty of care then demands the corporate managers to manage the corporate assets with reasonable skill and care.

It is the essence of fiduciary law that it imposes these duties, not as a mere rhetorical device, but as the real content of the law. The advocates of the contractual theory of the firm, however, identify the fiduciary law with "a standard-form penalty clause in every agency contract" and characterize it as the rules which "approximate the bargain that investors and agents would strike if they were able to dicker at no cost."[22] They thus argue that the fiduciary duties specified in corporate law are essentially "enabling" and can be and must be waived if the participants of what they call "the corporate contract" believe they can strike a better bargain among themselves. This is totally untenable. Fiduciary law can never be a substitute for private ordering. It is placed and ought to be placed at the foundation of the corporate governance system for no other reason other that any attempt to control corporate managers by means of contract or other forms of voluntary agreement would necessarily involve an element of managerial self-dealing. To make corporate law enabling and permit its fiduciary rules to be bargained around by insiders would be the surest way to destroy the corporate governance system.[23]

It is fortunate that the entire tradition of fiduciary law has so far been consistently hostile to viewing the fiduciary rules as implicit contracts.[24] The courts hold corporate managers liable for breach of fiduciary duties, even if some of these duties are expressly removed by corporate statutes, charter and bylaws, or by terms in contracts. They also refuse to delve into the subjective intentions of managers. Once corporate managers choose to become corporate managers, they owe fiduciary duties to the corporation and cannot waive the courts' supervision at will.

One may take exception to this entire discussion, on the ground that it deals only with a hypothetical self-owning corporation without any stakeholders. However, as long as the business firm takes the form of corporation with its characteristic two-tier ownership structure, it must have managers as its fiduciaries, thereby structurally giving rise to the possibility of fiduciary abuse of powers. Any attempt to control such abuse through contractual arrangement would necessarily involve an element of managerial self-dealing. And this is independent of whether the corporation occupies a position close to the "realistic" pole or the "nominalistic" pole of the legal menu of corporate forms we discussed in the section "Indeterminacy principle and two capitalisms." It is in this sense that I claim that the corporate managers' fiduciary duties to the corporation should lie 'at the foundation' of any corporate governance system.

## A sketch of the theory of comparative corporate governance

It is, however, neither wise nor practical to rely exclusively on fiduciary law for the governance of corporate firms. Implementation of such law requires a well-organized legal system in general and active courts in particular. But not every country has a well-organized legal system, let alone active courts. And even if the courts were active, the full implementation of fiduciary law would demand a large amount of human and non-human resources. All the more so since the "business judgment rule" very often works as a barrier to its applications unless courts are presented very strong cases.

For the efficient as well as effective governance of corporate firms, it is thus of vital importance to supplement the fiduciary law with other governance mechanisms. And it is as the agents of these supplementary mechanisms that various stakeholders, such as banks, employees, suppliers, customers, and others among shareholders, find their roles to play in the system of corporate governance. Indeed, there is a wide variation in costs and benefits of these supplementary mechanisms across countries, depending more or less on whether their dominant corporate form is "realistic" or "nominalistic." I believe this variation should constitute a starting point of the comprehensive theory of comparative corporate governance.[25]

In order to present a brief sketch of such a theory, let us now add "impurities" to our hypothetical self-owning corporation little by little, and see how they will open up room for supplementary governance mechanisms.

First, let us remove the supposition that our "realistic" corporation has no outstanding loans. Then, it can and may actually default on loans. And when on the brink of default, the residual rights over its assets are effectively transferred to the creditors, so that even a "realistic" corporation becomes a mere thing in the hands of the banks and other financial institutions.[26] And once a corporation actually files for bankruptcy, the banks and other creditors, at least some of the major ones, are forced to assume an active role in monitoring the managers' restructuring activities. True, such a governance mechanism operates only in a state of emergency and *ex post facto*, but that possibility may legitimize the banks and creditors to acquire a *de facto* right to monitor the managerial performance *ex ante* as a sort of preventive measure.

As a matter of fact, many business corporations in Japan and in some of the continental European countries have (or used to have) a long-term relationship with one particular bank (or a small number of banks) whose role extends far beyond that of the major supplier of loans. We will call such a bank the "main bank" of the corporation, though this designation seems to be used only in Japan.[27] The main bank daily watches over the financial position of the client corporation and periodically reviews its long-term investment plans. If it holds a substantial equity position as well, the main bank may use that power to directly intervene in managerial decision-making and even go so far as to dispatch a rescue team when the client corporation is in financial distress. It is because of these *ex ante* monitoring and *ex post* restructuring activities that some regard the existence of the main bank as "an important substitute mechanism for what in effect is a 'missing' takeover market."[28]

Many have, however, voiced skepticism toward such a view, and that skepticism arises from the too-obvious fact that the bank itself is a private business corporation that has a motive of its own. It is doubtful that the purpose of the main bank in monitoring and restructuring the client corporation coincides with or even approximates the best interests of the corporation, at least in normal times. Besides, who monitors the monitor? This suggests that the main bank system itself may turn out to be the paradigmatic corporate governance problem, not its cure.[29] Furthermore, we should also note that even if the main bank system really played an effectual role in the governance of corporate firms, if they can have easy access to various forms of external finances apart from bank loans, the way to use this supplementary governance mechanism is simply closed off. In fact, the government-led deregulation of financial markets and the market-driven wave of financial innovations in recent years, which have generated a wide variety of new means of external financing, are said to have weakened much of the efficacy of the main bank system both in Japan and in some of the continental European countries.

Second, let us introduce long-term employees into our picture of the "realistic" corporation. In several European countries employees have legal rights to participate in corporate management.[30] German law, for instance, requires a stock corporation (AG) of more than 2,000 employees to have representatives of employees and trade unions occupy 50% of the seats on the supervisory board which oversees the lower-tier management board. No such law exists in Japan; but a majority and sometimes the entire membership of the board of directors and the board of inspectors of a large Japanese corporation are promoted through internal competition from the pool of core employees who enjoy long-term employment, a seniority wage system and company unionism. Behind these laws and practices is a fact that the long-term employees have throughout their long working careers in the same organization accumulated a large amount of organization-specific human assets – skills and know-how not easily transferable to outside uses. If such skills and know-how were to contribute to the profitability of the corporation, the employees who embody them in their corporeal existence should have a *de facto* right to the management of the corporation. Again, however, we have to note that, even if the employees' voices actually played an important role in the management, they might not necessarily be the ones which would promote the best interests of the corporation as a whole.

Third, we have to let our "realistic" corporation maintain relational contracts with suppliers and customers. But their implications for corporate governance are somewhat murky. On the one hand, repeated interactions may promote cooperation from suppliers and customers; on the other hand, long-lasting relationships may encourage suppliers and customers to voice their opinions openly on matters related to their transactions. The balance can go either way, and nothing definite can be said on the effectiveness of this governance mechanism.

Up until now, we have been concerned only with the governance of the "realistic" corporation, and now it is time to move in the "nominalistic" direction along the long legal menu of possible corporate structures. For this purpose, we now have to unwind the tight network of cross-shareholdings among group corporations and expose the managers of each one of them to the harshness of the stock market. At least in Anglo-American countries, hostile takeovers are often regarded as the most effective disciplinary device against managers. Since there is huge literature on this subject and since I have already discussed the mechanisms in the section "How to make a 'nominalistic' corporation," I will touch on it very briefly. The basic argument is that whenever the share price of any corporation fails to reach the fundamental value of corporate assets, and as long as a majority of its shares are openly traded in the stock market, corporate raiders can easily employ the technique of LBO to wrest control from managers. Fearful of such takeover, the story goes, incumbent managers have little choice but to maximize the share price of their corporation. The stock market thus becomes a "market for corporate control." The bulk of empirical evidence indeed suggests that hostile takeovers generate substantial gains to the targeted shareholders.[31]

There are, however, heated disputes over the sources of these gains. The standard theory has attributed these gains to the increased efficiency of the raided corporation, due to such factors as the installment of better managers, realization of economies of scale and scope, improvement of incentive schemes, and tapping of free cash flow.[32] In opposition to this view, however, many argue that most of the gains of shareholders in hostile takeovers are no more than wealth transfers from other stakeholders. The raider may simply be expropriating long-term employees by effectively nullifying the implicit contracts the ousted managers have formed with them and forcing a substantial cut in their wages and pension funds.[33] The raider may simply be expropriating future shareholders and future stakeholders by slashing R&D and other future-orientated investments to finance current dividend payments.[34] The raider may, according to the so-called hubris hypothesis, simply be expropriating herself by setting a bidding price much higher than is justified by the rational calculation of the fundamental value of corporate assets.[35] What these expropriation theories suggest is a possibility that even the stock market discipline of corporate managers may sometimes end up with substituting one governance problem for another, rather than solving the first one.

Finally, let us go to the other pole of the legal menu of corporate forms and examine the problems of governing a purely "nominalistic" corporation. Such a corporate firm is of course the closest to the unincorporated business firm among all possible forms of corporate firms. And yet, even in this case the relationship between the dominant shareholder and corporate managers is not as simple as the relationship between the owner of a corporate firm and the managers she has hired as her agents. As long as a business firm retains a corporate form, corporate managers remain managers of the corporation, and it is only through her domination of shareholders' meeting, in particular through the exclusive power of appointing directors, that the dominant shareholder can exercise control over corporate managers. Of course, she can install a monitoring or bonding contract to discipline corporate managers; she can set up an incentive contract to motivate corporate managers. But these contractual arrangements cannot override fiduciary law. They are merely supplements to the legal rules which directly regulate the performance of the managers as fiduciaries of the corporation.

Moreover, even if the dominant shareholder has succeeded in controlling corporate managers completely, it does not mark the end of corporate governance problems. It merely changes the form they take. Indeed, the most important governance problem for the purely "nominalistic" corporation is no longer the corporate managers' abuse of fiduciary powers; it is now the dominant shareholder's abuse of corporate privileges, especially of her limited liability status, to the detriment of outside creditors, such as lenders, suppliers, employees, customers, and tort plaintiffs. As we have already seen, a purely "nominalistic" corporation is in reality a mere thing at the disposal of its dominant shareholder. Yet, legally, or rather nominally, it still has a personality, distinct from that of the dominant shareholders and capable of owning assets under its own name. What it is really is not what it is nominally. And it is not hard to see that this real/nominal discrepancy gives the dominant shareholder an easy opportunity for a variety of sham transactions. In particular, she can use her own corporation as her "alter ego" and have its managers transfer corporate assets and corporate incomes to her purse, with the intent to delay or reduce or defraud the payment of the debts the corporation owes to outside creditors. Indeed, it is to protect these unfortunate creditors from such fraudulent transfers that courts sometimes "pierce the corporate veil" and subject the dominant shareholder to personal liability for the debts of the corporation.[36]

## A concluding remark

The present chapter has been devoted to the stipulation of the legal structure of the corporate firm. A corporation is, however, not merely a legal entity but also an organizational entity that pools human skills, physical facilities and financial instruments and produces goods and services to market. Then, a question arises immediately. What is the relationship between the corporate firm as a legal institution and the corporate firm as an economic organization?

In organization theory there are two competing views of organization – one viewing organizations as collectivities rationally constructed to attain exogenously given purposes and the other viewing organizations as collectivities autonomously striving to reproduce themselves as going concerns. My suggestion here is not an unexpected one. There is a strong correlation between these two views of organizations and our "nominalistic"/"realistic" dichotomy of corporate structures.

When we lift the legal veil from a nominalistic corporation, what we find as its social substratum is a group of shareholders who control the managers for the sole purpose of maximizing their own returns. On the other hand, when we lift the legal veil of a realistic corporation, what we find as its social substratum is an autonomous organization whose internal members share a common interest in the survival and growth of the organization itself. Moreover, I would also like to suggest that the autonomous character of the "realistic" corporate organization is tied closely to the existence of intangible assets that have been variously called "firm-specific human assets," "organizational capabilities," "core competences," "managerial resources," etc. They more or less refer to "the collective learning in the organization, especially how to coordinate diverse production skills, integrate multiple streams of technology, maintain a reliable network of suppliers, and cultivate the goodwill of customers." In fact, these intangible assets have a very peculiar property – they belong to nobody but the corporation! No one outside of the corporate organization, by which I include not only creditors but also shareholders, can own these assets as their own properties. For these assets are inalienable human assets that are embodied in the members of the organization in the form of know-how and skills. No one inside of the corporate organization, by which I mean managers and core workers, can appropriate them as their own properties either. For these human assets are organization-specific and lose their economic values once they leave the organization. Here emerges a key insight into the role the corporation as a legal institution has played in the historical development of capitalistic economies – the legal personality of corporation has been able to act as the *de facto* owner of these intangible assets, thereby encouraging their accumulation within corporate organizations. Indeed, as has been documented so painstakingly by Alfred Chandler and other business historians, it is the development and maintenance of these assets, especially that of organizational capabilities of managers, that enabled modern firms to exploit the potential economies of scale and scope of their capital-intensive technologies and helped them to grow and continue to grow ever since the end of the nineteenth century.[37]

I, however, leave the fuller discussions on this topic to other articles.[38]

## Notes

1 This chapter is based on a lecture delivered for ISER XIII Workshop on ECONOMICS AND LAW, held from June 25 to July 6, 2000, at the Certosa di Pontignano, Siena, Italy. It is based chiefly on Iwai (1999). See also Iwai (2002).

2 Sec. 3.02 of the American Bar Association's *Revised Model Business Corporation Act* [*RMBCA*] states that

> unless its articles of incorporation provide otherwise, every corporation . . . has the same power as an individual to do things necessary or convenient to carry out its business and affairs, including without limitation power: [1] to sue and be sued, complain and defend in its corporate name; . . . [4] to purchase, receive, lease, or otherwise acquire, and own, hold, improve, use, and otherwise deal with, real or personal property, or any legal or equitable interest in property, wherever located;

[5] to sell, convey, mortgage, pledge, lease, exchange, and otherwise dispose of all or any part of its property.

3 There is a huge body of writings on this controversy. Some of the best-known works available in English are Savigny (1884), Maitland (1900), Machen (1911), Dewey (1926), Radin (1932), Wolff (1938), A. Hart (1954), Dan-Cohen (1986), and Teubner (1988). For a comprehensive review of various theories of corporate personality (before 1930), see Hallis (1930). In Iwai (1999) I have given a more extensive discussion on this controversy.
4 See, for instance, Coase (1937), Alchian and Demsetz (1972), Jensen and Meckling (1976), Easterbrook and Fischel (1991), Williamson (1985), Grossman and Hart, (1986), and Hart (1995).
5 See, for instance, Penrose (1959), Nelson and Winter (1982), Teece (1982), Wernerfelt (1984), Prahalad and Hamel (1990), and Chandler (1992).
6 Jensen and Meckling (1976), p. 310.
7 Winter (1988), p. 176.
8 See, for instance, Easterbrook and Fischel (1991), at p. 1445, and Posner (1992), at pp. 392–393.
9 We ignore all the informational difficulties associated with TOB operation discussed by Grossman and Hart (1980).
10 Moreover, if this hierarchical structure is combined with cross-shareholdings at each hierarchical layer, the capitalist family at the top can further enhance the leverage of their own capital.
11 See Prowse (1994) for an informative survey of corporate structures among large firms in the US, UK, Japan, and Germany.
12 I use the term "managers" to designate both directors and officers in the case of incorporated business firms.
13 America Law Institute, Restatement [Second] of Agency, sec. 1 [1].
14

> The agency cannot exist unless the "acting for" party [the agent] consents to the will of the "acted for" party [the principal]. The control need not be total or continuous and need not extend to the way the agent physically performs, but there must be some sense that the principal is "in charge." At minimum, the principal must have the right to control the goal of the relationship.
>
> (Kleinberger, 1995, at p. 8)

15 "Stockholders cannot withdraw the authority they delegated to the board of directors, because they never delegated any authority to the directors." Clark (1985), at p. 57.
16 According to Tamar Frankel (1983), the defining characteristics of fiduciary relations are (1) that "the fiduciary serves as a substitute for the entrustor" and (2) that "the fiduciary obtains powers from the entrustor or from a third party for the sole purpose of enabling the fiduciary to act effectively." (pp. 808–809). See also Frankel (1995) and DeMott (1991).
17

> It is important to emphasize that the entrustor's vulnerability to abuse of power does not result from an initial inequality of bargaining power between the entrustor and the fiduciary. . . . Rather, the entrustor's vulnerability stems from the structure and nature of the fiduciary relation. The delegated power that enables the fiduciary to benefit the entrustor also enables him to injure the entrustor, because the purpose for which the fiduciary is allowed to use his delegated power is narrower than the purposes for which he is capable of using that power.
>
> (Frankel 1983, at p. 810)

18 For a clear exposition of the orthodox principles, see Clark (1985); see also Clark (1986), at pp. 114–189 and Eisenberg (1989).
19 See Langbein (1995) as the representative of these recent attempts.
20 See Frankel (1983), at pp. 829–832 and Clark (1985), at pp. 75–79.
21 *Restatement [Second] of Trusts* (1959), for instance, lists 17 (!) such duties in §§169–185.

22 Frank Easterbrook and David Fischel (1982), at p. 737.
23 As has been witnessed by the Enron scandal in the year of 2001.
24 See, for instance, Frankel (1985).
25 For the previous works on comparative corporate governance, see, for instance, Mayer (1988), Aoki (1988), Franks and Mayer (1990), Coffee (1991), Baums (1992), Roe (1993), Aoki and Dore (1994), and Prowse (1994).
26 Because of the limited liability of shareholders, when the value of corporate assets cannot cover the value of debts, the rights over the disposal of the assets shift entirely to the hands of the creditors.
27 For the comprehensive account of Japanese main bank system, see Aoki and Patrick (1995). For the roles of German banks in corporate governance, see for instance Baums (1992).
28 Sheard (1989).
29 In fact, in Japan it is widely believed that it was the reckless speculative loans of the banks themselves, the supposed monitors of borrowers, that actually caused or at least fueled the so-called bubble economy in the second half of the 1980s. The bubbles then burst, and the majority of Japanese banks were left with a huge burden of bad loans.
30 See Hopt (1984).
31 See Jensen and Ruback (1983), Jarrell *et al.* (1990), and Bhagat *et al.* (1990).
32 "The market for corporate control is creating," claims one of its chief advocates, "large benefits for shareholders and for the economy as a whole by loosening control over vast amounts of resources and enabling them to move more quickly to their highest-valued use" (Jensen, 1988, at p. 23).
33 Shleifer and Summers (1988).
34 Hitt *et al.* (1996).
35 Roll (1986).
36 For the so-called corporate piercing cases, see for instance Clark (1986), pp. 35–92.
37 Chandler (1977, 1990).
38 See Iwai (2002) for such a discussion.

## References

Alchian, Arman and Harold Demsetz (1972), "Production, Information Costs, and Economic Organization," *American Economic Review* 62, pp. 777–795.

Aoki, Masahiko (1988), *Information, Incentives and Bargaining in the Japanese Economy* (Cambridge: Cambridge University Press).

Aoki, Masahiko and Ronald Dore (1992), eds, *The Japanese Firm: Sources of Competitive Strength* (Oxford: Oxford University Press).

Aoki, M. and Patrick, Hugh T. (1995), "The Japanese Main Bank System: An Introductory Overview," in M. Aoki and Patrick Hugh T. eds, *The Japanese Main Bank System: Its Relevance for Developing and Transforming Economies*, pp. 1–51 (Oxford: Oxford University Press).

Barca, Fabrizio, Katsuhito Iwai, Ugo Pagano, and Sandro Trento (1999), "The Divergence of the Italian and Japanese Corporate Governance Models: The Role of Institutional Shocks," *Economic Systems* 23, pp. 35–59; also published as "Divergence in Corporate Governance Models: the Role of Institutional Shocks," in A. Boltho, A. Vercelli, and H. Yoshikawa eds, *Comparing Economic Systems: Italy and Japan* (London: Palgrave, 2000), pp. 15–40.

Baums, Theodor (1992), "Corporate Governance in Germany: The Role of the Banks," *American Journal of Comparative Law* 40, pp. 503–526.

Bhagat, Sanjai, Andrei Shleifer, and Robert Vishny (1990), "Hostile Takeovers in the 1980s: The Return to Corporate Specialization," *Brookings Papers on Economic Activity: Macroeconomics*, special issue, pp. 1–72 .

Chandler, Alfred D. (1984), "The Emergence of Managerial Capitalism," *Business History Review* 58 (Winter): 473–503. Reprinted in *The Rise of Big Business (1992)* by Glenn Porter, John Hope Franklin, A.S. Eisenstadt Harlan Davidson Inc, USA, pp. 207–236.

Chandler, Alfred, Jr (1977), *The Visible Hand: The Managerial Revolution in American Business* (Harvard, MA: The Belknap Press).

Chandler, Alfred, Jr (1990), *Scale and Scope: The Dynamics of Industrial Capitalism* (Harvard, MA: The Belknap Press).

Clark, Robert (1985), "Agency Costs versus Fiduciary Duties," in Pratt and Zeckhauser ed., *Principals and Agents: The Structure of Business* (Cambridge, MA: Harvard Business School Press), pp. 55–79.

Clark, Robert (1986), *Corporate Law* (New York: Little, Brown and Co.).

Coase, Ronald H. (1937), "The Nature of the Firm," *Economica* N.S. 4, pp. 386–405.

Coffee, John C. (1991), "Liquidity versus Control: The Institutional Investor as Corporate Monitor," *Columbia Law Review* 91, pp. 1277–1368.

Dan-Cohen, Meir (1986), *Rights, Persons, and Organizations* (Berkeley, CA: University of California Press).

DeMott, Deborah A. (1991), *Fiduciary Obligation, Agency and Partnership – Duties in Ongoing Business Relationships* (St Paul, MN: West Publishing Co.).

Dewey, John (1926), "The Historical Background of Corporate Legal Personality," *Yale Law Journal* 35, pp. 655–673.

Easterbrook, F.H. and D. Fischel (1982), "Corporate Control Transactions," *Yale Law Journal* 92, pp. 1416–1448.

Easterbrook, F.H. and D. Fischel (1991), *The Economic Structure of Corporate Law* (Cambridge, MA: Harvard University Press).

Eisenberg, M.A. (1989), "The Structure of Corporate Law," *Columbia Law Review* 89, pp. 1461–1525.

Frankel, Tamar (1983), "Fiduciary Law," *California Law Review* 71, pp. 795–836.

Frankel, Tamar (1995), "Fiduciary Duties as Default Rules," *Oregon Law Review* 74, pp. 1209–1277.

Franks, Julian and Colin Mayer (1990), "Capital Markets and Corporate Control: A Study of France, Germany and the UK," *Economic Policy* 10, pp. 191–231.

Grossman, Sanford and Oliver Hart (1980), "Takeover Bids, the Free-Rider Problem, and the Theory of the Corporation," *Bell Journal of Economics* 11, pp. 42–64.

Grossman, Sanford and Oliver Hart (1986), "The Costs and Benefits of Ownership: A Theory of Vertical and Lateral Integration," *Journal of Political Economy* 94, pp. 691–719.

Hall, Robert E. (2000), "E-Capital: The Link between the Stock Market and the Labor Market in the 1990s," *Brookings Papers on Economic Activity* 2, pp. 73–118 (Massachusetts Ave; Washington, DC: Brookings Institution Press).

Hallis, Frederick (1930), *Corporate Personality: A Study of Jurisprudence* (Oxford: Oxford University Press).

Hart, H.L.A. (1954), "Definition and Theory in Jurisprudence," *Law Quarterly Review* 70, pp. 37–60.

Hart, Oliver (1995), *Firms, Contracts and Financial Structure* (Oxford: Oxford University Press).

Hitt, Michael A., Robert E. Hoskisson, Richard A. Johnson, and Douglas D. Moesel (1996), "The Market for Corporate Control and Firm Innovation," *Academy of Management Journal* 39, pp. 1084–1119.

Hopt, Klaus (1984), "New Ways in Corporate Governance: European Experiments with Labor Representation on Corporate Board," *Michigan Law Review* 82, No. 5/6, Festschrift in Honor of Eric Stein., pp. 1338–1363.

Iwai, Katsuhito (1999), "Persons, Things and Corporations: The Corporate Personality Controversy and Comparative Corporate Governance," *American Journal of Comparative Law* 47, pp. 583–632.

Iwai, Katsuhito (2002), "The Nature of the Business Corporation – Its Legal Structure and Economic Functions," *Japanese Economic Review* 53, pp. 243–273.

Jarrell, Gregg, James Brickley, and Jeffrey Netter (1988), "The Market for Corporate Control: The Empirical Evidence since 1980," *Journal of Economic Perspectives* 2, pp. 49–68.

Jensen, Michael (1988), "Takeovers: Their Causes and Consequences," *Journal of Economic Perspectives* 2, No. 1, pp. 21–48.

Jensen, Michael and W. Meckling (1976), "The Theory of Firm: Managerial Behavior, Agency Costs and Ownership Structure," *Journal of Financial Economics* 3, pp. 305–360.

Jensen, Michael and Richard Ruback (1983), "The Market for Corporate Control: The Scientific Evidence," *Journal of Financial Economics* 11, pp. 5–50.

Klein, Benjamin, Robert Crawford, and Armen Alchian (1978), "Vertical Integration, Appropriable Rents, and the Competitive Contracting Process," *Journal of Law and Economics* 21, pp. 297–326.

Kleinberger, Daniel S. (1995), *Agency and Partnership* (Little, Brown and Co.).

Langbein, J. (1995), "The Contractarian Basis the Law of Torts," *Yale Law Journal* 105, 625–675.

Machen, Arthur, Jr (1911), "Corporate Personality," *Harvard Law Review* 24, pp. 253–267, 347–365.

Maitland, F.M. (1900), "Translator's Introduction," to Otto Gierke, *Political Theories of the Middle Age* (Cambridge: Cambridge University Press).

Manne, Henry (1965), "Mergers and the Market for Corporate Control," *Journal of Political Economy* 73, pp. 110–120.

Mayer, Colin (1988), "New Issues in Corporate Finance," *European Economic Review* 32, pp. 1167–1183.

Nelson, Richard and Sidney G. Winter (1982), *An Evolutionary Theory of Economic Change* (Cambridge, MA: Harvard University Press).

Pagano, Ugo and Robert Rowthorn (1994), "Ownership, Technology and Institutional Stability," *Structural Change and Economic Dynamics* 5, pp. 221–242.

Pelikan, Pavel (1989), "Evolution, Economic Competence and the Market for Corporate Control," *Journal of Economic Behavior and Organization* 12, pp. 279–303.

Penrose, Edith (1959), *The Theory of the Growth of the Firm* (Oxford: Oxford University Press).

Posner, Richard A. (1992), *Economic Analysis of Law*, 4th edn (New York: Little, Brown and Co.).

Prahalad, C.K. and Gary Hamel (1990), "The Core Competence of the Corporation," *Harvard Business Review* 68, pp. 79–91.

Prowse, Stephen (1994), "Corporate Governance in an International Perspective: A Survey of Corporate Control Mechanisms among Large Firms in the United States, the United Kingdom, Japan and Germany," *BIS Economic Papers*, No. 41 (July 1994), pp. 215–239.

Radin, Max (1932), "The Endless Problem of Corporate Personality," *Columbia Law Review* 32, pp. 643–667.

Roe, Mark J. (1993), "Some Differences in Corporate Structure in Germany, Japan and the United States," *The Yale Law Journal* 102, No. 8, Symposium: Economic Competitiveness and the Law (June), pp. 1927–2003.

Roll, Richard (1986), "The Hubris Hypothesis of Corporate Takeovers," *Journal of Business* 59, pp. 197–216.

von Savigny, F.C. (1884), *Jurial Relations or, the Roman Law of Persons as Subjects of Jurial Relations: Being a Translation of the Second Book of SAVIGNY's System of Modern Roman Law*, translated by W.H. Rattigan (New York: Wiley & Sons).

Sheard, Paul (1989), "The Main Bank System and Corporate Monitoring and Control in Japan," *Journal of Economic Behaviors and Organizations* 11, pp. 399–422.

Shleifer, Andrei and Lawrence Summers (1988), "Breach of Trust in Hostile Takeovers," in Auerbach, ed., *Corporate Takeovers: Causes and Consequences* (Chicago, IL: University of Chicago Press).

Shleifer, Andrei and R. Vishny (1997), "A Survey of Corporate Governance," *Journal of Finance* 52, pp. 737–783.

Teece, D.J. (1982), "Towards an Economic Theory of the Multi-Product Firm," *Journal of Economic Behavior and Organization* 3, pp. 39–63.

Teubner, Gunther (1988), "Enterprise Corporatism: New Industrial Policy and the 'Essence' of the Legal Person," *American Journal of Comparative Law* 36, pp. 130–155.

Tirole, Jean (2001), "Corporate Governance," *Econometrica* 69 (1), pp. 1–35.

Wernerfelt, B. (1984), "A Resource-Base View of the Firm," *Strategic Management Journal* 5, pp. 171–180.

Williamson, Oliver E. (1985), *The Economic Institutions of Capitalism* (New York: Free Press).

Winter, Sidney G. (1988), "On Coase, Competence, and the Corporation," *Journal of Law, Economics, and Organization* 4, pp. 163–184.

Wolf, Harry D. (1938), "The Enforcement of Collective Labor Agreements: A Proposal," *Law and Contemporary Problems* 5, No. 2, Collective Bargaining under the Wagner Act (Spring), pp. 273–287.

# 15 Fiduciary duties, models of firms, and organizational theories in the context of relational interdependencies

*Fabrizio Cafaggi*

## Corporate law and corporate governance: re-locating the debate on fiduciary duties and relational interdependency

The idea that different types of constituencies affect organizational behaviour is at the core of both modern organizational theory and current debate in legal thought. The real question is not whether organizational behaviour is affected by a single category or multiplicity of categories of interests, but rather which legal instruments should protect which interests in order to have a proper design of organizational governance.[1]

The current debate on the juridical aspects of firms is beset by a fundamental drawback, namely: it focuses mainly on whether to use corporate law to protect all relevant stakeholder interests or to leave protection of constituencies other than shareholders, to other devices of a juridical and non-juridical nature.[2] Neither those who endorse the stakeholder perspective nor those who favour the shareholder perspective, focus their attention primarily on the causes, modes and consequences of the interdependency between the different explicit and implicit contracts that link organizational constituencies, but are more concerned with the design of organizational boundaries and with defining criteria to determine who insiders and outsiders are.[3] Whatever the preferred solution, my claim is that relational co-ordination is a fundamental goal for organizational governance, and the discussion should focus more on the comparative assessment of corporate law as a co-ordinating mechanism *vis-à-vis* other systems to co-ordinate various contracts within the organization.

It should also be stated at the outset that organizations have legal duties and obligations towards constituencies, for example in the area of environmental protection and product safety. The governance mechanism should therefore be perceived as a complex framework, requiring co-ordination of the contractual and legal obligations of the organization towards different constituencies.[4]

All these contracting and non-contracting parties are also claimants against the organization. They are generally distinguished between fixed and residual claimants, depending on how interests are prioritized. Obviously, trade-offs among claims occur in the lifetime of an organization. For example those concerning decisions on an acceptable level of risk may affect the creditor–shareholder relationship.[5] Decisions on the choice of investment projects may affect the shareholder–employee relationship. Different legal systems provide for different places within or without the organization where decision-making may occur and these trade-offs, or compensatory transactions decided.[6] These trade-offs exist regardless of the constituency to whom control of the organization is allocated.

An additional point should be made, especially relevant for the perspective of relational interdependencies adopted in this chapter. Firms, by their very existence also often require trade-offs to take place among stakeholders within which shareholders may be relatively neutral. A typical example is a trade-off between employment and environment. The adoption of a certain industrial project may increase the welfare or the number of employees at the expense of environmental protection. These are conflicts which arise through the operations of the firm and certainly cannot be solved by corporate law but they may have a significant influence on corporate governance design.

The main aim of corporate governance is therefore to provide an appropriate means for addressing the interdependencies of relationships between the firm and the various stakeholders consequential to contracts and as required by law, namely *relational interdependency*.

Relational interdependency can be modelled in different ways, the distinction between simultaneous and sequential models being worthy of particular note. In the simultaneous model, corporate and other contracts, for example those concerning creditors, change simultaneously.[7] In the sequential model there is a first mover, the corporate contract in general, and then the creditor, supplier and labour contracts follow, under the constraints defined by the corporate contract.

Whatever perspective one endorses on the theory of the firm, the fundamental issue concerns the ways in which control is allocated, and trade-offs among different interests are managed and resolved. Trade-offs imply conflicting interests but corporate governance should not be primarily thought of as a means to solve conflicts among different constituencies; its main goal should be perceived as producing innovation, sharing information, fostering co-operation, promoting mutual learning and, only within such a co-operative framework, defining distributive mechanisms within the organization that would preserve incentives to make specific investments.[8] These considerations depend on two premises:

1. the separation between allocative and distributive norms, defining surplus sharing among constituencies is artificial in that fairness of surplus distribution affects efficiency-based incentives and therefore;
2. one of the main goals of corporate governance is to ensure compliance with the fair agreement reached by constituencies (both initial and subsequent) in the course of the organization's lifetime. Furthermore, assuming that specific investments may not only be alternative but also complementary, equitable fair agreement concerning their protection constitutes the basis for a good project of corporate governance.

The debate on the role of stakeholders generally addresses publicly traded corporations, while lesser attention is paid to the role of stakeholders in relation to small and medium-sized enterprises, considered either individually or as part of a network.[9] This view provides a distorted perception since the role of stakeholders, and in particular that of local communities, has been shown to be particularly significant in the development of small and medium-sized enterprises.[10]

The significant feature in this case is the relationship between the stakeholders and the networks within which the firms operate, more than between stakeholders and the individual firm. Thence the different unit of analysis (the network) obliges a rethinking of the stakeholder/shareholder debate when shifting from the vertically integrated firm to the co-ordinated horizontal network of firms.

This chapter challenges the idea that corporate law and corporate governance are 'flip sides of the same coin'.[11] The claim is that corporate governance is the combination of different juridical devices of which corporate law is a prominent but not an exclusive one. This conclusion draws on the recent features of the debate concerning boundaries of firms.[12]

This approach highlights the need for a distinction to be made between corporate law and corporate governance, the former mainly concentrating on the relationship between shareholders and corporations, the latter encompassing other relationships also, for example those between stakeholders and the corporation, or among firms and the community.[13]

From what has emerged up to now some preliminary implications can be drawn. Organization theory applied to entrepreneurial organizations should consider the various tools of a juridical and non-juridical nature that give relevance to the interests of the various constituencies and may affect and/or constrain the decision-making process within that organization. The role of hierarchy and authority within organizations should be rethought in the light of the different instruments employed to co-ordinate alternative decision-making processes. It is often the case that hierarchical relationships between the firm and its constituencies are regulated by contracts. In many cases these are relational contracts, and the location of constituencies inside or outside the firm is either problematic or otherwise not particularly meaningful.

A comparison of various features of contract incompleteness in corporate, contract and labour law is beyond the scope of this chapter, the point being that corporate governance should be thought of as the answer to combining responses to interrelated incomplete contracts rather than coinciding with only one of these contracts. The creation of an organization in this perspective does not resolve contractual incompleteness, but it provides an alternative and often more successful co-ordinating mechanism than market transactions.

The focus of the remaining part of the chapter will be on the organizational interdependencies among these different 'incompletenesses'. It will highlight the need to create adjustment mechanisms both within the organizations themselves and, where relevant, among organizations, to ensure the effective completion of co-ordinated contracts and reduce constituencies' opportunism. In this framework the content and functions of fiduciary duties will be reconsidered.

## Fiduciary duties, ownership, control and agency

The debate on corporate governance has mainly focused on two issues as a way of evaluating how this interdependency can operate, namely the composition of the board of directors and the content and function of fiduciary duties.[14] Although I do not deny the importance of the composition of the board of directors for governance purposes, in the present chapter I wish to focus on fiduciary duties and other accountability systems.[15] As will be shown in this chapter, the issue of contractual and more generally relational interdependency requires more than simply voicing stakeholders' interests in the board room. In particular, both simultaneous and sequential contractual interdependencies may require contractual modifications and adjustments. The extent to which the term 'fiduciary duties' is applicable here is an open, although almost purely semantic, question if a sufficiently broad notion of fiduciary duty is adopted.

One central feature of this debate is the meaning of fiduciary duties and their functional equivalents in different legal systems.[16]

Fiduciary law and fiduciary duties are generally associated with relationships based on trust within organizations, as opposed to market relations.[17] Even within organizations, the role of fiduciary law and duties changes according to the ownership and the objectives of the organization. Recent analyses show the existence of a relationship between different ownership patterns and the nature of co-operative relationships between the firm and its stakeholders, in particular its employees.[18] In particular it is important to ascertain whether fiduciary duties actually change functions and content in different types of organizations and what the duties owed to outside stakeholders may be.[19]

Fiduciary duties are generally applied to relationships characterized by the discretionary power granted to one party (agent) and imply that the party on whom they are imposed, acts upon the authority, consensually attributed to or delegated by other parties.[20] The fiduciary may act in the interests of several parties (multi-principal organizations) and the organization as a whole or in his/her own interests and that of the party to whom the duty is owed. This notion is much broader than contending that the fiduciary is the party who acts on behalf of another party associated with the idea of agency relationship.[21] Only the broader view, however, is able to encompass the many situations in which one party is empowered to act both in his/her own interests and in those of other constituencies, or in the interests of the organization as a whole.[22] In this context the more traditional definition of fiduciary duty, as imposed on a party acting in the interest of others, constitutes only one particular subset of fiduciary duties.

The structure and content of duties owed to different constituencies are conventionally thought to have a common feature, namely they are aimed at protecting specific investments made by different constituencies and at defining correct procedures to define fair trade-offs when authority to make decisions affecting those investments is delegated to one constituency alone.

Specific investments made by different constituencies within one organization can either be alternative or complementary.[23] Fiduciary duties have an extremely important function when specific investments are complementary, thereby affecting the level of contract incompleteness.

A different but related point is that specific investments made by contracting parties are not always backed up by property rights, and their protection through fiduciary duties becomes extremely important when no property rights are associated with them.[24] As I will show the relationship between fiduciary duties and organization's ownership is quite relevant for the governance design.

A second point that should be clarified is that of enforceability. I disagree with the commonly held view that fiduciary duties should be enforced by recourse to judges. In many cases fiduciary duties should be self-enforced since resorting to judicial dispute resolution would imply the end of the relationship and often the dissolution of the organization.

The content and function of these duties change in relation to the gap between ownership and control. However, fiduciary duties also come into force when entities different from publicly traded companies are in place, for example in closely held corporations or partnerships. Co-ownership, associated with partnership, implies that each partner-owner owes fiduciary duties to the other partners and to the partnership. Here, there is horizontal separation between ownership and control (i.e. each managing partner has control beyond the amount of property he or she owns) and yet fiduciary duties still play an important role in protecting reciprocal specific investments. The function of fiduciary duties in co-ownership-based firms has some quite fundamental differences from that in publicly traded corporations.

Non-profit organizations are characterized by lack of ownership by members and donors.[25] The relevant organizational feature is the relationship between membership and control.[26] To the extent that a separation between membership and control occurs, controlling constituencies owe fiduciary duties towards members, whether individual or collective.

Such differences in features suggest that it would be difficult to apply a uniform standard of fiduciary duties with different functions to perform in organizational models characterized by various ownership patterns. Both in relation to the duty of care and the duty of loyalty legal systems display a remarkable level of differentiation among legal forms.

Two possible routes can be designed to regulate fiduciary duties: one more radical which does not contemplate a unitary standard of fiduciary duties in different organizational models, and one more moderate which, though recognizing significant differences, attempts to identify common functions. In accordance with the definition made earlier of fiduciary duties, I opt for the moderate approach and claim that a comparison among different organizational models is meaningful despite the considerable differences because the link between fiduciary duties and ownership is relevant but not decisive, while the need to co-ordinate relational interdependencies is a common feature of contemporary organizational law.

The unifying concept is the relationship between fiduciary duties, control of the organization and protection of specific investments.[27] Whatever the variable that influences control (be it ownership or something else) fiduciary duties become relevant when there is no overlapping between members of the organization and those who exercise direct or first-order control over the decision-making process within the organization.[28] They play a meaningful role when this separation translates into an allocation of decision-making power among different constituencies.

While a definition of fiduciary duties as 'duties owed by a party who acts in the interests of the beneficiary' would make fiduciary duties inapplicable to other constituencies, a broader notion, such as that suggested above, is compatible with different stakeholders even if no agency relationship is at work and co-ordination is the main goal.

If the function of fiduciary duties is to protect the investments of non-controlling stakeholders from the potential abuse of discretionary power by the controlling constituency in the organization, in particular managers or controlling shareholders, then these fiduciary duties should be analysed within the framework of contract incompleteness.[29]

Fiduciary duties may or may not be associated with other duties arising from the contracts. An organization that engages in financing contracts has duties and obligations arising from creditors' contracts. Depending on the level of delegation of authority that creditors have granted to the organization and its managers, those duties will be associated with fiduciary duties. Authority is a function of, *inter alia,* the degree of contract incompleteness in that the higher the degree of incompleteness the higher the need to delegate authority to complete the contract, especially when negotiation is costly.[30]

As we shall see, the existence and level of discretion associated with fiduciary duties is partly correlated to the incomplete nature of the contract linking creditors, employees or suppliers to the organization.

## Codes of conduct, corporate governance and enabling fiduciary duties

The debate on corporate governance and the role of fiduciary duties should not be limited to the study of the combination of different traditional legal instruments. Two interesting developments which occurred recently are influencing the content and roles of fiduciary duties. One is the growing phenomenon of codes of conduct enacted at the level of the single enterprise, industry or at the market level.[31] The other, which concerns the role of social norms, has developed more on the theoretical level but affects the interpretation of organizational structures and behaviours.

The first development can be placed within the debate on corporate governance stimulated by David Kreps' seminal article and by other subsequent contributions on corporate culture and business ethics.[32]

Codes of conduct generally regulate the relationship between the firm, its managers and 'external' stakeholders, suppliers, financiers, customers and local or international communities.[33]

Codes of conduct and more in general self-regulation constitute a complement of public regulation. This complementarity often operates as a mutually reinforcing system and less frequently as a compensating one. This means that more often than not a strong legal system is combined with strong self-regulatory mechanisms. Less frequently self-regulation is a response to legal failure, though it has happened that in the absence of regulation, private parties have supplied their own regulatory self-enforced scheme.

Codes of conduct are generally voluntary. Corporations, industrial and trade associations, public and private regulators or international organizations draft and approve to regulate profiles complementing corporate law and corporate charters.[34] They differ in relation to the extent to which they are binding.[35] Some are legally binding and associated with sanctions, either self-enforceable or judicially enforceable.[36] Others are not legally binding and the enforcement is left to non-judicial mechanisms and non-judicial sanctions (primarily, but not exclusively, reputation). The latter do not create any legal duty but may be used by parties and/or judges to fill gaps in the corporate charter or as an interpretive device to give content to standards (such as those related to the duty of care and the duty of loyalty). Compliance with the codes, either as a purely voluntary act or as a legal duty, is generally reported annually and used in different ways by financial institutions.[37] False or inaccurate statements concerning compliance may entail legal responsibility, relevant especially for third parties, that is potential investors, lenders, customers and suppliers.[38]

Legally binding codes of conduct define duties and obligations the organization owes to different constituencies, and they determine reciprocal obligations among constituencies themselves. They can be used as a powerful mechanism to reduce opportunistic behaviour and increase the level of trust within the organization or between organizations and their stakeholders.[39] Vertical integration may reduce but does not eliminate opportunism, and devices to protect organizational loyalty are still needed. For this purpose they complement other legal devices within the definition of the governance system.[40]

I would here like to examine the two main dimensions of corporate codes of conduct in greater detail:

1 Horizontal dimension: codes of conduct often implicitly draw a firm's boundaries substantially differently from the way corporate law does. By and large, they tend to increase the number of actors that affect the choices and the decision-making space of the organization encompassing customers, suppliers, communities and non-profit organizations related to the activity of the organization.[41] Furthermore, codes of conduct not only regulate relationships between shareholders and the other stakeholders, but they may also address conflicts and trade-offs among stakeholders which are generated by the operation of the firm (environmental protection and employment, for example). There are also, however, significant examples of codes of conduct that uphold the primacy of shareholders.[42] The general trend should not therefore lead to the belief that codes of conduct deny the primacy of shareholders;
2 Vertical dimension: codes of conduct have much deeper ramifications within the organization than corporate law.[43] Corporate law is still mainly concerned

> with the highest level of corporate decision-making, leaving lower-level regulation to labour law.[44] Codes of conduct refer to the overall organization and regulate employees' conduct.[45] From the codes of conduct perspective the boundaries between corporate and labour law blur and the organization regains a unitary structure. A deeper analysis shows that enforceable corporate codes of conduct may also deeply affect the internal balance of labour law.

Codes of conduct enlarge the scope of fiduciary duties to the benefit of categories other than shareholders and, especially in relation to loyalty, define an integrated system by co-ordinating different vertical organizational layers. The question then arises: are codes of conduct an empirical manifestation of a contradiction with the hypothesis that creditors, employees and suppliers are better protected by contract or labour law than they would be by corporate law? The answer is that there is no empirical contradiction insofar as codes of conduct are considered part of the corporate governance apparatus, but not part of corporate law.

Having stated the differences it is useful to briefly examine how the two 'regulatory' systems may complement each other *vis-à-vis* fiduciary duties.

The role of codes of conduct as a device to define relationships among firm's stakeholders varies according to the extent corporate law protects stakeholders. Another variable is the type of firm, namely the role and the influence of codes of conduct differ substantially from multinational to national firms and, within these according to whether the enterprise is big, medium or small, networked or not networked.

For simplicity's sake, two different polar legal frameworks can be identified to illustrate the different functions that codes of conduct perform in the definition of fiduciary duties. In the first corporate law plays a major role in stakeholders' protection while, in the second, stakeholders' protection is divided over a number of legal and non-legal devices for each class or subclass of stakeholders.

In the first, codes of conduct play a relevant yet supplementary role because the balance of different interests already occurs within corporate law. By enacting codes of conduct that recognize legal duties towards stakeholders, such as consumers, employees, local communities, suppliers and creditors, firms voluntary increase their level of accountability and signal that protection of specific investments will be ensured. To the mandatory fiduciary duties owed to stakeholders they add enabling fiduciary duties owed to other categories.[46] Insofar as they are legally binding the different constituencies may require the enforcement of these obligations before judges or before 'private dispute resolution' bodies.

In the second, codes of conduct can play a more direct role because they might become the locus of co-ordination of different interests, organized through different legal branches, that is, corporate, contract or labour law. Not only do they supplement the present insufficient legal protection for stakeholders, thus rendering explicit their influence on corporate governance, but they also become an important device for deciding how different interests in the organization should be protected and balanced. The division of tasks between corporate law and codes of conduct becomes clearer. Corporate law is specifically designed to regulate the relationship between organizations and shareholders; codes of conduct are designed to regulate the relationships between the organization and other classes of stakeholders, supplementing specific contractual arrangements but also balancing different interests affecting organizational behaviour. In this second framework, codes of conduct also may and often do contain rules concerning shareholders that have two functions:

1 they enhance the organizational framework by considering other stakeholders;[47]
2 they supplement norms that specify the content of legal duties.[48]

There are two ways of interpreting the provisions of fiduciary duties in codes of conduct:

1 One which contends that because of the mandatory nature of legal fiduciary duties, codes of conduct may only add new duties, without lowering the protection offered by law to stakeholders. They cannot contractualize the protection offered to stakeholders by mandatory contract, labour, consumer or environmental law.
2 A different interpretation is that shareholders, who approve codes of conduct, should be free to introduce new fiduciary duties and redefine the boundaries of different classes by increasing the level of stakeholders' protection even when that can decrease their own (i.e. shareholders') protection.

It is quite clear that shareholders cannot lower the mandatory legal protection of stakeholders by introducing weaker obligations in codes of conduct. This should not be possible even when codes of conduct are negotiated with the relevant stakeholders involved, given the mandatory nature of the norms concerning stakeholder protection. A more problematic question is to what extent shareholders, enacting codes of conduct, can decrease their own legal protection guaranteed by fiduciary duties in order to increase the protection of stakeholders. An answer, which I endorse, is based on the idea that legal fiduciary duties provide minimum standards of protection that can be increased by voluntary shareholders action, that is, enactment of a code of conduct.

To the extent that a code of conduct is formally approved by shareholders and not only by the board of directors, the second interpretation seems more consistent with the contractual foundations of corporate governance and in particular corporate law. On the other hand, the first interpretation appears more consistent with the idea that codes of conduct may only cover the contractual space not dealt with by mandatory provisions, not only when they concern stakeholders but also in relation to shareholders' protection.

As I shall show, a different account concerns networks of firms where the role of codes of conduct refers to inter-firm relationships. The difficulty here lies in deciding how to apply the conceptual framework of the stakeholder/shareholder debate to a very different organizational setup.

## Social norms and fiduciary duties for the protection of organizational interests

The debate on the relationship between social norms and legal rules, and their different combinations in regulating transactions in the market place and within the corporation, cuts across the discussion concerning the relationship between corporate governance and corporate law and more specifically the role, function and width of fiduciary duties. The question addressed in this section is whether social norms are to be considered substitutes or complements of fiduciary duties. Legal systems and doctrines provide different answers but a fairly commonly shared starting point acknowledges the existence of different functions of social norms in relation to the duty of care and the duty of loyalty.

The answer requires a brief *excursus* through the wide, rich debate concerning social norms in organizations and in particular in firms.

Two different yet not mutually exclusive perspectives have been suggested to address the issue of social norms in corporate governance. On the one hand, those who support a hierarchical theory of the firm have underlined the relationship between forbearance and corporate organizations.[49] On the other hand, those who favour a co-operative theory of the firm stress the role of trust and reputation as organizational devices. In both cases the consideration of social norms affects the policy implications of considering non-legally enforceable social norms for corporate governance design.[50]

One of the critical aspects of TCE (transaction cost economics) approach is the relationship between social norms and hierarchies. The firm is conceived as a hierarchical structure[51] and thus apart from market transactions where, supposedly, relationships are non-hierarchical.[52] The main governance norm is forbearance. It is worth noticing, however that according to this perspective, the relationship between social norms and fiduciary duties is different with respect to duty of care and duty of loyalty. While social norms reduce the role and function of the duty of care, they are not considered to be as effective as the duty of loyalty.[53]

If we consider the perspective that emphasizes the role of social norms in intra-firm transactions and legal rules in market transactions, we are led to the consequence that the relationship between firms and stakeholders, being predominantly market- or contract-based, is regulated through legal rules judicially enforced, while that between shareholders and firm, essentially intra-firm, is mainly regulated by social norms and self-enforcing governance mechanisms.[54] What would then be the main consequences stemming from this perspective? Not only are the relationships different, but so are also the regulatory devices. Intra-firm relationships are mainly regulated by corporate law which extensively defers to social norms, in particular forbearance.[55] Stakeholder relationships with firms, and inter-firm relationships are mainly regulated by contracts, and in particular by contract law, which adopts a more legalistic approach.[56]

A different perspective suggests that social norms also play a relevant role in contractual relationships between stakeholders and firms and that the use of social norms is not necessarily associated with hierarchy.[57] In particular social norms fostering co-operation in long-term contractual relationships, a widespread characteristic of the relationship between organizations and their constituencies, have long been identified and studied.[58] Some stress the idea that social norms, which tend to foster co-operation, may be a viable alternative to legal rules, since they favour a less adversarial approach to contractual relationships. Others suggest that social norms complement legal rules in regulating long-terms contracts. Whatever the correct interpretation, I believe that there can be no longer be any doubt that social norms play significant yet different functions (as compared to organizations) in contractual relationships, both long term and spot.[59]

The various roles social norms play in firms and market transactions may therefore be more a question of functionality than of degree. The functional differences of social norms, and the relationship between social norms and legal rules in firms and market relationships (i.e. in vertically and non-vertically integrated firms) may be linked to the different governance structures operating in firms and in contracts (though long-term contracts, such as those concerning creditors and workers should be distinguished from spot contracts, for example consumer contracts).

A possible explanation, consistent with conventional wisdom, is that, given the difference between market transactions and firms, social norms promote co-operation in the former and support hierarchy in the latter. This explanation infers recognition of the role of social norms in the definition of alternative institutions. However, it rejects the idea that social norms only play a major role in the life of hierarchical organizations while neglecting their function in contractual (i.e. market) horizontal relationships.

I fail to find this perspective entirely persuasive.

Social norms in organizations contribute to reducing the risk of abuse of power and thus complement and affect fiduciary duties. Typically, fear of reputation erosion would reduce the incentives for shareholders, were they endowed with appropriate power, to expropriate the percentage of surplus *ex ante* assigned to stakeholders. Likewise, reputation might be a factor in reducing managers' incentives to expropriate shareholders. Reputation also helps to create corporate culture.[60] Hierarchy is reinforced insofar as it needs a legitimate and not discretional ground for it to be exercised. Social norms, however, play a very significant role in determining the learning mechanisms within the organization.[61] It is crucial to underline that organizations and firms in particular are, or should be, designed to allow improvements in their performance and that the legal infrastructure can only provide a framework within which social norms can 'do the job'.

To the extent that fiduciary duties, both care and loyalty, have to foster organizational co-operation by enhancing trust within the organization and between the organization and its stakeholders, the role of social norms is crucial.[62]

Two preliminary conclusions may be drawn here:

1 Social norms may play different roles in the design of corporate governance by promoting or legitimizing hierarchy or co-operation in relationships between a firm and its constituencies;

2 The role of social norms for each relationship depends on the model of firm and the market structure. For example the change from a predominantly vertically integrated firm towards a firm that out-sources some of its relevant functions may involve a change in degree and type of the relevant social norms operating in the corporate governance design.

These two conclusions do not permit identification of a single specific role of social norms in the definition of fiduciary duties, but they certainly show that the content and roles of fiduciary duties are affected by the use of social norms as both a way of exercising control and of limiting the abusive use of hierarchical power.

## Organizational theory, contract incompleteness and relational interdependencies

There is a point of intersection between the governance debate and the problem of organizational contract incompleteness. As an example of this interplay I wish to dwell on the interdependence of specific investments and its influence on governance design. It has already been pointed out that specific investments made by different constituencies may either be complementary or alternative. Relational interdependence occurs in both cases but with slightly different features that affect the content of fiduciary duties.

Contracts affecting the structure and life of the organization, involving shareholders, suppliers, creditors and employees, are all characterized by the existence of some level of investments made by parties. The extent of the specificity of these investments may vary, but often all contracts share some aspects of transaction specificity and related hold-up problems.

A second factor concerning the role that specificity may play is the level of competitiveness at which the different constituencies operate in their own markets. Every constituency has its own level of competitiveness which not only affects the initial structure of its contract with the firm, but also the potential for opportunistic behaviour by corporate shareholders when exercising corporate power. Thus, if shareholders are given control rights, the potential to abuse them by performing or not performing the contracts with other constituencies, or opportunistically changing the governance structure of the corporation thereby reducing other stakeholders' welfare, is also a function of the level of stakeholders' competition (suppliers, creditors, workers) in their own market. For example, raw material suppliers who operate in a highly competitive market are potentially more exposed to corporate opportunism than if they were monopolists. Similar arguments can be put forward for creditors, workers and even for communities if we take into consideration the location of the firm.[63]

The incomplete nature of the contracts between stakeholders and firm poses co-ordination problems as yet insufficiently analysed. If financing contracts were complete, creditors' interests would have a greater likelihood of sound protection under contract or property law, and their potential for abuse by corporate managers would be relatively low.[64] These contracts and the obligations arising from them would represent constraints on managerial and, more generally, on organizational discretion.[65] The contractual duties owed to creditors would therefore limit corporate choices.[66]

Contracts with creditors, suppliers, customers and workers are incomplete and, to differing degrees, exposed to opportunistic behaviour.[67] The protection of specific investments, though purely illustrative, constitutes a good example of the interdependency to which corporate governance has to respond. The aim of a good corporate governance design is to maximize the incentives of each constituency to make specific investments insofar as they contribute to enhance the competitive advantage of the overall organization. The problem is to define a governance system able to provide sufficient incentives for every constituency even if residual rights of control are allocated to only one of them.

I will assume for the purpose of illustration that constituencies are internally homogeneous; however it should be borne in mind – and some reference will be made later to the fact – that constituencies may diverge greatly and their incentives may vary. In fact, very often constituencies are quite heterogeneous.[68] A complete study of contractual interdependencies should therefore take account of the internal balancing of incentives within each constituency as much as of the external balancing among constituencies.

If the assumption of a contract's completeness is relaxed, it is important to differentiate between endogenous and exogenous sources drawn from a contract's completion, for example as regards the financial contract between creditors and the organization. Internal corporate decision-making should be considered a relevant, possibly one of the most significant, exogenous variable for the completion of a financial contract.[69] In this case there is a bilateral contractual dependency to be governed, meaning that the completion of a financing contract depends on corporate decisions which in turn are affected by that contract's incompleteness. It is important to stress that interdependency exists both when contracts are complete and when they are incomplete, but it operates in different ways.

Furthermore, if incompleteness in financial contracts is attributable wholly or partly to corporate managerial discretion, then current co-ordination mechanisms between corporate and financing contracts may not be adequate. Similar reasoning concerning the difference between complete and incomplete contracts may also apply to labour or supply contracts.[70]

The conceptual framework illustrated above, encompassing more devices than just corporate law (i.e. codes of conduct, social norms etc.), poses a problem, namely: if stakeholders' interests are socially and legally relevant, in which way do they affect corporate structure and behaviour? In particular, if corporate contracts are conceived as incomplete, to what extent can or should different stakeholders participate in the completion process of the organizational contract? Is it a precondition of this function to be, legally speaking, a party to the corporate contract or can participation to the completion process be ensured through other devices? More specifically, to what extent can the content of fiduciary and non-fiduciary duties to parties other than shareholders (creditors, consumers, workers) be related to the completion processes of the contract?

It is important to clarify what I mean by participation in the completion process of the contract. Once direct participation is excluded, such as for example through participation in the board, creditors may indirectly participate in completion of the corporate contract by defining specific clauses in their contract or by protecting their property interests. In their contract they can impose limitations or procedural clauses that would subject specific corporate choices affecting their claims to consent or negotiation. Through the creation of security interests they may set constraints on corporate choices and affect the firm's decision-making.

According to one perspective, shareholders have greater incentives to make specific investments than creditors and employees.[71] From these differences among constituencies, the need arises for fiduciary duties in corporate contracting in relation to shareholders, but not for contracts of the firm with other stakeholders. Creditors, suppliers and employees would be better protected by specific covenants.[72]

As far as shareholders are concerned, incentives may depend on whether they are in a position of control or no control; for creditors one relevant difference is whether the credit is secured or not secured; in labour a significant difference is that between high- and low-skilled workers, and labour is also related to the adopted model of work organization.[73]

A different perspective is obtained by examining each constituency's specific investments with the firm in order to identify the governance structure and the legal and non-legal devices to ensuring their protection. The measure of investment specificity is provided by the combination between the resource and its use. If each constituency makes some specific investments the corporate governance problem is to ensure protection for these investments both when they are complementary (so that their protection be guaranteed simultaneously), and when they are alternative (so that protection of some specific investments reduces protection of others). The solution is not to shift from one governance structure to another, according to whether one or the other type of investment prevails, but to allow internal balancing and compensating systems among holders of debt and holders of equity when creditors are involved, or between capital and labour when employees are involved.

Fiduciary duties are one of the devices which protect these investments and minimize risks of opportunism and shirking among different categories. One of the dangers is for different constituencies to make specific investments at the time of their contract and then use the power to modify the corporate contract given to only one of them, the others suffering loss later. Again, if the contracts had been complete this contingency would have been factored into them but since they were not, an externality may be produced. In financial contracting the answer for some authors is simply to distinguish between fixed and residual claimants. Fixed claimants, being given priority, so the claim goes, get more protection. This on the one hand implies a high level of rigidity and, on the other, may not be sufficient to protect the so-called fixed claimants. The need arises to define adjustment mechanisms that would *in itinere* protect different constituencies (creditors and shareholders) from opportunistic behaviour stemming from the power to affect the changes in corporate contracts unequally distributed.[74] The flexibility needed can be provided by fiduciary duties.

A somewhat similar reasoning may be followed for labour. According to Williamson, the alternatives here are among different types of contracts since pure internalization leading to hierarchy presupposes ownership, something which is unacceptable in the case of human capital. It is worth noting, *en passant*, that labour contracts which led Coase to identify hierarchy as a distinguishing feature of the firm are recognized by Williamson as a limit to the level of hierarchy.

Here, again, different levels of specific investments generate different contractual arrangements in labour contracts which have to be co-ordinated with the firm's corporate contract.

In some models of firms, labour contracts tend to be more organization-specific, which poses new problems for corporate governance.[75] Transaction specificity for labour inputs does not necessarily have to be solved through a change in board representation but it does generate a higher level of incompleteness as well as increasing bilateral opportunism by recombining exit and voice. Protection of workers' specific investments requires that corporate decision-making internalize this interest.[76]

The problem is not so much about differing degrees of incompleteness but about different reasons for contract incompleteness and ways to complete contracts affecting and affected by corporate decision-making (corporate, credit and labour).

In short, the different functions of fiduciary duties in business associations, and those owed to different stakeholders discussed earlier, are the result of different types of contracts and ways of completing them. The need to co-ordinate incomplete contracts between the organization (the firm) and its stakeholders requires the use of fiduciary duties to discourage abuse of power by the constituency to whom the control is attributed. Needless to say, this conclusion applies to whoever has control, therefore workers who control the organization in a co-operative would owe fiduciary duties to the other constituencies.

It is important to point out that while the focus in the chapter has been on contractual interdependencies, relational interdependencies also encompass property regimes in which the partitioning of assets does not depend on contractual arrangements or other duties under law such as, for example, tort-related duties. Furthermore, it is clear that a study of interdependency would not only encompass legal rules but also social norms, thus affecting compliance with the contractual commitments and the sanctioning system.

## Operationalizing relational interdependencies: different complementing scenarios

I shall now move on to examine the different legal instruments available in order to recognize and give protection to relational interdependencies. If the corporate governance design is mainly focused on the systems of co-ordination of the relationships between the firm and its stakeholders, other, more suitable tools can be used. It is important to restate that co-ordination presupposes that interests have been prioritized, but also that conflict resolution is not the only aim of corporate governance, since a co-operative environment is instrumental to maximize the firm's value.

Having shown the existence of relational interdependency and framed it within the conceptual approach of contract incompleteness, I suggest that different institutional designs are available to solve the contextual incompleteness of contracts.

Recognition of interdependency among different contractual and non-contractual relationships implies that these should be read as different yet not alternative ways to render interdependency operational.

I will focus mainly on contractual relations. This interdependency must be addressed in different ways depending on whether a contract is assumed to be complete or not. In a simple scenario with only two contracts to be co-ordinated, and in which both are assumed to be complete, then interdependencies can be 'solved' by simply specifying the contingencies. If one is assumed to be complete and the other incomplete, then there will be unilateral dependency: the complete contract will be a constraint on the completion of the incomplete contract. The most plausible and theoretically sound scenario is that in which both contracts are incomplete and contingencies concerning one contract may affect the completion of the other. Many examples of relational interdependencies associated to two incomplete contracts, as be drawn from financing and supply contracts, as also from labour contracts.[77]

I can now address the question concerning the instruments needed to render interdependency operational. In describing the various interdependencies, a distinction should be drawn between instruments for affording the different constituencies legitimacy to express themselves and participate in the corporate decision-making process, as opposed to instruments for defining the balance among different interests and protecting them.[78]

Three alternative scenarios in which interdependency may occur can be used to illustrate the difference between these two goals. Each of them has a different combination of the two classes of instruments.

1. A corporate governance design which encourages participation by various constituencies may be based on procedural duties, owed by the organization to these constituencies.[79] These duties are principally dual, namely the duty to inform and the duty to consult or listen.

The duty to inform sets specific obligations to give information about corporate decisions and, in particular, there is a duty to report on decisions and occurrences and a duty to give information on forthcoming decisions. With regard to the former, there is an ongoing debate, and proposals have been made to improve the reporting system; the recently proposed annual corporate statement for listed companies would fulfil this aim.[80] A more focused means of pursuing this goal is to adopt a social balance, documenting the impact that decisions have on the welfare of other constituencies or the community at large in the light of the corporate social responsibility trend. Many other examples could follow. I suggest that a duty to inform should also be adhered to regarding decisions that have not yet been taken but that may affect the contractual relationships that the firm has engaged in. What is important, when rendering interdependency operational, is to bear in mind the distinction between information for shareholders, information for stakeholders and information to be given to the public. Each of these has different standards and entitles the recipients to different rights to be informed by the organization. This in turn affects the ways in which contract incompleteness can be solved taking into account rent extraction concerning the use of information.

A complementary duty is the duty to hear or, in a more intense form, the duty to consult.[81] In this case there are procedures to be followed for the appointment of representatives of the various stakeholders who are to be consulted on specific issues. These procedures are generally defined by the law but sometimes they are also regulated in codes of conduct. The corporate deliberation process would be affected, as it is in many public administrations, by the acquisition and assessment of the various interests influencing corporate decision-making. The interdependency here is purely procedural, and stakeholder interests may affect corporate decision-making only because they are given voice.

In the deliberative process, the regulation of which is the domain of shareholders, the corporation commits itself to allow – or even to require – other constituencies to express their opinions about choices which may affect their interests. This means that constituencies are to be fully informed about corporate issues that may influence their position and in particular their welfare. A duty to inform various constituencies is therefore necessary to implement a duty to hear or consult. A deliberative process in corporate decision-making requires hearing the opinions of creditors, consumers and employees on matters that may affect their position and welfare. Once the consultations are concluded, the board and/or the shareholders meetings are free to make their own decisions. In some cases they have a legal obligation to motivate their decisions in others they do not. The consultation process does not give the consulted parties the right to have their views accepted unlike the hypothesis of veto power considered later within the third scenario.

It is clear that to allow constituencies to express themselves would produce consequences on corporate policy and decision-making even if the highest degree of freedom is granted to shareholders, leaving stakeholder interests' protection to other legal instruments and to social norms. In this case, only the procedural aspects of corporate law would come into play but the decision-making process could be strongly influenced by the consequences in terms of reputation deriving from contrasting opinions expressed by different constituencies. This is a case in which legal duties constitute the preconditions for social norms to operate as a constraint for organizational decision-making.

There are a number of legal regimes which can be adopted; from those whose only requirement is the provision of adequate motivations (notice and comment) for the final decisions to those based on the 'comply or explain' principle. In the latter case the organization would be compelled to follow the suggestions and bound to explain if it decides not to adhere to them.

For example, creditors could be given voice to express their opinions but their legal protection in the case of a merger, a take over, an increase or reduction in capital, would be merely that provided by contract law, if at all. Consultation procedures are already functioning with regard to other constituencies. In Europe, worker consultation has been in force for a long time.[82] This model represents a possible method of implementing a deliberative process.

This scenario seems to be particularly promising concerning the duty of loyalty and self-interested transactions. Obliging the board to supply adequate and detailed motivations concerning the approval or rejection of a transaction which may be self-interested might increase transparency and enable both shareholders and external stakeholders to effectively monitor the decision-making process.[83] Many legal systems today require approval albeit nut with a publicly held deliberative process such as the one just proposed.

The wide divergence between shareholders and stakeholders means that the consequent weak interdependency will prevent legal repercussions, at least in the short term. The interdependency, however weak, may still be a decisive factor in determining corporate conduct through social norms. In this scenario the instruments are mainly aimed at legitimizing different constituencies, through the selection of those who are given an enforceable right to be informed and heard.

2 A second scenario is one in which the purely procedural voice is combined with other devices that take into account the structural interdependency between decision-making processes: those taking place within the corporation and those taking place in different contractual frameworks between the firm and its stakeholders. Here, the legal framework allows for the content of fiduciary duties and linked system of the corporation's and board's liabilities towards shareholders to be affected by the duties owed to creditors, employees and other constituencies. Symmetrically, the contractual and non-contractual duties owed by the corporation to other constituencies are affected by corporate decision-making not only *ex ante* (i.e. contracts signed by the corporation with other constituencies should comply with corporate charters and bylaws) but also *ex post* (i.e. a change in corporate strategy, for example to increase the level of equity, may affect the contractual relationship with creditors and its mode of completion). Here the interdependency is organized at two levels:

(i) Constituencies are given voice but no power in corporate decision-making. The results of the consultation are not legally binding but they produce effect through social norms;
(ii) The corporate governance design recognizes that there is a reciprocal influence among the various contracts the corporation engages in with different constituencies. This recognition is expressed by a revised version of fiduciary duties and a general duty to behave in good faith and adjust contracts when modifications so require.

Together with instruments aimed at legitimizing stakeholders' interests, there is a stronger recognition of legal instruments aimed at balancing different interests not only between shareholders and the others but also among stakeholders.[84] It is not *ex ante* defined how the balance should be struck, but it is clear that corporate decision-makers cannot ignore the effects of their decisions on contracts between the firm and its stakeholders.

3 A third scenario is that in which, in addition to these first two elements, substantive power is attributed to different constituencies to affect corporate decision-making. In this case, for example, creditors, consumers, environmental associations and employees are given power to veto certain decisions, to demand that their interests be adequately protected or, in cases where harm is likely to occur, that compensation be paid.[85]

Within this last scenario there is a continuum of legal devices that go from *ex post* compensation of external stakeholders damaged by corporate decision-making to *ex ante* veto power that would prevent the decision from producing any legal effect. One can express this distinction by referring to the distinction between property, validity and liability rules.

As already pointed out, the three scenarios illustrated define instruments that should be considered complementary and not alternative. In many cases the introduction of deliberative procedures may make the use of legal protection redundant and enable social norms to operate. The effect of a deliberative procedure will be clearly very different if it is coupled with a legal instrument that gives the dissenting constituency or contractual partner the power to resort to legal protection if the final decision violates its rights. When, despite a hearing which has documented the negative effects of the decision, no further legal protection is ensured, and firm still goes ahead, it will suffer losses in terms of reputation and market to the extent that its decision is perceived as unjust.

The scope of this chapter is not to provide a detailed comparative analysis of different ways to render relational interdependency operational, but to suggest that current organizational models are different responses to this problem. Even those conceptual approaches that advocate separation of corporate law from contract, labour and financial law should not fail to address the problem of relational interdependency.[86] In this perspective relational interdependency is a key variable when addressing comparative institutional analyses.

It is clear that this problem will be solved in different ways depending upon the degree of separation but it would be conceptually a mistake to believe that the higher the level of separation between corporate law and the other fields regulating contracts between the firm and other stakeholders, the lower the level of contractual interdependency.

Contractual interdependency obliges a rethink of the role of fiduciary duties. Fiduciary duties are located in the second and third scenario but the way to make them operational depends quite substantially on the decision-making process and its deliberative nature. The debate should focus not on whether fiduciary duties should extend to stakeholders but on the role fiduciary duties can play to render interdependency operational.

## Complementary models of industrial organization: network of firms, fiduciary duties and governance issues. A research agenda

Different models of firms have been developed in Western and Eastern capitalist systems.[87] The debate on the boundaries of firms reveals the necessity to reconsider the, by now traditional, dichotomy between vertically integrated firms and markets.[88] Not only have hybrids been shown to be the most diffused form of economic organizations, but some of the problems which were deemed to be solvable through vertical integration are often managed by horizontal co-operation.[89] Co-operation often translates into organizational networks. Many of the small and medium enterprises operate within formal or informal networks.[90] Within the label of networks very different models of firms have developed. For the purpose of this chapter, however, it is appropriate to consider them in a unified way in order to complement the standard hierarchical view of the firm.[91] Many analysts engage in comparisons of different models to identify comparative advantages. I will not consider the advantages or disadvantages of the network firms versus vertically integrated ones but will proceed to outline various reasons that in fact make some of the distinctive features of legal characterization of fiduciary duties in vertically integrated firms inapplicable to network firms.

The networks considered are characterized by a mix of co-operation and competition that allows a much more flexible choice in making a decision than the vertically integrated firm.[92] This higher flexibility enables firms to be competitors or collaborators depending on individual projects and circumstances. However, since these are long-term relationships, the legal framework should capture the idea that the same relationship can be simultaneously or sequentially characterized by both co-operation and competition.

These firms are characterized by high levels of resource-interdependence and complementarity features which imply that, even if each firm is a separate legal entity and owns some critical resources, if no vertical integration takes place the key governance tools are contracts or informal mechanisms that define the allocation of decision-making power in inter-firm relationships, more than in who owns the resources.

A second element is the organization of production and work. At the core of the transformation of models of firms there lies a fundamental change in the way production is organized and particularly the introduction of team work.[93] This change has been brought about mainly by the role that internationalized knowledge and learning mechanisms play in defining the core and boundaries of firms.

At the outset I should clarify that networks of firms can perform different functions according to the level and the type of integration among them. Networks of firms can be either purely regulatory or have some degree of industrial collaboration associated with resource-interdependence which leads to consequences in terms of governance and liability.[94] I shall leave aside regulatory networks and concentrate on networks of firms in which there is a reasonable or a high level of resource interdependence (this interdependence may relate to physical assets, capital labour or abstract resources such as knowledge or human capital, etc.). Here, relational interdependence takes on a very different form and the content and the functions of fiduciary duties models have to be rethought for a number of reasons.

To illustrate my point, I would like to offer a specific example and then generalize on the basis of the different features of fiduciary duties in network relationships. My example, which affects the function of fiduciary duties in networks of firms, is related to the control of opportunistic behaviour due to rent extraction connected to contract incompleteness and specific investments.

Networks are, at once, organizational devices to solve individual firms' contractual incompleteness while themselves posing a problem of contractual incompleteness. Contract incompleteness in a network environment is a phenomenon related more to the interaction between firms than it is to the constitutional contract of the single firm. The current approach, quite widespread in literature on fiduciary duties, is not applicable to networks for several connected reasons:

1 Most time-specific investments tend to be network-related rather than firm-related. For both capital and labour there are network-specific investments which are redeployable within the network, and less so outside the network. This phenomenon, at the very least, moves the exit frontier from the individual firm to the network.[95]
2 The problem of opportunism in networks becomes therefore more an inter- than an intra-firm problem.
3 The solution to contract incompleteness in networks may be provided by collaborative methods of production instead of the introduction of contractual safeguards or vertical integration.[96]

Two preliminary conclusions can be drawn:

1 The decentralized nature of decision-making within networks places control over the conduct of firms within co-ordination mechanisms of which the pre-requisite is mutual control instead of unilateral dependency, the characteristic feature of fiduciary duties generally associated with agency relations in vertically integrated firms.
2 The definition and function of fiduciary duties are therefore different from those typical of vertically integrated firms: they mainly hinge on relational interdependencies among firms and cannot be constrained within the boundaries of individual firms.

In addition, there are a number of structural factors that seem to point to the shareholder/stakeholder debate not being particularly appealing when the perspective is shifted from vertically integrated firms to networks of firms. This conclusion, if accepted, implies the need for a different conceptual framework for various suppliers of resources, fiduciary duties and alternative means of protection of the constituencies' interests within a network framework. These structural factors are:

1 In networks of firms, ownership of physical and non-physical assets may be shared and allocated among firms through contracts, joint ventures, strategic alliances, franchising, etc.[97]
2 Control of critical resources for the network is often shared out and at times dispersed among firms through the use of legal and non-legal devices.
3 The simultaneous or sequential presence of co-operation and competition makes the relationships more complex and changes the nature of the duties firms owe one another.[98] For example duties not to compete or to deal with rival firms, generally associated to the duty of loyalty, cannot be applied in the network's framework unless adequately adjusted since, at the same time, a firm may be a collaborator and a competitor. On the contrary a duty not to compete may apply to relationships with firms external to the network.
4 The circumstances under which some of the critical resources are externalized from the individual firm to the network pose different problems of governance and liability from those traditionally considered in the shareholder-stakeholder debate associated with the vertically integrated firm, which is mainly based on the form of a publicly traded corporation.

    (i) In particular on the one hand there is a need for a shared system of liability for decisions concerning shared or commonly controlled resources. On the other, a liability system for individual firms operating in a network cannot be devised with the same tools as those applied to firms that are vertically integrated.

At the very least these factors imply that the distinction between shareholders and stakeholders is redefined. Many agents who would qualify as shareholders in the vertically integrated firm become stakeholders or external suppliers in the network model. But the network model goes further than simply redistributing the number and quality of shareholders and stakeholders and thereby redrafting the boundaries of the firm. The core idea of the vertically integrated firm which defines the boundaries according to ownership of critical resources gives way, in networks, to boundaries of firms becoming blurred, and the set of duties and obligations owed by each organization to the other firms participating in the network becoming more interrelated than the clear-cut distinction presented by the literature on vertically integrated firms would suggest.[99] Even if the corporate form is maintained, to be residual claimants in the individual firm participating in a network does imply possessing that same power and control over the firms' decisions typical of the vertically integrated firm. The interdependency resource is such that each firm's operation is strongly influenced by other firms' decisions and behaviour. Insofar as this interdependency generates reciprocity and not unilateral power, risks of abusive behaviour and shirking are reduced. Other problems concerned with co-ordination arise and fiduciary duties are mainly aimed at defining co-ordination systems rather than at solving agency problems.

In order to identify the beneficiaries of fiduciary duties in networks of firms a distinction should be drawn between networks that are themselves legal entities, those created by contracts and those not formalized. Suffice it to say that when the network is a legal entity, either under corporate or another, perhaps non-profit form, duties are owed both to the network and reciprocally among firms, whereas duties are only reciprocal when there is no legal entity, that is, when the network is only informal, the two scenarios having in common collective assets to be safeguarded such as trust, reputation and social capital. Even when the network does not acquire a legal dimension, the informal structure supplies (or at least helps to generate) collective assets that may be legally safeguarded by reciprocal duties that firms and their individual components (boards, managers) owe to one another. This conclusion implies that firm A may owe duties of loyalty to firm B aimed at protecting not only the individual interest of firm B but also the collective asset of trust or reputation belonging to the network that may be violated by A. At times this reputation interest may be incorporated into an asset, for example a network trademark, other times it may simply be an interest worthy of legal protection through contract or tort law.

Considerations on collective assets may take different forms. B, who has a legitimate standing against A, would act not only in its own interest but also in that of all the network participants who could suffer an economic loss from A's conduct. The different levels of protection of individual and collective interests may, for example, affect the nature of remedies that an organization can ask for. If the individual interest alone has been affected, damages may be preferred to injunction. If a collective interest of the informal structure is threatened then injunction may be granted. The lack of a legal dimension of the network may pose a collective action problem when the behaviour of one organization harms the collective good more than that of the interests of individual firms. In this case the individual firm may not have sufficient incentives to act in the interest of the network and the harm may go unpunished. The question is whether the collective action problem should be resolved by providing a legal form to the network or whether other contractual forms may offer equally good solutions.

When the network has acquired a legal dimension then it is possible that each firm contextually owes fiduciary duties to the network and to other individual firms. The network may also owe fiduciary duties to individual firms. If the main function of the network is to co-ordinate, failure to co-ordinate or to facilitate co-operation by favouring one firm over another may translate into a violation of a duty of loyalty, in the form of a duty to fair treatment owed by the network towards each component.[100]

The question then becomes one of which interests should be protected by the network and which by individual relationships. The web of relational interdependencies becomes more complicated. The problem arises in cases of loyalty when the strong interdependency among firms belonging to the same network may make it difficult to distinguish between failure to co-operate between individual firms and failure to comply with social norms that may or may not have been codified in the network. The problem of competition and co-operation again offers a good example. Let us suppose that a firm within the network breaches a contract with another firm that belongs to the same network in order to favour an outside competitor. The breach of contract in this case is not only a violation of the specific contract that links the two firms but it affects the distribution of wealth within the network and decreases the general level of reciprocal trust. It may be the case that the decrease of trust is a greater harm than the breach caused to the individual firm and for this reason protecting this trust should not be entirely allocated to the individual organization which has suffered from its breach.

## Concluding remarks

In this chapter, I have tried to show that the current debate on corporate governance is relatively misplaced. The juxtaposition between the stakeholder and shareholder theories does not provide useful insights to define the features of a new design of corporate governance.

I have identified two major weaknesses:

1 The concept that the fundamental issue facing corporate governance is that of prioritising interests and solving distributional conflicts among different stakeholders.
2 The association of the legal features of the corporate governance debate with one only model of firm: the vertically integrated one.

With regard to the first point I have suggested that the main goal of corporate governance should be to encourage co-operation to protect specific investments and that the problem of solving conflicts among stakeholders should be addressed only secondarily. To promote co-operation in a web of incomplete contracts, linking the firm with different classes of stakeholders means focusing on relational interdependency.

I have defined the interdependencies among different relationships and then suggested different ways by which these contractual and organizational interdependencies can be addressed, by focusing on different legal devices, available particularly in European countries. In this framework I have attempted to provide a different account of fiduciary duties, aware that the legal content of the term itself varies in different legal systems and according to different legal cultures.

The critique on the current debate becomes even stronger when faced with different models such as the networked firm and the networks of firms. The historical debate concerning stakeholder and shareholder has always been referred to the American publicly traded corporation. Its transposition to different models is inappropriate and therefore a general debate on the legal features of corporate governance should address the complexity of different models of firms.

The distinction between shareholders and stakeholders blurs substantially when the unity of analysis becomes the network. Many shareholders of the vertically integrated firm become stakeholders in the network but they play a central role in the life of each firm. Interdependency is confronted with different legal entities, and legal boundaries of the individual firm become less significant. Therefore the meaning of fiduciary duties and its enforceability changes radically in the network environment. Furthermore, traditional contract law does not seem adequate to address the problem. The role of trust, loyalty and co-operation suggests the need to recombine legal and non-legal devices to ensure that these collective assets are preserved and that horizontal interdependencies among firms, and between them and their social environments, are well governed. The main aim of the chapter was to shift the relevant conceptual and institutional variables; the agenda for future work is to provide policy suggestions which, accordingly, will be able to improve the legal environment.

## Acknowledgements

This chapter a revised version of a lecture given at Siena Summer School on Law and Economics in June 2000. Useful comments were received by participants at the summer school. Thanks to Paola Iamiceli, Lorenzo Sacconi and Roberto Tamborini for interesting discussions on some parts of the chapter. The usual disclaimer applies.

## Notes

1 This point is made clear by Williamson (1986). Also in Williamson (1996)

> Transaction cost economics aspires to assess the contractual relation between each constituency and the enterprise symmetrically. The general argument is that each input will contract with the enterprise in a discriminating way. Specifically, inputs that are exposed to contractual hazards will either devise a contractual safeguard or the input will demand and receive a risk premium.
>
> (p. 313)

2 See Easterbrook and Fischel (1991); Romano (1996).

3 The problem of interdependency was acknowledged by Williamson (1984, 1986, p. 301). See on this point also Becht *et al.* (2002, pp. 16 ff.).

4 Deakin has correctly underlined that there are different concepts of enterprises depending on which legal aspect we view it from:

> Company law and labour law describe the enterprise from the point of view of the firm's relations with what we might call its 'internal stakeholders' that is, shareholders, employees and creditors. By contrast, tort law focuses on the claims of external parties such as accident victims, consumers and others that are affected by the firm's activities.
>
> (2003, p. 99)

5 There are several decisions that may affect wealth redistribution between debt-holders and shareholders. The conflict is well illustrated by Jensen and Meckling (1976) and then reproposed in the context of fiduciary duty analysis by Hart:

> If the firm issues risky debt as well as equity, then creditors' claims are no longer fully protected. In such a situation it is well known that managers, acting on behalf

of shareholders have an incentive to undertake risky negative net present value investments since these investments help shareholders in profitable states where the firm is solvent and do not hurt them in unprofitable states where the firm is bankrupt (they hurt creditors instead). These investments are not in the interest of shareholders and creditors taken together and would be avoided if management acted on behalf of both groups.

(1993, p. 305)

6 As will become clearer later 'trade-offs' does not mean offering greater protection to the specific investments of one specific constituency over another. When specific investments made by different constituencies are complementary, incentives to protect them should be guaranteed equitable allocation.

7 The contractual adaptation system is such that in the financing contract, contingencies are specified so that whenever a relevant change occurs in the corporation, not necessarily in the corporate charter, a co-ordinated change will occur in the contract with creditors. Symmetrically a co-ordination mechanism may operate when changes occur in a financing contract, for example due to completion.

8 See on this point Deakin and Hughes (1999).

9 See on this point, Sacconi (2000).

10 See Crouch *et al.* (2001). In particular see Crouch and Trigilia (pp. 212 ff.).

11 See for this perspective Romano (1996).

12 Holmstrom and Roberts (1998); Zingales (1998, 2000); Helper *et al.* (2000, pp. 471 ff.). With reference to asset partitioning and organizational boundaries see Hansmann and Kraakman (2000) and more recently Triantis (2004).

13 Legal systems differ in that some attribute to corporate law the task of pursuing higher level of stakeholder protection, while others, which endorse shareholders' primacy, provide stakeholders protection through different devices: contract law for creditors and suppliers, consumer law for consumers, tort or administrative law for environmental protection, labour law for workers, etc. In particular looking at corporate managers' duties and liabilities, it is clear that their choices are made accountable not only to shareholders but also to other stakeholders. Some level of protection especially in relation to creditors and mainly in the proximity of bankruptcy is provided by corporate law systems.

14 Romano (1996, pp. 279 ff.):

> Transaction cost economics offers the most compelling explanation of American corporate law's approach to the board of directors: the board represents the interests of shareholders and not other constituents. As Williamson explains this approach is appropriate because shareholders' investment in the firm is more vulnerable than that of other claimants: (i) equity is the residual claimant, the investments that stands at the end of the payout queue, and it is associated with no particular assets (in contrast to secured debt, or a worker with firm specific human capital, for example); (ii) equity alone is a claim with no periodic review or renegotiation right (i.e. there is no maturity of expiration date for stock as there is in debtor labour contracts, which enable bondholders and employees to take their resources and exit the firm if they do not like the firm's renewal offer price); and (iii) equity has no guaranteed interest payment or principal repayment.
>
> (Williamson, 1984, 1985)

These characteristics make equity investment akin to a transaction-specific asset, which is difficult to protect by simple contract. That is, the open-endedness of the claim makes it difficult to specify investment protection by contract at the time of investment, and, as circumstances change, the lack of renegotiation opportunities that accompanies the perpetual life instrument prevents it from addressing unexpected events that adversely affect share value. Corporate charter amendments follow the equity contract midstream, but there is no requirement that management propose amendments as particular events occur or contingencies realized and even if there were such a requirement, amendments are equally prey to the contracting problem encountered at the outset of the investment relationship, namely the impossible task of specifying constraints on a necessarily open-ended delegation of decisions rights. Consequently, the corresponding open-endedness of board representation and fiduciary duty law, which can flexibly adapt firm decisions to particular circumstances, is better suited for protecting equity (as opposed to other types of investments in firms).

Most investments in firms are not transaction-specific, and thus need no special protection device such as the board of directors. For most workers with general purpose skills and knowledge, special governance structures are unnecessary because they can quit without productive losses to either work or firm (Williamson, 1985, p. 302). This is also true of much debt, which is either short-term or financing readily redeployable assets that will not lose value if the creditor must repossess them (Williamson, 1985, p. 307). Where a transaction-specific component to the non-equity investment in a particular firm requires special protection, other governance structures beside the board of directors are more appropriate because of the more concrete specification of the claim on the firm. For example, fortransaction-specific debt and labour, equity collateral or contractual covenants restricting managerial actions and collective bargaining agreements requiring arbitration of grievances, respectively, are better-tailored mechanisms than board representation as they can pinpoint problems and responses without diminishing the value of the class claim. She then concludes:

> For safeguarding transaction specific investments, general purpose technologies, such as the board of directors, are less effective than specific technologies, such as protective covenants or grievance arbitration, and thus more expensive for firms (the inputs charge a higher price for the lower level of protection of their investments). But where the special purpose technologies are infeasible, the benefits of general purpose technologies are likely to exceed the costs in comparison to adopting no governance mechanisms.

See also Macey (1992).

15 For a detailed discussion of the different perspectives on board composition see Becht *et al.* (2002, pp. 48 ff.).

16 See Hart (1993); Macey and Miller (1993); Easterbook and Fischel (1993).

17 See the famous passage of Justice Benjamin Cardozo in *Meinhard v. Salmon*, 164 N. E. 545 (N.Y.ct.App. 1928): 'Joint adventurers like co partners owe to one another . . . the duty of the finest loyalty. Many forms of conduct permissible in a workaday world for those acting at arm's length are forbidden to those bound by fiduciary ties.'

18 See Deakin *et al.*

19 The definition of agency relationship and the content of fiduciary duties is highly problematic for several reasons. From a comparative perspective the terminology of fiduciary duties applied to relationships internal to organizations is typical of common law systems and much less so for civil law systems. Historically, in common law there has been a strong link between fiduciary duties, trust, agency and organizational law. This link has recently faded and fiduciary duties in organizations have defined different behavioural standards and different functions. Fiduciary law in civil law systems has played a different role and has rarely been applied to organizations where the standard of care and loyalty were borrowed from contract and tort law. There is still a double component of fiduciary duties based on loyalty and care. The combination of the two components changes as does the content of each, depending on the nature and form of the organization.

20 A strong connection between fiduciary duty, contractual incompleteness and managerial discretion is identified by Hart (1993, pp. 302 ff.). The relation between

fiduciary duty and contract incompleteness is long standing. See especially in relation to duty of loyalty, Easterbook and Fischel (1993).

21 There is no agreement concerning the relationship between agency theory and fiduciary duties. In Oliver Hart's perspective, fiduciary duties have no role in the principal–agent model of the firm:

> Given that the optimal principal–agent contract contains no gap or missing provisions, it is again impossible to make sense of fiduciary duty, board representation or voting rights . . . My conclusion is that if we wish to understand fiduciary duty, board representation and voting rights then we must depart from the comprehensive contracting world of principal agent theory and incorporate the transaction costs of writing contracts and the consequent contractual incompleteness.
>
> (1993, p. 301)

22 This conclusion allows us to identify situations in which even if directors have only a contractual relationship with shareholders they may be held to fiduciary duties to different constituencies with which only the corporation entertains contractual relationships. See Chapman

> Predictably, given Hansmann's insights on the nature of a fiduciary in the political context, restricted exit takes the form of management having a broader fiduciary obligation in the context of corporate control transactions than would be implied if management's obligations were those of an agent *contractually* bound to its principles and not really a fiduciary at all.
>
> (p. 549)

The reference to Hansmann is Hansmann (1991).

23 Different trade-offs may be required depending on whether specific investments are alternative or complementary, meaning that when they are complementary the productivity of specific investments made by one category depends on whether and how another constituency contributes with its own specific investments. Alternative specific investments do not mean that only one constituency makes specific investments but only that the protection of one category of specific investments may be associated with the reduced protection of another.

24 The relationship between ownership and specific investments is at the core of property rights theory of the firm. See Hart (p. 1707) and Hart and Moore (1990).

25 There is of course an ownership dimension in these organizations as well but it is referred to the organizations and not to the participants. On this issue see Hansmann (1996).

26 In these organizations, the basis of control is membership but as it is the case in profit organization, a high level of separation between membership and control may occur. Fiduciary duties towards members may reduce the risk of abuse by the controlling group. More often in these organizations social norms contribute to the definition of fiduciary relationships aimed at preserving correct incentives.

27 It should be remembered that the definition of specific investments encompasses not only pecuniary investments but also motivational investments.

28 I do not advocate granting control to one constituency alone by considering multiple constituencies in an organization nor that it should be allocated evenly among constituencies. As will be clarified later, an organization can have one constituency or one sub-constituency (majority shareholders) that exercises control while other constituencies may exercise indirect control by vetoing decisions or using liability rules.

29 The contemporary economic theory of the firm (Grossman, Hart and Moore in particular) suggests that the incomplete nature of the organizational contractobliges the allocation of residual rights of control to constituencies with the highest level of specific investment. To what extent this solution prevents from *ex post* expropriation of rent

due to authority is an open question. Two main problems are associated with exercise of discretionary power and the possibility of surplus' appropriation due to abuse: lower incentives to make specific investments when the risk of expropriation is high and organizational instability. Codes of conducts or ethical codes may be a partial response to the problem. On this issue see Sacconi (2000).

30 See Sacconi (2000).

31 See OECD-principles on Corporate Governance, Paris, 1999; The Combined Code of London Stock Exchange, London 2000; Code of Corporate Governance of Germany, 2002; Principles of European Association of security dealers, Bruxelles, International Corporate governance network (ICGN).

32 See Kreps (1990).

33 See for a specific example Royal Dutch/Shell group of companies, Statement of General Business principles, 1997. Article 2 (Responsibilities) states,

> Shell companies recognise five areas of responsibilities a) to shareholders, b) to customers, c) to employees, d) to those with whom they do business, e) to societies . . . These five areas of responsibility are seen as inseparable. Therefore is the duty of management continuously to assess the priorities and to discharge its responsibilities as best it can on the basis of that assessment.

34 See for example the Tripartite declaration of Principles concerning multinational enterprises and social policy adopted by the International Labor Organizations (ILO) and the Guidelines for multinational enterprises adopted by the Organisation for Economic Cooperation and development (OECD).

The OECD Guidelines are defined by article I.1:

> The guidelines are recommendations jointly addressed by governments to multinational enterprises. They provide principles and standards of good practice consistent with applicable laws. Observance of the Guidelines by enterprises is voluntary and not legally enforceable.

35 Codes of conduct can be binding either because a statute confers them this quality or on a purely contractual basis, by adhering to them. It should also be clarified that even when there is adhesion and therefore the company is bound to comply, there might be a principle of 'comply or explain' whereby companies have the possibility not to comply if they explain why they decided not to. The 'comply or explain' principle has been recently adopted in the German Code of Corporate Governance and has been indicated by the Report of the high-level group of company law experts on a modern regulatory framework for company law in Europe. The report states in the recommendation in chapter 3 on corporate governance (Item III.16 Corporate Governance codes-co-ordination): 'Each Member State should designate one particular corporate code as the code with which companies subject to their jurisdictions have to comply or by reference to which they have to explain how and why their practices are different.'

An important interaction is that with Regulatory Authority. See for example in relation to UK the City Code on takeovers and mergers that can be enforced by the Financial Services Authority.

36 Several factors affect the binding nature of the codes. A relevant yet not conclusive element to define whether or not the codes are binding is the procedure followed to enact them. Codes can either be unilateral act by the organization or can be negotiated with different constituencies and signed by all of them. A negotiated code of conduct is more likely to be binding than a unilateral one.

37 See Hopt (2003, p. 214 f.). Compliance with the codes varies. Empirical evidence reveals for example that compliance with the Combined Code of Corporate Governance is high. Yet it is pointed out that a high level of compliance has not translated into a higher firm's performance. See Armour *et al.* (pp. 19 ff.).

38 See Hopt (2003, p. 215).
39 It should however be emphasized that it is claimed that they can also increase managerial discretion and opportunism.
40 To complement means many different things:

they specify the content of duties and obligations that statutes intentionally leave open;
they add new obligations to those defined by legal systems;
they contribute to the definition of organizational boundaries;
they promote new regulations by identifying areas that are under-regulated.

41 See Principles of Corporate Governance by OECD title III the role of stakeholders in corporate governance stating: 'The corporate governance framework should recognise the rights of stakeholders as established by law and encourage active co-operation between corporations and stakeholders in creating wealth, jobs and the sustainability of financially sound enterprises.'
42 The UK is a good example of codes of conduct endorsing a primacy more oriented towards shareholders while the legal system, in particular the Company Law Act, has taken a more moderate approach. Compare for example the Combined Code of Corporate Governance and the Company Law Act. On this relationship also in a historical perspective see Davies (2002).
43 For example regarding the function of internal control, see Combined Code of Corporate Governance last revised version July 2003. Part C refers to Accountability and Audit and C.2 to Internal control:

> Main Principle The board should maintain a sound system of internal control to safeguard shareholders' investment and the company's assets.
>
> Code provision: C.2.1 The board should, at least annually, conduct a review of the effectiveness of the group's system of controls and should report to shareholders that they have done so. The review should cover all material controls, including financial, operational and compliance controls and risk management systems.

44 See, for example the new code of corporate governance in Germany where, in relation to the regulation of conflict of interest, legal rules concerning the 'Vorstand' and the same rules refer to the directors and employees. See §4.3, in particular §4.3.2.
45 The influence that codes of conduct have on industrial relationships can be extremely relevant. Breach by employees can trigger disciplinary procedures. A deeper analysis shows that codes of conduct in the corporate field, especially in relation to loyalty, work in two directions: they expand obligations in favour of employees but they also increase the obligations of employees towards the organization. See Cafaggi (2003).
46 See on this perspective, though not directly related to codes of conducts, Hart (1993).
47 For example if the board is called to perform duties towards other stakeholders, there might be rules concerning its internal functioning, its liabilities that need to be reformulated. Consequently the relationship between shareholders and the board may change and needs to be regulated in the code.
48 This is especially true in relation to loyalty when there are sections devoted to business ethics.
49 See Williamson (1996), ch. 4, pp. 95 ff.: before Williamson (1985) and more recently Williamson (2002b).
50 In both cases, hierarchy and implicit contracts, the main characteristic is that they are not legally enforceable. This does not mean that they do not affect the legal structure of the corporation and cannot affect judicial decision-making.
51 It is interesting to note that the hierarchical property of organizations derives from labour contracts (Coase, 1937; Barnard, 1938; Masten, 1998). This is a case in which an attribute of stakeholder contract (between employer and employees) has become,

according to an important yet not exclusive interpretation, an attribute of the whole organization. A complementary interpretation of hierarchy in organizations is based on forbearance (Williamson, 1991).

52 It is highly arguable that contractual relationships are not hierarchical. Contractual relationships can reflect a highly uneven distribution of power that translates into hierarchy. The real question is whether hierarchy in organization and hierarchy in a contractual relationship pose different governance problems.

53 See Rock and Wachter:

> The current state of the law raises two questions. First as compared to the enforcement of the duty of care, why is the review so intrusive? Second, as compared to trust law, why is the law so flexible? The answer to the first question is fairly obvious: the possibility of self-dealing provides too great a temptation to be controlled by the normal, socially acceptable internal firm constraints.
>
> (2002, pp. 669–670)

54 In relation to the social norm–legal rules debate in corporate law, this position is endorsed by Rock and Wachter:

> The choice between using firm or using market thus carries with it a choice of governance mechanisms. The relationships that are brought inside the firm are thus precisely those relationships that are best governed by self-governing arrangements. With only a touch of overstatement, market transactions are governed by contract and are judicially enforceable, while firm transactions are self-governed and are self-enforced, perhaps with the added protection of reputational effects. Taken literally, the boundaries of the firm represent a demarcation line or justification boundary, dividing judicially enforced market transactions from non judicially enforced internal firm transactions.
>
> (2001a, p. 1615)

See Rock and Watcher (2001b, pp. 1639–1640).

55 See Williamson (1996). See also Rock and Wachter:

> From our perspective, corporate law can be understood as a remarkably sophisticated mechanism for maximizing shareholder value. Since the corporation is largely governed by non-legally enforceable rules and standards, corporate law can also be described as a remarkably sophisticated mechanism for facilitating governance by NLERS. As a central tenet, corporate law creates and is protective of the corporation's hierarchical structure. Legal rules provide the default settings through which centralized management operates and non-pro-rata distributions are prohibited (a combination of ex ante and ex post duty of loyalty). Both create incentives for the controlling shareholders to maximize the value of the firm. The corporate form also mitigates the potential for opportunism by the board of directors and controlling shareholders toward non controlling shareholders. In providing for the hierarchical exercise of business judgement, almost entirely unimpeded by legal restraints, the corporate form protects centralized management form potential opportunism by minority shareholders and other stakeholder groups. In doing so, it is attentive to the firm's boundary as a jurisdictional boundary, within which NLERS governance predominates.
>
> (2001a, p. 1617)

56 See Williamson (1996, pp. 95 ff.). It should be pointed out that in the transaction cost economics perspective a significant difference between classical and relational contract is acknowledged. See ibid., p. 95; Williamson (2002b).

The somewhat paradoxical conclusion is that judges would intervene where contracts are complete but not where contracts are incomplete.

> When contracting is complete judges enforce those contracts ... but when contracting is sufficiently incomplete the enforcement is non-judicial: either self-enforcement or enforcement through non-legal means ... Contractual incompleteness and judicial abstention are two sides of the same coin. In these models contracts are incomplete when it is too costly to write complete contracts. The costs involved are – among others – the cost of judicial error. When, as in the firm, contracts are incomplete and the parties allocate the power of residual control by bringing the transaction within the firm, that power has not been delegated to third parties like judges.
>
> (Rock and Wachter, 2001b, pp. 1649–1650)

See Rock and Wachter (2002, p. 666).

It is fair to ask why, if contracts are complete, would judges have to intervene? Rational actors would not violate a complete contract. Litigation mainly occurs where contracts are incomplete and parties are not able to solve disputes themselves.

The difference is not so much between complete and incomplete contracts but between different types of incomplete contracts. Incomplete contracts that do not translate into corporate form, and therefore do not provide a complex governance structure, may need a very strong judicial intervention if litigation arises. The creation of an organization may need less judicial intervention. It is probably the way the conflict is structured that implies a different role for judges. To the extent that the use of an organization implies delegation of power to make decisions, allowing *ex post* control by the affected parties, the role of judges is weaker than when such a delegation does not occur, as it is the case in contractual relationships.

57 Moreover, where do contracts between firms and stakeholders stand in this picture? Can they all be treated the same way or do important differences arise concerning the role of social norms in labour, supply and financial contracts? Are they long-term contracts in which social norms have a mainly co-operative function or are they contracts that encompass hierarchical dimensions typical of the idea that associates firms and hierarchies?

It is quite clear, for example, that social norms play different roles in labour and financing contracts. I doubt that a general answer can be given to this question associating social norms promoting hierarchy in labour contracts with social norms promoting co-operation in financial contracting. In the definition of which primary goal is promoted by social norms in different contracts between firms and stakeholders, a fundamental variable is the competitive structure in which stakeholders operate (i.e. to what extent capital and labour markets are competitive). Social norms are also affected by the institutional environment they operate in (and in particular the market structure).

58 See Deakin *et al.* (1997).

59 The role of social norms is very important even in consumer transactions where the need for legal protection for consumers has raised the importance of legal rules.

60 In Kreps' words Corporate culture 'gives hierarchical inferiors an idea ex ante how the organization will react to circumstances as they arise; in a strong sense it gives identity to an organization ... Corporate culture also provides a means of measuring the performance of hierarchical superiors' (1990, pp. 126 ff.).

61 On different mechanisms concerning organizational learning see Simon (1997); Sabel (1994). See also Blackwell companion to organization, Blackwell, 2002.

62 It may seem far-fetched to mention the relevance of social norms on fiduciary duties but, in the sphere of loyalty, rules governing conflict of interest may be greatly affected by the role of social norms within the organization and its business environment.

63 The implicit contract that firms sign with local communities may be very strong and may affect corporate decision-making if no alternative locations are available, and therefore the community can be considered a monopolist. As we will see the role of the

community and the production of positive externality becomes even more important when we consider networks of firms.

64 See Hart (1993, pp. 305 ff.).

65 We could call this phenomenon unilateral dependency; that is, the corporate contract, because of claimants priority system, is constrained by the other contracts.

66 Current legal systems, however, do not recognize a wide possibility for firms to limit their own contractual freedom in the interest of stakeholders. With reference to close corporations and partnerships in the UK and US see Armour and Whincop:

> The second problem involves equity investors transferring wealth to themselves from existing creditors by altering the risk profile (either by switching from low-risk to high-risk projects or by devaluing the existing creditors by raising new debt of equal or higher priority). Neither partnership nor close corporations can give direct multital effect to a promise not to engage in a particular form of business activity or to raise further capital.
>
> (2001, p. 998)

67 On the incompleteness of employment contracts and the relationship with the concept of authority. See Simon:

> Commands do not usually specify concrete actions but instead define some of the premises that are to be used by employees in making the decisions for which they are responsible. If authority is used to transmit premises or make decisions rather than commands for specific behaviour, then many different experts can contribute their knowledge to a single decision. Information and policy can flow through the organization along many channels, serving as inputs, decision premises – for many organizational behaviours.
>
> (1991, pp. 24–25)

68 For example, the incentives of shareholders and their attitudes towards stakeholders may vary according to whether the shareholders are in the majority or minority. But even within minority shareholdings, there are significant differences in the relationship with stakeholders. Armour *et al.* claim that institutional shareholders, in particular pension funds, have an extended time horizon for assessing corporate performance and pay special attention to stakeholders suffering externalities from the firm. See Armour *et al.* (pp. 17 ff.).

69 Important corporate decisions such as increase or reduction of equity, asset partitioning, mergers and acquisitions, may affect creditors' rights and therefore make contractual adjustments necessary. From this perspective, corporate decisions and corporate contract modifications may affect financing contracts.

70 The possibility that corporate charters are designed to extract rents from employees is well known, see Aghion and Bolton (1987).

71 See Williamson (1986, ch. 12). Nonetheless it has been argued that employees may make important specific investments in the firm. See Mitu Gulati *et al.* (2000, p. 923), who have indicated at least four types of investment that can be made by employees: reputational capital, firm-specific capital, client-specific capital and intellectual capital.

72 See Macey and Miller (1993, p. 401); Easterbrook and Fischel (1993).

73 Protection of employees' specific investments from the risk of *ex post* expropriation has been analysed in the context of the debate concerning the composition of the board. All these relationships can occur in the same model of firms and many will often coexist. For simplicity here I will consider that constituencies are homogeneous, while being well aware that they are not. However, I believe that the argument of interdependency is made even stronger when heterogeneity of constituencies is factored in.

74 It is worth stressing again the point that the ways contracts should be adjusted depend greatly on how constituencies are organized internally. The initial structure of a

financing contract or subsequent modifications to it may have a greater effect on the protection of minority shareholders than that of controlling shareholders. Likewise, modifications of corporate contracts may have different effects on different creditors depending on their rating within the priority system.

75 On this issue Zingales (1998).

76 Specifically in relation to business restructuring. See in relation to the European directives on acquired rights and collective redundancies Armour *et al.*

> The ARD and cRD play a similar, functional role to the rules of insolvency law in protecting stakeholder voice. Employees' collective information and consultation rights, like those of the creditors in relation to insolvency, lie dormant until the point when they are activated by the employer's decision to engage on a restructuring. It is principally those events which put at risk employees' firm specific human capital or their entitlements to share in quasi rents – large scale redundancies, the sale of the employer's business to a third party, the outsourcing of parts of the employer's operation – which trigger the obligation to consult.
>
> (p. 13)

77 With regard to financing contracts, it is well known that several changes in corporate organizations can change the cost of credit directly or indirectly as is the case when the reputation of the organization falls along with its rating accordingly, and the cost of credit rises. Unless it is stipulated that financing contracts should not be adjusted or modified then the cost of credit and the security apparatus should change according to changes occurred in the organization.

78 The illustration of these instruments will be made by sampling current legal regimes but also by defining instruments that are not currently available.

79 For a brief summary see OECD Guidelines:

> The corporate governance framework should permit performance-enhancing mechanisms for stakeholder participation. Corporate governance frameworks will provide for different roles for stakeholders. The degree to which stakeholders participate in corporate governance depends on national laws and practices, and may vary from company to company as well. Examples of mechanisms for stakeholder participation include: employee representation on boards; employee stock ownership plans or other profit sharing mechanisms or governance processes that consider stakeholder viewpoints in certain key decisions. They may in addition include involvement in governance in the context of insolvency proceedings.
>
> (Sec. III C)

The issue has been considered from the perspective of information in relation to the board composition. It has been suggested that stakeholders could participate on the board without any voting power but for the sole purpose of being granted access to information. See Aoki (1984, p. 167) and Williamson (1986, pp. 303 and 308).

As mentioned earlier I do not consider this possibility in this chapter but I suggest that procedural duties to inform may be coupled with procedural duties to hear.

80 Among the recommendations made by the EU High Level Group of Company Law Experts, information plays a central role. See in particular the Recommendation contained in the Annual Corporate Governance Statement:

> Listed companies should be required to include in their annual report and accounts a coherent and descriptive statement covering the key elements of the corporate governance rules and practices they apply. This statement should also be separately posted on the company's website.
>
> The principles applicable to such annual corporate governance statement should be set up in a framework directive. The detailed rules should be set up by Member States in view of their national company laws but the EU should ensure

> a certain level of coordination. Such a statement should contain a reference to the designated national code of corporate governance and/or company law rules with which the company complies or in relation to which it explains deviations. Responsibility for the annual corporate governance statement should lie with the board as a whole.
>
> (ITEM III.1)

Notice the reference to codes of conduct and compliance with them as a social norm that contributes towards ensuring compliance. Previous suggestions along the same lines had been made in UK by the Company Law Steering Group in 2000. See Armour *et al.* (p. 8).

81 Consultation processes are envisaged both in general and in relation to restructuring processes. It is useful here to recall the European directives on restructuring processes and the roles that protection of employees plays. Particularly, in relation to the Acquired Rights Directives (Dir. Council directive 2001/23 EC 12 March 2001 on the approximation of the laws concerning the Member States relating to the safeguarding of employees' rights in the event of transfer of undertakings, businesses or part of undertakings and businesses), it is suggested that

> in the event of a transfer of employment, the rights and obligations of the transferor employer are automatically carried over to the transferee. In other words, the transferor's employment law obligations run with the assets and goodwill which are the subject of the transfer. Dismissal in connection with a transfer is automatically unfair and, in addition, a claim for compensation arises in the event of the employer's failure to consult with relevant employee representatives.
>
> (Armour *et al.*, p. 12)

82 See the most recent directive on information and consultation: CE 2002/14 of the European Parliament and the Council OJ L. 80/29, 23 March 2002. In particular recital 7 of the preamble states:

> there is a need to strengthen dialogue and promote mutual trust within undertakings in order to improve risk anticipation and make work organisation more flexible and facilitate employee access to training within the undertaking while maintaining security, make employees aware of adaptation need, increase employees' availability to undertake measures and activities to increase their employability, promote employee involvement in the operation and future of the undertaking and increase its competitiveness.

Article 4.2 clarifies the areas that information should cover:

(a) information on recent and probable development of the undertaking's or the establishment's activities and economic situation;
(b) information and consultation on the situation, structure and probable development of employment within the undertaking or establishment and on any anticipatory measures envisaged in particular where there is a threat to employment;
(c) information and consultation on decisions likely to lead to substantial changes in work organisation or in contractual relations, including those covered by the Community provisions referred to in Article 9(1).

Information and consultation procedures are mandatory for European society. See recital 6 of the preamble to directive 2001/86 which says: Information and consultation procedures at trans-national level should be ensured in all cases of creation of an SE. Article 3.1 of the directive states:

> Where the management or administrative organs of the participating companies draw up a plan for the establishment of an SE, they shall as soon as possible after

> publishing the draft terms of merger or creating a holding company or after agreeing a plan to form a subsidiary or to transform into an SE, take the necessary steps, including providing information about the identity of participating companies, concerned subsidiaries or establishments, and the number of their employees, to start negotiations with the representatives of the companies' employees on arrangements for the involvement of employees in the SE.

See also the European Works Council directive 94/45 22 September 1994, article 12.

83 For a more detailed analysis of the framework see Cafaggi (2003).

84 For example, interests for environmental protection and interests for increasing employment may diverge. These are formally external to the firm but they strongly affect the way decisions are reached by the firm.

85 There are different instruments that can be used to void *ex post* decisions due to violation of stakeholder interests. For istance veto power may be given to existing creditors against a certain project of asset partitioning. See the recent reform of company law in Italy, article 2447-*quater* of the Civil Code, as included by the decree 6 of 2003.

86 In particular, by considering the example of sequential interdependencies where contracts between the firm and its stakeholders are incomplete.

87 See Powell (2001); Helper *et al.* (2000), and from a different perspective Rajan and Zingales (2001).

88 See Holmstrom and Roberts (1998); Rajan and Zingales (2000); Roberts and Steen (2000).

Even the position of Oliver Williamson seems to have slightly changed. He has recently claimed that:

> Because added bureaucratic costs accrue upon taking a transaction out of the market and organizing internally, internal organization is usefully thought of as the organization form of last resort. That is, try markets, try hybrids and have recourse to the firm only when all else fails. Node D, the unified firm, thus comes in only as higher degrees of asset specificity and added uncertainty pose greater needs for cooperative adaptation.
>
> (2002b, p. 183)

89 See Powell (2001, p. 459): 'various forms of interorganizational collaborations have grown rapidly in recent years . . . So intensive are these partnering efforts that it may be more relevant to regard the interorganizational network as the basic unit of analysis.'

90 See ibid. See also Porter (1998).

91 See Helper *et al.*:

> The non-standard firm is federated, not centralized. Decisions of higher level entities are crucially shaped by the decisions of their constituent units. The federation is open, not vertically integrated: components or services crucial to the final product of one firm can be provided by independent companies and the firm's internal specialized producers can provide outsiders with crucial inputs . . . The fundamental unit of the new firm is the team or work group. This unit has the responsibility to achieve goals mutually agreed upon with its collaborators by means that are mutually determined through group deliberation. Thus, unlike the specialized subordinates in the hierarchy of a mass producer, the work group is free to change its internal organization and to choose inputs (tools, engineering services, components and so on) from either inside or outside the company that furnishes its members. The choice to buy externally rather than internally is not biased by the fact that the relevant product or service is available inside the collaborating firms, inside resources must out-compete outside resources to be selected. To the extent that it has this autonomy, the work group functions as it were an independent firm, whatever its formal legal status.
>
> (2000, p. 465 f.)

92 See Powell and Doerr (1994, pp. 368–402). See also Porter (1998).
93 See Sabel (1994) and Powell, Patterns in Western enterprises, cit. Citing Sabel, Powell states:

> Teams can determine their own internal organization, communicate horizontally within the organization instead of up a hierarchy, and build close relationships with suppliers, sharing information rather than hoarding it. Teams choose within broad parameters, the necessary tools, services and inputs needed to execute a task. Teams extensively monitor their own activities thus in a key respect they are self-managed . . . Just as the changed conception of work as organized around project teams, transforms firms internally, the growing involvement of firms in an intricate latticework of collaborations with outsiders blurs the boundaries of the firm. Making difficult to know where the firm ends and where the market or another form begins.
>
> (p. 58)

94 See Cafaggi (2004).
95 This observation does not imply that intra-network mobility solves the problem of opportunistic behaviour due to hold-ups. As much or even more than intra-firm mobility and redeployability there are obstacles for inter-firms intra-network mobility.
96 With reference to hold-up problems and their roles in different models of firms see Holmstrom and Roberts (1998, pp. 80 ff.).

For a more specific perspective that distinguishes standard and non-standard views of the firms see S. Helper *et al.* (2000). One key point is that the balance between asset specialization and resource redeployability is at the core of the different methods of production called pragmatic collaboration.

> The novel search routines and problem solving disciplines help develop this flexibility by breaking apart static procedures. Equally important is the capacity to reuse a high and increasing percentage of the capital equipment committed to one project in subsequent ones, by reprogramming computers that guide its operations or changing one type of tool bearing module for another. The greater a work team's command of the search routines, the problem solving disciplines and the re-configuring of flexible equipments, the more accomplished it becomes at the re-deployment of any resource. The effect is the product-specific resources are de-specified, coming increasingly to resemble general purpose assets, and thus no longer the instruments or objects of hold-ups.
>
> (pp. 471 ff.)

97 Ownership patterns in networks often reveal that stakeholders become owners of the firms. Suppliers or customers may therefore have a significant percentage of shares in the corporation. This may occur with creditors and employees as well. This is not to say that it does not occur in vertically integrated firms as well but it happens more rarely.
98 On the one hand, the perspective that a competitor may in the future be a collaborator and vice versa may reduce incentives to adopt opportunistic behaviour. On the other hand, since the legal duties that competitors owe to one another are significantly different from those of co-operators, the legal definition of these long term relationships needs to capture both aspects. A very formalistic shortcut is to consider these relationships separately as many short-term ones and change the structure of the duties accordingly. This configuration would miss the most important aspect which is precisely the ability to change the role of the firm in a flexible way.
99 See Holmstrom and Roberts:

> In property rights theory, the boundaries of the firm are identified with ownership of assets, but in the real world, control over assets is a more subtle matter.

'Contractual assets' can often be created rather inexpensively to serve some of the same purposes that the theory normally assigns to ownership: to provide levers that give bargaining power and thereby enhance investment incentives. What we have in mind here are contracts that allocate decision rights much like ownership ... With increased disintegration governance contracts seem to have become more nuanced and sophisticated. They place firms at the center of a network of relationships, rather than as owners of a clearly defined set of capital assets.

(1998, pp. 84–85)

100 A similar rationale to that concerning fair treatment of shareholders within the corporation.

## References


Aghion and Bolton, Contracts as barriers to entry, *American economic review*, 388–401, 1987.

Aoki, M., *The Economic analysis of the Japanese firm*, North-Holland, Amsterdam, 1984.

Aoki, M., *Comparative institutional analysis*, MIT, Cambridge, MA, 2001.

Armour, J. and M. Whincop, An economic analysis of shared property in partnership and close corporation law, in Symposium Unincorporated business entities, 26 *Journal of corporation law*, 983 ff., 2001.

Armour, J., S. Deakin and S. Konzelmann, *Shareholder primacy and the trajectory of UK Corporate Governance*, ESRC Centre for business research, University of Cambridge, Working Paper No. 299, 2003.

Augier, M. and J. March, *The economics of choice, change and organization*, Springer, Berlin/Heidelberg, 2002.

Axelrod, R., *Agent based models competition and co-operation*, Princeton University Press, Princeton, NJ, 1997.

Baird, D., Self-interest and co-operation in long term contracts, 19 *Journal of legal studies*, 583, 1990.

Barca, F., *Imprese in cerca di padrone*, ed. Laterza, 1993.

Barnard, *The function of the executive*, Harvard University Press, Cambridge, 30th anniversary edn, 1938.

Becht, M., P. Bolton and A. Roell, Corporate governance and control, ECGI, Finance Working Paper No. 2/2002, October 2002.

Bernstein, L., Social norms and default rule analysis, 3 *S.C. International law journal*, 99, 1993.

Black, B. and R. Gilson, Venture capital and the structure of capital markets: banks versus stock markets, 47 *Journal of financial economics*, 243–277, 1998.

Blair, M. and L. Stout, A team production theory of corporate law, 86 *Virginia law review*, 247, 1999.

Blair, M.M. and L.A. Stout, Symposium norms & corporate law: trust, trustworthiness, and the behavioral foundations of corporate law, 149 *University of Pennsylvania law review*, 1735, 2001.

Cafaggi, F., Riforma del diritto societario: il ruolo delle clausole generali, *Stato e mercato*, 45–67, 2001.

Cafaggi, F., Complementarità istituzionali ed evoluzione dei modelli organizzativi nella riforma del diritto societario, *Mercato concorrenza e regole*, 9–42, 2002.

Cafaggi, F., Organizational loyalties and conflict of interest, Paper presented at the University of Pennsylvania Law School symposium on conflict of interest, October 2003.

Cafaggi, F., Organizational models of networks of firms, in F. Cafaggi (ed.), *Le reti di imprese tra regolazione e norme sociali: nuove sfide per diritto ed economica*, Ilmulino, Bologna, 511–543, 2004.

Campbell, D. and H. Collins (eds), *Implicit dimensions of contracts*, Oxford, Hart, 2003.

Chapman, B., Trust, economic rationality and the corporate fiduciary obligation, 43 *U.T.L.J.*, 547–588, 1993.

Coase, R.H., The nature of the firm, 4 *Economica*, 1937.

Coffee, J.C., Contractual freedom in corporate law: articles & comments; the mandatory/enabling balance in corporate law: an essay on the judicial role, Jr., 89 *Columbia law review*, 1618, 1989.

Cooter, R. and M.A. Eisenberg, Symposium norms & corporate law: fairness, character, and efficiency in firms, 149 *University of Pennsylvania Law Review*, 1717, 2001.

Cooter, R. and B. Friedman, New York University Law Review, 1991.

Crouch, C. and C. Trigilia, Conclusions: still local economies in global capitalism?, in C. Crouch *et al.* (eds), *Local production systems in Europe: rise or demise?*, Oxford University Press, Oxford, 2001.

Crouch, C., P. Le Gales, C. Trigilia and H. Voelzkow, *Local production systems in Europe: rise or demise*, OUP, Oxford, 2001.

Davies, P., Shareholder value: company law and security markets Law – a British view, in K. Hopt and E. Wymeersch (eds), *Capital markets and company law*, OUP, Oxford, 262–288, 2002.

Deakin, S., 'Enterprise-risk': the juridical nature of the firm revisited, 32 *Industrial law journal*, 97 ff., 2003.

Deakin, S. and A. Hughes, Economic efficiency and the proceduralization of company law, Company, 3 *Financial and insolvency law review*, 169–189, 1999.

Deakin, S. and J. Michie, *Contracts, co-operation and competition*, OUP, Oxford, 1997.

Deakin, S., C. Lane and F. Wilkinson, Contract law, trust relations, and incentives for cooperation: a comparative study, in S. Deakin and J. Michie (eds), *Contracts, co-operation and competition*, OUP, Oxford, 1997.

Deakin, S., R. Hobbs, S. Konzelmann and F. Wilkinson, Partnership, ownership and control: the impact of corporate governance on employment relations, ESRC Centre for business research, Working Paper No. 200, 2001.

Deakin, S., Hobbs, R. Nash and G. Slinger, Implicit contracts and corporate governance: the impact of the city code on mergers and takeovers, in D. Campbell and H. Collins (eds), *Implicit dimensions of contracts*, Oxford, Hart, 2003.

Denozza, F., *Norme efficienti. L'analisi economica delle regole giuridiche*, University of Milano, Milano, 2002.

Easterbrook, F. and D. Fischel, *The economic structure of corporate law*, HUP, Cambridge, MA, 1991.

Easterbrook, F. and D. Fischel, Contract and fiduciary duty, XXXVI, *Journal of law and economics*, 425 ff., 1993.

Eisemberg, M., The conception that the corporation is a nexus of contracts and the dual nature of firms, 24 *Journal of corporation law*, 819, 1999a.

Eisemberg, M., Corporate law and social norms, 99 *Columbia Law Review*, 211–245, 1999b.

Frankel, T., The legal infrastructure of markets, 73 *Boston University Law Review* 389, 1993.

Gilson, R., Value creation by lawyers: legal skills and asset pricing, 94 *Yale Law Journal*, 239, 1984.

Goetz, C. and R. Scott, Principles of relational contracts, 67 *Virginia Law Review*, 1089, 1129–1130, 1981.

Grandori, A., Il coordinamento organizzativo tra imprese, (171)January–February *Sviluppo e Organizzazione*, 75–91, 1999.

Grandori, A., *Organization and economic behavior*, Routledge, Oxford, 2001.

Gulati, R., Alliances and networks, 19 *Strategic management journal*, 293–318, 1998.

Hansmann, H., When does worker ownership work? ESOPs, Law firms, codetermination and economic democracy, 99 *Yale law journal*, 1749, 1991.

Hansmann, H., *Ownership of enterprise*, HUP, Cambridge, MA, 1996.

Hansmann, H. and R. Kraakman, The essential role of organizational law, 110 *Yale law journal*, 387, 2000.

Hansmann, H. and R. Kraakman, The end of history, 89 *Georgetown law journal*, 439–468, 2001.

Hart, O., An economist's view of fiduciary duty, XLIII, *University of Toronto law journal*, 299–314, 1993.

Hart, O., An economist's perspective on the firm, 89 *Columbia law review*, 1119–1158, 1999.

Hart, O., Norms and the theory of the firm, 149 *University of Pennsylvania law review*, 1701–1707, 2001.

Hart, O., Financial contracting, *Journal of economic literature*, 701–733, 2001a.

Hart, O., Symposium norms & corporate law: norms and the theory of the firm, 149 *University of Pennsylvania Law Review*, 1701, 2001b.

Hart, O. and J. Moore, Property rights and the nature of the firm, 98 *Journal of political economics*, 1119, 1990.

Helper, S., J.P. Mac Duffie and C. Sabel, Pragmatic collabourations: advancing knowledge while controlling opportunism, *Industrial and corporate change*, Haas School of Business, Berkeley, CA, 443, 2000.

Hillman, R., Business partners as fiduciaries: reflections on the limits of doctrine, 22 *Cardozo law review*, 2000.

Holmstrom, B. The firm as a subeconomy, 15 *Journal of law, economics and organization*, 74–102, 1999.

Holmstrom and Roberts, The boundaries of the firm revisited, 12 *Journal of economic perspectives*, 74–89, 1998.

Hopt, K., Direzione dell'impresa, controllo e modernizzazione del diritto azionario: la relazione della Commissione Governativa tedesca sulla corporate governance, *Rivista delle Società*, 182 ff., 2003.

Hopt, K. and E. Wymeersch (eds), *Capital Markets and Company Law*, OUP, Oxford, 2002.

Hopt, K., H. Kanda, M. Roe, E. Wymeersch and S. Prigge (eds), *Comparative corporate governance. The state of the art and emerging research*, OUP, Oxford, 1998.

Jensen, M., *Foundations of organizational strategy*, HUP, Cambridge, MA, 1998.

Jensen, M., *A theory of the firm, Governance, residual claims and organizational forms*, HUP, Cambridge, MA, 2000.

Jensen, M., Value maximization and the corporate objective function, in J. Andriof, S. Waddock, S. Rahman and B. Husted (eds), *Unfolding stakeholder thinking*, Greenleaf publishing, 273–294, 2002.

Jensen, M. and W. Meckling, The theory of the firm: management behavior, agency costs and ownership structure, 3 *Journal of financial economics*, 305–360, 1976.

Kahan, M., Trust, collective action and law, 15 *Boston university law review*, 333, 2001.

Klausner, M., Corporations, corporate law and nexus of contracts, 81 *Virginia law review*, 757, 1995.

Kogut, B. and Zander, U. What firms do: coordination, identity and learning, *Organization science*, 7, 502–518, 1996.

Kraakman, R., The durability of the corporate form, in P. Di Maggio (ed.), *The twenty-first century firm*, Princeton University Press, Princeton, NJ, 630–665, 2001.

Kranton, R., The formation of co-operative relationships, 12 *Journal of law, economics and organization*, 214, 1996.

Kreps, D., Corporate culture and economic theory, in J. Alt and K. Shepsle (eds), *Perspectives on positive political economy*, Cambridge University Press, Cambridge, 90–144, 1990.

La Porta, R., F. Lopez-de-Silanesb, A. Shleifera, and R. Vishnye, Investors protection and corporate governance, 58 *Journal of financial economics*, 3, 2000.

Macey, J., An economic analysis of the various rationales for making shareholders the exclusive beneficiaries of corporate fiduciary duties, 59 *Stetson L.Rev.*, 23, 1992.

Macey, J. and G. Miller, Creditors as corporate stakeholders, XLIII, *University of Toronto law journal*, 401–424, 1993.

Masten, S., The great puzzle of the firm, in Stephen G. Medema (ed.), *Coesan economics*, Kluwer Academic Press, Boston, MA, 51–63, 1998.

Masten, S., Modern evidence on the firm, 92 *American economic review*, 428–432, 2002.

Mitu Gulati, G., W. Klein and E. Zolt, Connected contracts, 47 *UCLA law review*, 887, 2000.

Nicita, A. and U. Pagano (2003) 'Finance and technology: a comparative institutional analysis of the firm', Paper presented at the thirteenth Annual Meeting American Law and Economics Association, Toronto.

Noteboom, B., *Trust*, Edward Elgar, Cheltenham, 2002.

Noteboom, B. and Frederique Six, *The trust process in organizations*, Edward Elgar, Cheltenham, 2003.

Orts, E., Shirking and sharking: a legal theory of the firm, 16 *Yale law & policy review*, 265, 1998.

Pagano, U., Public Markets, Private Orderings and Corporate Governance, 20 (4), *International review of law and economics*, 453–477, 2000.

Porter, M., *On competition*, HUP, Cambridge, MA, 1998.

Powell, W., Neither markets nor hierarchies: networks forms of organizations, in B. Staw and L.L. Cummings (eds), *Research in organizational behavior*, volume no. 12, 295–336, Jai Press, Greenwich, CT, 1990.

Powell, W., The capitalist firm in the twenty first century: emerging patterns in western enterprises, in P. Di Maggio (ed.), *The twenty-first century firm, changing economic organization in international perspective*, Princeton University Press, Princeton, NJ, 300–332, 2001.

Powell, W., Patterns in Western enterprises, in F. Cafaggi (ed.), *Le reti di imprese tra regolazione e norme sociali: nuove sfide per diritto ed economica*, Il mulino, Bologna, xxx, 543, 2004.

Powell, W. and L. Smith Doerr, Networks and economic life, in Smelser (ed.), *Handbook on economic sociology*, Princeton University Press, Princeton, NJ, 363–402, 1994.

Rajan and Zingales, The Governance of the new enterprise, Working Paper No. 7958, 2000.

Roberts, J. and E. Van den Steen, *Shareholder interests, human capital investments and corporate governance*, Stanford university graduate school of business, Working Paper, 2000.

Rock, E. and M. Wachter, Introduction to the symposium on norms and corporate law, 149 *UPALR*, 1607, 2001a.

Rock, E.B. and M.L. Wachter, Islands of conscious power, 149 *University of Pennslyvania law review*, 1619, 2001b.

Rock, E. and M. Wachter, Dangerous liaisons: corporate law, trust law and interdoctrinal legal transplants, 96 *NWULR*, 651, 2002.

Roe, M., *Political determinants of corporate governance*, HUP, Cambridge, MA, 2003.

Romano, R., Corporate law and corporate governance, 5 *Industrial and corporate change*, 277, 1996.

Sabel, C., Learning by monitoring, in N. Smelser and R. Swedberg (eds), *Handbook of economic sociology*, Princeton University Press, Princeton, NJ, 137–165, 1994.

Sabel, C., The world in a bottle or window on the world? Open questions about industrial districts in the Spirit of Sebastiano Brusco, Note prepared for the conference on Clusters, the industrial districts and firms, the challenge of globalization, September 2003.

Sabel, C. Theory of a real time revolution, forthcoming, *Organization studies*, 2006.

Sacconi, L., *The social contract of the firm*, Springer, Berlin/Heidelberg, 2000.

Schwartz, A., *Incomplete contracts*, New Palgrave, New York, 1998.

Scott, R., *Conflict and co-operation in long term contracts*, 1987.

Scott, R., A relational theory of default rules for commercial contracts, 19 *Journal of legal studies*, 597 ff., 1990.

Simon, H., Organizations and markets, 5 *Journal of economic perspectives*, 133–154, 1991.

Simon, H., *Administrative behavior*, 4th edition, Free Press, New York, 1997.

Smith, T., The efficient norm for corporate law: a neotraditional interpretation of fiduciary duty, 98 *Michigan law review*, 214, 1998.

Tadelis, S., Complexity, flexibility and the make or buy decision, 92 *American economic review*, 433.

Tirole, J., Contract incompleteness, where do we stand? 69 *Econometrica*, 741–783, 2002.

Triantis, G., Organizations as internal capital markets: the legal boundaries of firms, collateral and trusts in commercial and charitable enterprises, 117 *Harvard law review*, 2004.

Uzzi, B., Embeddedness and the performance of organizations, *American sociological review*, 481–505, 1999.

Williamson, O., Corporate governance, 93 *Yale law journal*, 1197–1230, 1984.

Williamson, O., Assessing contracts, 1 *Journal of law, economics and organization*, 177–208, 1985.

Williamson, O., *The economic institutions of capitalism*, Free Press, New York, 1986.

Williamson, O., Comparative economic organisation: the analysis of discrete structural alternatives, 36 *Administrative science quarterly*, 269–296, 1991.

Williamson, O., *The mechanisms of governance*, HUP, Cambridge, MA, 1996.

Williamson, O., The lens of contract: private ordering, 92 *American economic review*, 438, 2002.

Williamson, O., Examining economic organization through the lens of contract, mimeo, August 2002a.

Williamson, O., The theory of the firm as governance structure: from choice to contract, 16 *The Journal of economic perspectives*, 171–196, 2002b.

Zingales, L., *Corporate governance*, New Palgrave, New York, 1998.

Zingales, L., In search of new foundations, 55 *Journal of finance*, 1623–1653, 2000.

# 16 Incomplete contracts and corporate ethics

## A game theoretical model under fuzzy information

*Lorenzo Sacconi*

### Introduction and motivation

Developing a corporate code of ethics amounts to something like playing the role of a 'constitution designer' on a small scale. It is an experiment of rational decision about the general and abstract norms that have to work as constitutional constraints on a 'corporate actor' – that is, a firm seen as a micro-constitutional order (Coleman 1990; Vanberg 1992). Codes of ethics in fact regulate claims and rights that several stakeholders may advance towards the organization, so that, when these claims are legitimate by the institution of a code of ethics, those who govern the firm must respond and to be accountable for them.

According to empirical surveys the corporate ethics phenomenon started to grow during the 1980, well before the time when it was sponsored by the base through the US sentencing guidelines (1991). In fact in 1980 only 8% of America's largest companies (the *Fortune 1000* list of industrial and service corporations) had a code of ethics. But afterward the phenomenon has been growing very fast in the US. According to surveys performed in 1985–1986 and 1990–1992 on *Fortune*'s first 1,000 US firms, those endowed with a code of ethics were respectively 77% and 93%. Although less extensive, nevertheless the phenomenon has been clearly recognizable also in Europe. A research performed in 1988 – the CEOs of the 600 largest industrial companies in RFT, GB and France were asked to answer a questionnaire and the level of acceptance was around 30% – concludes that at that time a code of ethics was present in 51% and 41% of the RFT and GB companies respectively. The very fast development of the field of business ethics in Europe in the last decade allows us to say that these levels have certainly grown in the meantime. Moreover, it seems clear that the different levels and timings of the spread of codes of ethics throughout US and European companies can be correlated to the different levels of state provisions and legally enforced social protections of the workers and the other stakeholders, and to the trends of liberalization and privatization of various national economies, which are obviously related to the empowerment of business in society. The best structured codes of ethics both in the US and Europe clearly reflect the idea of corporate responsibility towards all the firm's stakeholders, and are organized into separate chapters defining corporate fiduciary duties towards shareholders, customers, employees, suppliers, government agencies, competitors, local communities, political representatives, etc.

Corporations allocate to their corporate governance structures authority over a large part of the transactions they carry out, regulated both by (incomplete) labour contracts and by (incomplete) arm's length contracts with suppliers, customers, partners and capital lending organizations. These contracts are incomplete *per se*, but as the occurrence of unforeseen contingencies is anticipated, they are completed by residual rights of control allocating discretion upon *ex ante* non-contractible decisions to one party in the contract. Ownership and control structures respond to a need to minimize some transaction costs. But they also admit the overreaching risk of abuse of authority. This is true in particular when many parties involved in transactions make specific investments and face sunk costs. As a consequence corporations tend to be surrounded by the fear of abuse of power and by distrust on the part of those stakeholders that in principle might interact with them in the perspective of mutual gain. If this distrust does not end up with the collapse of these economic institutions, which on the contrary are overwhelming in the contemporary economies, it must be due to norms and institutions other than residual rights of control, which play the role of constraining abuse. Both empirical investigation and theoretical deduction from the theory of firms suggest that corporations need systems of self-regulatory norms of behaviour like codes of ethics exactly because of the 'abuse of authority' problem (Sacconi, 2000).

Let me state three main requirements for a code of ethics to play the role of a rational constraint on the abuse of authority:

1. It must reflect a reasonable and acceptable agreement amongst corporate stakeholders about how the surplus produced by their joint co-operation will be shared;
2. It must work as a self-enforcing social norm, as it should not be meant as a legal expropriation of the residual rights of control seen as a (second best) efficient economic institution;
3. It must answer the question of how those who hold authority in the firm may undertake commitments over events and situations that cannot be *ex ante* contractible or describable within contracts or detailed regulation. Such situations make contracts incomplete in the very sense that parties *a priori* do not even have an idea of the possible states that should be used in order to condition obligation or concrete commitment. Under such situations commitments tend to be empty, simply because they are mute regarding those states that were *ex ante* unknown.

Codes of ethics can satisfy these requirements because of the following:

1. They incorporate the ideal of a social contract amongst all the essential stakeholders of the firm (not only the shareholders), which opens the route

to identifying acceptable terms of co-operation in view of a hypothetical agreement amongst all the stakeholders.

2 As ethical norms, codes of ethics are meant to be self-enforcing. Norms of morality are complied with only because they are able to generate spontaneous adhesion or positive incentives in terms of reputation and social acceptation, so that they typically do not ask for an heavy legal enforcement.

3 They are sets of general and abstract principles, accompanied by rules of interpretation and precautionary standard of behaviour that are carried out when the interpreter recognizes that a concrete – even if *ex ante* unforeseen – contingency falls within the domain of the general principle. General abstract principles are wider than detailed regulation. They are universalizable, that is extensible to any (even if) unforeseen situations, which only might share or resemble a general characteristic or pattern of the principle itself. In order to recognize that a situation belongs to the domain of a general principle we do not need a complete description of it. Moreover, the way a general principle extends to unforeseen contingencies is a matter of 'grade,' not of yes or no. Thus, universality, abstractness and generality imply the 'wideness of application versus vagueness' trade-off.

The first two points are quite naturally amenable to a game theoretical analysis. Cooperative bargaining games provide the natural theoretical tool for understanding the social contract amongst the stakeholders of the firm, who are essential to the joint production of a surplus (Harsanyi, 1977; Brock, 1979; Gauthier, 1986; Binmore, 1991; Sacconi, 1999, 2000). Moreover, non-cooperative game theory provides games of reputation as the natural way of modelling codes of ethics as social norms that are put in practice only because they induce endogenous incentive to compliance, as they satisfy the conditions for the existence of a Nash equilibrium (Binmore, 1991; Sacconi, 2000). Requiring endogenous incentives to comply with codes of ethics suggests modelling them in terms of games of reputations – as far as quite naturally the code provides basis for defining the players' types in a game of incomplete information.

However, the third point – undertaking significant commitments under unforeseen contingencies – constitutes a serious challenge to current game theoretical modelling, as David Kreps puts forward in his pioneering contribution on 'Corporate culture and economic theory' (Kreps, 1990). Our understanding of incomplete knowledge – the label under which this point should be analysed – must go further than treatments where unforeseen contingencies are seen as a sort of statistical uncertainty over a qualified subset of states amenable to standard Bayesian modelling (Tirole, 1999; Anderlini and Felli, 2000; Al-Najjar *et al.*, 2004). What is needed are models of rational decision under situations such that (1) players are *aware* of the possibility of generic unforeseen contingencies (because of the limitation of their linguistic resources), but (2) they are also *ex ante* unable to figure out each of them. Thus the model of a player's reasoning must not assume that the complete and exhaustive set of the possible states of the world is already resident in the back of his mind.

This chapter elaborates on a first, very tentative, modelling of unforeseen contingencies I gave in a previous book (Sacconi, 2000) in terms of fuzzy sets theory (Zadeh, 1965; Zimmerman, 1991). Our incomplete knowledge about unforeseen contingencies is captured by defining some events as fuzzy sub-sets of the set of *ex ante* unforeseen states of the world – which are states that admit *ex post* only an incomplete and vague description in terms of the concepts formulated in our *ex ante* language. Such events correspond to terms of the language the players were able to use before coming to learn about the unforeseen states. By these terms we define the domain of general abstract norms, that is, abstract descriptive characteristics that have to be satisfied in order that a moral principle may be applied. Due to their generality, abstractness and universalizability, these terms admit of being at least in part satisfied by many situations, even though they do not share many details that we *ex ante* used to describe as belonging to their domain. The cost of their all-encompassing nature is vagueness. Membership into the set defining the domain of a general, abstract, principle of ethics is a matter of degree and this opens the route to defining domains of general norms as fuzzy sets of unforeseen states of the world.

This is only the first step, however. Then we have to model the practical reasoning that players are able to perform given this incomplete (vague) base of knowledge, by using the code of ethics as a deliberative procedure for jumping from vague premises to what has to be done in any unforeseen contingency. It is then suggested that a second tentative modelling of players' inferences be undertaken in terms of the logic of default reasoning (Reiter, 1980; Ginsberg, 1987). The intuition is that in many normative situations, given incomplete knowledge that does not allow refuting that the 'normal course' of things does in fact hold, we extend our belief that the 'normal course' does in fact hold also to the incompletely known situation, even if this belief is defeasible and as a whole the beliefs system results are non-monotonic. By this way I formalize the inference players are able to carry out within the code of ethics in order to conclude which actions are permissible and which are forbidden under any unforeseen contingency. As a consequence I can define the commitments a player conforming to the code is expected to carry out. This allows replicating within the new context some of the well-known results in the theory of games of reputation (Fudenberg and Levine, 1989, 1991). Thus, our elaboration on the logical structure of a code of ethics can be seen as the necessary preparatory step for applying standard results in the theory of games of reputation to the field of organizational decision-making under unforeseen contingencies

## The hierarchical transaction as a game

In order to explain how a set of general and abstract principles and norms – call it a code of ethics – may complete the gaps of an incomplete contract (Coleman, 1992), we need to define the context of strategic interaction under which a transaction takes place between two or more parties (the players). Because the contract is incomplete, some decision variables contingent upon unforeseen events are *ex ante* un-contractible. Thus, they are left under the control of some party in the *ex post* perspective – that is when the acceptance of the contract is over and some important decisions within the relationship will have already been taken. Such party will exploit such decision variables *ex ante* un-contractible in the resulting *ex post* bargaining in order to renegotiate the incomplete contract. Because this may generate transaction costs and inefficiency, an institutional design of the residual right of control over these *ex ante* un-contractible decisions variable is in order. The resulting situation is one where some transaction occurs under an incomplete contract cum residual rights of control (authority) over the *ex ante* un-contractible decisions allocated to one of the parties in the contract. This is what we call a hierarchical transaction (Grossman and Hart, 1986; Williamson, 1986; Hart and Moore, 1988; Kreps, 1990). A game theoretical model of the hierarchical transaction is our starting point.

### *A hierarchical transaction*

Consider two parties who may enter into a contract in order to carry out a hierarchical transaction. Player A may enter or not into a relationship of dependency with a second player B. This means that when A has entered the relationship with B, he will in fact agree to perform some *ex ante* unspecified task that B will discretionarily order him to carry out later on, against some pre-established payments. If A chooses 'enter' a relationship of authority is established. If 'not' is chosen by A the relationship is ended. In the course of the relationship between A and B unforeseen events can arise. They render the explicit contract, on the basis of which A decides to enter into a dependent relationship with B, 'mute'. The contract is 'mute' because it cannot contain explicit and concrete provisos contingent on the occurrence of the unforeseen events. This is exactly why the contract inherently builds up an authority relationship: B will be enabled to decide *ex post* discretionarily what to command A to perform, without having any specific decision automatically sorted out by the *ex ante* established provisos of the contract. But now A becomes afraid that B will abuse his authority. Moreover he realizes that an abuse, if it were to come, would not be easily checked on the basis of any existing contractual rules or provisos. The problem is: 'Why should A "trust" B and "enter"?'

### *The game in extended form*

The hierarchical transaction is depicted in Figure 16.1 as a game in extensive form. Player A (in short 'A') moves first. A has to choose out of a decision-set containing 'entering' (*e*) or 'not entering' (*non-e*) into an authority relationship with player B (in short 'B'). By choosing *e* A surrenders to B the right to decide at a later moment in the game one action within the set $a = \{a^*, a^C\}$. By choosing *non-e* the game is ended. If A chooses to enter, he incurs a specific investment $I_A$ with a fixed sunk cost $c(I_A)$ . If A enters, as a consequence B also incurs a specific investment $I_B$, with fixed sunk cost $c(I_B)$. Notice that in order to keep things simple we do not take these

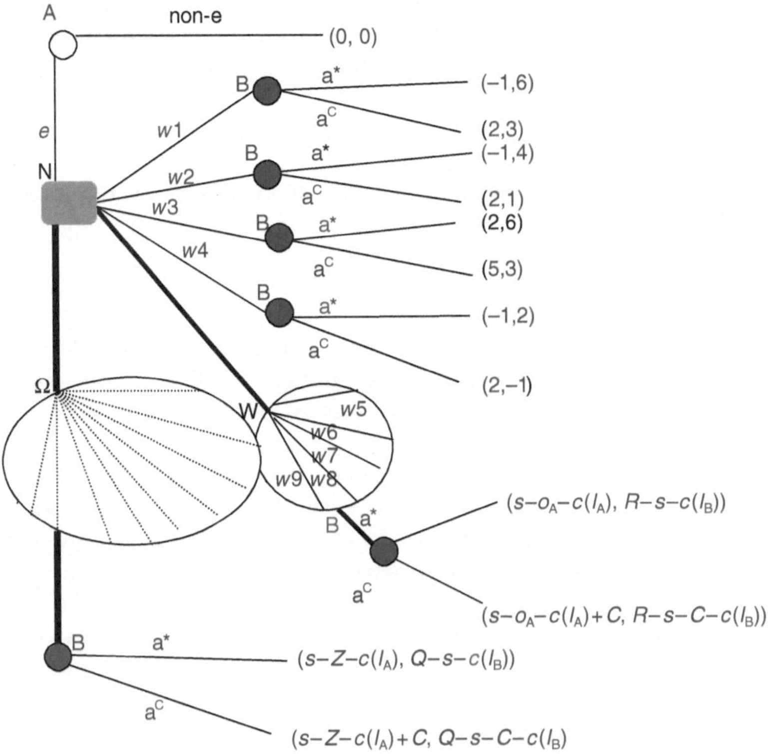


*Figure 16.1* A game of hierarchical transaction with unforeseen contingencies.

investments as separate strategic decisions within the game. They are assumed as the simple mechanical consequence of the only strategically relevant A's choice to enter. However, they shape the game in terms of the payoff-consequences of the strategic decisions (*e* or *non-e*, $a^*$ or $a^C$) the players undertake. In fact, specificity of investments is meant to signify that

$$V(e, a, I_i) - c(I_i) > r, \quad \text{for } i = \text{A, B}$$

where $r$ is the net benefit of any action $a$, given the investment $I_i$, when it is taken outside the relationship between A and B and $V(e, a, I_i)$ is the benefit of the action $a$ ordered by B and carried out by A, given $I_i$. That is, with respect to any other transaction outside A and B's relationship, there is a surplus attached to completing the transaction through a couple of actions $(e, a)$ within the relationship between A and B after the investment $I_i$ has been made. The global amount of wealth created by transacting between them, after the specific investment has been made, is higher than what could come out of transactions with any agent outside the relation.

Taking the utility function of the players linear in the money, this would also be true if measured in terms of each player's payoff functions. Moreover, we assume that the relationship between A and B is symmetrically cooperative, in the sense that the investments of both of them contribute additional value to the surplus:

$$S = V(e, a, I_A, I_B) - c(I_A, I_B) > V(e, a, I_i) - c(I_i),$$

where $I_i$ is the investment of A or B but not both. If A enters, he will receive a fixed salary

$$s - c(I_A) = p \geq 0$$

where $p$ is a constant. We assume that A's fixed salary covers the cost of A's specific investment but possibly *not* the cost of the variable levels of effort that are requested by the two actions that B can ask A to perform contingent over what may occur during the game.

At move two in the game tree Nature chooses a state of the world out of two sets W and Ω. States in W are defined as follows: each $w_i \in W$ is one of the alternative, jointly exhaustive, possible descriptions of the world, describable by a given set of linguistic resources **L**. **L** is a formal language made up of

- $N$ predicative letters $P_1, \ldots, P_n$,
- $M$ variables $x_1, \ldots, x_m$,
- $N$ individual constants $q_1, \ldots, q_n$,
- The usual logical connectives $(\&, \vee, \neg, \Rightarrow)$,
- All the formulae that can be generated by operating with the connectives and the rules of inference given these linguistic resources.

Formally said, each possible world $w_i$ is one of the maximal *sets* of (well formed) formulae of **L**, that is one set of formulae that cannot be increased by any formula without introducing a contradiction in the conjunction of the formulae belonging to it. To exemplify, given that we have $M$ free variables and $N$ predicative letters, one state $w_i$ will *first* consist, for each free variable, of the conjoint affirmation of as many of the $N$ predicates as does not imply a contradiction, and *second* of the conjunction of all of them over the set of $M$ variables. Take $U$ to be the domain of interpretation of the language **L**. Each state of the world $w_i$ made up of one possible maximal set of terms in **L**, can be seen as one possible way of describing, as completely as possible by means of **L**'s linguistic resources, any object belonging to $U$. It is an alternative description to any other state $w_j$ because for at least one variable, interpretable in the domain $U$, $w_i$ affirms a predicate which is negated by other states of $w_j$. To say differently, any state $w_i$ is an alternative description of $U$ within **L**. Within this framework we can define an event $E$ that a given object has a certain property $P_j$ as the subset of possible states such that each of these states, as expressed in **L**, affirms the predicate $P_j$ about the individual variable $x_i$ corresponding to the given object in $U$.

Let me now introduce the less conventional assumption that before playing the game players are *aware* that the set of possible states included in $W$ may be 'incomplete'. By this I mean that they *are aware* that the language **L** is limited and some properties could eventually be exemplified by events that may occur, which cannot be exactly described by predicates included in **L**. Thus, the domain $U$ will be 'completely' described by the states in W *only relatively* to what may be expressed through the resources of **L**. In general, however, the domain $U$ will contain some properties that the language **L** will not completely account for, so that any $w_i$ will neither affirm nor negate these properties. However, let us assume that the players are aware of that, but that they are not even able *ex ante* to say which properties these are nor even to imagine them. This means that the players are aware that, beyond the set $W$, there also may exist a set $\Omega$ of *ex ante* unspecified and undermined states, whose elements contain some properties that are incompletely describable in terms of the existing language **L**. For any $\omega_i \in \Omega$ players will be *ex post* able to find out some free variable, interpretable in $U$, such that they cannot exactly say whether some predicate in **L** is true or false for it. The reason is that predicates in **L** are inadequate for describing the unexpected proprieties of the state $\omega_i$, and this authorizes us to call it an 'unforeseen state of the world'. While eventually they will enrich their language by new terms, as far as the current linguistic resources are concerned, players cannot find in **L** predicates that describe exactly what happens under $\omega_i$.

Whereas in the context of $W$ an event $E$ is defined as the subset of all the states $w_i \in W$ in which a certain property is definitely true, on the contrary in the case of the elements of $\Omega$ an event $E$ may be defined as the subset of those states $\omega_i \in \Omega$ in which the given property can be affirmed only up to some degree. Being able to hold expectations only about events that they are able to formulate in **L**, there are no precise expectations on unforeseen events. Unforeseen events are things we cannot speak about directly within **L**. We may infer they exist from the fact that some *ex ante* known events appear with some vagueness under states in $\Omega$.

We are now able to define the state-set $\Omega$. States $\omega_i \in \Omega$ are possible descriptions of our domain $U$ other than $w_i$, containing properties that '*ex ante* the players are not in a position to anticipate, and that *ex post* they are not able to describe with full precision by means of the linguistic resources included in **L**'.

At the end, reached the third move in the game tree, player B chooses. B's decision consists of selecting one action to be ordered out of the set $a = \{a^*, a^C\}$, assuming that Player A, once entered, will perform whichever order B will have selected. (Remember that under this model, if B chooses a given action, then A will necessarily perform it later on. This permits us to focus on the unique strategic variable in the hand of A – deciding to enter the authority relationship or not.) Let us define the two alternatives:

- action $a^*$ maximizes the overall cooperative benefit $V(e, a, I_A, I_B) = R$ and takes entirely the return $R$ net of the costs already sustained by B (that is $c(I_B)$ and $s$);

- action $a^C$ is equally efficient to $a^*$, but it also provides for an additional fixed compensation $C$ to A.

Actions $a^*$ and$a^C$ represent variable costs to A as a function of the effort $o_A$ spent by A on performing the required task. Without any loss of generality, I call $o_A$ the cost of effort. In turn the cost $o_A$ is conditional on the state of the world selected by Nature, so that the same action under different states may involve high-, medium- or low-effort cost. *Anyway* B's choice may disregard these costs. This implies that, under some state of the world selected by Nature, B may choose an action that represents to A a cost hardly covered by the fixed salary $p$.

### *Payoffs under foreseeable states*

Consider now the players' payoffs under the case of foreseen states of the world. Remember that we assume that players have linear utility function in the monetary outcomes, so that in the game under $W$ players A and B have the following payoff functions respectively:

$$u_A(e, a^*, w_i) = s - c(I_A) - o_A; \quad u_A(e, a^C, w_i) = s + C - c(I_A) - o_A$$

$$u_B(e, a^*, w_i) = R - s - c(I_B); \quad u_B(e, a^C, w_i) = R - s - c(I_B) - C$$

To find out the effective payoffs, it is necessary to go back to the states of the world on which they depend. Assume that for every $w_i$ it is known by the players that:

- specific investments made by A and B are jointly indispensable to the production of the maximum surplus, and the resulting cooperative return is superadditive, that is

$$V(e, a, I_A, I_B) \geq V(e, a, I_i), \quad \text{for } i = \text{A, B}$$
$$V(e, a, I_A, I_B) \geq V(e, a, I_A) + V(e, a, I_B)$$

- parties make their specific investments $I_i$ without free riding one another.

Next assume that there are three possible descriptions of 'maximum return' $R$ (high, medium and low) conditional on some characteristics of the states

$$R = \{R_+, R_\approx, R_-\}.$$

To say it differently, the state space W is partitioned in three events as far as maximum return is concerned. Similarly, assume that each action $a$ may produce three possible levels of effort's cost (high, medium and low) contingent on some characteristics of the states.

$$o_A = \{o_{A+}, o_{A\approx}, o_{A-}\}$$

As stated above, the state space W is partitioned in three elements (events) as far as effort's cost is concerned. In sum, the language of our theory is capable of describing nine states of the world by multiplication of the two set of events: $w_1 = (R_+, o_{A+})$, $w_2 = (R_\approx, o_{A+})$, $w_3 = (R_+, o_{A\approx})$, $w_4 = (R_-, o_{A+})$, $w_5 = (R_\approx, o_{A\approx})$, $w_6 = (R_\approx, o_{A-})$, $w_7 = (R_+, o_{A-})$, $w_8 = (R_-, o_{A\approx})$, $w_9 = (R_-, o_{A-})$. Because we do not want to concentrate here on the intrinsic vagueness of qualitative terms such as 'high', 'medium' and 'low', whereas we will be concerned in the next section with modelling vagueness introduced by unforeseen states of the world, we take some cardinal values as representative of the three classes. Take for example

$$R_+ = 12, R_\approx = 10, R_- = 8,$$

$$o_{A+} = 5, o_{A\approx} = 2, o_{A-} = 0$$

The additional compensation C is a two-valued variable conditional on player A's action. I take it to be $C = 3$ if $a^C$, $C = 0$ if $a^*$.

Last, let the constants be

$$s = 5, c(I_A) = c(I_B) = 1$$

Payoffs can be then calculated according to the form of the utility functions given above, considering that nine states may occur under the choice of both actions $a^C$ and $a^*$ (in Figure 16.1 only the payoffs associated to states $w_1 = (R_+, o_{A+})$, $w_2 = (R_\approx, o_{A+})$, $w_3 = (R_+, o_{A\approx})$, $w_4 = (R_-, o_{A+})$ are depicted).[1]

I will confine my discussion to this particular example for more concreteness, but the result may be easily generalized. If A 'enters', B's dominant action is always to choose $a^*$ without more compensation. In all the situations in which the burden $o_A$ to A of the action $a^*$ chosen by B is high, this implies that player A, if she 'enters', obtains the payoff $(-1)$. Consequently in these cases $(w_1, w_2, w_4)$ A's best reply is *non-e*. Assume for simplicity that the burden $o_{A+}$ has near probability one. Contingent upon the states of the world now considered, the game is the *Game of Trust* (a sequential unilateral variant of the classic PD game): the only feasible outcome is the sub-optimal Nash equilibrium (*non-e*, $a^*$). In the remaining cases A's best reply is always *e*, with the Nash equilibrium outcome $(e, a^*)$.

## The game under unforeseen contingencies

The aim of this section is to consider the interaction between the two players when Nature selects a state from the state-space Ω. We show that, if the game is meant as one- shot, the solution is not only *ex ante*, but also *ex post* undetermined and ambiguous. In order to see that, first ask 'what do the players know about the game under Ω?' *Ex ante* (before Nature makes its choice) independently of the state $\omega_i$ chosen, they know that a generic return $Q$, described in terms of monetary gains, will follow (without loss of generality we can also assume that players know that $Q$ may take its values within a specified monetary interval $[0, n]$, where $n$ is a finite integer number). Moreover a generic action, in terms of a number $Z$ of hours to be worked, will be chosen by player B (as before, we may assume that players know that $Z$ lies within a definite time interval $[0, m]$, where again $m$ is a finite integer number).

At the same time they are aware that, if nature selects any state $\omega_i$ out of $\Omega$, this will imply the occurrence of events that they are not able to specify *ex ante*. In terms of what they are able to express within the existing language, in each state $\omega_i$ there will be ambiguity about:

1 *The joint nature of the return*: Is it still true that $Q$ is the output of the joint cooperation of both players carried out through their simultaneous specific investments and actions (as it was true under states belonging to W)?
2 *The size of the cooperative benefit*: How much, if any, of the observable $Q$ could be attributed to such investments and how much could be due to exogenous change of the environment? (The employee could result in not being necessary to the realization of surplus or, on the other hand, B may become superfluous).
3 *The existence of externality*: Are specific investments $I_A$ and $I_B$ in effect the fruits of independent decisions, or are some of the players' free rides the other's investment?
4 *The size of the burden of B's orders to A:* What does any value of $Z$ mean in terms of effort's cost of the action asked of A by B? (e.g. some unforeseen technological change would transform the burden of effort to a source of enjoyment).

We must keep in mind that in any state $\omega_i$ there will be ambiguity about (1)–(4), not because there is some uncertainty concerning which state occurs – so that the payers' information partition cannot separate states where (1)–(4) are true from those where they are false. On the contrary, in *each* $\omega_i$ there will be vagueness on whether the propositions (1)–(4) hold. This is so for players are incompletely able to describe *each* $\omega_i$, that is, the characteristics required to check whether (1)–(4) hold or not are not clearly specified in each $\omega_i$.

*Ex post* they learn the exact nominal value of the occurring $Q$ and $Z$ and the particular state $\omega_i$ selected out of $\Omega$ (and its possible alternatives). But what were *ex ante* true will still be true *ex post*. The players are *ex post* aware that 'in the presence of unforeseen states certain pieces of information remain vague', that is proposition (1)–(4) are not definitely true or false in the particular state $\omega_i$ selected out of $\Omega$.

As a matter of consequence the solution of the game under unforeseen contingency is indeterminate also in the *ex post* perspective. In spite of $Q$ and $Z$ being known *ex post*, the payoff functions have no determinate values conditional on states like $\omega_i$. Players are unable to understand their joint and separate contributions to the production of the surplus, whether each of them has effectively made a specific investment, whether the investment made by one free rides the other, and moreover how costly any action asked by B of A is in terms of A's effort costs. Understandably this will influence the players' incentives (Tirole, 1999). This translates to the ambiguity of the two basic variables $R$ and $o_A$ needed for specifying the players' payoff functions.

## Solution theory: social contract and the ethical code

Now, take the perspective of a repeated game of reputation amongst a long-run player B and an infinite series of short-run players taking in turn the role of player A. At each repetition the stage-game just defined in the sections above will be played again and again (Fudenberg and Levine, 1989, 1991; Kreps, 1990). The repeated game gives an elementary model of what we may call a 'firm', that is a series of hierarchical transactions amongst a potentially infinite number of employees and an institutional hierarchical superior who lasts potentially *ad infinitum*, that is, even beyond the life-span of a single individual owner – what seems at least necessary in order to understand the model as speaking about an institution like the firm. Can this change of perspective influence the solution? It is apparent that the bulk of the argument rests on the capability of player B to undertake commitments over his possible two strategies, which become 'types' in the eyes of the players successively taking on A's role. In such a way, these may function as the basis for the reputation effects mechanism. More precisely, what is needed is that player B may undertake commitments such that

- *Under the case W*: even though the prior probabilities were largely concentrated on states $w_i$ with $o_{A+}$ (high effort-costs), the sub-optimal outcome (*non-e*, $a^*$) is avoided nevertheless.
- *Under the case* $\Omega$*:* reputation also supports rational 'entrance' by player B under the occurrence of the unforeseen states $\omega_i$.

The second requirement is of course the most demanding. The point is that a commitment is normally understood as a conditional strategy, which can be announced in advance of any play of the game, stating which of B's actions will be selected contingently on the occurrence of any possible world. But there is no way for B to announce a commitment conditional on unforeseen states of the world, as he cannot describe the concrete conditions under which a particular action will be undertaken. This problem could be by-passed by adopting the same action in all the unforeseen states whatsoever – but this would amount to an inefficient *unconditional* commitment.

The *solution* here suggested is resorting to the *Constitutional Contract* of the firm as expressed by two types of norms:

- *With respect to W:* an *explicit incomplete contract* which establishes what must be done contingently upon a restricted set of possible worlds belonging to W, and leaves B with full discretion in relation to the remaining states in W.
- *With respect to* $\Omega$: a code of ethics containing

  1. a set of explicitly stated constitutional, general abstract principles,
  2. a set of interpretative rules that establish under what conditions a situation falls into the domain of a principle,
  3. the conditions for admissibility of $a^*$ or $a^C$.

Both types of norm are based on a unique abstract principle for solving games (i.e. a solution concept) that I identify with the Nash Bargaining Solution (NBS) for cooperative bargaining games (Nash, 1950; Harsanyi, 1977). Since our game is non-cooperative, NBS is not the obvious solution concept to be used here. It must be understood as a normative principle which does not simply follow from the individual rationality assumptions for non-cooperative games, and is meant as a constitutional rule purposively *ex ante* deliberated in order to give shape to player B's (the one in the position of authority) commitments. Suppose the players are able to posit themselves under an *ex ante* hypothetical stand point – the Archimedean point (Gauthier, 1986; Binmore, 1991) – from which they agree on abstract principles that will regulate their hierarchical transactions in general. This is the hypothetical bargaining position from which they agree on the social contract of the firm. I assume that in such a hypothetical position they would recognize the NBS as the general abstract principle for solving whatever strategic interaction among them may involve the joint production of a surplus (Sacconi, 2000). Moreover player B would accept (at least *ex ante*) to commit himself to follow this principle in any of the ensuing hierarchical transactions, where the joint production of a surplus is involved. Thus, NBS is the solution to which the parties *would converge*, if they *were* able to reason according to the *as if* format. Adopting NBS amounts to hypothesizing that player B will behave in the game – in fact a non-cooperative game – *as if* it were a cooperative one. Last, in the context of the social contract, this solution must be calculated on the basis of a fair *status quo*, which establishes the maximum level of concession of the parties without recourse to the use of force or fraud, threat or parasitism by one party on another (Gauthier, 1986).[2]

Take first the game under $W$, where the solution concept may be translated into a concrete incomplete contract. Computation of NBS is straightforward in this case. *Pareto Optimality* is guaranteed by both $a^*$ and $a^C$ by assumption. Parties must obtain payoffs at least equal to what they gain from the fair *status quo* $d$. Given linear utilities in the monetary payments, the *status quo* payoffs are

$$u_A(d) = c(I_A) + o_A$$

$$u_B(d) = c(I_B)$$

The variable $o_A$ figures in A's outside option since otherwise A would leave the bargaining table in a worse condition than the one in which she joined it. NBS requires

$$Max\ \Pi_h(u_h(V(e, a, I_A, I_B) - u_h(d))), \quad \text{for } h = \text{A, B}$$

The players' payoffs are given by participation in the cooperative return, respectively

$$u_A(V(e, a, I_A, I_B)) = s + C$$

$$u_B(V(e, a, I_A, I_B)) = R - s - C$$

NBS therefore requires that one action $a \in a$ is chosen so that

$$Max\,[((s + C) - (c(I_A) + o_A)) \times ((R - s - C) - c(I_B))]$$

The cooperative return is $R = V(e, a, I_A, I_B)$ and the surplus net of the *status quo* is

$$R - (c(I_A) + c(I_B) + o_A)$$

Were $C$ a continuous variable, the solution would be choosing $C$ such that

$$s + C = (c(I_A) + o_A) + 1/2[R - (c(I_A) + c(I_B) + o_A)]$$
$$R - s - C = c(I_B) + 1/2[R - (c(I_A) + c(I_B) + o_A)]$$

Given that the possible values of $C$ contingent on the action $a$ are only two, it follows that for all the states from $w_5$ to $w_9$ the NBS is satisfied by the action $a^*$. In states $w_1, w_2, w_3$ NBS requires that $a^C$ be chosen. When the Nash product is in tie under $a^*$ and $a^C$, as it happens in $w_4$, I assume that action $a^C$ must be used (this amounts to saying that the constitutional contract is biased in favour of player A, who must be convinced to enter the relationship).

An incomplete contract, with discretionary power being given to B, therefore consists of a simple function that permits action $a^*$, provided that the states of the world with respect to which it is explicitly prohibited do not occur:

$$f(a^* | w_i) = \begin{cases} 0 & \text{if } w_i = w_1, w_2, w_3, w_4 \\ 1 & \text{otherwise (that is for every other } w_i \in W) \end{cases}$$

Leaving B free to act according to his best reply in cases other than $w_1$, $w_2$, $w_3$, $w_4$, the contract of delegation ensures that the solution is always in line with NBS. This contractual rule may be employed to specify player B's conditional commitments. Compliance with them is observable in any $w_i$ state of the world. As a consequence, player A may rest on B's reputation effects related to his conformity to these commitments in order to trust B and enter.

## The role of 'vague' constitutional principles

In the case of $\Omega$ it is not possible to calculate *ex ante* the NBS for each possible state of the world. Why should a code of ethics succeed where the explicit contract fails? NBS is only introduced here as a general abstract concept of solution, like a constitutional principle without any concrete reference to the particular states under which the game is played. Rather than *ex ante* calculating the Nash product for each possible state, mere abstract characteristics are stated as descriptive preconditions for a game that can be submitted to the NBS. These are displaying 'in the appropriate way' (1) the existence of a cooperative surplus and (2) a fair *status quo* meant as the costs the parties independently undergo for making their investments and actions. *Ex post*, when unforeseen contingencies will have been brought about, we will be able to see whether the occurred state satisfies the requirements asking for an NBS-constraint over player B's choice.

In fact, general principles, 'formulated in universal abstract terms' of the current language **L**, are terms of reference both for *ex ante foreseen* and for *ex ante unforeseen* or simply 'new' states of the world. The form of reference is a *membership function*. Due to generality, universality and abstractness of the constitutional principles, any state of the world, even though unforeseen, belongs to the domain of a principle at least *to some degree* (between full membership and nil). Moreover, the requirements on the appropriate membership functions can *always* be specified, both in the *ex ante* and *ex post* perspective, as they are not contingent upon the description of *ex ante* unforeseen contingencies. Thus, by means of its general principles, the code of ethics *is never mute* in relation to events, including events that are *ex ante* unforeseen.

There is of course an important price in terms of vagueness to be paid to this all encompassing property of general and abstract principles. Unforeseen events in particular introduce vagueness in the membership relationship. I take for granted, even if this can not always be the case, that we mostly are able to clearly adjudicate a state of the world to the domain of application of a general principle as far as this state can be completely described with the same language in which also the principle is formulated. The hypothesis is that most vagueness is associated to unforeseen facts, because of the imprecision of the language **L** in *ex post* describing events that were *ex ante* unforeseen.

To state the point analytically, encode by $P$ an *abstract constitutional principle* and by $E$ the event 'the constitutional principle $P$ is fulfilled'. The event $E$ is equivalent to summing up all the *descriptive* features required to fulfil the principle.[3] The statement is that every unforeseen state can belong to the event $E$. Simply, this belonging must be defined in terms of *vague* membership. This allows for a fuzzy set modelling of unforeseen contingencies.

Take an ordinary set of objects $\Omega$. Intuitively mean $\underline{E}$ as a fuzzy subset of $\Omega$ such that the elements of $\Omega$ are member to $\underline{E}$ *up to a certain degree*. Degrees are given by membership functions $\mu_{\underline{E}}(\omega_i)$ with domain the set $\Omega$ and co-domain the real line [0,1]. Thus a fuzzy set $\underline{E}$ is the set of ordered pairs such that any element of the given reference set $\Omega$ is associated to the membership function assigning the degree up to which it shares the property referred to by the fuzzy set.

$$\underline{E} \equiv \{(\omega_i, \mu_{\underline{E}}(\omega_i))|\omega_i \in \Omega\}$$

Consequently it may be written

$$\underline{E} = \{(\omega_1, \mu_{\underline{E}}(\omega_1)), \ldots, (\omega_n, \mu_{\underline{E}}(\omega_n))\}$$

Let the set $\Omega = \{\omega_1, \omega_2, \ldots, \omega_n\}$ be the state-space, that is, the set of all the possible alternative descriptions of the state of the world and let $P(\Omega)$ be the power set of the subsets of $\Omega$, which is usually meant to be the collection of all the possible events, meant as subsets of $\Omega$. The bulk of our approach to unforeseen contingencies is the following proposition:

**Proposition 1.** Let $\Omega$ be the set of unforeseen states of the world. Then its power set $P(\Omega)$, defining the set of all the possible events, is the collection of the fuzzy subsets sets of $\Omega$ derived by associating to any $\omega_i \in \Omega$ its membership function to any fuzzy set representing any given event. With events defining the domain of universa application, abstract a general principles formulated in a given normative language **L** to induce membership functions with positive (not zero) degrees of membership for any state $\omega_i \in \Omega$.

Under this interpretation the elements of any fuzzy set $\underline{E}$ are meant as alternative descriptions of the state of the world, which are unforeseen *ex ante* and only partially describable *ex post*. An event $\underline{E}$ denotes the existence of an unforeseen contingency as it corresponds within $\Omega$ to properties that only vaguely can be traced back to the event $\underline{E}$. As a result, when the state space consists of unforeseen states of the world, its power set (the set of events) consists of fuzzy sets, that is, vague events.[4]

True, I do not characterize unforeseen states as such directly in fuzzy terms. What is properly modelled as fuzzy set are the events we are able to express in our existing language, whose members are unforeseen states of the world. By understanding unforeseen states through their imperfect membership function as fuzzy sets, we capture the impact of their being *ex ante* unforeseen on the precision and completeness of their *ex post* description by means of the existing language. To say it differently, being *ex ante* unforeseen implies vagueness in the *ex post* description, due to the inadequacy of the *ex ante* language **L**.

We are now able to draw important conclusions about the availability of commitments in the repeated game played under unforeseen contingencies. Although the player is not *ex ante* in a position to describe the set $\Omega$, he is nevertheless *aware* of its eventual existence. He cannot undertake commitments contingent upon concrete descriptions of elements in $\Omega$, for these are unforeseen. *But* he can undertake commitments regarding the occurrence *ex post* of a *certain membership relationship* between any generic element of $\Omega$ and the set $\underline{E}$, that is, about the degree up to which any generic $\omega_i$ is a member of $\underline{E}$. Notice that *ex ante* the player does not need any description of the particular $\omega_i$. He only needs to be aware that a generic $\omega_i$ may be selected out of $\Omega$, to know the set of conditions compounded in $\underline{E}$, and to establish the requirement that *if* any generic $\omega_i$ would belong to $\underline{E}$ at least up to some given degree, then the principle P (the NBS in our case) is to be carried out *ex post*. Thus B undertakes commitments on the basis of principles and criteria that can be understood in the *same terms* both *ex ante* and *ex post*. The occurrence of unforeseen contingencies no more creates any ambiguity and non-observability problems concerning compliance with them.

## First step in the ethical procedure of deliberation: vagueness of the constitutional principle

In this section I begin defining operationally the code of ethics as a procedure of deliberation able to decide for every state, included the unforeseen $\omega_i \in \Omega$, whether *ex post* a given action (e.g. $a^*$) is permissible in the light of a constitutional principle established *ex ante*. It fits the intuition of 'procedural rationality' as the decision is the output of a reasoning process addressed to respond to the decision-maker's limited knowledge of the alternatives (Simon, 1972). The procedure of deliberation contains many steps in order to decide whether:

- each state $\omega_i$ belongs to the set of situations (call it 'event $E1$' ) to which NBS does apply,
- the same state $\omega_i$ belongs to the set of situations in which, assuming that B chooses $a^*$, the outcome is *efficient/fair* (call it 'event $E2$'),
- given any $\omega_i$, the permissible action is $a^*$ or $a^C$.

First a better understanding of the event $E1$ is needed. Let $\Gamma$ be the game that I have just described in the sections 'The hierarchical transaction as a game' and 'The game under unforeseen contingencies' and let Gc be the codification for the conditions required for a game to be treated as one element of the class of cooperative bargaining games with fair *status quo*. $E1$ stands for the set of states where it is (at least vaguely) true that

'$\Gamma$ is a Gc'.

More precisely, $E1$ is understood as the set theoretic counterpart of a sentence resulting from the conjunction of the two following properties expressed in the language of our game $\Gamma$:

1 The return $Q$ has the nature (regardless of the extent) of a cooperative benefit;
2 Each player's specific investment cost (plus the effort cost in the case of player A) coincides with his fair *status quo*.

To begin with (*i*), define a return being the cooperative benefit produced by the two players through their specific investments as follows

$$R_\Gamma(\omega_i) = V(e, a, I_A, I_B), = R^*$$

where $\forall C \neq A, B$ and for each $a_i \in a$, $V(e, a, I_A, I_B) \geq V(e, a, I_A,) = V(e, a, I_B) \geq V(e, a, I_C)$. Take $R_\Gamma(.)$ to be the return function defined for the game $\Gamma$ in any state $\omega_i$. The set theoretic counterpart of $R^*$ is

$$R^* = \{\omega_i \in \Omega \text{ s.t. } R_\Gamma(\omega_i) = R^*\}$$

which is the definition of the event that 'return in game $\Gamma$ is $R^*$'. Consider however that *ex post* each unforeseen state does not admit a clear-cut description of the economic *nature* of the return. It only allows for an account in terms of a monetary value $Q \in [0, n]$, which is the clearly describable aspect of return in any $\omega_i$. Then the question is whether the observable returns $Q$ are also cooperative benefits $R^*$. In order to be expressed formally this question needs a set theoretic definition of the event that the return in unforeseen contingencies may at least be described by a number $Q$

$$Q^* = \{\omega_i \in \Omega \text{ s.t. } q_\Gamma(\omega_i) = Q \in [0, n]\}$$

where $q_\Gamma(.)$ is the return-numerical-description-function that for each unforeseen state *ex post* selects a number for the return in game $\Gamma$. Thus the first property is whether the intersection of the two defined sets is not empty

$$R^{**} = Q^* \cap R^* \neq \emptyset$$

where

$$R^{**} = \{\omega_i \in \Omega \text{ s.t. } q_\Gamma(\omega_i) = Q \in [0, n] \;\&\; R_\Gamma(\omega_i) = R^*\}$$

Notice that it is assumed that each state $\omega_i \in \Omega$ has the superficial describability property $Q \in [0, n]$, so that the set $Q^*$ coincides with $\Omega$. Thus the mentioned condition reduces to

$$\Omega \cap R^* \neq \emptyset$$

Moreover, because all the $\omega_i$ are describable by $q(.)$ but they do not necessarily contain the affirmation $R_\Gamma(\omega_i) = R^*$, the first condition we are interested in is whether the event that 'the observable return is of cooperative nature' is one of the possible events included in the power set of possible events defined on $\Omega$

$$R^* \in P(\Omega),$$

which reduces us to the condition that there are states $\omega_i \in \Omega$ that have a positive membership in the set $R^*$.

Now, consider more formally property *(ii)*. To be precise, define a cooperative two-player bargaining game Gc by the ordered pair $(R^*, D^*)$, where $R^*$ is the payoff space (i.e. we assume that it coincides with the cooperative return of the two players' joint investments and efforts), and $D^*$ is the two players' fair *status quo*. If the game $\Gamma$ may be interpreted as a cooperative bargaining game, we want to know whether the fair *status quo* for each player is

$$D^* = [c(I_A) + o_A, c(I_B)]$$

In order to find out the set theoretic counterpart of this property, define $d^*(.)$ as the function that for any $\omega_i \in \Omega$ selects the fair *status quo* $D^*$ of the cooperative game that may be construed out of $\omega_i$, so that $D^* = d^*_\Gamma(\omega_i)$ if the cooperative game played in the state $\omega_i$ has the parameters of our game $\Gamma$. Then

$$D^* = \{\omega_i \in \Omega \text{ s.t. } d^*_\Gamma(\omega_i) = [c(I_A) + o_A, c(I_B)]\}$$

is the event (understood as a set of states) that the pair $[c(I_A) + o_A, c(I_B)]$ coincides to $D^*$ in the cooperative bargaining game construable out of the game $\Gamma$.

Remember however that, as for return, the nature of player A's effort in each unforeseen state is not clearly *ex post* described. On the contrary we only have a superficial description of it in terms of the number of hours $Z \in [0, m]$ spent at work by A. The event that any unforeseen state, as far as A's effort is concerned, may be *ex post* described by an integer number $Z \in [0, m]$ can be expressed

$$Z = \{\omega_i \in \Omega \text{ s.t. } z_\Gamma(\omega_i) = Z \quad \in [0, m]\}$$

where $z_\Gamma(.)$ is the numerical-hours-at-work-description function that for each $\omega_i \in \Omega$ says how long player A is asked to work if he enters the game $\Gamma$. Thus the second property we are interested in corresponds to the question whether the situations superficially describable by the $Z$ values are also situations where the players' specific investments and effort define the fair *status quo* $D^*$ of the cooperative bargaining game construable out of $\Gamma$. In set theoretic terms

$$D^{**} = D^* \cap Z \neq \emptyset$$

where

$$D^{**} = \{\omega_i \in \Omega \text{ s.t. } z_\Gamma(\omega_i) = Z \in [0, m]\} \; \& \; d^*_\Gamma(\omega_i) = [c(I_A) + o_A, c(I_B)]\}$$

because we assume that $Z \in [0, m]$ gives a precise even though superficial description of the relevant aspect of each $\omega_i \in \Omega$, $Z$ coinciding to $\Omega$. Thus the condition above reduces to

$$\Omega \cap D^* \neq \emptyset$$

and this implies that the relevant condition is that the event that '$[c(I_A) + o_A, c(I_B)]$ is the fair *status quo* in $\Gamma$' is one of possible events defined on $\Omega$

$$D^* \in P(\Omega),$$

or alternatively that at least some $\omega_i \in \Omega$ have positive membership in the set $D^*$.

Therefore the event $E1$, corresponding to the joint two properties (i) and (ii), is the set of states resulting from the intersection of the two sets defined above

$$E1 = R^* \cap D^*$$

Remember that there is no vagueness about the two joint properties in any of the states $w_i \in W$, that is

$$\forall w_i \in W, \quad \mu_{E1}(w_i) = 1.$$

But consider now the membership of any state $\omega_i \in \Omega$ in the event $E1$. $\Omega$ is an ordinary set of elements that, although unknown *ex ante*, *ex post* turn out to be univocally describable as regards of the variables $Q$ and $Z$. But, because of the unexpected features of states $\omega_i$, these characteristics cannot be clearly traced back to the more basic properties $\omega$ defining $E1$. Therefore *ex post* we understand the membership of any unforeseen state $\omega_i$ in $R^*$ and $D^*$ in terms of fuzzy membership functions, as suggested in the section 'The role of "vague" constitutional principles'.

Take first the set of ordered pairs

$$\underline{R}^* = \{(\omega_i, \mu_{\underline{R}*}\omega_i))|\omega \in \Omega\}$$

where the membership function $\mu_{\underline{R}*}(\omega_i) = x \in [0, 1]$ associates to each $\omega_i$ a degree of membership in the fuzzy set $\underline{R}^*$. This expresses for any $\omega_i$ the degree of vagueness that the return $Q$ is a cooperative benefit $R^*$. Then take the second set of ordered pairs

$$\underline{D}^* = \{(\omega_i, \mu_{\underline{D}*}(\omega_i))|\omega_i \in \Omega\}$$

defined by the membership function $\mu_{\underline{D}*}(\omega_i) = r \in [0, 1]$ that associates to each $\omega_i$ a degree of membership in the fuzzy set $\underline{D}^*$. It expresses for any $\omega_i$ the vagueness that $\omega$the players' specific investments costs, together with the $Z$ value describing superficially A's effort, constitute the $[c(I_A) + o_A, c(I_B)]$ fair *status-quo* of the cooperative bargaining game construable out of $\Gamma$. Finally consider the set of ordered pairs

$$\underline{R}^* \cap \underline{D}^* = \{(\omega_i, \mu_{\underline{R}*\cap\underline{D}*}(\omega_i))|\omega_i \in \Omega\}.$$

It defines the fuzzy set resulting from intersection of the two fuzzy sets $\underline{R}^*$ and $\underline{D}^*$ in terms of membership function $\mu_{\underline{R}*\cap\underline{D}*}(\omega_i)$. Its results mean that the event $E1$ must be more properly understood as a fuzzy set $\underline{E1}$. Moreover,

$$\underline{E1} = \underline{R}^* \cap \underline{D}^*$$

stands for the event that initial conditions that asked for the application of NBS are satisfied, which – because its constituting elements are unforeseen states – is understood as a vague event. The membership of any state of the world $\omega_i$ in the fuzzy intersection event $\underline{E1}$ then is calculated by the MIN operator (corresponding to fuzzy intersection)

$$\mu_{\underline{E}1}(\omega_i) = \text{MIN}(\mu_{\underline{R}*}(\omega_i), \mu_{\underline{D}*}(\omega_i)).$$

In order to decide whether to treat any state $\omega_i$ 'as if' it were a situation to which Nash's solution must be applied, now let us introduce an $\alpha$*-cut set.* $\alpha$ must be understood as a vagueness "threshold" discriminating the states in which the game $\Gamma$ "sufficiently" satisfies the conditions for being a Gc, from the remaining states.

For $\alpha = 0.5$ define

$$\mu_{\underline{E}1\alpha}(\omega_i) = \begin{cases} 1 & \text{if } \mu_{\underline{E}1}(\omega_i) \geq 0.5 \\ 0 & \text{if } \mu_{\underline{E}1}(\omega_i) < 0.5 \end{cases}$$

This condition can be stated *ex ante*, so as to commit player B to treat the game as the appropriate domain of application of NBS whenever an unforeseen state were to belong to $\underline{E1}$ at least up to degree 0.5. Moreover its fulfilment can be checked *ex post*, when the players are also able to establish which of the *ex ante* unforeseen states exceed the ethical threshold of admissibility, simply by calculating the *crisp* (non-fuzzy) set

$$E1_{\alpha} = \{\omega_i \in \Omega | \mu_{\underline{E1}}(\omega_i) \geq 0.5\}$$

For example, *ex post* the players may learn about $\Omega$ and, given the imprecise knowledge on each $\omega_i$ due to its unexpected features, they generate the following fuzzy set

$$\begin{array}{lccccc} & \omega_1 & \omega_2 & \omega_3 & \omega_4 & \omega_5 \\ \mu_{\underline{E1}}(\omega_i) = & 0.1 & 0.6 & 0.8 & 0.4 & 0.9 \end{array}$$

Then the $\alpha$-cut set is

$$\begin{array}{lccccc} & \omega_1 & \omega_2 & \omega_3 & \omega_4 & \omega_5 \\ \mu_{\underline{E1}\alpha}(\omega_i) = & 0 & 1 & 1 & 0 & 1 \end{array}$$

The crisp set $E1_{0.5} = \{\omega_2, \omega_3, \omega_5\}$ is the 'admissible' set of states, and the players are allowed to conclude by default that NBS is applicable to it. The important implication is that commitments can be undertaken and verified on this basis:

- *Ex ante* B undertakes the commitment to treat the game as the domain of application of NBS in case any state $\omega_i$ should come out, which *ex post* falls into the 'admissible' $\alpha$-*cut* set $E1_{0.5}$.
- *Ex post* players learn the degree of membership of each state $\omega_i$ in the set $\underline{E1}$ and determine without any ambiguity whether NBS has effectively to be applied according to the already stated condition.

This fuzzy information can be used by each player in the role of A in order to check whether player B treats any stage-game under consideration appropriately. This is not enough, however, to define B's commitments to use particular actions $a \in \mathbf{a}$.

## Second step in the ethical procedure of deliberation: fuzzy measures of surplus and effort

Consider a subset of $E1_{\alpha}$ and call it event $E2$. By $E2$ we mean that 'the level of cooperative benefit $R_j^*$ associate to the observable return $Q$ and player A's level of effort $o_{Aj}$ are such that the outcome is "efficient/fair" in the sense of NBS, *if* the action $a^*$ is chosen'. To define the event $E2$ in set theoretic terms, we must consider actions contingent on states $(a^*|\omega_i)$. Thus, event $E2$ is defined as the set of states where the conjunction of any two properties $R_j^*$ and $o_{Aj}$ necessarily implies that NBS, defined on the cooperative payoff space $R^*$ and the fair *status quo* $D^*$ (containing the given $o_{Aj}$), is maximized *if* action $a^*$ is chosen *when* any of such states occurs. That is, for $h = \mathrm{A, B}$, and N levels of possible cooperative return $R_j$ and possible effort cost $o_{Aj}$,

$$E2 = \{(\omega_i) \in E1_\alpha \text{ s.t. } (R_j^* \& o_{Aj}) \Leftrightarrow (a^* | \omega_i)$$
$$= ArgMax_{a \in a} \Pi_h [u_h(f_a(R_j^*)) - u_h(D^*)]\}$$

where $R_j^*$ and $o_{Aj}$ are the levels of cooperative benefit and of player A's effort cost occurring in state $\omega_i$. Moreover the NBS is defined by player's $h$ utility function $u_h$ ranging over the possible allocations of the cooperative benefit $R_j^*$ calculated through the distribution function $f_a(R_j^*)$ associated to action $a^*$ such that, for utilities linear in the monetary payoffs,

$$u_B(f_a(R_j^*)) = R_j^* - s$$
$$u_A(f_a(R_j^*)) = R_j^* - (R_j^* - s)$$

and by the player's $h$ utility function $u_h$ ranging over the values of fair *status quo* $D^*$ of form $[c(I_A) + o_{Aj}, c(I_B)]$ as the level $o_{Aj}$ changes according to the different $\omega_i$.

The possibility that any $(a^* | \omega_i)$ has an efficient/fair outcome depends on some proportion between the *size* of the cooperative return $R_j^*$ (i.e. the *extent* of $R^*$), and the *size* of effort $o_{Aj}$ associate to the task $a^*$ in state $\omega_i$. Players however, when any $\omega_i \in \Omega$ occurs, do not see clearly $R_j^*$ and $o_{Aj}$ but their observable substitutes $Q$ and $Z$, and they remain in a condition of vagueness about the meaning of these two pieces of information in terms of the relevant variable $R^*$ and $o_A$. Thus they proceed by considering separately the two pieces of vague information before being able to compound them in order to evaluate whether and how any given $\omega_i$ belongs to $E2$.

The first component of vagueness of event $E2$ is indeterminacy of the causal relationship that links any size of return $Q$ (i.e. $Q_i \in [0, n]$) to any size of the cooperative surplus $R_j^*$. In fact, whatever the level of cooperative benefit $R_j^*$ considered, the set of the observable returns $Q$ (i.e. states $\omega_i \in \Omega$ exhibiting a level of $Q_i$ each) compatible with the given level of cooperative benefit, is a *fuzzy* set.

- *Example 1.* Assume that $Q$ can vary between 0 and 20, that is, there are at most 20 states $\omega_i$. Moreover assume the $R_j^*$ are not single values of cooperative benefit but the following five intervals

  $$R^*_{--} = 0 \leq R^* \leq 6;\ R^*_{-} = 7 \leq R^* \leq 9;\ R^*_{\approx} = 10 \leq R^* \leq 12;$$
  $$R^*_{+} = 13 \leq R^* \leq 16;\ R^*_{++} = 17 \leq R^* \leq 20.$$

Each interval of benefit defines therefore a fuzzy set of states. An example of the fuzzy sets defined by the various intervals of vague cooperative benefit is given in Figure 16.2.

| | $\omega_1$ $Q=0$, | $\omega_6$ $Q=6$, | $\omega_8$ $Q=8$, | $\omega_{10}$ $Q=10$, | $\omega_{12}$ $Q=12$, | $\omega_{15}$ $Q=15$, | $\omega_{16}$ $Q=16$, | $\omega_{18}$ $Q=18$, | $\omega_{20}$ $Q=20$ |
|---|---|---|---|---|---|---|---|---|---|
| $\mu_{B^*--}(\omega_i) =$ | 1 | 1 | 0.8 | 0.7 | 0.2 | 0.15 | 0.1 | 0 | 0 |
| $\mu_{B^*-}(\omega_i) =$ | 0 | 0 | 0 | 0.7 | 0.5 | 0.2 | 0.15 | 0.1 | 0.05 |
| $\mu_{B^*\approx}(\omega_i) =$ | 0 | 0 | 0 | 0.2 | 0.6 | 0.3 | 0.2 | 0.15 | 0.1 |
| $\mu_{B^*+}(\omega_i) =$ | 0 | 0 | 0 | 0 | 0 | 0.6 | 0.7 | 0.5 | 0.2 |
| $\mu_{B^*++}(\omega_i) =$ | 0 | 0 | 0 | 0 | 0 | 0 | 0 | 0.6 | 0.8 |

*Figure 16.2* Each state, characterized by a specified observable *ex post* return $Q_i$, is associated with every class of fuzzy cooperative benefit.

Figure 16.2 represents a situation in which we know that a substantial part of the return is a cooperative benefit, but its *extent* is vague. Vagueness is delimited by logical incompatibility between certain levels of observable return and certain sizes of cooperative benefit. On the contrary vagueness increases as the size of observable returns exceeds the given level of cooperative benefit, so that other sizes become more compatible with the observed ones. In fact, when the observable return is between 0 and 6 there is no vagueness that cooperative benefit must lie in the interval $R^*_{--}$. But when the observable return becomes larger the case becomes more and more vague as other sizes of $R^*$ seem more possible. At the same time a very large size like $R^*_{++}$ is incompatible to nearly all the levels of observable return, but it vagueness is at minimum when the return is very similar to the required value of $R^*$.

The second component of vagueness of $E2$ is the meaning of the variable $Z$ in terms of $o_A$. $Z$ is a description of $a^*$ in physical terms (hours required to carry out the task). But in order to understand whether and how a state belongs to the event $E2$ it is necessary to translate the value of $Z$ into a measure of A's effort cost $o_A$ (the tiredness or enjoyment experienced by A out of any action $a$). This evaluation is inevitably vague, because of the novelty of events occurring in $\omega_i$, some of which may translate a high value of $Z$ into a low effort-cost or, on the contrary, a low value of $Z$ into a high effort-cost.

- *Example 2*. Let us consider as in the section 'The hierarchical transaction as a game', only three possible values of effort-cost for $a^*$

$$o_{A+} = 5, o_{A\approx} = 2, o_{A-} = 0$$

These values are immaterial *per se*, and can be taken as numerical exemplification for 'high', 'medium' and 'low' effort-cost of a given task. However taking specified,

| | $\omega_1$ | $\omega_2$ | $\omega_3$ |
|---|---|---|---|
| $\mu_{OA-}(\omega_i) =$ | 0.2 | 0.4 | 0.9 |
| $\mu_{OA\approx}(\omega_i) =$ | 0.6 | 0.9 | 0.3 |
| $\mu_{OA+}(\omega_i) =$ | 0.9 | 0.2 | 0.1 |

*Figure 16.3* Each state, characterized by the same value of $\mathcal{Z}$, is associated with every level of fuzzy effort-cost.

even if arbitrary, numbers for the effort-cost entering the utility functions of the players will make possible the later computation of NBS. Moreover, take as given a value of $\mathcal{Z}$ (say $\mathcal{Z} = 8$ hours), in order to exemplify how the same value of $\mathcal{Z}$ may mean different levels of effort-costs. In Figure 16.3 fuzzy membership functions are understood as expressing the possibility that, given the value of $\mathcal{Z}$ in each of the states of the world (consider three of these) it happens that A must face each of the possible effort levels.

The example presents the case of three states that are inversely related to the three levels of player A's effort. Take $\omega_1$ first. This is a state where some unexpected features make the task very hard, so that it is quite clear that the effort spent is high, whereas it is much more vague that it is low. On the contrary, in state $\omega_3$ occurs some unexpected change that makes the task very easy, so that it is quite clear that effort is low, whereas it is much more vague if the effort requested is high.

Examples 1 and 2 illustrate how the pieces of information $\mathcal{Q}$ and $\mathcal{Z}$, which are foreseeable *ex ante* and are observable *ex post*, may give only vague knowledge about the relevant variables for evaluating whether in a given state the action $a^*$ satisfies the event $E2$. This vague knowledge concerning any level $j$th of cooperative return $R_j^*$ and player A's effort $o_{Aj}$ can be summarized by the corresponding fuzzy sets

$$\underline{R_j^*} = \{(\omega_i, \mu_{\underline{Rj}*}(\omega_i))|\forall\omega_i \in E1_\alpha\}$$

$$\underline{o_{Aj}} = \{(\omega_i, \mu_{\underline{o_{Aj}}}(\omega_i))|\forall\omega_i \in E1_\alpha\}.$$

## Vagueness of efficient/fair outcomes: third step in the ethical procedure of deliberation

How must the two components of vagueness mentioned above be combined in order to express an overall – albeit vague – judgement? Consider the conjoint properties ($R_j^*$ and $o_{Aj}$) where $R_j^*$ and $o_{Aj}$ represent the $j$th levels of cooperative benefit and effort. The event corresponding to ($R_j^*$ and $o_{Aj}$) is a fuzzy set defined as

$$\underline{R_j^*} \cap \underline{o_{Aj}} = \{(\omega_i, \mu_{\underline{Rj}* \cap \underline{0Aj}}(\omega_i)|\omega_i \in E1_\alpha\}.$$

whose membership functions are calculated as follows

$$\mu_{\underline{R}*j \cap \underline{0A}j}(\omega_i) = \text{MIN}\ [\mu_{\underline{R}*j}(\omega_i), \mu_{\underline{0A}j}(\omega_i)].$$

This establishes how vague it is that in any given unforeseen state the conjunction of the two properties $R_j^*$ and $o_{Aj}$ occurs.

Notice that vagueness lies in statements like 'in $\omega_i$ the cooperative return lies in the interval $R_+^*$ and the effort associated with the action $a^*$ is at level $o_{A+}$'. But, on the syntactic level, we are perfectly entitled to endorse an inference like

'if ($R_{i+}^*$ & $o_{A+}$) holds, then from $a^*$ follows $p$'

where $p$ may be some formal property of the payoffs. Vagueness lies at the semantic level, that is at the level where we ask whether, in any $\omega_i$, $R_+^*$ and $o_{A+}$ are *true*, whereas it does not jeopardize the syntactic inference that, if $R_+^*$ and $o_{A+}$ are assumed, then from $a^*$ follows $p$. Let $p$ be the following property of maximum Nash product

$$a^* = ArgMax_{a \in a} \Pi_h (u_h(f_a(R_j^*)) - u_h(D^*)) \quad (\textit{for } h = \text{A, B})$$

such that the solution payoffs are $[s - (c(I_A) + o_{Aj}); (R_j^* - s) - c(I_B)]$.

For every interval of cooperative benefit and every level of effort given in Examples 1 and 2, we can calculate $p$ or $\neg p$. Calculations of the combinations ($R_j^*$ and $o_{Aj}$) such that it is true that 'if $a^*$ is chosen then we have $p$', are summarized in the Figure 16.4.

Notice that $R_j^*$ and $o_{Aj}$ are intervals and numbers and not fuzzy sets as such. In order to understand whether the conjunctions of the two parameters' values, which imply p, hold, we must study the corresponding intersections of fuzzy sets. Thus, take the union of all the fuzzy sets intersections defining events corresponding to joint properties ($R_j^*$ and $o_{Aj}$) such that that p follows from $a^*$.

$$\mathbf{U}[(\underline{R}_j^* \cap \underline{o}_{Aj})^*] = \{(\underline{R}_{--}^* \cap \underline{o}_{A-}) \cup (\underline{R}_{-}^* \cap \underline{o}_{A-}) \cup (\underline{R}_{\approx}^* \cap o_{A-})$$
$$\cup (\underline{R}_{--}^* \cap \underline{o}_{A\approx}) \cup (\underline{R}_{-}^* \cap \underline{o}_{A\approx}) \cup (\underline{R}_{--}^* \cap \underline{o}_{A+})\}$$

| | $0 \leq R^*_{--} \leq 6$ | $7 \leq R^*_{-} \leq 9$ | $10 \leq R^*_{\approx} \leq 11$ | $12 \leq R^*_{+} \leq 16$ | $17 \leq R^*_{++} \leq 20$ |
|---|---|---|---|---|---|
| $o_{A-} = 0$ | $p$ | $p$ | $p$ | $\neg p$ | $\neg p$ |
| $o_{A\approx} = 2$ | $p$ | $p$ | $\neg p$ | $\neg p$ | $\neg p$ |
| $o_{A+} = 5$ | $p$ | $\neg p$ | $\neg p$ | $\neg p$ | $\neg p$ |

*Figure 16.4* For any couple of parameters the figure shows when it is true that the Nash Product is maximized if player B chooses $a^*$.

We call this fuzzy set event $\underline{E2}$. Intuitively $\underline{E2}$ is the union of all the situations such that choosing $a^*$ under any of them satisfies the NBS, that is, it is the event where NBS is satisfied (up to some degree) by choosing $a^*$. Thus we see that the proper notation for the above-mentioned event $E2$ is the fuzzy set $\underline{E2}$. Formally $\underline{E2}$ asserts for each state $\omega_i$ its membership to the union of all the events like $(\underline{R}^*_j \cap \underline{o}_{Aj})^*$ for which the *efficient/fair* NBS outcome is implied when $a^*$ is chosen. By definition, degrees of membership of any state $\omega_i$ into the set $\mathbf{U}[(R^*_j \cap o_{Aj})^*]$ are assigned by the MAX operation,

$$\mu_{\underline{E2}}(\omega_i) = \mu_{U[(\underline{R}*j \cap \underline{OA}j)*]}(\omega_i) =$$

$$\text{MAX}[\mu_{(\underline{R}*\approx - \cap \underline{OA}-)}(\omega_i), \mu_{(\underline{R}^* - \cap \underline{OA})}(\omega_i), \mu_{(\underline{R}^* + \approx \cap \underline{OA})}(\omega_i),$$

$$\mu_{(\underline{R}^* - \cap \underline{OA}\approx)}(\omega_i), \mu_{(\underline{R}^* - \cap \underline{OA}\approx)}(\omega_i), \mu_{(\underline{R}^* - \cap \underline{OA}+)}(\omega_1)_1].$$

Having this definition at hand, we are now able to work out formal conditions for committing player B to carry out action $a^*$ whenever doing that in an unforeseen state satisfies NBS at the 'appropriate' level. Within $E1_\alpha$, the set $E2_\beta$ is defined as the $\beta$-cut set of those states (unknown *ex ante*) whose grade of membership to the event $\underline{E2}$ is not lower than threshold $\beta = 0.5$.

$$E2_\beta = \{\mu_{\underline{E2}}(\omega_i) \geq 0.5 | \forall \omega_i \in E1_\alpha\}$$

Membership in this set is defined by the non-fuzzy membership function

$$\mu_{E20.5}(\omega_i) = \begin{cases} 1 & \text{if } \mu_{\underline{E2}}(\omega_i) \geq 0.5 \\ 0 & \text{if } \mu_{\underline{E2}}(\omega_i) < 0.5. \end{cases}$$

We therefore have a criterion for asserting in which states the action $a^*$ must be considered admissible, or be treated 'as if' it were efficient/fair. This criterion may be announced *ex ante* and be meant as the basis for committing B in face of the expected ambiguity of the relevant information under unforeseen states. Moreover it can be verified *ex post* as the membership functions take their values when the unforeseen states take place in practice.

## Default inference of admissible actions

Let $\pi$ be an evaluation function of actions, with domain the set {admissible, inadmissible} and co-domain B's conditional choice set, that is, actions conditional upon states of the world. Take the rule of inference

$$\forall \omega_i \in \Omega, \textit{ if } \mu_{\underline{E2}\beta}(\omega_i) \neq 0 \text{ then } \pi(a^* | \omega_i) = \{\textit{admissible}\}.$$

This rule is basically needed in order to define commitments conditional upon the occurrence of unforeseen states of the world, which may be undertaken *ex ante* and can be verified *ex post*, as far as vagueness concerning the satisfaction of a given solution concept does not exceed a given threshold.

The above scheme of inference is worked out by analogy with what in AI literature is called 'default reasoning' (Reiter, 1980; Ginsberg, 1987). A statement is allowed among the default conclusions of a theory when it follows from the base of knowledge plus the rule of inference about the 'normal course' of the relevant matter. Even though there is no proof that these statements are true, nevertheless they are added to the base of knowledge only because they are consistent in the simple sense that no refutations of them at the moment are known. Reiter (1980) by defaults means rules of inference like syllogisms, which extend the set of statements proved under a given theory and knowledge base by adding to them new statements derived through the application of default rules onto the basic set of statements of the theory and its default consequences. Given an incomplete collection of facts over the world, defaults are a way to 'complete' our belief system on the world by inferring what is allowed by basic beliefs (justified by our knowledge base) plus a set of 'reasonable' conditionals that cannot be falsified given our incomplete knowledge. Typical default rules have the following form

$$\frac{A(x) : M(A(x) \rightarrow B(x))}{\therefore\ B(x)}$$

where A($x$) is a precondition to the rule belonging to the knowledge base, MA($x$) $\rightarrow$ B($x$) is the conditional clause that is checked for consistency with the existing base of knowledge (and is assumed by default) and B($x$) is a consequence that is added to the base of justified beliefs if the clause is 'consistent'. According to the coherence interpretation of default logic (Reiter, 1980), in fact the modal operator M means 'it is consistent to assume that . . .' and clause MA $\rightarrow$ B can be interpreted as follows: 'in the absence of proof to the contrary it is coherent to assume that A $\rightarrow$ B . . .'. M can also be understood as 'normally . . .' or 'according to our best knowledge of the matter, it is reasonable to think that . . .'.

Default rules of inference permit adding more sentences to our base of knowledge and beliefs by assuming that any conditional is acceptable whenever we have an incomplete collection of positive examples of it and we have no constructive proof of the contrary to the conditional itself ensuing from the knowledge base. In the absence of a refutation, notwithstanding that we do not have conclusive proof of its truth but only some positive examples, we are permitted to assume the conditional sentence as part of the premises of an inference rule. By using the sentences of a knowledge base – a theory – as major premises of a syllogism, and by adding to them default conditionals, we derive new conclusions that add to the theory. In other words, as far as a proof of the contrary does not result, the 'consistent' clause put together with the base knowledge allows us to derive statements which shall constitute extensions of the basic theory. Of course default reasoning is 'non-monotonic' and its conclusions are 'defeasible': as more information comes out, some conclusion can be retracted in order to account for new information (McDermott and Doyle, 1980).

This is illustrated by the typical example of Tweety the penguin: in this case A($x$) stands for *Bird*($x$), B($x$) for *Fly*($x$), and it is part of our knowledge base that

$x$ (Tweety) being a *penguin* is also a bird. Read M as 'it is consistent that . . .', so that the conditional $M(A(x) \rightarrow B(x))$ represents that there is at the moment no evidence that contradicts that birds fly – that is, 'normally' birds fly. The result is a default inference that allows concluding that Tweety flies (even if Tweety is a penguin), which eventually will prove to be false and clearly reveals that the system of beliefs is non-monotonic.

There is a basic analogy between default reasoning and the rule given above for evaluating actions under unforeseen contingencies. The fuzzy-based inference establishes the admissibility of an act in a state if we 'do not have proof of the incompatibility' (this would amount to saying that $\mu_{E2\beta}(\omega_i) = 0$) between an unforeseen state of the world and a proposition of our base theory. The statement about the admissible action then follows, even though it remains vague under the current state whether the action fits the solution theory (we only ask that vagueness does not exceed a given threshold).

Let us illustrate in more detail the default inference rule applicable to our case:

$$
\begin{array}{ll}
(1) & \forall\Gamma, Gc(\Gamma) \rightarrow \Sigma(\Gamma) \equiv NBS \\
(2) & M(\omega_i \in E1_\alpha \rightarrow \omega_i \in E1) \\
(3) & M(\omega_i \in E2_\beta \rightarrow \omega_i \in E2) \\
(4) & \forall\omega_i, \omega_i \in E2 \rightarrow \pi(a^*|\omega_i) = \{admissible\} \\
\hline
\therefore & (a^*|\omega_t) = \{admissible\}
\end{array}
$$

Premises 1 and 4 are sentences of our knowledge base, that is statements belonging to our solution theory such that 'every game Γ that we may qualify as having the characteristics of a bargaining cooperative game Gc is solved according to NBS – where the symbol Σ means 'solution' and 'if the state with such as an action satisfies the conditions for an *efficient/fair* outcome in the sense of NBS, then that action is admissible'. Premises 2 and 3 are typical default reasoning conditionals, based on consistency. The first says that it is consistent with our knowledge to take the game *as if* it were a Gc in the state $\omega_i$ given that the 'degree of clarity' in the membership of $\omega_i$ to $E1$ is no less than $\alpha$. The second says that it is consistent to assume that action $a^*$ satisfies NBS in the state $\omega_i$ given that the 'degree of clarity' in the membership of $\omega_i$ to $E2$ is no less than $\beta$. All that is assumed in so far as it does not contradict the information at the disposal of the players. As far as any state $\omega_i$ belongs to the events $E1_\alpha$ and $E2_\beta$, it follows that there is no reason to believe that the two properties are not true in that state (more on the relationship between default logic and fuzzy logic in Sacconi and Moretti (2005)).

## Back to reputation effects

We now are ready for developing a reputation game model under unforeseen contingencies. The game defined in the section 'The hierarchical transaction as a game' now simply becomes the stage-game (called a *play*) of a repeated game. The stage-game is played repeatedly by the long-run player B against an infinite series of short-run players playing each for a single period (from now on I shall refer to them as player $A_i$ on the basis of their index of entry $i$). Thus the strategies of the long-run player B for the repeated game will become rules which establish his choice between $a^*$ and $a^C$ for each play, contingent on the previous history of the game up to the present play. Each $A_i$ will decide from the standpoint of the stage game in which he is taking part, whether to enter or not (*e* or *non-e*) contingent on previous history. In more general terms let $h^t$ be a history of the repeated game where $t$ is the number of repetitions of a stage game which has been played up to repetition $t$. Each history describes one possible sequence of actions the long-run player and the various short-run players may have taken up to repetition $t$. We can then define the set of possible histories of the game up to repetition t by $H^t$. A *strategy* of the long-run player B then is defined as a function that for each history $h^t \in H^t$ determines which action of the stage game will be used by the long-run player from repetition $t + 1$ on, where $t$ has any value (from 1 to infinity). Obviously, since a short-run player $A_i$ participates in a single repetition of the stage game, $A_i$'s strategy will be a function that, for all the possible histories of the game up to the repetition before the one he takes part in, determines the action $A_i$ will choose in the current stage game. The length of the history of which the short-run player $A_i$'s action is a function obviously depends on the point at which the player enters the game.

Since a short-run player $A_i$'s payoff depends only on the stage game he takes part in, each $A_i$ is interested in the outcome of that game only. He is thus *short-sighted* and tries to predict only the action the long-run player will take in the game he is involved in, ignoring any predictions about the further development of the game. The long-run player, on the other hand, has a payoff function which is built up as the infinite sum of the payoffs received from all the stage games; the payoff received from each stage enters into the sum multiplied times a discount rate which is 1 at the first repetition and $\delta$ (between 0 and 1) at the second repetition, $\delta^2$ at the third, $\delta^3$ at the fourth and so on. The discount rate is the value the long-run player attaches to future utility or, if you like, his 'impatience' level. Unless his impatience makes him evaluate positively only payoffs gained from the nearest repetitions, the long-run player is *far-sighted*, in that he is interested in predicting how the various future short-run players will act. Consequently his game strategy is chosen not only in order to produce a result in the current stage game, but also according to the effect this strategy will have on the short-sighted behaviour of the short-run players in any further repetition.

Games like this, but defined in the more traditional context of foreseen contingencies, have been studied by Fudenberg and Levine (1989, 1991) (see also Fudenberg and Tirole, 1991). The basic request for reputation effect that can be put at work in this kind of game is that *ex post* any $A_i$ must be able to check whether B conforms to his commitments or not. In order to see how this is so in our repeated game under unforeseen contingencies, let us define player B's types (which correspond to player B's commitments). Quite unconventionally, each type is not associated to the performance of an idiosyncratic act, but to the fulfilment or non-fulfilment of the conditions *ex ante* laid down by the code. Let's assume that there are three *types* of player B.

*Type* $\theta 1$ takes on the commitment to follow the ethical code in each play.

$$\theta_1 = \begin{cases} (a^C|\omega_i), & \forall\omega_i \text{ such that } (a^*|\omega_i) \text{ is inadmissible} \\ (a^*|\omega_i) & \text{otherwise.} \end{cases}$$

*Type* $\theta 2$ always adopts $a^*$ – his dominant action – in each state of the world

$$\theta_2 = \forall\omega_i, \quad (a^*|\omega_i).$$

*Type* $\theta 3$ makes his choice somewhat at 'random'

$$\theta_3 = \begin{cases} (a^C|\omega_i) & \text{with prob } 0.25, \forall\omega_i \text{ such that } (a^*|\omega_i) \text{ is inadmissible} \\ (a^*|\omega_i) & \text{otherwise.} \end{cases}$$

The code signals the *possibility* of a type, but compliance with the code depends on reputation effects. In order for the mechanism of reputation to be put at work, all that must be added is that the prior probability assigned to the type $\theta_1$ – who respects the code – should not be zero (plus the hypothesis that player B is not short-sighted). Assumed *prior* probabilities of the types are as follows:

$$p(\theta_1) = p, \quad p(\theta_2) = q, \quad p(\theta_3) = r$$

where $p$ can be very small and $1 - p = q + r$, small. The updating rule is Bayesian.[5] Read $(a^C \cap \omega_i|\theta_1)$ as 'the occurrence of the action $a^C$ in the state $w_i$ given that player B is the type $\theta_1$'. Likelihood functions of actions, *for each state* of the world given each type, are the following.

In the case of the *type* $\theta_1$:

$$p(a^C \cap \omega_i|\theta_1) = \begin{cases} 1 & \text{if } (a^*|\omega_i) = \textit{inadmissible} \\ 0 & \text{if } (a^*|\omega_i) = \textit{admissible} \end{cases}$$

$$p(a^C \cap \omega_i|\theta_1) = \begin{cases} 0 & \text{if } (a^*|\omega_i) = \textit{inadmissible} \\ 1 & \text{if } (a^*|\omega_i) = \textit{admissible} \end{cases}$$

In the case of the *type* $\theta_2$:

$$p(a^C \cap \omega_i|\theta_2) = \begin{cases} 0 & \text{if } (a^*|\omega_i) = \textit{inadmissible} \\ 0 & \text{if } (a^*|\omega_i) = \textit{admissible} \end{cases}$$

$$p(a^C \cap \omega_i|\theta_2) = \begin{cases} 1 & \text{if } (a^*|\omega_i) = \textit{inadmissible} \\ 1 & \text{if } (a^*|\omega_i) = \textit{admissible} \end{cases}$$

In the case of the *type* $\theta_3$:

$$p(a^C \cap \omega_i|\theta_3) = \begin{cases} 0.25 & \text{if } (a^*|\omega_i) = \textit{inadmissible} \\ 0 & \text{if } (a^*|\omega_i) = \textit{admissible} \end{cases}$$

$$p(a^C \cap \omega_i|\theta_3) = \begin{cases} 0.75 & \text{if } (a^*|\omega_i) = \textit{inadmissible} \\ 1 & \text{if } (a^*|\omega_i) = \textit{admissible} \end{cases}$$

Note that learning is allowed only when the code establishes $(a^*|\omega_i) =$ *inadmissible*. The conditional probability of types, given the act undertaken in the preceding stage game, with reference to each state of the world $\omega_i$is calculated by Bayes rule. For example in the case of *type* $\theta_1$

$$p(\theta_1|\omega_i \cap a^C) = \frac{p(a^C \cap \omega_i|\theta_1)p(\theta_1)}{\sum_{i=1}^{i=3} p(a^C \cap \omega_i|\theta_i)p(\theta_i)}$$

If player B chooses $a^*$ in a state in which the code establishes the inadmissibility of $a^*$, *then* the conditional probability of *type* $\theta_1$ is nil. After enough (say $n$) observations of $a^C$, in states in which the code requires it, the conditional probability of *type* $\theta_1$ increases to the extent that the decision to enter ($e$) becomes appealing for each $A_{n+1}$.

Fudenberg and Levine's results (1988, 1991) guarantee that in games like this, for a discount rate $\delta \sim 1$, the upper bound of the equilibrium set is given by an equilibrium that, except for an initial period of N plays, gives the long-run player the stage game *Stackelberg's payoff* for the whole duration of the repeated game. Hence, take the *ex post* perspective, when $\Omega$ has been revealed, and consider the subset of $\Omega$ of those states $\omega_i \in E1_\alpha$ such that $a^*$ does not maximize NBS, but nevertheless the player A's payoff remains positive. To keep calculations simple, I assume that the probability mass over such subset of unforeseen states measures zero. This amounts to saying that unforeseen states which are similar to the foreseen states $w_3$ of Figure 16.1 (where even if player B disobeys the code, entering is optimal to player A) will have practically null probability. Thus, in any state $\omega_i$ that we need to take care of, if $a^*$ is incompatible to NBS then the Stackelberg payoff in pure strategies to player B will be certainly given by the pair of strategies $(e, a^C)$. In fact if B's binding commitment fell on $a^*$ when the code would require $a^C$, $A_i$'s best reply would be *non-e*, with the payoff 0 for B. Moreover, the mixed strategy (0.75 $a^*$; 0.25 $a^C$) in general is not a Stackelberg equilibrium strategy of the stage game. Thus the optimal choice of binding commitments for a leader *á la* Stackelberg would always coincide with behaviour that conforms to the ethical code, or with the *type* $\theta_1$. This suggests the following proposition:

**Proposition 2.** Take the game of hierarchical transaction as the stage-game of an infinitely repeated game between a hierarchical long-run *superordinate* and an infinite series of short-run *subordinates*, in the presence of unforeseen events. Then an ethical code, to which is associated a 'compliant type' of the hierarchical *superordinate* with positive initial probability, allows the *superordinate* to induce a Nash *equilibrium* in the repeated game, such that *(i)* the total payoff of the hierarchical *superordinate* is identical to what he would obtain if he were able to take on binding commitments *à la* Stackelberg except for the N initial periods spent in accumulating reputation; *(ii) in* no period does the payoff of the hierarchical subordinates differ from that which conforms to the ethical code.

I only give here a sketch of the proof, as a more detailed one would be essentially analogous to (Fudenberg and Levine, 1989). An important difference is however the adaptation of that result to the completely new context of unforeseen states. This also implies that, as it will be clear in a moment, my proof can not be so clear cut as those in the reputation games literature are. Let $N$ be the number of plays that players $A_i$ employ in order to update the probabilities of the *types*, until a probability distribution over the actions of B is generated that induces player $A_{n+1}$ to enter. $M < N$ is the number of plays in which the players $A_i$ effectively learn, given that sometimes (precisely $N - M$ times) states may occur for which the code requires $a^*$. Let us suppose that until now player B acted as if he were the *type* $\theta_1$, that is, he used $a^C$ in the $M$ plays in which the code requires it. Given that players $A_i$ are rational, they will have refrained from playing $e$ until the period $N$, but from the period $N + 1$ on they will begin to enter. To choose his best reply player B will compare the expected payoffs from at least two strategies:

- *Strategy* $s1$: after having used $a^C$ in all the first $M$ plays in which the code required it, from the $N+1$th play on, when the code again requires it, continue to use $a^C$.
- *Strategy* $s2$: after having used $a^C$ in all the first $M$ plays in which the code established the inadmissibility of $a^*$, in the $N + 1$th play (and in any of the succeeding plays) in which the code again requires the use of $a^C$, use $a^*$ instead.

If strategy $s2$ were better than strategy $s1$ as a reply to player $A_i$'s choices, of course compliance with the code would never emerge as an equilibrium of the repeated game. Assume that by observing player B's strategy $s2$, any player $A_i$ becomes convinced that, notwithstanding that he observed player B acting according to the code during the foregoing $N$ plays, in fact player B is *type* $\theta_2$ (this can be the case if player $A_i$ may have a second thought, and he conjectures that he has been deceived during the first $N$ plays about the type of B). Strategy $s2$, after the initial series of $N$ plays in which the payoff is zero, on a single occasion offers player B the expected payoff of the dominant action $a^*$ of the stage game (calculated over the payoffs of $a^*$ in each of the possible states at that stage times the probability of each state). In the following periods however it has zero as expected continuation payoff (remember that the total probability of states where $A_i$'s dominant action in the stage game is $e$ whenever B chooses his action $a^*$, is assumed to be near to zero). After $N$ plays in which the payoff is zero, strategy $s1$ obtains in each play of the remaining infinite continuation game, in which the ethical code requires the action $a^C$, the expected payoff of $a^C$ calculated over the set of possible states in which $a^*$ is inadmissible. This must be multiplied times their probability (it should be remembered that, according to the hypothesis on the probability of states, player B predicts that in none of the remaining plays will a state occur which, according to the ethical code, requires the adoption of the action $a^*$). Therefore $s1$ dominates $s2$ simply if the continuation expected payoff of $s2$ counterbalances the single occasion on which $s2$ offers the payoff of the pair $(e, a^*)$. For $\delta \sim 1$, the strategy $s1$ dominates B's strategy $s2$, since it allows B to obtain an identical payoff in the $N$ initial play and a higher payoff in every play after $N$ except one, while the advantage that can be obtained from $s2$ in that unique play is more than counterbalanced by the series of higher discounted continuation payoffs.

Next, consider that starting from the play $N + 1$, player B chooses to simulate his *type* $\theta_3$. Hence, he chooses $a^C$ with probability 0.25 when the code declares that $a^*$ is not admissible, and $a^*$ otherwise – that is, he chooses $a^*3/4$ of the times the code does not allow it. After some players $A_i$ have seen B for a number of times playing both $a^C$ and $a^*$ against what is required by types $\theta_1$ and $\theta_2$, they will eventually become convinced that player B is in fact type $\theta_3$ (to be sure, under a simple Bayesian model even a single alternation of $a^C$, when requested, and $a^*$ when not allowed, should convince each $A_i$ that $\theta_1$ and $\theta_2$ are both false). Thus they will believe that thereafter the code will be complied with only up to probability 0.25 when it requires choosing action $a^C$. Remember the we have assumed that only states are positively probable such that whether the code asks for $a^C$ then choosing $a^*$ implies a negative payoff to the current player $A_i$. Thus there is no reason to believe that by developing a reputation of being $\theta_3$ player B will be able *in general* to induce generic players $A_i$ to ènter the hierarchical relationship. Although sometimes the contrary will be true, *in general* having the reputation of being *type* $\theta_3$ will imply that player B offers to each player $A_i$, in exchange for entering when the code asks for $a^C$, an expected payoff less than 0. Consequently, he must in general entertain the expectation of a zero continuation payoff after the first time he has played $a^*$ when the code asked for $a^C$, plus some gain reaped in cases that player $A_i$ will unpredictably enter. Notice that states such that the type's $\theta_3$ strategy happens to be able to induce entrance by any player $A_i$ are unforeseen. Given that *ex ante* player B can not predict the case nor the number of times this fortunate contingency will materialize – that is, the cases when 0.75 probability of a negative payoff will be counterbalanced by 0.25 probability of a positive one – he can not carry out the calculation of the discounted expected payoff of the strategy that simulates *type* $\theta_3$. In general this means that it is not possible to adjust *ex ante* the probabilities of the mixed strategy type to the particular payoff structure which will be revealed under each unforeseen state. The mixed strategy type thus degenerates to a idiosyncratic deviation from the pure strategy types' behaviour, and can not be seen as a type that player B may strategically simulate in order to adapt his behaviour to player $A_i$'s incentive to enter along the future repetitions of the game under unforeseen contingencies. Simulating *type* $\theta_3$ is a strategy with outcomes that are not *ex ante* under player B's rational control (he can not say whether the unpredictable cases in which it will induce $A_i$ to enter will balance the more frequent cases in which it will induce $A_i$ to stay out). Thus, we may only conclude that simulating *type* $\theta_3$ is not *rationally calculated* player B's best reply to the behaviour of the players $A_i$ who decide to enter after the first $N$ periods, as compared to the strategy $s1$, which assures an infinite series of positive NBS maximizing payoffs.

Fudenberg and Levine's theorems state that, for a discount level of future payoffs $\delta \sim 1$, there exists an equilibrium of the repeated game that, except for an initial period of $N$ plays, gives a long-run player like B the stage game Stackelberg's payoff for the whole remaining duration of the repeated game and this is the equilibrium which offers the long-run player the highest equilibrium total payoff. In our less predictable context for the most of plays in which $a^C$ is required by the code, the Stackelberg's payoff coincides with the pair $(e, a^C)$. In fact, if in the states with positive probability B's binding commitment fell on $a^*$, $A_i$'s best reply would be *non-e*, with payoff 0 for B, while choosing according to the mixed type (0.75 $a^*$; 0.25 $a^C$) would in general not even create indifference to $A_i$ between choosing $a^*$ or $a^C$, thus ending up again with the choice *non-e* by players $A_i$. Thus the optimal choice of a commitment for a leader *á la Stackelberg* would coincide with a behaviour conforming to the ethical code, that is, to *type* $\theta_1$. Summing up, apart from the initial $N$ plays which are spent in accumulating reputation, by adopting strategy $s1$ player B can generate an equilibrium in the game whose total payoff approximates the Stackelberg payoff; that is the same payoff he could obtain if the rules of the game permitted the announcement of binding commitments over the code of ethics.

## Discussion

It may be argued that the main result of the chapter (Proposition II) rests too heavily upon the choice of the set of possible types, and the 'mixed strategy' types in particular.[6] In fact, I introduced only type $\theta_3$ as a representative for these types essentially for two reasons. First, at least one mixed strategy type was needed in order not to let the probabilities of pure types change too dramatically after the single evidence of a choice by player B which was inconsistent with the hypothesis that player B is one of the two pure types. Note that this could be the case after a very few plays from the beginning of the game. Lacking any mixed strategy type, one single evidence of the choice $a^C$ made by player B, when the code requires it, would falsify type $\theta_2$, and would imply probability one assigned to type $\theta_1$. Type $\theta_3$ allows some learning dynamics to be associated to the emergence of the beliefs that induce players $A_i$ to play 'enter'.

Second, it seems reasonable to assume that player B may undergo idiosyncratic random mistakes in acting according to a pure type, so that he occasionally may act against his prevailing rule of behaviour. Thus acts that conform to the code can sometimes be carried out also by a player that normally does not conform to it. Assuming that there is a typical disposition to mistake the player's own conscious commitment, we may introduce this kind of disposition as a further 'type' of player B. One example of it is our type $\theta_3$. This would also justify the introduction of a mixed strategy type who randomly makes mistakes in complying with the code.

For simplicity I skip this hypothesis, but of course it should be kept in mind that a type who mistakes full compliance with small probability would nevertheless induce players $A_i$ to enter after some plays. As a consequence player B should optimally simulate exactly this type, for it gives him higher payoffs than a type of perfect compliance. Hence, a first limitation to Proposition II is that, under the hypothesis of random mistakes of the type conforming to the code, the upper bound of the equilibrium set in the repeated game would be given instead by a strategy of the long-run player that tolerates small random deviations from the code without inducing the players $A_i$ to stay out.

However, in my model there is no room for types that would express player B's ability to perform a fine tuning of the probability mixtures with respect to each situation – such that the players $A_i$ are induced to enter, while nevertheless player B can retain almost all the rent at stake. This would ask for types whose mixed strategy perfectly fits the expected utility of any player $A_i$ in each state of the world, which is clearly not the case in our context. True, in the classical context of reputation games 'mixed strategy' types should be more widely accounted for. Take for example the typical trust game (Figure 16.5) where the possible payoff vectors of the two players are $(0, 0)$ if the player A stays out ($\neg \boldsymbol{e}$), $(-1, 3)$ if A enters ($e$) and B abuses the first player's trust ($\boldsymbol{a}$), and $(2, 2)$ if, after A entering, he is not abused by player B ($\neg \boldsymbol{a}$).

Assume the one-shot game is a Stackelberg game where B can undertake binding commitments also on mixed strategies. Hence, consider player B's mixed strategy (2/3, 1/3), where the first component is the probability assigned to the action of abusing player's A trust, whereas the second component is the probability of not abusing. This strategy makes player A indifferent between his pure or mixed strategies. His natural best response then is the mixed strategy (1/2, 1/2), where the first component is the probability assigned to entering and the second the probability assigned to staying out. It gives the expected payoff 0 to A, but allows player B an expected payoff 1.32. Moreover it suggests that in a Stackelberg model

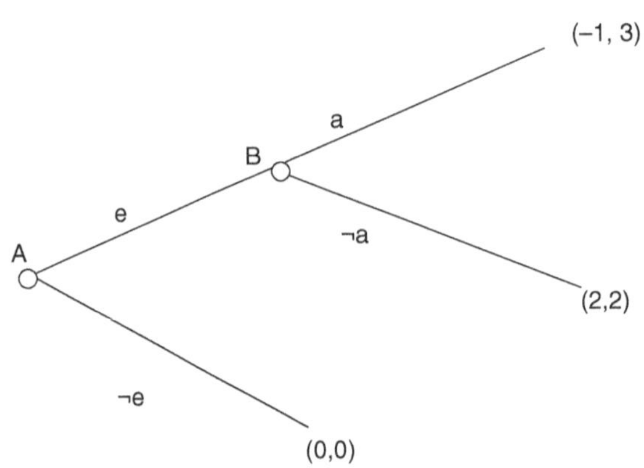


*Figure 16.5* One-shot trust game.

with the given values of parameters, where B was able to endorse genuine binding commitments on mixed strategies, player B could improve his outcome over the pure Stackelberg equilibrium strategy, simply by resorting to a commitment on the mixed strategy $(2/3 - \varepsilon, 1/3 + \varepsilon)$ (with $\varepsilon$ as small as possible). It gives in fact player B the expected payoff $2.64 - \varepsilon$, while leaving A the expected positive payoff $4\varepsilon$. That is the Stackelberg payoff of the game with mixed strategy commitments is associated with player B's commitment to this mixed strategy, which allows him to abuse A as long as this does not induce A to stay out. This would also translate in a different upper bound of the equilibrium set of the repeated trust game. Assume that the just quoted mixed strategy type is deemed possible by the players. If the long run player develops the reputation of being the (2/3, 1/3) type, why should not he adapt even more the probabilities of his strategy mixture by playing in the long run 'non-abuse' a little bit more in order to induce all the players $A_i$ entering from a certain play on?

It is an open question, however, whether this reasoning format can account for ethical commitments, like being the kind of players who conforms to a code of ethics. What does it mean to develop the commitment to comply with a code 'only one-third of the times'? Notice that we do not ask a question about a policy for enforcing the code, but concerning the very nature, character or identity of the player himself. It can well be the case that the only efficient policy of enforcement for a committed public authority is to inspect and possibly punish transgressors only one-third of the days at random, and nevertheless this would continue to be the behaviour associated with a type completely committed. Our question on the contrary is whether we can understand the very idea of an authority committed to a code only one-third, and not committed two-third. I guess anybody would say that this actor is simply not committed at all.

The reason for skipping nearly uniform mixtures of the two pure strategies is that types must represent commitments. Player A sees B as a player sticking to the rule of behaviour derived from the 'rational' solution of the stage-game, or nearly so, but also admits on the other hand that he may be committed to the code, or nearly so. While these rules of behaviour are understandable 'commitments', what seems to me to be 'nonsense' is the utterance that 'player B is committed to act x with nearly the same probability as not acting *x*' or worse – to say – with probability (2/3, 1/3). This should be better understood as avoiding committing oneself at all and remaining free to act arbitrarily.

These consideration can however be put aside when we leave the standard context of games of reputation and reach the new context of games under unforeseen contingencies. The reasoning underlying the adoption of the fine tuned mixed strategies is simply unrealistic under incomplete and vague knowledge. Consider player B who, having developed a reputation of being the type (2/3, 1/3), plans to play the code a little bit more in order to induce a correction of player $A_i$'s beliefs which later on will push him to enter every time. This move presupposes being able to calibrate the probability mixture in the light of the expected payoffs that any player $A_i$ will face later on under any contingencies. Under unforeseen contingencies this is a knowledge the players may have only *ex post*, and even *ex post* a lot of fuzziness will remain about the exact meaning of the monetary payoffs. However, in order to develop reputations in a repeated game under unforeseen contingencies commitments (i.e. 'types') must be established *ex ante* and must be announced unconditionally with respect to any specific description of the unforeseen states of the world. This was the very bulk of my construction of the code as a deliberative procedure capable of generating expectations of players that are aware of their incomplete knowledge of states, but are nevertheless not even capable of imaging further descriptions of the possible states. On the other hand, before knowing the current possible states there is no basis for calculating the mixed strategy that renders each player $A_i$ indifferent between his two pure strategies. If mixed types must be established *ex ante*, there is no room to tailor them as perfectly fitting the players' payoffs in each *ex post* state. For example, if before knowing that states will emerge in which the $A_i$ payoffs are not in the proportion $-1{:}2$, the type $(2/3-\varepsilon, 1/3+\varepsilon)$ were *ex ante* adopted, *ex post* this mixed strategy type would not be able to induce players $A_i$ to enter. Summing up, I do not see an alternative to assume that the mixed strategy types are only idiosyncratic deviations from pure types, not *ex ante* tailored to the specific numerical payoffs the players will obtain in each state of the world.

## Limitations and final remarks

There are two other apparently limiting assumptions implicit in my result. *First*, it is assumed that two agents $A_i$ and $A_{i+1}$ who participate consecutively in the repeated game, must share the same judgement regarding the observed action $a^*$. When a state that was not specified *ex ante* occurs, their judgement regarding the compatibility of the state with the two conditions of admissibility must be the same, that is to say the vagueness of the relationship between the state and the two events $E1$ and $E2$ must be measured identically by the two players. This assumption is assured by interpreting vagueness as objective indeterminacy or as vague knowledge, but not as subjective belief. It should be noted that both vague knowledge and subjective belief (subjective probability) intervene, but at very distinct points of the argument: when the state $\omega_i$ occurs, its compatibility with the events $E1$ and $E2$ is the subject of vague evaluation but is inter-subjectively invariable. Since the code contains a default rule of inference, the judgement about the admissibility of the action $a^*$ observed *ex post* is neither vague nor uncertain, but univocal although not monotonic. If the action in such circumstances is inadmissible B's behaviour appears to be incompatible with the hypothesis that he is a *type* who respects the code. Only at this point does probability come into play: each $A_i$ and $A_{i+1}$ will have an initial belief expressed via a subjective prior probability distribution regarding the *types* of B. The *type* is established without any vagueness, since it coincides with the behaviour prescribed by the default inference or its negation. Each *pure type* (i.e. the *ethical* and the *non*-ethical) chooses $a^*$ when the conditions regarding the membership of states in the sets $E1_\alpha$ and $E2_\beta$ are respectively $(1, 1)$ or $(1, 0)$. Then, the probability of all the *type* varies according to the evidence collected *ex post* via likelihood functions.

*Second*, in order that B may be able to foresee and anticipate the evolution in the beliefs of the other players, it is necessary that B comes to the same vague judgement as they do regarding the compatibility of the state known *ex post* with the events $E1$ and $E2$. What is required is not necessarily that B has at the beginning the same piece of information and therefore expresses the same judgement about the compatibility between the states and the sets $E1$ and $E2$. What is required is simply that B should have access to the common judgements expressed by $A_i$ and $A_{i+1}$, since it is from these judgements that $A_i$ and $A_{i+1}$'s short-run behaviour derives. Therefore the only relevant thing is the vague judgement in the state of information shared by $A_i$ and $A_{i+1}$.

Notice that strong assumptions such as the existence of a common distribution of fuzziness, or – worst – that it is common knowledge, are not necessary. What is really needed is much less than this: only any couple of players $A_i$ and $A_{i+1}$ must share the same fuzziness distribution on the unforeseen states, which have already transpired when they participate in the game. This same distribution must be also known by B at stage $i$ and $i+1$, without asking however that B agrees on it being an accurate representation of the vagueness at hand. On the other hand, player B has strong reasons for employing it when he is implementing the rules of the code. In fact, only if his behaviour conforms to what the code asks him, in the light of how things are seen by any couple of players $A_i$, $A_{i+1}$, will he benefit from the reputation effects that induce those players, participating in the stage games in the role of A, to 'enter'. To put it in other words, it is in B's best interest to take the fuzziness distribution assigned by any couple $A_i$ and $A_{i+1}$ for granted, in order to maintain the reputation effects mechanism at work.

## Acknowledgements

Previous versions of this chapter have been presented at the *International School of Economic Research* on 'Economics and the Law', Siena, June, 2000 and at the *4th Spanish Conference on Game Theory and Game Practice II*, Valencia, July, 2000. I gratefully acknowledge the support received by the MIUR under the national research project 'Economic comparative analysis of institutions and institutional complexity of governance structures in the perspective of incomplete contracts'.

## Notes

1 If A chooses $e$ and B chooses $a^C$ or $a^*$, then payoffs are:

$$\begin{aligned}
&[u_A(e,a^*|w_1),u_B(e,a^*|w_1)]=(-1,6); && [u_A(e,a^C|w_1),u_B(e,a^C|w_1)]=(2,3);\\
&[u_A(e,a^*|w_2),u_B(e,a^*|w_2)]=(-1,4); && [u_A(e,a^C|w_2),u_B(e,a^C|w_2)]=(2,1);\\
&[u_A(e,a^*|w_3),u_B(e,a^*|w_3)]=(2,6); && [u_A(e,a^C|w_3),u_B(e,a^C|w_3)]=(5,3);\\
&[u_A(e,a^*|w_4),u_B(e,a^*|w_4)]=(-1,2); && [u_A(e,a^C|w_4),u_B(e,a^C|w_4)]=(2,-1);\\
&[u_A(e,a^*|w_5),u_B(e,a^*|w_5)]=(4,6); && [u_A(e,a^C|w_5),u_B(e,a^C|w_5)]=(7,3);\\
&[u_A(e,a^*|w_6),u_B(e,a^*|w_6)]=(2,4); && [u_A(e,a^C|w_6),u_B(e,a^C|w_6)]=(5,1);\\
&[u_A(e,a^*|w_7),u_B(e,a^*|w_7)]=(4,4); && [u_A(e,a^C|w_7),u_B(e,a^C|w_7)]=(7,1);\\
&[u_A(e,a^*|w_8),u_B(e,a^*|w_8)]=(2,2); && [u_A(e,a^C|w_8),u_B(e,a^C|w_8)]=(5,-1);\\
&[u_A(e,a^*|w_9),u_B(e,a^*|w_9)]=(4,2); && [u_A(e,a^C|w_9),u_B(e,a^C|w_9)]=(7,-1),
\end{aligned}$$

whereas, if player A chooses non-$e$, payoffs are $(0,0)$ regardless of B's choice.

2 In this sense Nash Bargaining Solution (NBS) may seem at this point an exogenous principle superimposed on the game under consideration. Of course, our aim is making endogenous the principle by showing that this hypothetical reasoning can be supported by effective reputation effects that assures B will effectively carry out his part of the contract.

3 According to Richard Hare (1981) statements of ethics are universalizable. Hypothesize having a statement where some characteristics, carrying the moral value, are attributed to certain individual objects. Next replace all the individual objects with other individual objects that are completely new, except for being in a similar relationship to the morally significant characteristics. Then the new statement must retain the same normative meaning as the original one. Of course, the meaning is primarily normative, but the relevant characteristics, carrying the normative value, also have a descriptive content so that every time we find these characteristics in a situation where they are in the appropriate (analogous) relation to any individual objects, we also must have the same normative judgment. These descriptive characteristics, carrying the normative value, are the initial condition for applying the normative concept of solution to which we refer in the text.

4 At first sight fuzzy set theory presents us with an approach linked to the old idea that the set of states $\Omega$ is univocally determined, by means of a partition into mutually exclusive and jointly exhaustive states: we have a reference set which is clear cut. This would seem to leave no space for the idea of incomplete or imprecise knowledge of the basic possible alternatives. Nevertheless the fuzzy sets, insofar as they are subsets of $\Omega$, introduce exactly this characterization into the representation of the knowledge of the agents. A fuzzy set $\underline{E}$, to which a state $\omega_i$ 'imperfectly' belongs, means that that state is 'imperfectly' characterized as regards the property stated by the sentence corresponding to the event. Thus the description of the alternative states offered by $\Omega$ must not be the precise and exhaustive description of every characteristic that can be expressed using the resources of our language: we are not precise or univocal about the attribution of many characteristics to alternative states of the world (so that we cannot say that their description is devoid of ambiguity). Each $\omega_i$ represents a conjunction of the affirmation (or negation) of all the properties that can be expressed in language about any individual variables, but for many of these our 'state of the world' is not at all a precise and unambiguous description; in many ways it affirms that a given property is satisfied in that state *only to a certain degree*.

5 Introducing probabilities of unforeseen states of the world would ask for a clarification about the meaning of prior probability of states that *ex ante* were unforeseen, that is, were non-included within the states space. I leave this question to a further discussion. However, see Sacconi (2000, pp. 207–208).

6 I am indebted to Luciano Andreozzi (private communication, see also Andreozzi (2002)) for this and the following critical remarks concerning the matter of 'mixed strategy types' both in the one-shot and in the repeated trust game. Although they seem quite relevant to the standard case of games under foreseen contingencies, my reluctance to give wider space to mixed strategy types in my model depends on the fact that my main aim is to extend the reputation games technique to an epistemic context (unforeseen contingencies) in which the fine tuning of the probability mixture of pure strategies within the commitments devised by the Leader, in order to produce the desired response by Followers, is debarred by the very fact that the game is played under incomplete knowledge.

## References

Al-Najjar N.I., L. Anderlini and L. Felli (2004): Undescribable Events, Cesifo Working Paper Series No. 1092.

Anderlini L. and L. Felli (2000): *Bounded Rationality and Incomplete Contract*, Theoretical Economics Discussion Papers TE/00/47 STICERD-LSE.

Andreozzi L. (2002): *Moral Firms Require Moral Customers*, Mimeo.
Arrow K. (1988): 'Business Codes and Economic Efficiency', in T. Beuchamp and N. Bowie (eds), *Ethical Theory and Business*, 3rd edn, Englewood Cliffs, NJ (Prentice Hall).
Benson G.C.S. (1989): 'Codes of Ethics', *Journal of Business Ethics*, 8.
Billot A.: *Economic Theory of Fuzzy Equilibria*, Berlin (Springer).
Binmore K. (1991): 'Game Theory and The Social Contract', in R. Selten (ed.), *Game Equilibrium Models in Economics, Ethics and Social Sciences*, Berlin (Springer).
Binmore K. (1998): *Just Playing*, Cambridge, MA (The MIT Press).
Brock H.W. (1979): 'A Game Theoretical Account of Social Justice', *Theory and Decision*, 11, pp. 239–265.
Center for Business Ethics (1986): 'Are Corporations Institutionalizing Business Ethics?' *Journal of Business Ethics*, 5, pp. 77–89.
Coleman J. (1992): *Risks and Wrongs*, Cambridge (Cambridge University Press).
Coleman J.S. (1990): *The Foundation of Social Theory*, Harvard (Belknap Press).
Dubois D. and H. Prade (1995): 'Possibilistic Logic and Plausible Inference' in G. Coletti, D. Dubois and R. Scozzafava (eds), *Mathematical Models for Handling Partial Knowledge in Artificial Intelligence*, New York (Plenum Press), pp. 209–226.
Dubois D. and H. Prade (1996): 'Non-Standard Theories of Uncertainty in Plausible Reasoning', in G. Brewka (ed.), *Principle of Knowledge Representation*, Stanford, CA (CSLI Publications).
Fudenberg D. and D. Levine (1989): 'Reputation and Equilibrium Selection in Games with a Patient Player', *Econometrica*, 57, pp. 759–778.
Fudenberg D. and D. Levine (1991): 'Maintaining Reputation when Strategies are Imperfectly Observed', *Review of Economic Studies*, 59, pp. 561–579.
Fudenberg D. and J. Tirole (1991): *Game Theory*, Cambridge, MA (MIT Press).
Gauthier D. (1986): *Morals by Agreement*, Oxford (Clarendon Press).
Geffner H. (1992): *Default Reasoning, Causal and Conditional Theories*, Cambridge, MA (The MIT Press).
Ginsberg M.L. (1987): *Reading in Nonmonotonic Reasoning*, Los Altos, CA (Morgan Kaufmann Publisher Inc.).
Grossman S. and O. Hart (1986): 'The Costs and Benefit of Ownership: A Theory of Vertical and Lateral Integration', *Journal of Political Economy*, 94, pp. 691–719.
Hare R.M. (1981): *Moral Thinking*, Oxford (Clarendon Press).
Harsanyi J.C. (1977): *Rational Behavior and Bargaining Equilibrium in Games and Social Situations*, Cambridge (Cambridge University Press).
Hart O. and J. Moore (1988): 'Property Rights and the Nature of the Firm', *Journal of Political Economy*, 98, pp. 1119–1158.
Hart O. and J. Moore (1999): 'Foundations of Incomplete Contracts', *Review of Economic Studies*, 66, pp. 115–138.
Kreps D. (1990): 'Corporate Culture and Economic Theory', in J. Alt and K. Shepsle (eds), *Perspectives on Positive Political Economy*, Cambridge (Cambridge University Press).
McDermott D. and J. Doyle (1980): 'Nonmonotonic Logic I', *Artificial Intelligence*, 13, pp. 41–72.
Mansur Y.M. (1995): *Fuzzy Sets and Economics*, Aldershot, Hampshire (Edward Elgar).
Molander E. (1987): 'A Paradigm for Design, Promulgation and Enforcement of Ethical Codes', *Journal of Business Ethics*, 6, pp. 619–663.
Nash J. (1950): 'The Bargaining Problem', *Econometrica*, 18, pp. 155–162.
Reiter R. (1980): 'A Logic for Default Reasoning', *Artificial Intelligence*, 13, pp. 81–132.
Sacconi L. (1997): *Economia etica e organizzazine*, Roma-Bari (Laterza).

Sacconi L. (1999): 'Codes of Ethics as Contractarian Constraints on the Abuse of Authority within Hierarchies: A Perspective from the Theory of the Firm', *Journal of Business Ethics*, 21, pp. 189–202.

Sacconi L. (2000): *The Social Contract of the Firm. Economics, Ethics and Organisation*, Berlin (Springer).

Sacconi L. and S. Moretti (2005): 'A Fuzzy logic and Default Resourcing Model of Social Norms and Equilibrium Selection in Games under Unforeseen Contingiencies', University of Trento Economics Discussion Papers No. 13.

Sen A. (1993): *Moral Codes and Economic Success*, London (LSE, ST-ICERD Discussion Papers No. 49).

Simon H. (1972): 'From Substantial to Procedural Rationality', in C.C. McGuire and R.R. Radner (eds), *Decision in Organisation*, Amsterdam (North Holland).

Sims R.R. (1991): 'The Institutionalisation of Organizational Ethics', *Journal of Business Ethics*, 10, pp. 493–506.

Tirole J. (1999): 'Incomplete Contracts: Where do We Stand?', *Econometrica*, 67, 4, pp. 741–781.

Vamberg V.J. (1992): 'Organizations as Constitutional Order', *Constitutional Political Economy*, 3, pp. 223–255.

Willamson O. (1986): *The Economic Institutions of Capitalism*, New York (The Free Press).

Willamson T. (1994): *Vagueness*, London (Routledge).

Zadeh L.A. (1965): 'Fuzzy Sets', *Information and Control*, 8, pp. 338–353.

Zadeh L.A. (1978): 'Fuzzy Sets As a Basis for the Theory of Possibility', *Fuzzy Sets and Systems*, 1, pp. 3–28.

Zimmerman H.J. (1991): *Fuzzy Set Theory and Its Applications*, 2nd revised edn, Dordrecht and Boston, MA (Kluwer Academic Press).

# Index